MR 01 '01	DATE DUE		
FE 14 '02			

The Civil War World of Herman Melville

Herman Melville, 1861. By permission of the Berkshire Athenæum

The Civil War World of Herman Melville

Stanton Garner

University Press of Kansas

Published by the University Press of Kansas (Lawrence, Kansas 66049), which was organized by the Kansas Board of Regents and is operated and funded by Emporia State University, Fort Hays State University, Kansas State University, Pittsburg State University, the University of Kansas, and Wichita State University

Library of Congress Cataloging-in-Publication Data

Garner, Stanton.
The Civil War world of Herman Melville / Stanton Garner.
p. cm.
Includes bibliographical references and index.
ISBN 0-7006-0602-5 (hard : alk. paper)
1. Melville, Herman, 1819–1891. Battle-pieces—Sources.
2. United States—History—Civil War, 1861–1865—Literature and the war. 3. Melville, Herman, 1819–1891—Knowledge—History. 4. War poetry, American—History and criticism. 5. Melville, Herman, 1819–1891—Poetic works. 6. Authors, American—19th century—Biography. I. Title.
PS2384.B3G37 1993
811′.3—dc20 93-640

British Library Cataloguing in Publication Data is available.

Printed in the United States of America

10 9 8 7 6 5 4 3 2 1

The paper used in this publication meets the minimum requirements of the American National Standard for Permanence of Paper for Printed Library Materials Z39.48-1984.

To the memory of
Helen Marguerite Berry Jones

Contents

Illustrations

Acknowledgments

It has been said by a writer whom few know that a scholarly study is always a collaboration between the nominal author and all of those others, known or unknown, acknowledged or unacknowledged, who contribute to it by their earlier work. In the instance of this book, that includes, but is not limited to, those who have blazed the Melville trail and the path to the Civil War, whose books, essays, dissertations, and, in one case, masters' thesis, I have cited. In acknowledging by name others who have assisted me, I tender my sincerest apologies to any who, after all of these years of plodding along, I may have neglected to mention.

My thanks to the United States Naval Academy and its English department for a visiting professorship to which I attribute the inception of this study. Similarly, I thank the Newberry Library, with its generous and capable staff, for a summer fellowship that enabled me to use its extensive materials on Melville, the Civil War, genealogy, poetry, and other subjects encompassed by my work. I also owe thanks to the numerous persons, invariably courteous and efficient, on the staffs of institutions where I have gathered large quantities of material: the New York Public Library, the National Archives, the Federal Archives and Records Center, Bayonne (as it was at the time—now New York; particularly Tony Fantozzi), and the Library of Congress. My thanks also to the personnel of institutions where I have done more limited work; the Amon Carter Museum of Western Art (particularly Milan Houston); the Federal Archives and Records Center, Fort Worth, Texas; the Davenport, Iowa, Public Library; the Galena Public Library and the Jo Daviess County Courthouse, in Galena, Illinois; the Grand Army of the Republic Hall, the Winnebago County Court House, and the Rockford Historical Association, in Rockford, Illinois; the Hagley Museum and Library, Eleutherian Mills, Delaware; the Orange County Courthouse, Goshen, New York; the Pittsfield, Massachusetts, City Hall;

the U.S. Army Military History Institute, Carlisle, Pennsylvania, with its photograph collection of the Massachusetts Commandery, Loyal Legion of the United States; and the U.S. Naval History Institute, Washington, D.C., Navy Yard. I owe special thanks to the personnel of the Berkshire Athenæum, especially Ruth Degenhardt, whose research brought to light many of the Melville family photographs reproduced in this book. I must also thank separately the efficient, tolerant, and always willing interlibrary loan staff of the University of Texas at Arlington Library, particularly Mary Alice Price and Sheila Powell.

I am deeply indebted to all of those who have shared information, great or small, with me or who have assisted me by burrowing for it at my request, thus enriching this study. They include John Austin, of the Glens Falls–Queensbury Historical Association; Carolyn E. Banfield, of the Friends of Herman Melville's Arrowhead; John Bryant; John M. J. Gretchko; Alan B. Grieve, of Pittsfield, to whom I owe special thanks; Thomas F. Heffernan; Lynn Horth; the late Jay Leyda; Jean Melvill (a descendant of Herman Melville's Uncle Thomas); Hershel Parker; Margaret A. Ulrich, then a lieutenant in the United States Navy; Ila West, Ph.D., art consultant; Thomas Woodson, of the Nathaniel Hawthorne Edition; and Donald Yannella.

I am grateful to all of those, too many to name, who have given me advice and encouragement. The first, chronologically, was the late Wilson Heflin, a friend whom I knew all too briefly, who showed me the door where scholars enter the National Archives. Another is Harrison Hayford, who helped to arrange research support for my study. Among those colleagues with whom I have worked, and who therefore gave me their daily support, I include Charlyne Dodge, Robert J. Reddick, George E. Fortenberry, and Don R. Swadley. But above all, my debt to Merton M. Sealts, Jr., without whose example, counsel, and encouragement this work would have been unlikely or impossible, can never be fully repaid.

My thanks also to the New-York Historical Society, the Berkshire Athenæum, and the Rare Books and Manuscripts Division, the New York Public Library, Astor, Lenox, and Tilden Foundations, for their gracious permission to publish photographs and excerpts of manuscripts in their possession. I am equally grateful to Richard Manney for granting me access to the Edward Y. Lansing letterbook.

Finally, I wish to express my deepest gratitude to my family—my wife, Lydia, a rising scholar of history, and my sons, Stanton, Jr., George, and Edward, for their support and patience during the years it has taken me to write this book.

Introduction

This book is a study of the life of Herman Melville, perhaps America's greatest author, during the United States Civil War, perhaps the most crucial period in the history of the republic. It is also about *Battle-Pieces and Aspects of the War,*[1] one of the most underestimated of his works. When a book is entitled *The Civil War World of Herman Melville,* the reader is justified in expecting that it will detail the experiences of the author of *Moby-Dick* and *Billy Budd, Sailor,* during those convulsive years that transformed the United States from the agricultural and maritime confederation of Melville's youth into the industrial federation of his later life, that it will record and analyze his impressions and reactions to the events that unfolded before him, and thus that it will illuminate an important American intellectual landscape and an important moment in American history that has never before been placed in the context of that landscape.

However, those expectations must be tempered. Had Melville participated in the war in any official capacity, the voluminous archives and published records, public and private, of those years would contain an abundance of information about his experiences. But unlike Ambrose Bierce, Sidney Lanier, John William De Forest, and Walt Whitman, Melville did not join or make any attempt to join a branch of the army or the navy or the civil government. Nor did he leave behind him the kind of documentary trail that many other authors did. He was a private, elusive man; if he kept a notebook or a journal of the Hawthorne variety (other than a partial record of his 1860 sea voyage) between late 1859 and the middle of 1866, the period with which this book is concerned, it is not extant. Of the letters he wrote to others, only about two dozen, some of which contain little of biographical interest, have been located. To complicate the biographer's task further, it was his habit to discard most of the letters he received. Thus the available primary research materials reveal remarkably little about the man and his reactions to events. Moreover, he was a compulsively private person about whom relatively little was recorded in newspapers, magazines, and memoirs. His most telling statement about the war is *Battle-Pieces,* but the poems of that book only occasionally translate directly into biography. In short, what is known about this part of his life has been gleaned mostly from bits and snatches of information.[2]

In the face of that seemingly fatal impediment, the only useful biographical strategy is the methodology of Sam Patch in William Carlos Williams's poem *Paterson*: "Some things can be done as well as others." Thus if it is impossible to know much about the life of Herman Melville, it is possible to know a great deal about the world in which he lived. Granted that war is a communal experience, Melville's was that of several communities—his family, his friends, his neighbors, his fellow citizens of the North, and his Northern literary peers. Although he was an individualist with a talent and a personality peculiarly his own, idiosyncrasy has limits. He was also a Northerner at a time when common hopes, fears, defeats, and victories gripped the entire populace with a simultaneity and a commonality that have occurred only rarely in the nation's history. For this reason, knowing how those around him reacted to events, even when their reactions were likely to have been much different from his, is a means of knowing at least in part how he reacted, a large step toward understanding his Civil War experience.

Without that knowledge, it has been fashionable to conclude that there was essentially no Melville war experience. Thus Willard Thorpe remarked, "Many of the poems [of *Battle-Pieces*] deal so specifically with personalities and incidents of the war that the reader wonders naturally where the poet, who of course witnessed no battles, went for material to feed his imagination."[3] That is a fair question: the purpose of this book is to answer it.

The Politics of Families

Because this was a period in which political divisions and disputes were more dominant and more strident than they had ever been before or would ever be again in Melville's lifetime, one cannot know him without knowing his politics. Although he was notorious for not voting, he had strong sociopolitical opinions that must be understood in the context of the beliefs of his family.

One of the ties that bound American families together was their politics. Joel H. Silbey has described the general relationship of persons, families, and other communities to parties:

> Out of a network of primary-group relationships—family, racial,

> religious, nationality, class, and residential—individuals develop a set of values, beliefs, and interests that they often seek to advance or protect in the political arena. Individual parties come to be identified as favorable or not to these commitments. They are seen as standing for certain things in the voters' minds, general positions about the nature of society, its direction, and what government should and should not do. In a political world of great complexity and confusion, parties are the major instruments ordering events and articulating particular group desires. They establish for the average citizen "a point of reference" for political guidance. Parties thus become aggregations of persons sharing certain attitudes, assumptions, and commitments, evoked by the party label and to which they continually react.[4]

Silbey adds that in the Civil War era the extent to which family orientation and other formative conditions caused individuals to identify themselves with parties was even greater than this quotation suggests.

At the end of 1859, the minority Republican party had been in existence for less than a decade. It had first nominated a presidential candidate only in 1856, when John C. Frémont had been defeated by Democrat James Buchanan. The antislavery party, it was identified with the radical abolitionists, such as Ralph Waldo Emerson, John Greenleaf Whittier, and James Russell Lowell, whose single-minded opposition to slavery threatened the integrity of the union. The majority Democratic party dated, according to some criteria, from the origin of the nation. The Democrats were the conservatives, the conservators of values they believed they had inherited through the Constitution from the Founding Fathers. Since the nation was in effect a confederation, the single most important Democratic belief was that the authority of the national government should be subordinate to that of the states, particularly in relation to slavery.

Because the Democrats believed that the central government should not interfere in the lives of citizens, they feared its intrusion into the existing social system, regardless of its evils. They were intent upon preserving the union, with all of its quarrelsome diversity, and they blamed Republican agitation for the fact that its seams were pulling apart. For most Democrats, even those who opposed the institution, slavery was a constitutional issue: the citizens of one state had no right to interfere in the lives of the citizens of another. For others, particularly but not always those in the South, slavery was legitimized by racial considerations. They believed that the white race was superior and therefore that whites were justified in owning blacks and using them for labor and for service.

The Democrats feared that should the puritanical Republicans gain power they would centralize government and meddle in every area of citizens' lives, forcing their own narrow ideas of government, economics, culture, religion, and ethnicity on the populace. They suspected a Republican conspiracy to abrogate the rights of Southerners, even to destroy the union, if necessary, to reform the South. If they ever gained power, the Republicans would flout the Constitution by freeing slaves willy-nilly and would then compromise the national heritage by promoting the interests of blacks over those of whites. Democrats noted that for some years these scofflaw radicals had been smuggling slaves to freedom along the Underground Railway in defiance of the Fugitive Slave Act that had latterly kept the union together. Thus to oppose the Republicans was, in their eyes, to support the union.

These party beliefs were also family beliefs. Democratic families were likely to react according to the positions of their party and Republican families were likely to do the same, and within each a unity of purpose and belief resulted. For Melville's family that was true in one way but untrue in another, as the following discussion will suggest. As the relatives are introduced, it will no longer be possible to refer to Herman Melville using the traditional form "Melville." There were too many Melvilles and Melvills for that, and when the family wrote about "Melville," they meant his brother Allan, not "Herman," "Cousin Herman," or "Herman Melville," as they called him. Here family members will be referred to by the names they themselves used in reference to each other, despite the familiarity that results: Herman, Uncle Herman, Allan, Tom, Mother or Aunt Melville, Gus, Fanny, Uncle Peter, Uncle Nourse, Lizzie, and so on. The reader's indulgence is solicited.[5]

Forebears and Siblings

Herman descended from two Revolutionary War families. His Dutch maternal grandfather, General Peter Gansevoort, had fought in a number of campaigns and battles and had distinguished himself and earned the gratitude of the Continental Congress by his 1777 defense of Fort Stanwix, in the Mohawk Valley of New York, against the invading force of St. Leger. In the War of 1812 he was a general, though he died before he could participate in it. Because Herman was born after his death, he never knew this grandfather. His Scottish paternal grandfather, Major Thomas Melvill, had taken part in the Boston Tea Party and had served during part of the war in the Massachusetts State Regiment of Artillery, which saw relatively little action. Herman remembered him from childhood visits to his Boston home. Both grandfathers seem to have been Democrats (though the party then had other names, such as "Republican"), despite the fact that Grandfather Melvill had lost his position of naval officer of the port of Boston by supporting John

Quincy Adams for the presidency against Andrew Jackson. Both Jackson and Adams were Democrats of a sort.[6]

Closest to Herman were his mother, his siblings, and the spouses and children of his siblings. The men of his generation were successful and prosperous, with the signal exception of Herman himself. His oldest brother, Gansevoort Melville, a Democratic politician, had died as a young man. Now Herman was the oldest brother, forty years old at the end of 1859, but Allan, almost four years younger, was the wealthiest and the de facto family patriarch. Although the death the year before of his wife, Sophia Eliza Thurston, had forced on Allan the lonely responsibility for rearing his four young daughters, he was well able to afford a staff of servants to assist him. But he, too, was frail—during the winter of 1859 he was forced to travel to the South for his health.[7]

Like all of Herman's brothers and sisters, Allan had grown up in near poverty. After an experiment in reading law in the office of his uncle, Peter Gansevoort, an experience that ended in a rift between the two, he had moved to New York City. There he had entered the practice of commercial law and, probably with the advantages of his liaison with the well-to-do and socially prominent Thurston family, he had become well established in his practice and in society. Like most lawyers of the time, he was a politician, a Tammany Hall Democrat who as a younger man had run for the New York State Assembly. More recently, however, a persistent family tendency toward self-defensive diffidence (which included his late father and Herman) had asserted itself, making him reluctant to come forward as a candidate or as a leader of causes. Still, he was a loyal party member who preserved friendships with important Democrats. During the war he continued his practice and remained, like many others of his party, a loyal Unionist but a critic of the Republican administration.

Allan was a playful, good-natured bully who guarded his own interests without being overly offensive to others. He was especially close to Herman, whom he would not have dared to bully. The two believed that they were very much alike, though others chuckled at that conceit and insisted, correctly, that they were not. Despite being a man of affairs, Allan was no Philistine: a lover of luxury and ease, he was a patron of the arts and a member in his own right of the Duyckinck literary circle. Thus he probably appreciated Herman's art and encouraged it, perhaps sincerely and certainly because the writer was his brother. For Herman, to whom personal experience was often a source of literary inspiration and of typology and symbol, Allan, along with some of the other lawyers in the family, probably inspired the "bachelor" figure of his works. The bachelor is the untroubled man who, in a cozy retreat, does a snug business in rich men's bonds and holds remunerative offices. Married or unmarried, he sees the world not as one-third sunlight and two-thirds dark ocean, as Ishmael saw it in *Moby-Dick,* but as a comfortable Inns of Court replete with claret and roast beef dinners, as in "The Paradise of Bachelors." Allan seems to have resembled the lawyer of "Bartleby," a likeness that may explain why, of all Herman's fictional bachelors, that character receives the gentlest treatment.[8]

The baby of the family, just short of thirty years old, was Tom, who had gone to sea on a whaler when he was only fifteen and had risen rapidly in the merchant service from "the forecastle" (being a common seaman) to the captain's stateroom. For Herman, he was the type of the sailor, the frank larker of "John Marr" whom neither danger nor the inevitability of death can abash: "Taking things as fated merely, / Child-like though the world ye spanned" (165). At the end of 1859, Tom was on his first voyage as captain of the clipper ship *Meteor,* of Boston, sailing between San Francisco, Manila, and Calcutta.

Tom, still unmarried, was the darling of his mother and sisters. His frequent and long absences had made him a romantic figure in their imaginations, while his sailor dash and charm and his thoughtfulness in remembering them with exotic gifts to commemorate each voyage completed the conquest. The receipt of his letters, imperfect in execution as his limited formal education rendered them, was an exciting family event. Despite his youth, Tom's appearance was much like Herman's, including his impressive beard. He liked Herman's literary works, as he probably would have liked anything Herman did, and he carried a complete set of them in his cabin. Even though his travels carried him too far from national events to allow him to form political convictions of his own, he was a Democrat because that was what he understood himself to be.

The oldest of the siblings was Helen Griggs, forty-two years of age. Her husband, forty-six-year-old attorney George Griggs, had graduated from Brown University and the Harvard Law School, where he had been librarian. A friend of Herman's father-in-law, he had met Helen through that connection. The family sighed about the fact that "gruff" and "parsimonious" George was difficult to please, but as a matter of course they accepted him. And George *was* parsimonious. Although he was well able to afford a home for Helen, he would not buy one, instead moving her from rented house to rented house. At the end of 1859, they were living in Brookline, close to Boston, with George's younger brother, John William Griggs, a merchant, and his family. But despite the Melvilles' prejudice, George seems to have been fairly loyal to the family and even amiable at times. He was a Republican, well connected with important local political figures, and, as a wife was expected to do, Helen took her political coloring from him. That placed both of them in the family minority, but despite her apostasy, Helen's wit and charm made her a family favorite.[9]

Kate, almost six years younger than Herman, lived in Lawrence, Massachusetts, with her husband, John Chipman Hoadley, and her two small daughters, Maria Gansevoort, four years old, and Charlotte Elizabeth (Lottie), aged one. She acted the devoted and harassed wife and mother, always anxious about her children and her home and always short of household help; she was "born with what the Yankees call 'an anxious make,'" and had a tendency to "wear herself to an anatomy."[10] A year older than Herman and like Herman a native New Yorker, John matched Kate by being an equally devoted and anxious husband and father as well as a dutiful son who helped to support his widowed mother and his six sisters.

John was a remarkable man. Beginning at the age of fourteen, he had devoted his life to technology, studying when circumstances permitted and working successively as a surveyor, a mechanic, a designer, an engineer, an inventor, and an industrial manager. By 1848 he was a widower, working in Pittsfield as a partner in a machine shop which made railroad locomotives and textile machinery. Although family tradition would have it that at first Herman opposed the match, in 1853 Kate and John married and set up housekeeping in Lawrence, Massachusetts, where John had moved to help manage a locomotive manufacturing business. After 1857, John opened a plant in Lawrence to manufacture a portable steam engine of his own design. (Little wonder that during this decade inventors, textile sweatshops, and railroads appear in Herman's shorter fiction.) It has been said that John's invention was the first application of scientific principles to the design of high-speed engines, and it was a great success, particularly in Southern plantation applications. By 1860, John was a well-established and prosperous industrialist.[11]

John could also claim to be a man of letters. He had taught himself Greek, Latin, French, and German and had become something of an expert in the Homeric epics. It has been said that he knew the *Odyssey* as well as he knew the designs of his inventions. He wrote idealized verse that pleased the Melville family in a way that Herman's grittier poems may not have; in fact, one of the credentials he had submitted in support of his suit for Kate's hand was a small manuscript volume of poetry entitled "Destiny."[12]

But that did not alter the fact that he was the type of the new man, the man of machinery and metal and visions of a prosperous technological future for the nation, revealed best in the fact that he was one of the planners and an original trustee of the Massachusetts Institute of Technology and a donor of equipment for its engineering laboratory. In this sense, he was the antithesis of Herman, the man of oak and marble for whom the past marked the high tide of man's achievement. Little wonder that Herman withheld his approval until John's tender and loyal nature reached out to him. It is a tribute to those virtues that the two developed a strong and lasting mutual affection. John was consistently loyal to Herman, solicitous of his well-being and anxious to advance his interests, and Herman felt for him much of the affection that he felt for his natural brothers. John enjoyed and approved of Herman's literary achievements.

Although he had been born and raised in New York State, John fit the New England type of the Episcopalian Republican. Thus, despite his dealings with Southern planters, he was an unredeemed abolitionist. Not only was he a friend and supporter of the prominent radical Senator Charles Sumner, but in 1858 he had been elected as a Republican member of the Massachusetts legislature.

Herman's two maiden sisters, Augusta (Gus), two years younger than he, and Frances (Fanny), eight years younger, lived with Mother Melville and her widowed brother, Uncle Herman Gansevoort, on a farm at Gansevoort, New York. Gansevoort was a tiny village somewhat over forty miles north of Albany, accessible by train. Gus was pious, self-sacrificing, energetic, capable, good-natured, and outgoing, and, as her mother retreated into old age, increasingly the axis of family relationships and the center of family communication. Fanny shared many of these characteristics, but one senses that she was different, preferring that Gus lead and she follow. Nevertheless, there are occasional hints (not the least of which is the name given to Herman's youngest daughter) that she was a favorite of Herman. Mother Melville was approaching sixty-nine, but despite her increasingly fragile health she scandalized her family (or so they pretended) by her gusts of social activity. All agreed that she was a remarkable old woman. It hardly need be said that all three women were confirmed Democrats.

As a subunit of the larger family, Herman, his mother, and his siblings were especially close. In their earlier years, they had suffered privations, living largely on the charity of others in the family, with the result that, as Alice P. Kenney has said, their "early misfortunes had welded them into a proud, defensive clan."[13] They had demonstrated that closeness when, after Herman had married Elizabeth Shaw and Allan had married Sophia Thurston and the four newlyweds set up housekeeping together in New York City, Mother Melville and her daughters came to live with them, bringing the entire family, with the exception of Gansevoort and Tom, into the same home. That arrangement lasted for two and a half years or so. When Herman and Lizzie moved to Pittsfield, his mother, Helen, Gus, and Fanny came to live with them on their farm, Arrowhead, while Kate remained in the city with Allan and Sophia. Although the press of nine adults in the same house in New York and of six at Arrowhead must have taxed the patience of all, they bore the strain and seemed generally happy to do so. Helen moved out when she married in 1854, after which, in 1855, Mother Melville, Gus, and Fanny moved to Gansevoort, leaving Herman, Lizzie, and their children alone.

This communal living resulted in an intimacy between the Melville family and Allan's wife Sophia and an even greater intimacy between them and Herman's wife Lizzie. It also involved Herman's mother and sisters in his literary career. Safeguarding the sanctity of his study and making fair copy of his works from the vile orthography of his originals were family projects and his friends were their friends. There was a notable period in the early 1850s when Herman was a friend of Nathaniel Hawthorne and a fairly close acquaintance of Oliver Wendell Holmes, Sr., but it is no less true that Mother Melville, Helen, Gus, Fanny, and Lizzie knew them as well.[14]

One result of the congregation of the Melvilles in New York City was their relationship with the family of Allan's wife. The friendship of the Melvilles with the Thurstons did not end with the death of Sophia. The families were still tied together through Allan: with nieces and nephews of the Melvilles in the Thurston family, and with nieces and nephews of the Thurstons in the Melville family, the original relationship continued as though Sophia were still alive. Allan was still a brother-in-law to the younger Thurstons, and the special status that Herman, his mother, his brothers, his sisters, and Lizzie enjoyed with them continued as well.[15]

The most remarkable of the Thurstons, though a member of the family by marriage only, was Richard Lathers, a successful financier. Just over two years younger than Herman, he had been born in Ireland of a Protestant family but raised in South Carolina. In the South he was a Golden Boy who, at the age of twenty, was elected colonel of a South Carolina militia regiment and made a warden of the Episcopal Parish Prince George Winyah. Then he moved to New York City as commission agent for Charleston cotton factors, married Abby Thurston, and moved back to South Carolina for a year, where his firstborn was cared for by one of his slaves. After his return to New York City, he opened a commission and insurance business of his own and later organized the Great Western Marine Insurance Company. Being president of this firm made him a member of the city financial elite, and directorships in corporations, such as the New York and Erie railroad, followed. Richard's connection to the Thurstons gained him an entrée into the Bond Street set, made up of such notables as Senator John A. Dix and the literary lion Dr. John W. Francis. That in turn brought him into contact with such prominent authors as Washington Irving and James Fenimore Cooper, while the Melvilles introduced him to the intellectual circle formed around George and Evert Duyckinck. Richard's was not the self-conscious cultural dabbling of a businessman, but a patrician's interest in art. At one time or another he studied architecture briefly, collected art and painted, studied the flute, and practiced ornamental gardening.[16]

Richard was a fervent Democrat. A familiar figure at Tammany Hall, he gained a reputation as a Wigwam orator and he moved easily among the prominent figures of the state party such as Dix, Greene C. Bronson, and Horatio Seymour. However, he was an unabashed Southern Democrat who announced publicly that he agreed with the ideas of John C. Calhoun. Because Dixie was always in his heart, he argued the Southern point of view—probably with Herman—loyally and sincerely, as long as argument was possible.

By 1859 he had moved into a spacious estate, Winyah, in New Rochelle, whence he commuted to work by rail. He was well-to-do, with five Irish servants, a maid, a nurse and tutor for his son and three daughters, two cooks, and a coachman. Richard visited Herman in Pittsfield, Herman visited him in New York City, and other members of the Melville family were welcome at Winyah. There can be little doubt that Richard read Herman's works, and he probably admired them. Richard must have been Herman's model of the businessman. When in *Billy Budd* he excused businessmen from his class of adulterated "men of the world" (87), he probably had Richard in mind.[17]

The Thurston family matriarch, Rachel Thurston, was the widow of a Newport, Rhode Island, banker who had retired to New York City. She had been a friend of Mother Melville since the marriage of her daughter to Allan, she was a grandmother of Allan's children, and she still held a mortgage on one of Allan's properties. Her oldest son, Charles Myrick Thurston, Jr., was just Herman's age. He was a merchant in the city until 1856, when he retired with his wife Caroline to "Lathers Hill" in New Rochelle. As brother-in-law, neighbor, and companion of Lathers, he would have seen the Melvilles when they visited Winyah. A sister, Rachel, plays no part in this study, but she remained close to Allan and exchanged visits with him. She was the wife of Charles C. Barrington and the mother of a third Rachel, now a fifteen-year-old who was a favorite in the Thurston family. The youngest of the Thurston children was Alfred Henry Thurston, who in 1859 was twenty-seven years old. A graduate of Columbia University and the Medical College of New York, he practiced medicine in the city and served on the staff of New York Hospital. In 1856, he married Eliza Blunt, who bore him a son, Nathaniel.

Enates

Outside of the branch of the family headed by Mother Melville, the Dutch Gansevoorts were Herman's closest relatives, for after some indecision he and his siblings had finally concluded that they were more nearly Gansevoorts than they were Melvills. Of the sons and the lone daughter of old General Gansevoort, the oldest was Uncle Herman, who had inherited his father's badge of the Order of the Cincinnati and membership papers signed by George Washington. Herman was particularly fond of him and had dedicated *Omoo* to him. In 1859, Uncle Herman was eighty years old and able to do little more than to lie on his couch during the day while Mother Melville, Gus, and Fanny, cared for him. The next oldest was seventy-eight-year-old Uncle Wessel, "a strange excentric man" whose kinked personality was a trait that surfaced from time to time among the Gansevoorts. In 1859, he was living the life of a remittance man at Lapham's tavern in Danby, Vermont, where, in an obscurity so dim that Lapham did not even know whence he came, he was approaching the end of his years.[18]

The senior continuing line of the Gansevoorts consisted of the children of the third brother, Uncle Leonard, who had died in 1821. There were three surviving sons, all unmarried, and a daughter, Kate, who, despite indifferent health, was a woman of strength around whom her brothers gathered. Some five years older than Herman, she was said to bear a striking resemblance to Mother Melville. She was married to George Curtis, a Vermont native fifteen years her senior. During Herman's residence in New York City, nearly the whole of this branch of the family had lived in Brooklyn while George Curtis practiced law in New York City with his brother Edward. Politically, the Curtis brothers were powerfully connected: a Whig, Edward (now dead) had been a member of Congress from 1837 to 1841 and collector of customs for the Port of New York from 1841 to 1844. That suggests that by 1859 George Curtis may have been a Republican, but in truth nothing more is known about the politics of this branch of the family.[19]

Kate and George Curtis had three children, Edward (Ned), twenty-one, Mary, sixteen, and Martha (Mattie), eleven.[20] In 1859, they were preparing to move from Brooklyn to Glens Falls, New York, which was to be George's retirement home. Glens Falls was only about eight miles north of Gansevoort along the railroad, though after they were settled in the town the Curtises made the easy carriage drive to visit the Melville women and Uncle Herman. In a departure from the normal family unity, they were distant from the Albany Gansevoorts, described below, both because of their long residence in Brooklyn and because of an old financial quarrel that had left wounds.

The youngest of Kate Curtis's brothers was Stanwix, thirty-seven. Another of the family eccentrics, he was a graceless, irritable man who may have been given to drink. He had served in the navy for six years but had resigned, supposedly after fighting a duel with the son of Stephen Decatur. Now, afflicted with arthritis, he was living alone in a rented room in Glens Falls. The next older brother was forty-three-year-old Leonard. After a sea career somewhat like Herman's, ill health had forced him to seek a living ashore. No doubt through the good offices of his brother-in-law, Edward Curtis, he had been appointed an inspector in the New York Custom House in the spring of 1841. His removal for political reasons in January 1854 may have provided Herman with a model for the disillusioned "discharged custom-house officer" in chapter three of *The Confidence-Man*. Thereafter, Leonard does not seem to have been employed anywhere. Now he was moving to Glens Falls with the rest of his family.

The oldest of Kate Curtis's brothers, seven years Herman's senior, was Commander Guert Gansevoort, U.S. Navy. In terms of primogeniture, he was the ranking Gansevoort male of his generation, the one next in line to receive the Order of the Cincinnati when Uncle Herman died. The only living hero of the family, he was, excluding Herman, its most interesting member.[21]

After his appointment as a midshipman when he was only twelve years of age, Guert had served on most of the waters patrolled by the navy in most of the types of oak-hulled, sail-propelled warships then in service, from the smallest to the line-of-battle ship, and he also had limited experience aboard steamers. Like all of his naval contemporaries, he had endured extended periods of inactivity ashore awaiting billets at sea, to the point that in his thirty-five years of service he had been at sea only sixteen or so. What is unfortunately the best-known event of Guert's career occurred aboard the U.S. Brig *Somers* in the late fall of 1842, while Herman was at sea. While the brig was en route to the coast of Africa, Guert, then a lieutenant and the brig's executive officer, heard a rumor that Midshipman Philip Spencer, the son of the secretary of war, was plotting with two enlisted men to seize the ship and convert her into a pirate cruiser. The captain, Commander Alexander Slidell McKenzie, placed Guert in charge of an informal investigating board which, apparently under pressure from the captain, reluctantly substantiated the rumor. Then, without a trial, McKenzie hanged the three men.

The result was a scandal in which parties both sympathetic and unsympathetic to the ship's officers formed. Secretary Spencer was implacably among the latter, as were many others, including James Fenimore Cooper. The New York City newspapers reported developments daily, and the entire nation focused its attention on the case and on the officers who had presided over the melancholy event. When a court of inquiry recommended that Captain McKenzie be tried by a general court-martial, Guert, with the help of Samuel F. DuPont, an influential officer in Washington, arranged to be included as a defendant in order to forestall the civil suits that seemed inevitable. The court exonerated both men on the ground that naval vessels must be safeguarded from mutinies, but Guert was traumatized by the experience. Thurlow Weed, a family friend, claimed that it "had told fearfully upon his health and habits." Although Guert had been "a bright, intelligent, high principled, and sensitive gentleman, and a most promising officer of the navy," in later years he became "a sad wreck of his former self . . . moody, taciturn, and restless." Perhaps, as Weed hinted, this experience had brought on Guert's drinking. Guert would never discuss the mutiny with Herman. As a consequence, in his poem "Bridegroom Dick" Herman coined a name for him that memorialized both his silence and his drinking: Tom Tight (174–75).[22]

Guert redeemed himself when, on March 9, 1847, he led a landing party from the *John Adams* in the amphibious assault on Vera Cruz, Mexico. In an incident Herman recalled proudly in "Bridegroom Dick," Guert was among the first to raise the flag of the United States on the beachhead: "Where's Guert Gan? Still heads he the van? / As before Vera-Cruz, when he dashed splashing through / The blue rollers sunned, in his brave gold-and-blue, / And, ere his cutter in keel took the strand, / Aloft waved his sword on the hostile land!" (169–70). But in mid-1855, Guert's name came before a naval reform board charged with eliminating from the service those officers who were not competent to do their "whole duty." Most of those in peril had been reported for drunkenness, gambling, failing to pay their debts, and other ungentlemanly conduct, but some had simply spent too little time at sea. Curiously, the list included some of the greatest officers in the history of the service, Matthew Fontaine Maury, the noted scientist, John A. Dahlgren, distinguished ordnance pioneer and Civil War commander, Raphael Semmes, during the war the feared predator of the Confederate commerce raider *Alabama,* Henry A. Wise, a wartime bureau chief, and James H. Ward, an inventor and an early martyr of the war. Of all of these, Guert received the gentlest treatment, perhaps in part because his friend Captain DuPont was a member of the board. Although he was described as a "smart drinker," no one voted to remove him.[23]

Shortly thereafter, Guert took command of the U.S. Sloop *Decatur* at Seattle and of the other sea and land forces in Puget Sound. An Indian uprising in progress came to a boil on January 26, 1856, when Seattle was surrounded and attacked. Guert fought off the Indians, firing broadsides of grape, canister, and round shot from his ship and battling them from a blockhouse ashore. A newspaper correspondent wrote that "Capt. Gansevoort has proved himself as good a general as he is a thorough sailor. No one could have exceeded him in the skillful manner in which everything was arranged and conducted." Upon reading the official report, the secretary of war thanked the secretary of the navy.[24]

On the morning of August 18, 1856, while the *Decatur* was at the navy yard at Mare Island, California, the yard commandant, Commodore David G. Farragut, discovered Guert drunk aboard his ship. Summarily ordering another officer to take command, Farragut sent Guert home to await orders. When Guert's squadron commander heard the news, he wrote that he "was not surprised to hear of the circumstances, having long known indirectly that his [Guert's] habits in this respect are bad." Although the incident was common knowledge within the navy, Guert's family seems to have known little or nothing about it. Consequently, they did not realize that in his case awaiting orders meant that he was in disgrace. At the end of 1859 he was still awaiting them, preparing for permanent retirement by purchasing a sumptuous home and furnishings in Glens Falls.[25]

Herman felt a seaman's affinity with this well-salted cousin who had seen the blackness of darkness. Although he regarded Guert as an epitome of military gallantry, Allan was even closer to him, on one occasion acting as his attorney.[26] Guert's politics are not known, but beneath the neutrality that military officers affected lay a conservatism that differed little from Democratic dogma.

The youngest surviving son of the old Revolutionary general was his seventy-one-year-old namesake, Peter Gansevoort, the patriarch of the Albany, New York, Gansevoorts. At the end of 1859, he was traveling in Europe with his second wife, Susan, and the two living children of his first marriage, Henry and Catherine. The trip was both a result and a commemoration of Uncle Peter's retirement from his law practice during the year. Of the Gansevoorts of his generation, Uncle Peter was the best educated, a tribute to an intelligence and a steadiness of purpose that were not always combined in his family. After graduating from the College of New Jersey, or Princeton, he became a lawyer and a politician. Although in 1810 he had described himself as a Federalist of sorts—Allan Melvill, Herman's father, had earlier said the same thing, leaving later generations to wonder what he had meant by such an unlikely statement—Uncle Peter became active in the Democratic Republican party and in its principal successor, the Democratic party. His earliest loyalty was to Governor Dewitt Clinton, whom he served as private secretary, earning himself a two-year appointment to the post of judge-advocate general of the state of New York. Thereafter, in the usage of the times, he was permitted to prefix the title "General" to his name. When it suited his purposes he did so, affecting without shame the rank that his father had won through valor in the Revolution, and behind his back his children referred to him facetiously as "the general." Subsequently, he allied himself with Martin Van Buren in the powerful Albany Regency that controlled the state Democratic party. That made him a colleague of such men as William H. Seward, John A. Dix, and Thurlow Weed. Although by 1859 both Seward and Weed had joined the Republican party, they remained friends of Uncle Peter. An unquestioning loyalist to Democratic platforms and candidates, Uncle Peter held a number of offices, including seats in both houses of the legislature and on the court of common pleas of Albany County. As a result of this latter position he also used the more seemly title of "Judge."

He gradually assumed the Gansevoort family leadership, taking upon himself the joint obligations, perhaps impossible to fulfill, of preserving the memory of the family's heroic past (for the most part compacted into the one grand Revolutionary moment when old General Gansevoort had defended Fort Stanwix) and of perpetuating the family's prosperity. His home was filled with the old General's memorabilia, his uniform, his swords, his camp cot, his carriage, his portrait and that of his wife by Gilbert Stuart, the flag that his soldiers had brought him from the Yorktown surrender, and a tomahawk from the great defense. Although he suffered reverses, years when the volatile economy of the young nation turned his wisest investments into crushing debts, Uncle Peter managed to recoup his fortune. By 1859 he was as wealthy as he had ever been. In early 1861, he noted that his estate amounted to $60,000, not including $20,000 in stocks, and he kept three Irish house servants.[27]

For Herman, Uncle Peter, like Uncle Herman, was a symbolic presence of the old Dutch family. Over six feet tall, he was imposing, quick-tempered, sometimes cranky, persistently pompous—a figure who terrified Herman's youngest daughter, Fanny—but his shortcomings were mitigated by his winning manner. He had acted the part of a surrogate father to Herman and his brothers during formative years: after the death of Herman's father, Mother Melville and her brood had lived for several years on Clinton Square, only two doors from Uncle Peter. Uncle Peter was a trustee of the Albany Academy: the Melville boys attended it. Uncle Peter was a director of the New York State Bank: Herman obtained a clerkship there. As to his later relationship with Herman, it took some of its character from the fact that Uncle Peter, who at Princeton had been a member of the Cliosophic Society, a literary and debating club, and who had been a friend of James Fenimore Cooper, genuinely liked Herman's earlier fiction and called him "Typee." It may be, too, that Uncle Peter had an inkling that the future fame of the family, which concerned him greatly, might be secured as much by Herman as by anyone else in that generation.[28]

Uncle Peter's wife, Susan Lansing, was an old-fashioned Dutch housewife—the Lansings were Dutchmen, too—matter-of-fact and domestic. When Uncle Peter married her, his son Henry was only nine years old and his daughter Catherine four, so their upbringing was entrusted to her. Both of them treated her as though she were their natural mother.

At the age of twenty, Catherine (whom Herman called "Kitty" until she outgrew the nickname, then "Kate") was not long out of school—she had studied briefly at Mrs. Sedgwick's, in Lenox, Massachusetts, only a few miles from Herman's farm, but had finished her education in Albany. One of the reasons for the current tour of Europe was to augment that education. Young and romantic, she enjoyed the poetry of the historic lands as much as she enjoyed the shopping sprees in which she and Aunt Susan lavished Uncle Peter's money on souvenirs, clothing, and new furnishings for the family mansion. Following Uncle Peter's example, Kitty immersed herself in family tradition, venerating her father and worshipping her brother. Under the guidance of her father, she was a vehement Democrat.

Tall, self-confident, and engaging, Henry was twenty-five, well past the age at which, according to his father's timetable, he should have established himself as an industrious, responsible adult. Although he belonged to the same generation as Herman, he was young enough to have been a member of the succeeding one, and with the failure of male offspring that was endemic among the descendants of the old general it appeared that whatever children he sired might be the only ones to perpetuate the family name and to wear the Order of the Cincinnati. He was a Democrat, although he viewed politics less as the engine of government than as a useful system of connections and influence.

Henry was spoiled and rebellious. After a worrisome youth, he entered Princeton, where he, too, joined the Cliosophic Society. After he graduated with distinction in 1855, his father wanted him to become a lawyer. Henry was not convinced that it was proper for a gentlemen to engage in the requisite grubbing and groveling, but his father nudged him into an upstate law office. In 1856, Henry received a reprieve to attend the Harvard Law School, where he remained until mid-1858, when he was packed off to New York City to confront the law once more. Then, just as it appeared that he was condemned to a life of litigative drudgery, he accompanied his family on their Grand Tour, even though by doing so he risked being clasped in their uncomfortable embrace. At the end of 1859 he was with his parents and his sister in Rome.[29]

Henry was too independent to be obedient, but it is also true that the

Gansevoort tradition stifled him. If he was egotistical and selfish, he was also intelligent, romantic, and a victim of his father's insistence that because of their Revolutionary ancestry the Gansevoorts were aristocrats. What poisoned Henry for the life of endeavor that his father expected of him was his unwillingness to recognize the subtle distinction, clear to his father, between the hereditary aristocracy of the Old World and the renewable aristocracy of the New. Though his father was impatient for him to earn his own rank, albeit with the help of his family credentials, Henry wished to live the life of a gentleman, rejecting the labor among detail and the service to a peevish clientele that the practice of law entailed. Neither the attitude of the father nor that of the son was unusual, but Henry's rendered him nearly incomprehensible to his father and his sister.

Aunt Susan remained close to her lawyer brother, Christopher Yates Lansing, so much so that when the Gansevoorts and the Lansings were in Albany at the same time they dined together at least once a week. Yates had a twenty-five-year-old daughter, Anna, and four sons, Abraham, twenty-seven, twenty-six-year-old John, who had for some years been a merchant and U.S. consul in a Peruvian port, William, twenty-three, and Edwin Yates, nineteen.[30] Little is known of Will except that he followed in his father's profession. Abe, on the other hand, was especially close to the Gansevoort family. After attending Berkshire schools and the Albany Academy, Abe graduated from Williams College in 1855, and then read law in his father's office, graduating from the Albany Law School in 1857. He was capable, eventually earning his share of distinctions, but he was frail, sensitive, and delicately balanced. It need hardly be said that, granted the politics of those around him, he was a fervent and active Democrat. Not only was he Henry's cousin by marriage, but he was also his good friend, and through his family connection, strengthened by his eventual marriage to Catherine, Abe was also a friend of Herman. At the end of 1859, Edwin was probably already studying engineering at Rutgers College, which inspired the Albany Gansevoorts to tease him with the epithet "the eminent Engineer"—although, for no known reason, they also called him "the Major." Despite his youth, he was already tall, handsome, charming, and universally liked, though less substantial than Abe. Herman knew him, as, indeed, he knew all of the members of this branch of the Lansing family, and by the end of the war he knew him very well indeed.

Agnates

Less information is available about Herman's Melvill relatives, who, despite the orthographic affectation of Herman's branch of the family, retained the original spelling of the family name. His aunt Mary D'Wolf, who had died in July at the age of eighty-one, had lived on a small farm near Brighton, Massachusetts, with her eighty-year-old husband, Captain "Nor West" John D'Wolf, a cheerful old salt-water skipper. After her death, Uncle D'Wolf moved to Dorchester to live with his daughter, Nancy Downer, her husband, Samuel Downer, and his six granddaughters. He also had a son, John Langsdorff D'Wolf, and a daughter-in-law, Mary Davis D'Wolf, who were childless. In 1859, Uncle D'Wolf may have been writing his *A Voyage to the North Pacific,* which was published in 1861. Herman had another aunt in Boston, Priscilla Melvill, a spinster who, at the age of seventy-five, was nearing the end of her days. Then there was his Aunt Jean, seventy-one years old, who had married a man by the name of Knight and who also lived in Boston. The two youngest of the aunts were sixty-one-year-old Helen Melvill Souther and sixty-four-year-old Lucy Melvill Nourse. Aunt Helen resided with her husband, sixty-five-year-old Levitt Souther, a master carpenter, in a respectable house in Hingham, on the coast south of Boston. Living with her were two unmarried daughters, probably Souther's children from an earlier marriage. Aunt Lucy was living in Bath, Maine, with her second husband, Doctor Amos Nourse.[31]

Of all of these, Uncle Nourse, also sixty-five, was the most active and the most notable. A Harvard graduate who had become an obstetrician, a close friend of Herman's father-in-law, and an admirer of Herman's sea yarns, he had been a resident of Maine for over forty years. In 1846 he had been appointed lecturer in obstetrics at Bowdoin College and in 1855 professor, but he had also been both a Democratic and a Republican politician. From about 1828 to about 1842, mostly under Democratic administrations, he served as postmaster of Hallowell, Maine, and later President Polk appointed him collector of customs for the Port of Bath. But like his friend Hannibal Hamlin, his opposition to slavery led him into the new Republican party, and in early 1857 he was elected on the Republican ticket to serve out Hamlin's unexpired term (of a little over a month) as U.S. senator when Hamlin became governor of Maine. Although Hamlin changed his mind and reclaimed his Senate seat, Uncle Nourse was still entitled to use the title "Senator." Needless to say, during the war he had access to the Lincoln administration. Information about the Nourse children is sketchy, though there were at least two daughters. Clara, unmarried; was opening or had opened a school in Cincinnati, Ohio; Mary had married and was the mother of at least two children, Jeannie and Walter. She was living in or near Boston.[32]

The branch of the Melvill family with which Herman had historically been closest was the one that was now the farthest away, the family of his late Uncle Thomas. They lived in and near Galena, Illinois. As youngsters, Herman and his brothers were frequent visitors to Uncle Thomas's farm in Pittsfield, and in 1840, after the family moved to Galena, Herman and a friend visited them there. Uncle Thomas's widow was sixty-three-year-old Aunt Mary Ann Augusta Hobart Melvill. Orphaned as a child, she had been raised by her grandfather, Major General Henry Dearborn. Dearborn had been a distinguished public figure in the early days of the republic, an officer of field rank in the Continental Army, a congressman, the secretary of war under Thomas Jefferson, and the senior general of the army during the War of 1812. His close relationship with Herman's grandfather Melvill when both were officers in the Boston Custom House had resulted in Aunt Mary's marriage to Uncle Thomas. Her oldest natural son, Robert, was two years older than Herman and had in earlier years been his particular friend. Robert remained in Pittsfield with his wife Susan after the rest of the family went west and was still living there, along with his mother, his unmarried sisters, and his "idiot" half-brother, when Herman moved to town and boarded with him. Before long, however, Robert sold the farm to the Morewoods and moved the whole lot back to Galena. After a few tentative years there, Robert turned to the river, becoming a steamboat clerk and later a captain on the Galena to St. Paul route at the same time that Samuel Langhorne Clemens was working as a river pilot. For the most part, Robert's brothers were businessmen in Galena. Since none of them served in the armed forces during the war, their significance to this study lies mainly in the fact that they would of necessity have been acquaintances of Ulysses S. Grant, who for a year before the war belonged to their class of merchants and did business alongside them in Galena.

Although Herman had been close to these cousins, time and distance had dimmed the relationship. Nevertheless, he heard from them, and there is a strong possibility that he visited them in 1859, when a lecture tour took him through Illinois. He would have preserved pleasant memories of Robert and perhaps of a few of the others near his own age, but the youngest he had known only as small children. Also, the Galena Melvills were a different breed from many of the relatives to whom he was closer in time, space, and emotion: they represented a strain of New England culture that was recessive in his own family. Although they had been Democrats, in Galena Uncle Thomas had turned Whig, a politics that suited his Episcopalian background. By 1859 the whole family were probably Republicans.

There was another small group of relatives, distant ones, in Rockford, Illinois. Having failed to prosper in his native Maine, the brother of Aunt Mary Melvill, fifty-five-year-old Thomas Jefferson Hobart, or "Jeff," had moved to Rockford, where he had worked as a carpenter for several years.

His wife, Drusilla (or Drusella), was forty-nine years old, his son Randolph, a sickly man, was twenty, his son John was eighteen, and his two daughters, Mary and Ella, were sixteen and thirteen, respectively. Politically, the Hobarts' experience was similar to that of Doctor Nourse. Lifelong Democrats (as suited the name "Thomas Jefferson"), their antislavery sentiments drew them into the Republican party. There can be little doubt that Herman knew Jeff Hobart, who had attended school in Lenox, Massachusetts, near the Melvill farm in Pittsfield, and perhaps his sons and daughters, too, though he may not have known any of them very well. However, it is probable that Jeff had some part in arranging Herman's lecture stop in Rockford in 1859, and it is equally probable that Herman stayed at the Hobart home while he was there.[33]

The Shaw In-Laws

Herman's father-in-law, seventy-eight-year-old Lemuel Shaw, was chief justice of the supreme court of Massachusetts, though at the end of 1859 it was apparent that advancing old age would soon force him into retirement. A native of Barnstable, Massachusetts, Shaw had graduated from Harvard in 1800, after which he had been admitted to the Massachusetts bar. In addition to being a successful lawyer, he served in both houses of the state legislature and performed other public duties, such as drafting the city charter of Boston, before being appointed chief justice in 1830. Not a brilliant man, but intelligent, thoughtful, forceful, and uncompromisingly logical, he made himself a place in history through his seminal judicial decisions. In his presence, Shaw was well fitted for his office. Clean shaven and sober countenanced, he gave the impression of massiveness. On the bench that impression was heightened by his gruffness. When Ben Butler, a prominent Democratic attorney, was asked where he was going with his large mastiff, he answered that he was taking him to the courthouse to show him the chief justice "so as to teach him to growl." Or so the story went. Nevertheless, Shaw was kind and affectionate with his family.[34]

Herman's relationship to Shaw was more than simply that of a son-in-law. As a young man, Shaw had been close to Herman's Melvill family and had been engaged to one of old Major Melvill's daughters. The intended alliance failed with her death, but the relationship between Shaw and the Melvills continued almost as though he had married her. He was a friend and confidant of Herman's Uncle Thomas and later of Uncle Thomas's widow and children, and he was also a friend of Uncle Nourse and an acquaintance of Uncle Peter Gansevoort. Thus it was not by chance that in 1847 Herman married his daughter Elizabeth, nicknamed "Lizzie," and that thereafter the two men maintained a close personal and financial relationship. Herman's mother, hard put to support herself and her unmarried daughters, was not able to act the banker for her children, as parents often did and as she might have done under other circumstances, and Uncle Peter had his own family, and an expensive one at that, on which to spend his money—his generosity occasionally, but not often, extended beyond them. This being the case, Judge Shaw was the principal person who could and would act on behalf of Herman and his family.

Shaw had reason to sympathize with Herman's literary career. He had written poetry himself and had for a brief time been a journalist. Furthermore, his reading in English literature was extensive. Probably his major reservation about his son-in-law's career was that Herman's books did not sell well enough to provide adequately for his daughter and his Melville grandchildren.

Typical of his class, his place, and his time, Shaw was a Unitarian, a religious conviction that Lizzie inherited and Herman affected. It was also typical that Shaw had been a genuine Federalist in the first decade of the nineteenth century and that later by a natural transition he had become a Whig, but once on the bench he eschewed public political positions and party identifications. Still, his beliefs did not cease when he ceased to express them, though what they were at the end of 1859 cannot be known with certainty. Given his political origins, he should have made the transition to the Republican party, but if so he was remarkably unorthodox. A judicial decision (in 1851) to return a fugitive slave to his master and another (in 1849) to uphold racial segregation in Boston primary schools[35] could be explained as triumphs of legal principle over ideology, but a genuine abolitionist would have choked on such niceties. Finally, Judge Shaw's advocacy of renewed Northern enforcement of the Fugitive Slave Act as a means of averting Southern secession (see chapter 1) made him a bedfellow of the Democrats.

Of the Judge's second wife, sixty-six-year-old Hope Savage, there is little to say except that everyone who knew her liked her and considered her to be a sweet-natured woman—and that in private she was scornful of Herman's failure to provide better for Lizzie and her children. There were four Shaw offspring, two the children of the Judge's first wife and two the children of Hope. The elder two were John Oakes, a half year younger than Herman, and Lizzie; the younger were Lemuel, Jr., age thirty-one, and Samuel Savage, age twenty-six.

Oakes was a mediocrity who, during most of his adult life, depended for his livelihood upon government patronage, gained, in all likelihood, through his father's influence. After an early, unsuccessful attempt to establish himself in Chicago, at the beginning of 1849 he became an assistant coastwise clerk in the Boston Custom House. Although at some period in or after 1857 he seems to have been removed from office, he returned in or before 1861 and remained until 1881, at least. Oakes was married to Caroline Cobb and had two children, Josephine, age eleven, and another Oakes, age nine. He was civil to Herman, but he did not go out of his way to maintain a close relationship and he spoke disparagingly of Herman's fiction.

Lizzie's two half-brothers, Lemuel, Jr., and Samuel Savage, were embarked in more promising careers. Both were Harvard graduates, both were members of the bar, and in 1859 both were unmarried and living with their parents. Like Oakes, they had been brought up to think of the Melvills as friends of the family, nearly relatives. As a young man, Lemuel went through a brief period of enthusiasm for Herman, but as time passed the relationship cooled into the sort of cordiality that was expected between brothers-in-law. Furthermore, Lemuel's misunderstanding of Herman's fiction bordered on contempt. Without reading it, he consigned *The Confidence-Man* to "that horribly uninteresting class of nonsensical books he is given to writing—where there are pages of crude theory & speculation to every line of narritive—& interspersed with strained & ineffectual attempts to be humorous." On the other hand, beginning with a visit to the Melville home in New York City while he was still a schoolboy, Samuel developed a genuine affection for Herman. He continued to visit the Melvilles and to write to Herman, and Herman seems to have enjoyed his company. The two met in Europe in 1857, although they did not succeed in arranging to travel together, and soon after Sam's return to the United States he was visiting Arrowhead. If he had an opinion of Herman's fiction he left no record of it. Whatever their politics may have been, the younger Shaws were not moved by ideological fervor to participate in the war.[36]

Being a Democrat

Herman's family contained Republicans and suspected Republicans: the Hoadleys, the Griggses, and the Nourses certainly were, and the Shaws, the Glens Falls cousins, and the residue of the Melvill family could have been. The rest were solid, convicted Democrats: Uncle Peter and his family, Uncle Herman, probably, Herman's brothers, Allan and Tom, Richard Lathers, Mother Melville, Gus, and Fanny, and he bore in memory the stalwart role that his late brother Gansevoort had played in the party. As Augusta put it, "Herman has never been a politician, but he belongs to a Democratic family, & one which has done much for its party." That did not mean that they were slavishly orthodox. On one issue, nativism, on which Democrats demanded tolerance for the varied cultures that immigration brought into the country, Uncle Peter Gansevoort's family had reservations. When Henry wrote Kitty about the state of world affairs, suggesting that events might be leading toward Armageddon, she replied innocently that Armageddon would be different, a great battle pitting the Protestants on one side against the Mohammedans and the Catholics on the other—an idea far too parochial for a party that welcomed Catholics.[37]

The family cherished friendships among the white Southerners. The Gansevoorts had once owned slaves, and Henry and Kitty believed that blacks belonged to an inferior species. After a visit to Barnum's Museum, where Kitty saw a monstrous creature on exhibition, she described it as "a most disgusting object—supposed to be the link between the Negro & Monkey"; Henry, describing the low quality of the Union recruits, wrote that "Negroes, Germans and all the refuse of Gods Creation are now to fight for us. I fear the consequences much." Despite this bias, it is probably true that, with the exception of Richard Lathers, they did not altogether approve of black slavery. If the union could be held together in peace and good faith, in time slavery would wither and die, they thought. Despite her bigotry, Kitty Gansevoort espoused that view: "Let slavery stay where it is, for the present," she wrote. "Time will remove it in the South as in the North." The case was different with Richard Lathers. More fearful of the blacks than prejudiced against them, to the end of his life he argued the case for slavery—with prudence. He told the story of the supposed 1822 Charleston conspiracy, led by Denmark Vesey, in which thousands of black men planned to fire the city, assassinate the white men and black women, loot the city, and carry off the most desirable white women to Santo Domingo. Although the plot may never have been more than loose chatter among discontented blacks, and although Vesey may have had nothing to do with it, Lathers's story may have motivated Herman to write "Benito Cereno," despite the fact that the *source* of the story in the narrative of the historical Amasa Delano is well known.[38]

As was to be expected of a Massachusetts town, Pittsfield had its share of Republicans, but its proximity to New York, among other circumstances, insulated it from the radicalism for which greater Massachusetts was notorious. There were many Democrats, such as Herman's close friends, the Morewoods, and in 1860 some of them even voted the Southern rule or ruin Democratic splinter ticket. Herman's native city, New York, was notoriously Democratic; among his colleagues in the local literati, such as Evert and George Duyckinck, most were Democrats, and some of Herman's friends outside that circle were, too. Even though the Concord-Cambridge literati of Massachusetts were mostly abolitionists, Herman's one valued friend among them, Nathaniel Hawthorne, was a Democrat.[39]

Whether or not it is fair to call Herman a Democrat, it is nonetheless true that he saw the events of the war largely through the Democratic eyes of his family and friends. Uncle Peter may have overstated the case when he said that Herman had "always been a firm Democrat," but if so he was not far wrong. As noted above, families of that era formed political communities: one would not expect a Hoadley or a Griggs to be anything other than a Republican, for apostasy would have meant offending family and friends openly, brashly, ungratefully, and scandalously, and one would not expect the members of Uncle Peter's and Mother Melville's families—except for Kate Hoadley and Helen Griggs, wives who took the political coloring of their husbands—to be anything other than Democrats. And, indeed, the most telling evidence of Herman's political thought, the "Supplement" to *Battle-Pieces,* is clearly a Democratic treatise. That is not to say that Herman was active in any other way in the partisan struggles of the wartime years, or even that he engaged in normal political activity—Gus said that "it is well known that he has never voted in Mass., or taken any part in state matters." He was independent and politically negligent, but Democratically so.[40]

Oddly, the presence of Republicans in the family was not divisive. One countenanced Helen Griggs's occasional tirades because she was Helen, and one listened patiently to John Hoadley's rabid radicalism—and he did bring it into family discussions—because he was John Hoadley, and being either Helen or John was a powerful virtue. But it must also be said that Herman could not disagree with John's hatred of slavery, and in that he differed from the majority of those on his side of the political divide.

Like John, he opposed slavery and would not have condoned the racial prejudices of the young Albany Gansevoorts. As a young sailor on merchant and whaling ships he had sweated, skylarked, and berthed with men of all colors, and in his lectures he recommended travel as an education in sympathy with "people of all shades of color, and all degrees of intellect, rank, and social worth."[41] His affection and admiration for nonwhites is patent in much of his fiction, which includes a number of favorably depicted, sometimes noble dark-skinned characters. Some readers have claimed to find an antiblack bias in his "Benito Cereno," evil supposedly symbolized by the black skin color of mutinous slaves, but Herman simply did not employ that color convention, reserving other meaning for darkness and blackness. Another, more tenable reading of the story sees the slave leader Babo as a justifiably vengeful character who is also the philosophical spokesman of the work. To look at Herman's attitude in another way, it is all but predictable that a literary artist of his disposition, humanely curious about people of all sorts, will develop deeply felt, instinctive tolerances for his fellow man at his most exotic, and indeed it is difficult to find a wholly unsympathetic character in any of his works.

But as Carolyn Karcher has noted, Herman "could neither embrace abolitionism as a program nor abolitionists as fellow travelers." From the perspective of today, in which the tangled problem of black servitude in mid-nineteenth-century America seems to have had but one simple solution, that all men of good will *should* have demanded the immediate end of slavery, it is easy to criticize him, and thus to criticize the majority of the white Americans of that time. But Herman's refusal was a manifestation of two different aspects of his complex thought. First, his sympathies were too broad to distinguish black slavery as the special evil that in retrospect it seems to have been. For him, slavery was not only a specific evil but also, as Phillip Shaw Paludan has pointed out, "a metaphor for both chattel and economic bondage" of people of all races. The distinction between the particular exploitation and brutality to which slavery subjected the African in America and in many other places and the other tyrannies that he saw men visiting on their fellow men was only one of degree. He had made that clear in "Benito Cereno," both in his linkage of slavery to the rotting European feudalism represented by the *San Dominick* and in his subtle equation of the subjugation of the slaves of that ship with the subjugation of the "free" sailors of the *Bachelor's Delight*—both the skeleton of the slave owner and the American officer leading the attacking party of American sailors are associated with the deadly slogan "follow your leader," and in the assault mounted to subdue the mutinous slaves the white sailors and the blacks are slaughtered indiscriminately. Herman had made the same point in *White-Jacket: or, The World in a Man-of-War,* when he quoted a statement of John Randolph of Roanoke that "on board of the American man-of-war that carried him . . . he had witnessed more flogging than had taken place on his own plantation of five hundred African slaves in ten years," and when he caused White-Jacket to say that white men who had lived with the system of slavery were likely to have developed restraints in whipping sailors that were absent in others (141). In addition to the tyrannies that America had failed to eradicate, there were many other faults in the society, faults that irritated him sufficiently to write a series of reformist tales in the mid-1850s. In short, slavery was a noxious defect of the nation, but it was not the only one, not by far. Nor was he alone in thinking thus. Diarist George Templeton Strong, comparing slavery to the situation of some 200 women who perished in a Lawrence, Massachusetts, factory fire, wrote, "What southern capitalist trifles with the lives of his operatives as do our philanthropes of the North?"[42]

That said, Herman was committed to his country despite its failures, believing that the social perfection envisioned by the Founding Fathers could be approached only through slow, laborious effort, not by radical reform. He believed that, imperfect as it was, the United States still represented the great political hope for mankind. His conservatism was manifested in a desire to conserve the radicalism of the nation's founders, the revolutionary zeal of Jefferson and Madison. It is easy to forget that the Founding Fathers envisioned nothing less than the righting of all of the wrongs of old Europe, the establishment of a new, citizen-centered order to replace the old one that was hierarchy bound. Herman felt that the vision of the authors of the Declaration of Independence and the Constitution, embodied and perfected through the idealism and generosity of many generations of Americans, would reveal itself to be the new covenant with God. After all, if the exigencies of the moment had caused the framers of the Constitution to defer the elimination of slavery, they had also provided for its demise by granting suffrage to moral outrage.

This belief led Herman to Democratic orthodoxy on the export of American values. White-Jacket's vision of the destiny of the nation is hyperbolic, but it is nevertheless arguably Herman's:

> We Americans are the peculiar, chosen people—the Israel of our time; we bear the ark of the liberties of the world. . . . God has given to us, for a future inheritance, the broad domains of the political pagans, that shall yet come and lie down under the shade of our ark, without bloody hands being lifted. . . . We are the pioneers of the world; the advance-guard, sent on through the wilderness of untried things, to break a new path in the New World that is ours. . . . Long enough have we been skeptics with regard to ourselves, and doubted whether, indeed, the political Messiah had come. But he has come in *us,* if we would but give utterance to his promptings. . . . almost for the first time in the history of earth, national selfishness is unbounded philanthropy; for we can not do a good to America but we give alms to the world. (151)

In the light of this exhortation, Herman's celebration of the Mexican War, localized in the heroism of Cousin Guert at Vera Cruz, is of a piece with his conception of the American destiny; his outrage at the white colonization of the Pacific islands (as in his poem "To Ned," 200–201) was not an abrogation of his belief that the salvation of the world lay in its Americanization but rather a protest against the destruction, through the meddling of "Paul Pry" and his "Pelf and Trade," of primitive cultures and populations that had no tradition of European feudalism. In this commitment to the American experiment Richard Chase sees a search for a father that caused Herman to give filial allegiance to the Founders. Herman identified their spirit, Chase suggests, with that of "the St. John of the wilderness crying prophetic words of political wisdom," and feared nothing more, in a public sense, than the loss or perversion of that spirit. Thus his democratic ideals were linked to a deep respect for those who had institutionalized them and those who continued to do so. Lewis Mumford coined the word "aristodemocracy" for this posture.[43]

For Herman, America meant the North and the South together. In the late 1850s, the demands of the Northern radicals threatened to destroy the union by making it impossible for the two regions to coexist as one nation. In response, Herman questioned the merit of remedying one flaw in the national character at the cost of the nation itself. Would it not be better for the future of the slaves to preserve the grand experiment while working to remedy its defects? Was not gradual manumission preferable to irreversible rupture? What was the use of a victory now if it rendered unattainable a perfected world of tomorrow? If in modern times it is difficult to understand why a man of Herman Melville's generous nature would place any consideration above the immediate freedom of millions, to him there was ample reason for doing so. His position was not very different from that of Abraham Lincoln, who, although privately opposed to slavery, was willing to defer emancipation if by doing so he could preserve the United States.

The Mechanisms of Knowing and Caring

The experiences of Herman's family made up an important region of his Civil War world. Its members were remarkably well positioned—ideally, perhaps—to provide him with a comprehensive understanding of the conflict from the standpoint of the North. Guert Gansevoort performed a crucial service to the navy by helping to create the squadrons of warships that blockaded the Confederacy, but he also participated in the blockade, the navy's primary mission, as the captain of two of its ships. Also in the navy, Ned Curtis fought his way past the forts below New Orleans in Commodore Farragut's famous battle to open the Mississippi River. Early in the war Henry Gansevoort served in Washington as a militiaman, later in various Virginia campaigns as a regular army officer, and finally in the guerrilla-infested counties of northern Virginia as a colonel of volunteers. Henry Thurston served as an army surgeon, first in a militia regiment sent to Washington, then as a senior medical officer in the west, and finally in charge of a New York City hospital. For better or for worse, the Hobarts served in the western army as militiamen and volunteer infantrymen.

Among the civilians, Tom Melville captained a merchant ship in waters made perilous by Confederate commerce-raiders and Robert Melvill was an officer in the civilian riverboat fleet that carried supplies to army units along the Mississippi River. John Hoadley manufactured war materiel and traveled to England on a special government military mission. Uncle Nourse was a Republican politician, though he held no office in the federal government, and Uncle Peter was a prominent Democrat whose loyalty was impugned by the Lincoln administration. Richard Lathers was a Southern Democrat from the evil city of Charleston in the evil state of South Carolina—evil in the eyes of the North as the symbolic center of slavery and secession—but he also made a dramatic attempt to forestall the war and, later, made a speaking tour through Europe to defend the Union cause.

However, their experiences were relevant to Herman only to the extent that he knew of them and cared about them. That he did care was a function of the inner dynamic of the family. Although Democratic beliefs held many of them together, it is also true that a gravitational pull was exerted from within the galaxy itself. This was an age when the structural integrity of the group was valued and defended by its members: relatives were drawn together by an *a priori* assumption of the importance and permanence of their ties, by their geographical stability, and by an intense interest of each in the affairs of the others. This was especially true of Herman's large family, who were unified by their common descent from Revolutionary War veterans. Among them, Herman was particularly close to his relatives and he was scrupulous about observing family protocol, so much so that he was exempt from the reproaches that were occasionally meted out for perceived neglect. Privately, he might view the web of relationships critically and chafe under its constrictions, and he might view individual relatives with a critical eye, but he was loyal, tolerant, and affectionate toward them and they reciprocated his affection—if not always his tolerance.

Some idea of their closeness may be gained from the examples of the two cousins most active in the war. Henry Gansevoort interested himself in Cousin Herman's authorship when he was only twelve years old, and for the rest of his life he continued to notice and to comment, sometimes approvingly and sometimes not, but always with respect, on his cousin's works: he loved *Typee,* which he compared to Samuel Johnson's *Rasselas*. When he was attending Harvard Law School, he behaved as though the Shaws and the Melvilles were his next of kin. Cousin George Griggs called on him at the university and walked him the three miles to the Griggs home, where Henry dined. Then shortly after Herman's return from his travels through the Middle East and Europe, he brought Lemuel Shaw, Jr., to see Henry. The next night Henry attended a sumptuous banquet at the Shaw home with Herman, Oliver Wendell Holmes, Sr., and R. H.

Dana, Jr., who chauffeured Henry back to his student quarters. When Aunt Melville arrived in Boston, Judge Shaw sent Henry a note to make sure that he knew, and before long Henry dined with her at the Griggs residence. Being at Harvard did not mean that he was away from home; with Cousins Herman and Lizzie Melville and George and Helen Griggs present, he celebrated Thanksgiving with the Shaws.[44]

When in October 1858 Henry moved to New York City, Cousin Allan Melville took charge of him. When Henry was ill, Allan looked in on him regularly, and when Allan fell ill in turn, Henry reciprocated. In January 1859, when Allan was out of town, Henry sent a report to his family in Albany detailing the birth and the appearance of Cousin Kate Hoadley's new baby. In the middle of February, after Tom Melville gave him a tour of the *Meteor,* Henry wrote his family about the visit. During this period, Henry saw both Cousin Herman and Aunt Melville at Allan's home. By March 1859, Henry was denying his sister's accusation that he was spending too much time at Cousin Allan's home, and he followed this denial with continued visits there.[45]

If Henry was a good example of family interaction, Guert Gansevoort was a bad one, since his natural moodiness and his tendency to withdraw had over the years been exacerbated by the humiliations he had experienced in the *Somers* scandal and aboard the *Decatur,* and also by a sense that in the absence of a father the seniority of his branch of the family was not always acknowledged. Yet Guert was nonetheless a loyal family member and an object of its interest. To give a few examples from the year 1862 (detailed in chapter 4) when he took command of a new ship, the family was abuzz. When they read about his assignment in the New York City newspapers, the Albany Gansevoorts made sure that all of the other aunts, uncles, and cousins knew about it. Then Uncle Peter and his family visited the Brooklyn Navy Yard to see Guert, and Allan Melville brought his family, children and all, out to inspect the ship. Later, the movements of the ship as it was being readied for sea were reported daily by Allan's law partner. Naturally, there was no channel of information to keep the family informed about his subsequent adventures at sea, but when his ship was lost the news zigzagged around his relatives as soon as it was known. The report that he had salvaged family photographs from his cabin before abandoning ship was accepted by all as evidence of his affection toward them.

Somewhere between these two examples lies a measure of the closeness of the family. Its members were important to Herman: from the schoolyard exploits and childhood diseases of his nieces and nephews to the civilian and military experiences of their parents and grandparents, the events of their lives were part of the fabric of his. Still, the fact that he cared about them is not enough. The question remains, what did he know about them and when did he know it? The answer is that because of a family communication network that operated efficiently—relentlessly—he knew within days almost everything of interest and much that was not. News was exchanged largely through letters and occasionally through telegraphy. A member of each family subunit—typically but not always the wife—wrote regularly to a member of each other family unit—again, typically the wife—and failure to do so brought reproaches. In addition, a family member communicated news he or she had received to others who might not know of it, sometimes enclosing the original letter with instructions to return it or to pass it on. Aiding the process was the rapid postal service, in which one-day delivery was the rule rather than the exception. As Helen Griggs put it, "What a comfort and blessing these family letters are! We each know all that occupies or interests the others."[46]

Information was also exchanged through visits, which were confidently expected and affectionately made: one did not pass through a city without giving advance warning to the relatives who lived there, visiting them, and, unless one were hurried or rude, dining with them and if possible spending the night. During such visits, the one dependable topic of conversation was family news. Kate Curtis frequently exchanged visits with Herman's family in nearby Gansevoort, during which the Melvilles were brought up to date on their activities and those of Ned Curtis and Guert. Herman heard about Guert through this channel and from Allan, but when he was in New York City he must have visited Guert often at the Brooklyn Navy Yard. On a number of occasions in midwar Herman also saw Henry Gansevoort. Herman visited his mother and sisters in Gansevoort regularly, in the process seeing Uncle Peter's family in Albany and calling on his cousins in Glens Falls, and his mother and his unmarried sisters frequently visited him in Pittsfield and in New York City. There was an annual summer gathering of the Melville daughters at Gansevoort, which, before Herman moved to the city, would have meant stops in Pittsfield to see him on the way to and fro. Others, such as John Hoadley and Allan, were frequent visitors to Pittsfield. On such visits, as well as in letters, Allan brought news about Henry Gansevoort, Guert, and Henry Thurston.

Aside from the war experiences of his relatives, many other important sources of the information contributed to Herman's war experience. One critic has speculated about "how eagerly he had scanned the newspapers for word from the various fronts, how anxiously he had studied the bulletin boards when he was in the city, with what intensity of feeling he had watched the regiments of young volunteers march away to the South";

another has decided that he must have responded to these impressions of the war with "unusual intensity." Both are correct.[47]

Despite his rural isolation, he had access to the weekly *Pittsfield Sun* and the *Berkshire County Eagle*. Although he was a close friend of the editor of the *Eagle,* he probably read both. Because the *Sun* was a Democratic paper whose editorial policies conformed more closely to Herman's own attitudes, for the purpose of this study the reports of that paper have most often been noted. During the last year and a half of the war, when Herman resided in New York City, he was well served by the dailies there, but it should be noted that even in Pittsfield the remarkably detailed and comprehensive news summaries in the weeklies provided him with ample news from all parts of the country, often descriptions of actions involving units as small as individual regiments. Often a Pittsfield soldier in the field appointed himself an unofficial correspondent, sending the local newspapers neighborly letters about the experiences of his company or regiment. The papers even printed news from the Confederacy: a routine exchange of Northern and Southern newspapers was conducted at Richmond, where a Union flag-of-truce boat from Fortress Monroe called regularly for the purpose.

More immediate bulletins came via the telegraph which, from day to day or hour to hour, informed Herman of the progress and results of military and naval battles. This was a modern novelty that accelerated the transmission of communications at a rate that has not been equaled since. During the Mexican War, even to a young writer who had the advantage of living in New York, the news of an event at the front arrived at home weeks later; but in the period between wars the age of rapid communication arrived. Despite the awkwardness of the system, which consisted of numerous short relays that required that messages be transferred from wire to wire, telegrapher to telegrapher, the effect was still rapid communication from one distant part of the nation to another. An important occurrence in Congress early in the day was reported to Maine or Minnesota while the session was still in progress, and news of an event in Missouri reached the streets of Philadelphia in a correspondingly brief time. As Oliver Wendell Holmes, Sr., put it, "the whole nation is now penetrated by the ramifications of a network of iron nerves which flash sensation and volition backward and forward to and from towns and provinces as if they were organs and limbs of a single living body." During the war, this was especially true in Pittsfield, where a routine was established that allowed Herman to read or to listen to important news as soon as the telegrapher had written it down. The result was astonishing. Herman could follow the fighting at Gettysburg as efficiently or more efficiently than he could have had he watched evening television news reports. That presupposes that he came into town every day, which he did—to pick up his mail.[48]

Small as the town was, in Pittsfield Herman also had firsthand experience of many aspects of the war. Lizzie and the children worked to support the soldiers, and early in the war, while he was still living on his farm, Herman drove his family to town to participate in patriotic events and to watch the soldiers drilling at the local training camps and cheer them on when they left on the trains. Many of these recruits were local volunteers, whom he must have known. Herman also encountered a number of other soldiers in Pittsfield, notably William Francis Bartlett, his "College Colonel." Through other means and in other places he also met soldiers such as Colonel Charles Russell Lowell, who invited him to accompany a cavalry scout; Brigadier General Robert Ogden Tyler, with whom he became acquainted at Tyler's field headquarters; Lieutenant General Ulysses S. Grant, whom he visited at his field headquarters; Captain George Henry Brewster, Allan's law partner; and Brewster's younger brother, Lieutenant Charles Brewster. Then there were Private Toby Greene, his old shipmate, with whom he corresponded and perhaps talked, and others too numerous to name. In this experience he was like most other people: "Although few parts of the North would experience the war firsthand." Paludan notes, "it was constantly in their hearts and minds."[49]

That Book and This Book

Richard Harter Fogle has concluded that Herman Melville's poems will "never be widely read," and thus far that has been true of *Battle-Pieces*. If it were to continue to be true in the future, American culture would be the poorer for it. Yet there are explanations for its neglect. With his imagination crammed as it was with information and experience, Herman might have written a lively poetic recreation of the war, one reeking with the fumes of burnt powder and jostled by the sights and sounds of waves of infantry, ranks of cannon, flights of cavalry, and files of warships in action. Many contemporary poets did just that, leaving behind them an enormous amount of "newspaper" verse, some of which finds a place in this book, but little of permanent value. Newspaper verse fulfilled the desires of readers for battles they could refight, stirring lyrics they could sing, satirical attacks on the South and on political rivals they could savor, celebrations of favorite generals they could cherish, causes and martyrs glorified or sanctified they could renew their allegiance to, sentimental accounts of the bravery of old folks, pubescent drummer boys, and grateful former slaves they could make real in their imaginations, pictures of bereaved families they could weep for, and spiritual uplift through which they could purge the ugliness of battlefield brutality. The fact that *Battle-Pieces* does little of this has encouraged the notion that Herman was somehow so preoccupied with abstract considerations that he missed the excitement and the significance of the struggle. One respected commentator has said that he "surveyed the conflict from his own lofty crow's-nest"—Herman would have said "house-top" rather than "crow's-nest," but the idea is the same.[50]

One might explain the dearth of rowdy, slapdash enthusiasm and bias, to be expected of poems written in hot haste, while the stench of battle remained in the poet's nostrils, as a function of the date of composition of *Battle-Pieces*. According to Herman's preface, most of the poems were written after the fall of Richmond, over five years after the earliest event treated in the book. Whatever emotions of shock, elation, fear, or loathing he may have felt in the immediacy of an event, in his poetry were recollected in tranquility. But the better explanation lies in the fact that *Battle-Pieces* is quite different in kind from other books of Civil War poetry. Because Herman was a romancer-turned-poet, his verse takes its departure from his earlier prose fiction. Studied, symbolic, and encyclopedically allusive, it understands events as increments of a larger, unified experience of the nation in which the war was a product of the American past and an anticipation of the nation's future. This impulse toward grand synthesis is reflected in the form of the book: it is not simply a collection of poems comprehended within the parameters of war but rather a coherent literary entity in which discrete poems, often related to other poems, form parts of a larger whole. As William H. Shurr has described it, the book "has a unity of its own, yielding further meaning which is not accessible to a reader who knows only anthologized selections." A complex of metaphors and images begins, repeats, transforms, and returns, so that the reader is not fully aware of what the book is saying or how it is saying it until after he has read all of the poems. In other words, each one is a member of the larger, more trenchant structure. As another critic has said, the book can (and should, he might have added) be "grasped as an entity."[51]

In its versification, too, *Battle-Pieces* defies convention. Its technique is original, eschewing the received poetic norms to which Longfellow, Whittier, Lowell, and Holmes conformed. Modern critics have been most impressed by its cacophony, its clangor, what Robert Penn Warren has called "the violences, the distortions, the wrenchings in the versification," and what William Bysshe Stein has irreverently described as "ugly discordance and incongruity—in meter, rime, image, symbol, and language." Perhaps Caroline Karcher has described it best: the verse form, she says, is "harsh, grating, constricted, oppressive, like the perceptions it articulates about this unprecedented national bloodletting." Yet harshness is only one element of its versatile style, which varies from poem to poem, sometimes within a poem. Some of the poems startle by their polish, as in the compelling blank verse of "The House-top," others are crude, and still others are neither—they are rhythmical recreations of emotion or intellect, as in one instance ("A Utilitarian View of the Monitor's Fight") in which both a ship and an age of iron mechanisms are suggested by clanking, metallic prosody. Warren concludes that Herman was "aiming at a style rich and yet shot through with realism and prosaism, sometimes casual and open and sometimes dense and intellectually weighted, fluid and various because following the contours of his subject, or rather the contours of his complex feelings about his subject."[52]

Another barrier to easy comprehension lies in the difficulty of interpretation of certain poems. The narrative voice can be deceptive because it is not necessarily the voice of the author. Rachel Whitesides Stewart has identified eleven of the seventy-two poems as dramatic monologues, but her estimate is far too conservative. As Herman wrote in his brief preface, "I seem, in most of these verses, to have but placed a harp in a window, and noted the contrasted airs which wayward winds have played upon the strings." These wayward winds are the varied and conflicting perceptions and attitudes of different kinds and persuasions of Americans, including those of Southerners, which together made up the American consciousness of those tragic times, and to confuse many of their perceptions and attitudes with Herman's own is as unwise as confusing the character of the speaker of "My Last Duchess" with that of Robert Browning. Karcher notes, correctly, that "Melville wanted to include all Americans—northern and southern, pro- and anti-Negro, black and white, young and old, idealistic and cynical, hopeful and pessimistic—in a comprehensive statement about what the war had meant to them." To the reader familiar with Herman's other works, this medley of voices is akin to the multivocal narrative of *Mardi,* in which various points of view are articulated by Yoomy, the poet, Babbalanja, the philosopher, Mohi, the historian, and Media, the king; but in *Battle-Pieces* the voices are those of a nation. Thus the book is a public rather than a private literary event, a counterpoint played on the ostensibly neutral Aeolian harp of Herman's imagination by the crosswinds of the war.[53]

That is no more than to say that the book is ambiguous. Although the ambiguity of Herman's works is a commonplace of criticism, the origin of that ambiguity is seldom discussed. It stemmed from his understanding of the complexity of experience and of the conflicts of values within his society. In *Moby-Dick* he could celebrate both Ahab's defiance and Ishmael's compliance; in "Benito Cereno" he saw the justice of the fury of the slave, the ugliness of his revenge, and the suffering of the former slaveowner; in *The Confidence-Man,* he argued both the nobility and the folly of trust in one's fellow man; and the ambiguities of *Billy Budd, Sailor,* are sufficient to make fierce partisans of otherwise genial readers. In another man, such multiple vision might well have led to intellectual shortcircuit and paralysis; in Herman, it led to a literature of layered complexity. Yet the clash of contrasting, indeed irreconcilable, views does not preclude the emergence of a presiding and mediating intelligence: resolution out of diversity. Whatever use he made of this habit of mind in his other works, it was eminently suited to his treatment of the Civil War, in which a diverse conflict of convictions was comprehended within the larger unity of a nation at war with itself.

About this book, the author hastens to reassure the reader that its political bias is reportorial rather than programmatic. As a part of the spoils of war, the Republicans wrote its history, encouraging future generations to adopt a radical view of its events and its participants. But most of the principal characters of this study, including Herman Melville, were conservative Democrats who understood the war quite differently. Because this book presents the issues of the war as seen through their eyes, it differs in important ways from current historical scholarship without intending to challenge it. As a hero of Herman and his circle, General McClellan, who was anathema to the Republicans, is accorded extended and favorable treatment. Again, the New York City draft riots of 1863 are pictured as Herman and other Democrats understood them, as an unfortunate but understandable civic disruption rather than as a vast eruption of malignancy, as the Republicans saw them and publicized them. Today this is an unusual point of view which may disturb readers—to some it will be distasteful. Yet in their defense, those close to Herman, with one exception, and Herman himself, were not in favor of slavery per se: their denigration of blacks was often (but not always) no more than a byproduct of their unfamiliarity with them and of their disapproval of abolitionists. The portrait of Abraham Lincoln painted here may disturb those for whom the martyred president is an untarnished and unassailable hero, yet it is true that, as he invented a wartime presidency for which there was no precedent, he committed errors. In sum, the attitudes herein presented do not represent the opinions of the author, whose voice is the messenger rather than the message. Privately, he opposes all of the tyrannies that Herman Melville opposed and some that were not perceived in his time. Specifically, he would not prolong the servitude of any woman, man, or child by a single day, nor would he persecute, impugn, debase, or humiliate any honest person of any race or kind. He admires Lincoln as a great American leader and as a consummate orator who articulated values which Americans can forget only to their impoverishment. But he would not wish one side of this greatest of American stories to remain untold.

It is the purpose of this study to place both the poet Herman Melville and his book into the context of their time and place and to suggest the intent of individual poems and of *Battle-Pieces* in its entirety. That does not permit the luxury of exegesis, which must be sought in other studies of the poems. Occasionally samples of the large body of contemporary verse, including popular stuff, are included for comparison with Herman's different and more successful poetic strategies. As stated above, the story of the war is told in terms of Herman's attitudes and experiences, so far as they can be known or estimated, but it is also told in terms of the attitudes and experiences of his relatives, those of Northern Democrats in general, and those of all Northerners, since, Democrat or Republican, New Englander or Ohioan, many were the fears, joys, and bereavements which transcended party and geography. The reactions to events of other members of the Northern literary community are also noted, those of abolitionists such as Emerson, Lowell, and Whittier, those of conservative Democrats such as Whitman and Hawthorne, and those of Holmes, whose egotism defies classification. All in all, the following pages tell the story of a region, a family, and a poet during the Civil War. In the course of them, a Herman Melville somewhat different from the received picture of the author will emerge, one who is earthier and more concerned with everyday events than previous portrayals would suggest, but that is not intended as iconoclasm. It is, rather, an attempt to paint an ordinary picture of an extraordinary man who lived his Civil War one day at a time.

1

Before the Fall
1859–1861

For Herman Melville, as for the United States, late 1859 was a critical period. The life of the author of *Moby-Dick* had reached a stasis of irresolution and frustration. In his discontent, he quarreled not only with God—or Fate—but also with himself, his family, his rural exile in Massachusetts, and the path his country was following, though he continued to cling to them all. His congenital diffidence was threatening to mature into the self-defensiveness of his later years. When two college students, Titus Munson Coan and John Thomas Gulick, attempted to interview him, he refused to speak of himself, instead lecturing them about the Homeric Age, which, he asserted petulantly, was the only satisfactory one. He concealed his despair behind his wry humor, but according to family tradition it revealed itself in his irritability at home.[1]

Physically, Herman was manly, with sailor agility and power but with weak eyes. Only a year and a half earlier, a reporter for the *Cincinnati Daily Commercial* had described him as "a well built, muscular gentleman, with a frame capable of great physical exertion and endurance." Almost two decades later, he was still so imposing that people often believed that he was six feet tall, though he lacked two or three inches of that. But his pride in his physicality had ebbed. The sciatica and "neuralgia" that had besieged him in mid-decade had become chronic; according to Lizzie, he was never again the man he had once been. Sensing his mortality, he blandished his infirmity by refusing to list himself in the annual Pittsfield militia census, a muster roll of the fit men of military age. Those on the list were not required to join the militia or to drill, only to come to the defense of Berkshire should that be necessary. Surely he could have done that, but his hypochondria whispered no.[2]

In addition, he had failed as a writer. His early tales of exotic adventure had pleased both the general public and his own family. For example, although she did not wholly approve of them, his Aunt Priscilla Melville was proud of his achievement.[3] But with his adventure into metaphysics, so-called, during the decade that was closing, his career had withered and died. The reading public had repudiated him and some members of his family were uncertain. They may or may not have understood the inner turbulence that had impelled him to create an art that long after his death brought the recognition that his own age denied him, but they were products of their time. To them, lofty literary achievement meant the polished conventionality of Bryant, Macauley, Tennyson, Thackeray, Longfellow, and the great American historians such as Irving, Bancroft, and Motley. Privately, his mother and his sisters probably wished that his literary genius were more like that of John Hoadley, serene and pure. Henry Gansevoort's Cliosophic standards made him admire elegance and literalism and to regret what he called Herman's Emersonianism, by which he meant obscurantism. The family understanding of literary art was akin to that of Thomas Wentworth Higginson, who believed that it was decorous and honorable to patch and plaster Emily Dickinson's ragged verse.

This combination of neglect by the public, of the belief of some in his family that his works belonged in the byways of literature, and of the certainty of the Shaws that better writing would have resulted in higher income, had ended Herman's decade-long career as a romancer. Sadly, the titan whose ambition it always was to sit alongside Shakespeare, Montaigne, and Milton had also to provide for a wife and children and to struggle to maintain a taxing gentility in a family in which he was the sole unprosperous breadwinner—a struggle in which he was not successful, as the family suppers of bread and tea, the graceless homemade dresses of the girls that Mother Melville made fun of, and, perhaps, the dunning bill collectors described in "Cock-a-Doodle-Do," attested. The conflict between Apollo, on the one hand, and Mammon and Mrs. Grundy, on the other, had damaged his art, his psyche, and his relationship with his wife. Although Lizzie seems to have been proud of his achievements without always understanding them, she dreaded the emotional crises that his writing brought about and she resented the fact that she and hers were the only mendicants of the two families. Herman's return in May 1857 from his voyage to the Near East and Europe marked the end point of his career. Before he had understood the extent of the public rejection of *The Confidence-Man*, he had contemplated writing more fiction, but he was not long in abandoning the idea.[4]

When he decided to end the labors that had drained his inner resources for so long he also planned to sell Arrowhead, his farm, to abandon his "Vere de Vere" gentleman-farmer life in Pittsfield, and to remove to Brooklyn, New York. Neither he nor Lizzie was satisfied with life at Arrowhead. Although he could chop wood and do other farm chores, he was not gifted in the peasant arts and he had grown to hate the work. Similarly, Lizzie, although she was obliged to maintain the household, was poorly prepared by her upbringing for drudgery. Nor was she by nature a country woman. While others in Berkshire wore pastoral costume, she affected "a great flapping hat tied under the chin," pastel dresses, and Boston party slippers. In addition to the burdens of farm life on the family, Pittsfield had become a lonely Elba for Herman since the days of his friendship with Hawthorne, when his mother and his sisters had lived with him, gone on excursions with him, and played interminable games of whist with him, and Aunt Mary A. A. Melvill and some of her children had resided nearby. It was not that he lacked friends—the *Berkshire County Eagle* described him as "very popular"—but he needed more than that, the kind of intimacy that his mother, sisters, and cousins had given him and the intellectual and literary stimulation of a Hawthorne.[5]

Now closest to him was the Morewood family. His acquaintance with them dated back at least to the time when Hawthorne had lived in Lenox. John R. Morewood, or Rowland, as he was called, was an English-born merchant, thirty-eight years of age, Sarah was a thirty-five-year-old New Jerseyite, and there were three children, William, Alfred, and Anne. Sarah's older sister, Ellen Brittain, completed the family. Their home, to which Kate Hoadley had given the name Broadhall (Herman had named the Morewood cows Molly, Polly, and Dolly), was an old eighteenth-century house on a thirty-five-acre estate near Arrowhead. It had belonged to Herman's Uncle Thomas and then to his children, and the pond on the property was still known as Melvill Lake. Rowland Morewood had an extensive library, which he made available to Herman, and Ellen Brittain had a secure place in the Melvilles' affections, but Sarah was the one to whom Herman and Lizzie were particularly attached, though Herman, whose ideas about women were skewed by nineteenth-century preconceptions, underestimated her earthiness. Unconventional in life and religion, she was something of an existentialist, a local poet, a fisherman and outdoorsman, and a resourceful organizer of festivities and frolics. However, her health was declining, to the point that she was often a virtual invalid. Even so, she continued to be a true friend, a vivacious hostess, and, later, a dedicated worker for the Union cause. But fond as Herman was of the Morewoods, they alone could not slake his thirst nor divert his search for the transcendent relationship that he never again, after Hawthorne, found. He wanted to return to the place of his birth; he was, he insisted, a New Yorker. Neither he nor Lizzie enjoyed the relentless social pressures of the metropolis, and Lizzie would have preferred Boston, but when the farm did not sell that became moot.[6]

Herman found the state of the nation no more satisfactory. Despite the lofty visions of the Founders, young America, the "bachelor" nation, had exhibited the serious deficiencies that he had placarded in *Israel Potter*, "Benito Cereno," "Bartleby," "The Paradise of Bachelors and Tartarus of Maids," "Poor Man's Pudding and Rich Man's Crumbs," "Cock-a-Doodle-Do," "The Two Temples," and *The Confidence Man*. He shared the notion, popular among such intellectuals as Emerson, Thoreau, Whitman, Horace Greeley, Henry Ward Beecher, and Henry Bellows, that its people had eschewed patriotism, morality, and republican simplicity and become proud and avaricious. If the nation continued to tolerate its defects, they might become fixed in its character. But his warnings had gone unheeded.[7]

He had experimented with the Lyceum circuit. Lecturing had held the promises of income and of surcease from his rural isolation, but his makeup was ill suited to public performance, a remarkable fact considering that he was by nature a gifted performer. In small groups of congenial friends, he could spellbind with his monologues. On one occasion, he so mesmerized the Hawthornes with an account of a battle between a whaling captain and some Polynesians that Sophia believed that he had been wielding a war-club, though he had not. Had Herman exploited this gift on the lecture platform, he might have become one of the more popular speakers of his age. Sometimes he seems to have come close. Henry Gansevoort attended two of his lectures, one in late 1857 and one in early 1859, writing of the first that Herman spoke "with animation and effect," and of the second that "he was emphatically himself, and the lecture was to me like a quantity tied together of his vivid and colloquial sketches, (always too short) told under the inspiration of madeira after dinner—or drawn forth by some proper association elsewhere." But before an audience of strangers he could be stiff and formal, sometimes reading his lectures in an almost inaudible monotone. When this mood was upon him, he was not an entertainer who could sweeten the sour of instruction with a dollop of amusement, and thus keep the dull awake while the keen profited. As a result, he was sometimes used badly by the newspaper critics, as in Rockford, Illinois, where he was subjected to a denunciation of the sort that he never learned to tolerate. But with commendable courage he had endured two years of the grind, not enjoying the work but not always despising it. The experience had an unanticipated value: it allowed him to travel through the country as he never had before and would never do again, and the nation that he saw was about to declare war on itself and thereby to undergo irreversible change.[8]

At the end of 1859, Herman was forty years old and Lizzie was thirty-seven. Although their marriage had been a love match, it had not been made in heaven. Socially, the two were equals, but their similarity of character undermined the happiness of Arrowhead. Herman was congenial and thoughtful outside of his home, and "kind" was the adjective that Augusta prefixed to the name "Lizzie," but the atmosphere within the home was often tense. Both Herman and Lizzie had what Kitty Gansevoort called a "nervous temperament"; both were hypochondriacs of a sort, Herman succumbing to psychologically induced illnesses and Lizzie utterly abandoning herself to her annual summer allergies, the "enemy," as she called them. Each waged psychological warfare against the other: Herman challenged Lizzie for her intellectual shortcomings; in retaliation, Lizzie adopted the attitude—and disseminated it throughout the family—that Herman was unstable, incapable of managing his own affairs and of remaining alone for extended periods. Another source of tension was the household. The cooks, a never-ending parade, usually young Irish girls with little training for or dedication to the kitchen (but at the moment Frederika Schmidt, a thirty-six-year-old German immigrant), vexed Herman, who insisted on overseeing their work. He was finicky in petty matters, ordering his coffee made according to a new formula every day. Also, to an unknown extent, he drank. It is no wonder that during the winters, when the family was confined to the house, nerves were strung taut.[9]

Herman and Lizzie had four children who, the relatives agreed, were remarkable, though ill-behaved. The boys, Malcolm, age ten, and Stanwix (Stanny), age eight, were active and bright, both good scholars. Of the two, Malcolm, to whom Herman habitually referred using his full Christian name, was the most promising. Elizabeth (Bessie), six, and Frances (Fanny), four, who had not yet begun school, were less notable in a family overstocked with girls. In terms of health, practicality, and comeliness, Fanny was the more favored of the two. Herman loved them and was homesick for them during his travels. Although they were not permitted to enter his study, particularly while he was at work,[10] at other times he could be an attentive parent. His forte was organizing outings, drives and berrying parties, and, probably, taking them to events in town, such as performances on the local stage. But when wafted away by his musings he could become oblivious of them and he displeased Lizzie by his laxity in disciplining them, allowing them too much scope for their impishness. On occasion, his irritability caused him to frighten them with incautious outbursts. He was, on the whole, a devoted, well-meaning, but not very gifted father of the time.

During late 1859, Herman gave only one lecture. He had not been well, he had not stimulated his audiences enough to receive return invitations, and he had lost interest. However, he was writing again. As early as mid-1858, he had secretly begun composing poems—only Lizzie knew.

Elizabeth Shaw Melville, 1872. By permission of the Berkshire Athenæum

These were not the casual verses of the *Mardi* interludes but lyrics that inaugurated a new stage in his career. Fiction had been a suitable medium for a Herman Melville who had imagined that he might make a profession of art and thought. The kind of success that could give him a livelihood was no longer a reasonable expectation, but poetry was a noncommercial vehicle through which he could defy his failure and, with a new freedom from the marketplace, wrestle with the angel Art. Thus despair became his ally, permitting him to make peace with his pen. He had already submitted two poems for publication, though unsuccessfully, and, as though to placard his withdrawal from the literary marketplace, he had specified that he would not quibble about payment. By the end of 1859, he had accumulated enough poems for a volume.

For several years he had been reading the works of poets past and present—Francis James Child's *English and Scottish Ballads,* whose rough technique appealed to him, George Herbert's *The Temple,* the works of Robert Herrick, George Chapman's translation of Homer, and Ralph Waldo Emerson's *Poems* have been recorded.[11] His own poems would not be conventional; anyone who understood his fiction could predict that. Poetry was a craft, he believed, not a genteel emanation. He deplored Tennyson's "The Charge of the Light Brigade," a smooth-textured celebration of a pointless sacrifice of brave men written by a poet far removed in space, understanding, and emotion from the carnage of that day in the Crimea, noting that it was "stuff by a swell man." He would not write laureate poems; better gristle and meaning for him. In a late poem about art, "The Rose Farmer," he asked, "Shall I make me heaps of posies, / Or some crystal drops of Attar?" and answered, "this same Attar, I suppose, / Long time will last, outlive indeed / The rightful sceptre of the rose" (305). That was his goal, not the ephemeral color and texture of the flower but the distillation of its essence.

Other than such lecturing engagements as might be forthcoming, and surely he knew that without more dedication on his part there would be few, he had no plans for the future. Perhaps he intended to renew his application for a governmental appointment, but the advent of a new federal administration, the opportune moment for office-seeking under the Spoils System, would not occur until the end of the Buchanan presidency in 1861. Except for his poetry, he was drifting, just as his country was drifting.

A Portent

In October 1859, Herman could see that the United States was indeed drifting. The nation was approaching the end of a decade of intensifying suspicion and hostility between North and South. The turbulence of these years had been ominous. Kansas had been a battleground between proslavery and free-soil settlers; in a vicious display of intersectional rancor on the floor of the Senate, Preston Brooks of South Carolina had bludgeoned Charles Sumner of Massachusetts senseless; states in the North had enacted personal liberty laws in defiance of the compromise fugitive slave legislation negotiated by temperate men; and, in general, a continual succession of annoyances and confrontations had exacerbated the animosities between the two regions. Most ominous was the rise of the Republican party and the consequent fear of Southerners that, despite the reassurances of Northern Democrats, a Republican victory in the 1860 presidential election would result in an outright assault on their slave-based culture. To the Southerners, the abolition of slavery meant not only the end of a way of life but also the liberation of a large army of blacks who might be expected to exact bloody revenge, in the manner of the slaves in Herman's prophetic "Benito Cereno," for two centuries of enforced and often brutal servitude.

These fears were confirmed at Harper's Ferry on October 16, 1859, when John Brown and twenty-two followers seized the federal arsenal with its store of arms. Abetted by a group of abolitionists, mostly from New England, and funded by Northern money—a collection had been taken up at a mid-1859 meeting at the Concord town hall attended by both Emerson and Thoreau—Brown meant to establish a provisional government of the United States, to incite a general slave revolt, and to establish an insurgent headquarters within the national borders from which operations leading to the elimination of slavery could be generaled. The uprising ended a few days later when a company of marines led by Colonel Robert E. Lee retook the arsenal, wounding and capturing Brown and killing or capturing the members of his band. When the state of Virginia tried Brown, Edmund Clarence Stedman warned against his execution: "Virginians! don't do it!" he wrote, for Brown "may trouble you more than ever, when you've nailed his coffin down!" But on the second of December, Brown was hanged. Henry Wadsworth Longfellow protested: "This is sowing the wind to reap the whirlwind, which will come soon."[12]

To the abolitionists, Brown was a martyr. Louisa May Alcott referred to him as "Saint John the Just," and Emerson said that his execution would "make the gallows as glorious as the cross." But those who, like Herman, feared and perhaps foresaw the consequences of his "servile insurrection," as Kitty Gansevoort called it, did not celebrate. Although in early November Herman took Bessie to New York City for a week's visit with her cousins, her Uncle Allan, and her Aunt Gus, and delivered a lecture in nearby Flushing, he was sick. When his friend George Long Duyckinck complained about his demeanor, Sarah Morewood tried to put the best face possible on it: "Do not call him moody, he is ill." He probably was, if Sarah said so, but he was most susceptible to illness during moments of emotional stress, and this was one of those moments.[13]

Herman had good reason for bad nerves, for Brown's action threatened his priorities of union first and emancipation when possible. But there was more to it than that. A formal rupture between North and South could result in war, and despite his romantic admiration of martial display, Herman was a pacifist. War was evil, and if that was true of war, taken by itself, fratricidal war was monstrous. White-Jacket implores his readers, "whatever befall us, let us never train our murderous guns inboard. . . . Our Lord High Admiral will yet interpose" (400). But Brown's insurrection threatened to turn the nation's guns inboard before the admiral could intervene.

The family Democrats were shaken, but only those in New York City found a vehicle through which to act. Anxious to reassure their Southern friends, the conservatives there called a meeting at the Academy of Music for December 19, 1859. Their purpose was to deplore Brown's action and to reassert their traditional position that the rights of the Southern states must not be abridged. The call was signed by 20,000 citizens; the Mayor presided; the participants, such as John A. Dix, Richard Lathers, and, perhaps, Allan Melville, included the most prominent conservatives; and letters of support from Winfield Scott, the ranking general of the army, and ex-presidents Martin Van Buren, Millard Fillmore, and Franklin Pierce were read. Although the meeting resulted in nothing more substantial than symbolism, by participating in it Richard, and Allan, if he was present, became the first of Herman's relatives to take part in the series of events that led from the Brown raid to the Civil War.[14]

It is sobering to realize how many Northerners opposed Brown's radicalism. Many questioned not his end but his means. Walt Whitman sympathized with him:

> I would sing how an old man, tall, with white hair, mounted the
> scaffold in Virginia,
> (I was at hand, silent I stood with teeth shut close, I watch'd,
> I stood very near you old man when cool and indifferent, but
> trembling with age and your unheal'd wounds you mounted the
> scaffold;)

but addressing himself to the consequences of actions like Brown's, he also wrote,

> I will make a song of the
> organic compacts of The
> States—and a shrill song
> of curses on him who would
> dissever the union of The States.

Writing from the retrospective of midwar, when violence on a far grander scale had become the daily fare, Nathaniel Hawthorne could still deplore

Brown's adventure. "Nobody was ever more justly hanged," he wrote for publication. "Any common-sensible man, looking at the matter unsentimentally, must have felt a certain intellectual satisfaction in seeing him hanged, if it were only in requital of his preposterous miscalculation of possibilities." His private reaction was even more severe: "If Emerson chooses to plant John Brown's gallows on Mount Calvary, the moral and religious sense of mankind will insist on its being placed between the crosses of the two thieves, and not side by side with that of the Savior."[15]

Herman must have been alarmed and disheartened by the raid and by Brown's execution, but he may also have admired, if grudgingly, the insane gamble to win the black man's freedom. After all, he had told Hawthorne, he respected "all men who say *no*."[16] More to the point is the attitude that characterizes his poem about Brown, "The Portent (1859)." Had he composed it while the passions evoked by the incident were still fervent, he might have expressed alarm or admiration, but he did neither. That he wrote the poem at the end of the war, when the incident was a historical event five and a half years past, is suggested by its reference to and dependence on the bloody "future" of the Shenandoah Valley, a future that climaxed in 1864. By 1865, the Brown affair was no longer an issue, but, rather, what the name of the poem denotes, a recalled portent.

"The Portent" is so much a preliminary to the main body of *Battle-Pieces* that it is not even listed in the table of contents. Brief, substantial, and full of sinew and thump, it is justly admired. It announces a new poetic; the extent of its advance beyond the conventions of the times is notable. Contemporary standards demanded that such a poem tell the story of the insurrection in heroic, Tennysonian diction and meter, that it beatify or damn Brown, or that it claim divine sanction of his adventure. But with this beginning, this first poem of his first published book of poems, Herman broke free of the hobble of stale expectation.

It offers an iconographic glimpse of the just-executed leader, static except for the sway of his body. Its pendular movement counts off the diminishing months, days, and hours remaining before the consequences of his audacity are manifested in the outbreak of war. His injured "crown" refers literally to his unhealed head wound, but it also suggests the crown of martyrdom. Brown's martyrdom is not to a cause but to the imperatives of Fate: he may be "Weird" because of his mad audacity, but he is also Wyrd, or "fateful," John Brown. One of the principal assumptions underlying *Battle-Pieces* is that although men can intend and act, thus instigating the events of the day, the career of the world is preordained, predestined. Although we can propel events, God dictates the final outcome with no concern for our desires or our sufferings. As White-Jacket put it, "What we call Fate is even, heartless, and impartial; not a fiend to kindle bigot flames, nor a philanthropist to espouse the cause of Greece. We may fret, fume, and fight; but the thing called Fate everlastingly sustains an armed neutrality" (320). Thus a different handling of the John Brown affair might have caused a different outcome, but whatever happened would fit into Fate's heartless design.[17]

Despite the bitter national crisis that Brown's fanaticism fueled, the poem expresses sympathy for the addled, frantic conscience that had driven him to his desperate expedient. How could it be otherwise to a poet who had created the monomaniac Ahab? Even in death, Brown still expresses "the anguish none can draw" hidden beneath the cap that hides his face, just as the future of the land is hidden. His is the anguish of a nation driven by forces beyond its control toward an end it does not foresee, does not seek, and does not want.

The shadow cast across the valley of the Shenandoah by Brown's body is the portent to which the title refers. What does it mean? In one sense, it is a forewarning of an approaching conflict that will befoul and disfigure that green and growing region, transforming it (and many another fertile area of America) into a "valley of the shadow of death." From the beginning to almost the end of the conflict, the lovely Shenandoah verdure would be ripped and blasted by horses' hooves, caisson wheels, and smoking shot, its inhabitants would be impoverished, burnt out of their homes, and starved, and friends of Herman would be captured and killed there. In another sense, the dark shadow may be an allusion to the central issue, slavery, that caused both the John Brown affair and the war itself. That it may be is suggested by a question in the last poem of the book, "A Meditation," "Can Africa pay back this blood / Spilt on Potomac's shore?" The shadow has yet another significance. Light and its opposed darkness, "the blackness of darkness" of *Moby-Dick* (10), had a special symbolic meaning for Herman. In the "Try-Works" chapter, Ishmael explains that although the bright sun lights a gentle, glad world, there is also the dark of grief and sorrow that we ignore at our peril. Applied to the innocent America of 1859, joy under the sun meant an obliviousness to the potential tragedy that underlay the comfortable surface of life, and, in this case, to the radical depths of suffering, bereavement, and unalloyed brutality that are war. The shattering of that innocence is, in one sense, what *Battle-Pieces* is about.[18]

"The Portent" is iconographic not only in its imagistic vividness but also in its symbolism. Bits of imagery found here repeat, transmute, and accumulate throughout the book until they achieve symbolic force. For example, the green of the valley, another symbol of the stripling innocence of the North and the South, is repeated in the green forests of certain battle poems. Again, the downsweep of Brown's angular beard, the "meteor of the war," inaugurates a pattern of descent that threads through the book, the insistent plunge and soar pattern of *Moby-Dick* transformed.

As 1860 arrived, Herman faced the uncertainty of the coming political conventions and the national election. If the Democratic party could remain strong, the South might be conciliated for yet another decade, by the end of which slavery might have begun to wither. But with Brown's uprising that prospect had diminished, despite the fact that some men, such as Richard Lathers, remained confident of the fundamental reasonableness of the South.

Winter at Arrowhead could try Herman's soul. During the brief days with their dreary weather, the children rode their sleds, skated on frozen ponds, and made snow edifices. But when the slope behind the farmhouse was deep in snow and blizzards concealed Greylock in the distance, the house lacked privacy, with the children indoors much of the time, and, paradoxically, Herman was lonely. To seek congenial company, in late January he paid another visit to Allan in New York City. He probably saw Richard Lathers, whose office was just by Allan's, and called on literary acquaintances, friends, and relatives, including the Morewoods, who wintered there, and the Thurstons. Then he returned to Pittsfield with some new reading materials, which he could supplement with the installments of *Elsie Venner*, by his former neighbor Oliver Wendell Holmes, that were appearing in the *Atlantic Monthly*. He must have been amused by the likeness, perhaps intended, between the teaching experiences of Holmes's protagonist and those of his own youth. But except for this visit and two more lectures, the dying fall of his Lyceum career, he hibernated moodily in Pittsfield.[19]

Then at the beginning of February 1860, he was aroused from his winter torpor by the excitement of Cousin Guert Gansevoort's recall to active duty. The rustication that had begun at Mare Island in mid-1856 was at an end. By the eleventh of the month, Guert had assumed the duties of ordnance officer at the New York Navy Yard in Brooklyn,[20] ironically, just as Kate and George Curtis and their children and his brother Leonard were moving from Brooklyn to Glens Falls. Guert's was a post of responsibility suitable for a capable, experienced officer. The yard was a center of naval activity and authority. Not only did the commandant supervise the supply, repair, and construction of naval vessels, but he also exercised naval command in the vicinity and was the conduit of the orders of the Department of the Navy to the ships and individual officers present in his area. After the assistant commandant, Guert was next in command, responsible for providing, installing, and repairing the guns of the ships in the yard and for providing them with navigational materials and professional books.

Because the navy was small, Guert must have known the officers to whom he reported. Captain Samuel L. Breese, an old salt, was the commandant (and therefore addressed as "commodore"), and his assistant was Commander Andrew H. Foote, one of the most promising officers of his generation. Highly regarded throughout the service, Foote had been a member of the Naval Reform Board, whose scrutiny Guert had undergone. (It is unlikely that while at his new post Guert was guilty of any such indiscretion as the one that had damaged his career at Mare Island, since Foote was one of the navy's most vocal temperance advocates.) The officer in charge of the Receiving Ship *North Carolina*, Commander James H. Ward, was slightly senior to Guert and a fellow survivor of the reform board. Among the other officers in the area was William Budd, a thirty-year-old master in the Coastal Survey who lived near Guert's apartment, the Mansion House. Herman, who had every reason to call on Guert on his visits to the city, may have met these officers at one time or another.[21]

Guert's rehabilitation at this moment may have been motivated by more than the expiration of his punishment. There were those who sensed the dire seriousness of the tensions afflicting the nation: just at the time of Guert's assignment, a "Constitutional Union Movement" that sought to avert disunion by the formation of a compromise political party was gaining momentum. With this kind of apprehension abroad, the navy may have felt that Guert's ability and experience were needed at this important post.

Just after Guert's arrival in Brooklyn, Herman delivered his last two lectures, one at South Danvers, Massachusetts, on February 14, and the other at Cambridgeport on the twenty-first. For the better part of a decade thereafter, he had no gainful employment. It is difficult to imagine how he survived financially, even though during the following winter he loaned $600, a good round sum, to the town of Pittsfield. That, however, had come from the sale the year before of some of the Arrowhead acreage.

March passed uneventfully, giving way to a busy April. Brother Allan was engaged to Jane Dempsey, or "Jennie," as she was called, the pampered daughter of a well-to-do Philadelphia family, and on the eighteenth of the month they were married. Barring illness, Herman would have attended the wedding, along with every other family member who could possibly come and the Latherses and the Thurstons. The happy event caused some scandal. Because Allan's first wife had been dead for only a year and a half, Sarah Morewood was shocked at his hasty remarriage. "I am disappointed in Allan Melville," she wrote; "he is now only an acquaintance of the past."[22] Had Allan and Jennie known how soon Tom Melville would arrive home, they might have delayed their wedding: ten days later, the *Meteor* sailed into Boston harbor.

The Democratic national convention opened in Charleston, South Carolina, on April 23. Whatever token of good will toward the South was intended in the selection of this center of disaffection as its site, events soon proved that far more than a token was demanded. After a sectional quarrel, seven Southern states, led by South Carolina, deserted the convention and met in a separate one of their own. When the official convention attempted unsuccessfully to nominate a presidential candidate, the Northerners were still anxious to placate their Southern brethren in any way short of surrender, Ben Butler of Massachusetts casting fifty ballots for Jefferson Davis. Frustrated, they adjourned and the rump Southern convention followed suit.

The schism boded ill, making the election of the likely Republican candidate, William H. Seward, a credible possibility. If that were to occur, the nation would be ruled for the first time by a party that represented only one of its two regions, the North. This danger was the subject of conversation during a meeting between Northerners and Southerners in the parlor of a New York insurance office, probably that of Richard Lathers. A defiant Virginia planter insisted that if Seward were elected the South would abandon the union. One of the Northerners replied, "Then, sir, we shall nominate Mr. Seward. Mr. Seward is not my man; for I am a free trader and an old Democrat. But if Virginia, or any other state or states shall declare that, upon the constitutional election of any citizen of the United States to any office, the Union shall be broken up, then I nominate that man and vote for him on principle." All of the other Northerners present agreed.[23]

Jonah

Herman found the inexorable march of events toward tragedy unbearable. One of the defenses available to him was disengagement, and the pending departure of the *Meteor* made flight possible and convenient. What better escape than to sail away with Tom on a voyage to San Francisco and then on to the far reaches of the world, a voyage that would for a year insulate him from the post, the telegraph, and the newspaper? The sea, the flotsam, the fish, the whales, and the ocean birds spoke to him only of metaphysics, never of John Brown, Charleston, and disunion, and the pale sharks were an evil with which his imagination could grapple, one more bearable than that greater evil, fratricide, that was slouching toward America. And so when the news arrived from South Carolina he fled aboard Tom's ship. Although it was understood that the purpose of the voyage was to improve his health, there is little evidence that he was physically ill; his infirmity was spiritual.[24]

He had his sea outfit to assemble, including a plentiful supply of tobacco for his ubiquitous pipes and a number of old periodicals and books to pack—including Béranger's *Songs,* a Dante, a Milton, Chapman's Homer, Alexander Campbell's *Sketches of Life and Character,* Schiller's *Poems and Ballads,* the *Complete Poetical Works* of Wordsworth, Hawthorne's new romance, *The Marble Faun,* a gift from Sarah Morewood, and a New Testament and Psalms, which Aunt Jean Knight had given him years earlier. He also obtained a letter of introduction from the pastor of the Shaws' church, Orville Dewey. Doing her part, little Bessie made him a bag to take along. Because Herman's absence was to be lengthy, Judge Shaw wished to put Lizzie's financial affairs in order—just in case anything should happen to Herman. This was arranged by conveying Arrowhead and the Pittsfield municipal loan to Shaw in return for the discharge of Herman's debts to him—$6,900 or $7,000, Shaw was uncertain—and the further conveyance of Arrowhead from Shaw to Lizzie. Henceforth Herman was in the unmanning position of being a guest in Lizzie's home. His sensitivity on this point is evident in his response to an innocent remark about ownership made by little Fannie. Herman crushed her by calling her "Little Miss Property," and Lizzie had to calm the little girl by saying, "Papa doesn't mean anything. Run along to school."[25]

Then there were his poems, which were nearly ready for publication. He hurried his last-minute revisions and Lizzie performed the labor of Bartleby in making fair copies. While Herman was at sea, she was to send the manuscript "Poems by Herman Melville" to New York, where, with the aid of Evert Duyckinck, Allan would market it. Herman did not wish to give it to Harper's, probably because of the association of that house with his failed career as a romancer. He preferred Appleton's or Scribner's, and he gave instructions that whatever publisher might be found, the format be dignified and unostentatious. The title page was not to mention his other works, another way of distancing the Herman Melville of *Typee* from Herman Melville the poet.

To the extent that the voyage was intended as an escape, it came none too soon. While Herman was preparing his seabag, the Constitutional Union party convened in Baltimore. Since the single purpose of the delegates was to preserve the union (perhaps by forcing the outcome of the presidential election into the House of Representatives), they offered no platform but simply nominated John Bell, a slave-holding Unionist from Tennessee, and Edward Everett, president of Harvard University, an admirer of Herman's South Seas romances and a veteran laborer in the cause of union, for president and vice president. Representing themselves as a legitimate party, the "Belleverett" men later nominated state candidates, including Edward Dickinson, Emily's father, for lieutenant governor. However, Dickinson refused to run.[26]

That was harmless enough, but the next to convene were the Republicans. On the sixteenth of the month they met in Chicago, where they defied expectations by nominating Abraham Lincoln for president and Uncle Nourse's political ally, Hannibal Hamlin, for vice-president. With this political mischief brewing, was it not the duty of the bard, the unacknowledged legislator of the nation, to remain at home? Herman's imminent departure would not be a launching into the unknown of an Ishmael but rather a flight of a Jonah from his mission to Nineveh. What punishment might await him?

After a delay, during which Herman and Tom sat for a joint photographic portrait, in the middle of the beautiful morning of May 30 the *Meteor* departed from Boston harbor. The eight-year-old *Meteor* was a fine ship. A slender, graceful "medium clipper," she bore a figurehead of Atalanta picking up the golden apples. With her exotic equipage and decor, what Henry Gansevoort described as "the curiosities of the cabin, the mysterious lockers, the Eastern utensils, the cramped state rooms, and the [*undeciphered*] of oddities aboard," she had the appearance of a veteran of the Orient trade. She was carrying merchandise for San Francisco. Accompanied by sister Fanny and George Griggs, the two brothers boarded her in the stream, finding one of the owners, George Peabody, already there. The party lunched while the *Meteor*, under the command of a pilot, hoisted anchor and sailed serenely down the harbor. Just after lunch, the well-wishers transferred to a tugboat, which hauled the *Meteor* out to sea. Soon after one o'clock, the pilot left and the tug cast off. The brothers waved goodbye (to Fanny, Herman wrote in his journal, ignoring the presence of George Griggs), settled into the captain's stateroom, and began their voyage.[27]

A sailor who had been too long ashore, Herman was seasick for several weeks, and as the ship sailed easterly toward the Canary Islands the weather turned foul—cloudy, foggy, and rainy, but with a good breeze. Early in the voyage a passing vessel, a poorly officered English brig, collided with the *Meteor*. She inflicted little damage, but Herman's Jonah feeling must have been in the ascendant for the moment. Then his flight continued through alternating placid seas and gales. The course Tom set took him far from the world of affairs—he would be free of the relentless jangle of news until his arrival in California. After sailing halfway across the Atlantic, Tom steered south. As the ship neared the equator, it entered the "Doleful Doldrums," with "the whole ship's crew given up to melancholly, and meditating darkly on the mysteries of Providence" (132). Afterward, when the ship crossed "the line," Tom may have paused to allow the crewmen to perform the traditional rite in which King Neptune initiated the apprentice sailors into his realm. Then Tom navigated the ship southward around the bulge of

Brazil, far out of sight of the mainland. After passing between Argentina and the Falkland or Malvinas Islands, Tom intended to round Cape Horn and then to sail the standard course for San Francisco. The result would be that after leaving the cape the clipper would shun the land until it sighted Baja California.

It was good to be at sea, not crossing it to or from anyplace but sailing on out of sight of land like a planet hurtling through the great vacuum. Soon after leaving Boston, Herman read Campbell's *Sketches,* which he then gave to Tom, and later *The Marble Faun.*[28] A comet made an appearance among the southern stars—an omen, since comets and meteors held a special significance for Herman (John Brown was the meteor of the war) and since this one appeared among constellations that he had not seen since he was a young man. The ship's carpenter made a set of chess men so the two brothers could play in the evenings, and Herman read Tom his verses. On pleasant days he enjoyed being on deck with the wind taking the sails and the tackle creaking, and sometimes, as in olden days, he climbed a mast. On stormier days he sat in the cabin talking, thinking, and reading while the ship heaved, yawed, pitched, and rolled. He watched the ocean birds that always fascinated him, and in due time the official sow added nine official piglets to the ship's company. Far beyond the rail toy ships hove into view and then sank back into the abyss beyond the edge of the world.

Herman may have written poems during these indolent days and evenings. If so, some of them probably survive in *John Marr and Other Sailors,* published nearly three decades later. "Now the Polar Star sinks from sight / The Southern Cross it climbs the sky," he wrote in "Crossing the Tropics" (202), and "cut by slanting sleet, we swoop / Where raves the world's inverted year." Other late poems with their images of sea birds, storms, shipwrecks, sharks, and icebergs may have had their origins in these days. During this time he probably composed "The Admiral of the White" (404–6), which he may have read to Tom one evening.

As the ship careened southward it entered the latitude of winter. During one period it pitched in storms for forty or fifty days without relief, and sometimes waves washed men off their feet and nearly over the side—one was injured—and gale winds rent the sails. To combat the chill, the steward set up a stove which gave the cabin a moist snugness, and when topside Herman wore two flannel shirts, an overcoat, big mittens, and a thick leather hat known in sailor lingo as a "Russia cap." Then on August 7 the islands at the tip of South America hove into view, the first land Herman had seen since leaving Boston. In the distance he could see two other ships attempting the Cape passage. After sailing between the islands, the *Meteor* arrived where they had been. Herman had rounded the Cape years before, but it was an experience which custom could never stale. While hail, snow, and sleet drove the clipper on and the wind blustered through the abbreviated day, he buried himself in the cabin reading Schiller, Milton, Chapman's Homer, which included works by Hesiod, Musæus, and Juvenal, and the New Testament and Psalms.[29] In the course of the difficult passage, a seaman sent aloft to reef sail tumbled from the rigging to an instant death.

Both the scenery and the fatal fall affected Herman deeply. The sight of Tierra del Fuego and Staten Island on either hand while the ship passed through the Strait of Le Maire was appalling, an appropriate setting for such a soul-searing event. "Horrible snowy mountains—black, thunder-cloud woods—gorges—hell-landscape," he noted. Cape Horn was a "horrid sight," a "black, bare steep cliff," and, nearer, "awful islands & rocks" made "an infernal group" (133–34).

The death of Benjamin Ray, a Nantucket man, *was* soul-searing. About daybreak, he had lost his grip on the main topsail yard and struck his head on a spar before crashing to the weather deck. A few hours later, his still gory body, sewn in canvas and weighted with cannonballs, was slipped over the side while Tom read a prayer above the cry of the storm. For Herman, the death belonged "to that order of human events, which staggers those whom the Primal Philosophy hath not confirmed. . . . [I] read & think, & walk & eat & talk, as if nothing had happened—as if I did not know that death is indeed the King of Terrors—when thus happening; when thus heart-breaking to a fond mother—the King of Terrors, not to the dying or the dead, but to the mourner—the mother.—Not so easily will his fate be washed out of her heart, as his blood from the deck" (134–35). It was tragedy, but it was the kind of tragedy with which he could wrestle on paper: as Cambon says, he could come to terms with death because he fought it.[30] It had always haunted him, but writing about it gave him the opportunity to distinguish between its effect on its victim and its effect on the living, a distinction to which he would recur in *Battle-Pieces*. The next day the sea was calm, the sun was shining, the sky was blue, and the ship glided northwest toward San Francisco. Nature took away, but she also provided.

The rest of this last leg of the voyage was uneventful. Herman must have thought of Nukuheva and the valley of the Typees, to the left of the track of the northbound *Meteor*, and of the Encantadas, to the right—a modest change of course would have taken the ship to either place—but he contented himself with the salt air and with reading—Béranger, Wordsworth, more Milton, Dante—the "savage Tuscan" who chilled him—and Chapman's *Odysseys*. The nearest he came to renewing his acquaintance with the Typees was when he gammed for an hour or so aboard a passing whaleship, whose captain thought him "a gentleman in every sense of the word." There he saw nearly a dozen natives of Roratonga who had been recruited to fill out the crew. He knew why. It was to be expected that many of the American sailors would, as he and Toby Greene had done years before, desert their ships, leaving the captains to lure aboard whatever able-bodied men they could find, including islanders. Then after a long and tranquil transit from the Cape, the *Meteor* arrived at the Vallejo Street wharf in San Francisco.[31]

On October 12, after more than four months of confinement aboard ship, Herman set foot on land again and read letters (including one from Sam Shaw) and newspapers. That nothing had been happening at home was an illusion of the voyager. Shortly after the sailing of the *Meteor,* Lizzie had sent Herman's poems to Evert Duyckinck. Since at the time of his departure the making of fair copy had not yet been completed, and since Lizzie left it to Herman to punctuate his manuscripts, she asked Duyckinck to "overlook the sheets" for "little inaccuracies." Duyckinck did what he could to market the poems but Charles Scribner refused them, as did Rudd and Carleton. Lizzie suggested Derby and Jackson, since Derby was a brother-in-law of Toby Greene, but Duyckinck's efforts to find a publisher were at an end, though Lizzie seems to have assumed that he and Allan would continue indefinitely their efforts to peddle the poems. During this time, Lizzie had two of Herman's sisters, perhaps Helen and Fanny, to keep her company in Pittsfield. Then, just at the time when the *Meteor* had been rounding the Cape, Judge Shaw visited her. After his return home he bowed to old age and infirmity by retiring. Despite the fact that the hay fever season had not yet passed, Lizzie closed Arrowhead and took the children to Boston to be with him.[32]

While Herman had been escaping to the winter of the south, others had been returning to the vexed summer of the north—drawn in part by the very urgencies that had driven him away. On June 28, Nathaniel Hawthorne landed in Boston to end his seven-year exile in England and on the Continent and had settled into the Wayside in Concord. Concerning the crisis in which he found his country, he was a Democrat, but he was also Hawthorne. He does not seem to have had a clear idea of just what he did believe about it. He wanted the union saved, but he did not have great confidence in its viability. "If compelled to choose, I go for the North," he wrote Horatio Bridge, "New England is quite as large a lump of earth as my heart can really take in."[33] But if his heart had room for no more than New England, events would soon broaden the concerns of his head.

When correspondents at home had informed the Albany Gansevoorts that the fate of the union had become doubtful, they had left Italy for the United

States. After their arrival on August 31, Henry paid his respects to Aunt Melville. Then, with his excuses for delaying his law career exhausted, on the twentieth of September he straggled down to New York City in the custody of Abe Lansing to make yet another beginning. Although his attitude toward the law was similar to that of one of his relatives, who saw the profession as "full of mean, truckling expedients, unfit for any gentleman to resort to," Henry finally bowed to parental pressure by going into partnership with a Princeton friend, George Henry Brewster, in offices on Nassau Street. It was a cordial relationship, one that helped Henry to reconcile himself to his fate; he called Brewster "Bruce," and Brewster called him "Gans." For the benefit of the new firm, Henry asked Abe Lansing for help in obtaining an appointment as a notary.[34]

During Herman's voyage, the official Democratic convention had reconvened in Baltimore to nominate Stephen A. Douglas for president and Herschel V. Johnson of Georgia for vice-president, while the rump Southerners had nominated "rule or ruin" candidates, Vice-President John C. Breckinridge of Kentucky for president and Joseph Lane of Oregon for vice-president. Including a "people's" nominee, Sam Houston, that amounted to four candidates opposing Lincoln. As Herman had neared San Francisco, the campaign had approached its climax. In Albany, as elsewhere, there were parades—Kitty Gansevoort maintained loyally that the Little Giants, the Douglas paraders, were "fine," but she had no words of admiration for the Wide Awakes, the Lincoln men. Both consisted of platoons of youths who added spectacle and ardor to the party rallies, and by the end of the campaign the Wide Awakes, at least, were famous. In Rockford, Randolph Hobart became the only known Melville relative to participate in this electioneering hoopla. A local marching club, of which Randolph was a member, accepted Lincoln's invitation to join the Wide Awakes and marched through the streets whenever political excitement was demanded.[35]

The Return of Jonah

Having been advised by someone in Boston that Herman was aboard the *Meteor*, two San Francisco newspapers suggested that he give a series of lectures. But he was preparing to return home. Two reasons have been given, first that the voyage had done little to improve his health and second that it had been extended beyond its originally anticipated duration. The second has some foundation: as a result of new instructions that Tom must have received in San Francisco, the ship was to load wheat there and carry it to Falmouth, England, which would mean a near retracing of the route that

Herman had just traveled. As to the first, there is not the slightest evidence to substantiate it.[36]

Other than his early seasickness, during the voyage Herman did not complain of illness; on the contrary, he spent some of the time skylarking in the rigging. In San Francisco, he toured the burly and brawling city. He visited the bookstores, where he purchased a copy of Charles Mackay's *The Book of English Songs,* and he had at least one important social engagement. Using his letter of introduction from Reverend Dewey, he called on Thomas Starr King, a Boston clergyman and lecturer who had recently removed to San Francisco. King took him to Black Point, overlooking the Golden Gate, where the two called on Colonel and Mrs. John C. Frémont, he the noted explorer and unsuccessful Republican candidate for the presidency in 1856, she the daughter of Senator Thomas Hart Benton. During his enjoyable visit with the Frémonts, or, most notably, Jessie Frémont, Herman discovered that it was her nineteenth wedding anniversary. That led her to recall that at the time of her marriage all Washington had been shocked by its unsuitable nature. Now that Frémont's mills were producing $16,000 a year in gold, Washington might undergo a change of heart. That was the day before Herman's return home.[37]

There are two more credible reasons for his unscheduled return. First, he longed for his family, so much so that during the voyage he had made a fine sketch of the farm showing Lizzie and the children greeting him on his return. The second reason is the same as the reason for his departure: he was sick, but sick at heart. At sea he had received only stale newspapers and out-of-date verbal reports from the whaleship he had visited and perhaps from other passing vessels, and thus he had been spared the knowledge of the political chaos of his country. But in San Francisco, where the newspapers carried fresh bulletins brought by pony express, he had once more to confront the ills of his nation.[38]

On October 20, he bade goodbye to Tom and the Barbary Coast and sailed aboard the side-wheeler *Cortes*. The ship paused in the harbor to send ashore stowaways, then pushed down the west coast of Mexico, pausing at Manzanilla to pick up a cargo of silver and at Acapulco for coal, water, and provisions. Then, in the early afternoon of November 4, she landed at Panama City. Although this was Herman's first visit to tropical shores since his youthful adventures at sea, nostalgia did not delay him. He hurried across the isthmus on the Panama Railroad to Aspinwall (present-day Colon), and the next day, the day before the election, he sailed for New York City aboard the Vanderbilt steamer *North Star*, another side-wheeler. As the unkempt ship chugged through heavy gales and rough seas, he read lines from Schiller that echoed his own perturbed attitude toward the present and his sense that the worthiest days of man had passed: "Friends, fairer times have been / (Who can deny?) than we ourselves have seen; / And an old race of more majestic worth." On the night of the thirteenth of November, the *North Star* berthed at the piers of New York and, for better or for worse, Jonah had returned to share his country's agony.[39]

In the interval between Herman's departure from Aspinwall and his arrival in the city, the election had taken place. Many had eagerly anticipated a Lincoln victory and had voted for him without regard for the danger to the nation that his election posed. Among these were most of the Boston literati—always excepting Hawthorne. A week before the election, John Greenleaf Whittier wrote Salmon P. Chase, "For the first time in my life, I shall vote, I suppose, for a successful candidate for the Presidency, if I am spared to do so." Even Democrats believed that the Republicans would win: Henry Gansevoort wrote Kitty that Lincoln would carry New York. By the seventh of November, the telegraphic network had informed all of the states except those in the extreme west of Lincoln's election. He carried Massachusetts by a large margin and New York by a small one. However, his majority in Pittsfield was modest and there were even a few votes for Breckinridge. In fact, although he won in the electoral college, Lincoln did not have a clear mandate, having received nearly a million votes less than had his combined opponents. Had the Southerners sent their full delegations to the new Congress, the Democrats would have retained control of both the Senate and the House. Henry Gansevoort believed that the Congress would block radical actions by the new administration.[40]

Family Republicans, such as John Hoadley, George Griggs, Uncle Nourse, and, probably, the western Melvills, were elated. Whittier, now a Republican elector, was both enthusiastic and cautious: "Well, the election is over—Lincoln is elected! The slave power rebuked for once. I do not feel like *exulted*: I am not yet sure that we have gained as much as we hoped." The rest of the family in Gansevoort, Albany, and New York City tasted defeat, though Henry Gansevoort consoled himself with the idea that an honest man had won rather than a politician.[41]

Waiting for the End

When he arrived at the city piers, Herman faced the precise crisis that he had sought to escape. The moment that the nation had awaited with conflicting expectations and with varying degrees of hope and dread had come and passed with a dying fall—passions had already been squandered, and now the Southern states were methodically carrying out their threats. The day before the election the governor of South Carolina had recommended that the legislature secede in the event of a Republican success, and that is what it did. As that was occurring, and as Herman was debarking from the *North Star*, militiamen in Pittsfield were conducting target practice and parading before the citizenry.[42]

Surrounded by evidence of tragedy in the making, Herman called on family and friends before hurrying on to Boston to be with Lizzie and the children. Judge Shaw was not well, but Herman was. Far from exhibiting the illness that had excused his return, he visited relatives, friends, and acquaintances. He and Lizzie saw Helen and George Griggs, Kate and John Hoadley, and the Melvill aunts, and inspected the fine new house with its extensive grounds in the suburbs of Lawrence that the Hoadleys were purchasing. While Herman was in Boston, there were some curious occurrences that remained in his memory as symbols of the times. On Saturday evening, November 17, a furious windstorm swept across New England. In New Haven, it blew the steeple off the Wooster Place Church; in Durham, New Hampshire, it snatched the steeple from one of the Congregational churches there, inverted it, and dropped it like a spear so that it stuck in the roof upside down. What better emblem could there be of a country preparing to repeal the Sermon on the Mount?[43]

Herman and Lizzie then visited Herman's mother and sisters in Gansevoort and probably accompanied his mother and Fanny to Albany for Thanksgiving dinner with Uncle Peter.[44] Ed Lansing came up from Rutgers for the holiday, and Herman probably saw him, since the Lansings and the Gansevoorts customarily celebrated the holiday together. Upon his return to Boston, Herman was delegated to go to Pittsfield two days in advance of the rest of his family to open the farm.

Herman had been in Boston, away, and back again, for almost a month. Hawthorne, whom he had not seen in three years, was in Concord, only a short distance away, and Herman must have known that, since it was common knowledge. Considering that in Liverpool he had simply appeared at Hawthorne's door, why did he not now simply appear at the Wayside? Why did he never again see Hawthorne? The lapse in their friendship is a perplexing mystery, the solution to which is complex and, in all likelihood, ultimately unknowable. Herman wrote that neither was to blame, but it is probably true that both were, with the greater burden of guilt resting on Hawthorne because he was in the best position to extend his hand. But he had a difficult temperament, one that caused Emerson, who never succeeded in conquering his reserve, to write regretfully of his "unwillingness & caprice." Hawthorne rarely *made* friends; like New England matrons and their hats, he *had* friends. In contrast, Herman was sociable and generous to those he knew, and he was more willing to know people.[45]

By the time the two men met in Liverpool, their friendship seems already to have been failing. Because of his inability to secure a consular appointment for Herman, Hawthorne felt uneasy. He was also disturbed by Herman's philosophical wanderings, describing them as "morbid," "dismal," and "monotonous." Clearly, Herman no longer stimulated him as before. There is even a rather cruel note in Hawthorne's witticism about the heterodoxy—cleanliness—of Herman's underwear, something that loyalty would have forbidden him to say about Frank Pierce or Horatio Bridge.[46]

In the period of withdrawal that followed Hawthorne's return from Europe, he became increasingly irritated by even the slightest presumption, and he may have dreaded encountering Herman's spiritual aggressiveness once more. In turn, Herman must have been wounded by Hawthorne's silence. He was too proud to supplicate, especially now that Hawthorne had been acclaimed the foremost in the American literary parade while he himself had been forced off the route of march—he knew in his heart that he was as great a writer. Still, far from begrudging that success, he always regarded Hawthorne's literary heirlooms as sacred. The only contemporary writer to occupy such an important position in Herman's imagination and to bequeath him a literary legacy was Hawthorne.

When Herman arrived in Pittsfield in early December, he stayed for a day or two with the Morewoods. From Broadhall, he made preparations for his family's return, not only opening Arrowhead, setting up stoves, airing bedding, and preparing a dinner for his family, but also, since Frederika was gone, seeking a new cook. The rest of the family arrived shortly thereafter and Arrowhead was once again as it had been before Herman's voyage. Christmas came, and on New Year's Day, 1861, Herman's gift to Lizzie was his copy of Poe's works. She could have read it at any time before he gave it to her, but such were Herman's gifts.

Now he was in a good defensive position against whatever national calamity might come—fortified, so to speak, in the Berkshires. His musings of the moment were those inspired by his voyage—about Tom at sea and, by analogy, about his shipmates of old. He wrote of them and to them—a poem apostrophizing Tom, "To the Master of the 'Meteor'" (196), and letters to his old shipmates, Toby Greene, whom he invited to visit Arrowhead, and Oliver Russ. But nothing could defend him against the dark affliction of the North, the eerie sensation that unseen and inscrutable forces were at work. He recalled this time in "Misgivings (1860)" and in the first half of "Apathy and Enthusiasm (1860–1)." Although many of the narrators in *Battle-Pieces* are dramatic creations, the speaker of "Misgivings" is the poet himself communicating his reaction to the events preceding the war as he sits on his piazza observing Mount Greylock in the distance and knitting together images summoned from his creative storeroom. In fact, the elements of "Misgivings" so clearly stem from his experiences of 1860 that it would not be surprising to learn either that he wrote at least a preliminary version of it then or that he consulted a journal of impressions when he did write it.

"Misgivings" is the perfect beginning for the principal section of *Battle-Pieces*. In capturing the apprehensive mood of the North, the excruciating tension that followed Lincoln's election and the horror with which men peered down the bloody maw of war, it is brilliantly conceived. Images of alarm and warning crowd together as the "ocean-clouds" of the recent voyage "sweep storming in late autumn brown" of the Berkshire countryside, creating a cosmic tempest bursting "from the waste of Time." This tempest is more than a conventional symbol of approaching conflict; it is a welling from within man's nature of the cumulative malignancy of all of the past ages, of all time, assaulting the mountain height which in *Battle-Pieces* symbolizes the romantic innocence of the young nation. The storm topples a church spire in the town (an accident for which recent memory provided precedents) as Christ's peace and love give way to infernal emotions. Much later, his imagination created an analogous trope, Henry Ward Beecher consecrating a Christmas musket on the altar of his Brooklyn church. The assault batters "the world's fairest hope linked with man's foulest crime."[47]

To many modern readers it has seemed that "man's foulest crime" must have been slavery, but to a conservative such as Herman the disintegration of the union was the more foul, and he linked that disintegration to the worst crime of all, fratricide. As Robert Milder has said, "it is Unionism, not abolition, that *Battle-Pieces* presents as the Northern cause, as indeed it was for most Northern moderates, Lincoln included."[48] Yet the poem allows the reader to choose whatever crime best suits his preconceptions.

Then "Nature's dark side," prefigured by Brown's shadow in "The Portent," is heeded as the slope of the mountain merges with the awful scenery of Cape Horn to form the wrathful face and "moody brow" of a visage whose significance is yet to be revealed. The shouting torrents from this face descend violently through gorges, invoking and bringing closer the downward rush of the "meteor" of "The Portent" and announcing a succession of storms (seen later along the Pacific shore by Robert Frost) "formed behind the storm we feel." The downward rush is the descent of an entire people toward some violent destiny, while the many-battalioned storm suggests the manifold assaults to come. When the tempest shakes the hemlock rafter as well as "the oak in the driving keel," it is difficult not to read the symbols conventionally, the rafter the home and the keel the ship of state, and no doubt those ideas are intended. They are consistent with the symbolic woods, hemlock bringing death to families at home, and oak, as in the British "hearts of oak," or doughty sailors, meaning the courage and sacrifice of the nation. But there is also a personal meaning; Herman was recalling the pulse of the *Meteor* in a cape gale and the shiver of Arrowhead in the November wind.

The other poem, "Apathy and Enthusiasm," contrasts the numbness of the North after Lincoln's election with the "Easter" rising of the people the following spring. It is a curious poem, prosodically Poe-like (as in Poe's "A Dream," "Bridal Ballad," "Imitation," and "Lenore"). The impressive first half, which refers to this period and is here treated separately, is at the same time an excellent re-creation of mood and a philosophical preparation for the war to come. Four lines present emotion-laden images of dankness, blankness, lifelessness, and leaden sky, all re-creating the mood of the North; four offer a glacial symbol of the disintegration of the nation; four depict the numbness and paralysis of the North while the disintegration was in progress; and five final lines introduce a cracked hearth and a mother pleading with her sons not to part as enemies.

The mother and her quarreling sons are trite enough, but as a metaphor for the dissolution of the union they were probably unavoidable. Not only are they introduced by the fresh symbol of the cracking ice field (perhaps recollected from icebergs encountered on the transit through southern Pacific waters), but they also prepare for other poems at the end of *Battle-Pieces* in which the mother is transformed into an allegorical America renewed and her slain sons serve as the text of a sermon calling for a renewed brotherhood as a basis for a renewed nation.

The poem offers questions rather than answers. Together with "Misgivings," it provides images of approaching catastrophe without clarifying the nature of that catastrophe. In that sense, it is true to the events which inspired it. To fear the future and to sense its ominous nature is far different from understanding it, nor did the North—nor the South, for that matter—fully understand what lay ahead. A nation that did not understand the immanence of Herman's "darkness" was hardly in a position to read the mysteries of that darkness.

There is another question. To what "Fates" does the poem refer, and, conversely, what is meant by "The finality of doom"? In the conflict between the Cavaliers of the South and the Puritans of the North, must one side or the other be blamed? Do they cause events to occur, or are they merely instruments of destiny? As "The Portent" had suggested, Fate is the artisan of the future, which could mean that war was inevitable regardless of the efforts of men. That would render meaningless any thought of free will. The other possibility was that war, even though the result of human malfeasance, would somehow fit into a heavenly scheme to test, purify, and mature the nation. Herman would return to the subject in "The Conflict of Convictions."

Sweeping Back the Tide

Anxious as Herman must have been for the news of the day, in a sense there was little. The policy of the lame duck Buchanan administration was to do nothing in order to avoid exacerbating national tensions, and the Congress was almost as inert. Across the North there was apathy and gloom while the Southern states carried out with energy and optimism the ritual task of forming a new nation. Had the federal government done *anything* helpful, harmful, or even aimed wide of the mark, the tension would have been more bearable. But it did that most unbearable of all things—nothing.

Some put the best possible face on the crisis, one of Henry Gansevoort's Princeton friends writing him that "the election of Lincoln, although unfortunate & unjust is not casus belli." But knowing South Carolina as he did, Richard Lathers, Herman's interpreter of Southern thought, feared that the election might well prove to be casus belli. In letters to five acquaintances in Charleston, he implored the citizens of his home state to oppose secession. The currents of opinion were destroying sectionalism in the North, he promised, and he asked if Charleston would be willing to receive a delegation of leading New Yorkers. But the responses told him that the city would not.[49]

Chastened conservatism appeared in unexpected places in the North, even among the radicals. Whittier wrote, "With slavery in the States we have no right to interfere, and no desire to do so beyond the mild persuasion of the successful example of Freedom." Democrats were more aggressively conciliatory. "They circulated petitions," Silbey writes, "called state conventions to apply pressure, and began to prepare for forthcoming local and state elections to drive the Republicans from office." With sixteen other conservatives, Richard Lathers invited hundreds of distinguished New Yorkers of like sympathies, including Peter Gansevoort, to attend a peace meeting at his Pine Street office. At noon on the fifteenth of December, Richard opened the proceedings of the "Pine Street Meeting" with a brief speech, which was preliminary to many others. Then the participants agreed to send a three-man delegation, chaired by Millard Fillmore and including Richard and Greene C. Bronson, a former chief justice of New York State, to the South to deliver an address and resolutions modeled on a document that John A. Dix had written. In sum, the New Yorkers asked the Southerners to give up secession and to take their seats in Congress, thereby ensuring a

Democratic majority that could block any Republican rascality. But events were outpacing such measures. By New Year's Day, South Carolina had seized three U.S. military installations and a revenue cutter.[50]

Even so, men of good will continued their work. Judge Shaw, now confined to his home with asthma, published a letter countersigned by a number of other distinguished citizens of Massachusetts, including Edward Dickinson, asserting that some Massachusetts statutes, such as the inflammatory personal liberty law, were unconstitutional and should be repealed. In Pittsfield, petitions in favor of such a repeal were circulated. Lemuel Shaw, Jr., joined in a call for a Boston meeting to endorse the Crittenden compromise, a proposed amendment to the Constitution that would have protected slavery as a permanent institution. In the South, Governor Letcher of Virginia organized a peace conference, presided over by ex-President Tyler, to seek a compromise. The delegates, none of whom were from the states in secession, were received with cordiality by President Buchanan, but Henry Wadsworth Longfellow scorned the effort: "Perhaps the oddest and most grotesque feature of the melo-drama, is the re-appearance on the scene of Ex-President Tyler! It is really too droll!"[51]

To some radicals, the inaction of the administration was mitigated by the belief that the departure of the South was less of a loss to the Union than the conservatives and moderates thought. Longfellow objected to conciliation: "What I am afraid of is, not that they will go, but that the North will yield." "Tragic as secession is, it has also its ludicrous side. The six fugitive states look very much like six paupers leaving the Union Workhouse. Is it worth while to advertise them, and pursue them?" Whittier overcame his earlier heterodoxy on the slavery issue in a poem, "A Word for the Hour": the Southern states "break the links of Union," he wrote,

shall we light
The fires of hell to weld anew the chain
On that red anvil where each blow is pain?
Draw we not even now a freer breath,
As from our shoulders falls a load of death . . . ?

"Why take we up the accursed thing again?" he asked. Hawthorne, who was still Hawthorne, had a third point of view. "I am ashamed to say how little I care about the matter," he wrote. "New England will still have her rocks and ice. . . . As to the South, I never loved it." Then he stopped reading the newspapers.[52]

Herman watched with empty heart as the dissolution of the union continued through the winter, with secession, the resignation of Southerners from the federal service, the appropriation of national property by states in secession, and the lethargy in Washington. Large numbers of Southern officers left the armed forces, so many from the navy that Guert's seniority rose dramatically. This perceived disloyalty angered their Northern shipmates. Guert was unforgiving. He (or the commandant of the Navy Yard) referred to Matthew Fontaine Maury as "the late Commander Maury" and extended his contempt to the navigational advances that had contributed to the brilliant Virginian's reputation as a scientist.[53] Nevertheless, the unquestioning loyalty and the political neutrality which were hallmarks of the professional officer caused some Southerners, such as General Scott and Captain David Glasgow Farragut, to remain in the federal service even though that meant opposing their own states.

There is no way of knowing Herman's reaction to the defections of the Southern officers at the time when they occurred, but later in life, when he wrote "Bridegroom Dick (1876)," he looked at the subject with a rare understanding:

> We sailors o' the North, wife, how could we lag?—
> Strike with your kin, and you stick to the flag!
> But to sailors o' the South that easy way was barred.
> To some, dame, believe (and I speak o' what I know),
> Wormwood the trial and the Uzzite's[54] black shard;
> And the faithfuller the heart, the crueller the throe.
> Duty? It pulled with more than one string,
> This way and that, and anyhow a sting.
> The flag and your kin, how be true unto both?
> If one plight ye keep, then ye break the other troth. (170–71)

Since the passage concerns the ambiguity in human affairs that Herman conned so persistently, it is tempting to believe that he felt this way from the beginning.

The departure of Southern cabinet members made it necessary to appoint temporary replacements, such as John A. Dix. When Dix was made secretary of the treasury in January, the damaged credit of the government was revived despite a general atmosphere of economic panic. On January 27, he became a hero of the moment by ordering a loyal officer to relieve the rebellious commander of the revenue cutter *McClelland*, located in Louisiana, and to shoot on the spot any person who attempted to haul down the U.S. flag. The *McClelland* was subsequently surrendered, but the name of the vessel became a watchword around which the North rallied nevertheless.

Dix, whose prominence in efforts to placate the South has been noted, was one of the leading figures of New York City in an age when people so-called truly exercised leadership. He had served as an officer in the War of

1812, remaining in the army until poor health had forced him to resign. He had then become a member of the Albany Regency. He had been appointed adjutant-general of New York, after which he had served as the secretary of state of New York and as U.S. senator. Now the postmaster of New York City and a president of various railroads, he was wealthy and influential, one of the city's most distinguished citizens. Herman was associated with him in a variety of ways. Dix's membership in the Albany Regency had made him a friend and an ally of Uncle Peter. Politics, his connection to the Bond Street social set, and a close friendship with Dix's son Morgan, who was a minister of his church, had made Richard Lathers more than a casual acquaintance, and some of the same threads also connected Dix to Allan Melville. More to the point, during his time in the Senate Dix had endorsed Herman in an unsuccessful bid for federal office.[55]

Because of the financial crisis, commerce in the city faltered and failed, the financial market sagged, and real estate transactions were few, with the result that Henry Gansevoort and his partner Bruce had few title searches to make and few conveyances to draw up. In Pittsburgh, owners threatened to close their coal mines until March, and in Pittsfield lowered demand forced mills to reduce their working hours. Of greatest concern to Herman would have been John Hoadley's difficulties. Many of the buyers of the Hoadley engine had been Southerners, whose custom was now lost. That loss was compounded when Southern debtors took advantage of the national schism to repudiate their obligations to Northerners, with the result that John was unable to collect for engines he had delivered, even though agent banks in the South had already received the payments. He asked Richard to find friends returning to the South who would purchase checks on those banks, but the Southerners Richard knew had only enough money to pay for their transportation home. Thus John saw much of the wealth he had accumulated disappear just as he and Kate had begun to enjoy it.[56]

The most dominant and sinister variable in the equation of secession was the possibility of war. In Pittsfield, as elsewhere in both North and South, military preparations had been made. Because the Pittsfield Guards, a militia company, had fallen into decay, Thomas Allen had contributed $1,500 for its reorganization as the Allen Guard. By November it was up to its full complement of men, arms, and equipment, and under the able command of Captain Henry S. Briggs it had been drilled to an acceptable level of efficiency. In New York, Henry Gansevoort was quick to sense the likely importance of the military in the days to come. As he saw it, if Lincoln tried to hold the union together by raw power, the profession of arms would become preeminent, the Constitution would be suspended, and strength and weakness would replace right and wrong. The administration would introduce a new era of militarism, perhaps Napoleonic in nature, and if that occurred Henry intended to profit from it.[57]

Early in 1861, he joined the New York Seventh Regiment of National Guards, an elite militia unit that had gained international fame for its precision marching. To be a common soldier in this uncommon regiment was a social triumph; no private in the Seventh would exchange his position for a captaincy in the Allen Guard. The recruits came from the best families: West Pointers served in its lowest ranks, along with lawyers, artists, and businessmen. These included Robert Gould Shaw, a native of Massachusetts who had moved to Staten Island to live with his father, Francis G. Shaw. (The elder Shaw had acted briefly as Herman's publisher not three years earlier.) Henry Gansevoort suspected that in the event of war even the lowest rank in the Seventh would lead to a commission in the army.[58]

Worried by the vulnerable geographical position and the pitiful defenses of the federal capital, General Scott accepted the offer of the Seventh Regiment to stand in readiness. "That regiment, sir," he boasted, "can be relied upon." In Pittsfield, the Allen Guard, which had already been alerted by Governor Andrew, announced that it was ready. In Illinois, the Rockford Wide Awakes had transformed themselves into the Rockford Zouaves, a military company of which Randolph Hobart was first corporal and later a sergeant, and, somewhat later, they absorbed the South Rockford band, two drummers, one of whom was John A. Hobart, and a fifer. Like the Allen Guard, the Zouaves announced that they were ready. In Concord, Emerson asked the local captain of militia if his company were ready to march to Washington. When told that it was, Emerson noted, "I hope it will not need, but the readiness is wholesome."[59]

Guert Gansevoort was more actively engaged in the preparations for war than were the militiamen. The most pernicious irritant between the North and the South was federal property such as the *McClelland*—federal in the eyes of Washington but no longer federal in the reckoning of the state within whose borders it was located. But revenue steamers were not as likely to cause mischief as were land installations such as forts, which, to Southerners, were alien military outposts within their borders. Most mischievous of all was Fort Sumter, strategically located at the entrance to Charleston Harbor. Manned by artillerymen, including Major Robert Anderson and Captain Abner Doubleday, it was undermanned and undersupplied. Ultimately, the South would want to appropriate it and the North would want to keep it. General Scott quietly hired a steamer to resupply and augment the force there, and Guert and the other yard personnel in Brooklyn furnished what was needed by the marines and the artillerists she was to carry. But the mission was a failure; on her arrival, South Carolina batteries drove her off.

Tilting with Windmills

During these early months of 1861, Herman was privy to one of the most bizarre events of the prewar period. In New York City, the delegation of the Pine Street Meeting was ready to depart for the South, but only one of the three delegates remained. Fillmore, who from the first had doubted the likelihood of the mission's success, had pleaded feeble health, and Bronson, too, had declined to go. That meant that Richard Lathers was, by default, the entire delegation. His quest was the epitome of the quixotic, a lone New Yorker and his wife touring the Confederacy to persuade the states in secession to give up their new national experiment and return to allegiance to the United States. But that was precisely what he hoped to do when, in February, he and his Sancha Panza, Abby, bade farewell to their children, to Allan and Jennie, to Henry, and to the Thurstons, and departed to joust with the windmill of disunion.[60]

In Washington, Richard found the peace conference in session and discussed his mission with ex-President Tyler and with lame-duck Vice-President Breckinridge, who, along with other Southern leaders, gave him warm letters to influential Southerners, including Jefferson Davis. From there he and Abby went to Richmond, where they were received cordially, as they were, with one exception, everywhere along their route, but even though Virginia had not yet seceded, Richard was told unequivocally that he was too late. Undeterred, he and Abby took the railroad south to Charleston.

Toward the end of February, Richard had the bittersweet satisfaction of being once again in the city of his youth. There he argued his case, but in their excitement the Charlestonians were more anxious to talk than to listen. Civic leaders, old friends, introduced him to General Beauregard and Major Anderson, and he may also have seen William Gilmore Simms, who was excitedly devising plans for the attack on Fort Sumter. Through the good offices of some of these men, he and Abby witnessed the process of organizing the government: tariffs being instituted, fortifications being built, and an army being trained. They were taken to Fort Moultrie, where they saw raw Confederate soldiers drilling, and to the floating battery that had been built for the attack on Sumter. After they had listened to Richard's address at a dinner given by Governor Pickens, the local citizens told him that it was too late, although they expressed their appreciation. On March 1,

Richard Lathers, *circa* 1871, from a painting by Daniel Huntington. Frontispiece, *Reminiscences of Richard Lathers*

Richard unwisely wrote a letter to the friendly *New York Journal of Commerce* describing the progress of his mission. In the innocent belief that New Yorkers would applaud his effort, he meant to keep them apprised. He must have sent more informal reports to Allan, who would have relayed them to Herman.

The two emissaries next visited Savannah, Georgia, where they remained until the middle of March. In response to the governor's invitation, they accompanied a group of sightseers on a boat trip to Fort Pickens, which had just been abandoned by its federal garrison. As they returned, the other passengers entertained them by holding coattails and snaking around the deck to the tune of "Dixie." Richard wrote another letter to the *Journal of Commerce* on March 13, before he and Abby proceeded on their travels. They next visited Augusta, Columbia, and Macon, Georgia, before reaching the capital of the Confederacy, Montgomery, Alabama, where Richard mailed yet another report to New York. He received the impression that the South might eventually reunite with the conservative states of the North, such as New York, but that they would never again associate themselves politically with New England. He was introduced to Jefferson Davis, to whom, with part of the cabinet present, he delivered his address. Davis shook his hand cordially and invited the couple to an evening party at his residence. Appropriately, Davis wore gray.

While Richard was carrying out his forlorn mission, another journey was taking place, that of Lincoln to the nation's capital. From Chicago, Toby Greene had written Herman that he saw Lincoln often, and he predicted that, threats against the president-elect notwithstanding, he would take office on the Capitol steps. In February, Lincoln passed ostentatiously through the North. In the middle of the month Abe Lansing saw him at the Schenectady, New York, railroad station, where Lincoln spoke briefly from the rear platform of the train, but his namesake was not impressed. On Monday, February eighteenth, Kitty Gansevoort saw Lincoln in Albany. She thought that, though he was ordinary looking, his beard had improved his appearance. The next day, Lincoln appeared in the city, where Broadway was crowded with the curious—probably including Allan Melville and Henry Gansevoort. Then on the fourth of March, after Lincoln had been spirited through Baltimore without display, he took his oath as Toby Greene had predicted.[61]

After the inauguration, the new administration embarked on a calculated policy of procrastination and appeasement, in accordance with which Lincoln's inaugural address promised protection for the institution of slavery. After the inaction of the Buchanan administration, this was too much for some. Demonstrating that even the most detached of Northern writers was transfixed by the drama, Henry David Thoreau wrote a new set of beatitudes:

> As for my prospective reader, I hope that he *ignores* Fort Sumpter, & Old Abe, & all that, for that is just the most fatal and indeed the only fatal, weapon you can direct against evil ever; for as long as you *know of* it, you are *particeps criminis*. What business have you, if you are "an angel of light," to be pondering over the deeds of darkness, reading the

> New York Herald, & the like? I do not so much regret the present condition of things in this country (provided I regret it at all) as I do that I ever heard of it. I know one or 2 who have this year, for the first time, read a president's message; but they do not see that this implies a fall in themselves, rather than a rise in the president. Blessed were the days before you read a president's message. Blessed are the young for they do not read the president's message.
>
> Blessed are they who never read a newspaper, for they shall see Nature, and through her, God.
>
> But, alas *I* have heard of Sumpter, & Pickens, & even of Buchanan, (though I did not read his message).
>
> I also read the New York Tribune. . . . [62]

But for the Unionists, Lincoln's conservatism was welcome.

During this chaotic winter, Herman was understood to be in a precarious psychological state—at least Judge Shaw thought so. As usual, his condition corresponded to the troublesome events he was witnessing, for Pittsfield shared fully in the upset of the day. The topic of secession and worse was discussed in the parlor, in the pulpit, on the street, and in the newspapers, the *Sun* counting the Southern states as they seceded and reporting on both the formation of the Confederate government and the efforts in the North to appease them. The Allen Guard drilled as though its services would soon be required, sometimes to the music of Hodge's Band of North Adams, and once a month the public—Herman and his family included, probably, since they were in the habit of witnessing such events—watched their evolutions with admiration. In the middle of January, 150 guns were fired at Jubilee Hall, 100 for President Buchanan and 50 for Major Anderson. But the short drive from Arrowhead into town was sometimes difficult. The weather was cold and blustery, even worse when, on the thirteenth of the month, the temperature fell to twenty below zero, and when, on and after the twentieth, there was so much snow and rain that roofs collapsed. With the weather-imprisoned children downstairs, Herman continued his nostalgic correspondence with his old shipmates, but his attempts to bury himself in the past failed to shield him from the uncertainties of the present.[63]

These uncertainties were manifested variously. Some people, such as Richard Lathers and the two Lemuel Shaws, persisted in the hope that reason could avert war by checking passions. Others, Emerson, Longfellow, and Lowell, believed that in the event of hostilities, Heaven would intervene on the side of the right—the North. Yet a third party, the realists such as General Winfield Scott, anticipated the bestial nature and the staggering magnitude of the war that loomed before them and were already planning ways to win it.

Herman dealt with these responses in the pivotal, well-wrought poem, "The Conflict of Convictions (1860–1)." It captures a moment in history similar to that treated by T. S. Eliot in *The Wasteland*, a moment in which a soul-sustaining past was receding and a culture was fragmenting. It is hardly surprising, then, that in form Herman's literary reaction resembles Eliot's. A poem without precedent, "The Conflict of Convictions" is a disjunctive medley of images, characters, and contrapuntal voices. Placed in *Battle-Pieces* at the approximate point from which the battle poems take their departure, it summarizes what has gone before—images of mountains, storms, and downward rush—and accumulates a storehouse of materials on which the rest of the book depends. Although this study cannot provide a detailed analysis, cannot account for such perplexing elements as its peculiar typography and arrangement, for example, we may explore it in general terms.[64]

It is a poem of complexity, bafflement, and therefore irresolution that, divorced from its context in *Battle-Pieces*, makes little sense. In order to understand it, the reader must know what convictions are in conflict. Although one might expect them to concern states' rights or emancipation, no critic has been tempted to read the poem in such terms, for to do so would be to render it incomprehensible. Furthermore, the fact that it is Miltonic in reference—a battle between archangels—encourages readers to assume that it is a rewriting of the war in heaven of *Paradise Lost*, in which theological good and evil conflict. But the actual conception on which the poem rests is a familiar one, Ishmael's metaphor in *Moby-Dick* of the three-way fabric into which man's condition on earth is woven: "chance, free will, and necessity—no wise incompatible—all interweavingly working together" (215). The conflicting convictions are political, moral, and religious, facets of being which in Herman's imagination were always interrelated: God will not allow a fratricidal war to occur; should war occur, God will intervene in favor of the Union (or the Confederacy); or God will not intervene at all, leaving mortals to resolve their dispute through bloody struggle. With the kings of the Old World wagging their heads at the stumbling American experiment, the poem is about the "*Verge*" where the *"top of the ages' strife"* meets *"the last advance of life."*

Four figures define these convictions, God and three archangels, Raphael, Michael, and the fallen Satan. The poem begins with a confrontation between Raphael and Satan. Poised on starry heights, Raphael is, one might wish, an emissary sent by heaven to ensure that the crisis of the nation will pass with bloodshed averted and union preserved. The bugle that "wails the long recall" summons the nation back from the brink of war, as suggested in the contrapuntal stanza (spoken by a believer in Raphael) that follows his appearance: "*Battle no more shall be! / While the fields for fight in æons to come / Congeal beneath the sea.*" However, in his old age Satan, Raphael's opponent, "is strong and hale, / A disciplined captain, gray in skill." As events would soon prove, Raphael is no match for him in the sense that rational arbitration of differences is hopeless in the face of aroused passions. In the end, Raphael is a chimera, not an angel but a mere personification of the futile hopes and beliefs of the human "white enthusiast": war comes and Raphael appears no more on the pages of *Battle-Pieces.* Benign intervention is not God's way: "Heaven's ominous silence over all."

The fields beneath the sea are the place of inscrutable mystery, of the fates, of "Nature's last reserves" in "Timoleon" (213), of God's creation and predestination, as Pip learned in "The Castaway" chapter of *Moby-Dick*, "the unwarped primal world" where the little black "saw God's foot upon the treadle of the loom" (414). The link between the fates and slavery is forged in an allusion to the Old Testament account of the flight of the Israelites from their Egyptian bondage; as they approached the Red Sea, "the waters were gathered together, the floods stood upright as an heap, *and* the depths were congealed in the heart of the sea" (Ex. 15:8).

In *White-Jacket,* Herman had suggested that Satan, or the Devil, as he is there called, is not a mere symbol of evil but rather a personification of the spirit of war: "But as the whole matter of war is a thing that smites common sense and Christianity in the face; so every thing connected with it is utterly foolish, unchristian, barbarous, brutal, and savoring of the Feejee Islands, cannibalism, saltpetre, and the devil" (315). Not only does Satan symbolize war, but he is also the specific spirit of aggression and violence that is loosed in the warrior: "Soldier or sailor, the fighting man is but a fiend," White-Jacket says, "and the staff and bodyguard of the Devil musters many a baton" (320). Further hints about the nature of Herman's Satan are provided in *Billy Budd*, where he wrote, concerning the vocal defect which deprives the young sailor of the mediating power of speech, that it is "a striking instance that the arch interferer, the envious marplot of Eden, still has more or less to do with every human consignment to this planet of Earth" (53). To explain the precise nature of this diabolical interference, Herman specified that Billy's vocal defect is analogous to Georgiana's blemish in Hawthorne's "The Birthmark." The vocal defect is, then, like the blemish, an emblem of original sin and a proof that Satan is the agent responsible for it. Further, the nature of original sin is defined by Billy's makeup, which, on every occasion in which his vocal defect stifles arbitrative speech, leads him to violence. Thus original sin, which is the unmitigated spirit of violence in man, derives from Satan. Although in abstract terms one is justified in concluding that violence and war stem from the theological evil inflicted on man by the angel of evil, one can also see the matter psychologically. In Robert Milder's terms, the coming war would be "a descent into violence and thereby into a knowledge of evil."[65] Perhaps Satan is a genuine archangel—the existence of evil in the universe was as much a mystery to Herman as it has been to philosophers in general—but had one suggested to him that this Satan corresponds to the feral nature of man's deep-rooted resource of uncensored brutality, he might well have agreed.

With Raphael dismissed, there remains only one celestial champion, "Michael the warrior one," who in the clouds above girds on his sword. Although the principal model for this Michael is undoubtedly to be found in *Paradise Lost,* the poem must also refer to the biblical story of the Babylonian captivity. In an apocalyptic prophecy of a chaotic age in which the Kingdom of the South will battle the Kingdom of the North, there is this vision of the deliverer of the Israelites: "And at that time shall Michael stand up, the great prince which standeth for the children of thy people" (Dan. 12:1). As will be seen, the Book of Daniel is a source of allusion elsewhere in *Battle-Pieces,* as well. Michael is the angel of righteous war, the champion of most Northerners—and Southerners—who believed that their cause was God's cause and that God would intervene on their behalf. That was the message of Henry Howard Brownell's "Annus Memorabilis":

> This is not a war of men, but of Angels Good and Ill—
> 'Tis hell that storms at heaven—'tis the black and deadly Seven,
> Sworn 'gainst the Shining Ones to work their damnéd will! . . .
> But we all have read, (in that Legend grand and dread,)
> How Michael and his host met the Serpent and his crew—

Or, as Lowell wrote, "We have no doubt of the issue. We believe that the strongest battalions are always on the side of God." These were the people to whom, in "Apathy and Enthusiasm," "Michael seemed gigantical, / The Arch-fiend but a dwarf."[66]

Although Herman may have believed that God approved of and perhaps sponsored the noble and unique experiment in human governance that the union represented—and there is evidence that he did—he knew that the Confederates were not agents of a foreign tyranny but as much Americans as the Unionists, and he knew that the sins of the South were the sins of all America—his own family had once owned slaves. What in the name of reason could inspire God to favor red roses over white, or one region of America over another? And if God were to pick a favorite, what would induce him to champion the North over the South rather than the South over the North? As Lincoln later put it, the Southerners read the same Bible and prayed to the same God as the Northerners. Southerners also believed that they were the favored ones, a Louisiana woman writing that "our cause is right and God will give us the victory." In Herman's poem "The Swamp Angel," Michael is "the white man's seraph" who dwells in a church tower in Charleston, South Carolina, protecting the Confederates. A Confederate Michael made as much sense to Southerners as a Union Michael did to Northerners.[67]

Herman did not believe that God took sides in wars. In commenting on Jack Chase's contention that God was on the side of the British at the Battle of Navarino, White-Jacket says, "It would seem that war almost makes blasphemers of the best of men, and brings them all down to the Feejee standard of humanity" (320). In *Battle-Pieces,* Michael does not influence the outcome of battles. Whenever a battle poem suggests divine sanction or intervention, the reader can sense the Michael fallacy behind it and know that the thrust of the poem is ironic—delightfully so in the case of "Look-Out Mountain." Like Raphael, Michael is a chimera, not a warrior-angel but a personification of the popular desire and belief that heaven favored the North.

Since both Raphael and Michael are no more than unfulfillable desires, and since Satan may be no more than a pervasive psychological deformity in mankind, the one certain deity remaining is God. But He is remote. Despite His pastoral care of the Israelites in the lore of the Old Testament, He has withdrawn His compassion and His protection from His chosen people: "heaven with age is cold." Yet another covenant—the Declaration of Independence and the Constitution—has been broken by Americans in their frantic getting and spending. Herman had placarded their faults in his *Piazza Tales,* and now he reiterated the idea that they are "Mammon's slaves" who "spread like a weedy grass, / . . . And prosper to the apoplex," who have failed to cherish and to nurture the republican ideals they have inherited. They are a "rout" that "herds around the heart," the organ of beauty and love but also of greed and intolerance.

This God is not angry, vengeful, just, protective, generous, loving, or pedagogical. He is bereft of anthropomorphic characteristics and thus may be the "scheme of Nature" or predestination itself. That is what Herman meant when he wrote Hawthorne that "the reason the mass of men fear God, and *at bottom dislike* Him, is because they rather distrust His heart, and fancy Him all brain like a watch."[68] This clocklike God is indifferent to the small lives of individual men; he is not to be blamed for sufferings in war, nor does logic allow that he be credited with the rosy boons of peace.

God being remote, men are responsible for events. Mutual faith on the part of both North and South might bring about a Raphaelesque avoidance of war, but faith has been neglected. Depicted as an allegorical female sculpture related both to the mother of the quarreling sons in "Apathy and Enthusiasm" and to the later mother America, she stands alone:

(At a stony gate,
A statue of stone,
Weed overgrown—
Long 'twill wait!)

Without faith, war is inevitable. The struggle will have nothing to do with swords girded on in clouds but will be fought where Satan lurks—beneath the surface of the earth and in other dark and remote ambushes, most prominently in the depths of the forest. But in this poem the American brought down to Satan's depths is the miner in the tunnel, burrowing through the subterranean dark toward he knows not what:

(Ay, in caves the miner see:
His forehead bears a taper dim;
Darkness so he feebly braves
Which foldeth him.)

In historical terms, the miner was suggested by the 1864 "crater" episode in which Union miners tunneled under Confederate defenses at Petersburg, an event in which, as will be seen, Herman had a personal interest. But he had already equated war with tunnels in White-Jacket's vision of the ship's gunner, who, "like a Cornwall miner in a cave, is burrowing down in the magazine under the Ward-room" (67). The war must be fought to its end in Satan's underworld, dark, ambiguous, perilous, tragic.

Has God, then, nothing to do with the outcome of events? Although men control their own affairs, God is still the author of the divine plan, or Fate, that determines the final outcome of all things:

The Ancient of Days forever is young,
    Forever the scheme of Nature thrives;
I know a wind in purpose strong—
    It spins *against* the way it drives.

Men's actions will dictate the spin of the wind, that is, day-to-day events. At their best, they will defy the instinctual, Satanic urge to violence with which original sin polluted them and cause the wind to spin in a benign and constructive direction. At less than their best, they will succumb to those instincts, causing the wind to spin in a vicious, perhaps deadly direction. Either way, they are ultimately responsible for their own good or bad fortune. But however well or ill they fashion their destinies, in larger terms the "scheme of Nature," God's plan, will triumph.

Was the American experiment futile? Will God allow it to fail? At this point, it is too early to tell. The future of the union is symbolized by the iron dome, an image which recurs a number of times in *Battle-Pieces*. This anachronism—since it did not exist at the time with which this poem deals—had become fixed in Herman's imagination by the time he began sustained work on his book. While in Washington in 1847, he had visited the old Bullfinch Capitol, most of which is embedded in the present structure. Capped by a low wooden dome sheathed with copper, its design was republican, unpretentious but dignified, manifesting architecturally the virtues of the Founders of the nation. But as America grew large in size and giddy in pretension, the building was enlarged and, in the process, given a massy, imperial ostentation. This was the unfinished, domeless structure of early 1861. Crowning the palatial edifice was to be the present high dome raised on tiers of columns. In its effect the new dome would substitute papal pomp for the Jeffersonian restraint of the earlier design. In order to make the dome mechanically feasible, it was not carved of stone, as was the rest of the building, but manufactured of iron and painted white to give the appearance of stone. Symbolically, then, the new dome would suggest "an iron age to come, and perhaps in more than one sense," a new, technological, Hoadleyesque United States about which thinkers like Herman speculated uneasily.[69]

The future of the union, then, is linked to that of the dome. What would become of it? The promise of America may be renewed and its dross purged through the redemptive suffering of war:

> What if the gulfs their slimed foundations bare?
> So deep must the stones be hurled
> Whereon the throes of ages rear
> The final empire and the happier world.

That is the most optimistic note in *Battle-Pieces*. On the other hand, one pessimist foretells *"rust on the Iron Dome,"* an America weakened spiritually by the bitter struggle. Another foresees that the nation will emerge from the crisis mighty but wayward in spirit:

> Power unanointed may come—
> Dominion (unsought by the free)
> And the Iron Dome,
> Stronger for stress and strain,
> Fling her huge shadow athwart the main;
> But the Founders' dream shall flee.

This was the fear of the family conservatives, that the cherished republic would be transformed into the kind of European empire against which the Founding Fathers had rebelled, quite the opposite of a new beginning for mankind. Would that occur? In victory, would the nation lose its "consecrating sense of historical mission"?[70] The answer is neither yes nor no. An Olympian epilogue states the truth: none can know the future in which God's plan will mature. "WISDOM IS VAIN, AND PROPHESY."

Jonah Once More?

In Albany, the Gansevoorts wondered how Herman was going to pass the winter, as did his mother in Gansevoort. On the twelfth of January, Henry appeared at his family home for the weekend and Aunt Melville arrived for a three and a half week visit. Despite her age, she was full of the ambition of the country exile to "do" the city, so Aunt Susan and Kitty accommodated her with a whirl of social activity. That diverted her from her anxiety about Uncle Herman's health.[71]

At the end of the month it was still uncertain that Herman would appear to escort his mother home, but on Saturday, the second of February, he arrived, seemingly in good health for the moment. He attended Sunday services with the family and then, on Tuesday, took his mother to Gansevoort on the afternoon train. There he found Uncle Herman as well as might be expected, considering that he was feeble and that his knees ached. After a visit of nearly a week, during which he would have been expected to visit his cousins in Glens Falls, he returned to Albany, where he dined with the Gansevoorts. With his usual Delphic humor, which he described as "mine infirmity of jocularity," he sent Henry a message advising him to be "*sound*" on affairs of the country, leaving Henry to wonder what he meant by the word. Herman enjoyed treating his relatives to such conundrums, but in this case soundness meant conservatism. In the afternoon Herman boarded the train back to Pittsfield.[72]

There was reason for his revived health. When in "The Conflict of Convictions" one speaker warns, "Now save thyself / Who wouldst rebuild the world in bloom," he may be articulating Herman's own response to the crisis. Herman was already planning to act the Jonah again—not to avoid mutilation or death in the battles that might come, but to flee once more from his Nineveh, the spiritual agony of the impending crisis and the role he may already have foreseen for himself. He was about to begin the most vigorous campaign for public office of his life, with the object of securing a consulship at some overseas post such as Florence, Italy. In Florence, civilization was ancient and art was king. There he could bury himself in antiquities and seek the tranquility that evaded him at home.

In the face of the overwhelming competition for office, there were essential preparations to be made. Everyone seemed to want something from the new administration, including Whittier, who was asking for some of the federal spoils for his brother Matthew and specifying that a salary of at least $1,300 was needed. He succeeded in obtaining a clerkship in the customs service that kept Matthew comfortably situated for twenty years. Oakes Shaw, too, managed to obtain another patronage position, that of foreign clearance clerk in the Boston Custom House, and it may have been during this scramble that he did so. On a lighter note, George Strong gave the Columbia College Law School janitor his endorsement for a diplomatic post "in Mesopotamia, or that neighborhood" because "so inefficient a janitor may make a brilliant diplomat."[73]

The following week, Allan began working on Herman's campaign. Knowing how such things were done, he asked George Griggs to help and to enlist the aid of Judge Shaw. George was unwilling to bother Shaw, who was feeble, but he investigated the Florence position and found that it was worth only $500 per year, which he thought would pinch Herman and his family—Herman, to whom a regular income would be a novelty! When, despite George's solicitude, the judge learned of the project, he agreed that it would be beneficial for Herman to move away from Pittsfield, where he lacked companionship and exercise, and he suggested that Allan use his influence to find him a position in the New York Custom House. During the last week in February, Allan was absent from the city, perhaps visiting Herman to talk about the application, and John Hoadley began a three-week visit in Washington. Although John may have had business dealings and consultations there, he certainly meant to attend the inauguration of the first successful presidential candidate of his party. He would also have been alert for opportunities to mention Herman's case to influential people, particularly to his friend Charles Sumner.[74]

With the aid of his family, Herman collected an impressive list of endorsements. George Griggs obtained one from Representative Alexander H. Rice, one of the founders of the Republican party in Massachusetts and the first Republican mayor of Boston. John Hoadley got up a petition of prominent Lawrence men and contacted old friends in Pittsfield. Allan arranged a similar petition signed by prominent New Yorkers, including John A. Dix, who, as a result of his firmness as secretary of the treasury, had influence with the Republicans. However, Dix conditioned his support on the existence of a vacancy.

Herman also solicited endorsements in Pittsfield and received an especially touching one from Julius Rockwell, a justice of the Massachusetts Superior Court who had served in both houses of Congress. Rockwell stated pointedly that his letter was an exception to his policy against recommending applicants for federal office. However, Herman had somewhat less success with his friend and fellow writer of sea yarns, R. H. Dana, Jr., who was remaining aloof from the struggle for spoils, but after Dana discussed the matter with Judge Shaw he contributed something—not a recommendation, but a casual endorsement that praised Herman and expressed doubts about his physical condition. The day of that discussion, Herman received the kind of endorsement he would not have enjoyed had he known about it: Hope Shaw wrote in her diary that "I have no faith in sending away a *person* that is not able to see to his own business at Home." Judge Shaw joined in the pressure on Sumner, and George Griggs gave Herman letters to influential people in Washington.[75]

Probably Uncle Nourse also helped, but Uncle Peter, whose party was now out of power, was able to do little. In the evening of March 18, while on his way to Washington, Herman stopped in Albany. Uncle Peter's advice was that he should seek out Thurlow Weed, who was at the moment in New York City. The support of Weed, editor of the *Albany Evening Journal* and a powerful adviser to the Lincoln White House, would be invaluable. On the morning of the nineteenth, Herman boarded the train for the city, but it was not until Wednesday that, perhaps with Allan at his side, he called at the Astor to present his case to Weed. But Weed had returned to Albany, and Herman had to content himself with forwarding a letter to him in care of Uncle Peter. Before the letter could be delivered, Weed had left Albany again. The next day, in bitterly cold weather and just ahead of a blizzard, Herman departed for an expected eight- or nine-day campaign in Washington.

Back in Pittsfield, the blizzard left nine or ten inches of snow on the ground, the greatest fall of the season. In the city, Herman had just missed an accumulation of two feet—slightly less up the Hudson—which delayed train service and prevented Weed from going on to Washington. The 6:30 morning ferry had taken Herman to Jersey City, if his was the same schedule followed by Strong just five days earlier, after which he changed from railroad to railroad along the dogleg route to Washington. At six in the evening of March 21, he reached the capital and found boardinghouse accommodations. The weather was windy and unpleasant, as it was the next day, Friday, when he joined the crush of office seekers.[76]

Speaking of this crush, the Pittsfield *Sun* castigated the opposition party: "There never was such a disgraceful scramble for office as is now going on among the black republican 'patriots.'" The scramble *was* a disgrace. The hotel lobbies were crowded with office seekers. A week earlier there had already been up to 10,000 applications for post office jobs alone, and up to

700 more were arriving daily. Dozens of congressmen crowded into the White House anteroom each day to lobby for positions for their constituents. While Lincoln was working to end secession or, at least, to forestall hostilities, the demands for patronage were diverting his time and attention to the point that he found it necessary to set aside days when he would receive visits neither of friendship nor of business. Privately, he said that he felt like a man who was renting offices in one end of his house while the other end was burning down.[77]

John Hoadley had finished his heady inaugural business and had returned home without having had a chance "to shoot a rebel," he joked to Gus, but Uncle Nourse, "as facetious as ever," was still in the capital kicking up his Republican heels, looking for some patronage for himself and ready to help his nephew in whatever way he could. Herman's difficulty was that although he wanted to plead his case, the mandatory endorsements had yet to arrive. Consequently, he could do little for the moment but see the sights in the dismal weather and, under Uncle Nourse's sponsorship, find what amusement or enlightenment he could in official society.[78]

On the twenty-second, Herman visited the Capitol to watch the Senate in special crisis session. The building was an unsightly mess because of the unfinished state of its reformation, particularly the rotunda, which was open to the wind and the sky. Workmen were starting to finish off the space between the cornice, where the old dome had rested, and the tiers of columns that were to support the new dome. Scaffoldings and hoists marred the view of the exterior, though inside the marbles and the Brumidi frescoes, a novelty in the Western hemisphere, were impressive.

The enlarged and embellished building, old and familiar now, was new and exciting then. Its novelty and its abandonment of republican restraint can be sensed in this description by Walt Whitman, who was amazed by its variety of marbles and its elaborate metal work, "by far the richest and gayest, and most un-American and inappropriate ornamenting and finest interior workmanship I ever conceived possible . . . But . . . the style is without grandeur, and without simplicity." Herman's own description was far more abbreviated and somewhat more polite, but despite the disorder and the aristocratic presumption he must have been impressed: worked stone symbolized permanence and classical values to him. He left no record of his impression of the heroic paintings of national history that hung in the rotunda, paintings which Strong had wished to give away to South Carolina, but Herman must have preferred to keep them. The Yorktown ceremony depicted in John Trumbull's "Surrender of Cornwallis" had family significance, as did Trumbull's painting of the British surrender at Saratoga.[79]

Upstairs, the Senate galleries were crowded with spectators, both on the ladies' side and on the men's, muted in comparison with the noisy demonstrations that often took place during the regular sessions. With so many Southerners missing, the floor was sparsely populated. Senators were arguing over the legality of secession, the defensibility of the Southern forts, and the Democrats' talk of the powerlessness of the government. Herman thought these deliberations "nothing very interesting," and when the body went into executive session he had to leave the galleries.[80]

That evening, Uncle Nourse took him to the second public reception of the Lincoln presidency, from eight to ten. Herman was as dazzled as any tourist by the magnificence of the White House, the superb furniture, the flood of illumination, the magnificent flowers, and the music of the band. For an hour and a half, uncle and nephew stood in line with the horde of guests waiting to be greeted by the president. Herman was surprised to find Lincoln relatively young and, with his beard, comely, and he thought Mary Todd Lincoln "rather good-looking." "He shook hands like a good fellow—" he wrote Lizzie, "working hard at it like a man sawing wood at so much per cord." Sophisticated easterners thought Lincoln uncouth and beneath the dignity of the presidency—even Emerson's early acceptance of the raw westerner was qualified by his New England hauteur: "You cannot refine Mr. Lincoln's taste, extend his horizon, or clear his judgment; he will not walk dignifiedly through the traditional part of the President of America, but will pop out his head at each railroad station and make a little speech, and get into an argument with Squire A and Judge B. He will write letters to Horace Greeley, and any editor or reporter or saucy party committee that writes to him, and cheapen himself." He thought that Lincoln came very close to being one of the "leaders of the low," but that sort of thinking was foreign to Herman, to whom the ruggedness of the mountaineer and the Westerner was a virtue. Coming from him, the wood sawing analogy was a good-natured compliment.[81]

The next day the weather improved. In the continued absence of his recommendations, Herman again visited the Senate. The proceedings were tedious: the body chose a president pro tem and conducted other business of internal management. In view of his mission, Herman must have taken a wry interest in the fact that the Republicans were trying to fire the Democratic Senate clerks and the Democrats were deploring the cruelty of this application of the spoils system. Afterward, Herman called at Sumner's residence, which was just around the corner from Willard's, but the senator had left for dinner. Still later, Uncle Nourse exposed him to more of official Washington by taking him to a small party, apparently for the Maine contingent, at the home of an administration official. There were several senators present, perhaps William P. Fessenden and Lot M. Morrill of Maine, as well as Uncle Nourse's friend, Vice President Hannibal Hamlin. Uncle Nourse may have been promoting Herman's cause, but he had no need to apologize for his nephew, whom others regarded as an acquisition. Herman was still a well-known man of letters at a time when educated men attached great importance to literature, and the other guests must have felt as honored to meet him as he felt to meet them. Herman was at ease, and wrote home that Mrs. Hamlin was very pleasing in manner and that she resembled Lizzie.

The next day, Sunday, Herman was frustrated and homesick. Despite the driving dust, the worst in memory, he sat for some time in Lafayette Park, in front of the White House, smoking his pipe, no doubt. The park was notorious—two years earlier, Dan Sickles had murdered his wife's lover there. Herman could see the president's mansion, its landscaping, its greenhouses, its fruit trees, and its flower gardens, and he must have wondered about its occupant, how he would deal with the immense problems which faced him. What did Herman think about the man and the decisions he would be forced to make? Somewhere in the mansion before him was the untried Illinois lawyer who had been given the power to act and to dispose, wisely or unwisely. So far, he had eschewed the radicalism that his opponents had feared in him, but the experience of past millennia had failed to change man's quarrelsome nature, and Herman doubted that such a change would occur now.

On the other hand, the power of this man—or of any man—was limited. Free will, Necessity, and Fate! Lincoln could attempt to find a solution to the nation's crisis—that much Free Will was allowed him. On the other hand, if with their own Free Will the Confederates attacked, Necessity would propel Lincoln into war. But above all, an inscrutable and heartless Fate had the final say, and who knew what its purpose would be? Lincoln could make mistakes, bloody mistakes, or he could steer prudently and deftly, but in the end the predestined result would be the same. Regardless of his thoughts, Herman enjoyed the greening grass and the budding shrubbery, and he had for a companion the Clark Mills statue of Andrew Jackson—another secession gift to South Carolina, if Strong had his way.[82] For his part, Herman must have preferred that the North keep this memorial to the frontier president whom he had long admired.

Later he wandered over to "that hideous unfinished Washington Monument," as Strong described it. It was like the stump of a fallen Carthaginian column—and like the Bunker Hill monument, had been for so long that he had dedicated *Israel Potter* to it—and it stagnated forlornly in a boggy pasture amid grazing cows. Although he tried, he was unable to peek inside.

The new redstone Smithsonian building, a Mecca for the curious, was nearby, and his natural curiosity probably urged him on to see what Strong called its "stuffed penguins and pickled lizards." But he would not have gone on into the surrounding communities, the poorer of which were lawless and unsafe. All in all, Washington was not very pleasant, particularly since there was a strong undertone of hostility between the Unionists and a worrisome number of Secessionists.[83]

On Monday, the beginning of the last week of Lent, Herman was still awaiting his recommendations and paying the price in fatigue for his long walk the day before. What he did to combat his frustration and loneliness is not known, but the activity at the Senate may have drawn him back there. That day bickering continued about what should be done about secession, and Tuesday the same subject was taken up by Senator Breckinridge. Breckinridge fascinated Herman. Despite his unshakeable Southern sympathies, the former vice-president and presidential candidate had taken his Senate seat as though to remain with the union until the last possible moment—which is what he did.

It is likely that until his departure, which was scheduled for Tuesday, Uncle Nourse continued to maneuver Herman into the path of administration officials, but there was public entertainment, too. At the Washington Theatre, Joseph Jefferson was offering plays in repertory, "Rip Van Winkle," which would have interested Herman, "Mazeppa," and, on Monday and Tuesday, "Sea of Ice." As added attractions, there were operatic imitations and comic dances.[84]

On Wednesday, with Uncle Nourse probably gone, Herman's recommendations began to arrive—most important, the one from Rockwell, to whom he dashed off a letter of thanks—and on Thursday morning he took what he had to Sumner. However, Sumner was obliged to inform him that it was too late for the Florence appointment, as people in New York seemed to know already—George Strong, at least. Sumner suggested another consulship, perhaps Glasgow, and Herman retired to think the matter over. Later in the day he received an urgent message from Lizzie that her father was critically ill, and he knew that he must end his visit with little chance of making his application in person. He searched frantically for Sumner, but the senator had once more disappeared into the bustle of capital life. Herman had no choice but to leave him a letter in which he agreed to Glasgow and threw himself on Sumner's mercy. Then, early on a glorious Good Friday morning, March 29, he boarded the train for home.[85]

Sumner submitted the papers with a cordial recommendation that Herman be given a post at Glasgow, Geneva, or Manchester, but to no avail. One reason for the failure was that Herman had begun too late, after many of the consulships had already been spoken for. Another was that he did not ask for favors easily—did not put himself forward, as others were willing to do. Yet a third was that despite Sumner's prominence in the Republican party, Weed would have been the better advocate. After having been perceived as a radical candidate, policy had caused Lincoln to act the part of the moderate. Already he was identifying himself with the Seward wing of the party rather than the more radical Sumner wing, a position that gave him some hope of dealing successfully with the South, and he had appointed a bipartisan cabinet. Thus while the administration would hardly have repudiated Sumner, it may have preferred to distance itself from him. In contrast, Lincoln had embraced Weed. For whatever reason, fate dictated that Jonah would go to Nineveh.

Although by the time Herman reached Pittsfield he must have been exhausted, Lizzie was already packed to leave for Boston next morning. That night the former chief justice was restless. While his family watched at his bedside, his disturbed mind wandered aimlessly through imagined scenes in court, where he addressed ghostly juries. Then at 7:30 on Saturday morning, while he was sitting with Hope and Lemuel, Jr., he gently died. Lizzie arrived too late. There can be little doubt that Herman did what was expected of him, that he hurried on to Boston to be with Lizzie and the Shaws during that melancholy Easter Sunday. The next day was snowy, and there was a violent storm on Tuesday, when a large crowd gathered at the New South Meeting House in Boston to hear Reverend Dewey preside over the funeral of the great Massachusetts jurist. The governor attended, as did judges, the president and fellows of Harvard, members of the bar, delegations from other counties, the Shaws, and the Melvilles. He was buried in Mount Auburn Cemetery in Cambridge, and a week or so later Herman was back in Pittsfield, buying books—a set of Spenser and a set of Shelley.[86]

The passing of Shaw meant more to Herman than simply the loss of a father-in-law. His death was a part of the fundamental dislocation of the times; an era was disappearing into history as another was struggling to be born. Viewed that way, it provided Herman with the previously missing, more noble half of the equation of the innocent young country. There had been discouraging faults in the nation, but there had also been large men who had given shape to the new society. Like Andrew Jackson, John Quincy Adams, Henry Clay, and Daniel Webster, Shaw had been one of those dedicated artisans who had striven to chisel the features of the youthful republic. He had grappled with the public issues of his age, industrialization, urbanization, transportation, and penology, establishing precedents that would affect American life far into the future, and he had done so with a full sense of his role as a legal pioneer. It was not difficult to regard the loss of Shaw as the end of the age of the Founders. It was possible for Herman to redefine that age in his mind as a forerunner of a better America, which also suggested an exciting significance for the war that was approaching; it might be a tragic catalyst needed to cause the nation to flower into maturity.

In mid-March, with Commander Foote temporarily in command and Guert acting as his deputy, the Brooklyn Navy Yard busied itself preparing ships for relief expeditions to forts in the South, particularly Sumter. At the beginning of April, the group for Sumter was assembling and Strong noted in his diary, "Great stir in army and navy. Governor's Island, Fort Hamilton, and Brooklyn Navy Yard full of business. Troops moving, no one knows whither. Ships getting ready for sea in hot haste and sailing with sealed orders." The expedition to relieve Sumter left on the ninth of April. The flagship carried troops, including a battery of artillery, one of the officers of which was Lieutenant Robert O. Tyler, who later became an acquaintance of Herman. But by the time they arrived off Charleston, General Beauregard had already commenced his bombardment. The ships were forced to stand off, unable to do more than to watch the fearful scene and then, after the surrender, to evacuate Major Anderson and his men.[87]

It was the end of the waiting, as Herman wrote in "Apathy and Enthusiasm":

So the winter died despairing,
  And the weary weeks of Lent;
And the ice-bound rivers melted,
  And the tomb of Faith was rent.

The tomb of Faith *was* rent, and the war that many had believed impossible had begun.

2

War
1861

It was Saturday, April 13, 1861. As though to commemorate the day, the first thunderstorm of the season poured down on Pittsfield (as in "The Coming Storm"), swelling its streams. With Lizzie and the children in Boston grieving with the Shaws, Herman was alone at Arrowhead. Because of the weather, and because the news of Sumter did not arrive until late at night, he probably did not know about it until the next morning, unless rural heralds broke his sleep, but in New York Walt Whitman did. About midnight, as he was walking down Broadway after an evening at the opera, he heard paper boys hawking extras. Purchasing one, he crossed the street to read it under the bright lights of the Metropolitan Hotel. A crowd of thirty or forty others gathered, but no one said a word. Then they all went home to the new world that had been born.[1]

In the morning, the shocked silence ended as people everywhere learned the news. Many took their excitement to church. In New York, George Strong heard war prayers and a trumpet-stopped organ ("the spire falls crashing in the town"). In Concord, the Hawthornes held Sunday morning services at their Wayside chapel, and then, in an unheard-of departure from family protocol, Sophia accompanied her husband on his afternoon walk. In Rockford, as the Baptist minister delivered his war sermon, the American flag was displayed in the church for the first time in the history of the town. Even though Herman's church attendance was notoriously spotty, on this day he probably attended to sample the tension in the air and to mingle with the incredulous crowds after the service.[2]

By Monday, war was an established fact and the archangel Raphael, who had proclaimed that "Battle no more shall be," had vanished. Northerners came together in a unanimity that for the moment obliterated all conflicts of convictions. After the Confederates had fired on the flag and soldiers of the United States, people regretted any sympathy they may have had with their

Southern brethren. The single reality was that rebels had taken up arms against the constituted government and had attacked their brothers with mortal force. Had it not been for Sumter, many in the North might have accepted dissolution, but now the word "union" was spoken and displayed everywhere. Lowell compared the Sumter bombardment to the musket fire at Concord bridge.[3]

The majority of Democrats suspended party feelings and the rest muted theirs. This support for the government had nothing to do with emancipation: Lincoln had not called for that, so they rallied around the acceptable principle of defending their country. In one of his last statements before his death, Stephen A. Douglas spoke for his party: "I trust the time will never come when I shall not be willing to make any needful sacrifice of personal feeling and party policy for the honor and integrity of my country." Naturally, Republicans were overjoyed with the idea that loyalty to the nation was indivisible from loyalty to their administration. There could be only two parties, they gloated, one of union and one of rebellion. As Lowell put it, cynically, "It was certainly a great piece of good luck for the government that they had a fort which it was so profitable to lose."[4]

It was impossible to escape the war fever. Now that the tempest had broken, let it storm, as Whitman said in these preliminary jottings for a poem:

> Blow mad winds!
> Rage, boil, vex, yawn-wide, yeasty waves
> Crash away—
> Tug at the planks—make them groan—fall around, black clouds—
>   clouds of death
> Come now we shall see what stuff you are made of Ship of Libertad.

In Cambridge, Longfellow was startled by the fury that burst around him: "What a sudden uprising of a whole people!" In Amesbury, Whittier suspended his Quaker pacifism for the moment. "We have at last a *united North*," he wrote. "The old fires of Liberty are rekindled, and there is a spirit of sublime self-sacrifice pervading all classes. It is more than I had ever dared to hope for." In Concord, Hawthorne discovered that Emerson had an undersoul, as well as an oversoul, and was "breathing slaughter, like the rest of us; and it is really wonderful how all sorts of theoretical nonsense, to which we New Englanders are addicted in peaceful times, vanish in the strong atmosphere which we now inhale." He himself felt exhilarated: "The war, strange to say, has had a beneficial effect upon my spirits, which were flagging woefully before it broke out. But it was delightful to share in the heroic sentiment of the time, and to feel that I had a country—a consciousness which seemed to make me young again." "If I were younger," he wrote, tongue in cheek, "I would volunteer; but as the case stands, I shall keep quiet till the enemy gets within a mile of my own house."[5]

Aside from *Battle-Pieces,* Herman left only this reaction, spoken years later by "Bridegroom Dick":

> But ah, how to speak of the hurricane unchained—
> The Union's strands parted in the hawser over-strained;
> Our flag blown to shreds, anchors gone altogether—
> The dashed fleet o' States in Secession's foul weather. (170)

But in April 1861, the echo of the cannonade and the feeling of community with his fellow Northerners invigorated him with "a mingled effect of shock and exhilaration,"[6] as Arvin put it. Although he had always loathed the gore and the carnage of war, the contrary elements in his nature now condoned them. In one sulfurous flash, complexities had given way to simplicity, ambiguities to stark reality. The need to placate the South and the perplexity about how that might be done were moot. The union, in which so much of him was invested, was no longer disintegrating; the damage had been done and the struggle to salvage it was beginning. In inertia there had been no hope, only tacit complicity; now the war to resume the great experiment of the Founders might be won. Although the future would bring suffering, perhaps a vast conflagration, it might also forge a new, better era for him and for his country. In "Apathy and Enthusiasm," he linked the beginning of the struggle to the onset of fertility, the awakenings of spring, and the ascension of Christ after his crucifixion: "The rising of the People" is coupled to the "springing of the grass," and both are related to the resurrection. The young, stimulated by the excitement, invoke Michael and belittle the "Arch-fiend," while their elders mourn the end of an era. The poem concludes with the "old saw" of the Iroquois: *"Grief to every graybeard / When young Indians lead the war."* While it might have been true that the young overestimated Michael and underestimated Satan, at this moment almost everyone, Herman included, did the same. Only later, when the Satanic force was fully felt, would the wise become graybeards.

On the streets of the North that Monday, flags were flown in profusion, people wore red, white, and blue cockades, and crowds came together in excited groups to marvel and to exchange speculations:

> Then our hearts more fiercely beat,
> As we crowded on the street,
> Hot to gather and repeat
> All the tale. . . .

according to Edmund Clarence Stedman. Pittsfield shared in this display and excitement as the citizens boiled with the war fever and felt the wave of patriotism. The electricity persisted through the following days as clouds continued to bring snow and rain. The *Sun* proclaimed its loyalty by printing "The Star Spangled Banner" and an editorial affirming that all loyal citizens stood by their country. The Allen Guard drilled nightly before aroused spectators in preparation for the expected call to duty, and the Berkshire Life Insurance Company offered war policies for soldiers and sailors. A large flag with the motto "Constitution and Union" was suspended across North Street while a boisterous throng cheered. Wilson and Morris's Minstrels, who were performing in town, saluted the flag and sang the national anthem to another cheering crowd. At Plunkett, Clapp and Company, a giant flag was unfurled, after which speeches were spoken, songs were sung, prayers were prayed, and cheers were cheered. When it was reported that at six o'clock on Sunday afternoon a troop train was to pass through town, a crowd rushed to the depot, only to see the cars clatter by without stopping. Four Christian denominations joined to conduct a prayer meeting to "ask God, under a deep sense of our unworthiness, that he would spare our nation and not give his heritage to reproach, and make what was so lately the glory and admiration of the world a thing of scorn and contempt." Free of family obligations, Herman must have joined in.[7]

Surely one of the least fortunate of men in the North was that consummate Raphael, Richard Lathers, who reached home in the midst of New York's war hysteria, including a triumphal reception of Major Anderson and his men and a mighty rally in Union Square. After their meeting with Jefferson Davis, he and Abby had journeyed on to Mobile, where Richard had presented his address at a dinner of the local Chamber of Commerce. Just after he had finished, the news of Sumter had arrived, and with a vote of thanks to the speaker the meeting had ended. Confident of their safety, the two emissaries had proceeded to New Orleans. Richard had been invited there to speak about the affairs of the day and their effect on trade, but in the morning, while he and Abby had been breakfasting at their hotel, the mayor had appeared to demand that Richard "leave the city at once as an *alien enemy*." Despite Richard's protest that he was there by invitation, the mayor had been adamant: "After the capture of Fort Sumter, the first victory of the Confederate States, it ought to occur to such an intelligent gentleman as yourself that the discussions you refer to are clearly out of place. You would be mobbed should you remain." Then they had hurried to the train station and traveled night and day through "a most disturbed region crazy with enthusiasm" until the Confederacy was safely behind them.

When Richard reached home, he found that during his absence his published letters had outraged some New York newspapers, which had placarded him as a traitor. Privately, he grumbled that "Democracy [is] . . . at a discount and Republicanism in the ascendant." Publicly, he published letters professing his love for the Union and telling a half-truth, that he had been in the South on business. But the burden of proof was on him. He flew the flag at Winyah as a signal that he was "at home" and entertained Major Anderson there, and he subscribed to the city defense fund and took part in the raising of troops, but it was a battle he could not win: a New Orleans paper scoffed that "it is only a few weeks ago that this Mr. Lathers was in our city, making vast professions and [*sic*] love for the South," and that now he was contributing money to the Union cause and giving his employees paid leaves to enlist. To some on the Union side, he was never able to shed his reputation as a Southerner who had worked to conciliate the two regions. The supreme irony was that John A. Dix, not only the author of the address Richard had carried through the South but also a fellow supporter of the Southern rule or ruin ticket in the election, escaped opprobrium entirely.[8]

We Are Coming, Father Abra'am!

The national capital was nearly defenseless. Prior to the departure of the Southerners, the army in the east had numbered a little less than 4,000 officers and men, and few of those who remained were within reach of Washington. As if that were not alarming enough, the only regular officers who had ever commanded so much as a brigade were General Scott, seventy-five, and Uncle Peter's friend General John Wool, seventy-seven. In Albany, Kitty Gansevoort heard that Jefferson Davis was in Richmond preparing to attack,[9] and everyone in the District of Columbia, including those in the national government, expected an immediate invasion.

On April 15, Lincoln called urgently for militia regiments to guard the new borders for a three-month period. A town the size of Pittsfield could not supply a regiment, but it could send its company. At 7:30 on Wednesday evening, the expected telegram arrived: the Allen Guard was to join the 8th Massachusetts militia regiment to supply one of its missing companies. With the sky still stormy, Captain Briggs's men assembled their equipment and donned their handsome gray and gold uniforms. Meanwhile, a group of wealthy citizens met to pledge $5,000 for the comfort of the men and the aid of their families. That night and the following day, the town was caught up in a bustle of preparation unprecedented since the Revolutionary War. At noon on Thursday, the ringing of bells called the citizens to the town hall for the first of many wartime meetings. After the speeches, a motion was passed thanking the Guard and acknowledging a town responsibility to care for them and theirs. At about 6:30 that evening, the company marched through town to Railroad Square, where the citizens thronged to send them off. Nearest the platform were their families and sweethearts who, with no idea of what might await their men, bade them proud and anxious goodbyes. After the seventy-eight fledgling soldiers had boarded the cars, the train pulled out toward Springfield amid cheers. Probably Herman and the Morewoods were there to see them off.[10]

In New York City, Lincoln's call was answered by the Union Defense League, over which John A. Dix presided. Before he and General Wool, who had come down from Troy, New York, for the purpose, could dispatch any troops, two out-of-state regiments marched down Broadway on their way to the capital: the 6th Massachusetts, made up largely of Lowell and Lawrence factory workers, some of them probably John Hoadley's employees, and the 8th Massachusetts, with the Allen Guard attached and Brigadier General Benjamin Franklin Butler in command.

There were only two New York units that were uniformed, armed, and ready, one of them the Seventh Regiment. Because of its fame, all of the North watched its movements, none more anxiously than Lincoln. At four o'clock on the afternoon of the nineteenth, the veterans of the Seventh formed ranks in Lafayette Square and they, too, marched down Broadway. The onlookers were transported by the appearance of their own heroes. As the men of the Seventh crossed the river to New Jersey, they passed ships dressed with flags and pennants in their honor. In Jersey City there was another celebration, as there was at every other stop along the line, but when they reached Philadelphia they discovered that the route through Baltimore was impassable. As the 6th Massachusetts had passed through that city, which was largely Secessionist, it had been attacked by a mob that had killed three of them and injured two dozen others. After the regiment had entrained for Washington, the mob had destroyed the bridges and telegraph lines south of the city, isolating the capital from the rest of the North.[11]

At the Philadelphia Navy Yard, Commodore Samuel F. DuPont arranged for civilian steamers to transport the Seventh by sea, whereupon the troops disappeared from Herman's telegraphic reports. On the twenty-second of April, they arrived at the Naval Academy in Annapolis and began to make their way to Washington. Lincoln, who could learn nothing of the movements of Northern reinforcements until they reached him, was in despair: "I begin to believe that there is no North," he complained; "The Seventh Regiment is a myth." But on April 25, their band playing, the New Yorkers stepped out down Pennsylvania Avenue. Lincoln, Secretary of War Cameron, and Secretary of State Seward reviewed them, and Mary Lincoln presented them with a bouquet. Then the regiment was mustered into the federal service by Major Irvin McDowell of the regular army. As he inspected the New York aristocrats, he remarked that they were "officers instead of soldiers."[12]

The Seventh was followed by a host of other New York militia regiments. On April 21, when the 12th New York departed for Washington, Allan Melville's brother-in-law, Doctor Henry Thurston, left with it as regimental surgeon. No sooner had he gone than it was Henry Gansevoort's turn. After a hurried trip to Albany to equip himself for his adventure, Henry said goodbye on April 23 to those of his family and friends who came to see him off—Bruce presented him with a revolver—and fell in with seventeen other recruits of the Seventh who had been left behind by the regiment. To the cheering of a crowd that had not yet wearied of military display, he marched down Broadway to the piers in the company of another New York regiment. The following three days at sea were almost too much for Henry, to the point that a future for him in the ascendant military establishment that he envisioned ruling the land under Lincoln seemed improbable. When he reached Annapolis on the twenty-sixth, the surgeon hospitalized him briefly and considered sending him home, but after some delay he joined the main body of the regiment in Washington. There he was mustered into the federal service along with another recruit of his company, the noted painter Sanford Gifford.[13]

In the western states, the call to arms had a different urgency, since it was not the safety of the capital that was at stake but the integrity of the regional boundaries of this newer and cruder part of the union. On the sixteenth of April, the Rockford Zouaves received their orders. Immediately, the women of the town began making uniforms from donated bolts of blue flannel. On Wednesday, April 24, four or five thousand excited citizens flocked to the train station to see the hundred-man company, including Sergeant Randolph Hobart and his brother, Musician John Hobart, depart in their new regalia. On the thirtieth, at Springfield, the Rockford men were mustered into the federal service as Company D of the 11th Illinois militia regiment.[14]

In Galena, all business stopped and the citizens, probably including the Melvills, met at the courthouse and offered former army captain Ulysses S. Grant the command of a militia company that was to be raised. Wisely, he declined the position, since officers with his experience, if they were patient, could obtain the rank of colonel or even general. However, he did organize the Jo Daviess Guards and drill them on some of the more spacious lawns of the town. The sole local authority on military uniforms, he gave the lady volunteers who were to clothe the men specifications for regular army attire. In a few days, the company, uniformed and ready, marched through jammed streets to the railroad station. There, together with Grant, who was to be their chaperon, they departed for Springfield. After the company joined the Rockford Zouaves as part of the 11th Illinois, Grant remained for some time to guide them in their new military duties. On May 5, the regiment was sent—without Grant—to the vicinity of Cairo, Illinois, to guard the state's southernmost point.[15]

At Harvard College, the students were in the forefront of the uprising. William Francis Bartlett, a tall, slender junior who was approaching the age of twenty-one, seemed immature for a college student, more interested in youthful diversions than in intellectual pursuits. His politics made him a markedly unpromising champion of the Union: a Democrat who had steadfastly defended the South, on April 17 he stated that fighting against the Confederacy was contrary to his principles. But on the same day some other principle inspired him to enlist in the New England Guards, officially the 4th Battalion of the Massachusetts Volunteer Militia. So did many of the other undergraduates, including Oliver Wendell Holmes, Jr., and Charles Francis Adams, Jr. In his childhood, young Holmes had been Herman's Pittsfield neighbor. He is said to have admired the rugged sailor who had lived among the cannibals and to have read *Typee, Omoo,* and *Moby-Dick.* The battalion also accepted young graduates, such as Caspar Crowninshield.[16]

Harvard went not gently into that good fight but ostentatiously. Julia Ward Howe commemorated the scholar-soldiers:

Remember ye how, out of boyhood leaping,
Our gallant mates stood ready for the fray,
As new-fledged eaglets rise, with sudden sweeping,
And meet unscared the dazzling front of day?
Our classic toil became inglorious leisure,
We praised the calm Horatian ode no more,
But answered back with song the martial measure,
That held its throb above the cannon's roar.

For a week the students trained; then, on April 25, they embarked to garrison Fort Independence in Boston Harbor.[17]

The Artist at War

It was a rare person who was spared the beat of the drum and the clump of marching feet, for, as Longfellow wrote, "in these tumultuous days nobody can sing, but birds and children." He watched two regiments mustering on

Boston Common and the following day he noted, as the militiamen left for the war, that the streets were grim. "Ah, woe the day!" he mourned. At the same time, Emerson and Louisa May Alcott were witnessing the departure of militiamen from Concord. Art offered no escape. "When the times have such a gunpowder flavor, all literature loses its taste," Longfellow wrote. "Newspapers are the only reading." Hawthorne was similarly distracted: "The war continues to interrupt my literary industry; and I am afraid it will be long before Romances are in request again, even if I could write one." Later, he remembered that "I gave myself up to reading newspapers and listening to the click of the telegraph, like other people."[18]

Like Hawthorne and Longfellow and the ordinary townsman, Herman was ravenous for every morsel of information. As the *Sun* put it, "The desire for the latest news is unprecedented, and it seems next to an impossibility to appease the demand." Mr. Selden copied his telegraphic reports until late in the evening, sending them by messenger over to the Berkshire Hotel. When the crowds there grew too large, the messages were sent to the town hall and shouted to the multitude. Still later, when the excitement had become habitual, they must have been posted at the telegraph office, as described in Herman's poem "Donelson":

About the bulletin-board a band
Of eager, anxious people met,
And every wakeful heart was set
On latest news from West or South.

People of all convictions read the bulletins and exchanged opinions about the medley of truth and rumor that they offered. By these means, Herman could receive the report, fortunately not true, that the Seventh Regiment had been cut to pieces on its way to Washington.[19]

Anxiously, the town followed the adventures of the Allen Guard through the letters that men in the company wrote to the local newspapers. After performing its first duty, sailing the *Constitution* away from Annapolis to get her out of harm's way, the Guard occupied Fort McHenry, in Baltimore. There were no more battles in that city, but their service was important as Ben Butler's iron fist crushed the Marylanders into submission to the Union and reopened communications with Washington.

With vital points along the border manned by militiamen, anxiety gave way to calmer, longer-range preparations for war. On the day after the departure of the Allen Guard, the Pittsfield citizens congregated again to arrange for the formation of a second militia company. Known as the Pollock Guard after William Pollock, who donated $1,000 toward its outfit, the new unit grew rapidly. On Thursday, May 2, the recruits went into camp on the grounds of the Berkshire Agricultural Society, of which Herman's Uncle Thomas had in ages past been president. Less formally, a group of Pittsfield men formed a rifle company for home defense. With the countryside breathing war, it became a principal theme of children's play. The young boys of Pittsfield formed military clubs, such as the Springfield Zouaves and the Union Zouaves, just as, in Concord, Julian Hawthorne drilled with a company of youths, vowing to enlist as soon as he was old enough. The girls, too, played the game, forming the Campbell Guard. By Saturday, June 29, the game had matured to the point that two companies of children's Zouaves encamped for several hours at the Curtis residence.[20]

On Saturday evening, April 28, ex-President Franklin Pierce spoke from the balcony of the Eagle Hotel. Full of patriotism, his speech looked forward to a reunification of the states, a goal on which all parties could agree. Meanwhile, the flag epidemic was spreading—to the Pittsfield Bank, the Baptist church, the Western Railroad freight house, the Munyan shop, the Pomeroy Woolen Mills, and the Pittsfield Woolen Company. The workers of the Taconic Mill procured a fifty-foot flagpole, which they intended to mount on the mill's cupola, and private citizens raised a flag on a forty-foot pole in the center of Chester Square. To celebrate the latter, the Gilmore and Chester Bands played patriotic airs, the girls from the Everett School sang, and Edward Everett mounted the platform to thunderous applause. After a prayer, the flag was raised, the girls sang "The Star Spangled Banner," and Everett spoke.[21]

By mid-May, Lizzie had returned home and gone back to Boston, leaving Bessie and Fanny with Herman. The boys had been distributed among their grandmothers, Malcolm in Boston and Stanny in Gansevoort, where Gus tutored him in manners, virtue, and piety. So that Herman could join Lizzie at the Shaws', on May 22 Sister Fanny brought Stanny and little Lucy, Allan's youngest daughter, to Pittsfield so she could manage Arrowhead in his absence. Herman met them at the station, drove them to Arrowhead in the wagon, and the next day left for Boston. In his absence, Fanny proved to be as good a task-mistress as Gus, keeping school for Bessie, little Fanny, Stanny, and Lucy and exercising them by taking them up the hill behind the farm to gather flowers.

When Herman returned, Sister Fanny and the youngsters remained with him for a time. On the afternoon of the tenth of June, when the Pollock Guard was nearly ready to leave for active service, Herman drove Stanny—perhaps the entire household—to town to see the company drill. The day proved to be more exciting than he had anticipated. Despite the moral protection afforded by the ostentatious American flag flying above the Pittsfield Woolen Company, the factory caught fire. The Guardsmen hurried over to help the volunteer fire companies, but nearly everything was destroyed, including the firm's new machinery and the jobs of 150 workers. Using some morbid ingenuity, Herman made up for the loss of the military spectacle by improvising a tour of the cemetery. Early on Saturday, June 15, the Pollock Guard left for the war in their new cadet-gray uniforms. In appreciation of the assistance rendered them, the workers of the Pittsfield Woolen Company presented the company with the flag they had salvaged from the fire. Then the troops boarded the train for Springfield. Fanny probably stayed with Herman until Lizzie's return from Boston later in June, after which she took her little charges back to Gansevoort.[22]

The excitement continued to have a beneficial effect on Herman. He was happy to participate in the patriotic bustle, his ailments went into remission, and he was as merry as he had been in more carefree days. Sarah Morewood remarked that "Mr. M. our Neighbor is very social this Summer and is quite ready for pic nics and out of door pleasures." On the military side, although he did not consider joining any of the armed services, he entered his name once more on the militia list. This was more than a gesture, since there was a possibility that the enrollees might be called on to fight. People believed, correctly, that a Confederate military thrust could penetrate past Philadelphia and New York City, in which case those on the list would have to hold Fortress Berkshire as a final bastion. If that were to occur, Herman would be among the defenders.[23]

Only men marched off to war, but the women, many of whom (such as Kitty Gansevoort and Louisa May Alcott) wished that they could fight, too, volunteered to do whatever they could. This was not an idle diversion for bored females, but a matter of community leadership. Ladies were expected to shoulder such civil responsibilities. The maids could do the housework; their mistresses would serve the cause, even when the work was as menial as that of their servants. At first it was not clear what should be done. On one occasion, a New England woman presented a departing soldier with an umbrella, and in Pittsfield the girls of the Maplewood Institute presented troops with needle-books, as though men going into battle needed above all to be dry and well mended. But in time they learned to supply the real needs of the soldiers. On May 1, Louisa May Alcott was one of a group of 200 Concord women who sewed for two days making items needed by the soldiers.[24]

The women of Pittsfield had no formal organization. They met at the Town Hall, where they made linen caps, socks, handkerchiefs, and shirts. Later, they moved into a large hall in Martin's block, where they packed boxes for the Pittsfield soldiers, for the Sanitary Commission, for the hospitals, and, eventually, for the prison camps in the South. By common consent rather than by vote, their leader was a heroine of the Melvilles, Mrs. Deacon Curtis T. Fenn, a woman in her early sixties. Although she was straitened financially and of little social note, she had made a name for herself through her many good works among the ill and the poor and by service to the soldiers in the War of 1812. Now her ability and her resolute commitment brought her to the fore. She fixed meeting places and times, did much of the work herself, and tactfully enforced discipline whenever interest slackened or attention wandered. Under her leadership, the women stationed themselves at the railroad depot to greet regiments passing through, serving meals to the hale and lighter fare and wine to the sick and wounded. When conditions became difficult, Mrs. Fenn held the meetings in her own modest home to save money, and when the other women straggled, she published admonitions in the newspapers.[25]

Although Sarah Morewood was one of the most dedicated, she seems not to have joined Mrs. Fenn's army. She had her own agenda, lavishing attention, despite her poor health, on the successive waves of recruits passing through the town's training camps. When a military unit left for the South, Sarah was sure to present it with a handsome flag. At first, Lizzie was in a difficult situation. Being the daughter of the late Judge Shaw obliged her to be among the foremost, but there is no evidence that she joined Mrs. Fenn's group in the early days of the war. On her return from Boston she would have wished to participate, but she lived too far away and had too little household help to allow her to do much.

In contrast to this earnest patriotism, many merchants rushed to take what advantage they could of the sudden need for uniforms, food, and other supplies. One visitor to Washington was impressed by the abundance of "citizens in search of fat contracts." Nor were these entrepreneurs always scrupulous about providing honest goods at honest prices. Early in the war, the *Pittsfield Sun* clucked at their fraudulent practices, calling them "as infamous as privateering under the rebel flag, and robbing loyal merchants on the high seas." Herman referred to them (in "Bridegroom Dick," 171) as "the shoddyites a-toasting o' their toes; / In mart and bazar Lucre chuckled the huzza, / Coining the dollars in the bloody mint of war." Thus it will ever be in times of national need.[26]

Before the Catafalque

By its timely arrival in Washington, the Seventh Regiment could claim that it had saved the capital, though in truth the Confederate government was not planning an attack. Because Congress was out of session, the regiment moved into the Capitol, whose halls Herman had walked only a month before. When the Seventh camped in the chamber of the House of Representatives, the 6th Massachusetts in the Senate chamber, and the 8th Massachusetts in the domeless, scaffold-filled rotunda, the entire building, or the "Big Tent," as the militiamen called it, quartered troops. At first the men of the Seventh skylarked in the House chambers and marched to the most elegant hotels for dinner, but on the afternoon of May 2 they paraded through the city to a farm on Meridian Hill. At Camp Cameron, as they called their new home, they settled in as soldiers. Except for persistent poor health, Henry Gansevoort was enjoying himself. Only a year ago, he wrote Bruce, he had been a pampered child in Europe, but now he was a common soldier. Common was hardly the word for the Seventh, however, not with Matthew Brady as its photographer, Theodore Winthrop, a promising young author, as its scribe, and Sanford Gifford as its artist. Celebrities reviewed the regiment daily: Lincoln, Secretaries Cameron, Seward, and Chase, Major Anderson, Thurlow Weed, various senators, and the French and Brazilian ambassadors. Other militiamen visited the camp to ogle at what one of them called the nursery for brigadier generals.[27]

One of the most tempting targets for the 25,000 Union soldiers was Alexandria, Virginia, which, just across the Potomac, was both an irritant and a potential foothold on Southern soil. On May 24, the militiamen, with the Seventh Regiment in the lead, marched into Virginia unopposed, occupied the city and the surrounding area, and constructed fortifications at strategic locations. The gentlemen of the Seventh were excused from this manual labor, but they objected to preferential treatment. At their own request, the Broadway swells dug trenches for two days, after which they took their blistered hands and aching muscles back to Camp Cameron.

In recognition of the civilian obligations of its members—New York commerce needed its nabobs—the service of the Seventh was abbreviated. On May 31, the regiment returned home, this time taking the Baltimore route. Bruce meant to greet Henry on his arrival, but after waiting all afternoon he went home. Because Henry must have been exhausted, Bruce spoofed, "I concluded that it would not be advisable for me to stay over & hear an account of the moving incidents of flood & field, through which you have passed." Once home, many members of the regiment were commissioned as officers in new military units and Henry returned to Washington to try his luck with the regular army.[28]

Soon after the return of the Seventh, its members—and the Northern literary community—received a shock. Theodore Winthrop had left the regiment early to become military secretary, with the rank of major, to Ben Butler at Fortress Monroe. On June 10, Butler brashly engaged the Confederates in a bloody little battle at Big Bethel, Virginia, near the fort. In this

Seventh Regiment Soldiers at Camp Cameron, District of Columbia, May, 1861. U.S. Army Military History Institute

defeat for the Union forces, Winthrop was killed, and on June 21, just over two months after he had marched with the Seventh Regiment down the streets of New York, his comrades marched at his funeral. George William Curtis, Winthrop's neighbor on Staten Island, mourned his lost friend, and Longfellow wrote "What a sad affair. . . . This is one of the great tragedies of life."[29]

During these first months of the war, two naval events must have had a profound effect on Herman. The first involved him personally. With the passing of the years, most of the ships on which he had sailed, and from which he took his identity as a sailor, had foundered and sunk. The exception was the storied frigate *United States*, aboard which he had sailed from Honolulu to Boston in 1843 and 1844. Now obsolete, she was moored at the Norfolk Navy Yard along with a number of other ships of war, old and new, but it was apparent that when Virginia seceded the yard would fall to the Confederates. Some of the ships were all but ready for sea, but the *Merrimack*'s propulsion machinery was inoperative. The fate of this valuable steam frigate was of vital concern to the navy, but attempts to remove her failed. At the last minute, as navy Captain Hiram Paulding, a force of marines, and the 3rd Massachusetts militia regiment arrived from Fortress Monroe, just across the harbor, several of the ships were already sinking. Paulding was able to tow the *Cumberland* to the fort, but that was all. After ordering the remaining ships burned and the cannon spiked, he abandoned the yard. When Colonel Robert E. Lee inspected what remained, he found enough usable ordnance to provide coastal defenses for the state of Virginia. The *Merrimack* had burned to her waterline, but the Confederates were able to utilize the lower part of her hull and her machinery as the core of an armored warship. Because Paulding's men had not bothered to destroy the venerable *United States*, Lee ordered her into commission as the first ship of the Virginia Navy. When she was armed for harbor defense and in use as a school ship and receiving station, the last survivor of Herman's nautical past had gone over to the enemy—the "Confederate States," some of the Southerners called her.[30]

The other trauma occurred when Herman stood before the body of the first Union naval officer to be killed in action. The sequence of events that led to this scene had begun on the nineteenth of April, when Lincoln ordered a blockade of the Southern coastline. That was a part of the Anaconda strategy planned by General Scott before the war with the object of girdling and strangling the South. There was no time to build the necessary ships; they had to be obtained from the existing navy and from the merchant marine. With the loss of the Norfolk yard, the brunt of the work devolved upon Brooklyn, which became the scene of frenetic activity. Ships out of commission had to be made serviceable, and Commodore Breese was ordered to procure and arm five fast and sturdy steamers. Soon Guert had the additional task of refitting ships returning from foreign stations. Breese advised Washington that his wharves were full, adding that "Commdr. Gansevoort has perhaps more than he and his assistants can perform, in attending to his many arduous and legitimate duties in the Yard."[31]

Because qualified officers were in short supply, Breese was given authority to appoint to volunteer rank former naval officers and others with extensive sea experience. Master William Budd of the U.S. Coast Survey, a fierce, moustachioed man in his early thirties, was one of these. Not only was he ready for war, but he and Commander James Ward of the receiving ship *North Carolina* were planning a "flying flotilla" to secure the Potomac water route to Washington, to neutralize Confederate artillery along the river, and to blockade the Virginia shoreline. When the plan was approved, Budd was assigned to the Potomac Flotilla as an acting volunteer master. Ward selected three civilian vessels, two small, speedy steamers, the *Resolute* and the *Reliance*, and the larger side-wheeler *Thomas Freeborn*, all of which Guert armed. Budd took command of the *Resolute*, while Ward commanded the flotilla from the flagship *Freeborn*. Once on patrol in the Potomac River, Ward and Budd, both part pirate, enjoyed capturing unwary Virginia vessels and landing on the Confederate shore to see what mischief they could cause. On June 24, Ward bombarded Mathias Point, where, he suspected, a Confederate artillery emplacement was planned, and he returned on the twenty-seventh to capture the point for a battery of his own. But during the operation he was surprised by Confederate troops, whom he fought from close inshore. When one of his ship's gunners was wounded, Ward manned the cannon himself, only to be killed by enemy fire. With ceremony, his body was placed on a special train bound for the Brooklyn yard.[32]

Since Lizzie was back in Pittsfield to care for Bessie and Fanny, toward the end of June Herman went to the city, where he could absent himself from her annual hay fever attack, witness the bustle of metropolitan military activity, and visit Allan and his family over the Fourth of July. The streets of the metropolis were filled with the uniforms of men on leave, of visiting soldiers and sailors, and of new recruits. The store windows displayed military uniforms, weapons, and other paraphernalia; the war was all the talk, on the streets, in the parlors, and in the daily newspapers, and the death of Commander Ward was the principal topic of the day.

To honor the fallen hero, he was to lie in state aboard the *North Carolina*. On the evening of Saturday, June 29, the body reached the yard; on Sunday evening, about the time when a dazzling "war comet" appeared in the sky, it was arrayed on the poop deck of his former command. On Monday, Herman visited the yard to see Cousin Guert Gansevoort, to witness the frenzied activity there, and to view Ward's body. Evert Duyckinck accompanied him, as did, in all probability, George Long Duyckinck and Allan. The yard was no longer the quiet station that Herman remembered. At all of the piers were vessels in varying stages of repair and conversion, some nearly ready for sea, some in progress, and some barely begun, and the nearby anchorages were filled with others awaiting their turn. Cannon were being installed and pleas for more were being dispatched. Herman had found what he was looking for, a view of the real work of the war. Guert devoted what time he could to his visitors, but, with the double obligations of supervising the crush of work of the Ordnance Department and of marching in Ward's funeral procession, he had to hand them over to surrogates. They were escorted to the seawall to see the *Iroquois*, which had only recently returned from the Mediterranean station, and the *Savannah*, which was completing an overhaul. Aboard the *Savannah*, they were given a lecture on Commander Dahlgren's improved cannon.[33]

The flags of the yard and of the ships present were flying at half-mast as Herman's party visited the *North Carolina*. The area where Ward's body lay in state was set apart from the rest of the deck by walls of canvas draped with American flags. At the head of the coffin hung a red cross made of bunting and the national colors covered with crepe, wax tapers burned at both the head and the foot, and on the coffin itself lay Ward's sword, his dress chapeau, his uniform coat, and a cross of white flowers made by the wife of the ship's new commander. Few other experiences could have brought the war as close to Herman as did this scene. It was one thing to cheer the Pittsfield boys off to war and to raise flags on the village green, another to stand before the catafalque of a fellow man struck down by enemy fire. Since Ward had been a colleague of Guert at the yard, Herman may have known him, and there is a very strong possibility that Allan had, as close as he was to Guert. Ward belonged to Guert's generation of naval officers, and under slightly different circumstances, the body before Herman might have been that of his cousin. As Evert Duyckinck put it, matching his language to the nautical flavor of the scene, "Who shall fathom the iniquity of this rebellion?"[34] At 2:30 in the afternoon, the coffin was borne ashore by the *Freeborn* men, accompanied by the officers of the *North Carolina*. While the *North Carolina*'s battery fired minute-guns, a procession of mourners accompanied the body to a ship that was to take it to Ward's home in Connecticut. Foote was a pallbearer, and Guert marched in the procession.

Two days later, Herman must have risen early, for he had little time in which to make his purchase of the day, James Thomson's *Poetical Works*. Then he and a party similar to the one that had visited the navy yard took the Harlem Railroad to New Rochelle for what Allan Melville called a "strawberry festival" with Richard Lathers and, probably, Charles Thurston, adding an acquaintance named Siddons to the party en route. Richard was his usual courtly self, and Winyah was charming. The large Tuscan villa was filled with Richard's collection of art and set on a 300-acre estate laid out English-style, with a large orchard, a virgin wood, and the waters of Long Island Sound playing with its shore. All was muted and restful, excepting the antics of the children. For the moment the war was distant, though Richard and Abby must have had much to say about their forlorn quest for peace through the Confederacy and their hostile reception on their return. At such moments Herman's attitude toward secession was firmed, for under slightly different circumstances Richard would have been as loyal a Confederate as he was now a supporter of the Union. As Evert Duyckinck described the visit, it was "a happy relief to the war agitations of the times." Host and guests alike ambled through the woods, sat along the shore, drank blackberry wine, and lounged on Richard's piazza overlooking the blue water as they conversed. After dinner, the party declined an invitation to spend the night and returned on the last train to the city.[35]

In the evening of their return, the Fourth of July celebration began with firecrackers and rockets that exploded and arched into the sky until late. In the "hazy glory" of the next morning, cannon at the Battery greeted Independence Day with a salute, followed by the caroling of the bells of Trinity Church, and as the sun climbed into the sky, the day became brilliant and warm. At 7:30 a.m., the parade formed. Because so many of the city's regiments were absent, about 6,000 boys from the public schools marched in fiery red Zouave uniforms. Along the line of march, hotels and public buildings were decked out in American flags, and in the harbor ships were dressed with flags and pennants. Around noontime, the residents turned out to exchange visits, especially to the families of absent soldiers, and in the afternoon there were soldiers' relief benefits. In the evening, the fireworks were spectacular and patriotic. Aside from these events, there were calls to make—most interestingly on the Thurstons to hear about Surgeon Henry Thurston, who, unlike Henry Gansevoort, was still on duty in the South—and Herman may have had a chance to meet Brewster for the first time.[36]

After the holiday, Herman returned to Pittsfield to prepare for a visit to Gansevoort, and the Allan Melvilles left for their summer vacation. Allan rented a cottage at Edgewater Point, New Rochelle, near Winyah. That brought three "brothers" together, Allan, Charles Thurston, and Richard Lathers. There Jennie and the girls could escape the heat of the city and take advantage of the proximity of Richard's estate to visit, picnic, swim, and romp. When work called, Allan and Richard commuted to the city by train, a forty-five-minute ride.[37]

Herman found Pittsfield oppressively hot. The routine of daily life was by now interrupted by the sights, the sounds, and the tempo of the recruiting and training at "Camp Seward." That was common. Longfellow wrote that "everywhere in the air the warlike rumor of drums mingles discordantly with the song of birds." Hawthorne sought respite from the daily newspapers and telegraph reports at the seashore, but he could "hear the noise of drums, over the water, from Marblehead or Salem, and very often the thunder of cannon, which sometimes continues for an hour together; so that I begin to think the war has overspread the whole country except just this little precinct."[38]

Sadly, Herman was reminded that violent death was a visitor in the comfort of the home as well as at the front. On the morning of July 9, Fannie Longfellow, the wife of the poet, was making wax seals for her children when she dropped a match on her gown and was immolated. Burned beyond hope of recovery, she died the next morning. Herman and the nation mourned with the Cambridge poet as Herman's friend Henry T. Tuckerman put their grief into verse:

Nor to the camp alone his summons came,
  To blast the glowing day,
But heavenward bore upon the wings of flame
  Our poet's mate away. . . .

Longfellow was too broken to attend her funeral. Months after the tragedy, he was still saying, "How can I live any longer!" "I have not met him since his misfortune," Hawthorne wrote, "and tremble at the thought of doing so. . . . [I]t has been like a stroke of palsy; and he has grown old, even to outward appearance, and white-bearded at once."[39]

Forward to Richmond!

The popular voice demanded an immediate attack on Virginia. So gigantical did the Archangel Michael seem that *any* military adventure should bring a prompt end to the war. According to Morgan Dix, "The impression among the young and inexperienced—a delusion shared by some older heads—was that . . . all we had to do was to dash forward, seize Richmond, hang Mr. Davis, and return flushed with victory and crowned with bays. . . . The air was filled with the cry, *'On to Richmond!'*" When repeated in Congress by such men as Senator Sumner, the demand was irresistible. Even Hawthorne wrote, "I wish they would push on the war a little more briskly. The excitement had an invigorating effect on me for a time, but it begins to lose its influence." Some argued that an attack should be made before the ninety-day militiamen were discharged.[40]

General Scott correctly believed that the militiamen were not prepared for battle. They treated their service as a vacation from the constraints of home, brawling and firing their weapons in the streets of Washington. Henry Gansevoort was a witness: "Soldiers drunk and sober, lively and grave, crowd every corner. . . . Affrays are of daily occurrence. Yesterday there was a fight between many soldiers. I happened to be present; and, as revolvers are carried by all, there was a general whizzing of balls. One man was fatally injured. I had a bayonet run through my sleeve while innocently passing between two belligerents."[41] This was the army that Irvin McDowell, newly appointed its general, led to Bull Run.

It was an appalling error. Although the senior Union officers included many who would later be important army and corps commanders, they were untried and the militiamen they commanded, so combative in the security of Washington, were unprepared for the long, hot march to Manassas and for the rain of musket and cannon balls they encountered there. The Confederates were also led by generals who would later gain fame, and they won the battle. The apprentice warriors of the North fled back to Washington, their path impeded by fleeing government officials and socialites who had come to witness the anticipated victory. Whitman described the return of the "disorderly mobs, some in squads, stragglers, companies. Occasionally, a rare regiment, in perfect order." The war-startled soldiers were "queer-looking objects, strange eyes and faces, drench'd (the steady rain drizzles on all day) and fearfully worn, hungry, haggard, blister'd in the feet." Allan Melville, in Washington on business after a visit to Harper's Ferry, witnessed the retreat, called on Henry Gansevoort, and took home some souvenirs, a plume and a powderhorn, that Henry gave him.[42]

With its casualties and its injury to Northern pride, the defeat inspired one anonymous poet to call for revenge:

> I only feel the shameful blow,
> I only see the scornful foe
> And vengeance burns in every vein
> To die, or wipe away the stain.[43]

But for Herman, it was more a first stage of the transformation that the war would bring about in America than it was a humiliation. His fine poem "The March into Virginia, Ending in the First Manassas (July, 1861)" does not deal with the fighting at all. Following "Apathy and Enthusiasm" as it does, it concerns the innocent first days of the war when the "young Indians" were deaf to the warnings of the graybeards. It does not deplore the amateurism of the soldiers, their unpreparedness, or their misjudgment of what was required of them. Instead, it celebrates the mistaken impulse that animated them, the brash spirit of youth that clothes battle in glory despite its patent brutality. That, ironically, is the quality that will save the nation. The boy-soldiers are "The champions and enthusiasts of the state" and "Stimulants to the power mature, / Preparatives of fate." They will not win the future of America under the protection of Michael, but their clumsy defeat will steel them for future, more successful battles.

The poem's fame derives from its focus on a group of militiamen who tramp through a bright arboreal setting, the world of joyous light of the uninitiated bachelor. The subject is not victory or defeat, but youngsters of North and South who gambol unthinkingly through woods better suited to the rhythms of fertility than to battle. These are the many lads at the depot whom Herman had seen and was to see departing confidently for war with little idea of the carnage they would face. They are the youthful-spirited whose elation is nourished by fresh air and greenery:

> No berrying party, pleasure-wooed,
> No picnic party in the May,
> Ever went less loth than they
> Into that leafy neighborhood.

The intense irony of their blithe ignorance grips modern readers, and the fate of the boys to be "experienced" and "enlightened" by the fatal stings of muskets and blasts of cannon heightens and punctuates that irony.

Yet in the progression of battle poems that "The March into Virginia" begins, this irony serves another purpose, for the "leafy neighborhood" of war is as much a misconception of an entire people as it is of the militiamen. At this early moment, innocence blinds all to the truth that the boys march not into a pristine, friendly glade but into a dismal forest, a fatal wilderness, the empire of Satan. Herman's imagery is a model of artistic deceit behind which the mangle and gore of battle are concealed. It would be many battles and many poems in the book before it became clear that the forest of war is a horror of fire and slaughter. To journey into the forest is to confront that horror; it is also to probe deep into one's own psyche, to the region where brutal passions and snarling strife, the original sin of man, await their release. That reality would come later.

In the larger terms of *Battle-Pieces,* the leafy scene of "The March into Virginia" also recalls the green, fertile world over which John Brown's shadow fell in "The Portent." It is the old America, the farm and forest nation which was passing. The young soldiers are literally marching from the old, antebellum United States toward an unforeseen and unknowable future. Before they arrive, they will be "enlightened" on many another field of battle, but it is an enlightenment that will lead America to "power mature."

Herman's restraint and compassion for these victims of war contrast markedly with the bravado and outrage that the battle inspired in Hawthorne, who wrote that Bull Run would "dull the edge of many a northern appetite; but if it puts all of us into the same grim and bloody humour that it does me, the South had better have suffered ten defeats than won this victory." In fairness, that was an unconsidered reaction to the shock of the telegraphic bulletins, not one refined for publication. After his emotion had ebbed, he decided, like Herman, that wars are boyish, fought by boys. But his sardonic, chilly treatment of the "good fortune" of youth at war, written for publication, contrasts tellingly with Herman's sympathy: "The enervating effects of centuries of civilization vanish at once, and leave these young men . . . to kill men blamelessly, or to be killed gloriously,—and to be happy in following out their native instincts of destruction." Both writers were fatalistic about the human catastrophe they were witnessing, but Herman's fatalism was warmed by a compassion that Hawthorne either did not feel or did not wish to express. It is just here that the impressive achievement of *Battle-Pieces* begins to emerge.[44]

Shocking as Bull Run was to easterners, in Missouri, where the population was divided between Unionists and Secessionists, fighting had been going on since the opening of the war. News of the battles between pro-Union citizens and the Secessionist state government and its supporters was reported in every issue of the *Pittsfield Sun*, and Herman acknowledged its importance in two of his poems. As a border state, its retention in the union was problematical but strategically essential. In terms of irregular forces, Secessionists such as the "young Indian" Samuel Langhorne Clemens were opposed by equivalent Loyalist militia forces, civilians with guns but little training. Herman paid tribute to these amateur soldiers of the North who "fell not in vain, though in defeat" in a memorial stanza, "On the Home Guards who perished in the Defense of Lexington, Missouri." The battle on which the poem is based was of little importance, and the same judgment might be made of the poem if it were compared in terms of intellectual content and poetic intensity with many of the other poems of *Battle-Pieces*, but it must be understood in its context, the sixteen-poem section of the book entitled "Verses Inscriptive and Memorial" that is placed after the main body of battle poems. Often devoted to soldiers who died in defeat, these poems remember, reflect, and invite to generosity, effecting a tragic calm that precedes the end of the book. "On the Home Guards" is the first of eleven inscriptions or epitaphs of this sort, intended not to challenge poetically but to commemorate gently. They are slight, spare, and funereal.[45]

With its Secessionist government, it seemed likely that Missouri would join the Confederacy. However, a nucleus of Union men, such as Captain Nathaniel Lyon, of the regular army, were determined that the state should remain loyal. Lyon, who commanded the St. Louis Arsenal, moved his store of arms to Illinois, then drove the gathering Secessionist army out of St. Louis. After that he was promoted to the rank of brigadier general and given command of the Union troops in the state. With what forces he could gather, he pursued the Secessionists until, on the ninth of August, he met a strong enemy force at Wilson's Creek, just outside Springfield. The ensuing battle was in some ways a western version of Bull Run. Lyon's army, made up largely of ninety-day regiments approaching the end of their service, was about half the strength of its opponents. In the early stages of the battle, Lyon's horse was killed and he was slightly wounded. Later, while charging at the head of two companies of infantry, he received a mortal wound. Leaderless, his defeated troops retreated to Springfield.

Since there seems to have been no personal motive for doing so, Herman must have written the poem "Lyon: Battle of Springfield, Missouri (August, 1861)" because of the importance of retaining the state in the union and because of his admiration for those who worked steadfastly toward that end. But the result is the least fortunate poem of *Battle-Pieces*. Many pages could be devoted to analyzing and perhaps ridiculing its awkward meter and rhyme, its failure of proportion, and its regrettable invocations of Richard the Lion-Heart and the heavenly host, but it is nearly enough to paraphrase Sister Lucy Marie Freibert's summation: the repetition of Lyon's name, which is used as a refrain, does not produce poetic magic and the narrative is not dramatic enough to support that repetition.[46]

Still, the poem is intended to serve a purpose. At this crude stage of the war, a battle between crude armies of the crude west gave Herman a chance to reach back into the past of folk balladry. (In an attempt to emphasize the frontier aspect of the battle, Herman transplanted Indians fighting alongside the Confederates from the later Battle of Pea Ridge to this encounter.) The untutored narrator, one of the Union soldiers present, paints an extraordinarily romanticized picture of Lyon as a towering, melancholy leader instead of the feisty little redhead of history. Through this conception of a doomed but fearless martyr who fights with the foreknowledge that he will die (a bit of drama from the later Battle of Ball's Bluff), Herman must have intended to communicate the naive attitude toward war that pervaded the nation, for the narrator's attitude is Michaelic. But that is no more than a limp device for concealing the "darkness" of battle—few details are provided—by providing an uplifting ending for a day of slaughter. In defeat and death, Lyon is rewarded by a Heaven that favors the Union side: "his only flight / Was up to Zion, / Where prophets now and armies greet pale Lyon," a poor parody of the flights of angels invoked at the death of Hamlet. Perhaps the inept verse is intended to characterize the narrator, though doggerel remains doggerel, whatever the excuse.

After Bull Run and Wilson's Creek, the militiamen's service ended. Because Randolph Hobart's constitution had proved to be too frail for camp life, he had already been sent home with a disability discharge. After guarding Villa Ridge and Bird's Point, Illinois, the Rockford Zouaves and the Galena company returned to their homes. In Boston, the Harvard boys finished their garrison duty at Fort Independence, after which some of them returned to the classroom. When the 12th New York was sent home from its station near Washington, Henry Thurston resumed his civilian medical practice. On the second of August, the Allen Guard arrived in Pittsfield to an enthusiastic reception. Thousands of spectators greeted them at the depot, bells were rung, and cannon were fired. The heroes marched along the street accompanied by the Independent Zouaves, fire companies, the juvenile Zouaves, and private vehicles, and then the proud populace regaled them with speeches, presentations, and a luncheon. The ninety days of citizen-soldiering were over.[47]

Rally 'Round the Flag, Boys!

After the defeats of the militiamen, it began to occur to the public that the cost of the war in treasure, civil disruption, militarism, and bloodletting would be higher than they had thought. From the beginning, it had been the purpose of General Scott and the administration to employ the ninety-day volunteers for stopgap defense and to use the time to organize an army for extended service. To supply commanders, generals were commissioned from among politicians, such as Ben Butler, from among the middle-rank officers of the regular army, such as Lyon, McDowell, and George Meade, and from former military officers, such as William T. Sherman, Ulysses S. Grant, George Brinton McClellan, and John A. Dix.

Dix had put aside political partisanship in the interest of Union solidarity. In what was to become a schism among Democrats between oppositionists and War Democrats, he opted for the latter: "He considered the Federal Constitution as the greatest achievement of the human mind in the field of political science, and regarded the American nation as fortunate above all others in their system of government. To the maintenance of that system, as bequeathed to us by our forefathers, he postponed all other questions," his son wrote.[48] The same principle that had caused Dix to oppose Lincoln's election now led him to support him as president.

The government's reaction to its military defeats was to appoint two commanders for its armies, George B. McClellan in the east and, in the west, Herman's San Francisco host of a year earlier, John C. Frémont. Of the two, Frémont's tenure was the briefest; after embarrassing the administration by embarking on an abolitionist crusade, he was relieved. The case of McClellan was different. A young engineer officer who had left the army after the Mexican War, McClellan was a brilliant student of war and a capable organizer and administrator. The day after Bull Run, he was given command of the Division of the Potomac and, later, of the entire army. A small man with an admirable moustache, he was both articulate and charismatic: "Little Napoleon," he was called, and "Little Mac." The task awaiting him in Washington, as he recalled it, was staggering: "All was chaos and despondency; the city was filled with intoxicated stragglers, and an attack was expected." Many of the troops "were so demoralized and undisciplined that they could not be relied upon even for defensive purposes." He began to build what one historian has called "the finest army ever seen on the North American continent." That meant training officers and men and procuring vast amounts of materiel. Henry Gansevoort noticed the change almost immediately. The army, he wrote, "has a master spirit at its head now. There is order and silence in the streets of Washington. Soldiers are compelled to stay in their camps, liquor is forbidden them, and it really seems that there is to be some discipline in the army." For the moment, it appeared that the North had found its general.[49]

New regiments were needed, hundreds of them, and to that end Lincoln had called for 75,000 volunteers for three years of service. A number of well-known poets lent their inkhorns to the recruiting effort, though Herman did not. William Cullen Bryant issued "Our Country's Call," a solemn enlistment poem, and Oliver Wendell Holmes published "The Wide-Awake Man," which mocked the slacker as "my sweet little man." But the drawing room gentility of Parnassus lacked the bluffness demanded by the times. It was an unconsecrated songwriter, George Frederick Root, whose lilt and swagger touched the sympathies and pulses of the Young Indians:

> Yes we'll rally round the flag, boys, we'll rally once again,
>   Shouting the battle-cry of Freedom,
> We will rally from the hill-side we'll gather from the plain,
>   Shouting the battle-cry of Freedom.
>   The Union forever,
>   Hurrah boys, hurrah!
>   Down with the Traitor,
>   Up with the Star;
> While we rally round the flag, boys, Rally once again,
>   Shouting the battle-cry of Freedom.

To the accompaniment of such jolly ditties, regiments filled rapidly.[50]

Rank in the volunteers was determined largely by caste. There were exceptions, many of them, but in general gentlemen expected to serve as officers, while men of the lowest classes expected to carry muskets. Commissions went largely to men of pedigree, heirs of fortunes, lawyers, politicians, and college students, while clerks, artisans, bosses of labor gangs, and small tradesmen became noncommissioned officers. Farmers and field hands, mechanics and laborers, bullyboys from the taverns, and drifters enlisted as privates.

In New York City, recruiting had been brisk from the beginning. Those among the privileged class who could not or would not serve helped to raise regiments. Still bruised by the attacks on his loyalty, Richard Lathers contributed money to help Edwards Pierrepont raise the first one, the Pierrepont Rifles, then served on a YMCA committee that fitted out the Ironsides Regiment. Thomas Bangs Thorpe, author of "The Big Bear of Arkansas" and customhouse employee, was active in recruiting, and George Templeton Strong donated money for the equipment of a regiment. Whitman catalogued images of this activity in his "Broadway, 1861":

> The regiments arriving and departing,
> The Barracks—the soldiers lounging around,
> The recruiting band, preceded by the fifer—
> The ceaseless din.

Some of the regiments were distinguished only by their numbers, but others were colorful: the Free Academy (City College) Zouaves, the Tammany Hall regiment, and Irish, German, Polish, and Italian regiments.[51]

Men also joined in staff positions. Two months after his return from his militia duty in Washington, Doctor Henry Thurston was appointed a surgeon of regular army volunteers with the rank of major. Several weeks later, he was ordered to the staff of the Army of the Cumberland, in the west. The urge to be with the army reached as far as gentle Thomas Bailey Aldrich, who, in the fall, joined one of the division staffs of the Army of the Potomac as a war correspondent for the *New York Tribune*. He remained with it, accompanying a reconnaissance into Virginia, until early 1862.[52]

Recruiting in other states was similar. After returning from the Fort Sumter relief expedition, helping to clear the route through Baltimore, and taking part in an amphibious landing at Alexandria, Captain Robert O. Tyler took leave from the regular army to accept a volunteer commission as colonel in command of the 1st Connecticut Volunteer Heavy Artillery and trained it to man siege guns. In Massachusetts, Henry S. Briggs, late captain of the Allen Guard, was appointed colonel of the 10th Massachusetts Volunteer Infantry. The regiment had the distinction of securing Hodge's Cornet Band of North Adams, which had played often in Pittsfield, to be Hodge's 10th Regiment Band. Colonel William Raymond Lee, a West Point classmate of Jefferson Davis, raised the 20th Massachusetts Volunteer Infantry, known informally as the "Harvard Regiment." It was officered by young men of that college, many of whom had served in the 4th Battalion at Fort Independence. One of the first to join was Captain Frank Bartlett.

Despite his extreme youth, his lackluster performance in college, the fact that he was not yet near graduation, and his known pro-Southern inclinations, his natural leadership ability qualified him to command a company. Lieutenants William Lowell Putnam and James Jackson Lowell were both nephews of James Russell Lowell, Captain Caspar Crowninshield was a close friend of the Adamses, and the name of Lieutenant Oliver Wendell Holmes, Jr., needs no explanation. While the regiment formed and trained, both Holmes and Bartlett made recruiting visits to Pittsfield, where both courted Agnes Pomeroy. It is quite possible that Herman, who would have remembered Wendell, encountered them there, either on his own or through Sarah Morewood.[53]

In the west, Toby Greene caught the enlistment fever. Probably the child of immigrants from Northern Ireland, Richard Tobias Greene, three years younger than Herman, was a native of Rochester, New York. At the age of sixteen, he had signed aboard the whaleship *Acushnet,* where he had become Herman's shipmate and lifelong friend. While the *Acushnet* was at anchor at Nukuheva, in the Marquesas Islands, Toby earned a place in literary history by deserting with Herman and living with him among the Typee tribe; several years later, he was immortalized under his own name in *Typee.* He capitalized on that one distinction of his life by lecturing on "Typee, or, Life in the South Pacific" and by publishing newspaper accounts of his experience. After his return from the South Seas, he worked briefly in Buffalo, New York, as a sign painter before marrying a talented widow named Mary Stone, who bore him a son, Herman Melville Greene. He supported his family for a decade or so by working as a telegraph operator in Sandusky, Ohio (interrupted by occasional jobs in Lexington, Kentucky), and during part of that time he was an editor of the *Sandusky Mirror.* In mid-1858 he moved to Chicago, where he had difficulty finding employment. In 1860, he contemplated returning to New York, though in 1861 he was still in Chicago, working as a clerk and representing himself as a physician.[54]

Now thirty-eight, Toby was rugged, of middle height, with a dark complexion, black hair, and gray eyes, and he claimed to have been a Republican since the inception of the party. Although an older brother was a Methodist minister, there was a scapegrace element in Toby's character that he never mastered. The statement by Herman's former shipmate, Oliver Russ, that he was "not a very desirable patern for a husband and father," suggests his unreliability and, probably, his vices. In short, Toby never lost the sailor's devil-may-care immaturity that had endeared him to Herman. For a month or so after the outbreak of hostilities, Toby remained a spectator. Then, attracted by the turmoil in Missouri, he traveled to St. Louis, where, at Captain Lyon's arsenal, he enlisted for three years as a private and surgeon's orderly in the 6th Missouri Volunteer Infantry. On July 9, his regiment camped at a railhead at Pilot Knob and Ironton, south-southwest of St. Louis, where, together with a small group of pioneers, it held the position for the Union and checked a force of Confederates gathering in northeastern Arkansas.[55]

In Rockford, Jeff Hobart recruited a company of infantry. Although he had no military experience, few others had, either, and he believed that as a grandson of General Dearborn he was entitled to a position of leadership. He enrolled both of his sons, John as a private drum major and Randolph as a first lieutenant, despite the proven fragility of Randolph's health. As a reward for raising the company, Jeff was given the rank of major in the regiment of which it became a part, the 44th Illinois Volunteer Infantry. On September 14, the 44th left by train for the St. Louis Arsenal, where it received its arms. Then it began a series of futile marches to various locations in Missouri before going into winter quarters at Rolla.[56]

Although the Union army was to consist mostly of these state regiments, the federal government expanded the regulars by raising an additional 25,000 men. That provided a nucleus of well-equipped, well-trained, well-disciplined, and well-officered troops to anchor the volunteers. One of the first applicants for the new regular commissions was Charles Russell Lowell, the older brother of James Jackson Lowell of the 20th Massachusetts and a favorite nephew of the Harvard poet. While he awaited appointment as a second lieutenant in the artillery, he aided the War Department by slipping behind Confederate lines to observe the preparations of the Virginians. Secretary of War Cameron was so impressed by his exploits that instead of giving him the lieutenancy he appointed him a captain in the 6th U.S. Cavalry.[57]

When Henry Gansevoort went to Washington to seek a commission as a second lieutenant in the regulars, he neglected to obtain his father's sanction. Uncle Peter was alarmed. Did Henry intend to abandon his noble profession of the law? (Yes, he did.) In view of the fact that "the blood of the Hero of Fort Stanwix, courses through your veins," why did Henry not apply for a more appropriate rank, perhaps first lieutenant or captain? In reply, Henry "urgently" asked his father to procure the commission. The demand set in motion an awesome mechanism of influence—General Dix made an amiable exception to his vow not to write recommendations—one that must certainly have won Herman a consulship had it been applied on his behalf. Impatient with the bureaucratic delay, Henry threatened his father that if the commission were not forthcoming he would retire from "a treacherous and uncongenial world." That was too much for Uncle Peter. "How can a young man have rec'd a more liberal education, with health & a noble profession; good antecedents, birth & associations & numerous friends, become a '*Wanderer*'?" he asked. "If so, he seeks the Destiny—and no friendly arm, can save him from his folly—"[58]

In early August, Henry finally received his appointment as a second lieutenant in the new 5th Regiment of U.S. Artillery. He celebrated by requesting a transfer to one of the older regiments of light artillery, cavalry, or mounted rifles, enlisting John Hoadley, who was in town, in the campaign. If he remained in the new regiment, he argued, he might not be allowed to remain in the army after the war, though he was assured that he would. Nobody else was anxious to reopen the case, John telling him that the artillery was the most promising branch of the army.[59]

Death in a Rosy Clime

After enduring the pain of the Bull Run defeat ("Everything shines with us but the Washington news," Emerson had written), Herman was looking forward to a healing visit to his family in Gansevoort. Pittsfield was more barren of companionship than usual: in an attempt to improve her health, Sarah Morewood had left for four weeks at Long Lake. The parades of the Independent Zouaves and the Di Vernon Phalanx, a girl's cavalry company, were growing stale, and the Phalanx soon disbanded. On July 25, when Cousin Mary Downer married Malcolm Green in Dorchester, Herman and Lizzie may have been present, since that would have been expected. Later, there was some excitement when the Allen Guard returned, but the weather was stifling and Herman's imagination must have been overburdened with war images.[60]

Shortly thereafter, Herman and Lizzie left for Gansevoort. The visit to Herman's mother and sisters in the small community out of the way of the military rattle of Pittsfield and the city was wholesome. Herman always enjoyed seeing Uncle Herman, who was feeble but in as good health as could be expected, and he had a chance to be with Stanny before the end of the summer vacation season. He could gossip with his family about Henry's commission and about the Galena Melvills. Cousin Robert and his family were moving to Davenport, Iowa, the port from which Robert's riverboat sailed. The boat, which ranged at least as far south as St. Louis and at least as far north as Dubuque, was probably carrying war supplies. Quite likely, Herman and Lizzie visited with Kate Curtis and her family, since by this time the Curtises were seeing a lot of the family in Gansevoort. After a week or so, Herman wrote Uncle Peter to arrange a meeting between trains on his return trip. Uncle Peter replied with an invitation to stay for some time, but at almost the same moment he received word that Henry was ill in the city and that Bruce was nursing him. Kitty left immediately and Uncle Peter made preparations to follow, no doubt warning Herman of his impending departure. The result was that on August 14 Herman returned home without stopping, even though Peter did not leave until the following day. However, Herman made use of the time in Albany to visit the bookshops, where he bought Tennyson's *Poetical Works*. On the fifteenth of August, Herman and Lizzie were back in Pittsfield, leaving Stanny in Gansevoort.[61]

At the beginning of September, when there was a temporary reprieve from thunder and blood in the newspapers, the days became more placid than they had been all summer. In fact, it appeared that the most stirring event would be the appearance of General Tom Thumb at West's Hall, but on September 12, tragedy struck. Reaching into a closet, former Governor Briggs, one of the town's most prominent citizens, accidentally triggered a gun that was stored there, killing himself. As with the death of Fanny Longfellow, Herman was reminded that war is only one of the guises in which the enemy appears.[62]

After Herman and Lizzie left Gansevoort, Uncle Herman's health improved so much—he could walk with assistance—that Mother Melville felt that Gus and Fanny could manage him. Since Kate Curtis and her daughter, Mary, were going to visit the Hoadleys (Mary for the entire winter), Mother Melville decided to accompany them. They would not have passed through Pittsfield without stopping to see Herman and his family, so it is probable that in mid-month all three were there. Because Mother Melville still felt that she could not spare much time away from her brother, she must have passed through Pittsfield again a week or so later. But Uncle Herman's care became easier when Allan sent a young man, "Georgie," to Gansevoort to help. Because the time was nearing when Tom Melville might be expected home again, his mother and sisters in Gansevoort began collecting family photographs—Herman sat for a portrait during the year—for him to take on his next voyage.[63]

Although the events of the spring and summer had stimulated him, Herman was still dissatisfied with life in Pittsfield and less willing than ever to remain in its relative isolation. Not yet engaged in writing war poetry, he seems to have been writing nothing at all. Every issue of the *Sun* contained a topical poem, yet he contributed none of his own, nor did he compete for the prize for a national hymn, offered by a committee that included George William Curtis, John A. Dix, and Richard Grant White. Now back from her trip, Sarah Morewood won a prize for shell work at the agricultural exhibition, but neither Herman nor Lizzie entered any of the competitions.[64]

In late August, Henry Gansevoort, who was back in Albany, was ordered to report for duty. Brimming with pride, Uncle Peter presented him with epaulets and a sword worn by the Revolutionary general and subsequently by Uncle Peter himself. On August 29 Henry left for Harrisburg, Pennsylvania, accompanied as far as New York City by Abe Lansing. John Hoadley tried to locate him there, but perhaps no one other than a liberal-minded and attractive young woman could have. On the third of September, Henry reported at Camp Preble, apparently oblivious, then and later, to the fact that Herman's old friend, Charles Fenno Hoffman, was incarcerated in the local insane asylum.[65]

The odd man out was Bruce, who no longer had a partner. He had moved into a new, more expensive office not far from Allan's, and now he had no one with whom to share the expense. He was doubly burdened because after Bull Run business had ceased altogether. Following Henry's advice, he discussed his situation with Allan, who good-heartedly invited him to move, rent-free until he could rid himself of his lease, into one of his offices—a small one which had previously been occupied by Herman's friend Daniel Shepherd. In effect, Allan had a new partner, and soon Bruce was visiting the Melvilles at Edgewater Point. The process had begun through which Bruce became a friend of Herman, Tom, the Gansevoort Melvilles, the Albany Gansevoorts, and the Thurstons; in effect, a member of the family.[66]

The new partnership lacked one advantage. Allan wanted Bruce to be a notary, for the same reason that Henry had wanted the position, for the good of the partnership, but Henry, who had received it just as he had left for Washington with the Seventh Regiment, clung to it. When Abram Wakeman, an influential city attorney, promised to steer the appointment to Bruce should Henry resign it, Allan subjected Henry to some cousinly ragging. "Let me see—" he wrote, "you are a private in the 7th Reg. N.Y.M. Second Lieutenant U.S. Army and what else. Stopping here your name & additions may appear thus Henry S. Gansevoort U.S.A. P7 Reg N.Y.M. and N.P.—" With that, he ordered Henry to send in his resignation and Henry dutifully complied.[67]

On October 21, the Harvard Regiment took part in the most one-sided Union defeat of the early months of the war. It was encamped on the Maryland side of the upper Potomac River, not far from Leesburg, Virginia, when its brigade commander, Colonel Edward Baker, decided to make a "demonstration" across the river at Ball's Bluff. The objective was hazy, Baker's knowledge of the enemy's strength was deficient, some of the soldiers had been in uniform for only a month, and there were only a few small boats in which to ferry troops across the river. On the Virginia side, a high bank hindered any advance and impeded any retreat. But the weakest element was Baker, a senator from Oregon who had resigned from Congress to serve in the army. The night before the battle, he had a presentiment that he would be killed, a detail that Herman appropriated for "Lyon."[68]

Two companies of the 20th Massachusetts, commanded by Frank Bartlett and Caspar Crowninshield, crossed early in the morning and took position on the top of the bluff, where the rest of the force joined them as it arrived piecemeal over the jerry-rigged ferry. Then the battle began. With the concealed enemy volleying at them from the front, the Yankees fought in the open with their backs to the steep bank. While standing near Bartlett and Crowninshield, Baker was struck by eight bullets simultaneously—his blood so staining Crowninshield's coat that he appeared to be the wounded one. William Lowell Putnam was killed, James Jackson Lowell was wounded, and Wendell Holmes, after being bruised in the stomach by a spent ball, was shot clear through the chest by a minié ball. Of the 340 members of the 20th who had made the crossing, almost half were casualties. Two of the dead, Sergeant Merchant and Private Kelly, were Pittsfield men. With several of his officers, Colonel Lee fled up the river, where his whole party was captured. Frank Bartlett led those of his men who were unable to swim to a point up the river where, at pistol-point, they made an orderly crossing to the Maryland side, five at a time. Back at camp, Wendell believed that he was dying, though within a few days he was smoking and looking at girls' pictures. Later he went to Philadelphia, where his wound was attended to and where his worried father appeared to take him home. With so many of the regiment's officers taken prisoner, Frank Bartlett became second in command.[69]

The defeat reminded McClellan of what he already knew, that offensive operations must be delayed until his troops and officers were better trained. In Albany, Abe Lansing reported general indignation at the "inexcusable blunder of some one." Hawthorne was too closely touched to resort to his usual generalizations: "Lowell had a nephew (whom he dearly loved) killed, and another wounded, in one battle; and a son of Holmes received two wounds in the same. The shots strike all round us." Longfellow's reaction was eloquent: "I have no heart for anything."[70]

Herman responded with "Ball's Bluff: A Reverie (October, 1861)," one of his highly praised war poems. The opening lines,

> One noonday, at my window in the town,
>   I saw a sight—saddest that eyes can see—
>   Young soldiers marching lustily
>   Unto the wars,

reveal that it is a dramatic monologue rather than a recollection of experience, since Herman did not have a window in town, nor did he witness the departure of the 20th Massachusetts or any other regiment involved in the battle. Beginning with memories of the festive scenes of soldiers departing from the Pittsfield station and ending in a later mood of nocturnal melancholy that prefigures Robert Frost's "Acquainted with the Night," the poem comprehends in human terms the death-of-innocence months in which a nation began to learn the consequences of the war it had undertaken. In terms of Herman's personal experiences, through its verses march the feet of Henry Gansevoort, of Wendell Holmes and Frank Bartlett, neither of whom had yet reached twenty-one, and of the Pittsfield lads and the boys of the west at Wilson's Creek, while along the streets stand Agnes Pomeroy, the girl Zouaves, the mothers and wives of the innocents—all of the proud women of the North. Ahead await the innocents of the South, many of whose feet will also find pause by the cliffs of some Potomac.

Herman's reverie does not concern the blunder of Ball's Bluff but rather a graybeard narrator, lusty boys with hearts "fresh as clover in its prime," and the emotional riches of "ladies cheering royally," ladies who are exalted by the martial music and thrilled by the regimental flags bearing noble mottoes. Herman understood the sexual undertones of war, the urge to merit feminine compliance through valor. That urge was exploited by Lucy Larcom, who threatened to withhold her favors from shirkers: she was "not yours," she told them, "because you are not man enough / To grasp your country's measure of a man!" With plentiful images surrounding the marchers bespeaking their life force and the feminine approbation they seek, "How should they dream that Death in a rosy clime / Would come to thin their shining throng?" The question is answered weeks later when the graybeard awakens in the darkness of night to recall those marching feet that found eternal pause on the bluff and to listen in memory while "far footfalls died away till none were left." These are the footfalls of all untested warriors of every time and place as they echo down the halls of history, each marching toward his own Ball's Bluff.

In terms of *Battle-Pieces* as a whole, the poem, together with "The March into Virginia," brackets "Lyon." Both deny the posturing primitivism of "Lyon" by insisting that the youth of the nation are marching not toward heroes' receptions in paradise but toward experience, enlightenment, pause by Potomac cliffs, "battle's unknown mysteries." Yet "Ball's Bluff" moves no farther than does "The March into Virginia" toward an understanding of precisely what dangers and tragedies lie beyond the mask of martial display on hometown streets. It is well to speak in guarded terms of death, of the "crimson corse" of Lyon, but the blood of Colonel Baker splattered profusely on Caspar Crowninshield's coat is beyond the imagination at work here. It is too early in the war, too close to the lulling peace that has passed, for "the blackness of darkness" to color and inform the national consciousness. Grief is possible, but not yet the knowledge of what depths of the national psyche will be plumbed before the slaughter runs its course.

Ball's Bluff had been fought not by militiamen but by the green three-year soldiers of whom McClellan was forging his army. Nevertheless, it was the last of the amateur battles, the last instance in which young Indians would go into battle ignorant of what lay ahead of them. They would follow Michael's seductive banner, but never again would they believe that they were "immortal, like the gods sublime." In the east, they would submit patiently while McClellan organized and trained them; in the west, with its wider field of conflict and harder men, the army would fight its way into condition. With "Ball's Bluff," *Battle-Pieces* also reaches the end of its earliest conception of war and of the innocence of the nation. The fading sounds of marching feet were the fading away of a pastoral culture that was perishing on the bluffs of war.

3

The Anaconda and the Asp
1861–1862

During the late summer and autumn of 1861, Berkshire continued its patriotic demonstrations and its preparations for the fighting to come, but with a different, more chastened spirit from that of the innocent, exuberant spring and early summer. In mid-August, Sarah Morewood noted the "great change the Civil War has already wrought even in our quiet village," and in mid-September Fanny Kemble, a noted English actress who was living at Lenox, only a few miles from Herman, described that change:

> Our daily talk is of fights and flights, weapons and wounds. The stars and stripes flaunt their gay colours from every roof among these peaceful hills, and give a sort of gala effect to the quiet New England villages, embowered in maple and elm trees, that would be pretty and pleasing but for the grievous suggestions they awake of bitter civil war, of the cruel interruption of an unparalleled national prosperity, of impending danger and insecurity, of heavy immediate taxation, of probable loss of property, and all the evils, public and personal, which spring from the general disorganization of the government, and disruption of the national ties.

As Kemble suggested, the show of flags no longer promised a painless triumph.[1]

The waning summer was already hinting of the harvest and the gaudy poetry of brilliantly colored leaves shortly to come, but there was a heaviness in the air. The belief in a prompt, heroic victory had been canceled by Bull Run and Wilson's Creek, and was now an embarrassing and painful memory. The present was daunting: "The war . . . has assumed such huge proportions that it threatens to engulf us all—no preoccupation can exclude it, & no hermitage hide us," Emerson wrote. Emily Dickinson, caught up in the war mood, wrote "I shall have no winter this year—on account of the soldiers—Since I cannot weave Blankets, or Boots—I thought it best to omit the season—Shall present a 'Memorial' to God—when the Maples turn—" The new seriousness was evidenced by Henry Gansevoort, who was commencing his artillery training, and Guert, who was building a navy. Masses of troops were moving to camps near Washington and at numerous points in the west to train for serious battles to come, and in Pittsfield an entire regiment was recruiting at the Agricultural Grounds. The 31st Massachusetts Volunteer Infantry, or the Western Bay State Regiment, as it was called, was enlisting men for three years, and by now it occurred to men like Herman that perhaps all of that time might be needed.[2]

With that grim prospect and with the lack of movement by the army, it was difficult to maintain one's optimism. Whether or not Herman confronted the situation with the obstinate patience that is one of the boasts of *Battle-Pieces* (as in "The Fortitude of the North") cannot be known, but perhaps he did. His fatalism placed the ultimate outcome of events in the hands of a God whose distant purposes could only be surmised. He may have eased his apprehensions and doubts by musing that, in whatever contrary direction the gusts of war might blow, the path of the underlying storm must be toward a desirable conclusion. That would have been faith of the highest order.

The First Coils

Just as the temper of Pittsfield was modulating, so was the conduct of the war changing. The "Anaconda" strategy, intended to deny Confederate blockade-runners and commerce-raiders the use of the Atlantic and Gulf of Mexico seacoasts, required an extraordinary tonnage of ships. The procurement of merchant vessels had been intensified and systematized when, in mid-July, the navy began to examine every United States merchant vessel within reach of the Port of New York, purchasing all that were suitable for service; as they arrived at the yard, Guert examined them for fitness. When their armament and other conversion work was completed, they were sent to sea.[3]

One of the new officers that had been needed was Ned Curtis, Kate Curtis's son, who was commissioned a third assistant engineer on October 21, 1861. Many new officers were being appointed, but most to acting volunteer ranks. Ned, however, received a regular navy commission, probably through the influence of his Uncle Guert. He was assigned to the *Sciota,* one of the "ninety-day gunboats" built rapidly at the beginning of the war. A small, heavily armed, screw-propelled but schooner-rigged wooden gunboat, she was to be a part of the Western Gulf Blockading Squadron. Ned must have begun his navy career in Philadelphia, where the pugnacious little craft was launched and finished. Essential as were his duties, Guert was also pressing Washington for a sea assignment for himself. In wartime, navy men belonged at sea, and Guert's heroic moments had occurred there, on the Mexican coast and in Puget Sound, while shore duty had meant routine, torpidity, and failure. But Secretary Welles refused his requests, telling him that he was "doing his country greater service by his presence at the Navy Yard than if he was on ship board." That was true, but it frustrated Guert.[4]

In August, Commodore DuPont, who had been charged with planning the blockade, was appointed flag officer in command of the South Atlantic Blockading Squadron. He moved to the Brooklyn Navy Yard to select ships for an expedition to capture a base along the Southern coast and to monitor the work on them. The result was a typical old-navy reunion, two friends and former shipmates, DuPont and Guert, working together to make them ready. In the midst of this crush of activity, Captain Foote left the yard to command the gunboats on the upper Mississippi River, leaving Guert second in command.

In mid-October, DuPont sailed for an assault on Port Royal Sound, South Carolina, where a nearly impregnable deep-water port could be established. On November 7, he led a battle group into the entrance to the sound between Fort Walker, to the south, and Fort Beauregard, to the north. As his line of battle steamed slowly past Beauregard, DuPont opened fire on the gunners there, while the Confederates fired vainly at the moving ships. After that pass, the line swung left, reversing direction to steam seaward, and fired in turn on Fort Walker. Then it swung left once more to repeat the earlier cannonade of Fort Beauregard. After a number of such passes, the battered Confederates abandoned the two islands for DuPont's use. Port Royal became a comfortable, convenient, and strategically vital base for the Union blockaders. It was from this base that Acting Master William Budd, aboard his new command, the *Ellen,* conducted forays against the enemy.[5]

The news of Port Royal was received enthusiastically by a public that was sick of amateurish defeats and the casualty lists of futility. Herman, too, must have been overjoyed. Although at some point in the past Guert had probably revealed to him that DuPont had been so outraged by *White-Jacket* that he had attempted to organize a public rebuttal, Herman now had reason to forgive him. After Manassas and Ball's Bluff, the skill with which DuPont had captured Port Royal was reassuring, and in *Battle-Pieces* the poem about it opens a series of six contrapuntal sea poems that mark a juncture in the war. They express almost heart-rending regret for the passing of the old, heroic America and dogged hope for a new, better nation yet to emerge.[6]

Given Herman's commitment to rough poetics, it comes as a surprise that

"DuPont's Round Fight (November, 1861)" is technically fastidious and that it proposes that "in time and measure perfect moves / All Art whose aim is sure." Rhyme has rules as enduring as the laws that govern the "stars divine," it maintains. Both ideals are linked to the geometric perfection of DuPont's assault, and both are related to "Unity" and "LAW." Reading the poem without irony, as critics usually do, Edward H. Rosenberry believes that "what Melville the artist saw in this [DuPont's] maneuver was a Platonic principle uniting warfare, mathematics, astronomy, and poetry." Seen that way, the circular form of the battle invokes the traditional symbolism of the circle, eternity (hence eternal principles), with associative implications of symmetry, harmony, unity, beauty, truth, order, and classical clarity. It is God's way, revealed in the movements of the stars. The ships at Port Royal "in an orbit sailed" as they fought for the right, the unity, and the law of the covenant of America with God. The intermediary is the poet, whose trope suggests an ideal course of conduct for the nation, one consistent with the precise versification. In such a nation, God's way and the way of man would be as nearly identical as possible. In Herman's own terms, both the battle and the poem diminish or eliminate the distance between Plotinus Plinlimmon's "Chronometricals" ("Heaven's own Truth") and his "Horologicals" ("the earthly wisdom of man") of *Pierre* (210–15).[7]

But there is more than a suggestion of irony in the poem, a suspect and disturbing nuance, a note of deceptiveness of the kind that one detects whenever Herman—the later writer—offers slickly crafted poetry or prose. Surely a future in which man's ways and God's ways are coincident was desirable, but the poem is all abstract theory, no combat—all on the surface of the ocean, nothing below. It is a euphemism in which no shots are fired, no timbers shattered, no masonry tumbled, no seaman or artillerist harmed. If Herman studied the battle, as he must have, he knew that if DuPont's battle plan was immaculate its execution was less than perfect. Further, if all art whose aim is sure must be perfect in time and measure, then this is one of the very few poems in *Battle-Pieces* to demonstrate such a sure aim—Herman had to know that the rule condemned his own poetics. Finally, if man's horologicals were to become identical to heaven's chronometricals, then men would be gods, a boggy, soggy, squitchy idea. It is as though, through the poem's avoidance of clangor and splinter, he were satirizing Emerson's contention (in *Nature*) that by an act of the will ugliness can be eradicated. So much for transcendentalism and its principal American proponent. Striving for perfection is noble, but it is not to be found in Anarch war or even, perhaps, in peace. Nor would it be advisable for Americans to pretend that war is free of horrors. In short, Herman had his ideal two ways, as a goal and as a warning.[8]

In another sense, the poem is about a future given over to machinery, the engines of DuPont's ships and the mechanisms that might power a renewed America. However sad the loss, the glories of the past age of sail are not the models for the future. Efficiency has replaced gaudy display. But Herman would not allow "the great bluff brows" and the broad beams of the old ships to pass unmourned: hence his counterpoint to "DuPont's Round Fight," the poem "The Stone Fleet: An Old Sailor's Lament (December, 1861)." As another element of the Anaconda strategy, on December 20, 1861, the navy sank a "stone fleet" at the entrance to Charleston harbor. But these sixteen old whaleships, ballasted with rock and then scuttled to block navigation, were sacrificed in vain. As Herman noted, "the object proposed was not accomplished. The channel is even said to have become ultimately benefited by the means employed to obstruct it."

In a sense, the poem is one of the most personal in *Battle-Pieces,* though it is not directly autobiographical. The old sailor who has "scudded round the Horn" in the *Tenedos* is not Herman, who never sailed in that nor in any other of the sacrificed ships. Still, it was his own sailor past that was disappearing. Not only had the *United States* fallen into enemy hands, but now, less than a year later, two equally melancholy events were occurring. Tom was selling the *Meteor* in Bengal,[9] perhaps to avoid the danger of Confederate commerce-raiders, and the whaling ships of *Moby-Dick* were suffering the first of many depredations that would decimate them. Not only were the Confederates burning them at sea, painting the horizon with black swatches of oily smoke, but the Union was making stone fleets of them. There can be little doubt that he regretted keenly the "mission as pitiless as the granite that freights it," as he said in his note.

"The Stone Fleet" looks back lovingly at the disappearing whalers, "the Obsolete," and lovingly also at the romance of the past. That love makes this a better poem than "DuPont's Round Fight," though not as remarkable. With the "ghosts" perish the exotic "spices and shawls and fans" of the India trade and also a reverence for the past as the ships are "unkindly" destroyed. The narrator uses the arcane language of the sea to point out a moral loss, as well. To scud "round the Horn" was, in sailor lingo, to be tested, to gain experience, to achieve the wisdom of the dark, eternal sea. It meant that one had undergone the rites of passage, had matured as, metaphorically, only sailors can, had shed his white jacket, so to speak. As White-Jacket uses the metaphor, "sailor or landsman, there is some sort of a Cape Horn for all. Boys! beware of it; prepare for it in time. Gray-beards! thank God it is passed. And ye lucky livers, to whom, by some rare fatality, your Cape Horns are placid as Lake Lemans, flatter not yourselves that good luck is judgment and discretion; for all the yolk in your eggs, you might have foundered and gone down, had the Spirit of the Cape said the word" (109). This is what Herman meant when he expressed exasperation at Emerson's ignorance of the world of experience. Emerson had imagined that "the sailor, buffets it [the storm] all day, and his health renews itself as vigorous a pulse under the sleet, as under the sun of June." Herman replied in the margin of his copy of the *Essays,* "To one who has weathered Cape Horn as a common sailor what stuff all this is." In other words, a part of the American character known only to those who had gone 'round the Horn was at risk.[10]

But Herman knew that this past was beyond recovery, and in a political sense he did not want it recovered. Three names of the "patrician keels" stand out, Richmond, Leonidas, and Lee—suggesting the Confederate capital and Confederate generals Leonidas Polk and Robert E. Lee. Of all Americans, those of the South were the most wedded to a past that was also characterized by feudalism and slavery and the most reluctant to abandon it. But the future of the American experiment belonged to the future. Just as the innocence that had led youth a-berrying to Bull Run and Ball's Bluff had to disappear, so had the fleets of square-riggers to sail off into another era. It was a courageous admission for a man who suspected progress, but one of which his pliant intellect was capable.

Not long after DuPont's departure from Brooklyn, Uncle Peter and his family visited the city. By coincidence, Herman arrived there at about the same time, though he may not have encountered the Gansevoorts. He was taking advantage of the fact that the Allan Melvilles had just returned from their summer vacation to make a visit. While in the city, Herman visited the bookshops, buying Leigh Hunt's *Rimini and Other Poems* and Sir Henry Taylor's *Notes from Life,* but what he did aside from that is not known. The weather was fine and surely he took what advantage time allowed of the inexhaustible novelties of the city. On the other hand, it is known that Uncle Peter and his family visited the navy yard. When they arrived there, Guert was, by chance, acting commandant. He looked well, Kitty thought. Along with other sights, Guert showed his relatives the *Adirondack,* the construction of which he was supervising. She was one of fourteen new sloops-of-war a-building, handsome ships that flag officers wanted for their squadrons and that officers of Guert's rank yearned to command. She was destined for DuPont's squadron, Guert told his uncle, and he hoped to command her. Perhaps Herman and Allan accompanied Uncle Peter on this visit, or perhaps they made a separate visit of their own before Herman's return to Pittsfield.[11]

After ten days in New York, the Gansevoorts returned to Albany, where Uncle Peter encountered some relics of the family past. A week later he received a letter from his exiled brother, Wessel, who apologized for not telling Peter where he had been living. For this omission he blamed "a continued severe headache." Then while Peter was strolling down the street on the twenty-first of the month, he ran into another reminder of the old days, his friend Martin Van Buren. A week after that, Henry Gansevoort arrived home to spend Thanksgiving with his family and the Lansings. Augusta came down from Gansevoort to see him, but at the moment no one in New York City knew he was on leave. Allan, whose jaws were throbbing from a visit to his dentist, alleviated the pain by deviling (he thought) his artillery cousin in Harrisburg: "I am going home to get my spirits revived by wife children & dinner and a cheerful blaze in the grate, all of which must be denied you as a soldier at the wars." But Henry was enjoying similar amenities in Albany, a fact that Allan learned, much to his chagrin, when Henry dined with him on his way back to Camp Preble.[12]

Back in Pittsfield, Herman's life was measured out in coffee spoons. In the state elections early in November, the town gave a slight majority to the Republicans. At about the same time, news arrived that General Scott had retired from active duty because of infirmity (and because he was irritated with McClellan) and that McClellan had been appointed general-in-chief of the entire army. On November 13, the village was excited to learn that Secretary of War Cameron was coming to town on "the cars." However, he was on his way to Springfield to inspect the armory there and did not stop. The *Sun* reported that Jefferson Davis had visited his old friend, Colonel Lee of the Harvard Regiment, in his cell in Richmond, and had promised to do everything possible to make his stay comfortable. Thanksgiving, which arrived on the twenty-first of November rather than the twenty-eighth, as it did in New York State, was glorious. Pittsfield provided the Western Bay State men at Camp Seward with a great bounty of turkeys, chicken pies, and apple, mince, and pumpkin pies, and droves of citizens visited the camp during the day. Two days later, it snowed heavily enough for sleighing.[13]

That Hard Countermand

Herman and his family were planning to escape the winter isolation at Arrowhead by spending the season in New York City, but before they did, Lizzie wanted to be with her family on their first Christmas without Judge Shaw. Herman may have preferred Gansevoort, since he was concerned about Uncle Herman's health, but he also wanted to be in Boston when Tom arrived. Tom, who was returning home from Bengal as a tourist, was now en route by way of India, Arabia, Egypt, Malta, France, and England, whence he was to sail to Portland, Maine, then on to Boston for a reunion with his relatives there. Sometime before the twelfth of December, the

Herman Melvilles left Pittsfield; Lizzie, Malcolm, and little Fanny for Boston and Herman and Bessie for Gansevoort.[14]

Herman did not stop to see Uncle Peter, but he called at a brewery in Troy to order a cask of ale for Uncle Herman's holiday present. In Gansevoort, he found his uncle feeble, for several weeks unable to move from his bed to the sofa without assistance. Gus and Mother Melville wanted to knit "for our good soldiers," but, despite the assistance of Georgie, the burden of caring for Uncle Herman was too great. Herman found that Stanny had profited from his "strict course of mental training," but that he had not grown much. During the visit, Herman must have seen his Glens Falls cousins. He would have learned that Leonard was toying with the idea of a commission in the navy, in which Guert's influence would help, and he would also have learned of Ned's appointment, if he did not already know about it. Such news circulated through the family rapidly. On the twenty-third of December, Herman left Stanny at Gansevoort and, accompanied by Sister Fanny, took Bessie to Albany. They spent a pleasant day with Uncle Peter and his family, exchanging news and talking over the state of the country and the world. Although much of the conversation would have concerned Henry's artillery experiences, Uncle Peter may have talked about Uncle Wessel, since the subject was newly on his mind, and about Van Buren. After dinner, the travelers went on to Stanwix Hall for the night, as they often did when they intended to board the early morning train.[15]

By Christmas Eve, they had joined Lizzie and the other children at the Shaws' home. Because of the war, the Christmas celebration was probably muted, as it was in Concord, where Emerson reported that "no Christmas boxes, no New Years gift, this year to be offered by any honest party to any!" Later, the Hoadleys and young Mary Curtis drove down to Boston to see everyone and to take Sister Fanny, who was to spend the rest of the winter with the Hoadleys, back to Lawrence. It may have been at this time, too, that Herman's uncle, Captain "Nor West" D'Wolf, presented him with his just-published memoir, *A Voyage to the North Pacific and a Journey through Siberia, More than Half a Century Ago.* With her family depleted, Mother Melville did not spend Christmas at Gansevoort, but went to the Curtises' instead, leaving Gus, Stanny, and Georgie to tend to Uncle Herman and to celebrate as best they could. George Curtis picked her up in his sleigh and returned her late the next day.[16]

In Boston, Herman witnessed a Union humiliation near at hand. It was of particular interest to him because it involved Captain Charles Wilkes, a naval officer whom he had long admired. Wilkes had commanded the noted expedition to explore the South Pacific Ocean, an expedition that had fascinated Herman so much that he had purchased the old seaman's multivolume *United States Exploring Expedition, 1838–1842* and had used it as a source for *Typee, Omoo, Mardi,* and *Moby-Dick.*[17] While hurrying his warship from the Africa station toward Port Royal in the hope of joining DuPont's attack, Wilkes had discovered in Havana, Cuba, that two Confederate commissioners, James M. Mason and John Slidell, were there preparing to sail for Europe aboard the British steamer *Trent.* Mason, whom Herman had seen on the floor of the Senate earlier in the year, was accredited to Great Britain; Slidell, another former senator, was accredited to France. On November 8, Wilkes forced the unarmed *Trent* to heave to on the high seas and seized the envoys.

Many Northerners were elated—Emerson thought that such acts of will were notable—but the illegal and provocative seizure had been an awesome blunder. Whittier was frightened: "A war with England would ruin us. It is too monstrous to think of. May God in his mercy save us from it!" He was justified in his fear. With British troops on their way to Canada, a second war, with the right on the side of Great Britain, was a genuine possibility. But Secretary of State Seward meekly—and properly—agreed to return the two agents to British custody, much to the disgust of many Northerners, including Herman. It was only to be expected that Herman would be prejudiced on Wilkes's behalf and would believe that this fellow explorer of the Pacific was in the right. Now Mason and Slidell were at Fort Warren, nearby. On the first of January 1862, the emissaries were delivered to H.B.M.S. *Rinaldo* at Provincetown, Cape Cod. Herman vented his feelings in "Donelson," in which the narrator compares "The bitter cup / Of that hard countermand / Which gave the Envoys up" to "wormwood in the mouth."[18]

If that was a day of national humiliation, it was also a day of family rejoicing; Tom Melville arrived to spend his first New Year's Day in sixteen years in his homeland. His return was always a cause for celebration, even though his time at home might be short. He remained in Boston for only a few days, since he was scheduled to sail on a new ship, the *Bengal,* in a little over two weeks, and it was mandatory that he visit the rest of the family. Helen Griggs spent some time with him and then accompanied Tom and Herman on a visit to the Hoadleys in Lawrence. Soon after, Tom took the train to the city to see Allan and his family, and it is probable that Herman, who had the duty of finding rental quarters there for his family, accompanied him.[19]

On January 6, Tom left the city for Gansevoort to see his mother, sister, nephew, uncle, and, probably, his Glens Falls cousins. After a four-day visit, he paid the expected call on Uncle Peter in Albany, charming Kitty. She thought him "very much improved both in mind & personal appearance," now "the most agreeable of Aunt Melville's sons"—including, of course, Herman. Naturally, they talked about Henry and his new career and perhaps about Ed Lansing, who had recently joined the Albany Zouave Cadets to learn something about the military and was now anxious to enter West Point. But the big news was about Kitty herself: the previous Thursday, Abe Lansing had proposed marriage and she had accepted. Perhaps it was when she became engaged, with the implication of womanhood attached to the act, that Herman began to call her "Kate," as she will be known from this point on. Sunday was stormy, but Tom took Kate to church at St. Peter's anyway. The next morning, when the storm subsided, Tom left on the train for Boston to prepare for his coming voyage. Mother Melville wanted to accompany him, but she did not dare to leave for such a long time.[20]

On his arrival, Tom found that his sailing date had been postponed until the first of February. The delay gave him an opportunity to spend the weekend in Lawrence with Kate, Fanny, and Mary while John was in New Bedford negotiating for a new job. On his return to Boston, Tom met additional delays. On February 1, the Lawrence contingent visited the *Bengal* and lunched aboard, and on the eleventh the ship finally departed for Hong Kong. It had been a typical star performance; Tom had appeared, charmed his admiring family anew, and then disappeared, leaving them all to regret his absence and to hope for his prompt return.[21]

Herman had remained in the city to arrange quarters for his family at 150 East 18th Street, not far from Allan's residence. There he again experienced the war as New Yorkers were seeing it. Overall, the city was gloomy about the failure of progress in the war. As Hawthorne noted a month later, the streets were military. The store windows displayed uniforms and weapons, and on occasion one encountered a cannon parked at the curb. The daily papers still monopolized attention with their war news; Longfellow noted that "newspapers take up much time,—too much by a great deal; but one can hardly help it now when any moment may bring the greatest tidings." On the eighteenth of January, Lizzie and the children arrived from Boston just in time to nurse Herman: a few days after their arrival, both he and Allan contracted "rheumatism," probably sciatica, in Herman's case. During Allan's illness, Bruce assumed the burden of his legal affairs and reported to him nightly.[22]

By Saturday, February 1, Herman was well enough to leave his bed and search for books, and soon Allan, too, was on his feet. Herman's first resort was to ask Evert Duyckinck to lend him some collections of Elizabethan plays—Dekker and Webster, but not Marlow, whom he had read. On a more social note, he opened his "season" in the city by inviting Evert and George to visit him: "We will brew some whiskey punch and settle the affairs of the universe over it—which affairs sadly need it, some say." The reason the universe needed fixing was obvious. Ball's Bluff, the sinking of the Stone Fleet, the release of Mason and Slidell, all had depressed him and, worst of all, other than DuPont's capture of Port Royal, there had been little progress toward winning the war.[23]

Herman made his usual circuit of the city's bookshops. In February and March he bought a translation of Giorgio Vasari's *Lives of the Most Eminent Painters, Sculptors, and Architects,* a work which he had borrowed several years earlier from Evert Duyckinck, John G. Lockhart's *Ancient Spanish Ballads,* F. J. Vingott's *Selections from the Best Spanish Poets,* several works by Isaac Disraeli, two volumes of Emerson's essays, William Hazlitt's combined *Lectures on the English Comic Writers* and *Lectures on the English Poets,* Madame de Staël's *Germany,* and poetry by James Clarence Mangan, Thomas Moore, Thomas Hood, Robert Fergusson, Heinrich Heine, and Abraham Cowley. As winter turned into spring, he concentrated even more specifically on poetry, buying Matthew Arnold, Lord Byron, Charles Churchill, William Collins, and Henry Kirke White. He was studying his craft, but as always his restless mind took him elsewhere as well.[24]

Aside from the paraphernalia of war and the books, there were other attractions to make the winter worthwhile, relatives, friends, and writers with whom to exchange calls, and things to see—plays, operas, the painters' studios on 10th Street, and even a live whale at Barnum's American Museum—and he probably went to Brooklyn with Allan to see Guert. He may also have indulged in one of his favorite pastimes, riding the ferryboat across the Hudson River on crossing after crossing, moving about in order to see the maritime vista from every angle. Still, there is little evidence to suggest precisely how he and his household spent the winter. The record of these days is, instead, the record of the war, both near and far.[25]

The Old Ships' Hail and Farewell

Across the river in Brooklyn, Guert Gansevoort was involved in one of the most pivotal naval events of all time, completing the "Ericsson Iron Clad Steamer," or, popularly, the "pillbox on a raft." During the previous year, the government had learned that the Confederates were converting the charred carcass of the *Merrimack* into an armored steam warship that would threaten the destruction of the North Atlantic Blockading Squadron in Hampton Roads. Congress had responded by authorizing several experimental ironclads, one of which was the Ericsson battery. After she had been built at a private yard, the ungainly craft was towed to Brooklyn, where, on February 19, 1862, she was turned over to the navy for armament. Guert appropriated two eleven-inch Dahlgren guns from another ship and lowered them into the ironclad's single turret, then roofed them over with iron rails. On February 22, Commodore Paulding promised that the *Monitor,* the name finally given the gunboat, would be ready in four days. The same day, the *Adirondack* was launched.[26]

Despite the lack of evidence that he did, it is quite possible that Herman inspected the *Monitor* while it was at the yard.[27] His health had improved, the construction of the craft was well publicized locally, Allan and Guert were particularly close during this period, and Guert would have realized that his sailor-cousin would be fascinated by such a unique warship. In addition, Herman and Allan may have been interested in the launching of the *Adirondack,* which Guert might command. It is enticing to think of Herman and Allan meeting Lieutenant John L. Worden, the *Monitor*'s commander, and crawling over the little boat above and below, with Guert and Worden explaining its innovations—and it was mostly innovation.

When the *Monitor* was delayed, the newspapers called her "Ericsson's folly," but on the sixth of March, manned by a select crew, she was towed to sea en route for Hampton Roads. Two days later, the *Virginia,* the rechristened *Merrimack,* won the ironclad race. She steamed out into Hampton Roads, where she single-handedly defeated the powerful Union squadron there. Her two wooden sisters were helpless against her armor. One of them, the *Roanoke,* whose propulsion plant was inoperative, considered fighting, but her prudent commander instead ordered her pushed aground near the fort, where the deep draft of the *Virginia* prevented pursuit. Others followed her to safety, but the *Congress* was bloodied, forced to surrender, and torched. The *Cumberland* fought gamely, but, pummeled and rammed, she sank, carrying many of her crew down with her. She came to rest on the bottom with her masts above water and a pennant still flying from one of them. That accomplished, the *Virginia* retired for the night, expecting to renew her depredations in the morning, but when she returned the next day she found the *Monitor* waiting. A lengthy battle ensued in which the two ships battered each other at close range, shot after shot fired point-blank at unyielding metal, but neither could defeat the other. The smokestack of the *Virginia* was blown away and Lieutenant Worden was blinded temporarily, but otherwise there were few injuries to man or ship. In response to this painful lesson, the Union government set about building ironclads with Ericsson rotating turrets. One of its first moves was to send the *Roanoke* to the Brooklyn Navy Yard to be cut down to her waterline, armored, and equipped with three turrets on her leveled deck.[28] The armor and the removal of her masts were signals that the age of the wooden sailing warship was over.

These two days probably inspired more poems than any other single event of the war, but it was the sinking of the *Cumberland,* rather than the ironclad battle, that inspired most of them. There were grandiloquent and sentimental accolades to the brave captain and crew and celebrations of the flag that would not sink. George H. Boker imagined a mentally retarded black servant who faithfully clasped his captain's sword to his bosom as he sank to a depth far greater than was possible in the actual location. Longfellow wrote a tactless, beerhall ballad that unintentionally mocked the dead: "Ho! brave hearts that went down in the seas! / Ye are at peace in the troubled stream." Thus the popular and newspaper poets either failed to understand the larger implications of the event for the traditional man-of-war or they chose to ignore them, but a few authors were more percipient. Herman must have read Hawthorne's thoughts with interest:

> A whole history of naval renown reaches its period, now that the Monitor comes smoking into view. . . . That last gun from the Cumberland . . . sounded the requiem of many sinking ships. Then went down all the navies of Europe, and our own, Old Ironsides and all, and Trafalgar and a thousand other fights become only a memory, never to be acted over again; and thus our brave countrymen come last in the long procession of heroic sailors that includes Blake and Nelson . . . whose renown is our native inheritance. . . . [H]uman strife is to be transferred from the heart and personality of man into cunning contrivances of machinery, which by and by will fight out our wars with only the clank and smash of iron, strewing the field with broken engines, but damaging nobody's little finger except by accident.

That Herman did read this passage is suggested by parallel ideas in his four ironclad poems and in his invocation in *Billy Budd* (56) of the "naval magnates" of the past.[29]

Hawthorne distrusted progress and its technology. In his scriptural imagination, the fiery mechanisms in the bellies of railroad engines and steamships, with their stinking heat, soot, and cacophony, were infernal. That was true of Herman, too, except that his was the more adventurous imagination: he grappled with progress with both heart and head. In addition to the fact that Ned Curtis was now a navy engineer, Herman had close to him a prophet of the technological future, John Hoadley. If Herman's affections urged him back toward the gallantry and the grace of memory, yet he knew that the industrial might and the technological genius that had created the *Monitor* were strengths that might reunite and reinvigorate the union. This insight forced him to concede, reluctantly, that the technician-warrior of the armored ship possessed a dignity of his own distinct from the frank bravery of the old sea-warriors. He could not refrain from mourning the past; no more could he dismiss the future.

His response to the battle, therefore, continued the contrast between old and new established in "DuPont's Round Fight" and "The Stone Fleet." His four ironclad poems, the most extended treatment of any event in *Battle-Pieces,* are an able exposition of the meaning of what was, after all, a millennial event—millennial in terms of the revolution it caused in the conduct of naval warfare but also in terms of its encapsulation in a moment of time of a larger change in the fabric of the nation and of civilization. Taken as a series, they are symmetrical. The first and last, "The Cumberland (March, 1862)" and "A Utilitarian View of the Monitor's Fight," examine the battle in esthetic terms; the middle two, "In the Turret (March, 1862)" and "The Temeraire (Supposed to have been suggested to an Englishman of the old order by the fight of the Monitor and Merrimac)," examine it in terms of spirit and myth. These are the two questions of the heart that Hawthorne had raised, beauty and fable.

"The Cumberland" is a requiem to the ship which continued in defeat to fly its flag as a memorial to an age that had passed. Although it tells a fragment of the ship's story, an incident in which a gunner attempting to escape drowning was washed back into the ship, the battle as a whole is deftly encapsulated in the simple sentence, "She warred and sunk." Yet the meaning of the poem lies in the euphony of the ship's name. It is only fair to expect a poet to be sensitive to the sounds of words: to Herman's poetic ear, the name Cumberland, "rolling on the tongue," suggested the flowing water of the river after which it was named. It was music, modulated vowels and stately consonants. In contrast, certain other names, such as that of the ship "Bellipotent" in *Billy Budd,* were clipped, out of joint, and intended to be that way. The "telling sound" of "voweled syllables free" implies all of the other beauties of the old sailing ships, quiet swiftness, grace of carriage, gusting power, and sunlit splendor. With this ship disappear the laced gold of the old uniforms, the parti-colored flags that framed the tall masts during celebrations in port, and a hundred other colorful and romantic associations. And with the old warships disappears an entire past of color and romance.

It is useful to consider "A Utilitarian View of the Monitor's Fight" here, rather than at its proper place at the end of the ironclad series. If "The Cumberland" is a celebration of a retreating resonance, this poem is also about art. It is an acceptance of what Robert Frost called "a diminished thing," in life as well as in poetry. Deftly cast in crank and piston versification, the poem's opening hop-toad meter emulates and celebrates the mechanical, "grim and characterless efficiency" that Worden and his ship represented: "Plain be the phrase, yet apt the verse, / More ponderous than nimble." With this beginning, it comes perilously close to being the finest poem of the Civil War, and certainly it is one of the most inventive. As Hennig Cohen has noted, the lines "grind and clank like heavy machinery, and the rhythm pounds relentlessly," in imitation, he might have added, of the reciprocating engine of the little vessel. The style, Cohen says, is "antipoetic," which, if it refers to antipoetry, is the precise term needed; it is organically apt and a model of modernist experimental technique.[30]

The poem can be best read by making an esthetic comparison between the beauty of tall ships such as the *Cumberland* and the transcendent ugliness (more recently sanitized by calling it "quaintness") of both the *Virginia* and the *Monitor.* At first, the poem appears to mock that ugliness. "Ponderous" verse, not "the rhyme's barbaric cymbal" or "fans / Of banners," is suitable for a battle characterized by "zeal," cogency, lack of "passion," and "plain mechanic power." Instead of heroes thrusting swords and swinging cutlasses, "trades and artisans" do battle "by crank, / Pivot, and screw, / And calculations of caloric." What has been lost is elegance, "painted pomp," "gaud / of glory," and "lace and feather," despite the fact that the battle was "deadlier, closer, calm 'mid storm." But that loss Herman accepted. For too long war had been glorified and thus masked in idylls of kings and visions of knights—lace and feather—and that habit of glorification was still alive among the poets of the newspapers and in the imaginations of the Southern cavaliers. It communicated little sense of the truth, that the vestments of battle are grime and smoke and suffering and that victory is won by those most adept at killing. But now war reveals its true face: the grimy god, Satan, has found his liege knights in these artificers of destruction. Although one might accept such a war as the present one, it is "less grand than Peace."

But what of the resonance that was retreating, the fabled men-of-war on whose decks had stood the great sea-eagles, Don John of Austria, Andrea Doria, Blake, Tromp, Jean Bart, Nelson, and Decatur? Since the times demanded a farewell to their gallantry and display, Herman would make it grandly in "The Temeraire," a poem in tune with his "immense nostalgia for an older, simpler, more poetic time, an elder age of sail, . . . of an Eden before the fall." As suggested in Herman's note, the poem was inspired by a sister work of art, the painting "The Fighting Temeraire" by Joseph M. W. Turner. In it, the ghostly old legend, stripped of her regalia, is towed by a smoking steam-tug even uglier than the *Monitor* toward the berth where she is to be scrapped. As Herman put it,

A pigmy steam-tug tows you,
  Gigantic, to the shore—
Dismantled of your guns and spars,
  And sweeping wings of war.

It is a melancholy end for the ship that raced Nelson into the Battle of Trafalgar. From this beginning grows a poem worthy of Turner's painting.[31]

"The Temeraire" could well be two poems. The first three stanzas, cast in ballad meter, are a reprise of the lesson of Hampton Roads. The battle proved "that oak, and iron, and man / Are tough in fibre yet," but at a cost:

        The sea-fight yields
  No front of old display;
The garniture, emblazonment,
  And heraldry all decay.

In the last three stanzas, the verse form and the diction depart from this matter-of-fact comparison to mourn the passing of the old:

O Ship, how brave and rare,
  That fought so oft and well,
On open decks you manned the gun
  Armorial.

She is the great ship, the mythic ship, as the poem follows her into battle and her crew cheers. But here and in the painting she meets her end as her storied age departs:

O, Titan Temeraire,
  Your stern-lights fade away;
Your bulwarks to the years must yield,
  And heart of oak decay.

Gone were the open, frank, bold days. In the future, warriors would huddle in the armored bowels of their steamers and measure battle by "calculations of caloric." Regardless of the dominance of the new, Herman would not allow the old to pass without crying, "O, the navies old and oaken, / O, the Temeraire no more!"

When the old men-of-war sailed off into legend, did bravery depart as well? Could it survive in battles that damaged nobody's little finger except by accident, as Hawthorne thought? Herman's answer, the poem "In the Turret," is cast in the form of a brief narrative of the life of the *Monitor* from her journey south from Brooklyn to her loss, together with sixteen of her crew, off Cape Hatteras nearly ten months later. The point of the poem is that if the unseaworthy little gunboat was not grand and noble of form, and if Worden did not stand on an open deck shouting defiance to the gods of battle, the duel yet required other virtues, an "honest heart of duty," calm determination, and the daring to brave the danger of sinking while imprisoned in the turret.

In terms of myth, the poem invokes the legend of Hercules (here Alcides), who groped "into haunted hell / To bring forth King Admetus' bride." This is not the standard version of the rescue of the lady Alcestis, in which Hercules guarded her sickroom and grappled with Death when he approached,[32] but altering the story by grafting the myth of Orpheus and Eurydice onto it was not the first instance in which Herman changed "facts" to suit his purpose. By having Hercules descend into hell, Herman created an analogue to the miner of "The Conflict of Convictions," who descends into another hell, the hell of the battlefield, Satan's underworld. Thus Worden, who is "in the Turret walled / By adamant," has descended into a modern hell. There an "all-deriding" spirit, Satan, asks, "Man, darest thou—desperate, unappalled— / Be first to lock thee in the armored tower?" Had the prophecy of the spirit proved true, had the *Monitor* sunk then, Worden would have been trapped in the "goblin-snare" and carried down to the last reach of the unknown, the bottom of the sea. But Worden braved that danger: "First duty, duty next, and duty last." New perils and new myths for the warriors of the new.

Guns in the West

In the west, the Union finally succeeded in winning an important land battle. The object of General Grant's modest army and Flag Officer Foote's gunboats was to seize control of the Tennessee rivers used by the enemy for transportation; the plan was to capture two fortifications, Forts Henry and Donelson, that the Confederates had thrown up along those rivers. The preliminary event was the capture of Fort Henry on February 6, 1862, which Foote accomplished without the help of troops. But the attack on Donelson was hotly contested, the first notable occasion of the war in which adequately trained and organized troops on both sides fought to a decisive conclusion. On February 12, the Union soldiers took positions under the elevated fortifications. Both the weather and the terrain were unfavorable, and this time Foote's gunboats were ineffective; the Confederates punished the little fleet, disabling some of the boats and wounding Foote. Thereafter, Grant's army fought without naval support. It was a Tennessee winter, with freezing nights. Despite their inexperience, the western soldiers distinguished themselves by their courage and perseverance. Without winter clothing, they shivered through the nights and then fought again in the mornings. When they were beaten back, they accepted their casualties and retook the ground they had lost. On the sixteenth of February, the fort surrendered.

Whittier had been struggling against a dark night of the soul: "The shadow of this awful war rests heavily upon me," he had written. "I try to keep up my faith in God and my hope for man—but there are times when I am in great darkness." But the capture of the forts raised everyone's spirits. Citizens who were beginning to despair of ever seeing the Union army prevail were elated. In New York City, it inspired them to celebrate Washington's Birthday with gusto: artillery roaring, bells ringing, a parade, evening illuminations, and the first president's farewell address read throughout the city. "Glorious news," Kate Gansevoort wrote, and Albany celebrated with illumination and cannon salutes.[33]

Herman ignored the gunboat victory and instead wrote "Donelson (February, 1862)" about the land assault. Cast in rough, stumbling vernacular, it presents a reasonably accurate picture of the battle—the first poem in *Battle-Pieces* to follow soldiers into actual combat. Since Herman had no private account of the assault or personal interest in it—no known relative, friend, or acquaintance had participated in it—the poem is based entirely on news reports, including those reprinted in *The Rebellion Record*.[34] Taking advantage of that fact, he made news reports the basis of the poem's narrative form. It relates the reactions of various passersby who pause at a bulletin board to read the news of the battle as it is posted, then, gripped by what they read, remain until there is no more to be received that night, only to return the next day to read again. But the scene is imaginative, since at the time of the battle Herman could follow the events better in the city dailies than he could by waiting on the streets to read dispatches. It is likely that his memory of such a bulletin board scene came from a later event, the receipt in Pittsfield of the news of the Battle of Gettysburg.

The bulletins are similar to those described by Oliver Wendell Holmes, Sr.: "almost hourly paragraphs, laden with truth or falsehood as the case may be, making us restless always for the last fact or rumor they are telling."[35] Like these, the bulletins in the poem are ambiguous, sometimes misleading, on one occasion interrupted by a technical failure. What seems to be a report of today's battle may be no more than an amplified report of yesterday's. What is announced as a "GLORIOUS VICTORY OF THE FLEET!" may, when the details are clarified, prove to be a sharp repulse, instead. Fact is fact, but it is not always truth, as Herman would demonstrate many years later in *Billy Budd*. The result, then, is not so much a description of the battle as it is a learning process for the witnesses—and for the nation.

The poem focuses on a variety of civilians who respond to the news. A "cross patriot," made cynical by the repeated delays and defeats of the army, crossly doubts that any decisive result will ensue. Excitable children and Young Indians cheer excitedly for Grant, while a sour Copperhead sourly mocks their jubilation by warning that the Southerners are persistent foes. A solid merchant affirms his solid belief that "we'll beat in the end, sir." Together, the bystanders personify another kind of conflict of convictions.

That the narrator is a dramatic character rather than Herman himself is suggested by the epithet "the croaker" he applies to the Copperhead and his description of the man's face as a "yellow death's head," invective of a sort that Herman shunned. In his own voice, Herman would have been more tolerant of the doubter. The man may not have been a true Southern sympathizer at all: it was no more than the truth to say that the Confederates would not be easy to conquer, and his statement, "The country's ruined, that I know," might have come from Allan Melville or Evert Duyckinck. Further, although all of Herman's relatives and friends sincerely supported the Union cause, some were accused of being Copperheads. It was an odious accusation, emotionally loaded beyond all appeal to reason:

Red wrath on all *Copperhead* villains
  Who dare trail their blasphemous slime
On Loyalty's thrice-sacred flowers,
  That WASHINGTON sowed in our clime,

one poet fulminated.[36] Herman shunned such freighted terms, as was proper for a poet who sought to understand his fellow man. His world was populated by interesting people, not by heroes and villains.

Because it deals with the civilian response to the war, "Donelson" is a companion piece to "Ball's Bluff." The street scene becomes participatory as the experience of the assembled citizens parallels the experience of the soldiers in the distant battle. The crowd is drenched by the storm that had first gathered at Mount Greylock in "Misgivings," rain and sleet that take them in spirit to the weather and the storm of battle which the soldiers at Donelson experience. (The patriot's "battered umbrella" is "riddled with bullet-holes.") At Donelson, the fighting is desperate; correspondingly, at home the scene is dark as night. "Nature retained her sulking fit, / In her hand the shard." In Herman's other poetry, the shard is a broken piece of an Attic vase; here, held by Nature, the fragment suggests the nation shattered by fratricide.[37]

The bystanders, who had at first been content with a simplistic, friend-foe perception of the battle, begin to understand the darkness that engulfs them. In the beginning of the poem, both the crowd and the telegraphic reports are thoughtlessly partisan, as the Confederates are characterized as *"a yelling rout / Of ragamuffins"* led by Cavaliers in "gold lace," with a black piratic flag reported flying from the fort. But the crowd is chastened by the news that the Confederates have cared for fallen Yankees: *"The rebel is wrong, but human yet; / He's got a heart."* With this reminder that the enemy is a fellow man, the bystanders depart for the night, "Musing on right and wrong / And mysteries dimly sealed—." They see that the black flag is in reality their own "storm, whose black flag showed in heaven" above them and above all Americans, not a symbol of the evil of the Southerners, but an emblem of the nation's suffering permitted by an inscrutable heaven: "All fatherless seemed the human soul," says the narrator. At this point, Donelson is expanded from a single battle to a symbol of the Civil War as a whole.[38]

When in the following day's communique the counterattackers issue from the fort, they are no longer a rout of ragamuffins but infantry, cavalry, and artillery. This much has been learned, but there is more. When the news of the surrender arrives, there is jubilation: the North has won. But joy is mixed with apprehension, visions of light with those of darkness:

Grant strikes the war's first sounding stroke
At Donelson.
For lists of killed and wounded, see
The morrow's dispatch: to-day 'tis victory.

It is good to celebrate today, but tomorrow the cost must be totaled; "wife and maid" must scan the death list, which "like a river flows / Down the pale sheet, / And there the whelming waters meet." Now the river cascading down the hill in "Misgivings" has become a river of men named on a dripping list, the slain washed away by war.

For the newly chastened narrator, the battle has been a detail, death the whole. But the enlightenment is not complete. Some of the blackness of darkness has been shown, but the full meaning of war cannot yet be understood because news reports alone cannot reveal it—that would await a later vision. Still, enough is known to convince the narrator that Donelson, Satan's ramparts of war, must disappear. The ending prayer is that the flagstaff of Donelson may fall athwart the "curs'd ravine" that separates North and South so that the slaughter may be erased from the memory of man:

[May] naught
Be left of trench or gun;
The bastion, let it ebb away,
Washed with the river bed; and Day
In vain seek Donelson.

Streams of men, streams of rain and sleet, streams of river water. From the beginning of the poem, the rain has been washing the news of battle from the dispatch sheets as it drips down the pages, and finally nature will wash away the shame and level the battlements back to green Shenandoahs.[39]

With the fall of Henry and Donelson, the Confederates abandoned Nashville, which then became an important Union army hub. In March, Doctor Henry Thurston was sent there to take charge of the University Hospital. Since this was to be his permanent station, he sent for his wife, Lizzie, and his little boy, Nathaniel, whom he had left in the city. Although Lizzie was in the last trimester of her pregnancy, she came to Nashville to be with him. Not long after her arrival, she bore her second child, Helen Barrington Thurston, the family's first native of Tennessee.[40]

On Sunday, April 6, Grant's force, newly named the Army of the Tennessee, was surprised at Pittsburgh Landing, Tennessee, by a larger Confederate army under General Albert Sidney Johnston. By defeating Grant, Johnston hoped to regain the offensive so he could carry the war into the North. His assault was concentrated largely on green troops near Shiloh Church, a rustic log chapel. With many of its soldiers so inexperienced that they knew barely enough to load and fire their muskets, the Union soldiers were severely mauled. But on Monday, heavily reinforced, the Yankees turned to the attack, forcing the Confederates to retreat. Although the fighting was intense and bloody, neither side could claim that it had won. Nevertheless, Johnston was killed and the Confederates were prevented from invading the North.

"Perhaps the most delicate and moving lyric" in *Battle-Pieces,*[41] "Shiloh: A Requiem (April, 1862)" is a soft, elegiac, conciliatory poem that survives the technical difficulty of rhyming the name "Shiloh." Its double inspiration was the church that gave the battle its name and the Sabbath on which this part of the battle was fought. Shiloh Church reminded Herman that "the house of God was in Shiloh" (Judg. 18:31) and that the biblical Shiloh was a key to an incipient war that was nearly fought when one faction of Israelites became convinced that the other was worshipping false gods (Josh. 22).

A counterpart to "Donelson," it takes the reader to the scene long after the battle, after neutral nature has healed the land. The fields surrounding the church are hushed and swallows wing in circles of eternity, uniting symbols of spring—the swallows—and resurrection—the church. These turn memory back to the spring rains that on the battle evening of that Sunday fell on broken and waning lives. It had been a dark and brutal day in which men had frowned across the "curs'd ravine" at brothers whom they aspired to kill. But "what like a bullet can undeceive!" Divided as Israel was at ancient Shiloh, these modern disputants had learned late that causes—

"Fame and country"—paled before their own mortality and that their suffering was theirs alone. The rebirth of spring, the worship represented by the humble country church, the inviolability of the Sabbath, and the dedication to country that inspired both sides had become moot. Their prayers were "natural," and natural too was the friendship that resumed as enemies shared the brotherhood of pain and death. They were victims of the contrary spins of wind foretold in "The Conflict of Convictions"; while the storm itself was driving true, these men were felled by wayward gusts. When they were gone, nature's pitiless rhythms continued, and the green world was restored over their graves. As time washes Donelson away, so it returns Shiloh Church to the quiet refuge it had once been—as though these men had never lived and fought there. Through all of this, the poem takes *Battle-Pieces* a step forward, into that area of realism in which real men suffer and die on real battlefields.

Farther west, the Union Army in Missouri won a battle, this one with personal significance for Herman, since the Hobarts, in the 44th Illinois, were, or should have been, engaged in it. While in winter quarters, the regiment had suffered grievously and Lieutenant Randolph Hobart had again been sent home ill. He never returned. Although his illness was "incurable," he clung to his rank tenaciously, leaving his company with only one officer present for duty, until the repeated demands of the regiment induced him to resign so a healthy officer could take his place. Then late in the winter, the regiment, now a part of the Army of the Southwest, had pursued General Price's Confederate army into northwestern Arkansas. There they met Price, who had been joined by the Arkansas Confederates and a brigade of Indians, at the Battle of Pea Ridge. On the night of March 6, the Union army, expecting a Confederate assault from the south, was positioned with the 44th Illinois in a division near the far right. Unexpectedly, the Confederates circled around to flank them on the right and the rear. That began the battle, which continued throughout the seventh and the eighth of March, the 44th always in the heaviest fighting. Had it not been for their division, the Confederates might have won the battle, but as it was, Price was beaten and forced to retreat farther into Arkansas with the 44th in hot pursuit. It was the first decisive Union victory west of the Mississippi. But if the 44th Illinois behaved well, not all of its members did. Just as it advanced into battle, Major Jeff Hobart left. He was supposed to be leading his battalion, but he returned to his deserted campsite, where he hid until the fighting was over. As soon as his regiment returned to the camp, he was arrested, but he escaped punishment because the arrest was technically illegal.[42]

Like Guert's dismissal from the command of the *Decatur,* Jeff's conduct was hardly the sort of news that was mentioned in family correspondence, so it is unlikely that Herman knew the story. In fact, he may have had only the most general knowledge, gathered from his family and from references to the regiment in the newspapers, of the wartime adventures of the Hobarts. But that he was aware of their regiment's participation in this battle is suggested by the fact that he wrote "Inscription for the Graves at Pea Ridge, Arkansas." This slight stanza, spoken by the Union dead, is their self-justification: forced by traitors to do battle, they fought and won for "Man and Right."

During the winter and early spring, by far the giddiest triumph in the west was the capture of New Orleans, "the Queen City of the South," the gateway to the Mississippi River, and the largest and richest city of the Confederacy. It was significant for Herman, not only because it was a key to the control of the Mississippi River, but also because of the parts played in it by two of his relatives. General Ben Butler, who was to command the assaulting army, had been in New England raising troops for the expedition, the Eastern and Western Bay State Regiments. The state of Massachusetts donated the 26th Massachusetts Infantry as well, and the 14th Maine Infantry was also assigned to him.

Herman was familiar with the Western Bay State Regiment that had been recruiting and training in Pittsfield, but he also knew one soldier in the 26th Massachusetts. When John Hoadley had lived in Clinton, Massachusetts, he had invited his widowed sister, Sarah Pease, to move there with her daughter and two sons, and thereafter John acted as a father to the children. After John moved to Pittsfield, the Peases occupied his house in Clinton, where Henry Pease, Sarah's oldest son, grew up. When the 26th Massachusetts called for men, Henry, by then a seventeen-year-old mechanic, enlisted as a private, giving his age as eighteen. It is also likely that Herman knew someone in the 14th Maine, though who that may have been is not yet known. On February 12, 1862, after Sarah Morewood presented the Pittsfield company with a silk banner reading "By Courage not by Craft," the Western Bay Staters left Pittsfield for Ship Island, a barren location off the Mississippi coast, where the 26th Massachusetts and the 14th Maine were already encamped. Upon their arrival, the Western men named their bivouac area "Camp Morewood" in Sarah's honor.[43]

Captain David Glasgow Farragut, years earlier Guert's nemesis in San Francisco, commanded the Western Gulf Blockading Squadron, the naval force that fought its way to New Orleans. A Southerner, Farragut had been languishing on shore duty in New York, apparently because the Department of the Navy suspected his loyalty, but when his unquestioned abilities had been required, he was appointed the flag officer of this important operation. One of his gunboats was the *Sciota,* Ned Curtis's ship. She had been operating off the coast of Louisiana, capturing a blockade-runner, the *Margaret,* on the sixth of February, before joining Farragut. In the first stage of his attack, Farragut moved upstream, leaving the army transports astern. Beyond, Forts Jackson and St. Philip straddled the river, and between them a heavy chain was anchored to hulks. Beyond the chain waited Confederate gunboats, rams, and fire rafts. On April 18, Commander David D. Porter anchored twenty-six mortar boats below the forts and commenced tossing monstrous shells into them. The fire was terrible, but despite the punishment the Confederates stood fast. On the night of the twentieth, Farragut sent two gunboats in front of Fort Jackson to cut the chain. A devastating barrage from the mortar boats distracted the fort's gunners, allowing the gunboats to carry out the assignment.[44]

After the forts had been pummeled for six days, Farragut began his run. His squadron was divided into three divisions, the first commanded by Captain Theodorus Bailey, the second commanded personally by Farragut, and the third commanded by Fleet-Captain Henry H. Bell, Farragut's chief of staff, who flew his flag from the *Sciota.* At two in the morning, the gunboats battled the current before the forts, firing and being fired on. All but three passed the forts, but after surviving one hazard the squadron faced another, the Confederate ships. The lead Union gunboat, the *Varuna,* was rammed several times and sunk, and Farragut's flagship, the *Hartford,* was set ablaze by a fire raft, but in the end the Confederate ships were neutralized, and the fire aboard the flagship was extinguished. The casualties aboard Ned's ship were among the lightest, only two men wounded. On the twenty-fifth of April, the flotilla anchored at New Orleans, and on the twenty-ninth, Ben Butler marched into the city at the head of the Western Bay Staters to take possession. Henry Pease was not there; his regiment occupied the two forts until summer, when it moved to New Orleans.[45]

For readers who wished to participate vicariously in the battle, the only poem was Henry Howard Brownell's firsthand account, "The River Fight." Brownell set the entire sequence of events, from the beginning at the mouth of the river to the end at New Orleans, to vigorous verse with authentic nautical jargon and intimate pictures of the action and the participants:

> Bell and Bailey grandly led
> Each his Line of the Blue and Red—
> Wainwright stood by our starboard rail,
> Thornton fought the deck.

For a number of reasons, Herman would have read Brownell's poem.[46]

If nothing else did, Ned Curtis's participation ensured that Herman would write "The Battle for the Mississippi (April, 1862)," which recounts the events of the battle impressionistically, suppressing detail in favor of a sense of mighty struggle. As a "deep" ode "that hymns the fleet," it is a dignified tribute to Farragut's wooden-walled ships and the men who, even in an age of steam and armor, fought in the open like the sailors of the *Téméraire*. In doing so, it establishes a distant relationship, at least, with the grand three-deckers of Trafalgar and demonstrates that the virtues of the past have not been lost. Yet the battle is fought according to Satan's terms, in the dark of night and the obscurity of smoke. The poem also invokes the depths of Satan's *"fields for fight"* that *"congeal beneath the sea"* in "The Conflict of Convictions." Two of the warring ships, one Union and one Confederate, sank in the battle, carrying crewmen to their deaths; to these the narrator refers when he says that the ode is "deep," that the cannon pointed at New Orleans are "brooding deep," that the "glory slants her shaft of rays / Far through the undisturbed abyss," and, most pointedly, that "the living shall unmoor and sail, / But Death's dark anchor secret deeps detain." There is even a hint of Satanism in the quotation (Exod. 15:3) "The Lord is a man of war," which does not specify which is the correct reading, that God is a man of war or that the man-of-war is lord.

In its biblical and Miltonic allusions, the poem is most revealing. Herman had borrowed from chapter fifteen of the Exodus in the passage of the "Conflict of Convictions" quoted above, and he did so again in the opening passage of this poem:

When Israel camped by Migdol hoar,
  Down at her feet her shawm she threw,
But Moses sung and timbrels rung
  For Pharaoh's stranded crew.

That was to be expected, since there is a distinct parallel, though with the geographical pattern skewed, between the Israelites crossing the Red Sea with Pharaoh's army in pursuit and Farragut transiting the passage between the Confederate forts. It was such an obvious idea that Oliver Wendell Holmes, Sr., used it in "To Canaan! A Puritan War-Song":

What song is this you're singing?
  The same that Israel sung
When Moses led the mighty choir,
  And Miriam's timbrel rung![47]

But Herman's use of the passage has a dark meaning absent from Holmes's.

The allusion has two implications, that the passage of the ships led to the liberation of slaves from their Egypt and that the Lord protected the ships as

He had protected the Israelites. The latter is the main point. God protected the Israelites by swallowing Pharaoh's army in the depths of the sea, with the result that there were no Israelite casualties, but in the Mississippi, God abandoned Farragut's men to win or lose, live or die, as best they could manage. Similarly, the battle is likened to "Michael's waged with leven," or lightning, from Milton's *Paradise Lost*.[48] (Brownell also used the word "levin," but he spelled it correctly.) In a heavenly war waged with lightning there are no casualties—regardless of who wins or loses, all are immortal, all will survive—but for Farragut's men, the lightning flash of cannon is fatal. The point is clear: the remote God of *Battle-Pieces* will not intervene on behalf of these modern Israelites, nor do heavenly warriors have anything to do with ships battling on the Mississippi. When the Union crews "humble their pride in prayer," they pray for men killed in an earthly battle; their victory they have won unaided. If they pray that "there must be other, nobler worlds for them / Who nobly yield their lives in this," they can only hope that it is so.

The Democracy Reawakens

Toward the end of February, John Hoadley enlisted his technological expertise in the war by taking charge of the copper-rolling mill and other works of the New Bedford Copper Company, which was just commencing operations. Copper was essential to the North: large numbers of rolled sheets were needed for military purposes, the manufacture of percussion caps and the sheathing of the hulls of warships, for example. John arranged for his foreman and clerk to operate his factory in Lawrence; Kate and the two little girls remained there with young Mary Curtis and Fanny Melville for company until John could find a house for them in New Bedford.[49]

Sometime before mid-March, Guert went to Washington to ask Secretary Welles for the command of the *Adirondack*. After working long and well building, converting, and arming ships and supporting naval operations, he wanted this reward. Welles all but promised that he could have her, but others wanted her, too. Another officer lobbied a colleague in the Navy Department: "I think that I have quite as much claims as he has, for I have seen four years more sea-service, and he has had his Commander's command—that is the Sloop-of-War 'Decatur' in the Pacific until he had the command of her taken away from him on account of habitual Drunkenness, and his habits are not over and above steady and correct now." Despite this subversion, Guert won the prize.[50]

On March 18, Uncle Herman's heart failed at last. In response to Mother Melville's telegrams, everyone in the immediate family who was able hurried

John Chipman Hoadley during or just after the Civil War. By permission of the Berkshire Athenæum

to Gansevoort for the funeral. Herman, who was ill again, could not travel, but Allan and Jennie were there even though Allan still had a "game leg." The evening after the funeral at Uncle Herman's home, which was attended by neighbors from miles around, Uncle Peter, accompanied by Allan and Leonard Gansevoort, brought the body back to Albany for interment in the family receiving vault. During their conversations, Leonard told Uncle Peter about Guert's successful visit with Gideon Welles, adding that he himself was to be examined for a navy commission. That convinced Uncle Peter that Leonard was a "really noble fellow." Allan then went back to Gansevoort, where he and Jennie remained until they returned to the city late on the twenty-second of March. The day after, Herman, now back on his feet, took Bessie and Fanny to Allan's house to hear the family gossip and a report of the funeral; the death of this favorite uncle had been his second loss in Judge Shaw's generation in less than a year. In return, Herman could tell Allan the news of Richard Lathers's new daughter, Ida, who had arrived while Allan was out of town.[51]

Now that he knew that Guert's assignment was assured, Uncle Peter wrote him what was to become the standard Fort Stanwix letter. He had been anxious, he said, that Guert have an opportunity to exhibit his patriotism "in this unholy war against the integrity of the Union & against the great principles for which your grandfather manfully struggled in the war for independence & particularly in his noble & successful defense of Fort Stanwix." He added that he was going to send Guert the dozen bottles of old madeira, bottled thirty years before, that he had promised to give him when he received command of a ship. Curiously, he does not seem to have been aware that alcohol was not an appropriate gift for Guert, nor does he seem to have known that Guert had commanded the *Decatur,* despite the accounts of his bravery that had appeared at the time in the New York City newspapers. For reasons of his own, Guert neglected to acknowledge the letter. It was an almost unheard-of affront, but Guert may have resented being patronized by Uncle Peter.[52]

Since the Ball's Bluff disaster, the Army of the Potomac had been immobile as regiments arrived and trained in encampments spread for miles around Washington and its equipment and animals arrived from contractors and farms. In the first few months after taking command, McClellan had been enormously popular, both with the administration and with civilians. Richard Lathers, in Washington dining with the Prussian minister, witnessed a torchlight salute to the general: "The people seemed to have gone crazy with enthusiasm over 'Little Mac.' . . . He was the very god of war, judging by the speeches of Mr. Seward and other members of the Cabinet to the enormous outdoor assemblage gathered to do him honor. He was the young Napoleon; and the illustrated papers of the day were filled with equestrian portraits of him resembling those of Napoleon crossing the Alps."[53] But his most constant admirers were the men of the Army of the Potomac and Northern conservatives. When enthusiasm waned in other quarters, it did so for two reasons: McClellan was a traditional Democrat who did not conceal his politics, which alienated Republicans; and, foreseeing that the suppression of the rebellion would require a modern war that could not be fought using the haphazard means of the past, he built his army patiently, much to the frustration of the "on to Richmond" enthusiasts.

In the wake of the Sumter bombardment, political partisanship had all but disappeared. In this atmosphere of solidarity, about the time of McClellan's appointment to command the Division of the Potomac, Congress passed the Crittenden-Johnson Resolutions stating that the purpose of the war was to reestablish the union as it had been before secession. But in the following month it passed the First Confiscation Act, which allowed escaped slaves to be retained as contraband enemy property. With that, Democrats chafed in the uniform of no-partyism. The government embarked on a provocative series of actions, which eventually included the issuance of paper money and the imposition of an income tax, centralization and heavy-handed exercise of power, including the use of troops against the citizenry, suspensions of civil rights, such as banning unfriendly newspapers from the mails, surveillance of suspect citizens, and arrests, imprisonments, and banishments without due process. In August 1861, the editor of the *New York Freeman's Journal* was arrested for attacking the administration and incarcerated for eight months, without trial, in Fort Lafayette.[54]

At first, the *Pittsfield Sun* contented itself with criticizing the hypocrisy of the administration's call for no-partyism. Later, it kept vigil to discover radical tendencies in the government and to find opportunities to mock the abolitionists, whom it regarded as co-disunionists with the Confederates. It published a parody of Leigh Hunt's *Abou Ben Adhem,* beginning "Abo Bo Lition (may his tribe decrease)," in which a devil shows Bo Lition a list of those "who served Jeff Davis best, / And lo! Bo Lition's name led all the rest!" Despite its crudeness, the burlesque communicated the feeling of the conservatives that they, rather than the radicals, were the champions of loyalty and of union. Democrats rallied around McClellan as a champion of their cause, Kate Gansevoort calling him the "Washington of this war." Thus the general's position with the government must have eroded when, in March 1862, the Democrats in Congress issued a call for renewed political opposition to the administration.[55]

McClellan's policies, which were to insist on political neutrality within the army and to use his troops for the single purpose of restoring the union with as little controversy, bloodshed, and devastation to the South as possible, were consistent with judicious military thinking and traditional service professionalism. Still, army professionalism was generally conservative and Democratic. Thus the *Sun* was celebrating his orthodoxy when it boasted that he planned to use the army not "to obtain military glory but. . . to quell this rebellion by a mighty pressure and not by a mighty slaughter."[56]

It was inevitable that the radicals would turn against McClellan. What the *Sun* approved was precisely what hard-nosed Republicans disapproved, and in their belief that the South had sinned they wished to crush it. Nor did they approve of an apolitical army. Whittier spoke for the radicals: "The persistence of our Government and the people, in fighting for 'the flag' and not for Liberty, sometimes disheartens me."[57] McClellan's position was rendered yet more precarious by bipartisan disappointment in the tempo of the war in the east. War is a form of national dyspepsia for which successful battles are the only known palliative. Within the memory of most adults, the nation had fought the Mexican War with the puny regular army and some ragtag southern and western militia regiments, and many could not understand why the same thing could not be done now. Even after the defeats at Bull Run and Ball's Bluff, many were exasperated at the time required to build and perfect the Army of the Potomac. In the west, battles were being fought and won, while in the east the army drilled in camp.

McClellan was badgered not only by politicians but also by minor poets, such as W. D. Gallagher, who was certain that righteousness was more efficacious in battle than was readiness:

  No possible barrier can be
So fatal to a rightful stand,
  As wavering purpose when at bay;
  This way, or that—"At once! to-day!"
Were worth ten thousand men at hand.

George Boker accused McClellan of treason: "Are you waiting for your . . . / heart to soften, your bowels to yearn / A little more toward 'our Southern friends'"? Boker was not above accusing him of cowardice, as well:

Now that you've marshalled your whole command,
  Planned what you would, and changed what you planned;
  Practised with shot and practised with shell,
  Know to a hair where every one fell,
  Made signs by day and signals by night;
  Was it all done to keep out of a fight?

It was inevitable that some impatient soul would mock McClellan with a parody of Hamlet's to-be-or-not-to-be soliloquy.[58]

A Champion in the Lists

It was not a coincidence that Hawthorne chose this moment when political enmities were rekindling to visit the scene of the war in the east. His excuse was an invitation from Horatio Bridge, the chief of the Bureau of Provisions and Clothing of the Department of the Navy, who seems to have hoped that a closer look at the war might cure his friend's political heterodoxy. But an important motive was the opportunity to gather materials for a Democratic essay about the state of the nation and the course of the war. He told his publisher friend William D. Ticknor that the *Atlantic Monthly* had been "getting too deep a black Republican tinge, and that there is a time pretty near at hand when you will be sorry for it. The politics of the Magazine suit Massachusetts tolerably well (and only tolerably) but it does not fairly represent the feeling of the country at large; and it seems to me that it would be good policy to be preparing to respond to another, and wiser, and truer mood of public sentiment."[59]

On March 6, in Ticknor's company, he left for Washington. "The farther we go, the deeper grows the rumble and grumble of the coming storm," he wrote Sophia, "and I think the two armies are only waiting our arrival to begin."[60] As they neared Washington, they saw a guard at every station and tents, fortifications, and crowds of soldiers everywhere, and in the Washington station they passed through lines of musket-carrying troops. His reputation as the nation's foremost author ensured the success of the junket. He visited the Capitol several times to see the Congress in session and stopped at the White House, where he was introduced to Lincoln; at the invitation of the directors he traveled to Harper's Ferry over the newly restored Baltimore and Ohio Railway track; he watched a review of McClellan's troops and received a gracious bow from the general; and he visited Fortress Monroe as chairman of a committee charged with investigating certain civil and military matters there.

At Fortress Monroe, Hawthorne thought that the commander, General Wool, was a ludicrous figure. Shrunken by age and wearing what Hawthorne thought was the only surviving pair of epaulets in the army, he seemed useful only for training recruits and commanding impregnable fortresses. Hawthorne might have noted, though he did not, that Wool was growing senile. He also visited the *Monitor* and the flagship of the North Atlantic Blockading Squadron, the *Minnesota*. He thought that Flag Officer Louis Goldsborough was a naval version of Wool, but that was not fair. Although

Goldsborough was old and performed only limited combat service during the war, he had only recently commanded the naval forces in the capture of Roanoke Island. On the way to Newport News, the visitors saw the wreck of the *Congress* and the three masts of the *Cumberland* still showing above water with "a tattered bit of the American flag fluttering from the top of one of them." "I never saw anything so gloriously forlorn," he wrote.[61]

In Washington again, he joined a large party of civilians for a visit to the Bull Run battlefield. There he heard rumors, which he believed, that Southern soldiers had made souvenirs from the bones of Union soldiers, including drinking cups fashioned out of skulls, for their families and friends. Such atrocities, he thought, "show something so grotesquely hideous in the Southern character that our benevolent impulses are entirely non-plussed." In contrast, he thought that the innate qualities of the Union troops he passed along the way were noble.[62]

When he returned to Concord early in April, he summarized what he had seen in the perverse conclusion that whichever side prevailed all would be well. Then he began writing his memoir of the visit, "Chiefly about War Matters: By a Peaceable Man." In the essay, he told James T. Fields, the editor of the *Atlantic,* he "found it quite difficult not to lapse into treason continually."[63] It was not overtly disloyal; its subversiveness was mannerly—and *judicious.* Hawthorne was a deadly adversary, who slew his opponents gracefully and affably. His strategy was to act the sedate, good-humored but scrupulous observer giving reasoned opinions of scenes and persons. He wrote, in short, as though the country were at peace and the government were not at the controls of a giant engine of war. The result was a wicked combination of correctness, good humor, sober rumination, and brazenly Democratic propaganda against which one complained at the peril of being rude.

Republicans wished the nation to view Lincoln as the dignified commander of a great, historic crusade, though it was impossible for the man to be pompous. Hawthorne would not submit to that; his description of Lincoln was exactly what anyone who knew him would expect, a compliment couched in such iconoclastic terms that it would outrage the pompous and humorless. Abe, he said, was awkward, uncouth, unrefined, and uncultivated (in the sense in which the eastern upper class understood the terms), a man guided by native sense and craftiness. His hair was uncombed, he and his worn suit appeared to have a symbiotic relationship with each other, his slippers were shabby, and his face was coarse. He looked like a country schoolmaster, the kind of figure that a cartoonist might have drawn to represent a typical American of a certain class. For Hawthorne to describe the president in such terms as to make one think of a country-store loiterer was not only aggravating to supporters but also believable, since his earthy jokes and his vague physical resemblance to the traditional comic "Yankee" of the popular stage supported the characterization, despite his native dignity and the inner force that he radiated. The irony is that Hawthorne, like Herman, approved of the sort of person he described. Lincoln's serious but kindly eyes redeemed all else. It was strange that he had been elected, Hawthorne thought, but there was a certain fitness in it. "For my small share in the matter," he wrote, he "would as lief have Uncle Abe for a ruler as any man whom it would have been practicable to put in his place." In his own peculiar way, Hawthorne had praised Lincoln highly at the same time that he had offended Lincoln's supporters.[64]

Hawthorne also praised McClellan. At the time of his arrival in Washington, he had written Una that "unless he achieves something wonderful within a week, he will be removed from command, and perhaps shot—at least, I hope so. I never did more than half believe in him." But the essay indicates that his opinion changed after he had seen McClellan and heard the loyal cheering of his troops: "If he is a coward, or a traitor, or a humbug, or anything less than a brave, true, and able man, that mass of intelligent soldiers, whose lives and honor he had in charge, were utterly deceived, and so was this present writer; for they believed in him, and so did I. . . . I shall not give up my faith in General McClellan's soldiership until he is defeated, nor in his courage and integrity even then." That was conservative orthodoxy.[65]

Hawthorne did not feel at liberty to express in print his candid reaction to the Republican Congress. Instead, he spoke of the iron dome: "The freestone walls of the central edifice are pervaded with great cracks, and threaten to come thundering down, under the immense weight of the iron dome,—an appropriate catastrophe enough, if it should occur on the day when we drop the Southern stars out of our flag."[66] In addition to the conventional idea that the permanent loss of the South would destroy the American experiment, he also meant that any postwar vindictiveness by the North that had the effect of denying the Southerners full statehood would similarly damage the union.

In his treatment of the Confederates, Hawthorne made only a guarded reference to the grisly atrocities of which he had heard at Bull Run. Instead, he described the prisoners at Harper's Ferry, who varied from gentlemen to a "wild-beast of a man." He hoped that the war would free those of low intellectual development for education and cause "the regeneration of a people." The Confederates were people, and Americans, at that. He also wrote of the former slaves he had seen. Almost a year earlier, when he had considered the various supposed purposes of the war, emancipation had seemed to be the most justifiable: "If we are fighting for the annihilation of slavery, to be sure, it may be a wise object, and offers a tangible result. . . . [W]e should see the expediency of preparing our black brethren for future citizenship by allowing them to fight for their own liberties, and educating them through heroic influences." Arming blacks was not Democratic orthodoxy, but implicit in the statement is the idea that the black man was not ready for citizenship, requiring a transformation of character before taking his place alongside the white man. But now that Hawthorne had actually seen some of them, his reservations were more pronounced. "I would not have turned them back," he wrote, "but I should have felt almost as reluctant, on their own account, to hasten them forward to the stranger's land." This hesitancy to subject blacks to civil rigors without prior education or acclimatization to a life of freedom was characteristic of even the most liberal Democrats. He added, "whoever may be benefited by the results of this war, it will not be the present generation of negroes, the childhood of whose race is now gone forever, and who must henceforth fight a hard battle with the world, on very unequal terms." So much for abolition.[67]

When James T. Fields betrayed alarm at the heterodoxy of his essay, Hawthorne made some alterations, reserving the description of Lincoln for future publication and adding wicked footnotes, ostensibly the work of the editor, admonishing himself for offenses ranging from impropriety to disloyalty. "What a terrible thing it is to try to let off a little bit of truth into this miserable humbug of a world!" he mourned. Nevertheless, he received precisely the reaction for which he had hoped. George William Curtis wrote, "What an extraordinary paper by Hawthorne in the 'Atlantic'! It is pure intellect, without emotion, without sympathy, without principle. I was fascinated, laughed and wondered. It is as unhuman and passionless as a disembodied intelligence." It may have had another, unanticipated effect. It may have suggested to Herman Melville that serious writers, as well as poetasters, could make literary use of the war. Sometime around the end of the year, he began writing his own war poems.[68]

Henry Gansevoort Goes to War

Under other circumstances, George B. McClellan could have provided Herman with an excellent example of the ambiguities of human perception. There were two versions of the man: the hero, as Herman and his fellow conservatives saw him, and the incompetent, as the Lincoln administration and its apologists came to see him. The following narrative of his most important wartime service is based on the former view, as gleaned from his own statements and those of his supporters. It is what he seemed to Herman to be.

Thus far he had been a successful general in chief of the army, not only in creating the Army of the Potomac but also in supervising military operations in both the east and the west, including the capture of New Orleans. But when Lincoln and his advisers turned against him, it was inevitable that he would fail. As commander of the Army of the Potomac, he wished to ready the army and then to move it, jackrabbit fast, to a landing near Richmond, whence he would race to Richmond or a point south, such as Petersburg, to cut off the Confederate capital from the rest of the South before the opposing command could react. That strategy, as it finally developed, has been called "the only imaginative offensive ever mounted against Richmond." It held out the hope, as one cabinet member said, "of preserving the Union without destroying the nation."[69] In contrast, Lincoln's attitude combined two preoccupations. He was impatient for McClellan to attack Richmond in hot haste, believing, as many did, that a crushing defeat of the Confederacy would be the result. Also, because he never rid himself of the psychological scars left by those first few days after Sumter, when the nearly defenseless capital had been hostage to whatever Confederate forces had lain across the Potomac, he insisted that McClellan keep his army positioned between Washington and the Confederate power. His desire, then, was for McClellan to march directly from Washington to Richmond.

This disagreement would have been difficult enough to resolve without the intrusion of highly placed enemies of McClellan. One of these was Edwin M. Stanton, whom many judged to be a fickle, devious, and vindictive man. When scandal had forced Secretary of War Cameron to resign, the Democratic lawyer had been appointed to take his place. Once in office, he abandoned his conservative politics and became, in effect, a Republican, though he deceived his old friends and former allies in the Democratic party into thinking that he was still their ally. Now he was at Lincoln's side subverting McClellan's position. Impatient, Lincoln ordered all of the nation's armies to attack at once, whether prepared or not. Not wishing to fight his way through Virginia, McClellan countered with his own plan, only to be accused of plotting to surrender his army to the Confederates as soon as he was near Richmond. To guard against such disloyalty, Lincoln reorganized the Army of the Potomac by appointing corps commanders who were politically acceptable to the administration.

Faced with an order to attack, and knowing that the Confederates had withdrawn from Manassas, McClellan marched his army there. That gave the soldiers some practical experience in the kind of exertion they would soon be called upon to perform in a serious offensive. Many Northerners believed that the invasion was genuine; Kate Gansevoort reported that in Albany the news was greeted (together with that of the ironclad battle) with flags, cheers, and a 100-gun salute in the park.[70] But Bull Run was not McClellan's objective, and in a week the troops pulled back. In response, Lincoln fired McClellan as general-in-chief and performed the duties himself, a task for which he was suited neither by education nor experience.

With his authority reduced to the eastern theater, McClellan finally persuaded Lincoln to approve a variant of his original plan. He meant to push up the James Peninsula from Fortress Monroe while a large corps of his army under General McDowell marched down through Virginia to meet it. That way, he could confront the Confederate capital with such a preponderance of force that the South would be obliged to return to the union, and he could do so without fighting the unnecessary, punishing battles that would certainly occur repeatedly along the route that Lincoln had proposed. McDowell's force would shield Washington, even though the city was in little danger as long as the main part of the Union army threatened the Confederate capital. The plan was supported by his generals and accepted reluctantly by Lincoln. Soon his army was assembling near Fortress Monroe and preparing to commit itself.

The route from Fortress Monroe to Richmond was relatively short and direct. Nevertheless, it was a dangerous area for a Union force. The army would be surrounded in three directions by water and on the fourth by the Confederate army, much as the American army was choked in the Pusan perimeter of Korea in 1950. Near Fortress Monroe lay some cities and towns, Yorktown, where Washington had defeated Cornwallis, and Williamsburg, the colonial capital of Virginia. Between that area and Richmond the land was hostile, forest and pestilential swamp traversed by rivers and dotted with farms, crossroads, and tiny settlements. Unfamiliar to the Union generals, it was populated by Virginians who were anxious to aid their own and injure the Yankees. Once before Richmond, McClellan would face a military truism, that a determined and adequately armed defender placed in well-positioned defenses can hold off a much larger attacking force. But McClellan was prepared for that. His army was to consist of 155,000 well-trained and well-equipped troops, almost twice the available Confederate force, and a massive fleet of transports would make the waters there supply routes rather than barriers to retreat.

Since the preceding September, Henry Gansevoort had been training with his regiment at Camp Greble, a mile and a half from Harrisburg. Reasonably contented for the moment except for dissatisfaction with what he believed to be his unjustifiably low rank—his father had warned him about that—he reported that the life was healthy and exciting. He provoked a moment of sheer terror in Albany by asking permission to remount the blade of the sword that had waved gloriously during the Revolution and had clanked proudly through the political halls of DeWitt Clinton's administration. When the rumble of that shock rolled back to Camp Greble, he wisely abandoned the idea. Despite this indiscretion, Uncle Peter was pleased with Henry. "I am highly gratified by the assurance that you are now engaged fairly & fully in a congenial profession," he wrote.[71]

Unexpectedly, the spoiled lawyer became an able, enthusiastic artillery officer. The ideal of military service and the Olympian remoteness and impartial tyranny of the regular army suited him. His commissioned status conformed to his sense of his own aristocracy, and his unquestioning dedication to his new profession, which he manifested by thorough study of its principles and by full attention to his responsibilities, offered an arena for personal achievement that was not darkened by ancestral shadows. Furthermore, the service relieved him of troublesome ambiguities. As a committed Democrat, sympathetic to the South if not to secession, the prosecution of the war had threatened perplexities and contradictions, but for the professional officer there were no such threats. Henry was not required to admire his civilian and military leaders, nor to approve or disapprove of slavery or any political policy, nor was he expected to be elated by the success or discouraged by the failure of any general cause or specific event. He was required only to do his best to obey the orders given him with skill, courage, honor, and modesty. In short, Henry had found himself. He was somewhat more romantic about warfare than were his peers—while most of them wore the squat, visored cap of the soldier on the field, he affected the dashing, broad-brimmed cavalier style of chapeau, but there was room in the army even for his romanticism.[72]

Artillery regiments operated not as integral units but as detached batteries commanded by captains who were equivalent in authority to infantry and cavalry colonels. When the batteries of the 5th Artillery took the field, they were assigned to widely separated divisions, even on different fronts. After having been rotated through various duties during his apprenticeship, Henry settled in as the sole officer present and the acting commander, pending the arrival of the other officers, of Battery M. It was a "flying battery" of light artillery, one in which all of the personnel were mounted so they could maneuver like or with cavalry—though as yet they had no horses. The term "light" did not mean flimsy; it simply meant that the cannon were easily manageable, capable of being brought swiftly into action. The battery was divided into three sections, each commanded by a lieutenant; each section boasted two rifled ten-pounders and a line of caissons. Including the first sergeant and ancillary personnel, the battery contained over 150 men. When it was completely trained and equipped, it was a formidable machine of war, efficient and reliable.[73]

With the commencement of the Peninsular campaign, Battery M was ordered to the field. Uncle Peter was still convinced that the principal duty of the younger generation was to further adorn the family honor won in the Revolution: "I feel assured that you will, under all circumstances, sustain the glorious flag of the Nation—and the honor of your revolutionary name; in the spirit of a grandson of the Hero of Fort Stanwix."[74] But without horses that spirit would be impossible to sustain.

On March 24, Captain McKnight and the other two lieutenants arrived, though Henry continued to act as battery commander during the movement. After riding a special train to Baltimore, the battery boarded a steamer bound for the Peninsula. As it steamed into Hampton Roads, Henry saw what Hawthorne had seen, the *Monitor* lying in the calm waters with the *Minnesota* and the rest of the North Atlantic Blockading Squadron huddled around her for protection. Elsewhere, the water was choked with every kind of craft, particularly troop transports. Along the coast as far as the eye could see were campfires, and from all points Henry could hear medleyed bugles.[75]

The battery camped in the charred ruin of the village of Hampton. There were no tents yet, not even for the officers, and the rains had turned the earth into mud. Already the men were eating hardtack and salt horse. Further inland lay the Confederate forces, with whom the Union infantrymen engaged in sporadic duelling and skirmishing. The Harvard Regiment, with Captain Frank Bartlett still acting as second in command, was camped in a swamp not far from them. On April 24, while he was up with his pickets, kneeling and watching the Confederates through his field glasses, an enemy sharpshooter hit him in the knee with a minié ball. Frank was taken on a litter to a nearby house, where the regimental surgeon amputated his leg above the knee joint. Since his war appeared to have ended, he returned to Harvard to complete his degree.[76]

The army should not have been lying in camps; it should have been advancing rapidly toward Richmond to meet McDowell's corps, which should have been approaching from northern Virginia. McClellan was capable of rapid and decisive action, but at the moment he was a commander who had never fought a major battle, with an army that had never fought one, in a position where he was dependent for support on superiors he had reason to distrust, and without the presence of Union forces north of Richmond, the Army of the Potomac risked entrapment on the Peninsula. At just this time, Lincoln refused to release McDowell, holding him back in northern Virginia, and removed General Wool's 10,000 soldiers from McClellan's command. That reduced his force from the planned 155,000 troops to 95,000, a loss of 60,000 men. Then the administration restricted McClellan's authority to the immediate area of his operations. From the beginning of the offensive, then, McClellan was unsure of his authority, unsure of his strength, unsure that he could execute his plan of attack, and unsure of what further impediments the government might throw in his path. That was the beginning of a cautiousness that developed into paralysis.

Had McDowell marched toward Richmond, the Confederates on the Peninsula would have been forced back to defend their capital and McClellan would have been free to move his army unopposed. As it was, the Confederates took positions near Fortress Monroe. Yorktown was a sham fortification, sparsely manned and armed with "Quaker cannon," dummy artillery made of logs, but it fooled McClellan. He decided to besiege it with the seventy-one massive cannon that Colonel Robert O. Tyler commanded. At home, people were tense. "I feel a tremendous anxiety about our affairs at Yorktown," Hawthorne wrote. "It will not at all surprise me if we come to grief."[77] McClellan supporters blamed the administration for hampering his operations, while McClellan opponents marveled that, with so many men, he did not advance more rapidly.

"Camp 'No Where,'" as Henry's battery called it, was as quiet as Pompeii. The prospect of combat, added to the mausoleum-like atmosphere of Hampton, made Henry think of death on the battlefield, and, being Henry, he postured romantically about it. He did not fear death, he wrote his family, because "I see so little to live for, that to me there seems but little if any gulf between time and eternity." Perhaps that was the proper way for a regular officer to view life. Happy to escape Hampton, on several occasions he visited Fortress Monroe, where there were civilized amenities. Having mentioned Henry in a letter to General Wool, Uncle Peter insisted that he call on the ancient commander: Wool would be a "kind & faithful friend." An opportunity came when Henry went to the fort to dine with a companion, but Wool had difficulty remembering who Uncle Peter was, and Henry suspected that he did not remember him at all. When Peter heard this, he was incredulous. Had Henry referred to him as *General* Gansevoort, Wool would have recollected him instantly, he wrote.[78]

After dinner, Henry discovered that his horse was missing. A lengthy search located it in front of Wool's headquarters in the possession of the orderly of a "notorious desperado," a colonel who commanded an artillery emplacement out in the channel. Henry accosted the half-drunk thief: "I insist upon an apology!" he said. "Your conduct has not been that of a gentleman, sir! My name is Gansevoort, of the 5th U.S. Artillery. You have my card and the address at which your apology can reach me at any time!" The colonel, who was reputed to be a vicious duelist, vowed murderous revenge, but no harm came to Henry.[79]

The military stalemate allowed Henry and his battery commander to leave the Peninsula on a mission to obtain the missing horses and some recruits, and while in the North, Henry managed a visit to his family on April 21. Herman missed him, but Allan probably encountered him when he stopped in New York City to see Bruce. When he returned to the inactivity of Hampton, he mapped a new route to self-advancement. He would command a volunteer battery named after himself, and he asked his father and Bruce to work on the scheme. After the war, he argued, people would remember rank and deed without distinguishing between volunteers and regulars.[80]

He had already applied for a transfer to an active battery, but his chances improved when he visited the army headquarters near Yorktown. Several times he broke the monotony by carrying dispatches over the forty-mile quagmire of a road, and each time was an adventure. Once he rode with Professor Lowe, the balloonist who was McClellan's one-man air force, and every trip risked fire from Confederate snipers. At his destination, he met Colonels Hunt and Barry, McClellan's senior artillery commanders. Barry, who was from Henry's regiment, invited him to join the siege guns on temporary assignment, but just as the siege was about to begin, the Confederates evacuated Yorktown and retreated toward Richmond. One corps pursued them, provoking a sharp rear guard fight at Williamsburg in which the Union soldiers were bloodied. Then the Confederates continued to retreat and the Union army to pursue.[81]

Henry once again rode to Yorktown, where he applied to Barry for temporary reassignment to an active battery. Barry was happy to oblige, since a lieutenant of Captain Horatio G. Gibson's Battery C, 3rd U.S. Artillery, had just been killed at Williamsburg. With only the belongings he had with him, Henry joined the battery, which was assigned to the advance guard, a division of cavalry and of flying artillery. Now he was leading a real soldier's life, he wrote his father, sleeping on his blanket with his overcoat for a cover and a saddlebag for a pillow. "The enemy will meet us ere many days," he predicted. Peter was gratified. He had refurbished the flag that had "waved triumphantly at Yorktown on the surrender by Cornwallis to General Washington" and had hung it in his library to celebrate the second victory of Yorktown, he told Henry, and he spiced the letter with yet another version of his Fort Stanwix homily.[82]

Although the Harvard Regiment had the good fortune to be transported up the Peninsula by ship, other units, including Henry's battery, pushed

Second Lieutenant Henry Sanford Gansevoort (far right) with officers of the 3rd U.S. Artillery, June 1862, near the Fair Oaks battlefield. U.S. Army Military History Institute

through the rain and mud. For two and a half weeks, this part of the army, with the advance guard sweeping ahead, slogged up the Chickahominy River, mostly through woods and swamp. The cavalry fought the Confederate rear guard with their sabers, no large battles but dangerous skirmishes nevertheless, while Henry and his men were busy heaving their "flying" guns through knee-deep muck. Food was often in short supply, forcing officers and men alike to subsist on army biscuit and "fat pork, or odious beef served quivering from an animal heated by the long day's march and killed as soon as the day's march was ended." Their uniforms and blankets remained rain-sodden except when the fierce sun broke through to broil them dry. Finally, around the twenty-second of May, they reached a position so close to Richmond that Professor Lowe could watch the civilians on the streets from his balloon. Henry was happy to make camp at last: the exposure and the swamp insects had damaged his health, and he was dosing himself with quinine and drinking a gill of whiskey each morning.[83]

In the North, the agony of waiting was palpable. As the Army of the Potomac had pursued the Confederates up the Peninsula, the citizens had been held prisoner by the telegraph and the newspaper. Longfellow was optimistic about McClellan's success, believing that "slavery begins to reel and stagger," while Lowell felt that it was a mistake to fight for the limited objective of saving the union: "I fear we shall go on trying our old fire-and-gunpowder-cement over again, and then what waste of blood and treasure and hope!" Kate Gansevoort enjoyed the excitement. "How eagerly we read the papers & watch McClellan's movements," she wrote Henry. But despite the deliberateness with which McClellan's attack developed, Herman was patient. In a passage in his postwar "Major Gentian and Colonel J. Bunkum," the narrator mocks the buffoonish Bunkum for "chafing under McClellan's Fabian tactics," clearly an erroneous attitude. Herman saved his impatience for the Confederates. "Do you want to hear about the war?" he wrote Tom. "The war goes bravely on. McClellan is now within fifteen miles of the rebel capital, Richmond. New Orleans is taken &c &c &c. . . . But when the *end*—the wind-up—the grand pacification is coming, who knows. We beat the rascals in almost every feild, & take all their ports &c, but they don't cry 'Enough!'—It looks like a long lane, with the turning quite out of sight." Despite his disappointment that the Confederate "rascals" had not yet surrendered, Herman sensed that the end of the war might be long in coming.[84]

4

Wreck and Wrack
1862

In April 1862, the *Adirondack* was taking aboard her crew and making ready for sea, but Herman did not remain in the city to see Guert off. It was time to reunite the family for the spring budding and the summer plenty of Berkshire and time to put Arrowhead on the market again. Around April 15, he, Lizzie, and the two girls entrained for Gansevoort, where they visited Mother Melville and Gus for the first time since Uncle Herman's death had left the Melville women in charge of his estate. Although he did not see Fanny, who was still with the Hoadleys, Herman had an opportunity to visit his Glens Falls cousins and to hear the latest news about Ned Curtis from them.

About April 25, Herman cut the visit short and took Lizzie, the girls, and Stanny on to Pittsfield, where Malcolm joined them from his school in Newton. Then on Monday, April 28, Lizzie woke up ill and kept to her bed, leaving the children's clothing still packed and the household set to rights only to the extent necessary for family survival. The chaos was rendered even more disagreeable by the lack of a maid, though Herman had had the foresight the preceding day to advertise for one in the *Berkshire County Eagle*. He eased the responsibility for caring for the children by placing the two boys under Miss Drew's tutelage, Stanny in grammar school and Malcolm in high school—off at eight for the hour's walk to class and back at five after another hour's trudge. Both boys had to write compositions and declaim. Stanny studied geography, grammar, reading, and spelling, while Malcolm studied Latin, reciting his lessons at home every night in the hearing of his amused father: "'Hic—hei^{a}c—hoc'—'horum, horum, horum,' he goes it every night," Herman wrote Tom. Malcolm was an instant success, taking his place near the top of his class.[1]

Other than caring for Lizzie and doing household chores—to the extent that he did them—Herman was left relatively free. With Lizzie hors de combat, he probably reverted to type, allowing the children to misbehave at their pleasure, though during the day he had only the girls to neglect. When they were not at school, the boys took care of themselves, playing marbles and ball and roaming through the pasture, or, when other boys were handy, playing big ring, little ring, pea hole, and three hole. From time to time Herman took them on short walks—he lacked the stamina for long ones—and on rides into the village. He also called on Sarah Morewood, who was about to depart on a trip. She intended to leave her fields to be planted by the farmhands, which meant, Herman teased her, that they would "go to grass."[2]

During these ambling days, Herman sorted through his accumulated manuscripts. Reconsidering the poetry of his past was a natural consequence of his recent theoretical study, which was refining his ideas about his craft. It may also be that the idea of writing poems about the war was beginning to take shape in his mind and that this review was a part of his preparation. He probably discarded a number of earlier attempts, as he suggested when, in his poem "Immolated," he appears to be apologizing to them: "—spare, Ah, spare / Reproach" because "jealous of your future lot, / I sealed you in a fate subdued" (371). But he seems to have preserved many that found their way into print decades later in *John Marr* and *Timoleon*. He wrote Tom a wry account of his treatment of his "doggerel": "You will be pleased to learn that I have disposed of a lot of it at a great bargain. In fact, a trunk-maker took the whole stock off my hands at ten cents the pound. So, When you buy a new trunk again, just peep at the lining & perhaps you may be rewarded by some glorious stanza stareing you in the face & claiming admiration. If you were not such a devil of a ways off, I would send you a trunk, by way of presentation-copy." This was his "infirmity of jocularity" again, an inside joke akin to the incident in *White-Jacket* in which Lemsford's poetry is "published" by being fired from a cannon (191–92). The reference to the trunk-maker was a hoary literary witticism, by which an author meant only that his work had not sold well. Tom would have understood the coded message: Herman had been cleaning out his desk, nothing more.[3]

On the sixth of May, Henry David Thoreau, whose health had been failing, died in Concord. Hawthorne, who was still writing the essay about his Washington adventures,[4] attended the funeral with Sophia, Emerson read the eulogy, William Ellery Channing recited some occasional verses, and Bronson Alcott read excerpts from Thoreau's works. Stylistically, Herman had much in common with Thoreau, so much so that some paragraphs of *Walden* and *Moby-Dick* might be interchanged, but the two authors were not acquainted and Herman did not attend the funeral.

Though Lizzie was still puny, she was on her feet by the end of the first week in May, and the family was no longer at the mercy of a parent whose kitchen repertoire consisted mainly of chowders and duffs. She was recovering just in time. John Hoadley was moving his family to a home in New Bedford, which signaled Fanny's departure for Gansevoort, and Fanny was to be accompanied by Helen Griggs. Under normal circumstances, Herman's sisters would visit him whenever they passed through Pittsfield, but he worried that, in the name of charity, they might not stop if it meant taxing Lizzie's returning strength. "Dont write to Helen or Fanny or Kate about our affairs here," he instructed Gus, imperiling Lizzie's recovery in the bargain. Bringing Minnie Hoadley with them, they did visit for some days, bringing gifts from Kate Hoadley to the children, a slate eraser and a picture of General Burnside for Stanny. Herman responded by giving Helen his five-volume edition of Spenser and Fanny a volume containing the poems of Shakespeare and William Collins, a volume of William Shenstone's poems, and a volume of James Thomson's. About the time of his sisters' departure, Herman advertised Arrowhead for sale in the *Eagle,* as he continued to do for much of the summer.[5]

Lizzie's ego received a needed tonic when the *Sun* reported that a bust of Judge Shaw, as he had appeared twenty-five years earlier, had been placed in the Supreme Court building in Boston. By now, she and Malcolm were riding every day on Charlie, a new five-year-old horse Herman had bought. Occasionally, Lizzie may have ridden into town, where the ladies were meeting every afternoon to gather and package donations to the soldiers. When Mary, the former maid, was rehired, the family was back to normal. That was unfortunate for the girls, who had been subjected only to spelling lessons while their mother was sick and had now to pursue a sterner curriculum.[6]

As the spring matured toward summer, Herman continued to take the children on excursions to see what of interest could be found, in one case, some wintergreens. He may also have taken them to local entertainments. Bailey's French and American Circus appeared on the thirteenth of May, and on Saturday, the fourteenth of June, Sanford's Opera Troupe of Ethiopian Artists performed a minstrel show at West's Hall. For Bessie's birthday on the twenty-second of May, Lizzie gave her a stamp with a dog on it, while Herman gave her a napkin ring, a picture, and six envelopes. On the eleventh of June, with a chill still on the evening air, rockets were fired from Mount Greylock by a group of campers who stayed overnight to witness an eclipse of the moon; the Melvilles could see the display from the piazza. Otherwise, the spring in Pittsfield was uneventful.[7]

During this period, other family members were traveling. Early in May, Allan, Jennie, and Allan's youngest, Lucy, visited Gansevoort, probably too early to see Fannie and Helen. John Hoadley made a business trip to

Washington, where his warlike spirits must have been boosted by the massive movement of the army to the Peninsula. Richard Lathers also visited the capital as a member of a committee seeking government protection of New York shipping from the Confederate commerce-raiders. Lincoln told them that, with the demands imposed on the navy by the blockade, "the blanket is too short." Richard had a chance to talk to Secretary Salmon P. Chase, who took him for a tour of the treasury, where greenbacks had been printed since February. Chase reassured him that, rumors to the contrary, they were not being issued wholesale like the morning newspaper. In Albany, Kate Gansevoort was staying at home, sewing bed linens and clothing for the wounded in the federal hospital and awaiting news from Henry. But with all of this activity, family interest was centered on the Brooklyn Navy Yard and on the Peninsula.[8]

The Life and Death of the Adirondack

One cause of the excitement was Guert Gansevoort's assignment to the *Adirondack*. No longer shorebound, Guert now had the duty he had desired since the beginning of the war, the command of a warship. Allan reported that he was proud of her, one of the best and most modern vessels in the navy. Built of wood according to a well-tested design, she was handsome and large. Although a sailing ship, she was equipped with steam propulsion. By mid-June she had taken aboard most of her crew, and Guert was making final preparations for sea.[9]

On Sunday, June 15, Allan toured her. Guert was happy to show off his new command, and his eagerness to get to sea and to do battle with the Confederates was patent. When the two were alone in Guert's stateroom, he had Allan draw up his will. In the process, Allan persuaded him to pass on his grandfather's insignia of the Order of the Cincinnati and certificate of membership to Henry Gansevoort. Guert had received them upon Uncle Herman's death, but he had not bothered to apply for membership. It would require a casuist to decide who *should* have received the honor after Guert. Perhaps Leonard was the next in line, but Leonard had no sons and was unlikely ever to have any. Herman was ineligible because of his descent through a female Gansevoort, though he cherished the Order, as his unpublished "Burgundy Club" pieces reveal. Ned Curtis was ineligible for the same reason (though he eventually received it anyway). Allan and Guert may have rationalized the bequest on the ground that Henry was young enough to belong to the following generation, and he was also young enough to perpetuate the family name through a future marriage.[10]

Allan returned home under the impression that Guert would sail in two weeks. On the morning of June 27, Bruce spotted the *Adirondack* in the stream, trying her engines, it would seem, but because of difficulties with the engineering plant there were delays. On the morning of the Fourth of July, Allan visited again, this time bringing along Jennie and all four girls for an entire day and evening. The children had the run of the ship, cannon and all, and Jennie brought presents—pictures of Allan's girls and a small framed picture of Henry Gansevoort—which Guert put on his bureau to keep him company in his lonely hours at sea.[11]

The following Monday, the Allan Melvilles moved to New Rochelle for the summer. Their "cottage," loaned to them by Richard Lathers, was sumptuous—three parlors, a sitting room with velvet carpets, and a dining room on the main floor, six bedrooms on the second floor, and two bedrooms and two other large rooms on the third. Each morning Jennie drove Allan to the railroad station, and each evening she drove the girls down to pick him up. Despite their distance from Brooklyn, Allan and his family saw Guert once more, bringing with them two cans of ice cream. When Guert sailed at 2:30 p.m. on July 17, Allan rode down the bay with him, returning, probably, on a pilot boat. Then the *Adirondack* headed out to sea.[12]

Guert was ordered to British Nassau, where he was to search for the Confederate warship *Oreto* (later renamed the *Florida*), thought to be commanded by the "notorious Semmes." He was to ascertain her purpose and destination, or, if she had departed, he was to give chase. Since Nassau was a neutral port, though not very neutral, the mission was "delicate and highly responsible." Soon after her departure, the *Adirondack* encountered a gale, with heavy seas and almost continual headwinds, during which the acting master—the navigator—fell from a mast and broke his shoulder blade. On the twenty-third of July, just 120 miles north of the Hole in the Wall, a narrow passage leading toward Nassau, Guert boarded the schooner *Emma,* of Nassau. Discovering that she was a blockade-runner, he sent her back to Philadelphia under a prize crew.[13]

Eight or ten miles from Nassau Harbor, Guert sighted the *Herald,* which had just run armaments to Charleston and was returning with a cargo of cotton. Turning out to sea, where he could challenge her without violating British sovereignty, he signaled her to heave to. Instead, the low sidewheeler sped toward shore. Unwilling to allow the matter of sovereignty to interfere, Guert fired at her, hitting her several times, but with her superior speed she outran him and made the harbor. Just outside of Nassau, the British navy steamer *Greyhound* delivered a letter of protest addressed to "the officer in command of the federal vessel." Guert bristled at that: "I presume it is meant for me, although I have the honor to command a vessel of war of the United States," he replied, and answered that his action had been legal. As

U.S. Sloop *Ossipee,* sister ship of the *Adirondack,* in later years. U.S. Naval Historical Center

he entered the harbor, he heard a band playing "Dixie" for his benefit, and as he headed for the shore, in full uniform and with a pennant flying from his gig, the sailors of the *Herald* called out, "Here's your cotton, come and take it if you dare," and added offensive epithets about Yankees.[14]

In Nassau, Guert had constant difficulty with the port authorities and found open hostility in the streets (partly from men with Southern accents), but he collected a great deal of information. His executive officer prowled around the town in civilian clothing to find out what he could about Confederate blockade-running techniques. The *Oreto* was there, manned by a British prize crew. Guert asked permission to board her, but when that was denied he rowed around her to see what he could see. He was certain that the British were aiding the Confederates by closing their eyes to blockade-running, but, being low on coal and provisions and needing repairs to his rigging, he was diplomatic. Although he was given permission to remain in port, he was also handed a list of terms governing all United States warships approaching Nassau. In compliance with these terms, Guert left as soon as the *Adirondack* was ready for sea, and by the fourth of August he was in Hampton Roads.[15]

On the twelfth of August, he was ordered to Port Royal for duty with DuPont, but before he got underway he received emergency orders sending him back to Nassau by way of Port Royal. He was to alert the ships in the Nassau area to be on the lookout for Laird gunboat 290 (later the *Alabama*). Just before he sailed, his injured master was detached and his executive officer assumed the duties of navigator. By the eighteenth of August, he had reached Port Royal. DuPont was content to let him proceed on his mission, since the British had allowed the *Oreto* to sail from Nassau under the command of Commander Maffit—Semmes's assignment was to be the Laird gunboat. "Oh, if Gansevoort could only meet that pirate!" he wrote.[16]

On the nineteenth, Guert sailed for the Hole in the Wall. As the *Adirondack* steamed east above Man-of-War Quay, the executive officer made an error in plotting the ship's position. At eight in the evening, he and Guert together worked out the night's courses down the passage to the east of the island. As a precaution, Guert ordered the ship steered an extra point to port, away from land. Then he went to bed. At midnight, the officer of the deck steered southeast by east instead of southeast, which should have taken the ship still farther offshore, but because of the faulty navigation and the current, she was steaming into peril.

As August 23 began, the weather was rainy at first, then overcast with visibility of only about a half mile. Three times during the watch, Guert came on deck to check the situation, but at five minutes before four the ship ran onto a reef, ranging ahead one or more ship lengths before grinding to a stop. In the fire room, broken deck-plates were pushed up and jagged points of the reef jutted through.[17] Almost immediately, Guert arrived on deck in his nightshirt, and a moment later the chief engineer appeared in his drawers, trousers in hand. Despite their efforts, the engines would neither back up nor go forward. Soon all of the other officers were on deck in all states of dress, and the boatswain's mate called all hands to their quarters. Guert ordered the liquor in the spirit room destroyed.

He attempted to haul the ship off with the anchors, but they would not hold. Before long, a fleet of up to a hundred wreckers was headed in their direction. By daylight, Guert was attempting to get a large anchor out astern, but it was too heavy for the ship's boats. By cajoling and threatening, he succeeded in hiring one of the wreckers to carry it out. Then he made a final attempt to move the ship using the large anchor, but even though the sailors hauled in on the capstan until after dark, it was futile. When the topsails were set, the cables parted, the ship bilged, her back broken; her keel was forced up under the engine room floor nearly at right angles, and she took too much water to float under any circumstances. Guert then transferred the crew ashore, where they camped in tents. Before morning, Guert and the few other officers who remained on board were forced to fight off wreckers with hatchets and pistols.

The next day, the engineer and the executive officer returned with a working party to guard the ship and to accomplish what little remained to be done. By the day after that, the ship was thumping, the water was up to the berth deck inside, the weather deck was almost awash, and those aboard were spiking and jettisoning guns and destroying equipment that was too cumbersome to save. By nightfall, with the ship a complete wreck, Guert hauled down the flag. The following day, the other officers persuaded the "almost distracted" captain to leave the ship. He went down to his stateroom, salvaged the pictures of Henry Gansevoort and Allan's children, and then went ashore, the last man to do so. The grounding had been a disaster, but all of the ship's personnel had been saved.[18]

When DuPont heard the news, he was heartsick: "The loss of such a ship as the *Adirondack,* in the first place, is a national loss at such a moment—and then I feel so much for Gansevoort." But he had a predictable concern: "I hope he did not drink or has not since—he is one of those who cannot be temperate and to be safe must be abstinent." Then he dispatched the U.S.S. *Canandaigua* to the scene. When the *Canandaigua* arrived on September 1, the *Adirondack* was on fire. The next afternoon, the *Canandaigua* left for Port Royal with Guert and his crew and as much salvage as she could carry.[19]

Guert requested a court of inquiry and DuPont supported him: "I deem it my duty to you and but an act of simple justice, as your immediate commanding officer, to state that I can discover no want of vigilance on your part; on the contrary, having shown all reasonable caution. . . . you did all that I fully looked for from the energy and manliness of your character and skill as a seaman." Such an endorsement would help Guert's case.[20]

On the twenty-second of September, Guert's court of inquiry convened at the Brooklyn yard. The court was to decide whether or not he had conducted himself properly, but its real interest was in his drinking. A lieutenant was asked, "Do you know any instance of the want of sobriety on the part of the Superior Officers of the U.S. Steamer *Adirondack* during this cruise whilst on duty?" and answered, "I never have seen a more sober set taking them altogether." The surgeon was asked, "Was Captain Gansevoort at the time you saw him on deck in his right Clothes sober and self possessed, and every [way] capable of discharging his duties?" and answered, "He was." A midshipman was asked, "Was Captain Gansevoort sober and self possessed at the time he came on deck immediately after the vessel struck and in every way capable of discharging his duty?" and answered, "Yes Sir." Other witnesses answered similar questions the same way. On the first of October, the court found that Guert had behaved properly.[21]

That finding should have exonerated him, but Secretary Welles would not have it so. No doubt he was angry about the loss of such a fine new ship, but he may also have had private doubts about Guert's sobriety. On October 8, he forwarded all of the papers necessary for a general court-martial, and on

October 15 the court convened at the navy yard to try Guert for suffering the *Adirondack* "to be run upon a rock and wrecked through negligence." The procedure of the court-martial differed little from that of the court of inquiry, and on the twenty-eighth of October it found Guert innocent. Three weeks later, he was ordered to the navy yard to resume his ordnance duties. For the moment, he was beyond his family's reach. Command of the *Adirondack* had been his opportunity to erase the stigma of the *Somers* mutiny and the disgrace of his dismissal from the command of the *Decatur,* as well as to make a name for himself in the war, but as things stood, he had captured one blockade-runner, challenged the façade of British neutrality in Nassau, and lost a valuable ship. Now he was back where he had been at the beginning of the war.[22]

When the news of the shipwreck had raced through the family, they had been sympathetic and touched by the fact that he had saved the family photographs. Kate Gansevoort reported third hand what she heard from Allan: "It was a mortification to his pride[.] for full forty long years he had waited for the command of a vessel & when he had rec'd it, everything so complete—he was happy, but its loss has completely broken him down." She did not know about the *Decatur,* either. But when he had been brought before a court-martial, and the family honor was at stake, some of the relatives were less charitable than they had been. Henry wrote Kate that the court-martial "indirectly involves the feelings & fame of us all," and Kate agreed, replying that "as you say our name & family credit are at stake." But Herman never lost his respect or his affection for his hero-cousin.[23]

Seven Days

In obedience to his orders, General McClellan encamped on the north side of the Peninsula while he waited for McDowell's corps to join him for the assault on Richmond. After many delays, Lincoln finally gave him control of the corps, and it appeared that the attack would soon begin. But the Confederates found two ways to manipulate Washington. They played on Lincoln's fear for the safety of the capital by pretending to attack it; that was enough to disrupt any military operation that might be in progress. Also, they rode their cavalry around the Army of the Potomac, which, while it accomplished little militarily, made the Union commander look ridiculous and undermined the administration's faith in him.

By prearrangement, Stonewall Jackson rampaged through the Shenandoah Valley. Panicked, Lincoln called up the militia, clutched much of McDowell's corps to Washington, ordered the rest of it to the valley, and informed the amazed McClellan that the time was near when he "must either attack Richmond or give up the job, and come back to the defense of Washington." McDowell tried to persuade him that Washington was safe as long as McClellan was poised a few miles from Richmond and that the Peninsular strategy should not be abandoned. "It throws us all back," he protested, "and from Richmond north we shall have all our large mass paralyzed, and shall have to repeat what we have just accomplished." Then, while Lincoln was holding McDowell in the north, Jackson slipped away and force-marched his troops back to Richmond.[24]

When Lincoln called up the militia, Charles Emerson, nephew of the Concord sage, rushed from Harvard to New York City, where he left for Baltimore with the Seventh Regiment. In Pittsfield, the Allen Guard received its orders early in the morning of May 26 and accepted recruits at the armory throughout the day. At eleven the next morning they mustered, a prayer was said, and the 112 men marched to the depot. There a large crowd, including Herman and the boys, watched them entrain for Boston. Nine days later they returned, the psychological crisis having abated, and received a hero's welcome—fireworks as they marched to the armory and a dinner afterward. The Melvilles missed their return.[25]

A few days later, the Confederate commander, General Joseph E. Johnston, was deceived by an unimportant movement of McDowell's corps into thinking that Jackson's feint had not worked and that McClellan was soon to be reinforced. In response, he attacked a part of the Army of the Potomac at Fair Oaks and Seven Pines. The fighting was sharp but indecisive. Colonel Henry Briggs's 10th Massachusetts was in some of the heaviest. After Hodge's bandsmen lost most of their instruments, they turned stretcher bearers and helped carry Briggs, who was wounded in both legs, off the field. When Johnston was wounded and replaced by Robert E. Lee, the fortunes of the Union suffered a severe blow, but for the present, the two armies withdrew to their camps and waited, McClellan to see what Lincoln would do and Lee to see what McClellan would do.[26]

The Army of the Potomac had lain encamped close to Richmond for over a month. During that time, Henry Gansevoort rejoined McKnight's battery, which arrived with its horses. In Albany, Ed Lansing tried to join the army. With letters in hand, including one from Uncle Peter to General Wool, he made his way to the Peninsula, only to find that General Dix had replaced Wool at Fortress Monroe. Continuing on to the Army of the Potomac, he found Henry's battery in earthworks on the south side of the Chickahominy River, close to McClellan's headquarters and close to the "sickening details" of the Seven Pines battlefield. The battery was near the left elbow of the army, south of the river, while the far right, the reserve, was north of the river still waiting for McDowell. Ed lived in Henry's tent for nearly a week while he hunted for a position. After being rebuffed by one regiment, he called on the commander of the elite 50th New York Engineers. Although he was warned that social position and influence were no substitute for capacity, Ed talked his way into the position of regimental adjutant with the rank of first lieutenant. Then he returned to Albany to outfit himself.[27]

McClellan should have realized that his campaign had failed when, in mid-June, Lincoln ordered General John Pope, who had been successful in small engagements along the Mississippi River, to take command of a newly created Army of Virginia. Of what would this army consist, if not of McDowell's corps? Contemptuous of easterners and of McClellan in particular, Pope belittled the concept of the Peninsular campaign, to the delight of many in Washington, and mocked McClellan's meticulous logistics by announcing that his army would live off the land. When he boasted that his headquarters would be in the saddle, some joked that he was putting his headquarters where his hindquarters should be. Somewhat later, Lincoln brought in another westerner, General Henry W. Halleck, to assume the position of general-in-chief of the army. "Old Brains," or "Old Wooden Head," as he was called, was, like McClellan, a respected strategic thinker, and he had gained some success in the west. However, none of that altered the fact that he was a mediocrity.[28]

On June 25, Henry heard the sounds of fighting about a mile ahead, where a part of the army had become hotly engaged. He expected the general battle to begin as soon as the reserve had crossed to the south bank. That night he left his horses harnessed and hitched to the guns and caissons. The next day, the reserve, including Tyler's siege-train, skirmished with the Confederates near Gaines's Mills. On the following morning, in an attempt to cut McClellan's supply lines, the Confederates attacked in force, driving the reserve before them, though the reserve inflicted on them almost as many casualties as the South had suffered in the two days of Shiloh. The next morning, the reserve retreated across the river to join the rest of the army.[29]

Without McDowell's troops to hold his right, McClellan's supply base at White House, where steamers brought in food, forage, and materiel, was vulnerable, as Lee realized. Knowing by now that McDowell would not join him, McClellan decided to move his army to Harrison's Landing, on the James River side of the peninsula, where his supply lines would be secure and where the navy, newly freed by the destruction of the *Virginia,* could cooperate in an attack on Richmond. Already a base was being established there. The move was a hotly contested change of base—or retreat, depending on one's politics—which the North followed with fascination and apprehension. Lee attacked persistently, hoping to crumple the army as it marched across his front. These were the "Seven Days," a confused free-for-all in which there was almost continuous fighting at places named after single houses or crossroads. According to McClellan's critics, the week was a defeat for the large, well-equipped and supplied army that should already have taken Richmond—though the maneuver was, admittedly, well executed. According to his admirers, it was a success for their general, who, shackled by a hostile administration, did not allow Lee to destroy his army piecemeal.

Henry Gansevoort's battery went ahead to White Oak Swamp bridge, where infantry drove the Confederates off so that the artillerymen could cross. Once on the other side, they went into battery to protect the rest of the army as it in turn crossed. They remained until late on the twenty-ninth of June, when they joined the rear guard as it came up. The march was miserable, with oppressive heat and occasional cold rains. Henry had only hard biscuits to eat and little water to drink as he hauled his guns along the steamy, mosquito-infested route that had been torn up by the multitude of men and wagons ahead. The Harvard Regiment, once again under the command of Colonel Lee, fought every day and marched every night on short rations. On the third day, the Confederates attacked their part of the long column at Frazier's Farm, hoping to break it in the middle. Wendell Holmes waved across the line to James Jackson Lowell, who was reforming his troops. When Wendell glanced back, Lowell was lying on the ground mortally wounded. In the flux of battle, the regiment was unable to carry him away. Charles Lowell tried desperately to reach him behind enemy lines, as did Anna Lowell, a nurse on a hospital ship at Harrison's Landing, but neither brother nor sister was successful. Four days later, James died in Confederate hands.[30]

Before McClellan could reach his destination, he had to turn on his pursuers to prevent them from cutting up his army from the rear. About four o'clock in the afternoon of June 30, Henry Gansevoort, with the rest of the artillery reserve, went into battery in a grain field behind Malvern Hill while other army units deployed to receive the enemy. By the morning of the first of July, the last of the regiments and batteries had arrived and most had been arranged on the crest of the hill. Across this bend in the James River, both flanks rested on the river, where Navy gunboats, including the *Monitor,* waited to provide support.

Had McClellan been in favor with the administration, Malvern Hill would have been remembered as a successful major battle. The massed Union cannon did murderous execution on the charging Confederate infantry, leaving the battleground littered with their bodies. From his position in the reserve, Henry Gansevoort did not take part in the action, though his guns were shotted and ready in case they were needed. The Union forces prevailed, then, in a torrent of rain, scrambled toward Harrison's Landing, the gunboats firing to cover them. On arrival, Henry's artillery went into battery to protect the rest of the troops while they made camp. With that, the threat to Richmond was suspended. It had not endured the curious arrangement in which the campaign of the general on the field was at the mercy of a nervous political chieftain in Washington.

The Republicans perpetuated the idea that the Seven Days were a defeat for the Union, a curious notion in view of the facts: that there was little alternative to the march, that McClellan accomplished it with his army intact, that Lee failed in his attempt to destroy it, that the Confederates suffered far more casualties than did the Yankees, and that the Union won the only major battle. Still, in the sense that the assault against Richmond did not take place, it offered Herman little to celebrate. In fact, the main section of *Battle-Pieces* omits all of the battles in the east between this campaign and Gettysburg. Yet he wished to say something of Henry's part, even though his artillery cousin had not fired a shot during the entire odyssey. He did it obliquely, by attributing Henry's experience to a fictional major in "The Scout toward Aldie," "But through the Seven Days one [the major] had served, / And gasped with the rear-guard in retreat," and by making his College Colonel a veteran of the campaign.

Of the Seven Days battles, Herman memorialized only the final victory. Like "Shiloh," "Malvern Hill (July, 1862)" is spoken in retrospect by a veteran of the fight. In its treatment of its subject, the poem is fine, like "Shiloh" an elegiac memorial to those who perished. It also salvages what merit could be found in the Seven Days: at Malvern Hill, "with cannon ordered well; / Reverse we proved was not defeat." But in terms of the book as a whole, it also marks an advance in coming to terms with the realities of war. War occurs in the forest, the "wilds of woe," but now the reader is allowed a small glimpse of the horror of Satan's realm. Visions no more than implied in "Donelson," through smoke, dust, hunger, and fatigue that "pinched our grimed faces to ghastly plight—" are here specified in "beards of blood" and corpses, men whose gestures are made ghastly and futile by sudden death. "Our rigid comrades lay" as they fell along the march, their teeth still biting cartridges and their arms still stretching toward the haven to the south. *Battle-Pieces* takes another step in approaching the blackness of the darkness of war.

But the theological concern of the poem has been brooding since "The Conflict of Convictions." In the eyes of heaven and nature, how important was this suffering? Does Malvern Wood mourn the loss of these men? The elms reply that, although they remember everything, the "Wag" of the world is not their concern. Nature attends to the more important matter of its own rhythms, the filling of the twigs with sap and the annual renewal of the leaves; the griefs of men concern only men.

Partisans of both sides fervently believed that the mechanism of the universe responded to the march and countermarch of their armies, that every shot altered the divine plan in some way. But Nature "is passive and indifferent to their barbarous heroics and will not stoop to grant significance or honor to man's violence and destructiveness," as William H. Shurr says. This view was not peculiar to Herman: Thomas Bailey Aldrich approached it in his sonnet "Accomplices," repeated in full here because Aldrich gave some promise of becoming a major Civil War poet:

The soft new grass is creeping o'er the graves
  By the Potomac; and the crisp ground-flower
  Lifts its blue cup to catch the passing shower;
The pine-cone ripens, and the long moss waves
Its tangled gonfalons above our braves.
  Hark, what a burst of music from yon bower!—
  The Southern nightingale that, hour by hour,
In its melodious summer madness raves.
Ah, with what delicate touches of her hand,
  With what sweet voices, Nature seeks to screen
The awful Crime of this distracted land,—
  Sets her birds singing, while she spreads her green
Mantle of velvet where the Murdered lie,
As if to hide the horror from God's eye.

For Aldrich, nature is not *wholly* unconcerned: stopping short of indifference, she senses the shame in the human spectacle of crime, murder, and horror.[31]

An Interlude

After the Seven Days, Pittsfield shared the anxiety and gloom of the rest of the North as the Army of the Potomac lay inert at Harrison's Landing and as the casualty lists crowded the bulletin boards. Perhaps Herman's mood was similar to that of Kate Gansevoort: "It seems as if only for the past five or six months Albany has felt the horrors of war." But he must have been cheered when the gentlemanly impudence of Hawthorne's "Chiefly about War Matters" appeared in the July *Atlantic*.[32]

The Fourth of July was subdued because of the "unhappy" state of the nation. Baseball games were played on the town lot; in the morning, the South Adams Valley Base Ball Club beat the Pittsfield Taconic Mill Club, but in a memorable afternoon game Taconic won a silver cup by beating the Pittsfield Base Ball Club. In the evening, some private citizens lit fireworks on their lawns, but it was the Irishmen who salvaged the holiday. At ten in the morning, the St. Joseph's Mutual Aid Society marched through the streets, preceded by the Hancock Band riding in an omnibus. The Hibernians carried a banner of green cloth decorated with silver lace, bearing on one side a full-length portrait of O'Connell leaning on the Irish harp and a scroll inscribed "*Erin go Bragh,*" and on the other a rendering of Gilbert Stuart's painting of George Washington and the motto "The Father of His Country." After the parade, the Irishmen held a picnic. Ominously, the next day a lightning bolt smashed the Liberty Pole in the park and melted the telegraph wire at the depot, though Mr. Selden escaped harm.[33]

Pittsfield decided that it should have a military hospital associated with the Berkshire Medical College and set about to establish one, as it had during the War of 1812. On July 7, the "momentous crisis" on the Peninsula inspired a town meeting so large that it was adjourned to the park. McClellan's "masterly" change of bases was praised, his address to the Army of the Potomac was read, and three cheers were given for him and three more for the army. Home recovering from his wounds, Colonel Henry Briggs assured the citizens that his regiment had entire confidence in their general. When the town voted to sustain Lincoln's call for 300,000 more troops, twenty-two men volunteered on the spot. It was the recommendation of the meeting that an additional half-million men should be enlisted and sent at once to the field and that the town should offer a $100 bonus to each local enlistee. A similar meeting took place on August 2, at which the call was for a million draftees, one-half to be called at once.[34]

During the summer a new camp of instruction, Camp Briggs, was established on Elm Street, about a mile and a half east of Park Square. Its temporary commander was Colonel Lee, of the Harvard Regiment, who, after his imprisonment and his service during the Seven Days, had returned to New England to recover his health. Although he was in town less than two weeks, he attended the municipal meetings. On August 12, he was relieved by Adjutant Oliver Edwards, who was commissioned a major and given charge of forming the 37th Massachusetts Infantry. On August 25, Edwards paraded the regiment, already about 1,000 strong, into town, though as yet the men did not have muskets.[35]

Herman continued to study poetry and poetics and to invent amusements for the children, but he must also have participated in many of the events in town. Since he had lost interest in farming, Arrowhead was now little more than a country home—one that was inconveniently far from town. Despite her summer allergies, Lizzie may have spent some time doing war work.

The Allan Melvilles were contributing lint, shirts, and hospital wrappers, Kate Gansevoort was doing her share, and Gus was working with a group of women at the Methodist Church in Gansevoort, getting up a box of hospital supplies.[36]

For some reason, the spirit of the times brought a plague of confidence men to Pittsfield. On July 26, the "Hon. C. H. Clarke" gave a speech in the park announcing that, as the son-in-law of Sam Houston, it had been his sad duty to close the old Texan's eyes after he had died. Clarke claimed that he was carrying a bullet embedded in his lung, and that he wished to spend the short time remaining to him speaking on behalf of the Union. Then he headed west on the evening train. But Sam Houston, Jr., a prisoner of war in Illinois, wrote that Clarke was an impostor and that the elder Houston, who was alive and well in Texas, had no daughter and therefore could have no son-in-law. Sometime later, a "Madame Dombrofsky," a Polish physician, hired a horse and buggy from Chapman's Livery Stable and drove off to see a patient, leaving behind a number of debts. The horse was later spotted in Hoboken, New Jersey. In retrospect, some were of the opinion that the madame was actually a man in skirts.[37]

On August 25, Herman went on a short excursion with Sam Shaw, who had arrived two days earlier. He drove Sam into the mountains, proceeding part of the way on foot, and spent the night in an old house near Saddle Back. In the heat of the following day, the two descended to Cheshire, where they left the horse, which had gone lame, and returned to Pittsfield by train, just in time for the second Battle of Bull Run. During the trip the topic of conversation was the war—what was there more important to talk

Arrowhead, *circa* 1862. By permission of the Berkshire Athenæum

about?—the war in Virginia, the war in the west, the blockade, the generals, and such matters. After a week's visit, Sam returned to Boston.

In Albany, the Gansevoorts were worried about Henry, from whom they had received no letters since May. Kate approved of McClellan's change of base; at first she had thought it impractical, but later she decided that it was "splendid." Guert still had not answered Uncle Peter's letter, it had been some time since a letter had been received from Gansevoort, and Abe Lansing was away in Canada, seeking treatment for his lameness. However, Albany still had the heart for a Fourth of July parade and for gunpowder salutes, and Kate consoled herself in Abe's absence by attending a "Matinee Musicale" by the celebrated pianist Louis Gottschalk. On July 20, the whole family, Peter, Susan, and Kate, left for a vacation at Sharon Springs, where they found that Lieutenant Worden, hero of the *Monitor* battle with the *Virginia,* was a fellow guest at the Pavilion. His face was speckled with embedded powder and he had almost lost the sight of his eye, but he was well on his way to recovery and planning to apply for the command of another ironclad. Kate thought him very gentlemanly and danced a quadrille with him. After her parents' departure, Kate went on to Richfield Springs, where she was again in Worden's company. After socializing with him and some other recuperating officers, she became impatient at the fact that she could not defend a Fort Stanwix somewhere instead of knitting and making lint.[38]

On Uncle Peter's return to Albany, where he found that Martin Van Buren had died on the twenty-fifth of July, he received a letter from his brother Wessel. Wessel had emerged from his Vermont exile on July 22, come to Albany, and sent a letter asking to see Peter. After two days without a reply, he had returned to Danby without paying for his room and board. On August 7, Uncle Peter received a message from Danby saying that Wessel was dangerously ill at a boarding house four miles outside of town. The next morning, Peter and Susan went to Danby, but on their arrival they found that Wessel had died of palsy the preceding day. Despite their estrangement in life, Uncle Peter was determined that Wessel depart the world as befitted a son of the Revolutionary hero. He arranged to have the body sent to Albany, and he notified the family and sent a select group of friends discreet invitations to the funeral. At five o'clock in the evening of August 9, the service was performed at Peter's home, but not many came. Despite the fact that Fanny, Kate Hoadley with her two daughters, and Helen and George Griggs were in Gansevoort, the only family members who braved the stormy weather were Aunt Melville and Gus. But the Gansevoort pride and guilt had been assuaged. Two days later, when Kate Gansevoort returned home, Aunt Melville and Gus were still there. Although Kate knew little about Uncle Wessel, she reacted defensively to his death. "My Father can not blame himself for his conduct to Uncle W. or any other member of the family," she wrote Henry, probably reflecting some spoken or unspoken uneasiness lurking in the house. She was touched with the pathos of the exile: "What a lonely life his must have been, no wife to mourn his death & no one to share his many lonely hours." What Herman thought about the lonely life and death of his uncle is not known.[39]

Although Aunt Melville and Uncle Peter had shunned their brother in his later years, they were profoundly affected by his death. Coming as it did so soon after the death of their brother Herman, it left them the sole survivors of the six children of old General Gansevoort. Recognizing her dejection, Kate and Abe Lansing, who had just returned from Canada, took Aunt Melville and Susan for a brief holiday to a Catskill lodge. During the trip, the conversation turned to the war. Mother Melville wished to know everything about Henry's experiences and Abe bemoaned the fact that his lameness prevented him from volunteering. The day after their return, Aunt Melville left for Lansingburgh to visit the Peebles and Gus returned to Gansevoort, taking with her a party of the Van Rensselaers.

Just after the Battle of Shiloh, Toby Greene's regiment, the 6th Missouri Infantry, arrived at Pittsburgh Landing, Tennessee, where it was assigned to Grant's Army of the Tennessee. From there it campaigned in Mississippi before making camp in Memphis. In mid-August, the regimental surgeon sent Toby on an errand into town, where Toby was arrested by military police, probably because he did not have a pass. He managed to escape, but when he complained about his treatment the surgeon laughed at him. The insult reawakened the spirit of desertion that had remained latent in Toby since the old days with Herman at Nukuheva. About August 22, he slipped out of camp and ran away to Cairo, Illinois. There he enlisted as a regular foot soldier in the 11th Illinois Infantry, which had grown out of the old ninety-day militia regiment of the Hobarts. By this time, it was battle hardened, having fought at both Donelson and Shiloh. It was just moving from Cairo into Kentucky, where Toby spent much of the rest of the year.[40]

After the Battle of Pea Ridge and some feckless marching and countermarching in Arkansas, the 44th Illinois had been sent to Corinth, Mississippi, and then on to Rienzi, Mississippi. On the Fourth of July 1862, the 44th paraded, but Jeff Hobart languished in his tent, complaining of indisposition. Three days later, he departed without leave to spend a day and a half with friends in Corinth. On his return, his colonel charged him with misconduct and again ordered him court-martialed. On July 21, Jeff appeared before the court, but his accuser did not. After several days of waiting, the court dropped the charges, but in his ignorance of military procedures Jeff believed that he was still under arrest. When the 44th left, he remained in Rienzi. After appearing before an examining board, which determined that he did not understand the duties of an officer and had yet to learn infantry battalion tactics, Jeff returned home, still under the misapprehension that he was under arrest. While he was away, his regiment fought a punishing battle at Perryville, Kentucky. With its senior officers all absent for one reason or another, it was led into battle by one of its company commanders. In another brief appearance when the regiment was in Nashville, Jeff claimed that he was entitled to take command, but when no one agreed he went home again.[41]

During this period, there was a small Battle of Baton Rouge, Louisiana. Herman's interest in it stemmed from the involvement of the 14th Maine Infantry, although the identity of the Confederate commander must have interested him, too. Despite the fact that only about 5,000 soldiers were involved, the fighting was sharp and, in its own way, significant. Major General John C. Breckinridge, the former United States vice-president and senator, was attempting to recapture New Orleans. Through a dense early morning fog, Breckinridge threw his entire force on the camps of the 14th Maine and two other regiments. The force of the assault drove the Yankees back, all except for the Maine boys, who held their position. When the Union troops counterattacked, they drove the Confederates off, ending Breckinridge's hopes for his campaign. Casualties on both sides were great for such a small battle, the Maine regiment suffering thirty-six killed and seventy-one wounded, and the Union commander was killed. Herman's epitaph for the Maine men who had perished so far from home, "On the Men of Maine killed in the Victory of Baton Rouge, Louisiana," is a tribute to the men of the far northeast who fell battling for the exotic land of bayous and alligators. They had risked their lives because, however distant and alien it might seem, this place was still their country: "So vast the nation, yet so strong the tie." That was the true spirit of union.

With the exception of Ned Curtis, Herman's warrior relatives had as yet done nothing glorious. Guert had fired his cannon only in a futile sea chase, Henry Pease had done only garrison duty in captured forts, and Jeff and Randolph Hobart and Henry Gansevoort had not managed even that. Only John Hobart had fought in a land battle. Although Henry had served in the military from the first days of the war, the Seventh Regiment had missed Bull Run, and, although he had been present through the Peninsular Campaign and had made every effort to participate in it, by the time he had reached Harrison's Landing he had still not seen action. Then, at last, he had his fill of combat.

Chapter Four

From McClellan to McClellan, Part I

After its arrival at Harrison's Landing, the Army of the Potomac lay idle for a month while the unsanitary conditions of the crowded beach and the diseases of the Peninsula spread illness. On the fifth of July, Ed Lansing arrived to join his regiment, and soon he, too, succumbed to Peninsula fever. Charles Lowell left his cavalry regiment when McClellan appointed him his personal aide, and Henry Gansevoort was promoted to first lieutenant and reassigned to Battery C, 5th Artillery, which had lost its captain, wounded and taken prisoner, and two of its cannon, at Gaines's Mills. Pacified by his higher rank, Henry put on a show of newly restored virtue. Because of his separation from his family, he wrote Kate, he could not demonstrate his regret for his former shortcomings and his determination to be all that his family wished him to be.[42]

McClellan continued to ask for more troops, which he did not receive, nor does it seem to have occurred to Lincoln to order Pope, whose army lay idle north of the Rappahannock River, to cooperate in the Richmond assault—or, as McClellan himself mused in his perplexity, to order Pope to take command of the army on the Peninsula. The suspense in the North was brutal, with attitudes varying according to one's politics. "What shall one say?" asked James Russell Lowell, still shattered by his second loss of a nephew: "Who feels like asking more recruits to go down into McClellan's beautiful trap, from which seventy thousand men can't get away? Hasn't he pinned his army there like a bug in a cabinet?" Emerson combined his contempt with a prevalent, though hardly commendable, attitude toward women: "Strange that some strong-minded president of the Womans' Rights Convention should not offer to lead the Army of the Potomac. She could not do worse than General Maclellan." But the Democrats stood by their hero. Bruce wrote Henry that "the people here of the North . . . seemed to believe that it was only necessary to hoist the 'old flag' & give three cheers, & the day would be won." The Melvilles and Gansevoorts felt the same way.[43]

On August 3, Lincoln ordered the Army of the Potomac withdrawn to Aquia Creek, a landing on the Virginia side of the Potomac River not far below Washington. General Halleck assured McClellan that he would be the senior commander in northern Virginia, but he was lying: he intended to disband the Army of the Potomac, which was almost as unpopular with the administration as was its commander, and to transfer its troops to Pope's command.[44] It was an incredible blunder. Lee was waiting for Washington either to reinforce McClellan or to order him to northern Virginia, and he was poised to respond to either eventuality. As soon as he received firm intelligence that McClellan was to withdraw, he moved, catapulting the main body of his army north toward hapless Pope. Lincoln had managed to precipitate precisely the attack that he most dreaded. Washington and the Northern states were now in peril, not Richmond and the South.

Lee was closing on Pope, Pope was trying to hold his line on the Rappahannock River, much of the Army of the Potomac was afloat on ships scattered between the Peninsula and Aquia Creek, and those units that had already arrived were unsure of what was expected of them. That was the case with Henry Gansevoort and his battery. After a brief rest, they moved a few miles south to Falmouth, just north of Fredericksburg, where Burnside's corps, which had just arrived from North Carolina, was camped. Then their whole division was ordered west to join Pope. As each part of the Army of the Potomac arrived, it was also assigned to Pope until Little Mac had no army at all. The command structure was shattered. When McClellan reached Aquia Creek, he was helpless, uncertain of what his authority might be and ignorant of the locations of the armies of Pope and Lee. With desperately little information, Halleck was attempting to coordinate the army from Washington, but he had difficulty contacting McClellan by telegraph and no luck at all reaching Pope. Finally, McClellan went to Alexandria, where a part of the Army of the Potomac that had not yet joined the Army of Virginia was located. Although McClellan no longer commanded these troops, Halleck ordered him to send them to Pope. But even if his authority to do so had been clearer to him, he now knew that the Confederates had reached Manassas Junction, along the line of march to Pope, and he was unwilling to order soldiers into a bushwhack.[45]

From Falmouth, Henry Gansevoort marched west to Rappahannock Station, where Pope's rear guard was skirmishing. There he joined the retreat along the line of the Military Railroad. Because it was Pope's policy to forage off the countryside, and because retreating troops could not forage with an enemy in close pursuit, the soldiers lacked food and feed for their horses. Henry's battery, which often had nothing to eat but army crackers, became increasingly famished and exhausted in its day and night march. When news arrived that Stonewall Jackson had crossed the mountains from the Shenandoah Valley and had raided Manassas Junction—that he was between the Union soldiers and Washington—the retreat turned into a race for survival. On August 28, Henry's division encountered Jackson at Gainesville. As they advanced, Jackson's rifled cannon opened on them with a brisk fire and they went into battery in a field alongside the road. Just then a shell hit Captain Ransom's horse, killing the animal and stunning its rider. For some time Battery C duelled with the Confederates, Henry's first genuine fight, and then it marched to the old battlefield near Bull Run and made camp for the night.

The next day, August 29, Henry fought in the terrible second Battle of Bull Run. It was the same kind of defeat for Pope that McDowell had suffered the year before. Henry's battery joined after the fighting had begun and slept at their guns during the night. The next morning they were placed in a seemingly invulnerable position on a height on the far left of the army, whence Henry could look down on what appeared more like a panorama of the battle than the battle itself. "The amphitheatre was suitable for the tragedy to be enacted," he wrote. From his elevation he could see all of "the fight, dust, iron hail blood and glory [that] garnished the field." While the battery's cannon roared, Captain Ransom was slightly wounded and Henry's ankle was sprained by a recoil. The battle ended when the Confederates turned Pope's left flank, threatening the battery with capture, but the artillerymen fought their way out and retreated with regular army discipline. Because he was a soldier, not a citizen, Henry wrote, he could not speak freely about the defeat. However, he did say that the Union army would have won "if the same causes which defeated us at Manassas last year had not operated again"—bad generalship.[46]

With Pope stunned, shamed, and paralyzed, the army was leaderless and Washington was at Lee's mercy. Some regiments fell to pieces much as the militiamen had done the previous year, but others, particularly the regulars, held together. As one regular infantryman put it: "We were gloomy, despondent, and about 'tired out'; we had not had a change of clothing from the 14th to the 31st of August, and had been living, in the words of the men, on 'salt horse,' 'hard-tack,' and 'chicory juice.'"[47] Nevertheless, his regiment marched to Centreville and there, together with Henry's battery, took up a defensive position.

It was this aspect of the battle, the persistence of the army in adversity, that Herman memorialized in "The Fortitude of the North under the Disaster of the Second Manassas," although, as the title manifests, he was also speaking of the determination of an entire people. The storm of defeat took him back once more to Cape Horn and he pictured the Union as a cliff that would withstand the battering of any storm. No shame can come to the temporarily defeated because storms are to be expected. The refusal of the Union soldiers to abandon hope in the face of poor leadership, inept politicians, and Confederate bullets is for the moment their victory. Through these generalizations, Herman was also commemorating Henry's part in the battle without naming him.

The day after the battle, the two armies arranged a truce so the wounded could be cared for and brought away. Sixty ambulances, together with physicians and other authorized personnel, were sent in by the North. Some amputations were performed on the spot, and about half of the wounded were rescued. Unthinkingly, Henry took advantage of the truce to visit the battlefield, and what he saw gave him a dismal picture of warfare. Thousands lay where they had fallen, many still alive and in agony, and there were not enough physicians or medicines to treat them all. Henry realized not only that battle brought the danger of death or a "loathsome captivity," but also that a man with a crippling wound might lie "days and nights on the battlefield, until starvation renders him too feeble to survive even a trifling wound." He saw "many a wretch whose undressed wounds were covered with vermin, and who was gasping for water." Most gruesome of all were the bodies of officers and men who had been crushed under the wheels of retreating guns, caissons, and wagons.[48]

It was one of the most foolish things that Henry ever did. He had assumed that the truce entitled him to roam the battlefield freely, which he proceeded to do, mingling with the Union and Confederate medical personnel, but he was wrong. Under the cartel, had he been discovered he would have been taken prisoner, since he was within the enemy lines without authorization. As soon as he became aware of the danger, he disguised himself as an ambulance driver and escaped, convinced that otherwise he would have been hanged as a spy. That night his position was fired on, and the next day his battery marched toward Washington.[49]

From McClellan to McClellan, Part II

By chance, Richard Lathers arrived in Washington in time for the "fearful and disgraceful defeat of the army under General Pope," and soon thereafter he witnessed the frantic attempts of the administration to save itself. After the battle, Halleck wired McClellan, "I beg of you to assist me in this crisis with your ability and experience. I am utterly tired out." The next night, September 1, McClellan was in Washington, meeting with supporters to plan his personal strategy. Although Richard was not there, he was given the details by the person at whose home the meeting was held. It was argued that McClellan should accept the offer of command that was sure to be made only on condition that he be permitted to lead the army without interference, and late at night such a demand was drafted. Then it was abandoned. Considering the gravity of the emergency, the only honorable course was to accept without conditions.[50]

The situation was desperate. The bars were closed by government order, hordes of officers, from major generals down to captains, were milling about without the slightest idea of where their commands might be, the Treasury Department and the local banks were readying their money for transfer to New York, and a steamer at the navy yard stood ready, fully manned and fires lit, to evacuate Lincoln. At the breakfast hour next morning, Lincoln and Halleck called. Considering the fact that Washington was lost, would McClellan accept command? He replied that he would save the city. Halleck then ordered him to take command of the defenses of Washington, but not of any of the troops beyond them. The order would have been jesuitical had it not been addlebrained. Later in the day, two horsemen rode in the opposite direction along the line of retreat. When an officer shouted, "General McClellan is here!" dazed and bleared soldiers leaped to their feet and cheered, and as the riders proceeded down the road, regiment after regiment took up the cry. "The effect of this man's presence upon the Army of the Potomac . . . was electrical, and too wonderful to make it worth while attempting to give a reason for it." After giving heart to the shattered army, McClellan had just eleven days to prepare for battle.[51]

Lee believed that McClellan's army would "not be prepared for offensive operations—or he will not think it so—for three or four weeks." Thus deceived by the radicals' slander about McClellan's cautiousness, he invaded the Union. There were war meetings all week in Pittsfield, and it was time for Herman to contemplate defending Fortress Berkshire, but the next day McClellan was reestablishing control. Halleck stated, and subsequently insisted, that he was not the army commander and that his authority was limited to the Washington defenses, which meant that, since Pope and McDowell had been relieved, no Union officer in the field was empowered to order the army into action. Knowing that he must move and move rapidly, McClellan disobeyed Halleck. In the next few days, he reorganized the capital defenses, stationed a strong force on the Virginia side of the upper Potomac to prevent an attack from that direction, and reorganized the army, ending the confusion into which it had been precipitated by its withdrawal from the Peninsula and its subsequent defeat. On September 9, he once again began using the name Army of the Potomac.[52]

Henry Gansevoort's battery was assigned to General George Meade's division in Joe Hooker's First Army Corps, the force defending Washington on the Virginia side of the Potomac. At Leesburg, close to the point where Lee had already begun to cross into Maryland, Henry had the impression that the army had not recovered enough to meet Lee again, but he thought that the Confederates were probably in a similar condition. North of the Potomac, McClellan was hastening the rest of his army toward Lee, resupplying it as he went. By September 9, Henry's battery had crossed the river into Maryland and had been positioned on the right flank. In less than a week, Washington had been cleared of soldiers and army impedimenta, the stragglers, officer and enlisted, had been collected from the whorehouses of "Hooker's Division" and other sanctuaries, and the army was attacking.[53]

By then, Lee was in Frederick, whence he turned west. So confident was he that McClellan could not or would not overtake him that he sent Jackson on to capture Harper's Ferry, but on the fourteenth of September, two weeks after Bull Run, McClellan did overtake part of his army at South Mountain, just west of Frederick. The battle began in the morning and continued all day. Although Henry broke camp south of Frederick at daybreak, it took Meade until four in the afternoon to begin the assault up the steep slope of Turner's Gap, and the sun was setting by the time the infantry reached the Confederate positions. Although artillery was firing from the height, the Union guns were of no use. Henry's men muscled two cannon up the steep incline, but before they could go into action, night fell, and Henry slept among the Confederate wounded and dead. The Army of the Potomac had won the battle at both gaps, restoring their confidence that they could handle Lee. McClellan had also restored the confidence of Lincoln, who, after receiving the news of the victory, sent him belated orders to pursue Lee and "destroy the rebel army, if possible."[54]

The next day, McClellan dogged the Confederates toward the west. Henry's battery arrived at Keedysville, across Antietam Creek from Lee's army, on the sixteenth. Late in the afternoon, Hooker's corps crossed the creek to turn Lee's left flank, and at six o'clock it skirmished with enemy pickets. Then at dusk Henry's battery was thrown to the front to duel with some Confederate guns. The enemy had the range, but Battery C fought them until an hour after dark, when the Southerners withdrew. One of the battery's sergeants was killed and a few other enlisted men were wounded. Then rain began to fall.

It was an eerie night in which complete silence was ordered and no campfires were allowed. The two armies lay close to each other, the pickets firing sporadically. The next morning, September 17, was misty and cool, heralding a gentle September day in rural Maryland. Hooker on the right was to assault first, followed by attacks in the center and left. His corps was located in farmland, cultivated fields, and meadows interrupted by stretches of woods. In his front was a field of tall corn, and beyond that was a country road. There were patches of timber to the right and the left and a deep woods beyond the road. Early in the morning, as Hooker aligned his corps for the assault, with Meade's division in his center, the mist lifted. Henry's battery was parked in the rear and off to the right behind the West Wood, awaiting orders. The Confederate infantrymen had concealed themselves in the cornfield, where their position was given away by the glint of their bayonets in the morning sunlight.

Sometime before six, artillery opened from the rear of the corps. Then, when the infantry began to advance toward the cornfield, one of the bloodiest battles in the history of man commenced. As the soldiers moved forward, they were met by a fusillade of bullets, and soon the air was choked by clouds of acrid smoke. The attack was successful at first, until the Confederates countercharged. Then the initiative swung back and forth as each side made massive attacks and suffered massive casualties. Seeing where the danger lay, Lee moved troops from other parts of the field so that on this flank the two forces were equally matched.

It is impossible to describe the fighting precisely. In the confusion, regiments pressed forward, fell back, and mingled with one another in the smoky murk and the gale of ball and shell, and those who looked at their watches had different ideas of when events occurred. They could be certain only that shot flew so thick that the corn stalks were leveled to the ground and that bodies dropped everywhere. But it appears that the battle had been in progress for over an hour and a half when Battery C galloped up in full harness to a position behind the Union infantry. Then, at seven-thirty or eight in the morning, it was committed. Hooker led it to the front himself and positioned it. One cannon ball screamed past Henry's head and decapitated the swing driver of the cannon at his side, and Henry's horse was killed by a minié ball in its flank and a shell fragment. The men, horses, and guns halted at the extreme front, just before the cornfield, where they went into battery feverishly and opened fire on the swarm of charging Confederates. Behind the battery, the unhitched horses fell one by one.

How long Henry was there he did not know, though it would appear to have been an hour or more of steady fighting, during some of which Meade directed the battery's fire in person. In the course of it, Henry was grazed on the right cheek by a minié ball. At last the Confederate fury forced the infantrymen on either side and the battery to Henry's left to retreat. Captain Ransom would have ordered Battery C off the field, too, but because there were not enough horses left alive the artillerymen were forced to hold their ground alone. It was a single Union battery against the mass of Confederate assault troops, with capture the penalty for losing. As their enemies charged at them, they raked the field ahead with grape and shrapnel, choking in the smoke and deafened by the Confederate yells and the concussion of their own guns. When they ran short of ammunition, their caissons, which were lying under the cover of the wood behnd them, were brought up with fresh ammunition. Finally, a wave of Union infantry swept past them and the sweating, smoke-blackened gunners withdrew.

Shattered, the First Corps was no longer able to fight. Joe Hooker had been wounded, leaving Meade in command. Another corps had arrived on the field while Henry was still engaged, but its commander had been killed almost immediately, leaving his troops in confusion. Presumably, it was their retreat that had left Battery C alone on the field. Henry was probably saved by the arrival of Sedgwick's Division of the Second Corps, with Colonel Lee leading the Harvard Regiment for the last time. Sedgwick advanced his troops across the cornfield, but when they were flanked and attacked from the rear they had no choice but to run. While Wendell Holmes was retreating, he was wounded through the back of his neck, though the ball did miraculously little damage, missing his spine and coming out of the front.[55] He made his way to a farmhouse, which was filled with wounded. Soon, when the Confederates charged past the house, a rebel soldier threw his canteen through a window for the relief of the suffering men. When the Confederates retreated, the soldier reappeared at the window to reclaim his canteen. Soon after that, with both sides exhausted, the fighting ceased on that part of the field.

The calm on the right was followed by a lethal battle farther toward the center, and, in midafternoon, by Burnside's tardy attack on the far left. Burnside had been ordered to engage earlier while the battle elsewhere was still in progress, which would probably have put the Confederates to rout, but he had spent hours attempting to solve the problem of pushing thousands of men across a narrow bridge over a small stream under severe enemy fire. Had he forded the stream where it was shallow, he could have joined the battle on time, but he knew only how to assault head-on. By the time he established a toehold on the other side, he was too late to win the day, since Lee had been able to shift his troops from place to place to stave off disaster.

The heroics of Henry's battery did not go unnoticed. General Meade paid tribute to "the skill and good judgment, combined with coolness, with which Captain Ransom, his officers (Lieutenants Weir and Gansevoort) and men, served his battery. . . . I have described the advance of the enemy through the corn-field, and the check the column received from Captain Ransom's fire. I consider this one of the most critical periods of the morning, and that to Captain Ransom's battery is due the credit of repulsing the enemy."[56] At last Henry had proven himself in battle.

This apocalyptic struggle has been called indecisive, but that would have puzzled men like Herman, who thought that it was a Union victory. McClellan had reformed and reanimated a defeated army, bested the Confederates at South Mountain, halted the invasion at Antietam, and forced Lee's army back to its native soil. What more did Meade do at Gettysburg? McClellan did not renew his attack the next day, but Meade, for one, agreed with his decision. From the point of view of the present day, it is impossible to understand the conditions that prevailed following a Civil War battle that carpeted the landscape with corpses and filled houses and churches for miles around with wounded, but Herman would have known that never, during the entire war, did a general, Union or Confederate, pursue and destroy an opposing army after winning a major battle.

Obliquely, Herman remembered the enormous Union casualties in his memorial poem, "An Epitaph." In honoring a "soldier's widow [who] . . . Felt deep at heart her faith content," and who gave other civilians the courage to accept their losses, he honored all of the war-widows who, by their example, eased the bereavements of others.[57]

The Aftermath

Wendell Holmes wrote home asking that his father not come looking for him: "In a day or two . . . I shall start [for home] & I may remark I neither wish to meet any affectionate parent half way nor any shiny demonstrations when I reach the desired haven." He had ample reason to fear that, if not forestalled, the Autocrat would make his wound a topic of breakfast conversation throughout the North, but his request arrived too late. In the middle of the night after the battle, Holmes, Sr., received a telegram informing him that Wendell had been wounded. The next afternoon the Little Professor set out to find his son.[58]

Many other surgeons were rushing to the battlefield to care for the wounded, but the concern of the Harvard professor was limited to one casualty. In Baltimore, General Wool, who had other matters on his aged mind, affronted the Brahmin celebrity by his inattention. Wool had "Fort McHenry on his shoulders and Baltimore in his breeches-pocket, and the weight of a military department loading down his social safety-valves," Holmes wrote.[59] His ego wounded, he did not care that the confused old soldier was near the end of his military usefulness and would be sent home in a month or so. At Middletown, where the Battle of South Mountain had begun, he found a room for the night at a clergyman's home. That evening he toured the hospitals in the vicinity, located mainly in churches, and gave some advice to the surgeons, though he did not pitch in. At South Mountain, he saw the bodies of the dead being buried, if they were enlisted men, or being shipped home, if they were officers. At Keedysville, he learned that Wendell had been hauled away in a milk cart to Hagerstown. Assuming that his son was safely on his way to Philadelphia, the Autocrat toured the battlefield. Everywhere there were abandoned muskets, clothing, haversacks, canteens, ammunition, and dead bodies and horse carcasses yet to be buried. He collected souvenirs, some bullets, a button, and a belt buckle, and he stole a letter from the body of a Virginia soldier. Then he begged for a meal, probably for the first time in his life. That night he stayed with a doctor, but a wounded Confederate officer outside pleading for water kept him awake. Next he went to Philadelphia, but Wendell was not there. For a moment, he feared that his son had not survived, but in Harrisburg, he heard from Wendell, and the following morning father and son were reunited. At Keedysville, Holmes had been within ten miles of Wendell, who had suffered the pains of his wound in the company of a sympathetic young woman.

Despite Wendell's wish that his wound remain a private matter, Holmes wrote an essay about his trip. He might as well have made the journey to the battlefield to collect literary materials, and to one reading the essay that is just what he had done. From the beginning of the war, he had used it as an opportunity to advertise himself, filling the newspapers with glib verse. Now this, a witty account of the train rides, the wagon joltings, the meals, and the arrogance of a Boston Brahmin, published with the tragedy of battle as its stage scenery. It was a celebration of the Professor rather than of his wounded son, whose experiences in the battle are scarcely even mentioned, and it was an unintended confession that, surrounded by suffering and by selfless surgeons hurrying compassionately to the battlefield from far away, the cocky little doctor had failed to give of himself. It was not the kind of essay that would inspire Herman to emulation.

With the Army of the Potomac recuperating and resupplying near Sharpsburg, Herman was finally relieved of his almost continual anxieties about the safety of the army and the security of the northeast. From the moment when McClellan had moved to the Peninsula, there had been little surcease. Butchery had been a daily possibility, sometimes a daily fact, as the army had moved toward Richmond, as it had lain before the Confederate capital, as it had fought its way to its new base, and as it had been mired at Harrison's Landing. After Lee had moved north, there had been daily confusion about the location of the Union troops and about their fate, culminating in the Bull Run disaster. With Lee seemingly free to invade the Northern states at will, it had been impossible to feel safe in any one of them. Only Antietam and Lee's retreat had relieved the tension.

Responding to the fear and sad awe of these months, Emily Dickinson wrote:

> At least—to pray—is left—is left
> Oh Jesus—in the air— . . .
> Thou settest Earthquake in the South—
> And Maelstrom, in the Sea—
> Say, Jesus Christ of Nazareth—
> Hast thou no Arm for Me?

Hawthorne believed that the turmoil had prevented him from writing a new romance: "It is impossible to possess one's mind in the midst of a civil war to such a degree as to make thoughts assume life. . . . I feel as if this great convulsion were going to make an epoch in our literature as in everything else (if it does not annihilate all,) and that when we emerge from the war-cloud, there will be another and better (at least, a more national and seasonable) class of writers than the one I belong to." As he suspected, the shot and shell were killing not only the youth of the country but also its literature. The time of the romancers was passing; they were to be replaced by "more national and seasonable" writers, William Dean Howells, Mark Twain, and Henry James. Alienated from his imagination, Hawthorne turned to the expedient of converting his experiences in England into essays, writing he could still manage through the riot and rattle of war. Herman, on the other hand, was able in time to confront the turmoil and to become one of its poets.[60]

During these desperate days, Herman managed as best he could. After Sam Shaw's return to Boston, he visited New York State. He must have gone to see his mother, who was ill, but if he did so the family correspondence does not confirm it. In any event, he could not have stayed more than a day or so, since on the fourth of September he stopped to see Uncle Peter in Albany on his way to the Hudson River boat for New York City. The battle at Bull Run had just been lost, Lee was threatening the North, and during such periods of excitement and apprehension he gravitated toward the city of his birth, where he felt nearer the center of things than he did in Pittsfield.

The day of his boat trip, Allan and Jennie were in Boston attending the wedding of Annie Downer, "a sweet *Little* bit of a girl," and on their return to New Rochelle, Herman must have heard all of the details. A granddaughter of Uncle D'Wolf, Annie had married Doctor George C. de Marini, of Paris. "She married a *Roman,*" Jennie clucked, though when the de Marinis moved into a house on 34th Street, just around the corner, she found that their Catholicism did not prevent them from being pleasant neighbors. Allan and Jennie had intended to visit Gansevoort after the wedding, but apparently they changed their plans, which might account for the brevity of Herman's putative visit there.[61]

Immediately after Herman's return to Pittsfield, the Morewoods invited the whole family to picnic at Melvill Pond, on their estate. The children rowed out to fish, but the plentiful pickerel evaded their hooks. In the evening, Sarah invited them to visit the Morewood camp. Apparently they did, though Stanny had to stay behind with the other smallish children. On Sunday, September 7, in the panic caused by Lee's invasion, the 37th Massachusetts departed hastily, even though it was neither full nor ready. The Pittsfield churches canceled their services so that their parishioners could be present. By this time, a ritual had developed: Reverend Todd made a farewell speech under the old elm, Hodge's Band, just discharged after service on the Peninsula (and apparently with new instruments), played, Professors Ensign and Fedder sang the "Star Spangled Banner," and the regiment marched to the depot behind an elegant silk flag presented to them by Sarah Morewood. Fortunately, it was withheld from the Antietam fighting. Just as the battle was developing, John Hoadley must have stopped in Pittsfield on his way to Rochester to see his family. Kate Hoadley and Helen Griggs came down from Gansevoort to meet him at Uncle Peter's, after which they spent a week with the Albany Gansevoorts. John's return trip to New Bedford would have meant another stop in Pittsfield, but otherwise the rest of Herman's month passed in domestic quiet punctuated by a family tragedy.[62]

On September 26, school let out for a six-week vacation. That weekend, while the boys fished in the river, Herman went to the city again. It was unusual for him to make two such trips in the same month, but he had a compelling reason for this one. On the eighth of September, while Nashville had been braced for a Confederate attack, Lizzie Thurston had died there, probably of complications resulting from the birth of her daughter. Henry Thurston had informed his family of her death and of his impending return to bring her remains and his young son and infant daughter home. Allan immediately communicated the news to the Melville family, and it must have been this that brought Herman to the city, or, rather, to New Rochelle.[63]

Henry Thurston probably visited New Rochelle, and it is possible that he left his children there. He was particularly close to Richard Lathers, and Richard's estate, admirably arranged for children, was an ideal place for little Nathaniel and tiny Helen. In fact, two of Richard's children, Emma and Ida, corresponded with them in age. If he were able to do so, Herman would have attended Lizzie's funeral service, which was conducted at the Henry Thurston home on Madison Avenue. The whole family would have been present, old Mrs. Thurston, Rachel and Charles Barrington, Charles and Caroline Thurston, Richard and Abby Lathers, and Allan and Jennie Melville.[64]

During Henry's visit, Herman may have had a chance to chat with him about his experiences in Nashville. Apparently, Henry was attempting to arrange a reassignment to the Army of the Potomac, which would have permitted him to serve closer to his children and his family. When the attempt failed, he returned to assume the position of Medical Director in Nashville, which gave him charge of all of the army medical facilities there. Allan and Richard Lathers must have bombarded Herman with talk about

Guert's Court of Inquiry, which was in progress, with complaints and laments about the sins of the Lincoln administration, and with discussions of the Democratic gubernatorial nomination, a subject which was on Richard's mind. Allan must have shown Herman Henry Gansevoort's letter recounting his experiences at Antietam, which Bruce had loaned him—that would have given Herman his first idea of the heroic part Henry had played in it. But it would not be surprising to learn that Herman also spoke to Allan about Arrowhead, which had not been sold. It may be that in the past Allan had expressed some interest in having the farm as a rural retreat, and this would have been a good time for Herman to plant the idea of trading properties in his mind. At the end of the visit, Herman returned to Pittsfield with a basket of peaches from the Lathers orchard and a two-volume *Works of M. de la Bruyère*. In the margins he noted passages about the renunciation of greatness, injuries from parents and friends, the mixed emotions of the living toward those who die, and the worthlessness of some people in high positions—most of which corresponded to his concerns of the moment.[65]

Upon his arrival in Pittsfield, Herman found growing excitement about the raising of another new regiment at Camp Briggs. The 49th Massachusetts, enlisted for nine months, was known as the "Berkshire Regiment" because it was the first to be made up entirely from the local population. On September 20, Captain Frank Bartlett took command of Camp Briggs. Despite the loss of his leg, he had been recalled to duty because of his recognized abilities and assigned to the camp of instruction because the duties could be performed by a cripple. Even though he was a severe disciplinarian, he was popular with the recruits, who understood the need for rigorous training. As his biographer put it, "He was a born leader of the best men." At the time of Bartlett's arrival, the men had neither uniforms nor weapons, but Bartlett instructed them for hours at a time, standing rigidly erect on his single leg as they practiced musket drill with empty hands. When he put the regiment through battalion drill he rode along in a carriage. He was also popular with the townspeople; during his stay in Pittsfield he made a particularly strong impression on Herman, and Sarah Morewood became his friend. In a different way, he was also a favorite of Agnes Pomeroy, whom he later married.[66]

The camp was scrupulously clean and its streets were lined with tents decorated with evergreens. It was a popular gathering place for the townspeople, who acted as though it were their personal property. Despite the soldiers' growing use of profane and obscene language, women invaded the privacy of their tents to distribute the products of their ranges and ovens. Probably Herman took the children to see the soldiers' daily drill at two in the afternoon. Eventually, the regiment's uniforms arrived, dark blue trousers instead of light and black, high-crowned felt hats instead of the more familiar flat field caps. So pleased were the men that they marched into town to show off their regalia.[67]

Herman and Lizzie decided to simplify their lives by moving from Arrowhead to a house in town—perhaps an indication that Allan had shown interest in acquiring the farm. The move would benefit Herman by ending his rural isolation, particularly in winter, and by eliminating the need to drive into town every day. In town, he could keep his horse, his wagon, and his buggy at a livery stable, and he could have the hostler do the saddling and hitching for him. Lizzie would benefit, too, since it would be easier for her to participate in the Ladies' Soldiers' Relief Association, in which she had begun working regularly in August. By now, the whole family was involved in war work: Fannie later remembered them scraping old linen to make lint for dressing wounds.[68]

They must have rented "the square, old-fashioned house on South Street" in September, because on the first of October Herman had the initial load of the family *lares* and *penates* hauled in from the farm, and Lizzie was planning to use the boys' vacation time to get the house ready. Despite the pressures of the move, Herman half promised to take the children to the Berkshire Agricultural Fair that week. On the seventh of October, Helen Griggs passed through on her way to Boston, probably in the company of Kate Hoadley and the Hoadley children. The fair was in progress when the family moved in on or after mid-October, and Herman probably kept his promise to take the children to see the animals and the handicrafts. The moving continued until, in the latter part of the month, they were settled. All agreed that living in town was enjoyable.[69]

To try out the new freedom, Herman decided one night to take a pleasure jaunt. The next morning, he had the hostler hitch Charlie to the buggy and started out with Stanny for Lebanon Mountain. However, Stanny got more of a trip than he had bargained for. Herman made him get out and walk all the way up the mountain to lighten the load on the horse, and then walk down the steep descent. Before they returned, they drove past the Shaker village and up the New York State border through Lebanon Springs and Hancock. On October 27, Herman repeated the experiment, loading all of the children in the buggy to go chestnutting at Lulu Falls. When they arrived, he unhitched the horse and gave him his oats, then got out the bags that were to hold the harvest. Logs had been propped against the trees for climbing, but the yield was disappointing. On their way home, Charlie shied at a small bridge. Herman subjected him to the same persuasive power that had given the world a great whaling classic, but the Philistine animal refused to budge. Then Malcolm tried a few cuts with the whip, but the fear

The Melville home in Pittsfield, 1862–1863, taken in 1902. By permission of the Berkshire Athenæum

of the animal was greater than his sensitivity to pain. Finally, Herman unhitched him and gave him some decisive cuts, which carried enough rhetorical force to get him across. Then the luckless party returned home. Herman's attempts to entertain the children did not always succeed.

Meanwhile, in Albany, it was time to settle Uncle Wessel's estate. Uncle Peter sent the personal effects to Gansevoort for Maria to sort. Browsing through them, she found that her mother had set aside $4,000 for Wessel's support, from which thirty dollars per year in interest had been accumulating. Since she was perpetually poor, she asked Peter to abandon his claim against her share and that of her late brother so she could have the whole amount. That way, she said, she could pay off the mortgage on the mill. "You may have the impression that Allan aids me," she added, "as I know many have. He has now a very expensive family & for some time has done little for us. Were it not for Toms allowance I could not meet the insurance & interest." As usual, Tom was the hero. Clearly she expected no help at all from Herman, and she must have resented the opulent standard of living that Jennie expected Allan to provide her. Despite Gus's plea on her mother's behalf, Peter answered that unspecified losses in unnamed bank failures prevented him from complying.[70]

It was more pleasant for Peter to publicize Henry's heroism at Antietam. He showed Henry's letter describing his part in the battle to Judge Parker, who passed it on to Senator Harris. The Senator gratified the son of the Hero of the Revolution by praising the son of that son: "He shews the blood of Fort Stanwix," Harris wrote. So enthused was he that he gave the letter to the editor of the Albany *Argus,* who published generous portions. No doubt clippings went to the various branches of the family, as did pictures of Henry's battery. When he heard what had happened, Henry rebuked his father. It was unseemly for a regular officer to seek approbation in the press.[71]

The Victor of Antietam

The day after Antietam, Henry's battery began to regenerate itself, requisitioning horses from the baggage train and replacement soldiers from the regular infantry. The battery was camped near the battlefield, remaining in that gruesome, unhealthy location for more than a month while the new men trained.[72]

One of Lincoln's first acts after the battle was to issue a Preliminary Emancipation Proclamation, which provided that, as of January 1, 1863, all slaves in the Confederacy were to be considered free, and two days after that he abolished the writ of habeas corpus, depriving civilians of the North of their constitutional protections when they were brought before military courts. He visited Sharpsburg and treated McClellan just as though he were still the legitimate commander of the Army of the Potomac, rather than a maverick who had usurped authority, but he was not happy to have McClellan back. He renewed his nagging, urging and ordering McClellan to attack. McClellan argued that he needed time and materiel to refit the army, which, considering the mangled force he had received from Pope and the battles he had fought with it, was probably true. Just then, Jeb Stuart's cavalry rode around him, embarrassing him again. After further orders and counterarguments, on the twenty-sixth of October McClellan crossed the Potomac and marched down the eastern side of the Blue Ridge Mountains, shadowing Lee on the western side.

The comitragedy of conflicting aims and mutual distrust resumed. With the knowledge that he was at the mercy of men in Washington who had the power to frustrate his aims and strategy—including Stanton—McClellan became stubbornly immobile once more. Judging by Henry Gansevoort's comments, many in the army agreed that political interference had hampered their operations. The strategy in the east "has been a failure so far because we had not statesmen who were able to comprehend the war," he wrote. "The result is that at the eleventh hour we have to commence the war and have but a short time to settle the question."[73] But the resentment of the army stemmed from the Emancipation Proclamation, as well. To quiet that dissent, McClellan issued an order warning his troops against discussing emancipation. The people, he said, must decide the question at the polls.

At home, the most important political campaign since 1860 was in progress. During the summer, the New York State Democrats had been laying the foundations for the fall elections. On August 20, the editor of the *Journal of Commerce* had written Richard Lathers expressing doubt that Horatio Seymour, the favorite, was best candidate for governor.[74] Because of Seymour's opposition to the war, the party's chances might be better if it nominated a War Democrat like General Dix. Richard was deputized to confer with Dix at Fortress Monroe.

That was the reason for his presence in Washington at the time of Bull Run and McClellan's resumption of command. He applied for a pass to visit Fortress Monroe, but was told that because of the crisis travel there was prohibited. Then he called on Stanton, carrying a letter of introduction given him by Edwards Pierrepont, which specified pointedly that Richard was "a good Union man of the highest tone and character."[75] Stanton told Richard that it was unwise to bring a general into New York politics, even though that is what the Republicans were doing. However, he agreed to allow Richard to proceed on his mission, provided he deliver a letter from Stanton advising Dix not to run.

At Fortress Monroe, Dix listened with interest, although he preferred the Senate. He agreed to run, but said that he could not support an antigovernment platform. By the time Richard returned to New York, the convention was only a few days away and Dix could have been nominated only if the Seymour forces had yielded. When they refused, Seymour won the nomination. Then Richard called for Dix's nomination for the Senate, but without success. After the convention, Richard met with Seymour in his Pine Street office and persuaded him to include "the necessity of a vigorous prosecution of the war" in his campaign. Nevertheless, the Republicans maligned Seymour as a rebel sympathizer, and there were whispers among Democrats that he might be imprisoned at Fort Lafayette, in New York Harbor, on trumped-up charges.[76]

In Pittsfield, every issue of the *Sun* was filled with political reportage and editorials. Throughout the North, the Democrats presented themselves as the people's party and appealed to conservative Republicans and War Democrats, and former Whigs, Constitutional Unionists, and Nativists, to join them. One of the issues was McClellan. Democrats were outraged by the treatment of their general and insistent that he be allowed to pursue his own strategy without interference. They added the "Abolition Proclamation" to their list of Republican misdemeanors, as well as the suspension of habeas corpus. On the other side, the Republicans believed that McClellan's inaction after Antietam would aid the Democrats. "The election of Seymour as Governor of the State of New York would be a public calamity," William Cullen Bryant wrote Lincoln, "but it may happen if the army is kept idle. A victory or two would almost annihilate his party, and carry in General Wadsworth triumphantly."[77]

Using the slogan "The Union as It Was, The Constitution as It Is," Seymour won New York, though Republican Governor Andrew was reelected in Massachusetts. The Republicans retained control of both houses of Congress, but with reduced majorities. However, Pittsfield voted its own mind, giving the Democratic candidate a substantial margin over Andrew. About Seymour's election, Jennie Melville wrote, "Allan thinks this will assist in terminating the War—or may in some way influence it, but for my part, I know but little of Politics." If the election did not do that, it would at least restore the influence of the Gansevoorts in Albany.[78]

Although Lincoln wished to replace McClellan, he delayed in order to protect his party's candidates at the polls. Immediately after the election, he completed a purge of Democratic generals that he had begun two weeks earlier, firing McClellan, McClellan's top general, Fitz-John Porter, the commander at Gaines's Mills and Malvern Hill, and Ben Butler. Their removal was baldly political, both in motive and in timing, since two of them, McClellan and Butler, were possible Democratic presidential candidates in 1864. In the case of McClellan, it was patent that whatever general took Richmond could have the presidency for the asking. Lincoln appointed General Ambrose Burnside to command the Army of the Potomac. Knowing that he was unqualified for it, Burnside did not want the command, but he accepted in order to forestall the appointment of an even less qualified general.

That brought about a dangerous crisis. Henry Gansevoort wrote that "the intelligence of the removal of Gen. McClellan has created great feeling in the Army and I fear that it will lead to very bad results." There were passionate demonstrations in some of the camps, with many ready to march on Washington to remove the politicians responsible. One volunteer remembered that "sweeping denunciation, violent invective, were heaped without stint upon the Government. Subdued threats of vengeance, mutterings of insurrection slumbered in their incipiency. . . . The mails teemed with correspondence to friends and relatives at home denouncing the action of the War Department, raging at the authorities, and predicting the direst results." Meade observed that "the army is filled with gloom and greatly depressed. Burnside, it is said, wept like a child, and is the most distressed man in the army." He quoted Burnside as saying that "McClellan is the only man we have who can handle the large army collected together." One historian has concluded that there was a "very real danger of a military revolt against the government in Washington. . . . It was perhaps the greatest such danger the republic has ever faced."[79]

On November 11, McClellan and his staff departed. The 2,000 troops by the railroad broke ranks, surrounded McClellan's car, uncoupled it from the engine, pushed it back, and implored him to stay with them. At this critical moment, when the slightest gesture of approval might have ignited a general mutiny, McClellan stepped out onto the platform and asked that they support Burnside as they had supported him. The troops then recoupled the car and cheered as the train left. For the Army of the Potomac, "the romance of war was over." It would have commanders, but never again a leader.[80]

As McClellan returned through the North, crowds stopped his train at every station to catch a glimpse of him. When he arrived in New York City, where his wife had been staying, he declined a public reception, but he did accept Richard Lathers's invitation to a private one, but only if the party were managed discreetly, with only a few intimate friends present, and if the affair were not reported in the press. But the "intimate friends" turned out to be the mayor of the city, the president of the Chamber of Commerce, several bankers and merchants, and, probably, Allan Melville. During the complimentary speeches, Richard tricked the president of the chamber into making laudatory remarks. But *The Spirit of the Times* and other radical journals found out about the reception and claimed that Richard's hospitality was evidence that McClellan's sympathies were really with the South.[81]

McClellan was fortunate in having an important poet, Herman Melville, on his side. Apart from "Lyon," Herman wrote lengthy poems about only two generals, McClellan and Stonewall Jackson. "The Victor of Antietam (1862)" is a heartfelt tribute to a leader who deserved better from his government than he received. Although he presents the Democratic view of McClellan, the narrator does not glorify him, nor does he claim that McClellan was the great lost hope of the war. But despite its judicious tone, the poem is a statement in verse of "the feeling which surviving comrades entertain for their late commander," as Herman wrote in his note to the poem, and it lauds McClellan's achievements without the slightest concession to the criticisms of his enemies.

McClellan was the "grain" winnowed (after the first Bull Run) from the "bran," he whose leadership, because it passed through "storm-cloud and eclipse," was "unprosperously heroical." Dismissed after "a pall-cloth on the Seven Days fell," he was again needed when, after the second Bull Run, "staring peril soon appalled":

> You, the Discarded, she recalled—
> Recalled you, nor endured delay;
> And forth you rode upon a blasted way,
> Arrayed Pope's rout, and routed Lee's array,
>   McClellan. . . .
> Recalled you; and she heard your drum
> Advancing through the ghastly gloom.
> You manned the wall, you propped the Dome,
> You stormed the powerful stormer home,
>   McClellan:
> Antietam's cannon long shall boom.

The cannon are Henry's cannon, and the dome is, as always, the union itself.

In the only comment in *Battle-Pieces* on the Lincoln administration's conduct of the war, Herman's adverse criticism is unambiguous: "The Cause went sounding, groped its way; / The leadsmen quarrelled in the bay; / Quills thwarted swords; divided sway." The criticism is repeated once more when, in speaking of the Army of the Potomac, the narrator refers to the "maligner" of McClellan as an ally of the Confederates: "With you they shook dread Stonewall's spell, / With you they braved the blended yell / Of rebel and maligner fell." Yoking together the two enemies of the Union, the Confederates and the critics of McClellan, was pure Democratic politics.

Considering that the poem was composed late in the war or after its end, well after McClellan had lost the 1864 election and had left the country, Herman's praise is all the more remarkable. It stems from the trait in McClellan that Herman most admired, his ability to inspire men to love him and to follow him; in the terms of *Billy Budd,* he was a natural leader. The soldiers cheered him, both on the bone-weary retreat from Bull Run and on the battlefield of Antietam: "Along the line the plaudit ran, / As later when Antietam's cheers began." But even at the end of the war, the survivors of his army, "now so few," still render him tribute. When they

Meet round the board, and sadly view
The empty places; tribute due
They render to the dead—and you!
Absent and silent o'er the blue;
The one-armed lift the wine to *you,*
McClellan.

Herman later created a "one-armed" veteran, Major Jack Gentian. To the extent that the stainless Gentian, who lost his limb while serving in the Army of the Potomac, is a surrogate for his creator, Herman could imagine himself among those who toasted "Little Mac."

Although most radicals were happy to see McClellan go, many of his countrymen continued to believe in him, including some thoughtful abolitionists like George William Curtis. Curtis wrote that "a good deal [of the blame] must be shouldered by those who so attacked McClellan that he became the centre of party combinations." For the rest of the war, McClellan continued to symbolize the discontent of the conservatives. Kate Gansevoort, for one, was certain that he had a future ahead of him at least as great as his past—in the White House. Yet much as Herman and others may have regretted his removal, and much as the Army of the Potomac suffered as a result of it, there had been no other remedy. From a neutral perspective, McClellan was one of the most talented generals of the army, and Lincoln was a great wartime president, and surely both were committed to saving the union, but the two men could not cooperate to achieve that end. Because they differed politically, they differed strategically. One of the two had to prevail, and in a democracy that person is the president. As one contemporary wrote, "it would probably have been impossible to retain in command . . . a man who was not only a Democrat, but the probable Democratic candidate for the Presidency at the next election."[82]

While it is not appropriate to this study to debate the tangential matter of McClellan's generalship, it is necessary to defend Herman's tribute to him against the charges of ingenuousness and quaintness that have been made and the consequent belief that it is poetically flawed. It is enough here to point out that in Herman's own time, the thrust of his poem was to many judicious and insightful. McClellan's warrior-peers thought highly of him, as Burnside's statement at the time of the dismissal demonstrates. Grant thought that had he fought the entire war he would have "won as high distinction as any of us." One of his severest critics in the Army of the

Potomac ended a comprehensive condemnation with the caution that "it may appear a strange statement . . . , but it is none the less true, that there are strong grounds for believing that he was the best commander the Army of the Potomac ever had"—better, specifically, than Grant.[83]

Even more telling is the respect McClellan won from his enemies. At the beginning of the war, Confederate Lieutenant General Daniel H. Hill thought that the three Union officers most to be feared were William T. Sherman, William S. Rosecrans, and McClellan. Later, after fighting against McClellan on the Peninsula, at South Mountain, and at Antietam, he stated that "the light of subsequent events thrown upon the careers of these three great soldiers has not changed my estimate of them." The most convincing testimony came from Robert E. Lee, who stated that the greatest Union general was "McClellan by all odds." It is in this light that "The Victor of Antietam" should be read.[84]

5

Defeat, Dander, and Victory *1862–1863*

November 1862 began with a number of distractions, but none that presaged the accident that was about to disable Herman. On the first of the month, Aunt Priscilla Melvill died alone in Boston; since they were in the process of settling into their new home, Herman and Lizzie did not attend her funeral. Aunt Priscilla's death was followed in a few days by the state elections, and on the sixth the *Sun* carried Hawthorne's wickedly comical "English Women," an excerpt from the new book he was writing. On the seventh, McClellan received his dismissal order. In Brooklyn, Guert's court-martial was in progress, and in Pittsfield, Frank Bartlett, newly appointed colonel, was preparing to lead the Berkshire Regiment south, just as the Morewoods were preparing to leave for New York City. But in one moment on November 7, the outside world was canceled.[1]

That morning, Herman had the hostler hitch his horse to the wagon for a drive to Arrowhead with J. E. A. Smith.[2] On the way back with a load of family belongings, the two friends were passing along Williams Street near the home of Colonel George S. Willis when the ironwork of the wagon gave way. Charlie, the same horse that had been spooked by the narrow bridge several weeks earlier, bolted, throwing both men onto the hard street. Landing head first, Smith was stunned and bruised, while Herman fell where the street angled into the ditch, receiving a severe battering as well as dislocating or breaking his left shoulder. Colonel Willis took Herman home in his carriage, after which Doctors Root and Cady were called in to treat him.

During an afternoon blizzard that lasted through the following day,[3] Herman was in such intense pain that he could not even focus his attention on the bustle around his sickbed. Although Lizzie notified the family immediately, it was days before he could listen to their expressions of sympathy.

His psychic pain was even worse. The gods had sported with him, visiting on him the same violence that they had brought to the nation for a year and a half. He brooded on death and on his own life, which at moments seemed pointless. In time he began to recuperate, but it was more than a month before he could walk, write letters, and think of much more of the human race than himself.

Black Squadrons Wheeling Down to Death

But the earth had not stopped spinning. On November 5, Uncle Peter and his family had visited the city for two weeks or so, ostensibly to cure Peter's dyspepsia. On November 8, Allan and Jennie, back from their summer in New Rochelle, called on them at their favorite hotel, the St. Nicholas, which was noted for its elegant decor, its grand lobby, and its great oak staircase. That allowed Kate and Aunt Susan to meet Jennie for the first time. After paying a return call on Jennie, Kate concluded that her new cousin had more common sense than the family credited her with. Bruce, whom the Gansevoorts did not yet know well, paid his respects separately, sporting a walking stick, English whiskers, and a fashionable suit. He wanted to know everything about Henry, including his address, since he had not received a reply to any of his recent letters. After discussing Henry's demands for a volunteer commission, he and Peter decided that the rank of first lieutenant of regular artillery was superior to major or colonel of volunteers. The artillery was less exposed in battle than other branches (after his Antietam experience Henry might have disputed that), and the regulars were better cared for and were made up of a better class of men. Since Henry had suggested that he and Bruce might serve together in a volunteer regiment, Kate was offended by the fact that Bruce was in the service of Mammon rather than that of his country. Later, when her temper cooled, her opinion moderated.[4]

Kate wanted to visit the navy yard again, but even though she sent Guert a note in care of a convenient lieutenant she was unable to smoke him out. In her ignorance of his deep humiliation, she wrote, "I think it is so strange Henry that Cousin Guert Gansevoort should act so curiously, taking no notice of his family." The truth was that the only people Guert was seeing, with the possible exception of Allan, were his sister Kate and his niece Mary, who had come down from Glens Falls to be with him in his time of frustration and despair. On November 22, the family returned to Albany.[5]

In his pain, Herman had missed the departure of the Berkshire Regiment. Visitors crowded the camp to say goodbye to friends and relatives, especially the 140 soldiers from Pittsfield. In the chill of the morning of the fourteenth of November, the regiment marched to the station and took the cars to Worcester. Probably Lizzie, Malcolm, Bessie, Stanny, and Fanny—or some combination of the family—saw them off, the camp and the station being so close to home. The regiment was sent to the environs of New York for two months of provost duty, but in a way it never left home: the newspapers reported its activities just as though it were still at Camp Briggs and published letters from the soldiers describing their every experience.[6]

Still fighting her illness, Sarah Morewood had also left for the city. The doctors had advised her to travel to a warmer climate, such as Cuba, but she maintained that she had no disease of the lungs. She was in a strange state of mind, experiencing airy hallucinations. She wrote Gus a dreamy, poetic letter in which she spoke of clouds and mists that were always in her brain and cautioned Gus against religious fanaticism, which, in Gus's case, meant puritanical Christianity. But ill health could not halt her war work. She busied herself carrying gifts of delicacies to the Berkshire soldiers nearby.[7]

Near the mountains of western Virginia, Henry Gansevoort was now serving under Burnside. Warned by the fate of his predecessor, Burnside was doing what Lincoln had wanted McClellan to do: instead of going into winter quarters, as the army expected, he was advancing toward Richmond, first moving to a position north of the Rappahannock River near Aquia Creek. In response, Lee shifted his army to Fredericksburg, just across the river, where he took up positions squarely between Burnside and his objective.

In his new camp, Henry fell ill. Because his surgeon did not have enough medicines, he resorted to remedies that he had long avoided, including large doses of quinine. He lay in his tent by a glowing stove that made his fever and pains nearly insupportable, his discomfort intensified by the whistling, singing, and carousing of the other three officers of the battery. On his first day out of bed, Ed Lansing, who had filled out and had developed into a handsome young man, visited from his camp six miles away. But Henry was still not well: his teeth hurt from eating hardtack, he needed nutritious food, his stomach was constantly upset by the putrid water, and his health was hostage to the weather, which changed daily. Obtaining sick leave, he went home.[8]

On December 9, when Aunt Melville arrived at Uncle Peter's on her way to visit Herman, she was surprised to find Henry there. For a man who was supposed to be wasted by disease, he looked remarkably well. It is probably true that he was malingering, but, although he did not realize it, he was afflicted by an incipient illness from which he never entirely recovered. His months on the mosquito-infested Peninsula, compounded by the unhealthy conditions in which he had served since then, had damaged his health permanently. On the same day, a lieutenant from Henry's battery was writing him a hasty note describing the battery's twelve-mile advance toward Fredericksburg and advising him that "you had better come on *poste-haste* if you want to participate in the fun." It was too late for Henry to return in time for the Battle of Fredericksburg, even had he tried, but he was not in the mood to try.[9]

Burnside had sent for pontoon bridges for a river crossing and a wintry battle. Despite their delayed arrival, which gave the Confederates plenty of time to perfect their defenses, he planned to hurl his men directly at the enemy. He was a good general when not asked to exceed his capacity, but he was not competent to command a large, complex force in a large, complex battle, and he knew it. This sense of insufficiency, intensified by his natural obstinacy, made him intractable, proof against self-criticism, and unwilling to listen to advice. Thus his plan, which was faulty in its inception, could not be changed.

The Battle of Fredericksburg, one of the most tragic fought by the Army of the Potomac, began on December 11. The soldiers crossed bridges laid by Ed Lansing's regiment and skirmished through the town. Beyond, they found the Confederates waiting behind impregnable defenses. The assault began on December 13. Again and again the soldiers charged across an open field before Marye's Heights, and each time they were raked by intense fire from a sunken road and slaughtered miserably. Fallen men feigned death, knowing that if they stirred in the plain view of the Confederates they would be shot, and the night that followed was so cold that wounded men froze to death where they lay. In the Harvard Regiment, Private Stephen Longfellow, a nephew of the poet, was seriously wounded, and in one of the last attacks, Lieutenant Colonel Joseph Bridgeman Curtis, half-brother of George William Curtis, was killed while leading his Rhode Island regiment. The next day, Burnside made the compassionate decision to withdraw.[10]

Thomas Bailey Aldrich was the only poet to make literary sense of a tragedy that made no sense. In his haunting sonnet, "Fredericksburg," he achieved a clarity devoid of bravado, anger, self-righteousness, or bathos:

The increasing moonlight drifts across my bed,
  And on the churchyard by the road, I know
  It falls as white and noiselessly as snow.
'T was such a night two weary summers fled;
The stars, as now, were waning overhead.
  Listen! Again the shrill-lipped bugles blow
  Where the swift currents of the river flow
Past Fredericksburg,—far off the heavens are red
With sudden conflagration: on yon height,
  Linstock in hand, the gunners hold their breath:

A signal-rocket pierces the dense night,
  Flings its spent stars upon the town beneath:
Hark—the artillery massing on the right,
  Hark—the black squadrons wheeling down to Death![11]

With a little more craftsmanship, perhaps a revision which it never received, this might have ranked among the few really fine battle poems of the Civil War. In its muted vigor it says much of what could legitimately be written about such a terrible disaster.

Walt Whitman rushed to the front to nurse his brother, Captain George Whitman, who had been severely wounded, and whatever other victims he could. Louisa May Alcott was already in Washington, having received an emergency call to go to a Georgetown hospital two days before the battle. The casualties were enormous. Whitman reported that there were thousands of them, with hundreds dying every day, and he saw a cartload of amputated body parts heaped in front of a temporary hospital. On her third day in Washington, Alcott had to deal with forty ambulances full of wounded, and in New York City emergency measures were adopted to care for casualties who were brought that far north. So many were there that the army had to contract the services of local physicians, including Titus Munson Coan, who, as a student, had visited Herman at Arrowhead and who was now a surgeon at Bellevue Hospital. Coan spent most of January and a part of February in this temporary service.[12]

The North was aghast at the toll. Whitman thought the battle was the "most complete piece of mismanagement perhaps ever yet known in the earth's wars," and, in an editorial, William Cullen Bryant cried "How long is such intolerable and wicked blundering to continue?" By bringing discredit on its conduct of the war, the administration had wounded itself, and the Democrats hoped that Lincoln would be forced to recall McClellan. Wendell Holmes, who was hardly a partisan Democrat, wrote his family that "it is maddening to see men put in over us & motions forced by popular clamor when the army is only willing to trust its life and reputation to one man."[13]

But for "W. F. W.," politics paled before the real significance of the battle. In "Fredericksburg," he (or she) decried officialdom's abstract quantifications of "our losses." The bereavements were not "our losses," but rather the personal losses of those who loved the fallen—parents, wives, children, sweethearts, friends:

'T is *their* loss! but the tears in their weeping eyes
  Hide Cabinet, President, Generals,—all;
And they only can see a cold form that lies
  On the hill-side slope, by that fatal wall.

They cannot discriminate men or means,—
They only demand that this blundering cease,
In their frenzied grief they would end such scenes,
Though that end be—even with traitors—peace.

In the face of such truth, political bickering seemed shameful. Even some of Boston's Brahmins were learning the real costs of the war. Lowell, who had been sobered by the deaths of his two nephews, now made a sad point of showing their pictures to visitors. Longfellow, too, learned the lesson. After only two and a half months as a second lieutenant in a Massachusetts cavalry regiment, his son Charlie contracted "camp-fever." Alarmed, Longfellow visited Charlie in Washington, where he decided that the war, seen close, was horrible. He also visited a wounded officer of his son's regiment at a hospital that was presided over by Anna Lowell and another woman. There he saw his first gunshot wound and abandoned his flippant attitude toward the war.[14]

Returning from Pain

By the time Mother Melville arrived on December 11, Herman was much improved, though Lizzie was paying a price. Not only had the care of her husband made severe demands on her, but also the house was not yet fully settled. It may be that she was forced to miss some of Mrs. Fenn's three "soldiers days" each week; when she did attend, she made trousers, capes, stockings, mittens, and hospital clothing, work that continued throughout the winter. Herman had emerged from the isolation of his pain to communicate with the world once more. Even his wry humor had returned. His best excuse for living, he wrote Sam Shaw, was that "I consume a certain amount of oxygen, which unconsumed might create some subtle disturbance in Nature." Although he still carried his arm in a sling and experienced twinges in his cheek from his bruised nerves, he was able to walk around town. Since his social instincts had also returned, he tried to persuade his mother to lengthen her visit, but, satisfied that her son was out of danger, she seems to have returned to Gansevoort for Christmas.[15]

With Herman unable to take the children on excursions, they found their own amusements, skating on Silver Lake and on the river, and Malcolm made stilts for Stanny and himself. Except for a number of snowstorms, the attention of the household centered on a puppy. When a gray and white stray begged at their door, they made the common mistake of feeding him. Henceforth, he was theirs. Every day he returned for his food, until Stanny and Lizzie legitimized his family membership by making him a collar. The puppy was hardly the social equal of the noble black Newfoundland who had accompanied Herman on his visits to the Hawthornes' home a decade earlier, but he delighted the children, anyway.[16]

Herman's resurgent good humor must have been tested severely when Holmes's essay "My Hunt after 'The Captain'" appeared in the December *Atlantic.* It was the kind of war literature that he would not emulate. It was what Wendell must have hoped that his father would not write, the kind of response to the war that caused one of Wendell's most valued comrades to write that the Little Professor "is a miserable little manikin, dried up morally and physically, and there is certainly nothing more aggravating than to have such a little fool make orations and talk about traitors and the man who quarrels with the pilot when the ship is in danger."[17] Because Herman did not admire self-promotion, Holmes's exploitation of the tragedy of Antietam must have offended him. Placing the war in the context of one's own foibles and quiddities and inconveniences ran exactly counter to his conception of the role of the maker and seer. His own impulse to do the opposite must have been strengthened.

On Christmas Eve, the children hung up stockings, though this time not on the old Arrowhead mantel that was inscribed "I and My Chimney, We Smoke Together." The record of a few of their presents has survived: for Stanny, a pocket comb, a chain, two cents, and a paper of candy; for Bessie, *The Poetical Works of Mrs. Felicia Hemans.* The boys received a joint present from Gus and Fanny, a book entitled *Learning to Think,* the kind of gift they might have expected from their aunts in Gansevoort. On Christmas Day, Mrs. Brittain, who had been left behind in Pittsfield with the two youngest Morewood children, brought little Allie and Annie to the Melvilles' for dinner, and the next day, the Melvilles visited her at Broadhall. Allie fetched a suitable tree and the two children put together a celebration. There were no more presents, but Allie loaned Stanny *Dick Duncan* and *Guy Charlton.*

After the earlier snowstorms, the winter weather had become benign, with mild temperatures and only occasional snow. Lizzie was sewing on the soldiers days, now twice a week on Wednesdays and Fridays, and the children were conveniently close to their schools. Malcolm certified that living in the village was "first rate." He was being tutored in writing, and both of the girls were enrolled in Miss Sperry's school. However, not all of the domestic news was good. Stanny began the new year by contracting whooping cough, though it was not serious enough to keep him out of school. Far more dangerous was the illness of the Hoadley girls in New Bedford. Minnie, and soon Lottie, contracted scarlet fever and were miserably ill through the winter. Kate had help, including a nurse, but it was difficult to keep servants and to replace those who departed. As they came

Left to right: Malcolm, Elizabeth, Frances, and Stanwix Melville, *circa* 1863. By permission of the Berkshire Athenæum

and went, there were times when keeping house and worrying with John over the pale, feverish children pushed Kate almost beyond her limits.[18]

In Gansevoort, Mother Melville, Gus, and Fanny were excited about their letters from Tom Melville. The war had followed him to Hong Kong, where he attended a party in Shanghai at which a young lady of heterodox politics taunted him with a corrupt version of "The Star Spangled Banner," substituting "In *Davis* we will trust" for "In God we will trust." Following this desecration, he hauled a human cargo to Foo Chou, where he found other American ship captains and some of their wives more loyal company. From there he forwarded family presents on a ship returning to the United States before making his way back to Shanghai, where a river pilot allowed the *Bengal* to collide with another ship. The repairs left him fatigued, but, overall, he was lucky: he did not encounter any Confederate commerce-raiders.[19]

In Albany, Uncle Peter fell ill with rheumatism. Fierce John Hoadley sympathized, writing that the capture and obliteration of Charleston would cure him. With Henry out of town, Peter, Aunt Susan, and Kate spent Christmas at the Lansings', and at noon on January first they attended the ceremony in which Horatio Seymour took the oath as governor. Afterward they talked to Colonel Seymour Lansing, who had commanded a regiment at Antietam and who was now home to supervise the raising of regiments in New York City. He entertained them with anecdotes about McClellan and the "imbeciles" in Washington, and, like them, he had heard the rumor that McClellan was to be recalled.[20]

Guert Gansevoort continued to be the most elusive member of the family—he had to travel much of the time on yard business, though in part that was an evasion. Allan tracked him down at the Pierpoint House in Brooklyn, but he would not talk about the *Adirondack*. His siblings remained in Glens Falls, Stanwix in his usual egocentric isolation, Kate and George Curtis worrying about Ned, whose health seems to have been suffering in the Louisiana climate, and Leonard apparently reconciled to the fact that he would not receive a commission in the navy.[21]

Some of the girls of the family spent the winter traveling. Mary Curtis remained in Brooklyn, probably with Curtis relatives, after her mother returned to Glens Falls, and she must have been one of the few people outside of the navy who saw Guert. Cousin Nancy Downer's daughter Gertrude visited her sister, Annie de Marini, for a month or two, since her fiancé was established in the city. She brought little Alice Downer, ten years old, with her, and the three sisters must have visited the Allan Melville home frequently. At least, Annie took Alice there, where she could find plenty of little girl companionship. All three may have attended the party at Allan's on Christmas Eve, when a large group of ladies, gentlemen, and children—and probably Henry Gansevoort—were present.[22]

Through the traditional New Year family letters, Herman received word of yet another family bereavement. Aunt Mary Melvill wrote Mother Melville that she was thankful that Herman had recovered from his accident, but she reported that her son John, Uncle Thomas's favorite, had died in Chicago of "quick consumption" just before Christmas. The loss prompted her to tell Mother Melville that "we shall probably meet no more on earth." For Herman, it was the fourth death in the family in the past six months—Uncle Wessel Gansevoort, Lizzie Thurston, Aunt Priscilla Melvill, and now John Melvill. Other than that, Aunt Mary reported that Robert's steamboat had been commandeered by the government to carry supplies down the Mississippi River to the army in Tennessee. But the most exciting news was about Allan Cargill Melvill, who had joined a gold rush to an area just west of the Rocky Mountains. He left Galena for the mines about the first of May, traveling to St. Louis and thence on a steamboat up the Missouri River. But after spending several months in the Washington Territory, dangerous months amidst desperadoes and frontier vigilantes, he returned home through territory populated by hostile Indians, little richer for the experience.[23]

Aunt Nourse wrote that she was happy that Herman had regained the use of his arm and said that his move into town, in her opinion, was healthy: "While you were all *one family,* it was a delightful residence at 'Arrowhead,' but when Herman & Lizzie were left alone, it must have been very lonely, especially in the winter season." "Uncle D'Wolf is remarkably well," she added, "always in good spirits & looking on the bright side, every cloud has a 'Silver lining' for him." In addition to her letters, she sent photographs of the Gilbert Stuart portraits of Grandmother and Grandfather Melvill to all of the grandchildren, including Herman.[24]

Transfigurations

The advent of 1863 brought a change in Herman and in the country. Some elements of the transformation date from New Year's Day itself, since that was when the Emancipation Proclamation took effect. Longfellow called it "a beautiful day, full of sunshine, ending in a tranquil moonlight night. May it be symbolical of the Emancipation." For other elements, the day is symbolic, a convenient point of reference. That is the case with Herman. The suffering and recovery following his accident had been a sort of death followed by rebirth. His pain and depression had been severe enough to have marked him for life, and according to one observer, it did. J. E. A. Smith claimed that subsequent to the accident he developed a fear of driving. For some time, he is supposed to have refused even to enter a carriage, and thereafter, though in the past he had careened recklessly along the mountain roads, he drove timidly.[25]

Smith's statement obscures the more significant aftermath of the accident, the emergence of a rejuvenated Herman Melville. The despair into which his injury had plunged him vanished with his recovery. Soon he was in exceptionally fine spirits and health, optimistic and confident as one who had cheated the fates might be. Even his fear of driving, which could have been no more than temporary, benefited him. Because of it, he abandoned his sedentary ways and took to walking everywhere, which restored his stamina. He walked to the farm and back without complaint, which he could not have done the preceding summer.[26]

One can speculate that in his new fortitude Herman was no longer apprehensive about the outcome of the war. The fighting of the previous summer had inured him to transient disaster, to the point that Burnside's blunder at Fredericksburg was emotionally manageable. If Herman had equated his injury to the past year's reverses on the field, his recovery was equally a portent of Union success to come. The war might be long, but sooner or later the North would win, led by McClellan or by some other general. Even emancipation, though it affronted many in his family, was not an adverse development, taken by itself. He could hardly object to the liberation of the black man that he himself had desired, even considering the difficulties the freed slaves would face in coming to terms with a new, perplexing world. Nevertheless, he was irritated by the narrow focus of the abolitionists, who did not value union first and always.

In midyear, Lizzie expressed anger at her sister-in-law Jennie by saying "I *must* relieve my feelings—*Great fool!*—say it—or 'bust'—like 'Greely & the nigger.'"[27] Horace Greeley, the influential editor of the *New York Tribune,* was one of the most vocal and most partisan of the antislavery spokesmen. He was anathema in the Melville household because he had been willing to accept the existence of the Confederacy as the price of liberating slaves in the Union and because of his single-minded agitation for the Emancipation Proclamation. Lizzie's statement is remarkable evidence of Herman's attitude toward the abolitionists. At a time when married women customarily echoed their husbands' opinions on public issues, she would have been echoing Herman—the wording of her sentence was her own, but the idea behind it was probably his. Her word "nigger" should be read not as a slur on blacks but as an expression of displeasure with the abolitionists. She had probably encountered too few black people to have much of an opinion about them. Herman would have agreed with Greeley's opposition to slavery but not with his means for ending it. Nevertheless, Herman must have realized that the option of reestablishing the old America was now forever closed, that a radically new nation would be born out of the rubble of the battlefield. Even were McClellan to return to command, he could no longer reunify the states along the old lines. With the Emancipation Proclamation, the war had been transfigured, the fight for the union would have to continue until one side or the other capitulated, and as seer-poet Herman had to accept that.

January 1863 is as good a date as any to which to assign the beginnings of his war poetry. With those beginnings, he finally discovered his role as the poet of the war. During that month, the Pittsfield *Sun* published a slight but suggestive poem:

Painfully the people wait
For the news by flying car,
Eager for the battle's fate,
And the aspect of the war.

Although it cannot be proved, the author, "S," may well have been Sarah Morewood, even though she was in New York City at the time of publication. She often wrote for the *Sun,* never under her own name. Perhaps the best evidence that she wrote it, and that Herman began his war poetry at this time, is the fact that he adapted the last line as the subtitle, "Aspects of the War," of his book.[28]

It was also a likely time for him to have written "Inscription for the Slain at Fredericksburgh" (404), the only one of his war poems that was certainly composed in the midst of the long struggle. That it dates from this early time is suggested by the fact that he did not include it in *Battle-Pieces*—or in any other book—as though he decided that, as an apprentice piece, it did not belong in his works. Just before Fredericksburg, Emerson had written Thomas Carlyle, "Here we read no books. The war is our sole and doleful instructor."[29] In this poem, Herman was learning from that instructor.

The immediacy of his reaction to the battle and perhaps a touch of undigested emotion are betrayed in this brief stanza, which is a telling amalgam of sturdy Melville verse and a conventionality that allies it with the newspaper poetry of the day:

A glory lights an earnest end;
In jubilee the patriot ghosts ascend.
Transfigured at the rapturous height
Of their passionate feat of arms,
Death to the brave's a starry night,—
Strown their vale of death with palms.

It is surprising to find here a Michael conception of "glory" and an ascent of the ghosts of patriot soldiers as they are raptured in jubilation—itself enough to ban the poem from the "Verses Inscriptive and Memorial" section of *Battle-Pieces*. It is perhaps equally surprising to find amid this conventionality a fresh metaphor: "Death to the brave's a starry night." Yet charity suggests that Herman must have been hard-pressed to find an idea with which to respond to an abominable waste of life other than to assert that the earnestness and passion of the men who were "transfigured" were valuable wartime qualities. In *Battle-Pieces,* the gates of heaven do not open for the Union dead; nevertheless, it would be unwise to ignore the possibility that at this point in the war Herman genuinely meant what he wrote, that the ideas of glory and a caring God here suggested had not yet been expunged by sad experience. If that is true, then this poem shows what *Battle-Pieces* might have been had the war ended at Fredericksburg. But unsuitable for his book as it was, the poem was not wasted. When he wrote "Chattanooga," he recast it as the closing lines of that poem.[30]

Retrospectively, it would seem, he wrote a different poem about the battle, "Inscription for Marye's Heights, Fredericksburg." In it there is no glory or rapture, but tribute to those who followed "the heavenly flag" into the "deathful tumult." It is a more suitable, more modest epitaph that honors the soldiers for their fidelity rather than for a supposed heavenly reward that they might receive—the "heavenly" flag here being one containing the stars of the union. Through that fidelity, they won not victory but the greater merit of persistence in adversity.

Groaning Abe Lincoln

Despite Herman's new energy and purpose, the spirit of the new year was lowering. The Emancipation Proclamation had damaged the esprit of the army. Men who had volunteered for the sole purpose of preserving the union—nine out of ten, it has been estimated[31]—were now required, without their consent, to fight for another, the freedom of the slaves. Although radical soldiers were gratified by the change, conservatives believed that they had been swindled. Not only that, but few of any persuasion were happy with the experiment of appointing commanders because Lincoln liked them rather than because they were competent.

With no McClellan present to set and demand high standards of professionalism, officers of high rank in the Army of the Potomac openly declared that they would never have participated in the war had they known that it would be transformed into a crusade for emancipation. The same feeling extended through all ranks. Early in the year, the men of the Harvard Regiment passed their time "groaning Abe Lincoln and cheering Jeff Davis in the most vociferous manner." Others groaned with their heels: family and friends sent civilian clothes for soldiers to wear when they deserted, and in a week the army lost as many men as were killed in any battle. Adding soldiers who went home legally, half of the army, officer and enlisted, was absent. After visiting the Army of the Potomac, one senator estimated that about one quarter of the officers were missing.[32]

Still anxious to satisfy Lincoln, Burnside committed a second blunder, an attempt to attack Lee in the winter weather. When he went on the offensive on January twentieth and twenty-first, his "Mud March" mired his army so miserably that it took Henry's battery two days to haul its cannon back to camp, and during the humiliating maneuver the Confederates across the river brandished a plank with "Burnside stuck in the Mud" painted on it. A battery-mate wrote Henry, "it beat anything I ever saw."[33]

The moral deterioration of the Army of the Potomac was exacerbated by Burnside's vindictiveness. After the Mud March, he demanded the dismissal of several generals, including Joe Hooker, for disloyalty. Alternatively, he asked that his own resignation be accepted. Lincoln wisely accepted it, persuading him to continue on active duty in command of the Army of the Ohio. Although Burnside's removal brought loud calls from the Democrats for the restoration of McClellan, Lincoln appointed Joe Hooker to the job. Under "Fighting Joe," who was popular and not without charisma, morale revived.

One of the absent officers was Henry Gansevoort. He felt well enough to return to his battery, but he did not do it. He had had enough of close-range combat with screeching rebels; he confessed that although battle had excited him, he did not "hanker" after it anymore. But there was another reason. He wanted leave from the regulars in order to obtain a high rank in the volunteers. Now, with Governor Seymour in office, almost anything was possible for a Gansevoort. His comrades on the field did not criticize his failure to return. A battery mate wrote cynically, "if you will take my advice, you will continue to do so for some time—if *you can safely do it.*" Again and again, Henry misled his family into believing that he was returning to field duty, but instead he arranged a temporary assignment with his regiment at Fort Hamilton, on the Brooklyn side of the Narrows, and explained to his father that his health was not *wholly* improved. The army was in winter quarters, he said; if an offensive were to take place he would hear of it in plenty of time to return. But in truth he meant to find a volunteer commission before that time came. Bruce warned him to move quickly, and Abram Wakeman promised to help in any way that he could. General Dix was expected to be reassigned to New York City, and he would honor a request for assistance from Peter.[34]

During his time at Fort Hamilton, Henry enjoyed himself with Bruce and Allan and with less respectable society. He found one Englishwoman, Eleanor Wilson, who gratified his sexual desires. To protect his anonymity, he told her that his name was George Henry Brewster, though he later revealed his true identity. Eleanor was accustomed to such deceptions: "It is nothing strange to me to have *beaus so tell Me*." She had a confession of her own to make. She actually sympathized with the South, she said, though she stopped short of complete candor, as Henry's health soon proved.[35]

Partyism

What was true in the army was no less true in civil life. The Emancipation Proclamation caused the partisanship of the preceding year to mature into open hostility. The radicals were overjoyed. George William Curtis spoke for them when he said that "There are now none but slavery and anti-slavery men in the country." Emerson thought that every intelligent person must now become an abolitionist: "Our best ground of hope now is in the healthy sentiment which appears in reasonable people all over the country, accepting sacrifices, but meaning riddance from slavery, & from Southern domination." But Hawthorne had a different opinion: "Emerson is as merciless as a steel bayonet." Neither Curtis nor Emerson took into account the legitimacy of a third attitude, the union-first advocacy of a man like Herman, whose antislavery sentiments, though strong, were subordinate. In truth, Herman must have been happy with the prospect of emancipation, provided it was compatible with the restoration of the union, but that did not make him an abolitionist.[36]

The discontent of conservatives flowered into rage. Far from being won over to Emerson's point of view, they were quick to end any semblance of no-partyism. Hawthorne spoke openly of "such a miserable Administration as this." His ire was not directed toward Lincoln, "an honest man, I do believe, but with extra folly enough to make up for his singular lack of knavery," but toward those who served him. "I do not care a fig what powers the President assumes, . . . if he only used them effectually," he wrote, "but I must say that I despise the present administration with all my heart." He told his abolitionist sister-in-law, Elizabeth Peabody, that "you cannot possibly conceive (looking through spectacles of the tint which yours have acquired) how little the North really cares for the negro-question, and how eagerly it would grasp at peace if recommended by a delusive show of victory." His heterodoxy earned him the distrust of the radicals. "The war-party here do not look upon me as a reliably loyal man," he complained, "and, in fact, I have been publicly accused of treasonable sympathies."[37]

Hawthorne possessed a rare moral courage, as he demonstrated in his dedication of *Our Old Home* to the patriotism of Franklin Pierce. By this time, Pierce was anathema to the radicals, who damned him as a traitor.

When Hawthorne delivered the dedication to his publisher, James T. Fields, he faced a brutal test. After consulting with Emerson and Longfellow, Fields warned him that his praise of Pierce would ruin sales. Ellery Channing went so far as to persuade Elizabeth Peabody to give him a packet of newspaper clippings attacking Pierce. But although Hawthorne made slight revisions in the dedication, he left its spirit intact. He refused to bow to intimidation when loyalty to a friend was involved: "If he [Pierce] is so exceedingly unpopular that his name is enough to sink the volume, there is so much the more need that an old friend should stand by him. I cannot, merely on account of pecuniary profit or literary reputation, go back from what I have deliberately felt and thought it right to do; and if I were to tear out the dedication, I should never look at the volume again without remorse and shame."[38]

It was Hawthorne's finest hour, but the price was high. During August 1863, the Northern press published a report that there had been secret correspondence between Pierce and Jeff Davis which proved that for years he had conspired in the rebellion. It was a malignant but often imitated attempt to implicate the political opposition in an invented conspiracy that explained a national misfortune. Unfortunately, the scandal appeared just when it was most likely to poison the reception of Hawthorne's book. Charles Eliot Norton was quick to condemn the "dedication to F. Pierce,—the correspondent of Jefferson Davis, the flatterer of traitors, and the emissary of treason." Harriet Beecher Stowe wrote Fields, "Do tell me if our friend Hawthorne praises that arch traitor Pierce in his preface & your loyal firm publishes it. . . . I can scarcely believe it of you—if I can of him. I regret that I went to see him last summer—what! patronise such a traitor to our faces!—I can scarcely believe it." Much of the press denounced the book and *Harper's Weekly* complained about its "tone of doubt and indifference" toward the war, even though the book itself had nothing to do with that topic.[39]

Herman was inundated by furious expressions of partisan anger in the *Sun*. The paper caricatured abolitionists as having "long beards; lean, lank, and blank faces; slip-shod blue stockings; the wild, strange, indescribable air of the spiritualists, fourierites, free-lovers and transcendentalists run to seed"—as the descendants of the old cone-hatted Puritans, in short. It also published "A Plain Epistle to Uncle Abe" by an anonymous Berkshire poet who told Lincoln, among other things, that

Our mothers love their absent sons,
  Our wives their husbands true,
But no one cares a mouldy fig
  For Cuffy or for you

—Cuffy being a generic and unflattering denomination of the black man. He continued his diatribe with suggestions for some of the administration officers:

Send Stanton to the Feejee Isles,
  Give Welles and Chase the sack,
Swap Halleck for a Hottentot,
  And send for LITTLE MAC.[40]

Herman's family demonstrated the same partisanship, though they were careful not to wound feelings. Following Governor Seymour's inauguration and a subsequent brawl in the assembly over the selection of a speaker, Helen Griggs wrote her sisters in Gansevoort:

> Are you not ashamed of the proceedings in Albany? The whole country is crying shame upon the uncivilized mob law which holds it[s] own, without let or hindrance, at the *seat* of *Government,* forsooth. . . . I blush for my birthplace, & doubt the patriotism of Governor Seymour. A cause must be bad, which calls ruffians and rowdies to aid it, by threats and insults to peaceable men. Honesty & Truth are self reliant self-sustaining. Mere clamor, noise, and *bullying,* (if I may be allowed to use such an unfeminine word) never helped even a bad cause, & were never yet called in to aid a good one.

Gus and Fanny must have sighed, since such disorders were not uncommon and since Helen would probably have overlooked this one had it featured Republicans, but their sister could not be blamed. Her attitudes were those of her husband. Like Lizzie, most women did not *have* political opinions of their own—it was unladylike—but articulated those of their husbands or fathers or brothers.[41]

On the other side, Kate Gansevoort wrote Henry that Lincoln disgusted her with his uncouth jokes, but it was emancipation that bothered her most. "If we do not unite soon, & leave the Nigger alone," she wrote Henry, "we shall be a bye word to the world." Apparently, she was replying to Henry's analysis of the nation's woes: "There is a demoralization in our army principally apologised for by the demoralization of the Capital. . . . politicians are illustrating the depravity of man in all our capitals while patriotism is sneered at as a virtue of humble growth."[42]

The anger of the conservatives was rooted in more than the evil of emancipation alone. They were still incensed by the seemingly political dismissal of McClellan, the administration's suppression of civil rights, the failure of the army in the east under Lincoln's general, and a disastrous disagreement about what actions and attitudes the opposition party was entitled to. What was patriotic, and who was a patriot? Was it patriotic to support the administration, or was it patriotic to stand firm by the values on which the nation had been founded, as one understood them? One answer was supplied by the Union League clubs, political organizations formed by Republicans and War Democrats beginning in early 1862. According to one pamphlet published by their Loyal Publication Society, loyalty to the nation required that one support the contemplated draft, support emancipation, support the government's suspension of civil liberties, support the government against those who claimed to be neutral, and support the total conquest of the South. Had this been the opinion of a group of extremists, it might have been dismissed as such, but there was evidence that it was government policy, especially when Lincoln stated that anyone who did not speak out in favor of the government was supporting the Confederates.[43]

Despite Richard Lathers's work on behalf of the war, such criteria left him vulnerable to charges of disloyalty. One morning early in 1863, a three-man committee, headed by a leading member of the Union League Club, Lathers's friend Moses Grinnell, stopped by his office with a League affidavit of unconditional loyalty to the government. As a result of public dissatisfaction with the conduct of the war, which put the financial community at risk, they explained, the affidavit was being circulated. But Lathers would not sign. To do so, he argued, would be to impugn his loyalty by admitting that it required affirmation. Grinnell then remarked to the others, "I told you he would make a damned ingenious excuse, but that he would not sign the pledge."[44]

The most striking incident occurred in the west. In an odd, random way, Clara Nourse, the unmarried daughter of Uncle Amos, was associated with it. With her little niece Jeanie, she was living in Cincinnati, Ohio, in a large house in which she conducted a successful school. In March 1863 she fell ill, her condition so worrisome that her sister Mary, Jeanie's mother, hastened to Cincinnati to nurse her. Finally, Clara gave up, dismissed her students, leased her house to General Burnside and his staff, and went to Pittsfield to recover.[45]

Burnside commanded the Department of the Ohio as though he were the military governor of an occupied enemy territory. Shortly after his arrival in Cincinnati, he put into effect a Draconian regulation which provided punishments of death or exile for spies, traitors, and other persons who gave aid and comfort to the enemy. Anyone who so much as expressed sympathy with the South, which was "implied treason," was an offender. This raised the question of whether or not a person were culpable if he did no more than to advocate Democratic party principles. Clement L. Vallandigham, late congressman, principal Democratic candidate for the governorship of Ohio, and leading spokesman for the party in the west, stepped forward to test the order. Before he did, he visited Albany to consult with Governor Seymour and the other Democratic leaders there, including, perhaps, Uncle Peter. Then he returned home to put his opposition into practice.[46]

Since the beginning of the war, Vallandigham had opposed administration policies, but he stood firmly in favor of legal, nonviolent protest. In the present instance, he publicly stated his opposition to the war and to Burnside's order, adding that the administration had opposed a peaceful resolution of the conflict in order to pursue its abolitionist agenda. For that, Burnside arrested him and, since habeas corpus had been suspended, tried him before a military court which convicted him and sentenced him to imprisonment. Despite his protest that his case fell under the jurisdiction of the civil courts, the U.S. circuit court and the Supreme Court upheld the conviction. Lincoln changed his sentence to exile and had him delivered to Richmond, but at the first opportunity he moved to Canada, where he lived in Niagara Falls, just across the border, during the remainder of the war.

Vallandigham's conviction aroused widespread protests and caused some riots. To Democrats and to some high-principled Republicans, such as George William Curtis and Horace Greeley, Burnside had unnecessarily abrogated Vallandigham's civil rights. Most New York City newspapers agreed, the *World* deploring Burnside's "drumhead law." For this, some newspapers were proscribed and banned from the mails—the office of the *Chicago Times* was seized by Burnside's soldiers. Many citizens believed that such actions were more dangerous to the nation than were the Confederate armies. In the terms of *Battle-Pieces,* the iron dome was in danger of rusting.[47]

There were Democratic mass meetings across the North, the Albany meeting on May 16 being one of the largest of the kind in the history of the city. An appeal to Lincoln was adopted by acclamation and cosigned by party leaders, including Uncle Peter. It reminded Lincoln of the Democrats' loyal support of the war, both in men and in treasure, and of their intention to continue that support. However, it insisted that under the Constitution the civil authority took precedence over the military, and for that reason it condemned the persecution of Vallandigham. In his response, Lincoln claimed that he sought the same ends as the Democrats and that he had done nothing wrong. He did not brook opposition to the administration: "The man who stands by and says nothing when the peril of his government is discussed" "is sure to help the enemy; much more if he talks ambiguously—talks for his country with 'buts,' and 'ifs,' and 'ands.'" He defended drumhead justice for civilians. Had he arrested Southerners for expressing their intentions to commit treason early in the war, he said, he could have deprived the Confederates of the services of Generals Lee, Joseph Johnston, Breckinridge, and others, and of Commodore Franklin Buchanan. Vallandigham, he claimed, had attempted in his speech both to hinder recruiting and to encourage servicemen to desert; he could not punish a deserter and not punish the man who had encouraged him. It was a forceful but inappropriate response, since Vallandigham had not expressed any intention to commit treason and had not encouraged soldiers to desert, and it was ominously in agreement with the farfetched Union League definition of disloyalty and cynical belief that civil liberties were sacrosanct except when they were inexpedient.[48]

Swapping Places

Despite the woes of the Army of the Potomac and the vitriolic collapse of public civility, during this period Herman's family maintained a degree of normalcy. The attention of most of them, particularly on the Melville side, turned to portrait photography. In a sudden assault, the fad captured them, and they surrendered unconditionally. Everyone was sending photos to everyone else—almost—Henry Gansevoort, the Downers, the Latherses, the Allan Melvilles, the Griggses (although George was resisting), the Curtises, and the D'Wolfs. Kate Hoadley even sent one to Aunt Mary in Galena, and Kate Gansevoort distributed photographs of the Gilbert Stuart portraits of Grandmother and Grandfather Gansevoort. The most seriously wounded was Fanny, who decided to put together a comprehensive album for Tom to carry with him on his next voyage. Herman seems to have been allied to George Griggs in the resistance movement, but he had the excuse that he had had his portrait taken in 1861, and perhaps that was recent enough to satisfy his relatives.[49]

Nevertheless, the financial burdens of the war, including inflation and taxes, affected the whole family. In mid-1863, retail prices were up 43 percent from 1860. Helen Griggs wrote that fabrics were very expensive, all over a dollar a yard, and that the clerks in the stores simply muttered "*War prices;* War prices!" Among the women in Gansevoort, the problem became acute. With Uncle Peter's refusal to part with his share of Wessel's annuity, the money that Tom sent did not go far enough. They needed to make repairs to the barn, the mill, and the fences, and the helper, Mr. Sadler, had decided to quit. Lemuel Shaw sent the women a small amount of money, their share of Aunt Priscilla's estate, but that was only enough for the property tax, a special levy to pay bonuses and other military expenses. "*Taxes are heavy & purse light,*" Fanny moaned.[50]

It did no good to humiliate Herman by asking him for money, so his mother and sisters blamed Allan. When he failed to answer their letters, they complained throughout the family: "I would like to give this brother of ours a good shaking, he richly deserves something of the sort," Fanny wrote. "I have no patience with him." Allan defended himself through an intermediary, Helen Griggs. He "thinks you are very hard on him to accuse him of neglect because he don't write," she explained. "He says he is so tired at night, what with his business, and the excitement of politics & the war, he is too exhausted to do anything." When Allan did write, he said nothing about "The Repairs," which had become the litmus test for filial and fraternal devotion. Defeated, Allan sent a note scrawled on a scrap of paper giving June as the earliest date for beginning work.[51]

Life in Gansevoort was far better socially than it was economically. During the winter, the women there saw a great deal of the Glens Falls family, including a long visit by Mother Melville to the Curtises in February. Leonard Gansevoort was ill, Mattie Curtis was home on vacation from her school in Saratoga Springs, and Mary, weary of life in Brooklyn, returned to Glens Falls. "*Bully* for our Mountain home," George Curtis gloated about the victory over the big city. The news was that because of ill health Ned Curtis had resigned from the navy. In due time it was accepted, effective February 11, 1863, but conditional on his relief from his duties aboard the *Sciota*. When she heard that, Kate looked ten years younger, Fanny reported.[52]

With his newfound vigor and confidence, Herman was taking decisive steps to move back to New York City. Aunt Priscilla's bequest of $900, added to Lizzie's inheritance, made the move financially possible regardless of what was done about the farm. He wanted to talk to Allan about the trade for Arrowhead, but he was feeling his oats and wanted to visit the city anyway, just to be there. There were plausible excuses for going, including school supplies for Bessie.[53] Probably the Pittsfield stores could have furnished whatever Bessie needed, but about the first of February he packed up his rationalizations and took them with him.

His visit with the Allan Melvilles was lengthy, two weeks, it would appear, and enjoyable, even though Allan was not well. Allan must have been full of denunciations of the Lincoln administration and praise of the new Seymour governorship, but Herman had not come for that. During the visit the two brothers reached an understanding about Arrowhead. Jennie and Allan had contemplated the purchase of a summer residence of their own in New Rochelle, but the Pittsfield alternative was as good or better. Herman (or, to be legally correct, Lizzie) would take a house that Allan owned in the city in exchange for the farm, assuming the mortgage of $2,000 held by Mrs. Thurston and adding $7,750 to make up the difference in value. Herman and Lizzie would refurbish the house at their own expense, and Allan and Jennie would make whatever repairs and alterations they desired at Arrowhead at their expense. To formalize the exchange, Sam Shaw would draw up the necessary legal documents. Both men were satisfied. Herman's desire to return to the city amounted to more than mere homesickness. With the romance of anticipation that colors plans for the future, he looked back to his days before the writing of *Moby-Dick,* when he had enjoyed family, friends, and success there, as a measure of the times to come. Allan, who had lived in the city during his entire adult life and had commuted to his office from his various summer vacation retreats, envied Herman's hill country farm and looked forward to pastoral summers there.[54]

While in the city, Herman also saw his artillerist cousin several times. When Henry visited Allan's house on Saturday, February seventh, he saw the young hero in uniform and heard him tell of his experiences for the first time since the beginning of the war. ("He looked well and war-like," Herman wrote Kate Gansevoort, "cheerfully embarked in the career of immortality.") Something of what Henry told Herman can be inferred from what he was writing his sister at about the same time. The mud-march had demonstrated that McClellan had been correct in desiring to go into winter quarters, he said. "You see that my prophecy regarding the Army of the Potomac has been fulfilled. They cannot move. The change of Generals [to Hooker] I hope will be for the better altho' there is but little genius in the military shambles."[55]

But an oppressive amount of the conversation must have been about his desire for a volunteer commission, since that was the topic that was consuming him. To that Herman would have listened with outward cordiality and inner doubt. The maneuvers for personal gain and the tangled stratagems for achieving it that he saw in soldiers like Henry conflicted with his admiration for forthrightness and purity of motive. This generation of young heroes did not fight solely for higher principles, which was the only justification for this or any war. Instead, they adulterated the tradition of patriotism that they had inherited from the Founding Fathers[56] with an ambition that corroded and corrupted the nation as well as themselves. Herman could only hope that such motives would not characterize the new order that was coming. Perhaps Henry never realized that Herman used his flaw as an ingredient in his longest poem about the war, "The Scout toward Aldie," used it, as always in his works, with a humane understanding that could not wholly conceal his disapproval. Nevertheless, Herman liked his cousin and in other ways admired him. Ambiguous that attitude may have been, but Henry was a hero and, when not swaddled in his egotism, a good fellow.

Little else of what Herman did during these two weeks is known, but he must have spent some time inspecting the new house and visiting with Mrs. Thurston to discuss the assumption of her mortgage, and he could hardly have avoided seeing the de Marinis. Very likely, he also visited with Bruce, the Morewoods, and some of his literary friends. On one occasion, he demonstrated his newfound physical endurance by walking the distance from Trinity Church to Allan's home, perhaps on Sunday, the eighth of February. He also saw Henry again at dinner at Allan's house, probably the same day, and saw him on yet another occasion. Henry invited the Melvilles to visit Fort Hamilton, which they did on the weekend before Herman's return to Pittsfield—Saturday, the fourteenth. Jennie, Allan, and Herman made the two-hour journey to the fort, where Henry received them in the manner of a representative of the United States Army. He gave them the official tour of the installation, the ramparts, the guns, the quarters, in short, what the fort had to offer the uninitiated. The tour lacked the tragic interest of Herman's visit to the Brooklyn Navy Yard a year and a half earlier, but it was his first opportunity to see disciplined and hardened soldiers, in contrast to the recruits who trained at Pittsfield. Then, carrying Bessie's school supplies, he took the train home.[57]

While Herman had been away, Fanny and Bessie had been enjoying an unexpected two-week vacation from school. Despite the temperate weather, they occupied themselves by pulling each other on sleds, one day dropping in on Mrs. Colt. Lizzie was brooding over the fact that she had not visited her mother since the Christmas of 1861 and the fact that in the city she would be even farther away. "I do not think I shall ever be able to leave home again without some one here to over look things, and be company for Herman," she mourned. Her worry was about the children. "I cannot leave them and Herman alone—there were such 'goings-on' [the] last time I left them [and] *then* the boys were [no]t at home—and in the village it would be still worse." Her concern was that when Herman was preoccupied, wandering in his inner world, discipline lapsed.[58]

Gus had offered to stay with Herman sometime in order to make such a visit possible, and now Lizzie grasped at that straw. Some haggling ensued, in which Lizzie insisted that Gus come earlier than she wanted to, arguing that the visit to Boston must be made before the allergy season. In the middle of the negotiations, Helen Griggs intervened, suggesting that Lizzie bring the girls to stay with her and leave the boys with Herman. If Malcolm and Stanny were unable to stay with their father "without any startling outbreak of boyish outlawry," then "you had better send said boys to the House of Corrections." Eventually, Gus did agree to make a two-week visit, beginning on March eleventh. It was to this *fait accompli* that Herman returned.[59]

Soon Sam Shaw appeared at Allan's home to discuss the property transfer and, probably, to draw up the necessary documents. On Friday, the twentieth of February, he saw Henry, who came from Fort Hamilton through a snowstorm to dine there, and the de Marinis. On the twenty-fifth, Sam took the train to Pittsfield, where he completed the legal transaction before returning to Boston on the twenty-seventh.[60]

Herman was prompt in writing cheerful letters to the family about his visit to the city. A week and a half later, he sent the boys off to see Rumsey's Minstrels at West's Hall. The boys noticed that the performers were not black men but white men painted black, and Stanny was especially tickled by a joke about a dog that could add: "Why you see he is lame in one leg, and he puts down three, and carries one." Shortly after this, the notorious Madame Dombrowski was apprehended in Pennsylvania and returned to Pittsfield, where she was bound over in Police Court. Eventually Mr. Chapman's horse and buggy were returned to him. The following week was Malcolm's vacation, although he had to perform on stage at West's Hall, where the annual examination of Pittsfield high school students was held. The Sunday before Lizzie's departure, a severe storm, the worst of the season, inundated the town with a foot and a half of snow. That was enough to discourage most of the family from attending church, but Herman braved the weather with Malcolm. It would appear that Gus arrived on schedule, perhaps bringing some buckwheat Herman had requested, since, he said, there was nothing as good to be had locally. Lizzie must have been packed and ready to leave when she arrived. Lizzie took Bessie, Fanny, and Stanny with her, leaving Malcolm, Gus, and Herman behind in the quiet house with only the maid, Mary, to keep them company. As Emerson might have put it, it was "wholesome" for Herman and Lizzie to spend some time apart.[61]

On the Saturday following Lizzie's departure, John Hoadley, who detoured through Pittsfield on his way home from the city, arrived. He was probably breathing radical fire, but his main preoccupation was with his domestic situation. With the sickness that had prostrated their little girls for so long and the difficulty in hiring servants who would work in New Bedford, he and Kate were thinking about moving back to Lawrence. Then, on Tuesday, John left for Boston. In addition to John, Gus saw a number of the friends she had known when she had lived at Arrowhead. At home, she kept Herman company, listened to Malcolm's recitations—and gave him lessons in piety and diligence. She was threatened with housework when the maid, Mary, fell ill, but fortunately Mary's daughter filled in. For Herman, Gus's visit prevented the loneliness that he feared, while the depletion of his household rendered life more placid than usual. He always enjoyed "Miss Gusty," as Mary called her.[62]

The leave of absence was all Lizzie had hoped. Stanny, who still looked peaked from his whooping cough, stayed with his grandmother, while, as Helen Griggs had suggested, the girls were dispatched to Brookline, where Helen now had a rented house to herself. When Carrie, Oakes Shaw's wife, brought Oakie and Josie over to see Stanny, Oakie lured Stanny away on a four-hour lark that would have reduced modern parents to despair. The two wandered down to the wharves, visited Uncle Lem's office and Uncle Sam's, and finally trudged to the post office and other landmarks for young tourists. They even tried to climb to the top of the state house, but found that it was closed. Several days later, Lizzie and Carrie took the two boys to Brookline. Helen had the foresight to invite her nephew, Willie Griggs, to play with them, since Willie, who was just Fanny's age, knew where the local hilarity was to be found. The boys were, as Helen put it, "uproarious." Helen made them all a good dinner, omitting side dishes and dessert, "Being war-times," and afterward, as George left the house, the children screamed "Old Grandfather Stove Pipe" at him and pelted him with snowballs. George defended himself with snowballs of his own, but he was forced to withdraw to save his endangered hat. Back in Boston, Stanny distinguished himself by wallowing in a frog pond. Had he behaved with this abandon while Herman had been minding him, Lizzie would have blamed her husband mightily.[63]

After Lizzie's reluctant return to Pittsfield and Gus's departure, Mary, who was still ill, threatened to quit, but after Lizzie nursed her on bourbon and bitters she decided to remain awhile longer, a dubious blessing, Lizzie thought. After their return to school, Stanny and Malcolm decided that they wanted to collect stamps, not yet a popular hobby, and wrote Gus to save either foreign or revenue stamps for them. Lizzie had been back less than a week when an unusual display of northern lights appeared over Pittsfield, followed by a long streak of light arched across the heavens from east to west. As if there had not been omens and portents enough![64]

Familiar Faces in the West

Doctor Henry Thurston had for several months been back on General Rosecrans's staff in Nashville and Toby Greene was still on French leave with the 11th Illinois. Henry Pease's regiment was still in Louisiana, where it was relatively disengaged from the fighting, and Jeff and John Hobart were still members of the 44th Illinois, the former in name only.

Toward the end of December 1862, General Rosecrans marched his army from Nashville toward Murfreesboro, Tennessee, near which he met General Braxton Bragg's much smaller Confederate force. Bragg's preemptive attack initiated a bloody three-day battle in which, while holding their ground with obstinacy, all of Sheridan's brigade commanders were killed and his division was shredded. The 44th Illinois fought with Sheridan's division, though once again it was led by a company commander. After mauling the Union force, the Confederates retired, leaving Rosecrans to console himself by occupying Murfreesboro.

Herman may have believed that all three Hobart men had fought in the battle, but that was not his only motive for writing "Battle of Stone River, Tennessee: A View from Oxford Cloisters (January, 1863)," which gives no details of the fighting but says much about various matters that it suggested. The name "Rosecrans" inspired him to invoke the English War of the Roses, another fratricidal struggle that was bound to find a place in *Battle-Pieces*. The historical allusion is given meaning through a most unusual narrative point of view, that of an inhabitant of Oxford, England, who compares Stone River to the battles at Tewksbury and Barnett Heath, fought four centuries earlier. What deceived men in the War of the Roses, the narrator says, continued to deceive them in the Battle of Stone River. "Yorkist and Lancastrian" fought for political dominance disguised as theological right—the Michael fallacy. In order to arouse the passions of a holy crusade, both sides exploited the symbols of religion, thus shaming the faith under whose emblems they fought:

Our rival Roses warred for sway—
  For Sway, but named the name of Right;
And Passion, scorning pain and death,
  Lent sacred fervor to the fight.
Each lifted up a broidered cross,
  While crossing blades profaned the sign;
Monks blessed the fratricidal lance,
  And sisters scarfs could twine.
    Do North and South the sin retain
    Of Yorkist and Lancastrian?

An abomination of the England of long ago has been renewed in the present of America.

That motif leads to the most remarkable aspect of the poem when "Dark Breckinridge" is named as the opponent of Rosecrans, even though he was actually a subordinate commander. That was because to Herman he was the most important Confederate present. As at Baton Rouge, this former senator, vice-president, and presidential candidate of the United States had made war on the nation he had served long, faithfully, and well. Just before the war, Herman had seen Breckinridge on the floor of the Senate, clinging to his loyalty to the Union long after most other Southerners had abandoned theirs. Probably some family members—certainly Richard Lathers—had voted for Breckinridge for president. In the context of American fighting American, the fact that Breckinridge commanded enemy forces made him one of those "dark" figures, like Benito Cereno, who fascinated Herman. Herman was more interested in the dilemma faced by such Southerners, their entrapment in a moral quicksand of mutually exclusive fidelities that brought them face to face with the blackness of darkness, than he was in the fact of their apostasy.

Had Herman been a narrower partisan, he might have used the poem to accuse Breckinridge of treason. But that would have been short sighted, for, as the poem asks, "Shall North and South their rage deplore, / And reunited thrive amain / Like Yorkist and Lancastrian?" Such a reunification became more difficult when one of the South's most eminent men was condemned as a traitor and when each side claimed to fight for the right against the other's wrong. If that were to continue to be the case, how could brothers be brought together once more? Regardless, the nation must be reunited and the memory of Stone River must fade. The pauses in the battle-forest of man's depravity foretell a future quiet. Already the battle is becoming the distant stuff of legend, like the events of the War of the Roses, "a Druid-dream" as it "assumes the haziness of years." "The story dim and date obscure; / In legend all shall end," and the generals "shall fade away / Or thinly loom." The hope for the future lies in the conspiracy of Nature and Memory to mitigate, as at Donelson, Shiloh, and Malvern Hill, the memories.

Following that battle, Jeff Hobart reappeared in the camp of the 44th Illinois and submitted his resignation on the condition that all charges against him be dropped. His grounds for resigning were that General Sheridan had made statements "reflecting severely upon my character as an officer." Sheridan demonstrated what Jeff meant by leaving in Jeff's record two endorsements, one that said that he was "worthless and an eyesore," and the other that he was "worthless untruthful without *brains* or *vim*." A civilian at last, Jeff returned to Rockford for good, taking John with him.[65]

Other than this battle, there were no military events in the west prominent enough to merit Herman's poetic attention, but he did find one suggestive incident. It involved the continuing effort by the Union forces to secure the Mississippi River for navigation and by the Confederates to frustrate them. The attention of both was focussed on Vicksburg, where the narrowness of the river, its loop, and the height of its cliffs on the Mississippi side gave deadly ranks of Confederate cannon command of its waters. The fact that Robert Melvill's riverboat was engaged in transporting supplies to the area gave Herman a special reason for noticing that contest.

From time to time the navy ran ships past these batteries, a hazardous measure, but necessary to provide transportation across the river for Grant's army to the south. Although there were several such passages, the one that attracted Herman's attention occurred on the night of April 16, 1863, when Admiral Porter steamed seven ironclads, a ram, and three transports, each with a coal barge in tow and each protected by bales of cotton lashed to its sides, past the guns. With a gala ball in progress in the city,[66] the gunners ashore did not detect the vessels until they were abreast of them, but then they opened with their cannon. All of the ships were damaged, but with only one lost the maneuver was considered a success.

In personal terms, "Running the Batteries, As observed from the Anchorage above Vicksburgh (April, 1863)" commemorates the river service of men like Ned Curtis and Robert Melvill as well as honoring the bravery of Admiral Porter, "a brave man's son." By mentioning the "brave man," Herman also honored the father of the admiral, Commodore David Porter of the old days of oaken frigates. The older Porter, one of those "heart of oak" sailors who lived on in Herman's esteem, had won fame in battles against the Barbary pirates and, in the War of 1812, against the English. Herman had made extensive use of his *Journal of a Cruise Made to the Pacific Ocean, in the U.S. Frigate Essex, in the Years 1812, 1813, and 1814* in both *Typee* and "The Encantadas."[67]

In its form, "Running the Batteries" is the precise opposite of "Battle of Stone River" in that it is a narrative of the action on which it is based. Told in retrospect by one of several fictional seamen who watch the event from a distance, it is skillful in its evocation of the suspense while the ships attempted to steal past the battery and of the excitement of the duel that followed. Yet the poem is also a companion piece to "The Battle for the Mississippi." While the latter alludes to the Egyptian captivity of the Israelites, this poem alludes to the Babylonian captivity. Thus when taken together the two poems have the effect of marking the Mississippi River as a freedom route and a pathway out of slavery. Yet the biblical allusion is again ironic. When one sailor refers to the Confederate barrage as a "furnace," another responds, "Why, Shadrach, Meschach, and Abed-nego / Came out all right, we read; / The Lord, be sure, he helps his people, Ned." But when the biblical trio were cast into Nebuchadnezzar's furnace, a figure who appeared to be the Son of God protected them so that "the fire had no power, nor was an hair of their head singed, neither were their coats changed, nor the smell of fire had passed on them" (Dan. 3:21–27), while the Union ships and their men had no such protector and no such exemption from danger. Their survival was a result of their own skill and courage, and, though they were successful in their passage, that was not enough to save them from damage, casualties, and "the smell of fire."

Like "Battle of Stone River," the poem focuses on the Southerners as well as the Union men. When a fire is lit on the cliffs to illuminate the passing ships, one observer mistakenly believes that "The town is afire!" and, without thinking, he calls for "three cheers!" Another chastens him: "Nay, lad, better three tears." In war, where the object is to damage one's enemies, victory for one side is tragedy for the other. From the vantage point of the sailors,

> The effulgence takes an amber glow
>   Which bathes the hill-side villas far;
> Affrighted ladies mark the show
>   Painting the pale magnolia—

Behind the batteries lies a city full of innocent people, men, women, and children. Why should one cheer a fire that engulfs civilians and destroys their homes? The victory for the Union forces and the bravery of the crews of these ships were to be celebrated, but there should be no spirit of vindictiveness toward these other Americans. That would be a transformation of men into swine under the spell of "the fair, false, Circe light of cruel War."

Less than three months later, the Union army succeeded in opening the entire river. The passage of the batteries had been a preliminary element in Grant's plan to attack the city, which he proceeded to do. When his troops were arrayed against the Confederate defenses on May 18, Toby Greene's regiment was in the center of the line to the east of the city. That created a dilemma for him, since the 6th Missouri, the regiment from which he had deserted, was some distance to his right. There was always a chance that he might be recognized by one of his former comrades and apprehended as a deserter. On May 19, Grant ordered his soldiers forward against heavy fire, and on the twenty-second a general assault was mounted. Toby and his comrades almost attained their objective, but the resistance was too strong. A renewed attack was ordered, but without the success that might have justified the additional casualties. In this, Toby's first large-scale battle as a foot soldier, his colonel was killed while leading the brigade. Perhaps that shock helped him to decide to desert from his new regiment to return to the old one. As he may have seen it, he was not deserting but rather balancing the personnel books.[68]

After these assaults, Grant resorted to a siege. Finally, on July 4, the starving Confederates surrendered. It was one of the great Union victories of the war, one that inspired celebrations across the North, but Herman did not write a poem about it. As he indicated in "Running the Batteries," he could not approve of making war on civilians by reducing them to pathetic want. Tellingly, his only acknowledgement of the victory is in a later poem, "A Meditation," in which a magnanimous Northerner points out that "when Vicksburg fell, and the moody files marched out, / Silent the victors stood, scorning to raise a shout."

The final action in the struggle for the river occurred south of Vicksburg at Port Hudson, Louisiana, another point where passage by Union ships was interdicted by shore batteries. Here two regiments in which Herman was interested, the 14th Maine and the Berkshire Regiment, were in action. Perhaps he was also interested in the several Union regiments of black Louisiana troops, particularly the "Corps d'Afrique," that participated. The Berkshire Regiment arrived on May 24. The situation was similar to that of Vicksburg, with the Confederates well positioned and entrenched and, as at Vicksburg, on May 27 the Union soldiers attempted an assault. The terrain was difficult, choked with magnolias and underbrush and with ravines filled with tree trunks, making movement difficult and dangerous. Although Frank Bartlett opposed the assault and believed that it would fail, he led his regiment in the attack. Hobbled by his wooden leg, he went into action on horseback, the only mounted officer on the field. According to Confederate accounts, his conspicuous disregard for his own safety inspired the Southern officers to order their men not to shoot at him, but in the chaos of battle the order was impossible to obey. After the advance reached open ground, Bartlett was struck from his horse by one bullet that shattered his wrist and another that entered the right ankle of his good leg and exited through the sole of his foot, but he was not an exception. Among the casualties was Lieutenant Colonel Samuel Sumner, leaving the major, Charles Plunkett, in command for the rest of the regiment's term of active duty. Frank was carried from the field in an ambulance and sent by steamboat to Baton Rouge, where he was hospitalized.[69]

The assault had been unsuccessful and the army settled into a siege which continued until news arrived—just as another assault was imminent—of the fall of Vicksburg. Their position hopeless, the Confederate defenders surrendered on July 8. Despite his personal connections to the troops that took Port Hudson, Herman did not write a poem about the victory. As in the case of Vicksburg, success obtained through the privation and suffering by which sieges succeed, rather than through a frank contest between opposing armies, did not awaken his muse. Rather, he celebrated the opening of the

Mississippi River through poems about the doughty sailors who, challenging the Confederate batteries to do their worst, took command of the waters. That was the kind of warfare that Herman respected.

A Portrait of Jennie

At home, the remainder of the spring, the summer, and the early fall were filled with the kind of contentment that made Herman's life in Pittsfield less burdensome than it often was. Had it always been thus, he would have had less reason to move back to New York City. In mid-April, he paid another brief visit to Allan. He just missed seeing Richard Lathers, who, early in the month, had left the country for England and Europe. Richard planned to open branches of his insurance firm in European port cities, but that was not the only reason for his trip. With his loyalty continually suspect, he intended to address influential groups throughout Europe, but especially in England, to counter the sympathy toward the South and the hostility toward the North that continued to undermine the interests of the Union. He carried letters from Secretary of State Seward to Charles Francis Adams in London and to the U.S. ministers in France, Belgium, and Switzerland.[70]

With Richard absent from New Rochelle during the summer, Allan had every reason to try out his new vacation home in Pittsfield. Probably Herman encouraged the idea, seeing himself as a beneficiary of Allan's presence, and volunteered his services and Lizzie's in making Arrowhead habitable. He may also have given his new home another inspection, since it would require work before it would be ready for his family. After Herman's return to Pittsfield, Rowland Morewood stayed with him for a few days while Broadhall was being readied for the summer.[71]

In Glens Falls, Mary Curtis reported that Helen Griggs was trying to convince Kate Curtis to visit her, but that was difficult to do. Both her brother and her husband were recovering from illnesses, Leonard from dropsy and George from a lame back, and Kate herself was, as usual, ailing. But regardless of any other consideration, nothing could have enticed her to leave home until after Ned returned from the navy. Although at the beginning of May she was looking for him any day, he did not reach Glens Falls until the beginning of June—bringing her joy and relief, nevertheless. In Gansevoort, Tom's boxes of presents, which Allan had forwarded from New York City, arrived. As usual, there was a selection of exotic objects from the East, a dress, tea, a cabinet, a work box, fruit dishes, and ten idols. Another arrival was Herman's announcement that he intended to move to the city in the fall. "Herman . . . is not the first man who has been beguiled into the country," Mother Melville philosophized, "& found out by experience that it was not the place for him." Then Gus left for a visit to the Hoadleys, and, since she was unable to stop in Pittsfield, Herman and his family had a hurried visit with her at the railway station as she passed through. In New Bedford, Gus found that John had left on a week's business trip to Montreal, so she had Kate and the girls to herself. All were well, but Kate would not yet allow the recuperating girls to go outside.[72]

On Thursday, April 30, when Allan arrived in Pittsfield to inspect Arrowhead, the weather was so delightful that he telegraphed Jennie to bring the children up. The next day, when she arrived with the four girls, Arrowhead was not prepared for occupancy, so the whole family stayed with Herman and Lizzie. That meant that the house was crammed with four adults and eight children, enough to "shingle a house," as Mary the maid put it—and to challenge Lizzie's strength and patience. That night the walls must have groaned under the pressure of the high-spirited children, but on Saturday the two families drove out of town for an all-day picnic that reminded them of a memorable occasion when Tom had been with them. Feasting on tea, eggs, and fried ham in the open air was far more enjoyable than remaining indoors with the young shingles. All returned loaded with flowers.[73]

Sunday, while Allan and Jennie wandered off by themselves and Herman dozed in his room, Lizzie marched the six girls and two boys off to perform their Sabbath obligations. For Malcolm and Stanny, the next day was a black Monday—they had to attend school while the others continued the party. All but the two disgusted pupils went to Lebanon, where they dined at the establishment of "Sister 'Lazy Arms,'" as Lizzie called her hostess, after which Jennie shopped lavishly until it was time for the boys to return from school. On Tuesday, the visitors boarded the train for Hudson, New York, whence they took the boat to the city. Just after their departure, a storm broke and continued until the following day.

On Wednesday, Lizzie was worn out with nervous tension and fatigue, and on Thursday she was still recovering, though Sarah Morewood was expected to arrive from the city at any time. The Allan Melvilles had been so pleased with their visit that Jennie wanted to move to Pittsfield for the summer. Allan did not think that there would be enough of the season left to make it worthwhile, and Lizzie cattily confided to Fanny that she hoped that Allan would prevail. Although she scarcely knew Jennie, she did not like her; she resented her stylish frivolity and envied her the luxury in which she lived, an example of which she had just witnessed in the Lebanon shops. Her prejudice may have been increased when, although she and Herman had made a tasteful announcement of the property transaction within the family, Allan published the news in the *Berkshire County Eagle* that he had bought Arrowhead for a summer home. Perhaps she blamed Jennie for that. But despite her wish that she could have this last summer in Pittsfield free of her sister-in-law, Jennie won the battle and Allan returned to Pittsfield briefly to do some preliminary work at the farm.[74]

Pittsfield had on her best spring face. Not counting a few summery days in May, the weather was cool, so much so that there were fears for the corn crop. Sarah Morewood arrived and spent a night with Herman and Lizzie before moving into Broadhall. There was plenty to do and see in town. On May 28, Louis Gottschalk, accompanied by some local singers, gave a concert at the Maplewood Institute, and on June 2, Mme. Charlotte Varian, accompanied by pianist Edward Hoffman, sang Scotch-Irish airs at West's Hall. The town was treated to a distinguished visitor when General Fitz-John Porter came to Pittsfield in search of a summer home. Everyone of Herman's persuasion knew that, despite his valiant service on the Peninsula, Pope's vindictiveness had caused Porter to be cashiered from the army. There must have been general relief when the war income tax was delayed. It was supposed to be paid before June 1, but the collectors did not receive the forms in time.[75]

To celebrate the spring, Herman bought Malcolm and Stanny two more pets, a pair of rabbits, one black and one white, and he must have helped them put up the rabbit pen in the garden. For her part, Lizzie bought each of the boys catechisms and made them learn a lesson each week. Otherwise, she was busy arranging small matters for Allan and Jennie. She suggested that Jennie hire a hand to relieve Allan of some of the farm labor, but Jennie thought that with four young girls to look after, "one must be careful." Lizzie offered to buy a stove for them, to order coal, and to have food ready for their arrival, but Jennie wanted her cook to make the selection of stoves, so she asked Lizzie instead to buy a large quantity of vegetable and floral plants, since she intended to occupy herself with gardening—she was innocent enough to worry that in the country strawberries and other fruits might not be available for the girls, as they were in the city.[76]

Had Jennie known how much Lizzie disliked her, she might have been more careful about what she wrote. Expecting city visitors during the summer, she wondered what they would think of "poor, simple *Arrowhead.*" If Lizzie had been capable of murder, this might have inspired it. Regardless of what Jennie thought, Lizzie had not been raised a milkmaid in homespun. That Jennie should regard as poor and simple the home in which the daughter of the great chief justice had lived for twelve years was more than too much. But Lizzie had support within the family. Helen asked Gus, "How long do you predict that Madam will be satisfied & contented in such a quiet corner of the Earth?"[77]

On the first of June, Mary finally Levanted, leaving Lizzie both relieved to be rid of such a sloven and chagrined at having no help, but a week later a more competent Mary took the job, much to Lizzie's delight. Fortunately, the new Mary was installed in the household before the arrival of the New York Melvilles, the "great event of the season," Lizzie sneered. They reached Pittsfield on Thursday, June 11, a beautiful day, bringing with them several servants to do what Lizzie had always done with one, at most. Jennie and the two younger girls, Kitty and Lucy, spent the night with Herman and Lizzie, while Allan, the servants, and the two older girls, Milie and Florence, braved the new world of Arrowhead. The next day, Allan returned to shop with Jennie for furniture, kitchen utensils, and the stove, among other things, with a prodigality that further soured Lizzie's temper. That day the rains came, so heavily that streams flooded and roads were washed out, but Allan and Jennie bravely carted their mound of purchases back to the farm while Kitty and Lucy remained with Herman and Lizzie. On Saturday, Jennie returned in the rain with Milie and Florence for another day of shopping, notably for tomato plants. She stayed in the stores so late that she was afraid to return to Arrowhead alone, which meant that Malcolm had to ride with her and walk home early the next morning. Lizzie's temper was not improving, and it suffered another setback when a note from Jennie about entertaining guests arrived while Lizzie was sweating over her stove. "I think the lady is somewhat homesick already," she wrote Fanny, "and should not be surprised if she left the place in a month. Selfishly speaking, I hope she *will*."[78]

Herman's contentment in having Allan so near was increased by the arrival of Clara Nourse from Cincinnati. Clara settled into a room near enough—a three-minute walk—so that Herman and Lizzie could see her every day, though with the unusually cold weather Pittsfield may not have been as healthful as she had anticipated. It was the first time that Herman had had one of his cousins living nearby since Priscilla Melvill had died there in 1858, and Clara's presence—she was "pleasant" and "entertaining"—helped to recall the days when the town was well-populated by Melvilles and Melvills. Clara was in a position to give Herman a firsthand account of the temper of the citizens of the west. No doubt a devout Republican, like Uncle Nourse, she must have approved of Burnside's ironfisted rule in Cincinnati.[79]

At Broadhall, Sarah Morewood remained feeble and housebound, with frequent congestion of the lungs and head. Lizzie's summer allergies were not as severe as usual, perhaps because of the weather, but little Bessie was puny—pale, thin, and suffering from headaches. Despite the fact that she was doing well in her studies, her parents took her out of school. "I would rather she should grow up a perfect dunce than have her health suffer,"

Lizzie announced. The other children frequently walked out to the farm to play with their cousins, but Bessie was too weak to go with them. Then the cold drove Jennie and Milie back to the city, leaving the rest of the girls at Arrowhead with the servants. That was when Lizzie called her a "great fool" and compared her to "Greely & the nigger."[80]

Once More, Fortress Berkshire

Friday, June 26, was the semicentennial celebration of the Albany Academy, the school from which Herman had graduated, and he was expected to attend. As the president of the board of trustees, Uncle Peter had arranged that he be a member of the celebration committee and he expected him to be there: "Permit me to indulge the hope, that you will shew your gratitude to the Academy & your appreciation of the services it has rendered the cause of Science by participating in the celebration & favoring us with an expression of your feeling." He invited Herman to stay with him that evening, a kindness that was tantamount to a command. Herman dutifully agreed to attend and wrote his family in Gansevoort that he would pay them a visit afterward.[81]

On the day of the celebration, Herman took the train to Albany. There he met Uncle Peter, who was interrupting his vacation at Saratoga Springs, probably too late for the morning reunion at Academy Hall. However, he was present at the formal celebration in Tweddle Hall at three in the afternoon. He marched in the procession to the cadence of Wetron's "Grand March," after which Uncle Peter presided over the celebration with Herman, "whose reputation as an author has honored the Academy, worldwide," at his side. The proceedings, interspersed with band music, were lengthy, and at eight in the evening there was a meeting of the alumni at Academy Hall, complete with speeches, music, and refreshments. Herman attended, but he had no stomach for the food.[82]

Later, he relaxed in the luxury of the Gansevoort mansion and enjoyed his uncle's company, as he always did. The conversation gave him an inside glimpse of the political controversy that embroiled the North, a different and more sympathetic perspective on Vallandigham and his punishment from the one that he must have heard from Clara Nourse. The resolutions that Uncle Peter had endorsed agreed with his own beliefs about civil liberties, and Uncle Peter probably pointed out the fallacies in Lincoln's response. Perhaps the two commiserated over the fact that while Uncle Peter and his colleagues had the Constitution on their side, Lincoln had the armed forces on his. Still, in his own mind Herman did not attribute to Lincoln—or Jefferson Davis, for that matter—the same importance that

Peter Gansevoort. By permission of the Berkshire Athenæum

Uncle Peter did. Through its inclusions and omissions, *Battle-Pieces* makes the soldiers and sailors the principal agents of the struggle, while the presidents of the two sides busy themselves far away with less consequential matters.

On Saturday afternoon the two took the five o'clock train north, Uncle Peter back to Saratoga Springs, Herman to Gansevoort. Aside from his mother and Fanny, Herman had an opportunity to spend time with Helen Griggs. There was plenty of family news for him to hear. Tom had written that he was on his way to San Francisco, causing Fanny to alert everyone to write letters to greet him on his arrival. Mother Melville was concerned that he might encounter "the dread Allabamas," but Tom planned to evade the commerce raiders by sailing on to South America. John Hoadley had resurrected a book of poetry that he had published in 1855, *The Sounds I Love,* giving copies to various members of the family, including Fanny, Mother Melville, Kate Curtis, and "Gen. Peter Gansevoort." Mother Melville was enraptured: "It is got up in chastely simple garb & requires immaculate care to preserve its purity," she wrote. One wonders if Herman's verse ever received that sort of accolade from his mother.[83]

Mother Melville and Fanny were disappointed that Herman had not brought one or more of the children with him, but he had Bessie's illness for an excuse and he promised that if Gus stopped at Pittsfield on her way home from New Bedford he would try to send some of them back with her. Herman and his mother considered an overnight visit to the Glens Falls family, who had been in Gansevoort the day before Herman's arrival, and a trip to Saratoga Springs. In Glens Falls, illness was still the concern. Leonard Gansevoort was thinking of going to New York City for medical advice, which Helen Griggs thought wise. How much of that Herman was able to do in the six or so days he seems to have spent in Gansevoort is not known, but the weather was fine and it is difficult to imagine him leaving without talking to Ned Curtis, who was home by this time, about Farragut's passage of the forts and capture of New Orleans. He must have left for home shortly after the beginning of July.[84]

Despite the domestic tranquility of these days—always excepting Lizzie's pique—the North was in panic as Lee drove his army once again into Union territory. As had been the case the preceding September, no state in the northeast was safe from invasion and there was again a chance that Herman would be required to defend Fortress Berkshire.

Under Joe Hooker's command, the Army of the Potomac had regained some semblance of its splendid condition under McClellan. However, he did not prove to be adequate to the job. Although he had been and would continue to be a fierce and able corps commander, his luck—or his judgment—in this critical position was bad. Perhaps the root cause was the demands made on him by the administration, or perhaps it was Hooker himself. As soon as the weather was favorable, Hooker moved once more to carry out Lincoln's plan of marching down Tidewater Virginia toward Richmond, this time by crossing the Rappahannock River upstream from Fredericksburg. By April 30, Ed Lansing was throwing pontoon bridges across the river, after which Hooker crossed deftly. Because his army was stronger than Lee's, he believed that his movement would force the Confederates to retreat, and, assuming that they would, he halted just south of the river and crowded his army into a small open area where a tavern at a crossroads was called Chancellorsville. But instead of retreating, Lee attacked. Although the Union soldiers should have beaten the Confederates, Lee and Jackson made the most of their forces while the Union power was poorly used. The only victory for the North was the death of Stonewall Jackson, who was shot by his own pickets.

Down the river, while Wendell Holmes was marching his company through Fredericksburg in an ancillary movement, a shell exploded near him, piercing his heel. Discouraged by his many wounds, he prayed that his foot might have to be amputated so that he would not be required to return to combat. He was sent home once more, and never again rejoined the Harvard Regiment. The veterans of McClellan's army were, as Herman wrote in "The Victor of Antietam," dwindling.[85]

The telegraphic reports were confusing. As Morgan Dix wrote, "It would seem that Hooker has beaten Lee, and that Lee has beaten Hooker; that we have taken Fredericksburg, and that the rebels have taken it also." When the true outcome of the battle and the crushing casualties became known, public opinion turned against Hooker. Walt Whitman lamented that "it seems too dreadful, that such bloody contests, without settling any thing, should go on." The *New York Times,* hardly a Democratic organ, finally agreed that had Lincoln released McDowell's forces to him, McClellan would have taken Richmond a year earlier. Democrats expected that at last Lincoln would be forced to recall their idol, while the newspapers in the South predicted that Hooker would be beaten again and that Lee would then be free to invade the North with impunity. Already, preparations for the invasion were in progress.[86]

Herman found nothing to celebrate in the defeat at Chancellorsville, but he was courageous enough to write not one but two memorials to Stonewall Jackson. In the overall scheme of *Battle-Pieces,* these poems are linked to the two that precede them, "The Battle of Stone River" and "Running the Batteries," in that they deal with the enigma of the fratricidal, brother-as-enemy aspect of the war. Having looked at the conflict of loyalties of "dark

Breckinridge," and having refused to celebrate the suffering of fellow Americans in the Vicksburg siege, Herman wished now to write about the American hero who had fought for the Confederacy. This was an important subject for a poet who anticipated the postwar reunification of the nation. If a brother can be an enemy, can an enemy be a brother?

He could not praise Jackson directly. In the nationwide confusion of loyalties, to do so would have subverted the purpose of his book, yet his admiration for Jackson is patent. Jackson was an inspirational leader of the kind that Herman valued, and thus he was a memorable American. He was not one of those hotheads who had led the South into secession but one of the men who had fought out of loyalty to the people and the land he knew. From these considerations grew a poetic strategy through which Herman could affirm his allegiance to the Northern cause while still praising Jackson. He would write two poems from opposing points of view, one that of a Northerner whose partisanship allows him to give only qualified praise and the other that of a Southerner who is free to laud his leader. These two views would have to be reconciled in the new America.

The narrator of "Stonewall Jackson: Mortally wounded at Chancellorsville (May, 1863)" speaks in grudging admiration. In this traditional dramatic monologue, he cannot damn without praising. His portrait of Jackson acknowledges the earnestness, piety, and accomplishments of the general whose loyalty was mistaken and whose fame was, in the defeat of his cause, proscribed by officialdom. Unwittingly, he reveals a truth: if John Brown had been a dangerous radical, yet he had been true to his dream; similarly, if Stonewall Jackson had fought for the wrong cause (and Herman would have agreed that he had), he had been equally true.

The second poem, "Stonewall Jackson (Ascribed to a Virginian)," is narrated by a Southerner who, significantly, speaks at three times the length of the Northerner. He celebrates Jackson properly, through his illustrious career—the Shenandoah Valley and the Seven Days, Bull Run, Antietam, Fredericksburg, and Chancellorsville, in all of which Jackson and his men bore much of the burden. The poem opens with the claim that Jackson is the one Confederate general whose renown cannot be impugned by his foes, a surprising statement for a Southerner to make, since Lee's name comes immediately to mind as another. The life of Jackson, the "stormer of the war," "was charged with the lightning's burning breath"; he was "stoic," with "iron will and iron thew."

The most prominent element in the poem is the repeated idea that Jackson "followed his star," that he was one of those rare cynosures who feel that greatness is their fate. It is this, rather than the cause for which he fought, that gives him immortality. As to the cause, the narrator can say:

O, much of doubt in after days
  Shall cling, as now, to the war;
Of the right and the wrong they'll still debate,
  Puzzled by Stonewall's star.

Although the North won the war, Jackson bequeathed the legacy of his star to the South—though Herman intended to claim it for all America.

Both poems present identifiable attitudes of Herman Melville. In a man who was remarkably sensitive to ambiguities, those that he encountered in Jackson, and in his own response to Jackson, were bound to find expression. Where another poet might have avoided them for the sake of simplicity or consistency, Herman asked, in effect, two questions: Was Jackson right? and, Was Jackson great? As a loyal Unionist, he rejected Jackson's cause, but as an American he celebrated the American hero. The result is that the two contradictory poems together constitute the greatest tribute in *Battle-Pieces* to any single Civil War figure. It is probably true that of all of the American authors of the time, the only one, North or South, capable of such a performance was Herman.

The North was in a danger as great as the dark days of the preceding September. Once more Lee was free to invade the North, but now he was opposed by a demoralized general from whom he had little to fear—Hooker was no McClellan. The Confederates were already in Chambersburg, Pennsylvania, and there was panic in Pittsburgh and Philadelphia and throughout the northeast. The Pennsylvania militia mobilized, militia units elsewhere reported for duty, and once more the Seventh Regiment went to Baltimore.

The Importance of Being a Gansevoort

One of those who was hurried forward was Lieutenant Colonel Henry Gansevoort, New York State Volunteers. He had continued to seek such a rank and, although his family had not been enthusiastic, he had managed to enlist his father, Bruce, Allan, Abe Lansing, and Richard Lathers in the effort. Of these, he could badger only his father, who, because of his illness, had done less than Henry thought he should. Henry wept about his abandonment: "I am soon going back to throw away a humble life without the satisfaction of knowing that I have been enabled to gain such a position as to reward my efforts." Peter could hardly scoff at the maudlin appeal, as he had done in the summer of 1861, not after Henry's heroism at the cornfield of Antietam. He called on the adjutant-general, who assured him that if Henry could arrange a leave of absence from the War Department he would be considered favorably for a suitable position. Henry was offered the lieutenant colonelcy of the Horatio Seymour Cavalry, then being organized by Colonel Daniel Webb, and on March 10, 1863, he accepted. Then, with his battery pressing him to return to duty, he arranged for Richard Lathers and Allan to obtain the leave from Secretary Stanton. When it was granted, Henry was freed from his regular army obligations for the rest of the war. He took rooms on 23rd Street and commenced his new duties. Abe Lansing envisioned him at some future time grandly wearing the stars of a major general as he led the Army of the Potomac into Richmond. Kate, the spoilsport, carped about his imprudence in leaving a secure position for a doubtful one.[87]

Future major general or not, Henry had contracted a venereal disease, either from pro-secession Eleanor Wilson or from another of his doxies. Abe Lansing took the opportunity to sermonize: "In view of your precautions so long and persistently pursued the fact must be especially unpleasant[.] The safest way, I am now convinced is to sow your seed only in good ground. After your varied experiences I am sure you will now reflect seriously upon this advice." With the callousness of the soldier, a battery mate wrote that Henry must "pay the piper." Just what remedies Henry resorted to remains his own secret, but after a relapse Abe Lansing wrote, "I never believed in your doctrine of self torture and abstinence as a specific for your malady. At the same time I knew very well that you could not without danger be guilty of excesses. I hope you will be careful to avoid them until you shall be quite restored to health."[88]

Henry's single most important military duty was recruiting for the Seymour Cavalry. That rankled him, but the regiment had to be filled. If it were mustered into service full, the two senior officers would be given the ranks of colonel and lieutenant colonel, respectively; if not, they would begin with the temporary ranks of lieutenant colonel and major, instead. That was incentive enough to keep Henry working. As men were enlisted, they were sent to Camp Sprague, Staten Island. Abe Lansing expressed interest in a commission, but in the end he decided that his health was not good enough. However, Henry succeeded in recruiting Charles Brewster, Bruce's younger brother. Charles had been seeking his fortune in the new country in Minnesota, working as a law clerk. Since December 1862, he had sought an appointment as an acting commissary of subsistence of volunteers, procuring and managing provisions for an army unit, but he had been thwarted by civilian enemies, whose accusations of civil improprieties had held up his appointment until the time limit had expired. In desperation, Charles wrote Lincoln: "*I once did you a real and esteemed favor,* and since I need it, if you can, *will you not re-appoint* me,—my name not having been sent in." When that appeal failed, he came east to New York City, where Henry arranged a commission for him as a lieutenant.[89]

Since then, Henry's experiences had been bizarre enough to convince him that for the duration of the war his career would be far different from his well-ordered life in the regulars. On Saturday, May 23, his family arrived in the city to find him ill and under treatment by a Doctor George F Woodward. Then Henry suddenly disappeared. He had received a message saying that Colonel Webb was also ill and that he should take temporary charge of the regiment, and the next day Webb had died. It took him a day or two to understand the implications of the colonel's death. Then he rushed to Albany, where Will Lansing aided him in his attempt to secure the appointment as Webb's replacement, and on the first of June he was appointed colonel.[90]

Events were in the saddle. Because of Lee's invasion, the adjutant-general ordered the consolidation of all cavalry regiments in the eastern part of the state that could not be filled within thirty days. After some political maneuvering by Henry and Lieutenant Colonel Nathaniel Coles, the temporary commander of the Davies Cavalry, the adjutant-general and Colonel Seymour Lansing made one regiment out of the Seymour Cavalry, the Tompkins Cavalry, and the Davies Cavalry, with Henry in command and Coles second in command. Because the consolidated regiment, the 13th New York Volunteer Cavalry, was still under strength, Henry was given the rank of lieutenant colonel, Coles the rank of major. It had been an incredible exercise of nimbleness and influence in which the best-connected of the six original ranking officers involved had emerged as commander. Even Atropos had lent a hand.[91]

On June 20, the regiment was mustered into the federal service and ordered to Washington. Before his departure, Henry obtained Colonel Lansing's permission to carry on his roster his friend and his roommate in earlier years, George Lockwood, as a third major in charge of recruiting in New York City, and his physician, Doctor Woodward, as regimental surgeon in charge of screening new recruits. Henry attempted to contact Allan, who had returned from Pittsfield, but with Allan in New Jersey all that day he said his goodbyes to Bruce, instead. On the twenty-third, Henry, Coles, and 508 raw recruits, six companies in all, departed, leaving Company G, with Charles Brewster, to follow as soon as it could be made ready.[92]

Lee's army had turned east toward Philadelphia. The Democrats believed that, as in Lee's last invasion, McClellan's time had come, and Kate Gansevoort heard that he had relieved Halleck as general-in-chief,[93] but Lincoln gave command of the Army of the Potomac to Henry's former division commander, George Meade. The Battle of Gettysburg was only three days away.

When the battle was in its second day, the *Sun* warned that if Meade were defeated, the states north of Pennsylvania would be at risk, and the Army of the Potomac fought as though that were the case. Brigadier General Tyler, who commanded the artillery reserve, had two horses killed under him. Both senior officers of the Harvard Regiment were wounded, and all of the officers of Battery C, U.S. Artillery, were wounded, Captain Ransom mortally, it was feared. (General Barry offered Henry the command if he would resign his volunteer commission, but Henry declined.) In the end, the North was spared and Lee's army withdrew in grave peril of being trapped and captured.[94]

Allan and his family had returned to Pittsfield on the third of July. With the battle still in progress, the celebration of the Fourth was suspended for the second consecutive year. Some boys exploded firecrackers and there were some private pyrotechnic displays, but a morning rain dampened even those makeshift festivities. By the time of the heavier rain that night, the news of the victory had begun to arrive, continuing through Sunday morning, as did the rain. Herman must have hovered near the telegraph office reading the bulletins as they arrived, the scene described in "Donelson"—the rain streaking the ink of the reports as anxious citizens huddled to read them. Monday, when everyone knew that the invasion had been thwarted, a delayed celebration took place with bonfires and fireworks. Then on Tuesday afternoon the news arrived that Vicksburg had fallen.[95]

That was the day on which John and Kate Hoadley set out on a trip to Canada, leaving Gus in New Bedford to babysit. When the Hoadleys arrived in Pittsfield at 8:15 in the evening, Herman and Malcolm were at the depot to greet them and to bring their luggage home. They had arrived just in time to witness the eruption of elation with which the defeat-weary natives of Pittsfield greeted the news. John described the frenzy: "The village was all ablaze with bonfires, rockets were whizzing, streaming, flashing, exploding, and expiring in the air; roman candles popping, flashing, and dying away in infinity;—Bengal lights lending the usual effect of their spectral light to trees and houses and to the surging throng; bells were pealing from every steeple, groups of people on balconies were singing the Star Spangled Banner;—and through all these outbursts of joy for deliverance and victory, we drove to the house." At the Melvilles' home they found the rest of the family awaiting them at the front gate. Lizzie served light refreshments, or tea, as John called it, and then Kate Hoadley, perpetually close to the limit of her resources, went to bed. Bessie and Stanny followed her, while the rest, Herman and Lizzie, John, Malcolm, and Fanny, "as skirmishers, sallied out to the Common, to see the spectacle, which was kept up with great spirit to a late hour." John did not mention seeing Clara Nourse, the Allan Melvilles, or the Morewoods, but they were probably there. On Wednesday, Kate and John took a hack out to Arrowhead and then went on to the Morewoods' to pay their respects. After dinner they called on Mrs. Bigelow, then boarded the train to continue their trip.[96]

Herman's "Gettysburg: The Check (July, 1863)" begins as one of his ironic poems. The narrator, a Union veteran of the battle, sees the Northern soldiers as God's chosen people and the Confederates as infidels. Casting the conflict in terms of the biblical capture of the Holy Ark by the Philistines (1 Sam. 5:4–5), he likens the victory to the fall of the idol Dagon caused by the proximity of the defiled Holy Ark. Dagon symbolizes the Confederate cause, which is "impious"; the rebel Philistines charge with "hate," "scorn," and "ire," mouthing "screamings, taunts and yells," only to be defeated by the "sterner pride" of God's "Right."[97]

In other words, the poem records not an event but an attitude. Herman was, after all, chronicling the "wayward winds" that played on the strings of his poetic harp, as he said in his "Preface." Taken separately from the rest of *Battle-Pieces,* the poem may appear to embrace the God and glory partisanship that characterized so much of the war poetry of both sides. Perhaps this strategy was suggested by the partisanship of John Hoadley and the elation of the Pittsfield celebrants on the green. By no means should it be understood as an expression of the attitude of the poet, for the poem is yet another dramatic monologue in the Browning sense: the narrator tells more than he intends to reveal, and in so doing he effects a radical modulation in the import of the poem. Recalling the body-covered slope of Cemetery Ridge after Pickett's charge, his thoughts deepen into a true Melville metaphor:

Before our lines it seemed a beach
  Which wild September gales have strown
With havoc on wreck, and dashed therewith
  Pale crews unknown—
Men, arms, and steeds. . . .

The claim that Good has defeated Evil fades in the clarity of human tragedy. As in "The Battle for the Mississippi," the Confederate dead have plumbed the deeps of fate and are now human jetsam cast lifeless on the shore. That is the true meaning of battle, real men sacrificed in the rites of Satan. What, then, has become of the idol Dagon?

It has mutated. In the final stanza, it has become a "warrior-monument, crashed in fight." Historically, the referent was a monument erected to the memory of a Union officer killed on the Peninsula, which, in the fury of the strife, was toppled. It is a radically different image from the pagan idol that fell in the biblical allusion; it is a sad memorial to one of America's dead. Dagon has thus been transformed into a cemetery monument, a representation of the losses of both sides in the battle. That monument "shall soar transfigured in loftier light" and "a meaning ampler bear" in the new national cemetery at Gettysburg. By extrapolation, the monument acknowledges the spirit of Dagon, or Satan, but in human terms it honors all the dead who lay together on the field: "Soldier and priest with hymn and prayer / Have laid the stone, and every bone / Shall rest in honor there."

If the Michael tinge of the poem does nothing else, it expresses the optimism that the battle inspired. At last, the direction of the war seemed to be favorable, and the faith of the North, including Herman's faith that Fate would ensure a reunified nation, now seemed justified. The previously aimless flux of events appeared now to be transformed into determined movement in both east and west. With Lee all but trapped in Pennsylvania and the far western states of the Confederacy severed from the rest by Grant, the end might be in sight. Herman could only hope that it would come rapidly now, sparing the young manhood of both sides and leading to the better society for which he hoped. Perhaps now the "rascals" of the South would lay down their arms. If that were to occur, then 1864 might mark the beginning of a new, great era in the annals of mankind.

6

Farewell to Berkshire *1863–1864*

After the threat of invasion had passed and the victories at Gettysburg and Vicksburg had been celebrated, Berkshire returned to its wartime version of rural calm. When Herman appeared on the militia roll in July, he knew that it was for the last time. His Pittsfield years approaching an end, he and Lizzie were looking back on their lives there with nostalgia.

The rest of the summer promised the kind of content and interest that would preserve it in memory. Aunt Lucy Nourse had promised to visit, Hope Shaw and Sam were expected, and Gus had promised to stop by on her way home from New Bedford. But there was also to be a notable public event, the return of the Berkshire Regiment, now covered with glory from its charge at Port Hudson. Pittsfield was determined that its own heroes would receive the greatest reception in the history of the town and plans were already being made. Herman and Lizzie were excited, too, and planning to do their share, but they had other obligations, farewells to be said to mountains and fields, to cherished friends and places, to memories both sweet and bitter, and to Arrowhead.[1]

But the ubiquitous war would not relent. Relief and jubilation over the victories of July were tempered by the casualty lists that papered the walls in public places and by the wounded who poured into hospitals. In New York, Surgeon Coan once again offered his services to care for the masses of soldiers who arrived there. Meanwhile, Lee's army defied logic by slipping away from Pennsylvania with Meade's weary soldiers in pursuit. Although it was too late to assist in the attempt to cut off the retreat, Company G of Henry Gansevoort's 13th New York Cavalry was mustered into the service at Camp Sprague and ordered south. Then the draft riots began.[2]

Chapter Six

The Atheist Roar of Riot

In mid-1863, New York City was a social nightmare. Of its population of about 800,000, some 1,600 families enjoyed three-fifths of the city's income; for them, metropolitan life was as luxurious and as gaudy as that in the most fashionable European capital. Much of the rest of the money went to the well-to-do, such as the Allan Melvilles, and to small businessmen and skilled artisans; for them life offered less extravagant rewards. But for the poor, many of whom belonged to the somewhat less than half of the population who had immigrated from Europe, life was pitiful. Condemned to rags, cholera, smallpox, typhoid, typhus, malnutrition, violence, vice, crime, and housing squalid beyond remedy, they responded with resentment and despair—there were riots, large and small, almost every day, sometimes several a day.[3]

Prominent among these were the 200,000 or so Irish. To them, the despotic, meddling, and overbearing Republicans were enemies, reminding them of the British occupation forces in Ireland; the Democrats were friends and protectors. Already the war had taken a severe toll of Irish lives, life for Irish laborers had become even more straitened as inflation drove up rents and prices without increasing wages, and they were increasingly skeptical about the motives for fighting it. They suspected that it was being prolonged to profit the wealthy, and indeed, there were businessmen who were not anxious to see the end of their windfall profits; thus it was "a rich man's war and a poor man's fight." Its new justification, emancipation, had exacerbated whatever prejudice against blacks the Irish had previously felt, particularly because ward-heeling Democratic politicians had long warned them that freed slaves would pour into New York to take their jobs. Thus they were hostile toward the 10,000 or so blacks in the city.[4]

That was the situation when the draft riots erupted. There had been occasional state conscription since 1862, when the Militia Act had been enacted, but because the tempo of enlistments had lagged far behind the relentless consumption of human raw material, in 1863 the Enrollment Act became law. This was federal selective service, a measure that was anathema to Democrats, who felt that any kind of forced duty to the state was un-American. Not only had the war been perverted into a crusade for emancipation, but now the government intended to force citizens to fight and die in that crusade whether they approved of it or not. Principle aside, conscription was, as the Albany *Argus* warned, "flagrantly indiscreet and unwise," certainly unfair, and perhaps unconstitutional.[5]

It was indiscreet, unwise, and unfair because it proposed to force the poor and voiceless into the army while permitting the affluent and influential to escape the dangers and privations of service. Fairness would demand that all fit persons of suitable age, health, and circumstances serve, but all United States conscription laws have been class-biased: compulsory service has always meant conscription of the powerless and ample avenues of escape for the powerful. In 1863 the inequity was the most blatant of all. The law permitted three responses to selection: if a draftee had the means, he could hire a substitute to serve for him; if he could not find a substitute, he could still evade service by paying a $300 commutation fee, more than many a laborer earned in a year; if he could not afford to do either, he had to serve or be declared a deserter. Many citizens, including soldiers at the front, were outraged at this exploitation. One soldier (Joseph Osborn) wrote, "I hope they will resist it," another (William Pedrick), "i hope they will not Stand it." A sergeant (Henry G. Marshall), a Yale graduate, wished that Congress would "strike out the $300 clause & make *every* drafted man come."[6]

During the enrollment preceding the draft, conducted almost entirely by radical officials, there was bloody resistance, especially in border states and in regions, such as the Pennsylvania mines, where Irish immigrants were concentrated. Although New York City was relatively peaceful, there were warning signs elsewhere. The *New Haven Register* reported that a group of armed men had gathered on Goshen Mountain to resist, and Kate Gansevoort wrote that in Albany "the Irishmen [are] in a dreadful state of excitement." She quoted Samuel, one of the Gansevoorts' Irish servants, as saying, "down with the draft[,] let the *rich* men go & be shot if they wish it." It was not that the Irish refused to serve. A large number enlisted voluntarily, one of the two largest ethnic groups in the army. There were the Tammany Regiment, largely Irish, which had fought all the way from Ball's Bluff to Gettysburg; the Corcoran Legion, whose regiments were led by colonels named Murphy, McMahon, and McIvor; and the fighting Irish general, Philip Sheridan. Nor were they laggards in battle: by the time it had fought at Fredericksburg and Chancellorsville, Meagher's Irish Brigade had been reduced from around 5,000 men to 520. As they followed the brigade's green flags to their deaths at Marye's Heights, their enemies were so moved by their bravery that they cheered. But conscription was another matter.[7]

City spokesmen warned Lincoln that the draft lottery would foment disorder there. Governor Seymour asked the administration to postpone it until some of the city militia regiments returned from the Gettysburg emergency and complaints of inequities could be investigated, but without success. The Republicans, strangely unaware, it would seem, of the explosive situation, did not intend to accede to such stalling tactics.

On the day Lee's army escaped across the Potomac, riots erupted across the North. The worst was in New York, where names had been drawn without incident on Saturday, July 11. On Monday morning, July 13, there was an antidraft meeting of workers in Central Park, followed by some isolated violence. As work in the local industries dwindled and halted, members of the Black Joke Engine Company of firemen and other protesters, largely artisans, attacked the draft office where the name of one of the members of the company had been drawn. Angered because they had believed that firemen would be exempted, they smashed the office and burned it to the ground. At that point, the violence was directed at the draft itself, and James Gordon Bennett claimed in the *New York Herald* that a single regiment of militia could have halted the demonstrations before they became serious. However, no regiment was available.[8]

After the initial protest, the spreading riot took on the characteristics of social and political rebellion. With little opposition other than the police force and an ineffective detachment of the new army Invalid Corps, the violence spread throughout the city. Now the rioters were largely laborers, their wives, and their children, and the enemy was no longer simply the selective service, but all of their oppressors, real and supposed. In parties ranging from perhaps a dozen to several hundred, rioters attacked symbols of repression, the office of Horace Greeley's *New York Tribune,* which they left intact, the home of Postmaster Abram Wakeman, Allan's friend, which they burned, government offices, known Republicans, anyone in uniform, well-dressed "$300 dollar men," and blacks. They demanded gifts from individuals and shopkeepers as testaments of approval and they looted stores. They attempted to seize weapons from armories and depots, they tried to sever telegraph lines, they burned down the Colored Orphan Asylum, and, as their rage and, often, inebriation grew, they attacked, bloodied, and occasionally killed a perceived enemy.

As the riots continued the following day, marines from the Brooklyn Navy Yard, a small number of regular infantrymen from the harbor forts, a few gunners from the 5th Artillery detachment at Fort Hamilton, and personnel gathered from local recruiting offices reinforced the police. Major Lockwood, Henry Gansevoort's recruiting officer, was mounted and dispatched on various duties, and a new officer of Henry's regiment, Major Douglas Frazar, was sent wherever he was needed, once commanding a battery and again stationed with a small number of troops at the arsenal. Discharged veterans were asked to assist, though they were poorly used, and a call for reinforcements was sent to Camp Sprague on Staten Island. Henry's Company G, which was about to board the ferry for New Jersey, was halted at the landing and ordered back to the city, where it encamped in Gramercy Park. Placed under the command of an incompetent officer, a

Colonel Thaddeus Mott, it came under fire and the men were forced into defensive positions at their encampment until they were rescued by the police and regular infantry. In separate incidents, two of Henry's men were killed when they wandered away from the rest.[9]

The fighting continued through that day and Wednesday, though by Thursday it was subsiding, neighborhoods had organized to protect themselves, and the end was close. Late Wednesday and Thursday, regiments began to pour into the city. The War Department had sent two volunteer regiments from Fortress Monroe to augment the militiamen, who had completed their federal service in Maryland and Pennsylvania and would have been returning home anyway. After some of the militiamen did mop-up duty, the riots were over. A number of buildings had been burned, a considerable amount of merchandise had been looted, and over a hundred people had been killed—some policemen and soldiers, many rioters, some women and little children, and some blacks who had fallen into the hands of the enraged mob. Many others were wounded.[10]

People of all persuasions deplored the violence, but the city's leaders were divided on its causes and on the measures that should be adopted in its wake. The Union League Club of New York was at the center of the radical faction. In operation since April or May, it was made up of Republicans and their fellow-travelers, War Democrats. At the center of the membership were descendants of the "Old New York" families—John Jay, Theodore Roosevelt, and Moses Grinnell, for example—who, over the decades, had seen their influence wane. Now, with the addition of suitable newcomers, such as General Dix, Rev. Henry Bellows, and Francis G. Shaw, and a soupçon of the city's literati, Bryant, Bancroft, George William Curtis, and Henry T. Tuckerman, they meant to recover their former position as the ruling class. They would henceforth be the "true American aristocracy," the arbiters and enforcers of traditional culture, Protestant religion and values, and loyal politics, and they would preside over a subservient working class. They admired the self-assured aristocrats of the prewar South and of Britain, and they adopted some of their attitudes, but they were also Know Nothing nativists who despised the Irish and other Catholics. To them, the Irish were depraved papist hod carriers, traitorous Celts, "brutal, base, cruel, cowards, and as insolent as base." On the other hand, imagining that the blacks, "the most peaceable, sober, and inoffensive of our poor," could be molded into the kind of loyal, subservient class that they sought for the power structure they envisaged, they championed them and lavished their charity on them. These were the deserving poor, for whose benefit the Old New Yorkers had already created the Cooper Union for the Advancement of Science and Art and the Central Park, but the Union Leaguers despised the undeserving poor, who, they believed erroneously, had joined a conspiracy orchestrated by Confederate sympathizers to subvert the administration's draft. Acting on that belief, they had prevailed in their demand that the riots be suppressed by merciless force, which had further infuriated the mob.[11]

The opposition were the city's conservatives, such as Samuel J. Tilden, Samuel F. B. Morse, and Catholic Archbishop John Hughes, many of them remnants of the Young America movement of years past. Allied politically and socially with Evert Duyckinck, Richard Lathers, and Allan Melville, they were prejudiced against blacks and sympathetic to the Irish. Their aims were the same as they had been since the beginning of the war, to defend their civil rights, to oppose the political, social, and religious evangelism of the radicals, and to solve the city's problems through local action. They gave active support to the war effort and accepted the draft, but during the riots they attempted to conciliate the mob, appealing, often successfully, to conscience and reason.[12]

To forestall future riots, the Union Leaguers wished to resort to the ironfisted measures of Europe. They asked that the federal government intervene militarily in the city government and, specifically, that Ben Butler be assigned as military governor, as he had been in occupied New Orleans. Washington should garrison the city with troops ready to drown any future disturbances in Irish blood, and the conservative leaders should be arrested, tried for treason, and adjudged severe punishments, such as execution. Unwilling to go that far, Lincoln instead assigned General Dix to the command of the military department headquartered in the city. That was a partial defeat, since Dix, though willing to act the Draco, was no Beast Butler.[13]

In order to justify their position, the radicals concocted a vastly inflated version of the violence and its consequences. Thousands had been killed, they claimed, a far greater loss had been suffered in goods and property than had actually been the case, and the affair had been a race riot rather than an antidraft riot. Governor Seymour had encouraged the rioters, the troops that had been sent to reestablish order had been withdrawn from the Army of the Potomac, allowing Lee's army to escape, and these veterans of Gettysburg had again risked their lives in combat with the enraged Celts. Some of these fabrications have become so firmly rooted in national myth that one respected historian has written recently that the arriving regiments "poured volleys into the ranks of rioters with the same deadly effect they had produced against rebels at Gettysburg two weeks earlier," when in fact none of the regiments had fought in that battle.[14]

How would Herman react to the violence? Neither he nor Allan was present. Allan had not returned to New York since his departure on July 3, but had, as usual, left Bruce to run his errands while he luxuriated at Arrowhead, and Herman was simply not there. Therefore, Herman's understanding of what had happened was shaped by those, largely conservatives, who would have discussed the events with him. Unlike the radicals, they had no ideologically charged version. It was impossible to sanction anarchy, though they could sympathize with the rioters' grievances and thus retain some perspective on the events. The conservative *New York Journal of Commerce* reported that relatively modest numbers of rioters had been augmented by thousands of nonparticipants who collected on the streets to watch, making the rioters appear more numerous than they were. Bruce mentioned only the first day's disorders, telling Henry Gansevoort blandly that "great excitement prevails in the City about the draft—A large mob this morning visited one of the Districts where the drawing was taking place, and cleaned out the entire concern. . . . There may be some trouble yet before the draft is completely finished." His statement that the first day of riots did not amount to real trouble says much, as does his failure to comment in later letters on the subsequent days of rioting, despite the fact that his brother Charles was involved. Most telling is the attitude of Walt Whitman, who shared many of Herman's beliefs. Whitman was in Washington, where he was surrounded by irate civil servants and fire-breathing soldiers: "So the mob has risen at last in New York—I have been expecting it," he wrote, "the feeling here is savage & hot as fire against New York, (the mob—*"copperhead mob"* the papers here call it,) & I hear nothing in all directions but threats of ordering up the gunboats, cannonading the city, shooting down the mob, hanging them in a body, &c &c—meantime I remain silent, partly amused, partly scornful, or occasionally put in a dry remark, which only adds fuel to the flame—I do not feel it in my heart to abuse the poor people, or call for rope or bullets for them, but that is all the talk here." He was more offended by the calumny against his beloved city and its people than he was by the rioters and the riots. In Albany, Uncle Peter made a cryptic comment when, as the riots were ending, he cut off the beard that he had cultivated since his departure for England in 1859.[15]

Herman's poem "The House-top: A Night Piece (July, 1863)" is related to Whitman's reaction in that it investigates the attitude of the radicals toward the despair of the rioters. It is one of his most celebrated poems, largely because of the energy and polish of its blank verse. Yet this very polish, like that of "DuPont's Round Fight," is sufficient warning to the reader to suspect irony, and in fact it is a dramatic monologue in which Herman does not speak in his own voice but through a dramatic character whose opinions differ markedly from his own. This irony has ensured that the poem would be widely misunderstood. Its seductiveness encourages a literal reading that seems to condemn the rioters unrelentingly. Thus Edward H. Rosenberry writes, "To Melville this anarchy in the streets was a frightening parable of human depravity unleashed," Randall Stewart claims that "to Melville, such behavior showed that a jungle lust for violence is always active in man, to be checked only by the artifices of 'civil charms,' and 'priestly spells,'" and Richard Harter Fogle believes that "the poet utterly condemns" the riots. But the narrator is a Union Leaguer who, as Connor has correctly noted, expresses the aristocrats' view of the rabble on the streets, or, to quote Sister Lucy Freibert, he confronts the reader with "the selfishness of those who pass laws that protect the monied class." That is not to say that Herman approved of the riots. He deplored the satanic impulses that had been aroused in the mob, but was not the entire nation afflicted by the same evil?[16]

Because the poem concerns two different (though related) events, only the first eighteen lines will be discussed here. Looking down on the city from his elevated perch, the narrator describes the scene in savage and lurid terms. The silent, sultry atmosphere oppresses, banishing sleep, and images of "tawny tigers" in "matted shades" seeking "ravage" are mixed with those of Lybian deserts. Then sounds from afar, "a mixed surf" of "the Atheist roar of riot," introduce a vision of mayhem: "Yonder, where parching Sirius set in drought, / Balefully glares red Arson—there—and there." (Had Herman chosen to cast *all* of the poems of *Battle-Pieces* in such compelling lines, his reputation as a poet would have been long secure.) The unseen rioters are characterized as "ship-rats / And rats of the wharves." Having dismissed the common man, he welcomes the cannon with their "low dull rumble, dull and dead, / And ponderous drag that jars the wall."

The narrator is one of the privileged who, free of the danger of conscription and thus at liberty to dine at Delmonico's without risking salt horse out of a mess kit, positions himself safely on the top of a building to mull on the distant riots and to deplore them, since they threaten both his property and the military system which both exempts him and carries out his will. The idea of observing one's fellow man from a height too exalted to permit an understanding of his yearnings and sufferings, the crucifixion in his face, was repugnant to Herman, as a certain kind of understanding of Plotinus Plinlimmon in *Pierre* and of Captain Vere in *Billy Budd* reveals. To look down on one's fellow man from on high, as does the one, or from the elevated side of the quarterdeck, as does the other, (or from a Concord remove, as did Emerson), was to stand apart from the mass of men involved in the business of existence, earning sustenance, loving and hating, hoping and despairing, living and dying. That explains a peculiar aspect of the poem: the rioters never appear in it. However deplorable their violence, these real men with real grievances have no part in the poem. Too distant to see them, the narrator still characterizes them, a priori, as waterfront rabble. In contrast to Herman's own understanding of sailors, the Billy Budds, the Queequegs, the Tommos, the Toby Greenes, the Leonard Gansevoorts, and the Tom and Herman Melvilles, the narrator sees them as the jetsam of decent society, a debased class whose voice is "the Atheist roar of riot." Why do protests occur, why are there desertions and mutinies, overt and covert, in *Typee, Omoo, Mardi, Moby-Dick,* "Bartleby," "Benito Cereno," *Billy Budd,* and Herman's own experiences at sea? That question does not occur to the narrator. To him riots are caused by debased character, insubordination, a perverse refusal to live within the restraints imposed by "civil charms / And priestly spells," which were the manacles of feudal Europe. This Burkean but un-American idea continued to task Herman's imagination until, in *Billy Budd,* he made it the principle of government of Captain Vere.

If the sound of men protesting is an "Atheist roar," the atheist cannon that roll through the streets are greeted with a pious "Hail." Again, the muscle of the state sanctified by the jargon of devotion is the tool of pacification, though one that would have appalled the Founding Fathers. Thus the poem judges one of the many conflicting "aspects" of the war. It implies, in the larger context of the book, that the quasiaristocratic attitudes that had persisted in society despite the Revolution were inconsistent with the purification and renewal of which the Founders dreamt. Murder and arson, even as means toward desirable ends, were manifestations of natural depravity, of the Satan within, but Herman could forgive them when the perpetrators had been the victims of injustice. One need only turn to "Benito Cereno" to find a similar situation, one in which blacks, who have been brutalized by slavery, commit unspeakable atrocities against their former masters. The atrocities remain unspeakable, yet Herman found the means to understand them. In the same spirit, he understood these rioters when they committed atrocities that were racially the reverse of those in "Benito Cereno." In *Billy Budd,* the same sailors who mutinied at Spithead and the Nore won the gratitude of the British nation at Trafalgar.

Charleston

During the spring and summer the Union navy won no important battles, but in attempting to capture Charleston it lost one. As a preliminary to an assault on the port, Admiral DuPont was to run a line of monitors past the powerful batteries at the entrance of the harbor. Based on the performance of the *Monitor* against the *Virginia,* the Navy Department believed that monitors were invulnerable to cannon fire, though DuPont was less certain.

He believed that the navy could capture the port only in cooperation with an attack by land. Nevertheless, on the sixth of April, he crossed the bar before Charleston and ordered his ships to begin their run at dawn.

Forts Sumter and Moultrie were well positioned and heavily armed, and the gunners had anchored range buoys in the water to perfect their aim. The Union ships received a terrible shelling, exchanging measured volleys for a gale of ball and shell. The Confederate fusillade blew bolts dislodged from armor around the insides of the monitors' turrets and fragments of metal were catapulted into men and machinery. Finally, having received far more damage than they had inflicted, the monitors limped back to their anchorage. When his captains reported the baleful condition of their commands, DuPont realized that another attempt would fail at best and at worst deliver some of his ships into Confederate hands. With the concurrence of his captains, he terminated the engagement.

The Navy Department ordered him to renew his assault, and when he refused, ordered Admiral Foote to relieve him. However, Foote, who had never completely recovered from the wound he had received at Donelson, died in New York while on his way to Port Royal. Admiral Dahlgren was the next to be selected, and on July 6 he received the command of the South Atlantic Blockading Squadron from his old friend. Then DuPont retired to his home and to official neglect, repudiation, and ignominy. The nation had lost two of its most distinguished naval leaders and Guert Gansevoort had lost two friends.

Immediately after the draft riots, with their antiblack undertone, another attempt to breach the Charleston defenses enlightened conservatives about black men. Many who had originally been well disposed toward blacks had become less so when the war for reunification had been redefined as a war for emancipation. In a heated political atmosphere in which logic could warp and fail, they blamed blacks for the fact that the altered purpose of the war seemed to be to reduce the Southern states to miserable subjection, to scramble their societies and to destroy their economies. They objected to putting the interests of blacks ahead of those of Southern whites, and they believed that the most villainous manifestation of this inversion was the enlistment of blacks into the Union army, where, armed and trained, they were in a position to exact terrible revenge against their former masters.[17]

The conservatives accused the radicals of wishing to use black men to reduce the quotas of whites, but some black regiments had been raised relatively early in the war in states where they could not have been counted against quotas. Colonel Thomas Wentworth Higginson, Emily Dickinson's editor, had been given command of the black 1st South Carolina Volunteers, inspiring Whittier to write, "How strange to think of him so fresh, so beautiful in his glorious manhood, with his refinement, culture, and grace—leading that wild African regiment," and Dickinson to write, opaquely, "War feels to me an oblique place." In Louisiana, both "Native Guard" and "Corps d'Afrique" regiments had been enlisted, and at Port Hudson several of them had distinguished themselves, paying a price in casualties high enough to satisfy the doubts of skeptics. At Milliken's Bend, Louisiana, an "African Brigade" of Grant's Vicksburg army fought well in a small but sharp engagement in which they sustained severe casualties. Yet the valor of these black troops had failed to alter the conservative belief that the inferiority of blacks rendered them unreliable as soldiers.[18]

Now more of these regiments were being raised, in the course of which Henry Pease left the 26th Massachusetts to become a second lieutenant in the 14th Regiment of the Corps d'Afrique, later the 86th U.S. Colored Troops.[19] They were fearless fighters among whom desertion was almost unknown, but, although a significant number fought alongside white volunteers, many saw little or no action. Conditioned to despise the former slaves and then attacked by regiments of them, Confederate soldiers committed atrocities on the black troops they encountered, including massacres. Fearing repetitions of this brutality, fearing that they might be accused of placing black troops in the forefront of battle in order to spare the lives of white soldiers, and aware that black prisoners would be returned to servitude, many Union commanders were reluctant to commit them. The Colored Troops proved themselves in combat, but often they were relegated to garrison duty.

The 54th Massachusetts Volunteer Infantry was different. One of the proudest achievements of the Massachusetts radicals was the formation of two black regiments, the 54th and the 55th, the enlisted ranks of which were filled entirely by black men—mostly ordinary citizens, farmers, laborers, artisans, tradesmen, and others from Massachusetts and as far away as Canada—very few former slaves. In other words, except that the soldiers were black, most of them were not very different from other volunteers. However, because Secretary of War Stanton had prohibited the commissioning of blacks, all of the officers were white, including the colonel of the 54th, Robert Gould Shaw.[20]

The son of Francis G. Shaw and the brother-in-law of George William Curtis, Robert Gould Shaw had spent a part of his childhood at Brook Farm and had later attended schools in Switzerland, Italy, and Germany before entering Harvard. After garrisoning Washington with the Seventh Regiment, he had joined the 2nd Massachusetts Infantry and had fought with it until 1863. When the organization of the black regiments was decided upon, Governor Andrew offered him the colonelcy of the 54th. On May 28, 1863, there was great excitement in Boston when he led his men through the streets to the piers. Longfellow was among those who cheered them along, feeling that there was "something wild and strange" about the sight, "like a dream," and Frederick Douglass, who had two sons in the regiment, addressed them on their way down the bay.[21]

At Charleston, the black soldiers were to take part in an assault on Battery Wagner, which was located on Morris Island, a short distance seaward from Fort Sumter. On July 18, Union artillery and naval cannon bombarded the battery until twilight, when, leading eight other regiments, the 54th assaulted the fortifications. Under the fire of Confederate artillery from other locations and intense fire from Wagner itself, the black soldiers advanced doggedly while suffering severe casualties—Shaw was killed on a parapet. The attackers took and held a portion of the works, but in the darkness the Union soldiers were forced to retreat, and the second attempt to seize Charleston had failed.

The 54th sustained heavier casualties than any other regiment on the field. Three officers and 31 enlisted men were killed, 11 officers and 135 enlisted men were wounded, and 92 were missing. It was reported that in their rage the Confederates threw Shaw's body into a mass grave with his black soldiers, but what was a gesture of contempt for the Southerners was a symbolic triumph for Northern abolitionists. The man who had led them down the streets of Boston now lay in the same grave with them in South Carolina.[22]

The great significance of this bloody attack lay not in the death of the leader but in the fact that the soldiers of the 54th Massachusetts had dispelled the misconception that blacks could not or would not fight well. Before the assault, the *Pittsfield Sun* had published a steady stream of disparagements of black troops, and those in command of them, like Colonel Higginson, knew that "a single miniature Bull Run, a stampede of desertions, and it would have been all over with us; the party of distrust would have got the upper hand, and there might not have been, during the whole contest, another effort to arm the negro." But now the question was moot. Walt Whitman said, "Wherever tested, they have exhibited determin'd bravery, and compell'd the plaudits alike of the thoughtful and thoughtless soldiery." It was a terrible price to pay for respect, but the soldiers of the 54th had paid it. As the *New York Tribune* put it, Wagner was for American blacks what Bunker Hill had been for American whites. It was a minor battle, but so was Bunker Hill.[23]

Although Herman did not write a poem about Battery Wagner, he did find a symbol, the Swamp Angel, through which to celebrate the black soldiers who fought there. In August, Union troops placed an eight-inch,

200-pound Parrott rifle in the marshes of Morris Island, not far from the scene of the charge. The Confederates were given an ultimatum: evacuate Fort Sumter and the batteries on Morris Island or expect a bombardment of Charleston, less than five miles away. When they refused, the bombardment began on August 22, with the point of aim just to the left of the steeple of St. Michael's Church. When explosive and Greek fire shells landed in the city, the panicked citizens rang bells and blew warning whistles, but the bombardment lasted only a day. Frequently overcharged, the barrel fired only thirty-five times before it blew out its breech. Although that was the end of the original cannon, smaller Parrott rifles, known generically as the Swamp Angel, subsequently fired on the city.

Both the note to "The Swamp Angel" and its placement in the 1864 section of *Battle-Pieces* suggest that the cannon that is its subject is an imaginative construct that includes both the original swamp battery and its later namesakes. To be historically precise, the lyric should have been placed just after "The House-top," but Herman wished it to appear in the part of his book that refers to the final onslaught of the war, and with good reason. This cannon is black revenge, "A coal-black Angel / With a thick Afric lip" located in the swamp where, in times past, "hunted and harried" black refugees had shivered. Since that image and the setting of the poem (close to Battery Wagner) relate it to the soldiers of the 54th Massachusetts, all of whom must have been the descendants of slaves, it properly belongs with the late actions of the war that ended black slavery.

It was not Herman's custom to celebrate attacks on civilians, but in this case the poem deals—like "Benito Cereno"—with the violence wrought by the former slaves in retaliation for the violence to which they had been subjected. Thus it is one of only two poems in *Battle-Pieces* that deal explicitly with the experience of the black man who, to those of a different persuasion, was the principal figure of the war. Yet the cannon is more than a representation of the black; it is an African avatar of Satan, who personifies the black man's thirst for revenge. The revenge is horrifying, the chilling scream of each missile as it rises into the sky medleyed with the "wails and shricks" of the civilians as it descends, a glowing comet. The terror of the inhabitants must owe something to Richard Lathers's stories about the Denmark Vesey rebellion:

> They live in a sleepless spell
> That wizens, and withers, and whitens;
> It ages the young, and the bloom
> Of the maiden is ashes of roses—

Fear of the bombardment is equally fear of the blacks, and as the missiles drive farther and farther into the city, tumbling walls and leaving weeds to grow where men had lived, there is no refuge from them.

Charleston is the "proud City," "the scorner / Which never would yield the ground." Because it had "mocked at the coal-black Angel," reprisals were inevitable. The citizens trusted in their white angel, Michael, the divine guardian of supposedly just causes and the symbol of romantic delusions, not realizing that Satan is the true divinity of warfare. But Michael the chimera has fled, leaving the town to face the reality of the black angel it has summoned. The poem concludes with a caution:

> Who weeps for the woeful City
>   Let him weep for our guilty kind;
> Who joys at her wild despairing—
>   Christ, the Forgiver, convert his mind.

He who mourns the fate of Charleston should, instead, mourn for all white Americans, since all share the guilt of slavery—it persisted not because of the evil of this one city but because of the flaw in the American character exemplified in Captain Delano's approving response to slavery. On the other hand, to wish for and to celebrate the suffering of civilians is to fail in brotherhood and charity. The suffering of Charleston was as deplorable as was the suffering of Vicksburg, even though it was morally explicable.

Guert's Last Chance

In the summer bustle and travel in Herman's family, the lone enigma was Guert Gansevoort. In March, Allan had inquired after him in Brooklyn, where he had been told Guert could be found, but without success. Finally he tracked him down in a rooming house in the city, but if the discovery made Guert any more accessible Allan left no evidence of the fact.[24]

What Guert needed was another command. Fortunately, at just this time he was given the *Roanoke.* Built in 1856 as a steam frigate, she had been, along with the rest of her class, superior to any other warship in the world. But less than six years later, her sister, the *Virginia,* had rendered her obsolete. Her conversion to an ironclad had taken sixteen months, during which, with the exception of the period during which he had commanded the *Adirondack,* Guert had been intimately involved with it. The radical alteration had made her into a supermonitor. Her tall masts had been removed, her high sides had been cut down, and she had been plated with armor along her sides. Her propulsion plant and her steering had been improved, but the most telling alteration had been to her armament. Her broadside guns had been removed and replaced by three rotating Ericsson turrets mounted along her centerline, making her the prototype of the modern battleship. In June 1863 she was recommissioned, and on July 15 Guert was detached from the navy yard to command her.[25]

Although his reprieve was welcome, for the most part it was empty. The *Roanoke* was a disappointment. The weight of her turrets made her top-heavy, causing her to roll excessively in brisk swells and expose her wooden hull below her armor. The rolling not only made her vulnerable to enemy fire, but also caused her turrets to work against her wooden frame, threatening to spring it or to force out her bottom. In this kind of weather, her guns had to be braced by timbers to prevent them from "fetching away." When her guns were fired, the recoil threw them back off their slides against the sides of the turrets, bending the metal plates. Guert was ordered to join the North Atlantic Blockading Squadron in Hampton Roads, but, unable to fight at sea and too deep of draft to enter the shallow water of the James River, the *Roanoke* could do little more than ride at anchor in the deep water off Fortress Monroe, a floating artillery platform. Appropriately, there was none of the family fanfare that had greeted Guert's command of the *Adirondack*. When Uncle Peter learned of the assignment, he asked Henry in a few laconic words, "Have you observed that your Cousin Guert Gansevoort is in the Command of the Roanoke."[26]

Guert's most important duty was to act as the second senior naval officer in Hampton Roads, and in that capacity he was the area commander whenever Flag Officer Lee was absent. It was an important enough position; on July 26, Secretary of State Seward, on a tour of the area, called on Guert, partly because he wished to see the new design of the *Roanoke,* partly because Guert was the nephew of his old friend Peter Gansevoort, but primarily because of Guert's position.[27]

While Lee was away, the commanding general at Fortress Monroe asked Guert to join him in a reconnaissance up the James River. On August 5, they were aboard the gunboat *Commodore Barney* above Dutch Gap, not far from Richmond, when the *Barney* was sent careening by an enormous explosion under her starboard bow. In the surge of water over her deck, twenty men either jumped overboard or were washed away, and only eighteen were recovered. With her hull damaged, her steam pipe severed, and her engine partly disabled, the *Barney* lay dead in the water. She had been the victim of a Confederate mine. Lt. Hunter Davidson, the genius of the Confederate Submarine Battery Service, had sunk a torpedo containing a half ton of gunpowder, with electrical circuits to detonate it, at that location. As the *Barney* approached, the Confederates lay in wait to calculate the precise moment at which to blow her up. However, in their eagerness, they closed the circuit too soon, else the gunboat would probably have been destroyed.[28]

A tug towed the *Barney* back to Dutch Gap, where, during the night, her crew made temporary repairs. Late the following afternoon, as the small armada reached a sharp bend, it came under fire from Confederate shore batteries and small arms. A shell hit the *Barney*'s side below the waterline, piercing her boiler. When she drifted aground, the tug pulled her off while a monitor duelled the enemy. After that, the monitor took the *Barney* in tow, assisted by the tug, until an army tug arrived to take over. Near Turkey Island Bend, the Confederates opened fire once more, hitting all of the ships repeatedly but without inflicting significant damage. After that, the battered force returned to Hampton Roads. To Guert's thinking, the reconnaissance had been a success despite the fact that the captain of the tug had been killed, two men had been drowned, several had been wounded, and the *Barney* had been so badly damaged that Guert had to ask permission to send her to Baltimore for repairs. It had been the kind of shot and shell melée on which Guert thrived, but it was the last significant action of his career.

When Johnny Comes Marching Home

Herman lost Allan's company when, after the draft riots, the truant lawyer returned to the city for several weeks, it would seem, to relieve Bruce of some of the office work and to appease his mother and sisters by paying for "The Repairs" in Gansevoort. While he was absent, the Pittsfield weather was rainier than usual and Herman and Lizzie had company. On Tuesday, July 27, Hope Shaw and Sam arrived for a four-day visit. Despite the rain, Herman treated them to his repertoire of rural amusements, driving them along a bumpy road to Mount Washington on the twenty-eighth. As Lizzie put it, they were "riding about early & late." From there the Shaws went on to Gansevoort to see Mother Melville, Fanny, and Helen Griggs. Malcolm and Bessie probably accompanied them.[29]

With Gus due shortly from New Bedford, Lizzie warned her that the house was too crowded for her to bring anyone with her. The scarcity of room suggests that Aunt Lucy and Uncle Nourse were visiting them, since they did visit that summer. That was another advantage of having Clara Nourse in town—it meant an opportunity to see her father and mother. On the evening of Tuesday, the fourth of August, one of the few clear days of the season thus far, Herman met Gus at the railroad station. Gus stayed for several days, giving Lizzie a chance to make up for missing her in the spring. In the hot spell that followed the rain—temperatures in the eighties and nineties—it may be that Herman took her for one of his carriage tours through the Shaker community and beyond—at least, John Hoadley spoke of her "travels in Berkshire."[30]

Jennie was up to her old tricks. On Friday morning, she invited Gus, Lizzie, Herman, the children, and any other guests who may still have been with them to a picnic at Arrowhead.[31] She did not invite them in person, since she did not dare to expose herself to the heat, but she sent the invitation with Milie and one of her younger sisters, who were instructed to hold parasols over Lizzie and Gus on their way to Arrowhead. Better yet, she offered to pay for a covered carriage, though Herman's buggy must have had a roof, as was usual. Lizzie must have shaken her head once again over the imagined fragility and the real foolishness of her citified sister-in-law. Soon after, Gus left for Gansevoort.

With their visitors gone, two of the children in Gansevoort, and the anticipated return of the Berkshire Regiment still two weeks away, Herman and Lizzie concocted a mischievous plan. Before moving to the city, they would make a grand tour of the countryside they would soon be leaving, a reprise of the trips they had been making for some thirteen years. Herman laid out an adventurous route, one that, in its comprehensiveness, they may never before have followed. With Allan still in the city, Jennie agreed to keep Stanny and Fanny at Arrowhead.[32]

On Monday, the tenth of August, they set out in the buggy. The weather was hot, but they were headed for the cool of the mountains. Their first stop was Great Barrington, where they lunched before continuing south. By nightfall, they were near Mount Everett, the "Dome of Taconic," as Lizzie called it, where they spent the night at "Smith's." The next day they drove east to Bash Bish Falls, an inspiring and perilous waterfall some 200 feet high. After spending Tuesday night there, they drove across the New York State border to Copake, where Lizzie sent a letter to Malcolm. From there they drove north, then east to re-enter Massachusetts. They passed through Great Barrington again in time for lunch, then drove east to Monterey, by Lake Garfield, where they spent Wednesday night. The next day they could easily have returned to Pittsfield, but they were not anxious to. Instead, they skirted it to the east on their way to North Becket (presentday Becket), then entered the Berkshire Hills region, "a very wild mountain spot very thinly settled," as Lizzie described it, and spent the night at Peru Hill, due east of Pittsfield. On Friday they continued north to East and West Cummington, where they met the Westfield River, then drove north along its banks to Savoy Hollow, where they again spent the night. On Saturday the excursion ended when they returned to Pittsfield, reclaimed Stanny and Fanny, and saw Allan, who returned that day from New York. On their way home they passed the triumphal arches being erected on the streets. In two days Helen was to bring Malcolm and Bessie back from Gansevoort, and in three Malcolm's school was scheduled to start. Along with socializing with Helen between trains and readying Malcolm for school, Herman and Lizzie did their part in preparing for the great parade, decorating their house with flags and festoons.[33]

Herman's marriage had not always been idyllic, but during that week he and Lizzie behaved like young lovers. Perhaps they had forgotten the pleasure of being together, away from family, friends, the war, and the obligations of being Typee and the Daughter of the Judge. For five and a half days, they had lurched along behind their horse, talking, laughing, and falling silent with each other, and eating and sleeping in romantic surroundings as though their private world had been born anew. They must have discussed the familiar things that make up the practiced conversation of husbands and wives, the war, the family, the times past in Pittsfield and the times to come in the city, and perhaps now and then one of them revealed a shy thought that might otherwise never have been spoken—but the overwhelming presence was that of pastoral scenes and unspoiled nature. As Lizzie said, "Both Herman and myself enjoyed it very much—We passed through some of the wildest and most enchanting scenery, both mountain and valley[,] and I cannot sufficiently congratulate myself that I have seen it before leaving Berkshire." Not a word about her allergies.

The triumphal arches a-building and the complementary bustle of the town manifested Pittsfield's excitement about the return of the Berkshire Regiment, an excitement so great that Mrs. Fenn had to remind the women that every troop train passing through town bore sick and wounded and that they were still needed at the station to serve refreshments. The town had been preparing since July 20, and Lizzie had already contributed. Mrs. Fenn had decided that some kind of hospital was needed for the sick and wounded, and the women had appropriated a vacant store on the south side of the park for Sanitary Rooms. Lizzie had contributed an American flag—a decoration appropriate for recuperating patriots. She had specified that when the rooms were finally closed, the flag was to go to Mrs. Fenn in recognition of her dedication to the war effort. One of the soldiers was already a patient there.[34]

Before the arrival of the regiment, Herman had ample opportunity to see Frank Bartlett, who had sailed on a steamer from New Orleans to New York, whence he had returned home. When the recuperating colonel arrived on Wednesday, August 19, he was greeted by a salute from the Pittsfield battery, two brass cannon which had been seized from a British blockade runner. He was a guest of the Morewoods—Lizzie reported that Sarah was "pretty well just now"—and a guest of the town. The evening of his arrival, the Liederkranz Singing Society appeared in front of Broadhall to serenade him, Bartlett made an impromptu speech, the leader responded, and Sarah served refreshments. A reporter discovered that he had been offered command of the 57th Massachusetts, a three-year veteran regiment that he was to raise in western Massachusetts, and noted that he was recuperating nicely, though he still carried his left arm in a box sling.[35]

After the surrender of Port Hudson, the Berkshire Regiment had been ferried down the river to Bayou La Fourche. At noon the day of their arrival, they had fought a small, fierce, inconsequential battle, their last of the war, in which twenty-two men were killed or wounded. Then the regiment had traveled from New Orleans to Cairo, Illinois, by boat before boarding the train for home. By prearrangement, they sent periodic telegrams announcing their progress. When they reached Buffalo, New York, the cannon were fired in Pittsfield to alert everyone that they would arrive in twenty-four hours, and trains brought kinsmen, friends, and admirers to Pittsfield from other Berkshire locations. At Albany, the volunteers washed and changed into their best uniforms, then, at ten in the morning of Saturday, August 22, their train pulled into the Pittsfield station carrying 676 of the 1,003 members who had departed the previous year.[36]

As the soldiers left the train, bells pealed, the cannon boomed once more, and the great crowd cheered. When Frank Bartlett appeared mounted on the horse he had ridden at Port Hudson, his left forearm still in the sling, his crutch visible by his saddle, it was the soldiers' turn to cheer. The ensuing parade was made up of citizens, bands, fire companies, the St. Joseph Mutual Aid Society, and, last, the regiment itself. The crowd lining the streets numbered about 10,000, including, probably, the Herman Melvilles, the Allan Melvilles, and Clara Nourse.

The regiment marched with its best military precision, interrupted by delirious bystanders who broke through the ranks to clasp their loved ones. Along the line of march, residences, stores, and the spaces between were decorated grandly, beginning with a banner just by the depot that asked "How are *you* 49th." On North Street, the soldiers passed under large flags suspended across the street and banners that read "Welcome Home, Gallant Forty-ninth" and "Ain't you glad you've come." Next there was a triumphal arch, covered with red, white, and blue colors, wreaths, and flags, all of which had been arranged by the ladies. Over the bank flew a Union flag with a Confederate banner that the regiment had captured reversed beneath it, and between the bank and Backus's Block there were more flags. As the soldiers marched beneath a large banner trimmed in black and bearing the motto, "*In Memorium. The Fallen Brave,*" they raised their hats in salute. When they entered South Street, near the Melville home, they passed under an arch of evergreens and wreaths of flowers suspended overhead with "W.F.B." worked into the center. The Melvilles' decorations were not elaborate, but they received notice in the newspaper. Banners nearby announced "Receive our Gratitude" and "Old Berkshire." Down East Housatonic Street there was an arch of evergreens surmounted by a portrait of George Washington and the slogan "Our Country's Pride." On East Street there were more banners trimmed with evergreens, and at Thomas Allen's home a banner proclaimed "Free Navigation of the Mississippi." From the Sanitary Rooms, the ladies had suspended a banner reading, "Know them which labor among you. Esteem them very highly in love, for their works' sake." Between these rooms and the park, the Louisiana flag taken from the New Orleans Custom House on the arrival of Farragut and Butler was displayed.

At 11:30, the soldiers halted in the park opposite the Congregational Church. There was an address, after which the parade marshal read the ladies' invitation to dine on the prodigious feast they had laid out with a sign that punned, "Only the brave deserve the *Fare*." After the soldiers' appetites had been satisfied, the spectators took their turn, but even after all had had their fill there was still enough left to feed a regiment that was expected to pass through in the evening and to give to the poor. The reception over, the Berkshire boys were dismissed. The sick, about fifty in all, were taken to the Sanitary Rooms, where the ladies cared for them. Lizzie was among the foremost, hovering over the men and bringing them beef tea.[37]

One of the stars of the day was a twelve- or thirteen-year-old boy who had attached himself to the regiment at Worcester. Known as the "Little Major" and clad in a sort of Zouave uniform, he had marched with the regiment and shared the soldiers' rations throughout its service. Now he was the pet of Pittsfield.

Herman recalled the return of the Berkshire Regiment in one of his finest poems, "The College Colonel." It is particularly interesting because, although it is an eyewitness account, it is demonstrably fictionalized. It is anachronistic in including Bartlett's later experiences as well as those prior to August 1863, and for that reason Herman located it in the 1864 section of his book. Like "The House-top," the poem will be discussed both here and later in this study.

The description of Bartlett is taken from the time of the Pittsfield parade. As he rides by, his crutch and his splint catch the eye. The men, too, are wartorn,

> a remnant half-tattered, and battered, and worn,
> Like castaway sailors, who—stunned
> By the surf's loud roar,
> Their mates dragged back and seen no more—
> Again and again breast the surge,
> And at last crawl, spent, to shore.

This is and is not an accurate picture. The soldiers had fought, but they had been away only nine months and a week or so, not two years, as the poem states, nor did they return shabbily dressed. As one soldier said, "To have marched into Pittsfield in all our dirt and rags would only have been an affectation of heroism."[38]

Herman was recording a vision of the heart together with his memory of the event. Crispness of appearance and a brief term of service would not have been consistent with the ravage of war that he wished to evoke. He was more interested in his nautical simile, which relates the poem to "The Battle for the Mississippi" and "Gettysburg" by depicting Satan's domain not as a forest or an abyss but as a sea where men are imperiled by shipwreck. Some fortunate ones are stunned by the surf and exhausted by the repeated struggle to reach the safety of the land; others do not survive the struggle and are dragged back to sink to the bottom of the sea. The survivors are marked by the experience, "half-tattered, and battered, and worn." It is a fine metaphor. It is also a tribute to Herman's poetic tact that he did not take advantage of the sentimental possibilities of the "Little Major."

Having the Heart to Make an End

There were few goodbyes remaining to be said. After the tour through Berkshire and the reception of the Berkshire Regiment, the sole scheduled event—if the family remained there long enough—was the Agricultural Fair, with its deep roots in the Melvill family history. Otherwise, the time would be passed in tidying up family affairs and in preparing the furniture, appointments, and clothing for the move. But, unexpectedly, fate demanded one more farewell.

For some time, Lizzie busied herself in tending the soldiers in the Sanitary Rooms, but she had other things to do. She presented the bar of Berkshire with a statue of her father, made in Boston some fifteen years before, which was to adorn the Lenox courthouse. In addition, she sent photographs of her camera-shy husband around the family. She and Herman also took care of a religious duty that they had neglected for some years, having Doctor Dewey of Boston come to Pittsfield to baptize Bessie, Stanny, and Fanny—Malcolm had been baptized in his infancy. During this time, Clara Nourse probably left for Cincinnati, as she had planned to do, to reclaim her house from General Burnside's staff and to reopen her school.[39]

On Monday and Tuesday, September 14 and 15, delightful weather graced the festival of the Liederkrantz, which included a concert at West's Hall with the Albany Brigade Band, a ball, and a picnic. But more meaningful to Herman was the visit of Commodore Charles Wilkes. Wilkes had been taking the waters in Brattleboro, Vermont, for six weeks and was now sightseeing in Pittsfield. He arrived on Monday early enough to visit Lenox, took calls at his hotel that evening, and, after visiting the Shaker Village and New Lebanon, departed on Tuesday. Herman did not hesitate to call on anyone who interested him, so it is possible that he took advantage of this opportunity to talk to the explorer of the South Pacific who had also been the captor of Mason and Slidell. Frank Bartlett was in and out of town, staying with the Learneds before a recuperative visit to Saratoga Springs, and with the Pomeroys afterward.[40]

On the third of September, John Hoadley had stopped in New York to purchase a steamship ticket and had spent a few days with Allan, who had promised that he and Jennie would visit New Bedford in the fall if the Hoadleys could resolve their servant problem. In the middle of the month, Kate Gansevoort and Anna Lansing visited the Melville women and Helen Griggs in Gansevoort. Mother Melville had wanted Abe to come, too, and had wanted the young ladies to spend the night, but they came alone and left the same day. Then late in the month Helen Griggs left Gansevoort for New Bedford, probably stopping in Pittsfield on the way.[41]

John Hoadley's voyage came about when the state of Massachusetts decided to purchase artillery for coastal fortifications. On September 16, Colonel Harrison Ritchie, of the military staff of Governor Andrew, sailed for England to oversee the manufacture and to take charge of the contracts, but because Andrew also wanted someone with engineering expertise, he asked the directors of the New Bedford Copper Company to lend him the "distinguished engineer" for two months. When they consented, Andrew appointed John an assistant quartermaster of state militia with the rank of captain. He was to collaborate with Ritchie and to study the machinery and the techniques employed to see if the guns could be manufactured in the United States. John was also to inspect English coastal fortifications and draw up a plan for the defense of Massachusetts. In response to John's plea, Helen agreed to stay with Kate until Fanny's arrival in midmonth. On September 23, with Allan present to see him off, John sailed from the city piers aboard the steamer *Scotia,* arriving in Liverpool in early October.[42]

After John's departure, Allan returned to Pittsfield intending to bring his family back to the city on Tuesday, October 6. Jennie wrote Mother Melville that she would take the girls to Gansevoort on the way, even if it meant traveling alone, and perhaps she did. That would explain how Stanny got there to live with his grandmother and his aunts over the winter. Herman had hoped to take Stanny and Fanny there himself to see their grandmother once more before the cold weather set in, but already his household was being dismantled. He and his family were not able to move to the city with the Allan Melvilles, since the New York house needed attention before it would be ready for occupancy, but he went with them, or perhaps with Allan, if Jenny went to Gansevoort, to supervise the work. While there, he had a chance to see Henry Thurston. Henry had arranged leave from his duties in Nashville in order to be with his children and his family, whom he had not seen in a year, and now he was recovering from a fortuitous illness that kept him from returning to duty—a malady endemic among soldiers on leave. Herman expected to return to Pittsfield on Thursday, the fourteenth of October, to fetch his family, but the work delayed him.[43]

It was fortunate that Lizzie remained behind. On Tuesday, October 6, Sarah Morewood attended the cattle show, seemingly as well as usual. Just after that, her physician informed her that she was dying. Although she rebelled against the idea, she made preparations, tidying up the end of her life by instructing Rowland about how to manage without her. Then her condition worsened rapidly. On October 15, Lizzie was feeling frustrated and a little guilty about having missed Fanny at the railroad station when, just after breakfast, she strolled over to the Morewood house. On her arrival, the doctor sent her up to Sarah's room with a warning that death was only minutes away. It was Sarah's wish to have friends but no clergyman present, and Lizzie had arrived just in time. With only Lizzie, Rowland Morewood, and her sister Ellen Brittain present, Sarah clung to life, only partly conscious, until 2:30 in the afternoon, when she died. Then Margaret, a favorite servant, Lizzie, and another woman who had been called in, dressed her for burial. For Lizzie, who had never before seen a person die, it was "a very solemn and eventful day," and she believed that Providence had delayed her departure so she could be with Sarah. She recalled that "for thirteen years we have been on the most intimate terms with out the least shadow of a break in our friendship." Sarah's death was a shock to Mother Melville and all Herman's siblings, the *Sun* extolled her indefatigable war work, and many a regiment mourned her passing.[44]

With her husband and the Allan Melvilles in the city, Lizzie was the only adult member of the family to attend the funeral, which was conducted in the Episcopal church on October 21. Herman, who was invited to be a pallbearer, must have wished to attend, but he could not leave the contractors to work on the house without supervision. Lizzie sent a wreath, Allan and Jennie sent a cross, and Herman sent an all-white wreath. With Sarah laid out in a rosewood coffin decorated with silver, a Stockbridge minister read the service. Lizzie was disappointed that there was no eulogy, though the lack was no doubt Sarah's wish, and she regretted that the Episcopal service did not reserve time for silent prayer, as did her own Unitarian Church. Nevertheless, she had said her last goodbye to Berkshire.[45]

Sarah Huyler Morewood. By permission of the Berkshire Athenæum

Herman included a subtle eulogy to Sarah in *Battle-Pieces,* or, better, a eulogy to all of the women, especially Sarah and Mrs. Fenn, who gave of themselves to care for the soldiers. Placed in the "Inscriptive and Memorial" section of the book at the approximate chronological point of Sarah's death, "The Mound by the Lake" commemorates their service in a brief narrative about a spinster, now dead, who devoted her life to tending the sick and wounded soldiers who passed by her door: "So warm her heart—childless—unwed, / Who like a mother comforted." In this story, the features of the women at the train station tending to the regiments as they passed through Pittsfield, the childless Mrs. Fenn devoting herself single-mindedly to the young men of the army, and Sarah Morewood sending delicacies to her regiments even as she slowly died, are plain to see. It is a memorial to them placed alongside the memorials to the men whom they nursed and comforted.

The Once and Future New Yorker

Much to Kate Hoadley's relief, on October 21 the family received word that Captain John had arrived in England without falling into the hands of a Confederate raider and was on his way to London. On the evening of October 28, Herman finally returned to announce that the great move would take place on Monday or Tuesday, November second or third, shortly revised to the middle or end of that week. That meant some days of hard labor for Lizzie, made easier by the vision of being settled once more. "I am out of all patience living in this forlorn condition," she wrote, "—carpets up window shades down, & everything in boxes."[46]

Herman, Lizzie, and the two girls left early the next week, as Herman had originally planned, and moved, bag and crate, to their once and future home. They were reminded of the realities of city life when they found, to their dismay, that they had to pay as much to transport their belongings across town to the new house as they had paid to bring them all the way down from Pittsfield. They moved in with Allan and Jennie until their house was ready for occupancy. Lizzie could hardly have failed to enjoy the luxury of the Allan Melville household, in which she was freed of the constant tedium of "women's work," but she must have spent much of the day at 26th Street, where, despite Herman's lengthy preparations, there was still work to do—repairs to be made and furniture to be purchased. All that would be paid for with the $1,000 that Aunt Priscilla had left to Herman. Eventually the family settled into the new home and Bessie and Fanny entered the Quaker School in Stuyvesant Square.[47]

Although she would have preferred to live in Boston, Lizzie must have been happy to be in New York again. For one thing, she was close to relatives. Although she had been intolerant of Jennie in Pittsfield, Jennie's hospitality and some living together in Jennie's natural habitat may have mitigated her resentment. After all, she was going to be in more or less continual contact with her sister-in-law for the foreseeable future. Moreover, if in Pittsfield Lizzie had scorned Jenny's urban fastidiousness, she herself was a daughter of the city, more comfortable walking the sidewalks than she was plodding along rural lanes. Of the inhabitants of the new house, it may be that only Bessie and Fanny missed the pastoral world they had left.

Sarah Morewood's death just as he was leaving Pittsfield had cut the last of Herman's strong ties to Berkshire, and as the closing scene of one important epoch of his life, it was tragically appropriate. As he said, he was returning to his home after a thirteen-year sojourn on foreign soil. When he had moved to Pittsfield, he had wished to test his paternal heritage, to contact and to understand the Scottish, Melvill element of his nature. His return to the city after over a decade was a tacit recognition that the Dutch Gansevoort element had triumphed. Now Pittsfield would fade into memory as an experiment well worth the heavy cost. It would be a memory of joys and fulfillments he had experienced there at intervals from childhood on and of failure, despair, and loneliness. The next time he saw the town, he would be a casual visitor.

He recognized now that his identity had always been rooted in his native state and city, even when he had been far away, but in his absence the city had changed. The novelties that he had glimpsed as a frequent visitor now gained the substance of permanency. In his childhood, New York had been little more than a large town, with streets whose names recorded its history and boundaries which relegated portions of Manhattan Island to suburbia and bucolica. When he and Lizzie had lived here in his earlier adulthood, the growth of that old Dutch town had not yet rendered it unrecognizable. Now it was a different place. Impersonally numbered streets stretching far to the north were consuming the suburbs, and as that happened the heart of the city and the piers along its flanks were also creeping north; Herman's 26th Street location was now one of the most desirable sections. Even his church had migrated uptown. Before they had moved to Pittsfield, he and Lizzie had belonged to the fashionable Church of the Divine Unity, as Rev. Henry Bellows's Unitarian congregation on Broadway and Crosby had been named, but now it was All Souls Church, located at Fourth Avenue and 20th Street. A basilica-like structure of layered red brick and limestone, it was often referred to as the "Beefsteak Church" or the "Church of the Holy Zebra." Elsewhere in the city, new buildings contained new institutions, and now there was the novelty of Central Park, where Allan and Jennie liked to ride in their carriage. While Herman's attention had been diverted, the city of his birth had grown out of its adolescence.[48]

The war also gave a new character to the city, which was a center of its manufacture, its finance, and its opposition—some burnt-out buildings stood as reminders of the recent riots. The metropolis grunted as it fabricated war materiel, and the navy yard over in Brooklyn growled at the task of making and mending warships. In what had been storefronts, recruiting offices hung out hopeful banners to compete with the draft for the dwindling remainder of healthy young men, and they were increasing as regiments approached the end of their three-year enlistments. Store windows displayed military uniforms and paraphernalia, pistols, sabers, and insignia, and the streets were dotted with the men who wore and carried them. Across the river on Staten Island, newly formed regiments were drilling at Camp Sprague, preparing for the front. Some prominent figures of the war were now residents of the city—General Frémont, General McClellan, General Fitz-John Porter, and Admiral Farragut. For a man who wished to be in close contact with the struggle, this was the place.

If Herman had been tasked and heaped by the isolation of Pittsfield, he could hardly have wanted for company here, even though he no longer lived along the Gansevoort–Boston shuttle that his mother and sisters traveled on their visits back and forth. Allan and Jennie and their parcel of girls lived only about a mile away, as did the young de Marinis. Herman could see Allan almost daily, at home with his family or at his office, where Herman developed a friendship with Bruce that lasted until the end of his life. There were also the Thurstons and their Barrington subbranch, with whom he had not been in regular contact since his earlier residence in the city. As a matter of course, he had his old literary friends with whom to visit and argue, with the melancholy exception of George Long Duyckinck, who had died at the end of March. Down on 10th Street were the studios of many of the most notable artists of the day, including Sanford Gifford, now back from his summer service with the Seventh Regiment. How many of these artists did Herman know? Bayard Taylor assumed that he was widely acquainted among them, and his deep interest in art suggests that Taylor was right. But if there were artists whom he did not know, their galleries, at least, were open to him. From time to time he must also have met officers of Henry's regiment as they passed through the city on leave and on business. In addition, New York was a crossroads where travelers from all points converged, so that one was likely to encounter distant family and friends at unexpected moments. When human companionship palled, the ferryboats, the bookstores, and the libraries beckoned.

Then there were the Latherses, whose rambling estate Herman and his family visited on occasion. Richard and Herman had many opportunities to meet and to compare their ideas about the war. At present, Richard was just back from his speaking tour abroad, and in the evening of October 29, just before Herman's move, he had visited Allan's family to report on his voyage. For several months he had spoken on behalf of the Union in London, Manchester, Edinburgh, and cities in Switzerland and Germany. Always the busy factotum of the local financial community, now that he was home Richard was making representations in Washington on behalf of the principal New York merchants about Confederate cruiser raids on merchant shipping. Gideon Welles told him that the navy would do what it could, but that there were too few vessels left over from the blockade to secure the sea lanes.[49]

But the city also had its darker side. The attacks on Franklin Pierce and James Buchanan—and on Hawthorne—and the manipulation of the facts of the draft riots had been continuations of the outrages against Democrats and their civil rights that had, symbolically, begun with the persecution of Vallandigham. The vendetta had continued when, in mid-September, the proprietors of the *Baltimore Republican* had been arrested for publishing disloyal poetry and exiled to the Confederacy. The Democrats responded with the charge, similar to that of the draft rioters, that the true reason for the continuation of the war was the "Republican party and its greedy retinue of contractors." But when the elections took place, they did not do well against the Republicans, who ran as the Union party.[50]

The assignment of General Dix as the district commander was not wholly a result of the draft riots, since Henry Gansevoort had known of it six months earlier.[51] It may be, as some Democrats suspected, that it had been long planned but delayed until the riots had given the administration an excuse to order in a strong general who would keep the always suspect city in his grip. It was a brilliant strategy. A powerful nabob and a man of culture, Dix was enormously popular. As a longtime Democratic leader and an ally of Richard Lathers's faction of the party, his actions could hardly be blamed on the Republicans, nor, in view of his military position, could he be held personally responsible. Furthermore, with the suspension of habeas corpus whatever measures he adopted were exempt from civil appeal or constitutional redress.

Upon his arrival on July 18, immediately after the riots, the administration had garrisoned the city with troops, ostensibly as a precaution against a recurrence of the disturbance when the draft resumed on August 19. The amount of force was overwhelming: volunteer infantry, volunteer artillery, and every regular infantry regiment in the east, save one. It amounted to an entire army corps, the most awesome military occupation force ever inflicted on an American city. Some of them were still present when Herman arrived, and some continued to garrison the city until the following spring. As their commander, Dix became a military interventor and a counterforce against the authority of Governor Seymour. Under his rule, a secret police system was instituted in the city as perfect, Morgan Dix boasted, as any domestic intelligence bureau in Europe, a comparison that had its roots in the Union Leaguers' admiration for European techniques of civil repression. Agents slunk along the streets and alleyways and reported to Dix's headquarters those whom they suspected of disloyalty. As a result, some citizens were exiled. "There was no such thing as hiding from the vigilant eyes which, during those months of peril, were watching every one to whom the slightest suspicion was attached," young Dix gloated.[52]

One of the employees of Richard Lathers was recruited to spy on him. That meant that Richard was suspected of subversion, though in the end the agent found no tangible evidence with which to impeach him.[53] But the corollary was that Richard's close friends and relatives, including Herman and Allan, were likely to have been subjected to surveillance, too. Since they often met Richard in town and exchanged visits with him at their various homes, it would have been necessary for the snoops to ensure that Richard was not conspiring with them. It was testimony to the perversion of friendships and principles that the war brought about. In 1860, Dix had drafted the conservatives' appeal to the South, but now he was spying on his longtime ally whose most obvious act of treason had been carrying it there! And his son, Richard's pastor at Trinity Church and one of his good friends, boasted of it! In justice, Dix should have been as much an object of suspicion as was Richard.

Herman knew this by the time he wrote the last lines of "The Housetop," in which he commented on Dix's stewardship in the city. The coming of "Wise Draco" corroborates "Calvin's creed / And cynic tyrannies of honest kings." Although Draco is a personification of the abrogation of civil rights by the federal administration, Dix is the specific figure involved. By giving him the name Draco, Herman advertised the irony of the poem, for "Draco" is one of those names that evoked a predictable and unequivocal response in educated people. In Herman's time, as now, the name of Draco, or the idea of Draconian law, was never invoked honorifically; it always signified an unjust and indefensible harshness in controlling a population. For instance, had Burnside been accused of being a Draco in Cincinnati, he would have been offended. Thus Draco, or Dix, is wise only to one who believes, contrary to the principles on which the nation was founded, in controlling supposedly free men through terror.

Were the riots a slur on the Republic's faith and proof that man is not naturally good and that the American is not "Nature's Roman, never to be scourged"? That is the narrator's idea, not Herman's. Had Herman believed that, he could never have invented a ship in *Billy Budd* named the *Rights-of-Man* in which the crew learns to govern itself through the virtue of a Handsome Sailor. Nor in a book that condemns scourging could White-Jacket have said: "Is it lawful for you to scourge a man that is a Roman? asks the intrepid Apostle, well knowing, as a Roman citizen, that it was not. And now, eighteen hundred years after, is it lawful for you, my countrymen, to scourge a man that is an American?" (142). No, the whole burden of *White-Jacket* says, it is not. In later years, Herman's Jack Gentian, always an embodiment of the author's ideals and a reliable spokesman for his thinking, discussed the idea of a Roman America. Gentian is asked, "Art thou such an old-fashioned Roman in thy patriotism that thou wouldst consign to oblivion the fact that thy countrymen, claiming the van of Adam's alleged advance, were but yesterday plunged in patricidal strife?" The answer is, yes, Gentian is precisely that kind of Roman patriot, and yes, he would consign that struggle to oblivion. Americans *are* never to be scourged—that would corrode the iron dome, subvert "the genius and principles of republican government." But that conception of American citizenship is lost upon those who view America from the remote vantage point of the housetop.[54]

If one were to search through Herman's life for an experience that might have prompted him to create the shipboard world of the *Bellipotent* in *Billy Budd,* the search might well end with General Dix's New York City. Beginning with a commander who shows two faces, one perhaps fatherly and the other that of a "martial disciplinarian," and adding to that a subordinate office which manages "wires of underground influence" through a staff of ship's corporals, one has the *Bellipotent* exactly. Then there is Richard Lathers. Not a rebel himself, but an object of suspicion because of the rebellion of others, he was, in that sense, a Billy Budd. Was that lost on the former "Vere de Vere" of Pittsfield? As Fogle has said, "the treatment of Law and the People in 'The House-Top' has a strong bearing upon the interpretation of . . . *Billy Budd*."[55]

The situation provoked Herman's ambiguity of attitudes. He had strong reasons to like and to be grateful to Dix, who had twice recommended him for public office and who would later, perhaps, assist him to obtain a position in the customhouse. Certainly Dix's methods were distasteful, but at the same time Herman's fair-mindedness must have understood Dix's motives. But the well-intended policy of a good man whose loyalty is to civil order rather than to the human heart can result in persecution of the innocent, including an ally, Richard Lathers, whom Dix had trusted in the past and had every reason to continue to trust. Of such stuff is ambiguity made.

Mother Melville fell ill and remained so for the entire winter. In fact, the infirmities of her generation were alarming. Aunt Helen Souther was in the poorest health: she had declined to the point that she was forced to ask Aunt Lucy Nourse to come to Hingham to care for her. Aunt Lucy came, but to do so she had to leave Uncle Nourse confined to the house with a lame foot. With legs swollen and body thin, Aunt Helen lay on her parlor sofa most of the time with Aunt Lucy massaging and bandaging her. Everyone in the family knew that her illness was terminal, but, bright and cheerful nevertheless, she lingered. Nor did the youngest generation escape. Ned Curtis suffered an accident and was confined to his bed for some weeks.[56]

As Christmas approached, so did John Hoadley's return from England. His business finished, he sailed from Liverpool on the first of December aboard the Cunard steamer *Hecla*. It was a remarkably slow voyage, nearly three weeks, but on Sunday, December 20, he arrived at the city piers. He would have spent the night with either Herman or Allan, but whichever brother he stayed with, the other would have appeared to hear about his experiences and about the attitudes of the English toward the Union cause. Then John had to hurry to reach New Bedford before Christmas. On the twenty-fifth of December, Herman's family, Stanny back from Gansevoort, Malcolm back from Newton Center, and the girls liberated from the Quaker School, had their first Christmas in their new home. Only one of the children's presents is recorded—Stanny received a toy cannon and a top from the Hoadleys. On New Years' Eve, Herman and Lizzie entertained a small group who were to "come early, stay socially & go early." The guest list included Allan and Jennie and their girls, Mrs. Brittain, down from Pittsfield, Evert Duyckinck, who was celebrating his first Christmas without his brother, and a few others, probably including the de Marinis.[57]

From Chickamauga to Chattanooga

It is likely that Herman had received a letter from Toby Greene just after the fall of Vicksburg. After his return to the 6th Missouri, Toby had fallen ill with diarrhea, a ubiquitous malady in the army and one that pestered him for his remaining service. Because of his illness, Toby was assigned as a clerk to General Grant's headquarters of the Army of the Tennessee. With his proven writing skills, he must have been one of the most qualified soldiers in the army for the duties, which, with changes in the headquarters and the general involved, he performed for the remainder of his enlistment.

In his letter, he must have told Herman about the siege, about his charge against the Confederate fortifications, and about his present assignment, and he must have asked Herman to send him several copies of *Typee.* His excuse was that he wanted one for his son, Herman Melville Greene, but he probably wanted the other two to impress the generals whom he was serving. It would not hurt his position for them to recognize him as the immortal Toby who had basked in the Polynesian sun with the famous Herman Melville.[58]

On August 10, Herman ordered three copies of the book sent to Toby at Vicksburg, and if he followed his usual practice he also sent his old shipmate jocular congratulations on the capture of the strategic city. But by the time Herman's letter and the copies of *Typee* arrived, Toby was in Chicago recovering from his illness and seeing his wife and son for the first time since he had enlisted, and he did not return to duty until October 16. On his arrival, he received Herman's communication, but for several days he was unable to acknowledge it. During his absence, his place on Grant's staff had been filled, leaving him to scramble for a new position. Fortunately, he obtained one at General Sherman's corps headquarters. Perhaps Sherman received Grant's copy of *Typee,* though Toby may have given copies to both. Then, not long before Herman left Pittsfield, he received another letter from Toby promising to visit the following June, when his enlistment was due to expire. He also reported that his headquarters was on the move.

Previously, the Army of the Cumberland had attempted to drive the Confederates out of Tennessee. In September, Braxton Bragg's army was concentrated in Chattanooga, not far from the Georgia border. General Rosecrans went on the attack, but Bragg turned on a part of his army at Chickamauga Creek. During the two days of fighting on September 19 and 20, Rosecrans lost over 16,000 casualties, while Bragg lost nearly 18,000. The Union force was nearly routed, but General George Thomas hung on tenaciously until his troops were able to withdraw. It was a defeat, but it was a personal triumph for Thomas, who became known as "The Rock of Chickamauga."

Although the 44th Illinois took part in the battle as part of Sheridan's Division, Herman knew none of the current members of the regiment. In addition, because he was in the city on leave, Doctor Thurston was not in Nashville to tend to the casualties that arrived there. Still, Herman wrote one of his slight memorials to the Union soldiers who had been killed, "On the Slain at Chickamauga." "To those who survive battles to enjoy the peace at war's end," he wrote, "the wreath be given, / If they unfalteringly have striven." They will live with memories of right restored, and they will remember their fallen comrades of Port Hudson, Vicksburg, and Gettysburg. But the defeated dead go uncelebrated; their valued lives were surrendered in futile battles and humiliating routs—here at Chickamauga and in other places that men will prefer to forget. But Herman would not allow their memory to die. The "will" and the "aim," not success, "Make this memorial due."

The plight of the Army of the Cumberland, now besieged by Bragg in Chattanooga, became increasingly desperate. The soldiers were in need of food and clothing, and their artillery horses died of starvation. Some of the blame lay in the army organization, since no commander on the field had the authority to coordinate the available Union resources. Then in the middle of October the administration gave Grant command of a new Military Division of the Mississippi, which placed all operations in the western theater under the control of a single able commander. Grant named his own generals, the reason for the upheaval that Toby had found on his return from Chicago. He gave command of the Army of the Cumberland to Thomas and chose Sherman to command the Army of the Tennessee. That meant that Toby served under Sherman, while he was a corps commander, for only a week or so, after which he served under a number of other generals who succeeded Sherman.

Well suited to his new position, talented, informed, unexcitable, determined, and experienced in organization and battlefield command, Grant promptly resupplied and reinforced Chattanooga. General Joe Hooker arrived with one corps of the Army of the Potomac and part of another, and Sherman's army, including Toby Greene, arrived from Memphis. The Confederate positions extended much of the way around the city, from Lookout Mountain in the southwest along Missionary Ridge on the east and on to a point well to the northeast of the city. The river enclosed the rest. Grant ordered Hooker's troops to a point fronting Lookout Mountain; in the center, facing Missionary Ridge, lay the revived Army of the Cumberland; across the river almost north of the city, Sherman's men were concealed.

On November 23, Thomas's men drove in the Confederate pickets and captured their outer works of Missionary Ridge, and that night Sherman's men moved into position at the northern end of the ridge. But the day belonged to gallant Joe Hooker, who assaulted Lookout Mountain. The "Battle above the Clouds" was supposed to be no more than a feint, but, capturing the spirit of their commander, the soldiers pressed on until all but the impregnable crest was in their hands. During the night, the Confederates abandoned that last bastion. The next day the grand assault began. The Confederate losses, particularly in prisoners, were around twice those of the Union army, and by nightfall Bragg's army was in full retreat and in danger of capture. From then on, the Union army controlled Tennessee. Although as a clerk Toby did not participate in the assault, he was present, probably writing tactical messages and performing other communication duties. This vantage point would have allowed him to describe it to Herman far better than he might have had he been engaged in the front-line fighting. But the man who almost certainly gave Herman an eyewitness account was General Grant.[59]

The first of Herman's two contrapuntal poems about this victory, "Look-Out Mountain: The Night Fight (November, 1863)," treats Hooker's battle as though it were a separate engagement rather than merely a preliminary to the assault. It is unique in *Battle-Pieces* in that it is a spoof disguised as a celebration. Why he wrote it in this way is difficult to know. Perhaps he disapproved of Hooker, or perhaps he was offended by the glorification of this battle in a war that canceled old ideas of the glory of combat.

The spoof originated in an unintended but well-publicized bit of military comedy. The Twentieth Corps that Hooker had brought to Chattanooga had been created from two earlier corps, the Eleventh and the Twelfth, that had been shattered at Gettysburg. The badge of the Eleventh had been a star, while that of the Twelfth had been a crescent. When the two corps were merged, the two insignia were combined into a single star and crescent badge until the army realized its mistake—the star and crescent being a powerful Muslim symbol. In an age when Kate Gansevoort could envision Armageddon as the final battle between the Protestants, on the one hand, and the Catholics and the Mohammedans, on the other, the army eliminated the crescent, leaving only the star as the badge of the new corps.[60]

The result is a Michael poem about "the war of Wrong and Right" narrated by an enthusiast who believes that the war between North and South pits God's chosen instruments against the forces of evil. That was the burden of much of the newspaper poetry of the day, such as the question of five-year-old Little Willie, who, looking up at the night sky, asks,

> And away up, up in the sky,
>   Is such a little bright star;
> Why, God is for the Union,—
>   Isn't He, mamma?[61]

That was reason enough for satire. Herman's poem pictures Hooker's men embarked on a holy crusade, but instead of depicting the daylight fight in obscuring mists he set the attack at night, with the mountain glowing with the "lurid light" of evil and surrounded by thunder and blight. Even at that, the poem might yet have seemed sincere had not Lookout Mountain been compared to Kaf, the Caucasian peak that rises above the Moslem Hell, the "evil height" of Eblis, who is the Muslim Satan.

It is in this translation of an invalid Christian idea into Muslim terms that the satire lies. If the public demanded the sanction of a god for such a battle, Herman made sure that it was not a Christian god or any other god satisfactory to a Christian of the times. In addition, he inverted the symbolism of "The Conflict of Convictions," where the height is the territory of an archangel and the depth the lair of Satan, and he inverted a biblical allusion (Isa. 57:13–15) in which God Himself is on the height. Even if the arrangement is true to the historical battle, the fact remains that in the poem the forces of evil are at the top of the mountain, the forces of good at the bottom. By obscuring his meaning thus, Herman was able to mock the Michael fallacy without denigrating the brave soldiers who fought there and without embroiling himself in a religious quarrel.[62]

In contrast, the lengthy "Chattanooga (November, 1863)" belongs in the mainstream of *Battle-Pieces:* its "heaven" refers to the bracing atmosphere in which the battle took place rather than to divine intervention. Here the fighting on Lookout Mountain pits two dimly seen ghost armies against each other in the obscurity of gray mists. The bulk of the poem describes the fighting of the following day, the character of the commander, the spirit of the soldiers, and the casualties. The Union soldiers outrun their orders, striving to be the first to reach the top of Missionary Ridge:

> one flares highest, to peril nighest—
> *He* means to make a name:
> Salvos! they give him his fame.
> The staff is caught, and next the rush,
> And then the leap where death has led.

These are the soldiers of the west, spirited, plucky, and determined, but their esprit costs many their lives. This was Herman's first opportunity to write proudly of a successful large-scale assault and his first opportunity to suggest the flood of Union troops that would increasingly sweep the North toward victory.

The narrator's admiration for the commander, "Grant, who without reserve can dare," is patent. Grant is a master rider who can give his men their head because he knows and trusts them. As he stands silhouetted on a cliff, his calm conceals "mastered nervousness intense." The attackers who appear on the crest of the ridge in "sharp relief" are compared to

> sky-drawn Grant,
> Whose cigar must now be near the stump—
> While in solicitude his back
> Heaps slowly to a hump.

This is gritty verse. Readers will disagree about the poetic tact of introducing Grant's cigar, but it is a part of the book's poetry of democracy. This is the real Grant, not a sanitized, scrubbed-up victor of conventional poetry. Popularly, the image of the cigar had become attached to Grant through anecdote and photograph, and it was preferable to his equally famous whiskey bottle—the only surprise is finding it in a poem. Similarly, readers may object to the image of Grant's humped back, but the last two lines of the quotation are carefully considered. In later days Grant became notorious for the cost in casualties of his battles, to such an extent that he was nicknamed "Butcher Grant," but that had to be balanced against the fact of his success, that is, that he was not a retreating general. It is Herman's own fancy, perhaps a sense that grew out of the meeting between the two men, that Grant agonized over the suffering of his soldiers. Be that as it may, Grant is the new hero of the new America, plain, blunt, efficient, masterful, and filled with compassion for his men.

Typical of *Battle-Pieces,* it is the dead with whom the end of the poem is concerned. In a stanza added after the first publication of the poem, one adapted from "Inscription for the Dead at Fredericksburgh," those who were felled on the slopes, "eager, ardent, earnest there— / Dropped into Death's wide-open arms." These men are not haloed or glorified by any power other than their own youthful spirit, their determination to gain the height whatever the cost. The word "height" accrues a meaning greater than that of the crest of a ridge; it is the lofty aim of the "young and fair," in the pursuit of which many of them were "Quelled on the wing like eagles struck in air." "Their end attained, that end a height: / Life was to these a dream fulfilled, / And death a starry night." Death has no abstract meaning here. Like the death of Billy Budd in Herman's last romance, it takes its significance from the mystery of life, from the existential beauty of youth in its heedless and vigorous dreamlike march toward its starry end.

Envy and Slander

Herman seems to have passed the winter in good physical health and moody temperament. An inevitable reaction to the dislocation of his move had set in, the idea that his native city was viewed as a hotbed of disloyalty did not cheer him, and the war in Virginia had again been going badly. When Evert Duyckinck asked that he review a book, he replied that his spirits were too low. As had been anticipated for some time, on January 20, 1864, Aunt Helen Souther died. It is reasonable to assume that Herman and Allan attended her funeral, not only because that was expected but also because there were not many aunts and uncles left.

Early in February, Henry Gansevoort appeared in the city, where he could bring Herman up-to-date about his activities since he had rushed south just before Gettysburg. During the summer and fall, he had been striving to make his regiment battle ready under deplorable circumstances, circumstances so aggravating that most of the time he had been ready to resign. The 13th New York Cavalry was hardly the fulfillment of his sanguine expectations. As John Hoadley summarized it, it was made up in equal parts of bounty-jumpers, future bounty-jumpers, invalids, and "the best men in the country, strong, brave, patriotic, and devoted, but raw and undisciplined." Ed Lansing recalled that "in a few hours [the officers had] found themselves transferred from the sidewalks and bar-rooms of New York to the rank and dignity of cavalry officers,—to command and to be commanded." Many of the new troopers were immigrants scarcely able to speak English.[63]

On its arrival in Washington, the 13th had been ordered to oppose Jeb Stuart's cavalry, which was reported to be at Fairfax, only fourteen miles away. The green men were issued tents, stores, carbines, and horses and sent out to defend the city, but Stuart did not attack. Then, immediately after Gettysburg, four companies had been ordered to the Cavalry Corps of the Army of the Potomac to assist in cutting off Lee's retreating army, but some compassionate general withheld them from the fighting.[64]

During this time, Henry had relapsed into malarial fever and returned to the city to recover under the care of Doctor Woodward, to visit Allan, and to spend time at the seashore. Then on October 1 he had rejoined his regiment at Centerville, where he had met his brigade commander, Colonel Charles Russell Lowell, "the son of Prof. Lowell of Harvard and a very excellent officer though young," Henry reported, confused about Lowell's parentage. After having served in the regular cavalry and on General McClellan's staff, Lowell had been appointed colonel of the 2nd Massachusetts Cavalry. Now he was in command of the Cavalry Brigade, Corcoran's Division, Department and Defense of Washington. The other regiments of the brigade were the 16th New York, which was awaiting its commander, Colonel Henry M. Lazelle, a West Point graduate and a regular captain of infantry, and Lowell's 2nd Massachusetts, commanded in Lowell's absence by Lieutenant Colonel Caspar Crowninshield, who had fought with the Harvard Regiment at Ball's Bluff. All three regiments were new, and their assignment to this station just outside the capital fell short of the visions of glory of their commanders. "Not very magnificent," Lowell had quipped.[65]

With water so filthy that Henry drank liquor instead, and with an ominous vulnerability to attack by the guerrillas of John Singleton Mosby's partisan ranger battalion, the location of the camp had been untenable. In

Colonel Henry Sanford Gansevoort (seated, second from left), with senior officers of the 13th New York Volunteer Cavalry, 1864(?). By permission of The New York Public Library, Gansevoort-Lansing Collection

August, the rangers had ambushed a small party of the 13th New York nearby, and in the same month they had captured a sutler's wagon of the 2nd Massachusetts. On August 24, they had penetrated the camp perimeter, captured 100 horses, and escaped. "I expect to be in Richmond ere long if we do not make better dispositions than we have," Henry had written his father. "I hope you will save up some gold for me if I ever take that trip." On October 5, Henry had commanded the brigade while it moved to Vienna, a defensible area with adequate water and a newly opened stretch of the Alexandria, Loudoun, and Hampshire Railroad to bring in supplies from Alexandria. There Henry worried less about visiting Richmond.[66]

With his regiment reassembled at last, Henry was happier with it than he had been. Major Coles proved to be a trustworthy second in command and Charles Brewster's eyes and ears helped Henry to monitor the doings of the company-grade officers. But wary of the politics of the volunteers, Henry wanted more allies, such as Ed Lansing. Never having managed a permanent position in the 50th New York Engineers, Ed had finally been sent home. When Henry wrote offering him a commission in the 13th, Ed was happy to accept.[67]

Periodically, Henry suffered recurrences of "malarial fever," but otherwise life was reasonably pleasant. He was able to visit nearby Washington frequently on the many pretexts offered a regimental commander. One of his favorite companions was Charles Brewster. A type of the eastern boy who had gone west to seize what he could of the frontier plenty, Charles had been coarsened by the experience. He drank too much, cursed volubly, and exercised his libido with an abandon which made Henry seem celibate. One of Charles's Washington amusements was to meet an actress in a theater box and "drink &c" with her. One can only imagine the consequences of his influence on Henry, or, perhaps, their influence on each other. Certainly Henry continued his fornication as though he had learned nothing from his disease of the preceding winter. Later, when Ed Lansing teasingly warned one of Henry's feminine friends to be cautious of "King Bee," she clucked that "the warning comes *rather* late in the day."[68]

Henry had another opportunity to command the brigade when Lowell married Josephine, or "Effy," Shaw. On October 27, he handed Henry the temporary responsibility and left for home. But Henry was in no condition to command anything: he was in bed, sweating and in pain. Privately, he recognized that if his illness continued he would be unfit for the responsibility of any command. "The truth is that the fever has got into my system and there it remains to bother me," he wrote.[69] After ten days, Lowell returned with Effy in tow. He moved her into a cottage within the camp limits and there the two did their best to begin their married life.

The beginning of 1864 brought changes in Henry's division. The commander had been Brigadier General Michael Corcoran, an Irishman whose Irish brigade, the Corcoran Legion, guarded the northern stretches of the Military Railroad, the main supply line to the Army of the Potomac. When Corcoran was killed in an accident, General Robert O. Tyler was transferred from his artillery duties in the Army of the Potomac to Fairfax Court House, with the result that Henry now served in Tyler's Division. Colonel Lazelle, who had arrived to take command of the 16th New York, went on leave, returning in mid-January with a bride whom he settled in the house he had been occupying in his regiment's section of the camp. Not to be outdone, Henry also moved into a house, a good idea, considering his health. During this time, the cavalrymen were relatively inactive, but because of Mosby they did not go into winter quarters. At one o'clock one night fifteen rangers slipped into the camp three times to steal horses and mules.[70]

In February, Charles and Effy Lowell departed for a month or so of temporary duty in charge of the great cavalry depot at Giesboro Point, Washington, leaving Colonel Lazelle in command of the brigade, but by that time Henry was in New York recruiting. There could be no promotion to full colonel until his regiment was full, and it was losing an average of a man each day to Mosby's bullets, to illness, to discharge, and to desertion. Recruiting was so ineffective that the strength of the regiment was actually waning rather than increasing. It became apparent that the problem centered on Major Lockwood, Henry's friend, who, it was reported, was more intent on enriching himself at the expense of recruits than he was in helping the regiment. Finally, Henry fired Lockwood and asked for recruiting help—from his father, Abe Lansing, Bruce, and Allan—and obtained a petition signed by William Cullen Bryant, Parke Godwin, and others asking that the regiment be filled with men raised in Queens. Herman may have helped circulate it for him, since Bryant was a member of his church congregation and Godwin was Bryant's son-in-law.[71]

There was a genuine danger that if the regiment were to remain undermanned the colonelcy would be purloined by someone else who promised to fill it. Furthermore, Henry became aware that some officers who had been dismissed, including Major Lockwood, were plotting to have another officer appointed colonel. Detained in camp by a court-martial, Henry sent Major Coles to Albany with two letters. The first was an endorsement by Lowell, who praised Henry for his qualities as a commander and the regiment for the progress it had made; the other was from Henry to his father, asking him to use his influence with Governor Seymour, Judge Parker, and anyone else he could think of. In Albany, Coles surprised a delegation of the conspirators in the act. Then he and Uncle Peter talked to Governor Seymour and General Sprague, each coming away from the meetings with a different conception of the details of the conspiracy. The truth was that Doctor Woodward, who had never intended to be more than a recruiting station surgeon, had become convinced that Henry meant to order him to the field. For that reason, he had agreed with the conspirators to certify that Henry was physically disqualified for command, a charge which combined malice and truth. The certification would be enough to send Henry home to civilian life. Upon hearing from Coles, Henry sped north, arriving in New York on February 8 and in Albany the next day. That left Major Douglas Frazar, a Massachusetts man who seems to have been Henry's enemy, in charge of the regiment. Rumors flew around the 13th that another officer was certain to obtain the colonelcy, and Frazar began to report Henry absent without leave every day. Ed Lansing spied on the other officers and reported their mischief to Henry.[72]

After doing what he could at the state capital, Henry returned to New York to supervise recruiting. That gave Herman his first opportunity since his visit to Fort Hamilton to see his young cousin regularly and to chat with him about the war. In turn, Henry had an opportunity to renew his acquaintance with Herman, who, although he had always interested his young cousin, had for so many years been out of the way in Pittsfield. One of the things that tickled Henry was the fact that, although Herman and Allan believed that they were much alike, he could see that they were very different—Allan the frail, self-assured, facetious, tyrannical man-about-town, Herman the rugged, philosophical, independent, and impecunious humorist and melancholic. He decided that although they would not admit it, they were "the antipodes." During their social hours with him, he must have invited them to visit his camp—provided he retained his command.[73]

It did not take Henry long to set matters right with Doctor Woodward. After he assured him that he would not have to go to the front, Woodward withdrew his certification. He had been misled about Henry's condition, he lied, but now that he had had an opportunity to observe him further he believed him to be fully qualified for field duty. In payment for that untruth, Henry replaced Woodward as regimental surgeon with Doctor Benjamin Rush Taylor.[74]

Under Henry's personal supervision, recruiting prospered. His prize catch was Captain George Henry Brewster. Charles Brewster had never wanted to be a line officer: he was a commissary of subsistence at heart and had expected to fill that position in the regiment. With Henry's blessing, he had renewed his application for an appointment as commissary in the U.S. Volunteers, which he received during Henry's absence. Henry then persuaded Bruce to join the regiment in his brother's stead. Nothing could have pleased Henry more than the prospect of having his longtime friend and former partner with him to share his confidences and his tribulations.[75]

With Henry putting out fires at home, others were igniting them in Vienna, but Major Coles was keeping the regiment "snug" in his absence. One of the officers who was resigning preferred charges against Henry, claiming that he occupied a house in camp, that he consorted with prostitutes in Washington, that he was physically incapable of performing his duties, that he dismissed officers unjustly, and that he was guilty of various other offenses, such as not getting out of bed at reveille. Coles knew how to handle that: he withheld the resignation so the officer could not go to Washington to submit the charges. Again, a New York buffoon who had never succeeded in raising a regiment of his own appeared in camp to circulate a petition to make himself the colonel. All things considered, Coles advised, Henry should not return from New York until after he had mustered in as colonel.[76]

While Henry completed his last company, his father continued the struggle in Albany. Peter was in Governor Seymour's office when a certificate arrived saying that the regiment was complete, at which point Seymour and Sprague issued the orders to promote both Henry and Coles. Henry was mustered in as colonel immediately, and the following day, March 29, 1864, he returned triumphantly to camp "with the Eagles on"—too hastily for Herman and Allan to see him off. Now Henry was in control of events. The charges against him had been entered formally, but, seeing that he was defeated, the complainant asked that they be withdrawn as "frivolous." Major Frazar, whom Henry credited with being deeply implicated in the plot, offered to make a new start, to which Henry agreed. With that, Henry's life and the regiment's returned to normal. Ed Lansing had been appointed adjutant to Colonel Lowell, a post which Henry thought suited him better than line duty. Charles Brewster left shortly for his new assignment as commissary to General Custer's cavalry brigade, and on the fifth of April, Charles and Effy Lowell, the latter now pregnant, returned to camp.[77]

Henry's presence in the city had meant that Herman and Allan had been privy to the conspiracy-counterconspiracy drama, outlined in melancholy detail by Henry. It was this kind of treachery so close to him, together with other like memories, surely, that led Herman to write in a late poem, "In a Bye-Canal" (239–40), about seeing "following me how noiselessly, / Envy and Slander, lepers hand in hand."

Although everyone was proud to have a full colonel in the family, the most immediate effect of Henry's visit was that Allan was about to lose his partner. Bruce received his commission[78] and began to assemble his uniforms, weapons, equipment, and cavalry mount and to put his business affairs in order. With that, the relationship between the partners was reversed. Now Allan would have to manage Bruce's affairs, which, under the circumstances, he could hardly refuse to do. Patriotism demanded as much.

Relief

Although the tempo of the war was sluggish during the cold season, Northerners were excited about the Sanitary fairs, the sort of community endeavor, almost unknown in peacetime, that the common purpose and determination of wartime inspired. Some cities had already held theirs. Those in charge of the Great Western Sanitary Fair in Cincinnati had conceived the idea of selling autographs of celebrities and had asked Herman to contribute some from his files, but, although he was anxious to help he had to confess to his "vile habit" of discarding most of his correspondence. The Cincinnati folk had better luck with Hawthorne, who sent three autographs. Then in midwinter Herman was asked to contribute a manuscript to the Baltimore fair. John Pendleton Kennedy had proposed the publication of a book, *Autograph Leaves of Our Country's Authors,* to be made up of lithographs of pages by prominent authors and sold to raise money for the Sanitary and Christian Commissions. Each author was to submit a short piece, complete, if possible, made up and signed so as to be suitable for reproduction. Although Herman's files contained a number of unpublished poems from his aborted book, he chose to contribute "Inscription for the Slain at Fredericksburgh," possibly the only Civil War poem he had completed by that date. By mistake he sent a superseded version and had to rush a replacement to the editor. He was insistent that the earlier version not be published, probably because in minor ways it no longer represented his view of the war. The new title was to be "Inscription for the Dead at Fredericksburgh" and the "glory" that "lights an earnest end" was to become a "dreadful glory." "Slain" was too much a euphemism for his present mood, and by now he believed that any glory in death on the field was dreadful. But the substitute poem arrived too late.[79]

For the Albany fair, or "Army Relief Bazaar," Aunt Susan was to be both a patroness and one of the ladies in charge of the United States booth and the Holland booth, and Kate contributed her services enthusiastically. She made an afghan, to be raffled off for two dollars a ticket. There were 100 tickets to sell; Aunt Susan bought some, sending one to Mother Melville, and other charitable folk, such as Doctor Woodward, took their chances. In her work for the "Post Office," which was to assemble and sell letters and literary pieces, Kate solicited letters from a number of the officers of the 13th Cavalry, including Majors Coles and (in her innocence) Frazar, Ed Lansing, and Charles Brewster. It is difficult to believe that she did not obtain something of value from Herman, since he was a willing contributor to the cause. During the bazaar she was to work in the United States booth, wearing a red, white, and blue costume and a chaplet of stars.[80]

On February 24, two days after the bazaar had opened, Herman passed through Albany without stopping, despite the fact that he wanted to see it. Though both he and Allan were concerned about Mother Melville's illness, which had alarmed the family, Allan claimed that he could not get away from his business. Herman brought a parcel of "delicacies" that he thought might stimulate her appetite and found that Fanny had just arrived after spending most of the winter with the Hoadleys. Mother Melville's face was thin and pale and she was weak from pain, but she announced that seeing Herman made her feel much better. Soon she was sitting up.[81]

Catherine Gansevoort (seated under eagle) in costume for the United States booth, Albany Sanitary Bazaar, *circa* February 1864. By permission of the Berkshire Athenæum

After a five-day visit, Herman returned to Albany. He arrived at nine in the evening of Leap Day, February 29, and felt obligated to leave on the afternoon train the next day, which would give him no opportunity to see the booths—not even the Oriental booth, where the ladies wore alluring costumes.[82] With snow falling the next morning, the best he could do was to accompany Uncle Peter and Aunt Susan to the studio of the eminent sculptor Erastus Dow Palmer to see the art exhibit there. After lunching in town with his aunt and uncle, he left for home.

He returned in time for the departure of the first New York black regiment, the 20th U.S. Colored Troops, on March 5. Although there was still much antiblack feeling in the city, expressed in various ways, the Union Leaguers presented the regiment with its colors in Union Square and marched protectively at its side as it proceeded down Broadway. Even though the league had sponsored it as a slap at the city conservatives, it was a remarkable event to have occurred only a half-year or so after the riots.[83]

Thus far, Herman's life in New York had been uneventful, useful but limited in its opportunities for immersion in the stuff and event of the war.

But there was a stir in the air. The city was anticipating a spring offensive and preparing for its own Sanitary fair. In a little over a month, Herman would be caught up in an excitement for which nothing in his previous experience had prepared him. In short, he was about to go to the war to see it for himself, to extend by far the sum of the wartime experiences that were his imaginative grist for *Battle-Pieces*.

7

A Portrait of the Artist as a Man of War

1864

In the late winter and early spring of 1864, Herman responded to three potent forces. The first was his creative genius: he was preparing for what he hoped would be a great literary work of the war, a historical record of its agony, a philosophical study of its horror and its purpose, and a vision of a meliorative future that the catharsis of carnage might bring. The second was the spirit of New York City, with its instinctive loyalty, its disorderly opposition, its busy industry, its dogged optimism, and its determination in the face of repeated military defeat. The third, called by Herman the "Abrahamic river," is difficult to define. Northerners in general, and Herman in particular, sensed that the great climax of the war was near. They had been heartened by the victories at Gettysburg, Vicksburg, and Chattanooga, and the coming campaign was about to pit the seasoned Union and Confederate armies against each other in a desperate confrontation. Northerners everywhere felt that with justice on its side, the great Abrahamic flow of Northern soldiers and civilians would somehow prevail.

But there remained the vexing problem of defeating a general as skilled as Robert E. Lee. Good fortune had deserted the Army of the Potomac after Gettysburg. Meade had camped south of the Rappahannock River while the priceless days of late summer and early fall had drifted away. Then he was duped by a Confederate feint into rushing his army back to Washington, where Henry Gansevoort waited to fight a battle that never came. Then Meade moved against Lee before the weather forced him into winter quarters, but the attempt was futile and cost casualties. Several days after his father, Henry Wadsworth Longfellow, and his brother, Ernest, reached Washington, Charlie Longfellow arrived with a wound from a bullet which, passing through both shoulders, nicked his spine. His father and brother took him home, but even though his condition proved to be less than dangerous, his recuperation was so lengthy that he lost his volunteer commission.[1]

Not long after, the administration appointed Grant general-in-chief of the army. His management of the forces at Chattanooga, where he had turned military disaster into victory, had been a welcome success that ratified his already established reputation. He was also promoted to lieutenant general, the first officer since George Washington to attain that rank. The Democrats would have preferred McClellan, but even if McClellan and Grant were equally suited to the task, as many thought, Grant was the better general in the most crucial respect: although he was not brilliant, basing his strategy on aphorisms developed from experience rather than on a supple intellect, the administration trusted him. He did not threaten Lincoln, as McClellan did.

Apart from his military skill, Grant's success at Chattanooga had resulted from his freedom to select his generals and to direct his campaign without political and bureaucratic interference. Now he was given that freedom in his management of the entire army. He appointed Sherman to the command he was leaving, the Military Division of the Mississippi, chose James B. McPherson, a leading commander at Vicksburg, to replace Sherman as head of the Army of the Tennessee, and promoted Sheridan from his division command in the Army of the Cumberland to command of the Cavalry Corps of the Army of the Potomac. He enlisted the abilities of capable generals who had been discredited as top commanders, ordering Meade to continue in command of the Army of the Potomac, bringing Burnside east to command the independent Ninth Corps, giving Hooker command of the Twentieth Corps in Thomas's Army of the Cumberland, and even finding make-work for Halleck—though he could do nothing to reinstate the purged Democratic generals. It appeared that the means of winning the war had been found.

The Metropolitan Fair

The New York City Metropolitan Fair had been long in the preparation. It was largely the work of the "benevolent ladies" of the city, perhaps including Lizzie, whose minister, Henry Bellows, had been instrumental in founding the Sanitary Commission and who was not hesitant to recruit from his congregation. It had been delayed, with the result that as the opening day approached spring was in the air and Grant was in Washington and Virginia adjusting his machine of war. That heightened an anticipation that needed no heightening. The event was to be, as the *New York Times* asserted modestly, "the greatest fair the world has ever known." $140,000 had been raised in Boston and $60,000 in Chicago, but New York aimed at $1,250,000.[2]

On Sunday, April 3, 1864, the mayor proclaimed the following day, when the fair was to open, a holiday, and the Stock Exchange, the banks and insurance companies, and most other businesses complied happily. On Monday, the sun came out after a week of rain. Flags bedecked the city, the ships in the harbor dressed in flags, and precisely at two in the afternoon a grand parade, led by General Dix, stepped off. With 10,000 soldiers and twenty-seven bands, it was the largest parade in the history of the city.

The fair was held in two buildings constructed for the purpose, one the Palace Garden, the other at Union Square. The opening ceremony, presided over by Dix, began in the evening when the Seventh Regiment band played "Hail Columbia!" and the fair band and massed choirs performed "The Star Spangled Banner." After the ceremony, the guests mingled and ogled at the exhibitions as speeches continued through the evening. Generals McClellan, McDowell, and Burnside were present and a glimpse of the diamonds and dresses of the ladies was said to be worth the price of admission.

The exhibits at the Palace Garden were dazzling. In the Grand Hall, there was a breathtaking display of flowers, evergreens, columns, mirrors, gas jets, and national emblems. Elsewhere was a re-creation of the summer house where Washington Irving and the other Salmagundi notables had congregated. Uncle Peter had loaned the fair his father's sword, the American flag from the surrender of Cornwallis, and a hammer (probably a tomahawk) from the Indian wars,[3] but their interest was dwarfed by trophies of the present war and artifacts that illustrated the battle history of the nation, uniforms of Generals George Washington and Andrew Jackson, the first "Bowie" knife ever made, an impression of the stamp of the Stamp Act, and the most important flags of the nation's past. There was even a drinking cup of the sort that Hawthorne had reported in 1862, reputedly fashioned by a Rebel from the skull of a Yankee killed at Bull Run. The Picture Gallery, with artist John F. Kensett in charge, exhibited 600 paintings. The 400 or so American canvasses represented a history of the national art, particularly that of New York City; canvases by West, Stuart, Cole, Durand, Kensett, Cropsey, Church, Bierstadt, Mount, Thomas Hicks, and Eastman Johnson, and Leutze's heroic *Washington Crossing the Delaware* dominated. Albert Bierstadt superintended a show of aboriginal life, with Onandaga and Cayuga Indians who still lived according to the traditions of their forebears. They wore aboriginal clothing and paint, and in periodic performances they acted out their way of life, including dances and rites.

One could purchase curiosities, including an American eagle woven from the hair of Lincoln, his cabinet, and seventy members of Congress. There was a restaurant where filet mignon with truffles was served for a dollar and lobster salad for a quarter. One could buy manuscripts by Beethoven,

Mendelssohn, Rossini, Irving, Dickens, Walter Scott, Napoleon Bonaparte and his generals, autographs of Washington, Hancock, Kossuth, and Garibaldi, and a sheet of paper containing the signatures of both Whittier and Barbara Frietchie. One could purchase the *Spirit of the Fair,* containing such items as General Dix's essay on "The Six Writers of the Augustan History,"[4] and, probably, the volume to which Herman had contributed, *Autograph Leaves of Our Country's Authors,* since its copyright was owned by the Sanitary Commission.

Two Tiffany swords, one naval and one military, were on exhibition. One paid to vote for the officers to whom they were to be presented. The motive was patriotic, and so it turned out in the case of the navy sword. After three days of polling, the votes were about equally divided between Commander Stephen Rowan, an early war hero, DuPont, and Farragut. But the voting for the army sword was certain to arouse political passions. At the end of the same three days, the city's favorite, McClellan, led Grant, as he continued to do throughout most of the fair. So exciting was this contest that the *New York Times* soon began omitting the navy vote count.[5]

Entertainment was the motif at Union Square. For children, there was a playground outside and inside a stage, a skating rink, and a toy shop—dolls, tops, toy cannon, and other favorites. One could also attend a concert by several dozen of the finest local musicians. But the great attraction was the Knickerbocker Kitchen, which transported the visitor back to the days of Peter Minuit. The ladies of the old Dutch families had ransacked their homes for the authentic clothing, furniture, paintings, place-settings, and recipes of New Amsterdam. While sitting at the rough old tables and chairs and looking at portraits of the early colonists, one ate lunch or tea cooked over an open hearth from old, heavy crockery. Managing the room were ladies of Dutch descent, such as the Roosevelts, and black women impersonated the slaves of the old city. The fare included *olykoek, kröller, roliltjes,* mince pie, head cheese, and smoked ham.

Nathaniel Hawthorne, sad and feeble, was in town for some days prior to the grand opening. He had been infirm for a year or so, but during the winter he had failed badly. In early March he had been unable to summon the energy and the spirit to put on his boots and coat or even to read. He had failed creatively, too, unable to follow any coherent fictional path to a successful conclusion, and socially he had retreated far within himself, available only to his family and his few intimate friends. He had responded poorly to the intolerance and ill will of which he had found himself the object. Emerson spoke for many when he said unforgivingly that recently Hawthorne "had removed himself the more by the indignation his perverse politics & unfortunate friendship for that paltry Franklin Pierce awaked."

Sophia Hawthorne put it this way: "The state of our country has, doubtless, excessively depressed him. His busy imagination has woven all sorts of sad tissues." It was under these conditions that William D. Ticknor, convinced that it would benefit his health, prodded him to travel.[6]

On the morning of March 29, the two men had arrived in the city, where they had remained at the Astor House for about a week. Perhaps Hawthorne did not know that Herman had moved to the city, but in any event he would not have called on him any more than he would have accepted Jessie Frémont's invitation to call on her. On the opening day of the fair, they left for Philadelphia, stopping at the Continental Hotel. Their next objective was Baltimore, which meant that, whether it was apparent to them or not, they were gravitating toward Washington and toward a repetition of their visit of 1862. Hawthorne had been gaining strength, but the day after their arrival Ticknor fell ill. Then, early Sunday morning, he died, the first such scene that Hawthorne had ever witnessed. Grieving and helpless, Hawthorne remained in Philadelphia for a few days after Ticknor's son had sent his father's body home and then allowed himself to be taken back to Concord.[7]

On Monday, April 4, just as the fair was opening, Bruce received his commission and wrote Henry Gansevoort that he would leave for Washington on the Thursday evening train. He asked Henry to meet him at the Ebbitt House on Friday, but volunteered, if that were not possible, to find his way to the cavalry camp on Saturday. Then Allan decided that it was time, before the spring offensive began, to visit Henry. He, Jennie, and Milie, his oldest daughter, would accompany Bruce to Washington. That required another letter to Henry to arrange appropriate facilities should the women wish to pass the night at the camp.[8]

But that plan did not take Herman into account. When he heard about the anticipated visit, he decided to go along. There was nothing haphazard or frivolous about the decision. Despite his statement in the preface to *Battle-Pieces* that he was motivated by the fall of Richmond to write most of his war poems, by April 1864, he had already begun, as his "Inscription for the Dead at Fredericksburgh" demonstrates. Now he wanted to see troops on the field and to gather useful insights and vignettes—to enrich his understanding of the war for the poetic task that lay ahead. As Allan put it, probably paraphrasing Herman, as a literary man he "should have opportunities to see" the army that he might "describe" it.[9] Had the visit to Henry's camp not taken place, Herman would have devised some other means of peering over the parapets of the war. With Grant poised to begin his campaign, the timing of the visit could not have been more opportune. Grant had announced that his headquarters would be—not in the saddle, which was by now a stale joke—but both in Washington and on the field. For the moment, the field meant Culpepper, Virginia, not far from Meade's headquarters. He was anticipating the day, fast drawing near, when the push to the south would begin, and further delay would have rendered Herman's visit impossible.

When Herman decided to accompany Bruce and Allan—too late to warn Henry—the plan changed. Jennie and Milie were still to see the cavalry camp, but they would not accompany the men to Washington. After giving the men a few days of freedom, during which they could travel to the Army of the Potomac, the women would meet them in Washington, and then all would visit Henry together. If Herman wished to see the fair, he had to hurry, since it was possible that it would close before his return. It may have been during the brief time remaining before his departure that Lizzie decided to take the girls to Boston in his absence. Then Herman threw together his traveling kit, sailor-fashion, and on Thursday evening, April 7, he left with Bruce and Allan.

To See That He Might Describe

The railroad journey was more expeditious than it had been in 1861, but it was no more comfortable. To accommodate the heavy wartime traffic, an arrangement had been made so that trains could travel through or around cities express, without requiring passengers to change from train to train and from station to station, but endurance was still needed to survive the discomforts of the eleven-hour trip, not the least of which was the horrid clatter of the train. Although there was a dining car at the rear, promoted by a barker who went from car to car, drinking water was difficult to locate. During the all-night journey, each car was lit by a single dim sperm candle, "which, had there been two, would, by Irish reasoning, have created total darkness," as one lady put it. "This route is a disgrace to the country," she added. When Herman passed around Philadelphia on the recently completed spur, Hawthorne and Ticknor were there at the Continental Hotel.[10]

After the train arrived at the Washington station around 6:30 the following morning, Herman, Allan, and Bruce went through the rain to the Ebbitt House, on the corner of F and 14th. On newspaper row just across from the new Willard's Hotel, it contrasted markedly to that elegant monument to upper-class pretense. With its imperial architecture better suited to the Holy See in Rome than to the capital of a republic, Willard's was where the rich, the celebrated, and the ostentatious stayed, but the Ebbitt was racier in both architecture and clientele. A homely brick structure created by joining together four old buildings, it was low-keyed and comfortable. Men with a purpose stayed there: newspapermen, military officers, politicians, and, it would appear, visiting authors. Longfellow had recommended it to a friend, adding that "it is three doors from Sumner."[11]

Henry was not there to meet them. Bruce had his own agenda to follow prior to reporting the following morning, and Herman and Allan had to arrange their visit to the front. Under ordinary circumstances, that would have been easy, but at the moment arrangements proved to be unexpectedly difficult. Grant was sending excess baggage, regimental sutlers, and most other civilians to the rear and restricting travel in order to strip the camps for battle. For civilians without documents, visiting was forbidden. In every issue, the Washington newspapers carried notices that passes could be obtained only from a Major Pelouze and that no appeal of his refusal would be accepted. Pelouze's office was just up the street from the Ebbitt, but the brothers must have thought it unwise to appear there without sponsorship. Unfortunately, the office closed at 1:00 p.m., and Friday was the last day of the working week. In their reactions, the brothers were, as Henry Gansevoort had said, the antipodes. Resorting to his usual channels of influence, Allan rushed off a note to Richard Lathers. Stating that Herman was anxious to visit the front for literary reasons, he asked Richard to send his endorsement to Willard's, which suggests that the brothers were planning to move across the street after Bruce's departure.[12] Herman's more practical idea was to locate Senator Sumner.

During the mile and a half ride to the Capitol, Herman saw a city quite different from that of 1861. As in New York City, the shop windows displayed swords and insignia. Amidst cars with tinkling bells and trains of government wagons and ambulances, military police patrolled the streets searching for soldiers without passes. The sidewalks were crowded with blacks and with soldiers of all kinds—some happy to be on their way home, some haggard and sick, some crippled. In front of the drinking establishments and oyster bars were officers' horses, tied or tended by servants or orderlies.[13] Military offices were everywhere, as were hospitals—at times there were as many as 50,000 patients in them—and "Hooker's Division" was stocked with whores who cared for the soldiers' earthier needs. In short, the capital was now a military post characterized by all of the endless bustle and perverse gratifications of an army at war.

The entire capitol dome, with the effigy of Freedom Triumphant mounted on its top, was in place. Now that the scaffolding was gone, the enlarged building revealed a pretentiousness that contrasted vividly with the modest republican structure that Herman had seen in his young manhood. In the interior of the dome, Constantino Brumidi was just beginning his fresco, "Apotheosis of Washington." Herman must have wondered what the building had been like while Henry Gansevoort and his militia colleagues had been quartered in it. In the Senate chamber, the constitutional amendment abolishing slavery was passed on this day. Senator Sumner was busy maneuvering over substitute bills, but he was cordial to Herman and Allan, pausing long enough to write a note to the provost marshal general in which he described Herman as "a loyal citizen & my friend." That enabled the brothers to obtain authorization from Secretary Stanton himself for either or both men "to visit the Army of the Potomac & return."[14]

It was too late in the day to leave for the south, they were fatigued by their journey, and etiquette required that they remain in the city long enough to send Bruce off to war with friendly gravity and facetious levity. With Sumner living so near the Ebbitt, they may have paid him a more social visit than the hurried meeting during the day, but there was also entertainment, notably Edwin Forrest's *King Lear* at Ford's Theatre, which the Lincolns and Secretary Seward planned to attend that night, and an opera at Grover's Theatre, *La Dame Blanche,* by Boieldieu.[15]

Early the next morning, Bruce left for Vienna, stopping at Fairfax Court House to muster in at the division headquarters. From 1:00 to 3:00 in the afternoon, Mrs. Lincoln held a reception at the White House, and that evening there was a new choice of entertainments: at Grover's, Carl Maria Von Weber's patriotic opera *Der Freischutz;* and at Ford's, *Señor Valiente: or, The Soldier of Chepultapec.* Throughout the day, a downpour inundated the city.[16]

This prodigious spring storm altered the Melvilles' plans by interrupting travel in northern Virginia. Four miles down the Orange and Alexandria Railroad from Alexandria, tracks and a bridge were submerged, while the Bull Run bridge was washed out. At Harper's Ferry, the Potomac was so swollen that the railroad bridge had to be taken up and was not relaid for well over a week. Nevertheless, on Sunday morning the brothers departed for "the front," leaving a note at the Ebbitt advising Jennie and Milie that they would be back by Thursday but not specifying their itinerary. Because of the flooding, they could not have visited Henry's camp or the battlefield at Bull Run or the Army of the Potomac, nor could they have visited Harper's Ferry. They could not have visited the battlefields at Fredericksburg or Chancellorsville, which were behind the Confederate lines. They could have reached the battlefield at Antietam, but the weather was unsuitable for wandering over the countryside of western Maryland and they were away from Washington for a longer time than that trip would have required. They could have visited Annapolis, where Burnside's corps was encamped, but rear area soldiers were not the object of their trip.[17]

Virtually the only place worth seeing that they could have visited without difficulty, and that would have required a trip of five days, was the anchorage of the North Atlantic Blockading Squadron off Fortress Monroe. They had good reason for going there to see Captain Guert Gansevoort. He would welcome them, and a visit to his ship would be the naval equivalent of a visit to Henry's camp and even more congenial to the sailor in Herman. Furthermore, Herman was aware that Hawthorne had made the trip in 1862 and had used the experience in writing about the *Monitor,* the *Virginia,* and the *Cumberland.* Hawthorne continued to influence Herman—perhaps he was an unacknowledged rival. In sum, although there is not the slightest proof that the Melvilles visited Hampton Roads, there is every reason to think that they did. Their pass would by implication have entitled them to visit any forward area, and there was a steady traffic of government vessels plying the route to Fortress Monroe from Baltimore, Annapolis, and the Washington Navy Yard. From the fort, a visual signal to the *Roanoke* would have brought one of Guert's boats to the landing to pick them up.

In the previous few days, the monotony there had been broken by a Confederate attack. On the day of the great storm, Lieutenant Hunter Davidson had steamed down the James River in a partially submerged torpedo boat, or "David," and in the murk of night had maneuvered through the fleet until he had reached the wooden flagship *Minnesota.* When his torpedo exploded against the frigate's side, the concussion tumbled officers and crewmen out of their bunks, destroyed ammunition, damaged three guns, and crushed the ship's shaft alley, disabling her propulsion machinery. Then, under fire, Davidson escaped upstream. To close the barn door, the tug *Violet* was now guarding the *Roanoke* from dawn to dusk.[18]

Taking travel time into account, Herman and Allan would have had two or three days in the area. They would have had a number of novel experiences, not the least of which would have been staying in the officers' quarters of the turreted battleship and hearing Guert's accounts of the various naval operations up the river, the Saturday attack by the David, and the spring offensive that was about to begin. Guert may have taken them for a tour of the ships present—busy with make-work as he was, not much was really happening—and introduced them to Flag Officer Lee. On their way down or back they may have visited Ben Butler at the fort and conversed with him about the capture and subjugation of New Orleans. Herman's social status and his reputation as a writer entitled him to audiences with commanders such as Lee and Butler; conversely, commanders were flattered by the attentions of literary celebrities. Apart from everything else, Herman was the son-in-law of the late Judge Shaw, who figured large in Butler's memories. Around the fort, the troops under Butler's command readied themselves for the spring offensive. Near Fortress Monroe, the brothers would have seen the masts of the sunken *Cumberland,* which still flew a remnant of her pennant as a ghostly symbol of her defiance of her iron nemesis. Nearby Hampton Roads was the scene of the ironclad battle, where in the imagination one could still hear the clatter of iron ball and shell against iron. Herman would have wished to see Malvern Hill, in honor of Henry Gansevoort, but that battlefield, only a few miles from Richmond, was out of the reach of Northerners.

Speculative as this visit must remain, it probably took place. Of all of the poems in *Battle-Pieces,* those about the ironclad fight and the ramming of the *Cumberland* are the most varied in method and among the most heartfelt. The idea that Herman may have brooded over the historic waters, as Marius brooded over the ruins of Carthage, places that part of his book in an interesting context. But above all, if the Melvilles did not visit Hampton Roads, where else could they have gone?

While Herman and Allan were touring, Jennie and Milie arrived in Washington ready for their visit to the cavalry camp. Jennie had sent letters and telegrams ahead, but not in time to reach Allan. On Tuesday morning, carrying boutonnieres from the fair to present to their personal army, Henry and Bruce, they arrived in Washington. Jennie picked up Allan's letter at the Ebbitt House, but, unwilling to stay at that *"poor place"* (characterized by energy rather than gentility), she checked in at Willard's. She was thrilled to find that General Grant was occupying a suite on an upper floor, and at one point she caught a glimpse of him.[19]

Two women in a strange city without escorts were limited in their mobility, and Jennie's helplessness was compounded by her ignorance. She did not know where Allan and Herman had gone or precisely when they would be back. She did not know where Bruce was, and she did not even realize that he was in Henry's regiment. She did not know the number of the regiment, though she knew that it was stationed in the vicinity. Women were not required to know such things; it was Allan's duty to escort his wife and daughter to the camp. After two days of waiting, Jennie was at her wits' end. Taking matters into her own hands, on Wednesday evening she wrote Henry, using the best address she could invent, explaining her plight and asking him to tell Allan where she was, if he could, and warning him that she and Milie intended to visit him. "Don't be alarmed," she added, "we can endure more than Allan & will think anything nice." As an afterthought, she invited him to dine with her in Washington. However, the letter lay unclaimed in the post office for almost a week.[20]

Fortunately, Allan and Herman soon returned. Because they had the neglected women to placate, they must have spent Friday in social atonement as well as in recuperation from their travels. They may have taken

Jennie and Milie to see Forrest in *The Broker of Bogota* at Ford's or to Beethoven's *Fidelio* or Verdi's *The Merry Wives of Windsor* at Grover's.[21] Their most difficult task was to tell Jennie and Milie that they could not accompany them to the camp, since their pass provided only for the two men. At about the same time, Henry Gansevoort checked in at the Ebbitt. Although he knew from Bruce that Herman and Allan had been there the preceding weekend and that they intended to visit him at Vienna, he did not search thoroughly enough to find them. He remained in residence across the street from all or some of the Melvilles for three days without checking at Willard's and without encountering them on the streets.

In Pursuit of Mosby

On Saturday, April 16, Herman and Allan made their delayed visit to the cavalry camp. The conventional route was via the Military Railroad. One crossed the Potomac River to Alexandria on a ferry from the 7th Street pier. Once in Alexandria, any question of ways and means could be answered by Brigadier General Henry Briggs, the former captain of Pittsfield's Allen Guard, who was now in command there. The journey to Fairfax Station was brief and relatively safe from Mosby's guerrillas, although a little farther down the track Grant had narrowly escaped capture the previous day. Fairfax Station was guarded by the Corcoran Legion, made up of the same Hibernians whose countrymen had been made the villains of the draft riots. From the station, there were four bumpy miles of corduroy road (road made passable and uncomfortable by logs laid across it) to Fairfax Court House, which Herman and Allan could have traversed on one of the many government wagons that lumbered to and fro along it. A short distance beyond that was the cavalry camp, which the brothers must have reached about midday.

Vienna was not a city or a town but a settlement, much of which was now enclosed by a defensive abatis, a fence constructed of a snarl of woody shrubs and tree limbs intended to deny Mosby's rangers informal access to the camp. At intervals were entrances manned by sentries. Apparently because of the laxity of these sentinels, Herman and Allen entered without hindrance, motivating Colonel Lowell to issue a special order that day calling for more rigorous control of ingress. Once inside, Herman and Allan saw for the first time what the life of the trooper on the field was like.

The clouds were just lifting from what had seemed an endless rain. What had once been peaceful rolling countryside was now trampled by men and horses and partially denuded of its trees, some of which had been burned to warm the chilled troopers during the winter, others of which had, in the words of Herman's poem "The Scout toward Aldie," been "leaned / In antlered walls about their tents." "What was late a vernal hill" was "now like a pavement bare." The hotel down by the station was the brigade hospital. In the southeast of the enclosure was the camp of the 2nd Massachusetts, tents with board floors, brick fireplaces, and makeshift chimneys, arranged in neat rows that enclosed the stables, and to the west of that was the brigade headquarters. Then came Henry's 13th New York, similarly tented, and beyond that the 16th New York.

As the Melvilles wandered about in search of Henry, they passed soldiers working and idling, the sounds of their activities and banter interrupted at intervals by bugles that informed and demanded in shrill voices: "The morning-bugles lonely play, / Lonely the evening-bugle calls— / Unanswered voices in the wild." From the stables, hundreds of horses could be heard snuffling and stamping their hoofs. Life in camp was military routine interrupted from time to time by the dispatch of scouting parties, but during the neutrality of night Mosby's rangers claimed equal ownership of the land. Only a week before, Mosby had made a personal reconnaissance of Fairfax Court House to report the activity there to Lee.

Mosby was the principal reason for the presence of the camp. A thirty-year-old lawyer from Bristol, Virginia, he had been a cavalry scout before receiving authorization to conduct guerrilla operations in northern Virginia. In January 1863, he had established himself there, bringing with him volumes of Shakespeare, Plutarch, Irving, and Hazlitt, and had recruited the 43rd Virginia Partisan Ranger Battalion. His men were able, daring, fierce, and elusive, and they profited from their plunder, but they were also con-

Encampment of the 2nd Massachusetts Volunteer Cavalry Regiment, Cavalry Brigade, Vienna, Virginia, February 1864(?). U.S. Military History Institute

vivial, jaunty, witty, and on occasion gallant. Mosby himself was much like Lawrence of Arabia, a man who, though in peacetime he might have lived his life in obscurity, was brilliant in his wartime role. In short, fate had made him the greatest of the Confederate guerrilla leaders and a pioneer of modern warfare.

One of Mosby's most powerful weapons against the Yankees was their ignorance. They believed that his rangers numbered in the thousands and that they operated from a camp with cook fires, pickets, tents, stables, and headquarters. But Mosby never commanded as many as five hundred men and he had no headquarters and scarcely any camp. His men were civilians by day, rangers by night, never very fastidious about whether or not they wore uniforms or what uniforms they wore, Confederate or Union. Men met by prearrangement or in obedience to word-of-mouth orders, junior officers acted independently as they saw fit or as they understood Mosby's intentions to be, and, when called, larger groups mustered within hours or minutes. So pervasive and so dangerous was the ranger presence in and around Loudoun County that it was known as "Mosby's Confederacy."

Although they had a serious purpose, Mosby's raids could be comical. Early in 1863, Brigadier General Edwin H. Stoughton had been sleeping off an overdose of whiskey at Fairfax Court House when his bedclothes had been ripped off, his buttocks had been slapped, and he had heard a Southern voice telling him that he was a prisoner. Along with thirty-two others, he had made the regrettable march to a Richmond prison while Mosby disposed of the arms, equipment, and horses he had captured. It was not long before such exploits created the anxiety—almost superstitious—that the Union forces in the area felt and that permeates Herman's "Aldie" poem.

The Melvilles must have gone first to the camp of the 13th, but neither Henry nor Lieutenant Colonel Coles was present. Bruce, just beginning to acclimate himself to the life of a cavalry troop commander, was there to greet and provide for them, though Ed Lansing was probably at the brigade headquarters. Bruce would have introduced the brothers to the regimental officers, particularly to Major Frazar, who was in temporary command, and found them accommodations. Herman probably shared Ed Lansing's tent,[22] while Allan probably bunked with his former law partner. It would be interesting to know what Herman thought of Frazar, who was a villain in Henry's accounts of his troubles in the regiment. At the moment, Frazar was the president of a general court-martial, which, although it was in recess for the weekend, technically barred him from exercising command. He was commanding, regardless.

Protocol demanded that Herman and Allan visit the Lowells, who were the models for the newlywed young couple of Herman's poem "Ah, love in a tent is a queenly thing" (poetic license having converted their cottage into a more fitting camp abode). Charles Lowell must have impressed them, as he impressed everyone. His Harvard education had been supplemented by his acquaintance with his uncle's circle of authors and intellectuals, including the "schoolroom poets." He was an acquaintance and an admirer of Emerson and a reader of Matthew Arnold, Sir Thomas Browne, Byron, Carlyle, Cervantes, Hawthorne, Milton, and Shakespeare—a reading list after Herman's heart—and, like Herman, he was interested in Greek philosophy, so much so that his favorite oath was "By Plato!" He was an ideal soldier. Lean and handsome, he had matured into an experienced and capable commander, cool and inspiring in action and fearless to a fault. Henry referred to him as "my model in arms."[23]

The wife was as impressive as the husband. Barely out of her teens, Effy was intelligent, witty, educated, athletic, and strong, though small, and beautiful and gracious. When he had seen the two together at a dress parade of the 54th Massachusetts, William James had thought that "they looked so young and victorious."[24] In camp, Effy interested herself in the well-being of the soldiers and made daily trips to the brigade hospital, where she cared for the sick and wounded, read to the patients, wrote letters for them, and comforted the dying. With patients who knew little English, she spoke French, German, and Italian. For recreation, she rode around the camp with her husband.

The Lowells knew who Herman was. Charles must have heard of him from his Uncle James, and he had probably read at least some of Herman's works—his regimental library contained *Typee* and *Omoo*. Effy must have known of him through her family. Even if her father, Francis G. Shaw, had never mentioned Herman, living near her brother-in-law, George William Curtis, must have made her familiar with his name. Lowell was able to converse with his visitor on equal terms, and with her well-equipped mind there was no need for Effy to sit silent. Lowell could help to bring the war to life for Herman by recounting his experiences on the Peninsula and at Antietam and telling anecdotes of his present duel with Mosby.[25]

Whether he heard it from Lowell or another source, such as Ed Lansing, one of these anecdotes remained in Herman's imagination for the rest of his life. The incident concerned a young soldier named William E. Ormsby. Born in Massachusetts twenty-four years earlier but a resident of San Francisco, Ormsby had led a reckless life in the west before returning east with the California Battalion, which was now a part of the 2nd Massachusetts. He had succumbed to the charms of a Virginia woman, he claimed, and had deserted his picket station, taking with him two horses and six pistols. Then he had joined Mosby's rangers. He was drunk when, on

February 5, 1864, he led a small group of rangers in an attack on the rear guard of a Union scout near Aldie. The other rangers dispersed, but Ormsby was captured. The following morning, the scout brought Ormsby back to the cavalry brigade camp.[26]

At five o'clock in the afternoon of the same day, Ormsby was tried by a drumhead court-martial. His chosen counsel, Chaplain Charles A. Humphreys of the 2nd Massachusetts, pleaded for clemency on the grounds of his youth and his seduction, but the court found him guilty and sentenced him to be executed before the entire brigade. In the morning, Lowell issued an order saying that "for such an offence death is the only punishment and the Comdg officer hopes and believes that the Summary execution today will prevent forever the necessity of the repetition in this Command." At eleven o'clock the brigade was drawn up on three sides of the execution area. The band played a funeral dirge as Ormsby appeared leaning on the chaplain's arm, his former messmates carrying his coffin ahead of him. After Ormsby made a short speech acknowledging his guilt and expressing his faith in the Union cause, Humphreys prayed with him, blindfolded him, and carried his request to the firing squad that they aim at his heart. While Ormsby sat on his coffin, the six troopers shot him. As Ed Lansing put it, the punishment was very impressive and had an excellent effect on the men. The similarity between the trial and execution of Billy Budd and the experience of Ormsby is striking. The theme of mutiny (desertion and joining the enemy), the haste of the drumhead court-martial, the desire of Lowell to make him an example for the other troopers, the promptness of the execution, and Ormsby's loyal last words suggest the extent to which Herman used the story in *Billy Budd*. In addition, the name Ormsby is echoed in the names of both Daniel Orme, in one of Herman's late manuscript fragments, and the Orm of the poem "Pebbles" (205–6), in Herman's *John Marr and Other Sailors*.[27]

For her part, Effy may have talked about the death of her brother, Robert Gould Shaw, in the attack on Battery Wagner, and some mention of George William Curtis was inevitable. It would have been appropriate for her to invite Herman and Allan to tour the brigade hospital. It was in the charge of the brigade surgeon, Doctor Oscar C. DeWolf, a graduate of the Berkshire Medical Institute who had later returned to it as a faculty member. In the small community of Pittsfield, he was probably an acquaintance of Herman.[28]

Anticipating Henry's return from Washington on Sunday, the Melvilles remained overnight. That gave them time to hear the regimental gossip, particularly from Ed Lansing, who was its most prominent exponent now that Charles Brewster was gone. Ed could have given them even more

Chaplain Charles A. Humphreys, 2nd Massachusetts Volunteer Cavalry Regiment. U.S. Military History Institute

details than they already knew about the insurrection that had so threatened Henry's career and of Major Frazar's supposed part in it. In addition, Herman and Allan were able to observe the regimental routine Henry had established, beginning with first call to reveille at 5:15 in the morning and ending with taps at 8:30 at night. On the ordinary weekday, the working hours were filled with stable calls, guard mountings, drills, and meals. Much of this routine was observed even on Sunday.

Henry did not return when expected. What happened instead was something for which Herman must have wished but that he could not have anticipated. A few days earlier, Lowell had reported to General Tyler that Mosby's men were in the vicinity of Leesburg, which had not been visited by Union forces that season. There was hostile activity there, to the extent that Union travelers had been refused entry to the town. The truth is that Mosby's quartermaster was there requisitioning the grain that had accumulated on the Virginia side of the Potomac when the flooding had interrupted transport across to Maryland, and then hiding it in dispersed locations. In addition, Mosby's new Company D was being formed there. Sensing an opportunity to damage the rangers, General Tyler gathered a large expedition for the purpose. Five hundred men, divided fairly equally between infantry and cavalry, were scheduled to leave Monday morning under two brigade commanders, Colonel Arthur H. Grimshaw of the infantry and Lowell. Grimshaw's men were to march from Fairfax Court House about twenty-five miles up the Little River Turnpike toward Aldie, just short of which they were to establish a picketed camp for the cavalrymen. Simultaneously, the troopers were to ride to Leesburg to accomplish whatever mischief they could. Perhaps because he understood Herman's literary mission, or perhaps because of Ed Lansing's intercession, Lowell invited him, and perhaps Allen, too, to accompany the cavalrymen.

Herman accepted, setting in motion the train of events that resulted in his "Aldie" poem, but Allan did not. Allan must have recognized that the physical demands of an extended adventure into disputed territory would be too much for his health, and he may also have had the excuse that Jennie and Milie were still in Washington, expecting him to return after the weekend to salvage their visit. But Herman welcomed the opportunity, which was exactly what he wanted and needed for his book. Bruce, who was still too inexperienced to ride on the scout, loaned him warm clothing and his horse. By the following morning, Herman was ready for the saddle and the dangers and hardships of the field. Of his two personalities, the hypochondriac and the robust sailor, the latter was in the ascendant.

Early Monday morning, April 18, when the bugles sounded "Boots and Saddles" and "To Horse," the scouting party formed. There were detach-

Major Douglas Frazar, 13th New York Volunteer Cavalry Regiment. U.S. Military History Institute

ments from all three regiments, each man, including Herman, carrying two days' rations for himself and three days of forage for his horse.[29] Lowell chose as his second in command Major Frazar, who suspended the court-martial until his return. There is a good chance that, as Lowell's adjutant, Ed

Lansing also went along, and it is likely that the new surgeon of the 13th New York Cavalry, Doctor Taylor, was present: the 13th sent extra horses and Herman's poem includes a surgeon—Doctor DeWolf, the only other surgeon in camp, did not accompany the scout. Effy would have been present to wave goodbye to her husband, and neither Allan nor Bruce would have missed the opportunity to send Herman off with bantering cautions and sincere wishes. Colonel Lazelle of the 16th New York, who was to act as brigade commander in Lowell's absence, was there to receive last-minute instructions, and his bride may have accompanied him to provide moral support for Effy, since female solace was scarce for a wife in an army camp. Probably Lieutenant Colonel Crowninshield of the 2nd Massachusetts was also present to see his former regimental commander off.[30]

The column that snaked its way through the opening in the abatis between nine and ten o'clock was impressive, even though the inclusion of an ambulance rendered it cumbersome. There were perhaps three hundred troopers in smart blue uniforms with field caps and waist-length jackets embellished with gold, each wearing a saber and carrying a carbine, though because of the grim business at hand the guidons of the troopers were not flying and the bugles ceased their blare as soon as the camp was left behind. The force was about equivalent in number to Mosby's entire battalion, although the Yankees were not aware of that. In the lead, behind the advance guard, was the brilliant colonel, "light, active, and tough" and seemingly "incapable of fatigue," Herman, Major Frazar, Doctor Taylor, "Yankee" Davis, the guide, and perhaps Ed Lansing. Lowell customarily defied established practice by wearing his crimson officer's sash, and the other officers may have emulated him.[31]

It cannot be stated with certainty that any of the characters in Herman's poem is an exact rendering of an actual person, but there is, at least, a remarkable resemblance between the guide and Yankee Davis. The guide, "in frowzy coat of brown, / And beard of ancient growth and mould," rode a "bony steed and strong." He was "a wheezy man with depth of hold." A Union man from the vicinity of Aldie, Davis had been persecuted by his secessionist neighbors and, the poem suggests, even by his son and his wife. Thus his desire for revenge was bitter. He was valuable to the cavalry because he knew both the countryside and the loyalties of many of its inhabitants, but Herman suspected him. How could one be certain that Davis's impeachments of his neighbors were reliable? "A grudge? Hate will do what it can."

In a reprise of his vision of the Bull Run and Balls Bluff innocents marching off to battle, Herman described the troopers riding out into the spring morning. In the gold of the sun and the green of the countryside, opal vapors from the still-sodden ground rolled about the prancing horses and riders:

How strong they feel on their horses free,
  Tingles the tendoned thigh with life;
Their cavalry-jackets make boys of all—
With golden breasts like the oriole.

Just then Chaplain Humphreys rode up. A novice clergyman barely out of divinity school, he wished to share the dangers of the field with the soldiers in order to earn their confidence. When he had heard "Boots and Saddles," he had obtained permission from Crowninshield go along and had galloped after the column on Jaques, known in the regiment as the "Parson's Old Cob." When he arrived, he was surprised to find "the noted traveller Herman Melville" there. He was thrilled to be in Herman's company, but like many other contemporary readers he thought of Herman not as a seeker of metaphysical truth but as a sailor-raconteur along the lines of R. H. Dana, Jr., though he thought *Moby-Dick* "a classic among whaling stories." "He was out now to learn something of the *soldier's* life and to see a little campaigning with his own eyes, preparatory to the writing of the book which appeared two years later," Humphreys remembered.[32]

Herman's encounter with Humphreys did nothing to mitigate his long-standing literary prejudice against clergymen: his poetic chaplain "went to the wars for cure of souls, / And his own student-ailments." He thought deeply about the role of the man of God in uniform and remembered the scout when he wrote *Billy Budd*. The chaplain aboard the *Bellipotent,* who attended Billy before his execution as Humphreys had attended Ormsby, is "the minister of the Prince of Peace serving in the host of the God of War" (122). Like that chaplain, Humphreys lent "the sanction of the religion of the meek to that which practically is the abrogation of everything but brute Force."

With guards ahead and to the rear, the column probably rode west along the abandoned railroad track as far as Guilford Station, where it turned up Church Road toward a mill along Goose Creek between Aldie and Leesburg.[33] That was where the column was to meet the infantry detachment. Along the route, the cavalrymen stopped every hour and a half to rest their horses and to adjust their saddles to prevent abrasions. In Herman's poem, scenes and buildings along the road were ominous reminders of earlier engagements with Mosby in which comrades of the troopers had fallen. During the ride and the rest stops, Herman must have spoken with members of the party about the military business at hand, and he may have had a chance to talk about more homely matters with some of the half-dozen

Pittsfield men in the 2nd Massachusetts. Of particular note (in the poem, at least) was a hospital steward with a carefree demeanor. The steward, "A black-eyed man on a coal-black mare," teases and gambols along the way: "A healthy man for the sick to view; / The taste in his mouth was sweet at morn; / Little of care he cared about." Unlike the others, whose anxious awareness of the mythic Mosby is expressed at the end of every stanza, he was in little danger; he was protected from the enemy by "the caduceus, black and green" on his uniform. Still, he had learned the grimness of war from treating "others, maimed by Mosby's crew."

At four in the afternoon the column reached Goose Creek. There the troopers left the road for the woods, where they halted for an hour across from the mill. It was time for the riders to dismount and feed their horses, whose care always came first, and then to eat their own dinner. Some, like Chaplain Humphreys, unsaddled their mounts to allow them to refresh themselves by rolling on the ground. Certainly Herman took his cue from the others and rested Bruce's horse as they did theirs. Herman lit his pipe and then, if he followed Humphreys's example, he built a fire of cornstalks and cooked his dinner over it. The food was utilitarian—Humphreys's was ham and dry bread. At five o'clock the column remounted and forded the creek, which, swollen by the rains, could be crossed only by men on horseback. That meant that Herman had to perch on the back of his mount with his feet raised to keep them out of the water. He must have chuckled when Humphreys, attempting to do the same, accidentally spurred his cob and stampeded the animal in midstream, but he was forgiving enough to refer in his poem to "wild creeks where men have drowned."

The column then rode north on the Old Carolina Road, nearing Leesburg, "the hot-bed of secessionism in those parts," by dusk. As the troopers veered onto the pike they expected trouble, and they found it. When the men of the advance guard were fired upon, they sent word back to Lowell that the enemy battle line was drawn up in the wood just ahead—a typical exaggeration, where Mosby was concerned. When Lowell ordered a charge, the entire column broke into a trot and then a gallop. Herman had no choice but to charge with the rest when the officers shouted "Steady! Wait for orders! By platoons left, gallop, march! By fours, march!" loud enough to be heard above the clattering of sabers and of horses' hoofs on the hard road. With sabers drawn, the first squadron prepared to engage, while the others behind them, with whom Herman must have thrown in his lot, rode with carbines at the ready. Considering the gravity of the advance guard's report, he must have felt that these could be the last few moments of his life, but there was no vintage Mosby attack, no surprise charge from concealment intended to stampede the Yankees. The enemy probably consisted of no more than a few of the new men of Company D showing their bravado. After their token volley, they had the good sense to retreat and disperse. None of them were taken, even though the momentum of the charge took the column all of the way into town. Nor, after this forewarning, did a search of Leesburg yield any prisoners.[34]

When Lowell's inquiries revealed that Mosby's commissary officer had already made away with most of the town's corn, he decided that as long as the Potomac remained impassable nothing could be done to prevent him from taking the rest. It was best to adhere to his plan, to bivouac for the night on the road just outside of town in anticipation of the work of the morrow.

The night tested Herman's stamina. He could doze, but the cold prevented sleep even if he dared to surrender to Morpheus. Intermittently, the sky was lit by enemy signal rockets fired from the hilltops ahead and the quiet of night was interrupted by rangers firing at the pickets. Under these tentative conditions, Herman could neither unsaddle his horse nor light a fire to temper the bitter chill, which must have pinched him through his borrowed clothing. His horse remained in column with the others, four abreast on the narrow road, while he lay vulnerable at its feet, bridle in hand in case he had to mount and ride at a moment's notice. It required courage to lie alongside the iron-shod hoofs of a stamping cavalry horse, but the animals were amiable. They avoided stepping on their riders, though when lonely they nuzzled them awake for company and when sleepy they lay down beside them. What naps were possible were interrupted by the rattle of small arms fire, which brought the recumbents abruptly to their feet, ready to mount. Standing was the only alternative when bones ached from lying on the hard ground, and many of the party gave up and resigned themselves to "sleeping" erect. It was a tortured night during which Herman probably thought more than once of the comfortable bed in which Allan must be lying, but at least it did not rain.

Before dawn, Herman ate a cold breakfast and mounted his horse once more. Assured by the events of the night that Mosby's men were still in the vicinity, Lowell sent out search parties. When a group of mounted men was spied on a nearby hill, Lowell dispatched Major Frazar with a much larger force to circle around them. The inexperienced rangers were captured easily by the main force, all except one, who rode into Frazar's trap. Considering the nature of the countryside and the many avenues for escape, Lowell felt fortunate to take them. In all there were eleven captives, including one officer. Herman observed the prisoners and listened to their conversation, which he wove into his poem in such a way as to suggest that captive and captor were siblings, teasing each other as brothers might. Had it not been for the intervention of the officers, these enemies might have become friends.

While the attention of the trooper guarding him was diverted, the ranger who had earlier attempted to evade capture dashed for the nearby wood. Before he could escape, the negligent guard overtook him and tackled him headfirst against a tree. Seeing that he was seriously injured, the troopers made him a grass pillow, while Doctor Taylor treated the injury and Humphreys attempted to comfort him. Herman decided that the surgeon, "the kindliest man / That ever a callous trade professed," was the more effective chaplain of the two. When it became apparent that the man could not be saved, he was left where he lay with a flask at his side.

According to the poem, another incident occurred at about this time. At a farmhouse in the vicinity, where the troopers stopped to leave word about the injured rebel, Yankee Davis pointed out a man who, he claimed, played the part of an innocent farmer by day but rode with Mosby by night. The man was taken into custody, but Herman was skeptical. The captive might well have been a ranger, but, on the other hand, there was nothing to prevent Davis from abusing his summary power.

Considering subsequent events, one other incident in the poem may be founded in fact. The cavalrymen halted a veiled woman in a wagon drawn by a lame horse and driven by an old humpbacked slave. After interrogating her, Lowell discovered a letter in her possession revealing that there was to be a ranger wedding, which many of Mosby's battalion were expected to attend, in Leesburg that night. For reasons of security, he detained the wagon and its human freight. Although the event may be fictional, adapted from a different incident Herman must have learned about during his visit, in one way or another Lowell did learn of the wedding.

In his poetic account of this putative episode, Herman made an antiabolitionist statement. When questioned about Mosby, the old slave replies, "Let we go." "Go where?" asks Captain Cloud, whose name betrays him as an airy idealist. "Back into bondage? Man, you're free!" But the old man answers, "Well, *let* we free!" This dramatization places Herman on the side of Hawthorne, who had questioned the abolitionists' idea that all slaves desired their freedom and were prepared for it. A majority did; about them there was no argument. But for others, an acceptable life in slavery was preferable to the maltreatment and neglect that were often the lot of freedmen.[35]

Around ten o'clock in the morning, Lowell abandoned his search and led the column back down the Old Carolina Road to Goose Creek, which the riders forded once more. By then, Colonel Grimshaw's infantry had arrived at the rendezvous, allowing Herman and his weary companions to halt in security, if not in comfort. Still, Herman could not unsaddle his horse and light a cooking fire—the stop was no more than a respite in anticipation of the night's work. There would be time for relaxation and a satisfying meal at nightfall, when Lowell planned to send a party westward through the Aldie gap toward Middleburg and Rectortown, thought to be Mosby's headquarters. The afternoon was for anticipation.

It was during such moments that Herman talked "metaphysics and mental philosophy" with Lowell and Humphreys, though the unfortunate chaplain may have found himself outmanned by the other two. This was not the usual occupation for a colonel of cavalry commanding a raid into country disputed with the enemy, but it was in character for Lowell, who took advantage of such opportunities for discussions of philosophy and the social sciences. It would have been fascinating to hear the two admirers of Plato debate and, probably, bring Emerson into the discussion, while the young chaplain struggled to hold up his end.[36]

At four o'clock in the afternoon, while Herman was eating cold rations, an informer reported that Mosby and a companion had just been seen riding through a field less than two miles away. Although the countryside was well adapted to concealment, Lowell decided to pursue him, and, since Mosby must have known of the presence of the cavalry, Lowell ordered the bugler to sound "Boots and Saddles." The entire cavalry contingent swallowed their food and took to horse. A lieutenant and ten troopers rode off in direct pursuit while the main column, with flankers sweeping a half mile on either hand, rode from Goose Creek toward the Little River Turnpike, which passed through Aldie, to head off their prey. But when they reached the pike they learned that Mosby had preceded them by three quarters of an hour. The troopers who were sent into Aldie reported that Mosby had been reconnoitering the cavalry column and that before melting into the countryside he had left messages expressing his regards for his enemies. Apparently, the only thing the guerrilla leader did not know was that riding with the column was an eminent author whose works he may have read. Since there was now no possibility of surprise, Lowell canceled the night raid beyond the hills.

Back in their temporary camp, the troopers prepared for the night. For the first time since he had left Vienna, Herman could unharness his horse and warm himself with hot coffee. There was time to gather boards and dried leaves for a makeshift bed, a luxury compared to the hard road of the preceding night, but Lowell was improvising an action based on the information he had gathered during the morning. If Mosby had eluded him this time, he might still be captured at the wedding. Lowell dispatched a force of seventy-five dismounted troopers toward Leesburg to surprise the rangers. Together with the others who remained behind, Herman lay down thankfully on his bed.

However, his slumber was broken when, at two o'clock in the morning,

John Singleton Mosby, Commander of the 43rd Virginia Partisan Ranger Battalion. U.S. Military History Institute

the raiders returned, the worse for their experience. When they had reached Leesburg, they had found the hotel lit brilliantly, but they were a half hour late for the wedding. The crowd was dispersing, and there was noisy celebration in the streets. In a brief, confused skirmish, one attacker was killed and three others wounded before their opponents disappeared into the night. If the Confederates suffered any casualties, the troopers were unaware of them. In his poem, Herman gave this fictionalized account of the event, cast in hypothetical terms: Mosby will

> be found in wait.
> Softly we enter, say, the town—
> Good! pickets post, and all so sure—
> When—crack! the rifles from every gate,
> The Grey-backs fire—dash up and down—
> Each alley unto Mosby's known!

The troopers had left their dead and wounded in the hotel where the wedding had been celebrated and had marched back to camp with nothing but the gaps in their ranks to show for their effort.

In the first loom of dawn, the cavalrymen returned to Leesburg. Doctor Taylor and Chaplain Humphreys, and perhaps Herman, went to the hotel, where they found the three wounded men well tended. At ten o'clock, after the casualties had been bandaged and loaded into the ambulance, the scout started home. Once past Goose Creek, the boundary of their fear of enemy attack, they paused to feed their horses and themselves. Then, while Grimshaw's infantry marched the weary twenty-five miles back to Fairfax Court House, they rode back to their camp. Herman's description of the end of the scout sounds authentic: "Foot-sore horses, jaded men; / Every backbone felt as nicked, / Each eye dim as a sick-room lamp."

The principal literary consequence of Herman's experience is the long narrative poem "The Scout toward Aldie," which is typeset after and separate from the "inscriptive and memorial" verses of *Battle-Pieces*. Although many of the minor characters may be based on actual people, the Major, the Colonel, and Mosby are not, nor does the route of the poem correspond with the actual route of the scout. In other words, Herman's poem is, like his romances, literature woven out of fact.

It is a small-scale version of *Moby-Dick* adapted to the events Herman had witnessed.[37] In place of the infinite sea, the travelers wind through the eerie forest, as ambiguous in its tangled fertility and its peril as the whiteness of the whale. In place of the whale, at once hunted and hunter, there is Mosby, the figure who, without ever appearing in the poem, dominates it. As the cetological chapters of *Moby-Dick* enlarge the idea of the whale through iteration, so does the repetition of Mosby's name in nearly every stanza enlarge the idea that he represents. But this Mosby is so clearly not the historical warrior that Herman felt obliged to explain the difference between art and life in a footnote. Mosby, he said, was "shrewd, able, and enterprising, and always a wary fighter. . . . To our wounded on more than one occasion he showed considerate kindness. Officers and civilians captured by forces under his immediate command were, so long as remaining under his orders, treated with civility." This is the warrior whom Herman respected; the Mosby of his poem is the infernal spirit whose homily is that *"Man must die."*

He is a mythic figure, the principal avatar in the book of the Satan of "The Conflict of Convictions." He is a shape-changer, of no certain form. Perhaps he is the wounded prisoner or perhaps the bent slave—or perhaps, in another time and in another wilderness, the inscrutable whale. Certainly he is the shark, the Nemesis of Herman's later poems. It is he who mocks Michael and Raphael, he who knows that war belongs not on the heights but in the depths of the wilderness, he who lures the young braves into his snares, he who fires sudden death out of the darkness. Who pursues Mosby pursues his own destruction.

The glory-hungry Colonel bears no resemblance to Lowell, despite the fact that Lowell's bride and his later death suggested the ending of the poem, nor does the experienced Major resemble Major Frazar. Rather, disparate elements in Henry Gansevoort's character are personified in both "Hope" and "Experience sage," as the two figures are called. In his hunger for glory and advancement—*"Names must be made and printed be!"*—the Colonel exhibits that part of Henry's nature that caused his constant dissatisfaction with his rank and assignments and motivated his constant levies on his father's influence. Like the boyish troopers, the Colonel of the poem is one of the youthful enthusiasts who, unaware of the significance of the forest and of Mosby, contrast with the older, cautious sages—a contrast first seen in "Apathy and Enthusiasm." He is a latter-day version of the young militiamen who thoughtlessly entered the forest in "The March into Virginia." But Henry was also the experienced, battle-hardened warrior of the Seven Days, Bull Run, and Antietam. This other aspect is given to the Major, as Herman indicates in the lines "through the Seven Days one [the Major] had served, / And gasped with the rear-guard in retreat." Those gasps were Henry's.

The Colonel and the Major act the parts of an innocent, unmaimed Ahab and a respectful but skeptical Starbuck. Both are brave warriors, but the Major has been enlightened by experience. In battle he has learned the meaning of the forest and the identity of its monarch, has seen "truth," as it is defined in *Battle-Pieces*. The one is bent upon capturing Mosby through a daring stroke, while the other argues caution. Is it really necessary to imperil lives in a direct challenge to Mosby-Satan or might it not be better to keep him in check through more prudent means? When the Colonel speaks "of the partisan's blade he longed to win, / And frays in which he meant to beat," his motive is a vision of glory rather than a desire to further the Union cause. The Major's advice is sensible: "I'd beat, if I could, Lee's armies—then / Send constables after Mosby's men." At another point he becomes more specific: "Save what we've got," he says, "Bad plan to make a scout too long; / . . . These rides I've been, / And every time a mine was sprung." But the Colonel replies, "Peril, old lad, is what I seek."

Youth is beautiful, but because youth is also ignorant, impetuous, and in this case self-serving, Mosby—Satan—war—death—lures it away from the young man's business of love into the fatal traps of the young man's dream of glory, and therein lies the tragedy. In the climax, a foray to Leesburg, the Colonel leads a full-column, mounted raid. When the advance guard encounters a tree lying across the road, the Colonel rides on until he is killed from ambush. Like Moby-Dick, Mosby has turned on his pursuer with deadly fury, leaving the bride, if she "should see threescore and ten," to "dream of Mosby and his men." "The bullet of Mosby goes through heart to heart," Herman wrote, echoing Edward Willet's soldier's wife, who says, "But the bullet that slew my darling / Is piercing my poor heart through."[38]

Herman returned to Vienna excited, inspired, fatigued, and appalled. The troopers and their poet-guest were greeted by their comrades and loved ones and by a band playing patriotic airs. Effy Lowell was there along with Henry Gansevoort, who had learned of Herman's adventure-in-progress on his return from Washington. Doctor Taylor took the wounded to the brigade hospital, while the prisoners remained under guard awaiting transportation to Washington and prison. As Chaplain Humphreys put it, "We had been out three days and two nights, and I had slept only two hours, and was so stiff from a cold caught the first night that it seemed as if I could count by its special ache each muscle in my body."[39] But Henry thought that Herman looked well and that he had enjoyed his experience. Where had his sciatica, his neuralgia, and his bad nerves gone?

It is likely that General Tyler rode over to Vienna to meet the scout on its return so that he could learn its results from Colonel Lowell. The scout was the most important activity of his division at this time, and Colonel Grimshaw would not return for some hours. Perhaps, also, Tyler knew by this time that Herman Melville had accompanied it. One way or another, he met Herman—and Doctor Taylor—in Henry Gansevoort's tent, and while there he probably invited Herman to visit him that evening.[40]

Herman's weariness was hostage to his excitement. He must have marveled with Henry at the coincidence that had kept the Melvilles from encountering him in Washington, and Henry must have asked about the scout. The cavalryman would have been both curious and amused, and in fairness he should have been impressed by his cousin's endurance. On

Herman's part, his appetite for war information and image was unabated. Henry must have told him about the resolution of the conspiracy against him and speculated about the coming spring offensive and the part his regiment would play in it. In talking about the regiment, he may have mentioned the shipwreck of the transport *Fairhaven,* which had been carrying some of his men, on Cape Henry three weeks earlier. Fortunately, none had perished.

This incident was only one of many instances, often grim in their consequences, in which ships carrying soldiers foundered. Herman took note of them in the inscriptive and memorial poem, "A Requiem for Soldiers lost in Ocean Transports." It is so fine in its way that one reader has called it "one of the most remarkable poems to come from nineteenth-century America" and another has mentioned it in the same breath as Milton's "Lycidas."[41] It is one of those poems that, like "Shiloh" and "Malvern Hill," reminds the reader that heedless nature continues her processes of living and renewal despite man's tragedies. Yet its origin lies in the symbol of the ocean-bottom as the location of the inscrutable secrets of eternity, as in "The Battle for the Mississippi" and "The College Colonel." War is a storm from which nature shrinks. Robins and meadowlarks withdraw, insects hide in nooks, and fish retreat to the depths, while men's frail barks founder. After the storm, the birds and insects revive to cavort in the "atoning dawn" and the fish and sea-mammals play in the "delightsome sea," but for the human victims there is only the fabled shore, the pale stream, the dark, and the reef of bones. War is a shipwreck which nature survives, though men may not. They cannot heed "the lone bird's flight / Round the lone spar where mid-sea surges pour"; only the flotsam of their wreck remains as testimony to their existence.

Since Henry had left the City pell-mell, this was his first opportunity to show off as a commander of troops in the field before one of his civilian relatives. Herman probably received a tour of his domain, which he did not need, and in the evening Henry took Herman to the division headquarters at Fairfax Court House for his visit with General Tyler, a ride that Herman also did not need. Tyler was charming, curly-headed, cherub-faced, and slightly overweight. He was the sort of man who appealed to Herman, an affable, whiskey-drinking, cigar-smoking lover of books. But he was more than that, one of the most experienced of all of the Union officers in the east. Conversing with him was like thumbing through the pages of the war, Fort Sumter, rebellious Baltimore, Yorktown, the Seven Days, Fredericksburg, Chancellorsville, and Gettysburg.

It was a convivial evening. Probably the conversation included chat about Mosby and about interesting events, such as the capture of Mrs. Carter and Miss Bissell, two Confederate agents. A month and a half back, these women had appeared at Fairfax Station with two wagons and an official pass. The sentries became suspicious because their pass did not mention baggage, although the ladies were accompanied by a large load. When an album marked "C.S." and correspondence with Confederate officers were found in Miss Bissell's belongings, the guards expanded their search, discovering cloth, clothing, and "enough medicines incl. quinine to stock a small apothecary shop." The ladies were arrested and sent to Washington under guard.[42] That could have inspired the incident of the intercepted lady in "The Scout toward Aldie."

As a West Pointer of the era when Edgar Allan Poe and James Abbot McNeill Whistler had been attracted to the academy, Tyler was interested in literature; Herman earned his interview by allowing Tyler to interview him in return. Tyler presented him with two books, Jean Paul Richter's *Titan* and a translation of Terence. All in all, Tyler impressed Herman as "an accomplished General & jolly Christian"—apropos for a man who boasted both that he was descended from Jonathan Edwards and that he had never read Edwards's sermons.[43]

Back in Vienna, Herman was more than ready for the sleep he had sacrificed during the previous two nights. The next morning he left. Henry had business to attend to—such as clarifying for Major Frazar the legality of an officer commanding a regiment while detached as president of a court-martial. Herman had not yet seen the Army of the Potomac, and the spring offensive was less than two weeks away. If Herman returned to Washington briefly to enjoy a bed intended for sleep, he could hardly be faulted. Probably Henry provided him with ambulance transportation, as he often did for his guests. Herman may even have traveled with the prisoners from Leesburg, who were delivered to the capital prisons that day. Apparently he did go to Washington, since he attempted unsuccessfully to contact a doctor there, probably Doctor Taylor, and he appears to have claimed a letter that awaited him at the post office. He could have read a *Washington Evening Star* description of the scout that contained as little truth as the naval chronicle account of Billy Budd's service aboard the *Bellipotent:* "A scouting party sent out on Thursday from the cavalry brigade stationed at Vienna, overhauled a party of White's rebel cavalry near Leesburg, and captured eleven of them." Since so many of Herman's memories of this period found their way into *Billy Budd,* this one may have, as well.[44]

The Armies of the Wilderness

Herman's further travels are almost completely undocumented, for the most part traceable only through his poem "The Armies of the Wilderness

Brigadier General Robert Ogden Tyler. U.S. Military History Institute

(1863–4)." However, it would seem that he was soon on his way down the Military Railroad to the camps of the Army of the Potomac, following in the footsteps of Walt Whitman, who had made a similar visit in February. He could have traveled on Grant's train, since the general went to Culpepper at about the time of this visit. Just whom he knew at the front, whose letters of introduction he carried to whom, and who guided him and furnished him accommodations are matters of speculation. Tyler could have given him letters to most of the commanders, Henry Gansevoort knew Meade and General Hunt, the artillery commander, Lowell had many connections, and Bruce would not have neglected to suggest that he visit his brother in the Cavalry Corps.[45]

It would appear that when he reached Rappahannock Station he paused to visit the small battlefield where Meade's men had attacked and captured a Confederate force the previous fall. The fighting, much of which had occurred at night, is referred to in the poem as the "Moonlight Fight." The most striking image is the hand of a dead soldier which reaches out of a shallow grave "as begging help which none can bestow," while others are a rusted canteen and the drum of a dead drummer-boy. Even a poet of Herman's stature could not escape the sentimental idea of the martyred drummer-boy, though to his credit he did not exploit it.

Beyond the Rappahannock was Brandy Station, headquarters of the Army of the Potomac, and beyond that was Culpepper Station, Grant's headquarters. Herman's visit to the Cavalry Brigade had not prepared him for the broad carpet of regiments, brigades, divisions, and corps laid over mile after mile of open land. The soldiers had erected comfortable buildings, "streets of beechen huts," for their winter quarters, where, not yet sobered for the fighting to come, they had, as Whitman put it, "more fun around here than you would think for"—band concerts, theatricals, and other entertainments. A fine spirit prevailed among the soldiers "for endurance & work" that boded well for the offensive.[46]

Herman visited one or more of the headquarters. If he saw Wendell Holmes at the Sixth Corps staff, he could have listened to Stewart's Cornet Band of North Adams, which had taken part in the parade celebrating the return of the Berkshire Regiment. It was in great demand among the soldiers. Of all of the corps commanders, General Winfield Scott Hancock impressed him most. A West Pointer five years Herman's junior, Hancock was a natural leader of men who, unlike most of the other senior generals, had fought long and well without ever incurring suspicion of over-caution or mismanagement. Herman commemorated him in "On the Photograph of a Corps Commander." Assuming that Herman really did see Hancock at this time, that title is an example of his elusiveness, disguising his personal experience by claiming that the narrator saw Hancock's photograph rather than the man himself.

Hancock's features are "manly," but it is "the soul," "the spirit" that "moulds the form," that matters. He is the ideal American field commander, as his "eagle mien" announces. An ancestor of his, perhaps a "noble" in decorative armor or a "Yeoman" in leathern garb—no matter which—must have fought with King Harry at Agincourt. Hancock is the natural leader that a democracy is capable of producing, not a man born to rank and position but one who is worthy of it: "Nothing can lift the heart of man / Like manhood in a fellow-man." In this Hancock anticipates Herman's conception of the "Handsome Sailor," in *Billy Budd* the figure of Admiral Nelson, the modest minister's son, as opposed to that of Captain Vere, the nobleman who has inherited his rank.

At Culpepper, Herman may have visited Charles Brewster at General Custer's headquarters. Charles was avoiding life in a tent by boarding at a private home, where he could have arranged overnight quarters for Herman. Although Charles missed the "Washington fun," he had found local women who, suffering wartime deprivation, were willing to trade intimacy for sustenance. In fact, he had written to offer Henry Gansevoort a go at them, noting that "they are uniformly fond of whiskey! which at present this Brigade enjoys in abundance."[47]

The high point of the visit to Culpepper was Herman's meeting with Grant.[48] Immersed in important duties and responsibilities as Grant was, Herman's authorial credentials entitled him to preferential consideration. Aside from that, as a merchant in prewar Galena, Grant had been associated with the Melvills and may have felt obligations of courtesy toward their cousin. It is also possible that he had received one of the copies of *Typee* that Herman had sent Toby. Any one of these motives, or any combination of them, could have induced him to receive Herman graciously and perhaps to arrange accommodations for him at his headquarters. Grant occupied a house surrounded by the tents of his entourage. As the lieutenant general sat "by the Culpepper hearth / With the slowly-smoked cigar," Herman conversed with him about the various battles he had fought. Later, he recalled Grant's statement about the spontaneous charge of the Army of the Cumberland at Chattanooga. "I never saw any thing like it," Grant told him. From his impression of Grant, the "taciturn Commander," Herman decided that those few words were "equivalent to a superlative or hyperbole from the talkative."

Herman's admiration of Grant is notable. In the early days of the war, before the capture of Donelson, Grant had played the dandy, wearing an ornate uniform and affecting an artfully coifed beard and a generous moustache. But by 1864 he had remade himself into a democratic icon with "homely manners, dislike for military frippery—for every form of ostentation in war and peace," as Whitman put it. "Grant was the typical Western man—the plainest, the most efficient; was the least imposed upon by appearances; was most impressive in the severe simplicity of his flannel shirt and his utter disregard for formal military etiquette." Whitman's description is of a piece with a story in circulation that when Grant had first glimpsed Meade's headquarters flag, emblazoned with a golden eagle in a silver wreath, he had demanded sarcastically, "What's this!—Is Imperial Cæsar anywhere about here?"[49]

Herman was of two minds about the opposites of democratic simplicity and knightly blazonry, a conflict which he never resolved. His heart preserved a romantic longing for the lace and feathers of a Chevalier Bayard and an admiration for leaders like Nelson, who placed martial display ahead of prudence. Yet plain Grant was the product of the evolution of the democratic military hero that had begun with gentleman farmer George Washington, and in this sense he was an heir of the Founding Fathers. It may be that in Herman's imagination Grant and Lincoln were prototypical of a new, unpretentious America to come. By the time of *Billy Budd,* it was the commoner Nelson who loved military display and it was the aristocrat Vere who affected plain appearance, but in 1864 Herman honored Grant's democratic dowdiness.

Where one expects the keen penetration by a poet into the character of a leader of the age one finds instead the poet clearly seduced by his encounter with the commander, so much so that none of the later criticism of the bloody cost of Grant's offensive, even from members of his own family, found its way into *Battle-Pieces*. Herman remembered him as a "quiet Man, and plain in garb," with "a heart as calm / As the Cyclone's core." The times and the principles of the war demanded the "meekness and grimness" that met in him, determination wedded to humility. Far from seeing him as the butcher who was spendthrift of human lives, Herman believed him to be the kind of man who, had he been given the larger management of affairs, would have prevented the suffering. If all men were like Grant, *"War would be left to the red and black ants, / And the happy world disarm."* Whether or not Thoreau himself would have associated this metaphor (from the chapter "Brute Neighbors" in *Walden*) with Grant, he would have approved of Herman's humane intention.

Valuable for his purpose as such interviews were, perhaps more valuable was the opportunity to witness the two massive armies counterpoised across the Rapidan. The first twenty stanzas of "The Armies of the Wilderness" contain a wealth of images gleaned from this visit. Herman was impressed by the ruined countryside, trampled fields, ravaged groves, and empty houses: "Ah! where shall the people be sought?" and *"Where are the birds and boys?"* (Lost somewhere between Bull Run and the camps of central Virginia.) For miles around, the forest had been hewn to stumps.

He was aware that he was visiting two armies, not one, two armies that lay facing each other in a stagnation of anticipation. On the one side of the river lay the Union encampments, while on the other side lay the Confederates, separated, literally and figuratively in Herman's emblematic imagination, by "the vale's deep rent." Across that rent one could see the Southerners, mounted pickets patrolling lazily and soldiers playing football, a game in which, in a world in harmony with itself, the Northern boys would have joined. Elsewhere, rebel soldiers in battle-worn uniforms were digging fortifications in the red earth, a presentiment of the blood that would soon dye the soil. In his imagination, at least, Herman heard a captured Confederate soldier identifying the campsites of Georgians, Carolinians, Virginians, Alabamians, Mississippians, Kentuckians, Tennesseans, and ten unidentified regiments, across the river. On the Union side the pickets waited tensely in secure locations, since the Confederates were known to steal across the river to harass them. It could have been on such a mission that the prisoner had been captured. Herman's fellow feeling for this enemy is patent. In the poem, the Union captors admire their prisoner: "'True-blue like you / Should wear the color / your Country's, man!'" But the rebel soldier had been *"foully snared / By Belial's wily plea"* and was entrapped in *"Feudal fidelity"*—the discredited feathers and gold lace that were to disappear from the new America, to be replaced by the plainness of Grant and the ironclad sense of duty of Worden.[50]

In addition to being a guide to what Herman may have seen and done on his visit, "The Armies of the Wilderness" is an index to his intellectual and emotional response, and as such it marks the most important crossroad in *Battle-Pieces*. For the first time, the truth of the war—the Satanic state in which the rule of law and civility is mocked by violent armies bent on feral destructiveness—is seen. This is ripened war, all pretense of nobility of purpose and chivalry of deed stripped away to reveal the ugliness beneath. History and learning are canceled as campfires are fueled by "indentures and bonds, / And old Lord Fairfax's parchment deeds; / And Virginian gentlemen's libraries old." The church is despoiled and the call of religion unheeded as the soldiers' huts are furnished with chapel pews. Justice sleeps as horses are stabled in courthouses. Tradition and human dignity are despoiled as an old gravestone is toppled for use as a hearthstone. In short, the symbols of ordered lives and peaceful civilization have been misappropriated, overturned, debased, ravaged, and burned. *"Has Time / Gone back? or is this the Age / Of the world's great Prime?"* What remains but savagery? Are these men, stripped of the patina of enlightenment and civility, swarming in tribal warfare as they had in primal times? They camp and march where the dead of earlier battles moulder, half-buried or not buried at all. The shattered forests testify to rape by weapons and warriors, the civilians who once lived on the land are dispersed, and the instruments of harmonious society are desecrated. This is Satan's wasteland: *"Man runs wild on the plain, / Like the jennets let loose / On the Pampas—zebras again."* What of the men who had sacrificed themselves in the Revolution to overthrow the ancient wrongs? Was that sacrifice not enough to prevent this present wrong? *"Can no final good be wrought? / Over and over, again and again / Must the fight for the Right be fought?"* The worth of the Union cause remains, but the quarreling brothers of "Apathy and Enthusiasm" have become beasts girding for slaughter. No other poet looked this closely at the ghastly truth of the war.

By the time of Herman's departure, the trains from Washington had finished their work and the army he was leaving was stirring into action. In about a week, the offensive would begin. However, his tour had not quite ended. On his way home, he visited "several battlefields," according to Lizzie. That should not be taken too literally, since many of the important battlefields were still impossible to reach. Most likely he visited Bull Run, as Hawthorne had done, since it was a stop along the track and it combined two battlefields in one. He would have rambled over fields still littered with human bones and other jetsam of the war. There, where new fighting had welled and ebbed over the graves of the dead from the previous battle, Herman would have received additional inspiration for "The Armies of the Wilderness." But he did not tarry long.

He returned to the city better equipped to write his book. As Whitman had told his mother, "You dont know what a feeling a man gets after being in the active sights & influences of the camp, . . . he gets to have a deep feeling he never experienced before."[51] And Whitman had never ridden out on such a scout as Herman had, nor had any other major author of the North.

May *Is the Cruelest Month*

While Herman had been visiting the front, the Metropolitan Fair had ended. Its financial success had come close to matching expectations—a preliminary estimate indicated that it had raised over a million dollars. It was an esthetic success, too, its art exhibit leading New Yorkers to contemplate the establishment of a metropolitan museum of art. But toward the end, the voting for the army sword had become a main focus of interest. General McClellan had led General Grant almost every day, and when Grant had pulled ahead briefly, Mrs. James Gordon Bennett had bought 300 votes to restore McClellan's lead. When the voting booth had closed, McClellan's lead had been 2,256 votes. But from the beginning the Union Leaguers and other Republicans had been withholding their money in order to mislead the McClellan supporters, and at the last minute they stuffed a makeshift ballot box with envelopes containing huge donations for Grant. By eight o'clock in the evening, when the final vote was tallied, Grant had received 30,291, McClellan only 14,509.[52]

But none of this interested Herman until long after his return, for when he reached the city he was ill. Fortunately, Lizzie was back from Boston to nurse him. The immunity to fatigue and illness that had sustained him through his journey had dissipated, and now he was paying in full the physical price of his excited hyperactivity, lying in bed suffering from "an acute attack of neuralgia in the eyes."[53] He was too ill even to pay attention to the opening of Grant's offensive on May 4.

The illness also prevented him from visiting Uncle Peter to report on his visit to the cavalry camp. Instead, on May 2, Allan and Jennie called on the Albany Gansevoorts, where they were able to see Mother Melville, as well. She had been there recuperating while her sons had been traveling, and now Allan was making restitution for his failure to visit her at the height of her illness. He and Jennie gave a full account of their visit to Washington: Jennie told of missing Henry and seeing Grant, and Allan described Henry's camp and told of Herman's departure on the scout and of his present illness. It appears that Herman had been too sick to tell Allan about his further adventures, since Allan said nothing about them—no mention of his visit to the Army of the Potomac or his interview with Grant.[54]

It took Herman over a week and a half to recover, but by the tenth of May he was up and about, able to bear the excitement of the campaign in Virginia and to deal with his memories of the army which was engaged in it. Always prompt to fulfill his letter-writing obligations, he took the first opportunity to thank his army hosts for their hospitality. His letter to Henry Gansevoort was full of his usual warmth and wit. He was especially tickled by the metamorphosis of Bruce, the swell lawyer, into a military officer: "Coke on Lyttleton, and Strap on the Shoulder." For Ed Lansing's attentions he sent his warm thanks. Believing that General Tyler was still at Fairfax Court House (though he had already joined the Army of the Potomac), he continued his literary discussion with him through Henry. Henry was to tell Tyler that the worst thing Herman could say about Richter's *The Titan* was that "it is a little better than 'Mardi.'" Tyler would surely have known enough not to take that seriously, authors being what they are. Since Herman did not ask Henry to deliver a message to Lowell, and since he would not have failed to thank the man who had made possible one of the important adventures of his life, he must have written another letter, no longer extant, to the young brigade commander. Herman inflicted his "infirmity of jocularity" (or jocular hyperbole) on Henry. He did not admire people who put themselves forward as Henry did, but he would not offend a family hero. He pictured himself at attention, saluting: "May two small but choice constellations of stars alight on your shoulders. May your sword be a lesson to the despicable foe, & your name in after ages be used by Southern matrons to frighten their children by. And after death (which God long avert, & bring about after great battles, quietly, in a comfortable bed, with wife & children around) may that same name be transferred to heaven—bestowed upon some new planet or cluster of stars of the first magnitude. Farewell, my hero & God bless you." That said one thing about Henry's ambitions: "The Scout toward Aldie" would say the other.

Whether or not he was on his feet in time to see Surgeon Henry Thurston as he passed through the city is problematical. For nearly two years now, Henry had served in Nashville. After the death of his wife Lizzie, he had fallen in love with Mary Sullivan Bankhead, an Arkansas-born resident of Nashville. At the beginning of 1864, he had been reassigned to field duty as the Medical Director of the Twelfth Corps in Tennessee, but he did not want that post. He told the Surgeon-General that because his children were still in the city he wanted to be transferred there or to Philadelphia. Instead, he was ordered to the staff of Joe Hooker's Twentieth Corps in Tennessee, but on the day of his relief, April 25, he married Mary Bankhead in a Catholic ceremony and brought her to the city, apparently in violation of his orders. He spent some days moving his reassembled family into his home before reporting to the Surgeon-General's office in Washington. The Surgeon-General must have been satisfied to have him there, since he immediately sent him to an army hospital at Belle Plain, Virginia, where casualties from the Army of the Potomac were arriving. For a month and a half Henry served as needed there and in Washington until, on July 1, 1864, he assumed command of Grant General Hospital at Willett's Point, New York City. If Herman had been too ill to see him in early May, he had plenty of opportunities to do so later.[55]

While Herman had been ill, battles had been fought and the two armies of the east had locked into a combat that would continue until Lee's surrender. On the first of May, General Tyler was recalled to the Army of the Potomac, not to resume his artillery command but to lead an infantry brigade that included the Corcoran Legion. In addition, just as the offensive was about to begin, Burnside brought up his corps, which included Frank Bartlett's 57th Massachusetts. As they paraded through Washington, Lincoln joined Burnside to review them from the balcony of Willard's. Just before George Whitman passed Lincoln, his brother Walt arrived to march beside him and visit. Distracted, George neglected to salute the president. Then the corps moved down the railroad to Rappahannock Station.[56]

On the fourth of May, Grant had slipped across the Rapidan. On the fifth, Ben Butler moved swiftly up the James River to Bermuda Hundred, near Richmond, where he was trapped by a smallish Confederate force that held him there until Grant was able to rescue him. On the seventh of May, Sherman's troops, including Toby Greene and John Hobart, marched on Atlanta.

Although Grant eluded Lee in his river crossing, by the time he arrayed his army for the march toward Richmond, Lee was there to cut it up on the march, as he had tried to do to McClellan on the Peninsula. Grant turned to fight him in the Wilderness, next to the Chancellorsville battlefield, and a bloody battle ensued, fought by men who could not see the enemy fifty yards ahead and by Union generals whose confusions were paralytic, resulting, among other sad occurrences, in the shattering of the Harvard Regiment—Stephen Longfellow received a wound that crippled him for life. In the tangle of forest, fires added their smoke to the clouds from the gunpowder and burned wounded men to death. On the morning of the sixth of May, Frank Bartlett and his men, in the foremost brigade of Burnside's corps, pushed up. Soon after his regiment was committed, Frank was struck above the right temple by a ball. As he fell, he wrenched what remained of his truncated leg so that he could not support himself on his artificial limb. "The crippled, a ragged-barked stick for a crutch, / Limp to some elfin dell," Herman wrote in "The Armies of the Wilderness." Bartlett returned to the Fifth Avenue Hotel in New York City, where he was received with cheers. He remained there with his father and mother from the thirteenth to the nineteenth of May, during which time Herman may have called on him, and then left for Boston to recuperate and to be fitted with a new leg. Whittier took note: "I see Harriet Bartlett's brave young hero is again wounded,—I trust not severely."[57]

By the time the news of the renewal of the fighting at Spotsylvania arrived, Herman had recovered. As good as his word, Grant was pressing the attack, and as good as his reputation, Lee was frustrating him. In each battle, Lee lost a substantial portion of his smaller army, but he was punishing Grant mercilessly. When Spotsylvania ended Grant had already lost 33,000 men and he was still far from Richmond. That battle was followed by yet another at the North Anna, where the Army of the Potomac again lost hordes of men. So continuous and so fatal was the fighting that soldiers carried slips of paper into battle to identify their corpses.

The people of the North could hardly help being shocked by the staggering casualty lists, which were now arriving daily. There were calls for the removal of both Grant and Lincoln. The day after the bloodiest fighting at Spotsylvania, Greeley's *New York Tribune* demanded the nomination of some other Republican for the presidency, and a little over a month later Kate Gansevoort wrote that Grant "will scarcely bring back a man if he meets with such heavy losses as every battle has been to him." But Herman imagined Grant's back heaving to a hump in solicitude.[58]

As if his illness and the crushing casualties were not enough to depress Herman's spirits, the irritation of rotting garbage tasked him. Sometime around the fifteenth of May, the New York City collectors went on strike for a week, and there in front of the house lay spoiling waste to greet him with its awful stink whenever he opened a window or a door to let in the spring air. Lizzie described the odor as "villainous." In addition to this annoyance, "wise Draco" rode through the city once more. In the afternoon of Wednesday, May 18, just as the bloodletting at Spotsylvania was ending, some local newspapers were victimized by an "official" telegram that had been forged by two employees of the *Brooklyn Daily Eagle* in order to manipulate the gold market. When Richard Lathers arrived at work the next morning, he found the financial community in a frenzy about the news in the *New York World* and the *New York Journal of Commerce* that as a result of military disasters in Virginia Lincoln had proclaimed a day of fasting, humiliation, and prayer and had called for the immediate enrollment of 400,000 more men. In view of the magnitude of the casualty lists, the forgery was credible.[59]

After an investigation, General Dix wrote Stanton exonerating the newspapermen, but Stanton obtained Lincoln's order to arrest the editors, proprietors, and publishers of both papers pending a military trial, to shut the papers down, and to station troops in their offices. That evening, Richard—unaware that he was under surveillance by Dix's footpads—called on the general in the company of Supreme Court Justice Barbour, but the military was not to be challenged. Although Dix did not agree with the arrests, the good soldier intended to carry out his orders. Richard could remonstrate and Dix could sympathize, but no one could challenge faraway Washington—that was the devilish beauty of having Dix in command. Fortunately, the next day the order was rescinded, and after three days the soldiers withdrew from the press offices, leaving only the shaken sensibilities of New York conservatives and a futile lawsuit as reminders of the incident.

With garbage at the door, long casualty lists on the walls, and the man on horseback in the streets, Herman was ill-prepared for the death of Hawthorne. Hawthorne had continued feeble and dispirited after Ticknor's death, so much so that Franklin Pierce had taken him for a carriage trip through the New Hampshire countryside. Hawthorne had survived only a few days, dying in his sleep in a Plymouth inn during the small hours of the nineteenth of May. Whittier's reaction was filled with critical insight and, for an abolitionist, generosity: "And so Hawthorne is at rest—the rest that he could not find here. God—the All-Merciful—has removed him from the shadows of time—wherein he seemed to walk himself like a shadow—to the clear sunlight of Eternity."[60]

In a single moment, there was no Hawthorne and never again would be. Herman did not attend the funeral. He had not seen his friend in over seven years, and he was not able to overcome the habit of alienation, even at such a moment. He was deeply shocked personally, though it was a loss for his mother and his sisters, too. It was the disappearance of the one friend to whom he had felt that he could bare his inmost heart. The relationship had lapsed, but its memory remained; a perusal of some of Herman's letters from their early, excited times of more or less mutual discovery gives the reader a guilty feeling of intruding into a privacy that was not meant for him.[61]

There is disagreement about whether or not Herman's impeccable poem "Monody" (228–29) commemorates Hawthorne, and even about the depth of their friendship, but there are strong reasons to believe that it does.[62] It is a simple, eloquent expression of loss:

To have known him, to have loved him
  After loneness long;
And then to be estranged in life,
  And neither in the wrong;
And now for death to set his seal—
  Ease me, a little ease, my song!

By wintry hills his hermit-mound
  The sheeted snow-drifts drape,
And houseless there the snow-bird flits
  Beneath the fir-trees' crape:
Glazed now with ice the cloistral vine
  That hid the shyest grape.

Herman's heartfelt expression of grief would be a better tribute to his friend than the uneasy gestures of the Concord-Boston literati who, having condemned Hawthorne for disloyalty while he lived, gathered with solemn expressions and uneasy hearts around his grave.

In after years, Herman was true to Hawthorne's memory. In his poem "The Rose Farmer" (303–10), in which rose-growing is a thinly disguised metaphor for literary creation, he paid tribute to "a friend, whose shadow has decreased . . . / A corpulent grandee of the East." The friendship had begun, according to the poem, when the narrator had "prepared a *chowder* for his feast," as Herman had dedicated his "chowder," *Moby-Dick,* to Hawthorne. In return, the narrator became his heir: "Well dying, he remembered me: / A brave bequest, a farm in fee / Forever consecrate to roses." This legacy became clearer when Herman used Hawthorne's tale "The Birthmark" as a benchmark of meaning in his last great tale, *Billy Budd.*

During May, there were also two causes for rejoicing. One, the result of another bereavement, came from Doctor George Hayward, probably a cousin of Judge Shaw. Hayward, credited with being the first to use ether as an anesthetic in a major operation, was a distinguished surgeon. His death on October 7, 1863, while she had been preparing to move from Pittsfield, had grieved Lizzie, but the legacy of $3,000 with which he had remembered her was welcome. She used part of it to pay off Mrs. Thurston's mortgage on the house, giving her ownership, free and clear.[63] The other cause for celebration was the marriage of Gertrude Melvill Downer, Anne de Marini's next younger sister, to James D. Scudder on May 26. Whether or not the two New York Melville families attended the ceremony is not known, though with the de Marinis living nearby it may have been difficult to avoid.

There was no surcease from the casualty lists of the Army of the Potomac. As Wendell Holmes put it, the "butchers bill" had been "immense." The first two weeks or so of the offensive had "contained all of fatigue & horror that war can furnish."[64] Grant had continued to sidle toward Richmond, but Lee had been agile enough to remain in his front. This minuet had forced the Army of the Potomac to circle the Confederate capital toward the battlefields of the Seven Days. Finally Grant's army arrived near McClellan's old battlefield of Gaines's Mills, but Lee, now reduced to only a third as many men as Grant, arrived at the same time and placed his men in strong breastworks and entrenchments. The two armies fought the Battle of Cold Harbor in the exact location where Henry's battery had guarded the rear of McClellan's forces at the beginning of their march to Harrison's Landing.

At dawn on June 3, in a drizzling rain, the Union soldiers attacked, but the Confederate works were so ingeniously placed that the slaughter was terrible, reminiscent of Fredericksburg. One of the most prominent brigades in the fight, Tyler's Corcoran Legion, succeeded in taking an advanced Confederate position. Colonel James P. McMahon seized the regimental flag from a fallen color-bearer and planted it on the enemy parapet, then, his body riddled, fell dead—so much for the Irish "rats of the wharves." Tyler had to leave the field with a bullet through his ankle. For three days, the army lay under Confederate fire, listening as the shrieks and gasps of the Union wounded left between the lines diminished into silence because Grant refused to request the customary truce that would have saved them. All in all, the Army of the Potomac lost nearly 13,000 men, having inflicted relatively few casualties on the Confederates.

Because he did not know earlier how to address the letter, it took Herman over a month and a half to send an expression of sympathy to Tyler. He wrote that he was gratified that the wound had not been more serious than it was and he added the hope that as Tyler recovered he would enjoy cigars, books, and admiring feminine attentions. He added his home address so that Tyler might visit him in the future, which Tyler may well have done, since he had plenty of opportunity. But Herman did not know at the time that, superficial as the wound may have sounded, Tyler would never fully recover from it.[65]

The offensive had been a ghastly failure. Grant had reached McClellan's old position close to Richmond by squandering 55,000 casualties, half the number of men with whom he had crossed the Rapidan. The reason, thought the Confederate officers, was that he was not a strategist, depending instead on direct, mutually punishing assaults with overwhelming resources of men. That method was too primitive for the brilliant Sherman: "Its glory is all moonshine," he said, "even success the most brilliant is over dead and mangled bodies, with the anguish and lamentation of distant families." That Grant could have avoided the slaughter by following McClellan's example was not lost on the army. Wendell Holmes noted that "theres no use in disguising that the feeling for McClellan has grown this campaign," and a high-ranking officer serving with Wendell said: "Two years before, this same army had been placed much nearer Richmond with comparatively little loss. . . . [Grant] had the advantage, of which he freely availed himself, of ordering troops to his assistance, not begging for them as McClellan did in vain." Even one of the Confederate generals agreed; Grant could have reached the Richmond area, he said, "in a much shorter time and without any fighting at all." It is true that, according to Satan's reasoning, the sacrifice of the flower of Northern manhood helped to bleed Lee's army to death, but families and sweethearts on both sides wept.[66]

Then Grant decided to stanch the flow of blood. Leaving Lee confused about his plans, for once, he "changed his base," following McClellan's trek across the Peninsula in order to move south of Richmond, as McClellan had wished to do early on. The Army of the Potomac positioned itself near

Petersburg, through which Richmond's rail lifeline from the south passed, and there it dug in.

Herman's visit to the front enabled him to portray the fighting in Part 2, the battle section, of "The Armies of the Wilderness." Although the name associates the poem with the opening battle of the campaign, these stanzas deal with the slaughter—on both sides—as a whole. They follow and relate to the camp scenes that depict the Union soldiers as men robbed by war of the appointments and values of civilization, as tame animals gone wild on the pampas. In "The March into Virginia," men had tramped into the inviting wood as though they were enjoying an outing. In "Donelson," the victorious assault on the Confederate fortifications had been filtered and sanitized through the reports of newspaper correspondents. But here the soldiers, like the night winds, are *"at the height of their madness."* The fighting, in the real and symbolic tangle of wilderness, is the truth of war stripped of all noble pretentions. "Plume and sash are vanities now," the poem warns, and with a realism that appears nowhere else in Civil War poetry it portrays the primitive brutality with which soldiers fought in the wilderness of battle and in the wilderness of their primal impulses. As in the forest of "The Scout toward Aldie," Satan is the master and the Valley of Death the setting: "Pursuer and pursued like ghosts disappear / In gloomed shade," and the dead of the past are present:

In glades they meet skull after skull
  Where pine-cones lay—the rusted gun,
Green shoes full of bones, the mouldering coat
  And cuddled-up skeleton.

The hellishness of battle is emphasized by a biblical allusion. The Pillar of Smoke that in scriptural times had led the Israelites in their Exodus (13:21) now cremates the dead and chars the wounded in the forest fires that erupt during the fighting: *"the Pillar of Smoke that led / Was brand-like with ghosts that went up / Ashy and red."* These men are not led and protected by God but are enticed and immolated by the deity of destruction. Battle this horrible cannot be known by anyone who has not experienced it: "The entangled rhyme / But hints at the maze of war," a maze "of which the slain / Sole solvers are."

This unspeakableness is also the subject of the memorial poem "An uninscribed Monument on one of the Battle-fields of the Wilderness," a coda to "The Armies of the Wilderness." No monument can express the "din" and the "striving of the multitude," only the "Silence and Solitude" and the rusting detritus of battle can hint of it. If the visitor understands the meaning of the silence, he will "silent stand— / Silent as I, and lonesome as the land." After the cacophony of shrieks and explosions, after the tragedy of pain, death, and immolation, sermons and eulogies are useless. Only the still of the wilderness hints at the meaning.

He counterpointed the animalistic elements of "The Armies of the Wilderness" by showing their other side in "The Eagle of the Blue." The poem is about "Old Abe," of the 8th Wisconsin Volunteer Infantry, or "Eagle Regiment." Garbed in red, white, and blue ribbons, during three years Abe survived twenty battles and numerous skirmishes, delighting in the firing. When the fighting was at its most intense he flapped his wings and screamed. At the end of the war, he was retired to the Wisconsin state house.[67]

Old Abe is an "Emblem" of the battle spirit of the North—the Union must be rescued despite the cost—much as the rooster in Herman's "Cock-a-Doodle-Do" symbolizes the enduring human spirit. This grim determination is of a piece with Hancock's "eagle mien" in "On the Photograph of a Corps Commander." It may be that it is of divine origin, as the natural habitat of the bird in the heights suggests, but it is not a spirit of heaven intervening on the side of the just. It is that other divine spirit, remote but all-powerful, whose plan will be fulfilled regardless of men's errors and successes.

In relation to "The Armies of the Wilderness," the poem originates in the lines "Heaven lent strength, the Right strove well, / And emerged from the Wilderness." Whereas the men who fought there revealed a dark, brutal nature nurtured in warfare, the eagle expresses another aspect, their mitigating purpose. Yet he is in no way sanitized. Like the Wilderness soldiers, he is a feral creature, glaringly aggressive in a way that caused Benjamin Franklin, according to tradition, to suggest the substitution of a peaceful bird like the turkey as the national symbol. He is an "unhappy fowl," as Hawthorne called him,[68] remembering his menacing effigy perched over the entrance to the Salem customhouse. No longer soaring in the heights, no longer joying in the wind, the creature screams in joy as the battle for the right is fought below. A creature of the primal wilderness, bereft of romantic claptrap, historical sense and deliberation, and social constraint and pity, he is pure battle—ball, bayonet, and saber, fatigue and suffering, cake of sweaty grime and snarl of utterance. Death for him is a companion, life an endless campaign. In short, he is the nation at war in earnest. This was the time for the spirit of the eagle to dominate. The sufferings of the past had punished; the sufferings of the present wilted the faint of heart. As the men of the North and the South fell in the grand harvest of death, nothing but this spirit could hold the people steady to their purpose until the chasm that separated the states could be closed. In the end, they, like "The Eagle of the Blue," would retire to their peaceful homes.

The College General

Henry Gansevoort's excitement about the offensive had cooled when his regiment had not been ordered to the Cavalry Corps. Other than that, his position was satisfactory. He was pleased with Bruce and believed that he would make an excellent officer. On May 9, he and Bruce accompanied Lowell on a long patrol along the idle Military Railroad. Shortly after, the Cavalry Brigade moved to Falls Church, whence Effy Lowell returned to her parental home on Staten Island. With so few troops left behind to guard Washington, the cavalrymen had been pulled in closer to the city.[69]

But Henry's health continued to be poor—at times he was so sick that he was barely able to sit at his desk. Before long, the same was true of Bruce, whose constitution was not strong enough to withstand camp life. Henry assigned him temporarily to courts-martial, but his malarial fever did not improve. By July 4, he was unable to leave his quarters, and on August 6 he was discharged. His army career and Henry's dream of having his old friend in the regiment over, Bruce returned to his partnership with Allan.[70]

Back home, Kate Gansevoort sewed for the soldiers while Aunt Susan sent them pickles—between vacation trips. Despite Henry's hopes, Kate was anxious that he avoid duty with the Army of the Potomac because of the immense casualties and because she did not want him to fight for "the Negro." On June 15, she joined a small party for a trip to West Point to witness the dedication of the Battle Monument, a memorial to the regular soldiers killed thus far in the war. For the occasion, General McClellan spoke of the need to prosecute the war to a successful conclusion. Toward the end of the month, she and her parents left for two weeks at Saratoga Springs, where Mother Melville joined them.[71]

Elsewhere, Allan and Herman's sisters were preparing for their summer travels. Kate and John Hoadley planned to leave their two girls at Gansevoort in the middle of June while they visited John's family in Rochester. On their return, Kate and the girls were to remain at Gansevoort while John returned to New Bedford. George Griggs was planning a trip through Canada, followed by a 160-mile tramp through the woods to St. Paul's, Minnesota; Helen refused to accompany him because that would mean giving up her summer in Gansevoort. Since the end of April, Allan and Jennie had been preparing for the summer at Arrowhead. Jennie and little Kate Melville had gone to Pittsfield to make arrangements, after which, following the Fourth of July, the family moved for the summer. Before their departure, Henry Thurston reappeared to assume his new duties in the city. Although he was ill, he was home with his new wife and with the children from whom he had been separated for so long.[72]

In the wake of his visit to the front, Herman must have been pondering the form and content of the book he was to write. What else he did during this period is little known, although he did buy a two-volume set of the poems of Elizabeth Barrett Browning—perhaps he took his family to Arrowhead to relax with the Allan Melvilles. Richard Lathers and his family may have visited Allan and Jennie in their summer home, too, since Richard learned to like the area enough to build a home there shortly after the war. After the Herman Melvilles' putative visit, Lizzie would most likely have taken the two girls to Boston while Herman took the two boys to Gansevoort.[73]

By this time, Kate Hoadley and her girls were in Gansevoort, with Helen due to arrive later. Aside from the peaceful holiday, with the children playing at all hours and the family gossiping and inventing amusements, all were concerned about the Glens Falls Gansevoorts. Leonard was seriously ill, some days better and some days worse. He had improved in the spring, but by early July he was weak, emaciated, short of breath, and without appetite or interest. Because Kate Curtis and Stanwix Gansevoort were occupied with nursing him, Gansevoort had little intercourse with Glens Falls.[74]

Mid-July brought another Hoadley family crisis. Lottie, who had been bright, comical, and indefatigable, fell ill, refusing to play and clinging to her mother. John dashed for a train, rode all night on the Rutland route, and arrived at Gansevoort desperate with anxiety, but it was a false alarm. With Lottie out of danger, John made the best of the situation by remaining in Gansevoort so Herman could enjoy two weeks of his company. John was the right person to be with at this time, since he was certain to have firm opinions about the campaigns; for his part, Herman's account of his pursuit of Mosby and his visit to the Army of the Potomac would have found an eager audience in John.[75]

Upon John's departure, Herman, Gus, and the boys visited Leonard in Glens Falls. It was a good thing, because it was the last time Herman ever saw him alive. The patient had been diagnosed as having "dropsy of the heart" and had been given a month or two at most to live. The visit also provided Herman with a good opportunity to inquire about Guert, whose recent activities, however, were scarcely worth reporting, and to talk to Ned. Had the visit taken place only a few days later, Herman and Ned could have celebrated Farragut's victory at Mobile Bay.

When Herman returned to Gansevoort, Helen had arrived. That meant that the end of his vacation, which had been timed to give him a few days with her, was approaching. On August 8, he left for New York City with Gus for company, since Lizzie and the girls were apparently still in Boston, while the two boys remained behind in Gansevoort. A little less than two weeks later, Lizzie arrived at Gansevoort with the two girls and stayed there until September 9, when she brought all four children back to the city. Gus then returned to Gansevoort.[76]

If Herman did visit Pittsfield in the early summer, he may have seen Frank Bartlett, who appeared in the village a time or two. Newly promoted to brigadier general and fitted with a new leg, he visited the Pomeroys before returning to the army. Somewhat after the middle of July, he took command of a brigade of the Ninth Corps at Petersburg, where a novel experiment was under way. A Pennsylvania regiment made up mostly of miners dug a tunnel under the Confederate lines in order to plant explosives beneath a particularly strong and irksome fortification. In the wake of the explosion, an attack was to be made through the gap in the defenses to spearhead a general assault. But at the last moment the specially trained assault force of U.S. Colored Troops was replaced by white troops, including Frank Bartlett's men.

The sight of the explosion on July 30 was spectacular, people, weapons, and dirt propelled high into the air and then falling so close to the attackers that some ran to avoid being struck. While the division commander remained in the security of a "bomb-proof" far away, drinking, Frank and the other brigade commanders led their men forward. At the rim of the crater, they paused to gaze into the magnificent hole, the like of which they had never imagined, thirty feet deep, sixty feet across, and one hundred and seventy feet long, with the bodies of Confederates, many still alive, protruding from the rubble at the bottom. Then they charged on, but the regrouped Confederates forced them back into the crater. Without the division commander present to coordinate the attack, Union troops behind them also poured in and soon the bottom of the pit was crammed. Finally the Colored Troops were ordered to attack, but though they fought well and took severe punishment, they too were repelled. With the Confederates firing at them from the rim, the men trapped in the crater were helpless. When a large lump of earth crushed his artificial leg, Frank asked to be helped to sit up. One of his men remonstrated, "But you are wounded, General, aren't you?" To which Frank replied, "My leg is shattered all to pieces." "Then you can't sit up, you'll have to lie down." "Oh, no!" Frank answered, "it's only my cork leg that's shattered!" Under other circumstances, it would have been a bully joke, but because Frank could not move he was captured along with 1,100 others. The next day he was shipped by train to the Danville prison, where he suffered from deprivation and dysentery until it was necessary to hospitalize him. On August 27, he was transferred to Libby Prison in Richmond, where he nearly died. Fortunately, he was exchanged on September 24. He had served as a brigade commander for less than two weeks and had been a prisoner for some three months.[77]

Bartlett's imprisonment is included in the latter part of "The College Colonel." Although the parade in the first part of the poem had occurred in Pittsfield in 1863, and Bartlett returned from his imprisonment at the end of the summer of 1864, the poem is located in *Battle-Pieces* in late 1864, where it fits into an "Abrahamic River" sequence that begins with "The Armies of the Wilderness." It is a tribute to General Bartlett, not Colonel Bartlett, a study of his change (and the changes in the other youthful Indian braves of innocent courage) into an enlightened warrior who, as Herman wrote in "The Coming Storm," reaches "Man's final lore." Although the poem fictionalizes his war experiences (Frank had not served "all through the Seven Days' Fight"—Henry Gansevoort had), he is nevertheless an important example of the aware Melville hero: "There came— / Ah heaven!— what *truth* to him." His amputated leg relates him to Ahab, on the one hand, and to Major Jack Gentian (whose arm has been amputated) on the other—two contrasting versions of this character. Bartlett stands somewhere between the two, neither consumed by revenge nor benign in his acceptance, yet one whose dark experience has awakened his understanding of the wisdom of Ecclesiastes, that all earthly things are vanity and woe: "Self he has long disclaimed." As Milder says, he "is an image for all those youths from Manassas onward whose lessons have been both physical and metaphysical, and who now stand as instructors to the uninitiated reader in the realities of war and life."[78]

The futility of his brief command and long imprisonment was mirrored in the position of the Army of the Potomac. Despite all of the casualties of the spring, the Union soldiers lay immobile before Petersburg. Before them were seemingly impregnable defenses from which the Confederates could not be dislodged, while the enemy marksmen forced them to cower in trenches and bomb-proofs. Short of food and ill-clothed though they were, the Southern soldiers held their positions with a persistent stubbornness. In the capital just to the north, the Confederate government conducted business as usual, seemingly indifferent to the presence of the great Union army. The spirit of the eagle was demanded, but in truth it was flagging. There was only one step to be taken before the war would end and the Union would be restored, but the question "how?" was baffling.

Yet Herman could look back on the preceding six months, the most intense of the war for him, with some satisfaction. Although they had begun with the disgraceful struggle for power in his cousin's cavalry regiment, that had been followed by the great exertion of New York City to support the soldiers. Then, at last, he had seen the war for himself, the chase

Brigadier General William Francis Bartlett, 1864–1865. U.S. Military History Institute

after Mosby and the immense Army of the Potomac and the grisly details of its surroundings. He had crept to the edge of Satan's murky chasm, and if he had not seen clearly what lay below he had at least rid himself of any last vestiges of peacetime innocence and romantic illusion. With that cleansing, he was prepared to write his book. The subsequent battle reports that followed him back to the city were ghastly, heartbreaking, but they intimated that the war would end with the union intact. Now was the time for some final patience.

8

De Year ob Jubilo
1864–1865

While Herman's battle summer wore on, Sherman's offensive in the west was achieving greater success than was Grant's in the east. Shortly after Grant crossed the Rapidan, Sherman marched into northwestern Georgia. His campaign was brilliant, subtle, and daring. For a month and a half he played cat and mouse with Confederate General Joseph Johnston, fighting almost daily, often sharp and bloody battles with unfamiliar names like Resaca and New Hope Church, but for the most part dodging Johnston's strength, thus avoiding a full-scale battle while forcing the Confederates relentlessly back to the outskirts of Atlanta. There, like Grant's, his offensive stalled.

Just before and during the campaign, the enlistments of many of the three-year regiments expired. Not long after its service in the Battle of Chattanooga, the 44th Illinois returned home to discharge those who wished to leave the service and to recruit for the battles to come. One of the new men was John Hobart, who, after a year in Rockford, decided to rejoin his old regiment. Then the 44th returned to Sherman's army. Toby Greene participated in the Atlanta campaign in his usual staff position. The expiration of his enlistment on June 24, 1864, found him at Big Shanty, Georgia, a little over twenty miles from Atlanta. There he was discharged from the 6th Missouri and returned to Chicago, where he must have remained with his family for a decent period of time while he rested and attempted to recover from the various chronic maladies of camp life. It is difficult to believe, considering the firm promise that he had made, that he failed to visit Herman. The period when Herman was in the city with Gus would have been as good a time as any for the reunion, though Toby remained a civilian throughout September and part of October before enlisting in Battery A of the 1st Illinois Light Artillery. Thereafter, he did garrison duty, though in later life he boasted, truthfully but misleadingly, that he had participated in Sherman's march through Georgia.[1]

It would have been appropriate had Toby's visit occurred just after September 2, when Sherman's army finally entered Atlanta. The reunion would not have been a temperance meeting, since Toby was a confirmed drinker and Herman was no teetotaler.[2] Herman would have wished to resurrect memories of the *Acushnet* and of the valley of the Typees, since these were the bonds that held their friendship together, but Toby would have been full of yarns about Missouri, Vicksburg, Chattanooga, and Georgia.

Such a visit may have inspired Herman's "A Dirge for McPherson, Killed in front of Atlanta (July, 1864)."[3] General James B. McPherson, the young commander of the Army of the Tennessee, was the highest ranking Union officer killed during the war. He fell near Atlanta on July 22, between the date of Toby's discharge and any likely date for a visit to Herman. McPherson had commanded the assault on the works at Vicksburg in which Toby had taken part, and at the time of Toby's discharge his corps was a part of McPherson's army, making it likely that Toby had encountered him. In his note to the poem, Herman praised the fallen general as "one of the foremost spirits of the war," a man "hardy, intrepid, sensitive in honor, full of engaging qualities, with manly beauty," qualities comparable to those of General Hancock in "On the Photograph of a Corps Commander." Yet the poem may be a roundabout tribute to Toby as well as to Toby's former commander, and it may be that the promise of a resurrection for the fallen hero, "There's a trumpet that shall rend / This Soldier's sleep," is a concession to Toby.

Framed in stately, solemn, and ritual terms, the poem imagines McPherson's funeral. Arms are reversed, flags are swathed in black, drums are muffled, and the coffin, bearing McPherson's sword, is drawn by white horses. Thus the North mourns a hero. Yet the poem makes another point. The eulogy is to "this Soldier," not to a titled aristocrat, as might have been the case in old Europe, and the frippery of feudal extravagance is absent—no bays and laurels, no ranks of men who owe fealty, no knighthoods or titles. McPherson was "the warrior / Who led," a democratic leader chosen out of the citizenry, a man whose rank was justified by his virtue, his ability, and by the willingness of his soldiers to follow him. He is mourned for this rather than for his exalted station, for in death he is no more than any of his soldiers, as the lesson read at his funeral proclaims: "Man is noble, man is brave, / But man's—a weed." This is how an American leader should be mourned.

Another recognition of Sherman's army at the point of Toby's discharge is the inscriptive and memorial stanza "On Sherman's Men who fell in the Assault of Kenesaw Mountain, Georgia." Despite its distance in *Battle-Pieces* from "A Dirge for McPherson," the two poems are thematically similar,

Richard Tobias Greene, 1865. By permission of the Berkshire Athenæum

suggesting that Herman saw a special democratic quality in the western troops. Writing at a time when the reading public devoured narrative poems by Tennyson and Lowell about Round Table knights, Herman wrote of citizen-warriors reared with "gentler hearts," ordinary men of peace rather than paladins of the lance and the broadsword. But if glory means anything, it characterizes these men who, without girded armor, withstood hails of fire that the knights of old could not have imagined. The dead of Kennesaw Mountain are one with Herman's vision of the new republican warriors in ragged coats who might a bard restore, the rededicated bard of America's destiny.

Victory and Humiliation at Sea

After the capture of New Orleans, the Union navy had achieved no glittering successes, though it had performed its essential, unspectacular duties of patrolling, blockading, and supporting the army. What feats of derring-do there were belonged to the Confederate sailors in their commerce-raiding cruisers, such as the *Alabama*. But then the Union sailors won three successive victories.

In June 1864, off the coast of France, Confederate Captain Raphael Semmes lost the *Alabama* in an old-fashioned broadside battle with the U.S.S. *Kearsarge*. Herman did not commemorate this celebrated event, even though he was given reason to do so when New York City was threatened by another Confederate cruiser. On August 10, the *Tallahassee* appeared off the harbor to capture and burn Union shipping. The captain even considered entering port to burn ships alongside the piers and to attack the Brooklyn Navy Yard, but instead he continued his depredations for a while before sailing for Nova Scotia.[4]

On August 5, Admiral Farragut caught Herman's attention by fighting his way into Mobile Bay, Alabama. With Ned Curtis at home, Herman had no known family or friends involved in the battle, with one exception. On October 27, 1863, Surgeon Titus Munson Coan had joined the navy and had been ordered to the U.S.S. *Sebago,* a small but heavily armed wooden gunboat that was about to be recommissioned at the Brooklyn yard. Leaving at the beginning of December, she reached the Western Gulf Blockading Squadron well in advance of the battle. Whether or not Herman knew that Coan was there is not possible to say, though Coan claimed that he maintained a relationship with his literary idol during the New York City years.[5]

Mobile was a Confederate blockade-running port. Landward it was defended by earthworks and seaward it was protected by obstructions, mines, and two forts straddling the channel. For some time the Union commanders had wished to close it to enemy shipping and to use it as a base for their own ships, for which New Orleans was inconveniently far upriver. Although these considerations paled before the necessity in 1862 of seizing New Orleans, the navy hoped that a victory at Mobile would also be a victory in the Northern press, reviving interest in the war at sea.[6]

At the beginning of the attack, Surgeon Coan's gunboat was stationed on the seaward side of powerful Fort Morgan, the principal defense of the channel, to deliver enfilading fire. Farragut also sent four monitors up close to engage the water battery on the channel side. Then he brought up his eighteen wooden-hulled warships, lashed together in pairs so that only one of the two was exposed to enemy fire. Three Confederate gunboats took station up the channel to join the gunners of the fort in fighting them off.

When the passage was in its early stages, the lead ship and her companion stopped because they were drawing abreast of the monitors, which were supposed to run ahead to neutralize the Confederate ram *Tennessee*. That stalled the whole column just before the muzzles of the fort's guns. While the ships in the van were being pummeled, the monitor *Tecumseh* struck a mine and sank with all but twenty-one of her crew. Farragut, who was again lashed in the rigging, ordered his flagship, the *Hartford,* to pull out of line with her companion and run past the halted pair into the bay, thus breaking the jam. Once past the fort, the column proceeded to an anchorage up the bay. There the *Tennessee*, reputed to be the strongest warship in existence, bore down on the *Hartford*. The *Hartford* turned toward her and escaped her ram while the entire force pummeled her, disabling her steering mechanism and forcing her to surrender. When the accompanying infantry force starved the Confederates out of Fort Morgan, the bay, but not the city of Mobile, was in Union hands.

The bloody battle elevated Northern spirits. Farragut tied to the mast and Farragut exclaiming "Damn the torpedoes" became instant legend. Henry Howard Brownell celebrated the romance in his "The Bay Fight," a lively poem that justifies his selection as the admiral's poet laureate. Spoken by a narrator who has experienced the battle, it captures the sailor's bluster in the face of peril: "Ha, old ship! do they thrill, / The brave two hundred scars / You got in the River-Wars?"[7] But Herman's poem was different and, surprisingly, inferior.

"The Battle for the Bay (August, 1864)" is a long, disunified, ultimately incomprehensible poem. At times vivid in detail, it falls into three poorly integrated sections. Unlike "The Battle for the Mississippi," in which the conclusion is justified by the beginning, the three sections of "The Battle for the Bay" are essentially immiscible. The seven earliest of the fourteen stanzas pay tribute to Farragut (or, perhaps, to all experienced salts), who, through years at sea, has gained that awareness which, through other means, came to the College Colonel.

O mystery of noble hearts,
  To whom mysterious seas have been
In midnight watches, lonely calm and storm,
    A stern, sad discipline,
And rooted out the false and vain,
  And chastened them to aptness for

Devotion and the deeds of war,
And death which smiles and cheers in spite of pain.

The discipline of the old sailor's long exposure to elemental life at sea, so reminiscent of the knowledge of blackness that is the subject of the "Try Works" chapter of *Moby-Dick,* renders him a thoughtful, devoted, fearless warrior. Later, Farragut is certainly the subject when he takes the lead of his column and "his action is a stirring call; / He strikes his great heart through them all, / And is the genius of their daring deed." But as the narrative proceeds, it changes into a Michaelean vision of good opposed to evil, a jarring note, considering the sophisticated revelations of "The Armies of the Wilderness." The enemy ships have "dark hulls," their animating spirit is "guilt," and the *Tennessee* is "strong as Evil, and Bold as Wrong, . . . / A pestilence in her smoke." She is a "Man-of-Sin," "the bad one," whose crew "spat ribald curses." On the other hand, as the Union sailors prepared for battle, "Behind each man a holy angel stood— / He stood, though none was 'ware." Surely this idea is not Herman's, and, more the pity, it is also not consistent with the opening theme of philosophical ripeness.

On what note, then, could the poem close, a reaffirmation of the educative powers of the sea or a crescendo of God-on-the-side-of-the-Union hokum? Both are abandoned when, unaccountably, the poem shifts its focus to the stricken monitor. Since the only previous mention of her is the aside, "A cheer for the Tecumseh!—nay, / Before their eyes the turreted ship goes down!" it is perplexing to find the poem concluding with only a passing mention of the casualties suffered by the squadron, "pale on the scarred fleet's decks there lay / A silent man for every silenced gun," followed by a memorial to the lost monitor. She will inspire navies forever:

decks that now are in the seed,
And cannon yet within the mine,
Shall thrill the deeper, gun and pine,
Because of the Tecumseh's glorious deed.

Precisely why a ship that—on the periphery of the poem—had the misfortune to detonate a mine should be thought of as having earned a glory that will thrill the timbers and the cannon of navies throughout eternity is left to the reader's perplexed imagination.

The poem is more about a poet in creative difficulty than it is about a battle. Confused about the point of the action, perhaps, in attempting to write one poem, Herman wrote fragments of three—one about moral maturity, one about moral and divine values in conflict, and one about the men of the *Tecumseh,* who, as in "The Battle for the Mississippi" and "A

Requiem for Soldiers lost in Ocean Transports," have been carried down to the bottom of war's waters. Had he focused on any one of the three, the poem might have succeeded. For example, the evocation of the *Tecumseh* may have been intended to illustrate the courage required of a Worden to imprison himself "in the Turret," but if that is so Herman failed to make the point.

The third naval victory, over another formidable Confederate ram, the *Albemarle,* did not involve Union ships, nor was it a major event in the war, but it was celebrated. The ram lay at Plymouth, North Carolina, a threat to Union ships throughout Albemarle Sound, since no vessel capable of opposing her could be brought in across Hatteras bar. Then navy Lieutenant William B. Cushing attacked her with a small party of men. A twenty-one-year-old who had gained notoriety by operating behind Confederate lines, he conceived the idea of attacking the *Albemarle* with a Union version of the Confederate Davids, a small steam launch mounting a torpedo at the end of a boom. As he approached the ram on the night of October 27, he discovered that she was protected by a cordon of logs and illuminated by a fire on the shore. Through a hail of small-arms fire, which ripped his clothes to rags, Cushing ran his launch up over the logs, and, with an enormous cannon muzzle pointing at him just ten feet away, fired the torpedo. As the cannon discharged and the boat sank, he and his crew jumped into the river. Some died and some were captured, but Cushing escaped.

The adventure inspired the fine poem "At the Cannon's Mouth: Destruction of the Ram Albemarle by the Torpedo-launch (October, 1864)." After a brief description of the attack, Herman addressed the question, "Had Earth no charm to stay in the Boy / The martyr-passion?" Why should a young man risk death rather than seek youth's "Paradise of opening joy"? Life "puts forth a share / Of beauty, hinting of yet rarer store," and when it is over, "who shall tell the rest?" But like General Hancock, Cushing is an eagle: "What imps these eagles then!" With the warlike spirit of "The Eagle of the Blue," they "fling disrespect on life by that proud way / In which they soar above our lower clay." In this almost angelic disregard for self, Cushing is an archetype of the Young Indians who saved the union, and perhaps his example mitigates the terrible sacrifice of the nation's youth. He conquers death by scorning it.

In musing over Cushing's contempt of profane delights, Herman recognized his own kinship to the brash young man:

In Cushing's eager deed was shown
A spirit which brave poets own—
That scorn of life which earns life's crown;
Earns, but not always wins.

As an artist Herman had made similar sacrifices of the joys and successes of ordinary life. Cushing's deed was a correlative of his own years of little-rewarded wrestling with the angel Art. In the still of his study, he had assaulted his own *Albemarle,* as he revealed in his poem "In a Garret":

Gems and jewels let them heap—
  Wax sumptuous as the Sophi:
For me, to grapple from Art's deep
  One dripping trophy! (228)

He had endured the impatience and intolerance of those committed to "life" by dedicating himself to his ideal of beauty, so much so that even his own family considered the accomplishments of Allan and John Hoadley to be more valuable than his. He had lived at the cannon's mouth and had risked perishing there.

Herman could see that his own family, now represented by Guert Gansevoort alone, would play little part in the victory at sea. Guert was in disfavor. When the spring offensive had begun, Admiral Lee had moved up the James River. Too deep in draft to accompany him, the *Roanoke* lay at Hampton Roads with the other large ships. As senior officer there, Guert was responsible for receiving and relaying messages, managing personnel, repairing ships at the Norfolk yard, reporting the status of the vessels present, and coordinating the shipment of supplies to Lee upriver and to Port Royal. This routine did not bring out the best in him. He was a fighter, a stormer of beaches, a queller of Indian uprisings, a pursuer of blockade runners—in Herman's terms, a pirate. The stagnation made him inefficient. At the Brooklyn yard his work had been essential and his support had been adequate. Here, he did not have the flag officer's staff that he needed, and he was bored. Perhaps he was drinking, or perhaps he was distressed by Leonard's illness, or perhaps symptoms of his own fatal disease had begun to appear, but for those in the Navy Department who knew him, the likely culprit was alcohol.

By July 2, Secretary Welles had given up on him. "It seems impossible to obtain any replies from you to the Department's telegrams," he complained. "Report all information which the Department ought to know, as is customary in the service, and inform the Department the reasons for these constant and persistent omissions." Guert could only reply, "I have but one clerk to assist me in my correspondence, and if I have made any omission it was not done intentionally, as I have a great deal to do." But Welles had already convicted him *in absentia* and had ordered Lee to "send the *Roanoke* to some convenient anchorage above Newport News, and direct the commanding officer of the *Minnesota* to make reports to the Department: and to him, in your absence, information and orders from the Department will be directed." Once again, Guert was in disgrace.[8]

Discovering a Confederate plan to liberate prisoners of war at Point Lookout, Maryland, the Navy Department sent the *Roanoke* there. But however important the assignment may have been, to Guert it was another personal reproof, which it probably was. Perhaps at his own request, on September 14 he was detached from the *Roanoke* and ordered to his old position at Brooklyn. While he visited his Glens Falls family for a week or so, he was given the option of returning to the *Roanoke,* but his days at sea were over. He chose to spend the rest of the war at his old quarters at the navy yard.[9]

That gave Herman his first chance to see his navy cousin since his putative visit to Hampton Roads. Guert's dark moodiness must have been at high water, but Allan would have returned from Pittsfield at about this time, which might have kept communications open. Herman and Allan did not measure Guert against the hero of Fort Stanwix; they offered him friendly approbation. These were the last months of Guert's life during which he and Herman were near neighbors, and it was during this period that Herman's memories of Guert took their final form.

Shenandoah

Startlingly, the Confederates attacked in northern Virginia. With the Union offensive stalled before Petersburg and the Pennsylvania miners burrowing under the Confederate entrenchments there, General Lee took advantage once more of what he called "the well-known anxiety of the Northern Government for the safety of its capital."[10] In the past, that anxiety had scattered armies and discredited commanders; perhaps another such threat might panic Lincoln into recalling the Army of the Potomac to the north. It was not beyond the limits of reason that there might be yet another Bull Run, a Confederate victory over a temporarily disorganized Union army that might win the coming election for the Democrats and permit a negotiated peace through which the Confederacy might survive.

General Jubal Early's orders were to interrupt communications between Washington and the rest of the North, to capture the capital if he could, and to free the Confederate prisoners at Point Lookout—the latter being the excuse for sending Guert there. At Falls Church, the Cavalry Brigade watched as Early disposed easily of his opposition in the Shenandoah Valley. Uncertain of the enemy's intentions, in early July Lowell ordered out a scout of 150 troopers to observe the passes through the Blue Ridge Mountains. Since a surgeon could not be spared, Chaplain Humphreys went along with bandages and brandy to dress wounds and stupefy senses. But near Aldie, while the troopers were feeding themselves and their horses, Mosby fell on them at full gallop, routing them and exacting a severe price in dead, wounded, and captured. One of Henry's lieutenants was captured, another was wounded, and the fourteen-year-old brother of Georgie Bedell, Henry's most dependable procuress, was wounded. Humphreys fled as fast as his horse would carry him. Mistaking the Parson's Old Cob for Yankee Davis's horse, some rangers pursued and captured him. He may have hoped that his service to the Prince of Peace would exempt him from the treatment accorded to combatants, but Mosby dispatched him, together with forty-nine others, to prison camps.[11]

Early continued north, crossed the Potomac, and marched through Maryland to the outskirts of Washington. However, the Sixth Corps, with Wendell Holmes on its staff, arrived at the capital from Petersburg just in time to thwart him, and Early faced about and headed back across Maryland. By that time, Lowell was after his army with the 2nd Massachusetts, leaving Henry behind at Falls Church. Coming upon Early's force, Crowninshield led a battalion charge on the rear guard, but when two brigades turned on him he broke off. Lowell then dismounted the troopers and held off several charges until the Confederates returned to their main business, retreating.[12]

With that, Wendell Holmes's war was over. As early as the second week of Grant's offensive, he had decided that he would not return to his regiment, telling his parents that if he were still alive at the end of the campaign he would resign his commission. One reason was that "nearly every Regimental off[icer] I knew or cared for is dead or wounded," and, in truth, the 20th Massachusetts was by now so decimated that it was a regiment in name only. When his father remonstrated, Wendell added another reason: "I am not the same man (may not have quite the same ideas) & certainly am not so elastic as I was." He had grappled with Satan in the wilderness, had seen the shark gliding through the sea, and, no longer fit physically or spiritually for combat, he had informed Governor Andrew that he did not wish promotion. He returned home on July 17, leaving the last battles of the war to those who could bear to fight them.[13]

Before the end of July, Charles Russell Lowell left to command a brigade in Sheridan's Cavalry Corps, taking the 2nd Massachusetts with him. Colonel Lazelle took command of what remained of the Cavalry Brigade and retained Ed Lansing as his adjutant. It was beginning to occur to Henry that he might not be ordered to the front at all. He tried every means at his disposal to have his regiment transferred to the Cavalry Corps, and Charles Brewster claimed to have spoken to Custer on his behalf. Henry wrote to Senator Ira Harris and Judge Parker asking for their intervention, and eventually he enlisted Lowell's aid. He even asked his father to arrange a transfer to the volunteer artillery with the rank of colonel, but nothing availed.[14]

In early August, the Cavalry Corps, augmented by two army corps and the small Army of West Virginia, moved into the Shenandoah Valley, where it became the Middle Military Division or the Army of the Shenandoah. Sheridan's responsibilities were both to prevent a recurrence of Early's raid and to destroy the crops and herds in the area. Now that Mosby had an entire army to harass, he attempted to kidnap Sheridan, and with a little better luck he might have succeeded. In response, Sheridan sent the veteran 8th Illinois Cavalry into Loudoun County to search for him, but the rangers had, as usual, disappeared. The next morning Mosby attacked one of Sheridan's wagon trains, burning materiel and supplies and capturing large numbers of men and animals.

Henry had better luck with Mosby than did the 8th Illinois. On September 13, several rangers crept into his camp and captured the brigade butcher and a beef that he had slaughtered to feed the troopers. Henry's revenge came two days later. As he was returning from a long scout, he ordered two corporals and three privates to check for rangers at Centerville. On the way, they overtook Mosby and two of his officers. Mosby shot two of the troopers' horses, but one man wounded Mosby in the groin. It was a serious and painful wound, though it was not long before the ranger chieftain had recovered sufficiently to return to his battalion. The myth lived on.[15]

On September 27, a German woman, "Mother Wise," stopped at the Gansevoorts' Albany home. She was the washerwoman of the 13th Cavalry, she said, the beloved "Mother of the Regiment" who had been mustered unofficially into one of its companies. The Gansevoorts called Anna Lansing over and whiled away the day with their honored visitor, as Mother Wise showed them her muster papers and Henry's *carte de visite* and told anecdotes of the regiment. Their generosity touched, the Gansevoorts gave her some winter clothing and fifteen dollars, which she promised to repay, and gifts to take back to camp. Anna sent Ed a basket of cake and jellies and the Gansevoorts sent a large basket of pears and grapes to Henry. Then the old scoundrel disappeared down the river. A week later, Lieutenant Colonel Coles called. Mother Wise, he laughed, had been dismissed from the regiment some six months since. Back in camp, Henry joked at his family's gullibility: "Mrs. Wise has not reported, so your good works will not bear *fruit* after all. She is too wise to return here. I thank you for the gifts although they reward Mrs Wises palate: As these are voting times in the army we will consider it done by proxy." None of them ever heard of her again.[16]

Since it had entered the Shenandoah Valley, Sheridan's army had been battling Early. On October 15, with his men camped at Cedar Creek, Sheridan was called to Washington. Shortly after daybreak on October 19, the Confederates overran encampments where the soldiers were undressed and unbreakfasted, panicking them into headlong retreat. The main resistance came from the cavalry; at one point Lowell's brigade checked the enemy by fighting on foot from behind stone walls. During that action, Lowell was wounded. Returning to his army, Sheridan galloped his horse, Rienzi, from Winchester to the battlefield, where he restored order and counterattacked. As the Confederates broke, the cavalry pursued them until night ended the fighting. Defeat had been transformed into victory, but in the final charge Lowell had received another wound, this one mortal.

Sheridan's ride became instant myth; the idea of the young general galloping to the front to turn the tide of battle was stirring and romantic. The poet who profited most was T. Buchanan Read, much of whose "Sheridan's Ride" focuses on Rienzi:

Under his spurning feet the road
Like an arrowy Alpine river flowed;
And the landscape sped away behind
Like an ocean flying before the wind;
And the steed, like a bark fed with furnace ire,
Swept on with his wild eyes full of fire.[17]

It was nicely adapted to the tastes of the times and was read by school children for generations. In the tradition of Tennyson, it re-created for the reader the drama and hurry of the moment.

Herman's poem, "Sheridan at Cedar Creek (October, 1864)," is less effusive but far richer, and his rougher, plainer diction is better suited to the texture of this punishing war than are Read's soaring river and ocean similes. It is more apropos because it deals both with the ride and with the subsequent events, whereas Read treats the ride as though it were a victory in itself. And though both poems celebrate Rienzi, Herman's uses homage to the horse to keep in check his homage to the man—to celebrate valor without adulation. "Shoe the steed with silver" for the desperate ride to "retrieve the day"; "Wreathe the steed and lead him— / For the charge he led" to rout Early's men, thus turning the "cypress" of defeat into the "amaranths" of victory." The tactic is successful, sparing the narrator the need for bestowing silver and wreaths on Sheridan himself, as though the general were a demigod. An analogy between Sheridan and Philip of Macedon accomplishes quite enough of that. But it is also necessary to "shroud the horse in sable— / For the mounds they heap!" in burying the dead. Herman insisted, as other poets were loath to do, that the tragedy of battle be known and remembered, that many of those who fought were not spared to exult in the admiration and gratitude bestowed on the survivors:

> There is glory for the brave
> Who lead, and nobly save,
> But no knowledge in the grave
> Where the nameless followers sleep.

They lie in the gaunt shadow cast by weird John Brown across the Shenandoah green. Herman's tribute to Sheridan—and to the fallen soldiers—elevates the heroic to the height of the true.

Herman's visit to Vienna and his scout through Loudoun County had given him a special reason to mourn these dead. The memory of Lowell, the stainless soldier, was as vivid in his mind as it was in Sheridan's when he said, "He was the perfection of a man and a soldier. *I* could have been better spared." There was something poignant about this death that Herman pointed out in "The Scout toward Aldie." Unlike Wendell Holmes, Lowell did not live to be the great American some had anticipated, he never saw his daughter Carlotta, who was born soon after his death, and he never even received his brigadier general's commission. For James Russell Lowell, this third death among his nephews was a culmination of the tragedy of which he spoke at Harvard at the end of the war:

> I strive to mix some gladness with my strain,
> But the sad strings complain,
> And will not please the ear:
> I sweep them for a pæan, but they wane
> Again and yet again
> Into a dirge, and die away, in pain.
> In these brave ranks I only see the gaps,
> Thinking of dear ones whom the dumb turf wraps,
> Dark to the triumph which they died to gain:
> Fitlier may others greet the living,
> For me the past is unforgiving;
> I with uncovered head
> Salute the sacred dead,
> Who went, and who return not.

To honor the warrior who had discussed philosophy with him, Herman wrote a classic memorial, "On the Grave of a young Cavalry Officer killed in the Valley of Virginia." It is a simple yet elegant tribute: "Beauty and youth, with manners sweet, and friends— / Gold, yet a mind not unenriched had he." He also expressed his peculiar view that it is better to die well than to live meagerly: "His happier fortune in this mound you see." That idea remained with him until he dramatized it in the death of Billy Budd.[18]

The Return of McClellan

The 1864 presidential campaign began in Baltimore on the seventh of June when the Republicans, who named their meeting the National Union Convention in order to attract War Democrats, renominated Lincoln. For the same reason, the convention chose as its vice-presidential nominee Andrew Johnson, the firm-handed Democratic military governor of Tennessee. The party platform was simple and predictable—victory, union, and emancipation.

There were objections to Lincoln's candidacy: he had offended both conservatives and radicals, the war news was dreadful, and the casualty lists from the Army of the Potomac disheartened citizens of all persuasions. The culmination at Cold Harbor of the costly Grant campaign and other failures since then (including Sherman's stalled army at Atlanta) dimmed Lincoln's hopes. James Russell Lowell, for one, was spiritless. Even before the death of Charles Lowell, he had written that "the war and its constant expectation and anxiety oppress me. I cannot think." Some Republicans had wanted to replace Lincoln with Salmon P. Chase, Grant, or even former Democrat Ben Butler, and in May a convention of dissident radicals had favored General Frémont. Whittier, who preferred Frémont, wrote that Lincoln "is not the man of my choice."[19]

When Uncle Peter passed through New York just after mid-August, he may have forewarned Herman of the likely results of the Democratic Convention, which was scheduled for August 29 in Chicago. Because of the broad dissatisfaction in the North and the fact that a one-term presidency had become the norm, the Democrats could be optimistic. They nominated McClellan for the presidency and George H. Pendleton for the vice presidency. On September 14, Uncle Peter presided over a massive meeting at Albany's Tweddle Hall—15,000 of the faithful, the largest he could remember—that ratified the national nominations and renominated Seymour for governor. Closer to Herman, New York City was wild with enthusiasm for the general.[20]

But it was possible for the party to defeat itself, and it did. Doctrinaire Purist Clement Vallandigham subverted the platform by inserting a call for the restoration of the union without victory. That would return the South to the union without further fighting and without any alteration to its prewar ways. The plank played into the hands of the Republicans, who had at-

Sketch of Charles Russell Lowell. U.S. Military History Institute

tempted to paint the Democrats with the color of treason and had made progress in equating loyalty to the North with loyalty to the administration's policies. On September 8, McClellan met Governor Seymour, a party Legitimist, or pragmatist, to plan a repudiation, which was, simply, to insist on union *before* peace. McClellan did, but he was unable to escape the stigma of what Whittier referred to as "that traitor platform."[21]

Eventually the dissident Republicans supported Lincoln. Even before Chicago, James Russell Lowell had written, "If Mr. Lincoln is re-chosen, I think the war will soon be over. If not, there will be attempts at negotiation, during which the rebels will recover breath, and then war again with more chances in their favor." On the other hand, most of those to whom Herman was closest supported McClellan, Uncle Peter, as always, voting a straight party ticket. Allan would have been a McClellan man, too, as Richard Lathers is certain to have been. Mother Melville rejoiced at McClellan's nomination and hoped that he would be elected. Bruce also would have supported the Democratic ticket.[22]

There is no evidence that at this time Herman favored Lincoln, and he admired McClellan, as his poem "The Victor of Antietam," probably written after the election, demonstrates. Nevertheless, he responded to his mother's McClellanism by sending her a copy of *Harper's* containing "a most melancholy picture headed Compromise with the South. Dedicated to the Chicago Convention."[23] That was an objection to the platform rather than to the candidate, and he probably sent the magazine before McClellan's repudiation became known. He would not have accepted a compromise with the South after so much blood had been shed to make possible the future he envisioned. Thus he may have supported McClellan, but there is a real possibility that he looked to Lincoln as the man who would end the war on the most favorable terms. Whatever complaints others might have had, he had been steadfast in his determination to reunite the states, and Herman did not yet know that a part of his family was under surveillance by the administration's secret police. Whichever his preference, his reaction to the platform demonstrates how badly it hurt McClellan.

Several years earlier, his attitude and that of the North probably would have been different. At the beginning of the war, the ideas and emotions of peace prevailed. In April 1861, the Seventh Regiment had vowed not to fire on its old comrades, the Richmond Grays, unless fired upon first, but the reality of war had transformed disagreement into hostility. The soldier may have entered the military service bedazzled by the tinsel of glory, chivalry, and fidelity, but soldiering had brought separation from loved ones, exposure to and injury from enemy and sometimes friendly weapons, filth and pestilence, an unpalatable and often inadequate diet, penetrating cold in thin clothing and canvas shelter, and subordination to the whims of competent and incompetent officers. For civilians at home, war had brought anxiety, pain, want, and taxation, and for many the death or mutilation of a brother, father, husband, son, lover, or friend. For all it had brought a litany of real or imagined atrocities. In *Battle-Pieces,* these are correlated in the figure of Satan. The only acceptable recompense for the painful investments on the war exchange was victory, and peace without victory rendered the suffering meaningless—many, like Whitman, had decided that "the war *must* be carried on," and some actually approved of it: "I shall always respect War hereafter," Emerson wrote.[24] Yet the Democratic platform proposed to close the war market before any dividend had been declared.

Henry Gansevoort's attitude demonstrated the change. He wrote Allan, "I hope you are all right—a war Democrat—determined to carry on this fight until we are able to show some result for the carnage of four bloody years." He regretted that there was to be an election and supported Lincoln. As he said later, "I did not sustain that platform. As a soldier I could not. It said the war was [a] failure and that all the bloody battles I had participated in were vain. I could not believe it so." In his poem "Riding to Vote (The Old Democrat in the West)," John James Piatt demanded that the carnage be justified by victory. Speaking as an ancient who had once voted for Andrew Jackson, the narrator is now casting his vote for Lincoln on behalf of himself and his two slain sons:

I go to give my vote alone—I curse your shameless shame
Who fight for traitors here at home in Peace's holy name!
I go to give my vote alone, but even while I do,
I vote for dead and living, all—the living dead and you!

The North could not be expected to listen to Democratic reason when it was fighting with a passion that had long since mutated into obstinacy—something resembling Herman's spirit of the "Eagle of the Blue."[25]

New York was McClellan territory, which only enhanced its reputation as a hotbed of treason. Whitman, who had come home to arrange the publication of *Drum-Taps,* was so disgusted that he decided he would make his home elsewhere. "I don't know what move I shall make," he wrote, "but something soon, as it is not satisfactory any more in New York & Brooklyn—I should think nine tenths, of all classes, are copperheads here, I never heard before such things as I hear now whenever I go out." Herman must have been more tolerant of his native city than was Whitman, who had become an ardent admirer of Lincoln. In the frenzy of the campaign—an August rally for McClellan was supposed to have been the largest in the city's history—Herman may have become involved as a witness, despite his dislike for crowds and politicking. Partly because of the momentous consequences of the election and partly because of the spectacle, his appetite for experience may have drawn him out. Even Whitman enjoyed the display. "The political meetings in New York & Brooklyn are immense," he wrote. "I go to them as to shows, fireworks, cannon, clusters of gaslights, countless torches, banners & mottos, 15, 20, 50,000 people."[26]

The election campaign cost Henry Gansevoort his reputation with the War Department and nearly cost him much more. At the new Falls Church camp, he had lost his friend and ally, Colonel Lazelle, who had resigned in disgust at a homosexual scandal involving his second in command. Now the brigade commander, Henry was away from the camp guarding the rebuilding of the Manassas Gap Railroad, which was to facilitate the transportation of men and supplies to Sheridan. Because of Mosby and other obstacles, the work was not completed in time, but it kept Henry busy just across the Blue Ridge Mountains from the Army of the Shenandoah, where he could hear the roar of artillery during the Battle of Cedar Creek.[27]

There he gained his only distinction as a cavalryman. He learned that Mosby had established an artillery park somewhere in the Cobbler Mountains, and in the evening of October 14 he captured a bivouac of nine of Mosby's gunners, including a captain. After he had forced one of the captives to reveal the location, his men crawled a mile and a half up the side of Little Cobbler, where they found four cannon, ammunition, and harnesses concealed in a thicket. A triumph over Mosby was so rare that Henry was formally commended for it and as he lay dying Charles Russell Lowell expressed his satisfaction.[28]

On October 24, sickness forced Henry back to Falls Church and to his bed, one of the most damaging moves he ever made. Unknown to him, his regiment had received its absentee ballots, and while he lay in bed two of his officers conducted the election, urging the troopers to vote for McClellan, it was said. Unaware of what had happened, Henry returned to the field the following day, but the damage had been done—he had been physically present during the balloting, he was responsible for it, and there was no other senior officer present in the brigade to defend him.[29]

Political partisanship was running high in the army. The unofficial War Department policy seemed to be that voting for the Democratic ticket was evidence of disloyalty, and the attitude infected the ranks. A scribe in a local regiment noted that one Samuel Snyder "died of drinking Democratic Campaign Whiskey." Quick to find fault and to dismiss officers who committed crude offenses like drunkenness on duty and stealing out of camp to whore in Alexandria, or who proved to be incompetent, Henry had forged a cabal of enemies more deadly than the one that had contested his appointment as colonel. Even before the election incident, charges of "Copperheadism" had been made against him. Now the War Department began to investigate his loyalty.[30]

A Broadway Swell in Castle Thunder

During the early fall, with Lizzie and the children home again, Herman's days were gentler than they had recently been. On August 14, Richard and Abby Lathers added yet another girl, Julia, to their family, but with new life came death, as well. On October 8, Leonard Gansevoort's heart finally failed. His remains were shipped to New York for burial at Greenwood Cemetery, where the family congregated to bid him goodbye. Herman and Allan and their families must have been present, and Uncle Peter and his family came from Albany. The Curtises and Stanwix Gansevoort were probably there, and certainly Guert was. Kate Gansevoort regretted that she had not known Leonard during his lifetime, but noted that "the Gansevoorts are a strange family." What she really meant to say was that Guert was strange. When he had passed through Albany without calling, she had sulked, "How strange it is that he so entirely gives up all his family ties." Now, at the burial, she added, "Guert certainly behaves *strangely*." That meant that he was remote and inattentive. It did not occur to her that even though her branch of the family was the wealthiest, Guert's was the oldest, and that his new disgrace exacerbated his unwillingness to pay the usual family homage to Albany.[31]

Bruce had been back in the office with Allan for several months, but now that his health was again sound he felt adventurous. In the quiet that followed Early's defeat at Cedar Creek, his brother Charles invited him to visit Winchester. Charles was still the commissary of subsistence of a cavalry brigade, but Custer was no longer his commander. Happy at the idea of seeing his brother and visiting the scene of the recent battle, around the second of November Bruce left for the Shenandoah Valley. He must have expected to return to the city in time to vote, but he, too, had made a bitter mistake.

On November 3, Charles met him at the Winchester station. During an evening of fraternal reunion, the two decided to visit Cedar Creek the next day.[32] It was raining in the morning as they set out in the company of two enlisted men. They all wore waterproofs, which disguised Bruce's civilian clothing, and Charles was carrying a wallet containing nearly $2,000. As they rode past Newtown, another soldier on his way to pick up his discharge papers joined them. A few minutes later, fifteen mounted men wearing Union overcoats approached them. Charles's cook rode ahead to have a look, but by the time he realized that they were concealing drawn pistols beneath their capes it was too late to warn off the others. The squad of Mosby's rangers, for that is who they were, forced them to ride over a hill while a large party of Union cavalry passed by, then robbed them and took them across the Blue Ridge Mountains into Mosby's Confederacy. As they rode along, the rangers discussed the Union election. They hoped that Lincoln would win, since they believed that McClellan would steal their victory from them by offering an honorable peace, while Lincoln would continue the war until the Confederates triumphed.

When the party stopped at Ashby's Gap, Mosby rode up and inquired if any of the prisoners had ever served with Custer. Custer had hanged seven of his men, and Mosby intended to retaliate, man for man. Charles said that he no longer served under Custer, but Mosby was not impressed. Forewarned, the others denied any connection with the Michigan regiments of Custer's old brigade and Bruce, trying to appear as valueless a prisoner as possible, claimed that he was a clerk.

That night, while the captives were being held in a barn, Charles concealed his money in his clothing and Bruce's. For most of the next day, they were confined in a filthy storeroom with other prisoners, altogether about twenty-two soldiers, four newsboys, and one city lawyer, all by now aware that some of them were to be hanged. Then on Sunday morning, November 6, they were marched to Rectortown and confined to a corn crib while Mosby's battalion held one of its rare assemblies. Mosby called out the prisoners, sent Bruce and the newsboys off to one side, and formed the rest into a double rank along the wall of a building. Then Willie Mosby, the ranger adjutant, read the order to hang seven of them selected by lots. After twenty prayerful minutes, the drawing began. As each fatal slip of paper was drawn, the victim was asked his name and was sent to one side, where the red-bearded ranger in charge made remarks such as "We'll give *you* a chance to stretch hemp," and "You can shake the dust off *your* feet." Two of the enlisted men who had been captured with Charles and Bruce drew fatal slips, but Charles did not. After the drawing, the seven victims were marched off to be hanged where Sheridan would find their corpses. However, four of them escaped.[33]

Bruce was surprised to be sent to Richmond with the rest of the prisoners. On the way, he and Charles agreed to attempt to escape independently, if necessary. Then at one of their stops Charles walked out into the night and entrusted himself and his money to an underground railroad operated by the slaves of the vicinity. They passed him from place to place, occasionally disguising him in blackface, until he reached Sheridan's army.

Bruce was marched on to Richmond, where he was confined with political prisoners in Castle Thunder. A local newspaper reporter noted the incarceration of one of the "swell mob" of Broadway in his "baggy trowsers." When the reporter asked Bruce what he thought of his situation, Bruce growled that it was "too damned bad."[34] It was November 11; he had missed the election.

On election day, Herman and Allan had no idea what had happened to Bruce except that he had not returned from his visit. The weather was rainy and muddy, with fog between the storms. The city was quiet, but it was a sullen quiet. Having received a report of a Confederate plot to burn down the city and to seize it during the ensuing panic, Dix had called in troops. Ben Butler arrived from Petersburg with several thousand combat-hardened soldiers, drew his ships up along the piers, and stationed local soldiers at the battery. He sent spies into every district, arresting suspects and sending them to Fort Hamilton. That was not what Dix wanted, but under Butler's guns the election was peaceful. His candidacy buoyed by favorable war news, including Cedar Creek and the capture of Atlanta, and his opponent damned by the Democratic platform and imprudent Democratic campaigners, Lincoln won the national election by a wide margin. Though he did not win the city, the Republicans maintained their heavy majority in Congress and Reuben E. Fenton defeated Horatio Seymour for governor. Longfellow noted, "Lincoln re-elected beyond a doubt. We breathe freer. The country will be saved." For their part, the Democrats realized that there could be no peace short of total victory.[35]

A week later, Herman and Allan learned from a *New York Times* interview with Charles Brewster's cook, one of those who had been condemned in Mosby's lottery, the astounding news that their vacationing friend was a prisoner of the Confederates. On November 17, they learned from the *Herald* that Bruce was being held in Castle Thunder, and a few days later Allan received a frantic letter from Charles Brewster verifying the newspaper accounts. Military prisoners were the business of the federal authorities; Bruce was a civilian for whom the government would feel little responsibility. Those of Herman's family who were closest to Bruce set about trying to rescue him. Herman might have worked on his behalf had he been a man of affairs, but Allan was in the better position and he had the greater obligation to his partner. Researching the means of effecting an exchange, Allan found a blockade-runner at Fort Lafayette and convinced himself that Bruce could be recovered promptly.[36]

It turned out that the blockade-runner was reluctant to return to the South. Frustrated there, Allan wrote Henry Gansevoort. He urged action on behalf of "our friend Brewster of whom you spoke so playfully in your letter"—Henry must have joked about Bruce's plight. That reprimand delivered, he asked Henry to find out what could be done in Washington and volunteered to go to the capital himself if Henry could find anything concrete to work on. Henry had already received a plea from Charles to do something "for God sake," but his inquiries were fruitless. When Allan wrote Henry again on the sixth of December, the blockade-runner had still not made up his mind. In the meantime, Charles had discovered a possible candidate for exchange, a Winchester clergyman named Boyd who was supposed to be the brother of the Confederate attorney-general. It would be up to Henry to interview Boyd in Washington, where he was being held. Allan offered to hire an agent to handle the matter.[37]

When nothing availed, Charles was in despair. "I fear it is doubtful whether we ever see him again," he wrote Henry. His fears for Bruce's life were justified. Like all Union and Confederate prisoner-of-war facilities, Castle Thunder was brutal and critically unhealthy—insufficient food, clothing, and sanitation. Captain Alexander, the officer in charge, was, according to complaints against him, harsh, inhumane, tyrannical, and dishonest. His assistant was Hero, a gigantic Russian bloodhound who weighed some 180 pounds. Hero had been imported to fight bears and had beaten them. With him on guard, escape attempts were unwise.[38]

Various people wrote to friends in Richmond and Charles enlisted Custer's aid. Custer asked Secretary Stanton to effect Bruce's exchange for reasons "of interest to the U.S. Military Service." Bruce was also working on his own behalf. He contacted a prominent Richmond attorney who helped him to obtain an order from the Confederate secretary of war for his release. Bruce wrote home that he expected to be aboard the next flag-of-truce boat leaving Richmond, but when he gave the order to Captain Alexander, Alexander confiscated it and refused to release him.[39]

On the fourth of January, there was an escape attempt in the "citizens' room." The prisoners had obtained knives and revolvers and had made holes in the building. At moonset that day, they were to rush for the holes and escape, no matter what, but the plan was betrayed by an informer. Then in late January, the defense of Richmond became so tenuous that Bruce was sent to Salisbury, North Carolina. While their train was taking on wood, the prisoners in Bruce's car overpowered their guard and fled. Other prisoners were recaptured, but Bruce had the same good fortune as his brother had several months earlier, being passed from slave family to slave family until he reached the Union lines near Norfolk. Considering the goodwill of the slaves and the terrible punishments they would have faced had their disloyalty been discovered, Bruce's racial attitudes must have undergone a revolution. By the time he returned to the city, weak and emaciated, the war was nearly over. On February 17, 1865, having had scarcely enough time to recover, he visited Henry at Falls Church, trusting that he would not again be captured by Mosby, and in March he resumed his interrupted partnership with Allan.[40]

Bruce was the only person Herman knew intimately who had ever actually seen Mosby and he was one of the few Northerners who had ever witnessed an assembly of Mosby's rangers. He must have described his entire adventure to Herman, who used the hanging incident in "The Scout toward Aldie." Poetically, it is an anachronism, since the scout Herman had accompanied had taken place long before the cycle of execution and retaliation had begun. Nevertheless, Herman made the hangings a topic of conversation between the Major and the young Colonel. Affected by the eeriness of the forest, the Major fancies that the tree limbs are gallows:

> "what's that dangling there?"
> "Where?" "From the tree—that gallows-bough["];
> "A bit of frayed bark, is it not?"
> "Ay—or a rope; did *we* hang last?—"

Integrated into the poem, the menace of the reciprocal executions adds to the atmosphere of feral violence in the forest. If killing is an evil rite for the Satan-Mosby of the poem, and a path to renown for the Colonel, then hanging for the purpose of keeping score loses its bizarre character—or adds to the bizarre balance of the poem. And so it had been during the ordeal of Bruce and Charles.

That Herman's poem "In the Prison Pen (1864)" was suggested by the experience of Frank Bartlett is evident from its placement just before "The College Colonel," but its subject is more general. Herman knew and knew of a number of men who suffered Confederate imprisonment: Bruce, Chaplain Humphreys, some of Henry Gansevoort's officers and men, the brother of Lieutenant Colonel Coles, Henry's second in command, and probably others. But the poem also concerns the many prisoners whom Herman did not know. For example, Captain George Whitman, Walt's brother, was captured on September 30, 1864. The lot of these prisoners had become desperate when Grant had halted exchanges of military personnel.

Other prisoner-of-war poems appeared, but, as the following lines illustrate, they ignored the desperate plight of the victims: "In the prison cell I sit, / Thinking Mother dear, of you, / And our bright and happy home so far away." From his acquaintance with men who had survived Confederate prisons, Herman knew that captives suffered from more than mere homesickness. Neither romanticized nor sentimental, "In the Prison Pen" is about the plight of a representative prisoner who faces death of mind and body. The setting is an open-air compound, walled in by palisades and patrolled by sentries, in which are incarcerated

plaining ghosts
Like those on Virgil's shore—
A wilderness of faces dim,
And pale ones gashed and hoar.

These are milling throngs of the living dead like the unsanctified of the *Aeneid* who plead for admission into Hades. His quarters are "his lair— / A den that sick hands dug in earth / Ere famine wasted there." Now surviving listlessly within the walls of his only world, dulled by an idleness far worse than boredom—"vacant hands" and "idiot-pain"—blurred in mind so that he can neither think nor remember, and a participant in shared suffering, he awaits he knows not what. This time he may totter once again back to cringe in his earthen trench, or he may fall in his tracks "till forth from the throngs they bear him dead— / Dead in his meagreness." Imprisonment reduced survivors of epic battles to ghosts enduring their exile from the world of the living not with determination but with hopeless tenacity. No other poet of the age could have written this unadorned and audacious truth.[41]

Postwar revelations about the suffering of Union captives at Andersonville prison, where some fifteen thousand died, inspired Herman to write yet another poem, the memorial "On a natural Monument in a field of Georgia."[42] It is a tribute to the soldiers who did not die in battle but wasted away in durance, "The nameless brave whose palms are won" in this faraway place. Their memorial is not a trophy but a natural stone placed there by geological chance. Other soldiers died "in cheer of hymns that round them float" and "in happy dreams," but these were victims of "withering famine" and "fell disease." They could not think of home

Lest wreck of reason might befall.
As men in gales shun the lee shore,
Though there the homestead be, and call,
And thitherward winds and waters sway—
As such lorn mariners, so fared they.

Trust Herman to cast the sanity of the captives in terms of Bulkington's "Lee Shore" of *Moby-Dick!* But the poem does offer the mitigating idea that if there was little for these prisoners, at least their endurance, lonely and otherwise uncelebrated, made them memorable.

Home Is the Sailor

Despite the death of Leonard Gansevoort, the humiliation of Guert Gansevoort, the political peril which engulfed Henry Gansevoort, and the captivities of Frank Bartlett and Bruce, the fall brought a happy event. On the same day that Herman read the story of Bruce's arrival at Castle Thunder, Tom Melville landed at the New York City piers aboard the *Bengal,* safely home and beyond the reach of the Confederate cruisers. His return and his promised year ashore had been anticipated for some time, but he had not been expected so soon. He may not have planned it, but he was home permanently.[43]

When he was not working aboard the *Bengal,* Tom would have stayed with Allan and Herman, who had much to tell him about the war. Because he had been at sea since early 1862, the United States of the later war years was terra incognita to him. Reading whatever stale newspapers opportunity had placed in his hands was far different from seeing the armed camp of the city and reading the daily dispatches in the papers. Eager to learn about the war for himself, he probably visited Guert, who could hardly have avoided being civil to the second saltiest member of the family, and he wished to visit Henry's camp, too.[44] One of the reasons why Allan volunteered to come to Washington to work for Bruce's release was that he could do so in the company of his young brother.

Since Tom was required to unload cargo and to look after his other command responsibilities, it was impossible for him to leave the city to see his relatives. When Mother Melville was notified of his arrival and of his inability to come to Gansevoort, she decided to go to the city for the first time in five years. John Hoadley would be there on his way to West Virginia to evaluate the investment possibilities of the new petroleum fields, which caused Mother Melville to announce proudly that she expected to celebrate Thanksgiving with her four sons—consciously or unconsciously omitting her fifth son, George Griggs—and with eight of her grandchildren. After coming to Albany with Gus to spend a day with Uncle Peter, she went on alone to New York, where she was met at the 26th Street station by Herman, Allan, Tom, and John—but not George Griggs.[45]

Some Confederates in Canada had been planning to work mischief across the border. On October 19, twenty of them slipped into St. Albans, Vermont, killed a man and wounded several others, robbed three banks, and attempted to burn the town before retreating across the border. But another rebel plot touched Herman more closely. His Thanksgiving Day with the united family was joyous, but the following day, Evacuation Day, was not. In the evening, fires broke out in many of the principal hotels as six

Confederate officers, the ones who had planned to torch the city on election day, did their work. The panic could hardly have failed to touch Herman and his family, since the first fire broke out in the St. James Hotel, just down the street from him at Broadway and 26th, across Madison Square. However, the arson was controlled efficiently and there were no serious casualties, even though Uncle Peter's St. Nicholas Hotel suffered extensive damage. Then the Confederates escaped to Canada.[46]

Mother Melville stayed until early spring, first with Herman and then with Allan. As usual, everyone pretended to be scandalized by her socializing. "She goes everywhere & sees everything," Tom reported, including, he snickered, a dancing school ball. After she moved to Allan's home, she sleighed in Central Park and, when the ground was bare, rode down Broadway to the lower city. She would have visited old friends, such as Mrs. Thurston, and she may have been a guest at Winyah. Her visit was enlivened first by the return of Allan's prisoner-of-war partner and second by a smallpox epidemic which sent everyone scurrying to be vaccinated. Tom, too, remained in the city much of the time to prepare the *Bengal* for sea pending the arrival of her new captain.[47]

As always, Tom had brought gifts for the family. As Christmas approached, he visited his sisters in Gansevoort, where he delivered their New Year presents, and then returned to pay the expected visit to Albany. He must have received a quick course in politics and the war from Uncle Peter when he delivered Chinese tea to Aunt Susan and a "curious" Chinese tea set to Kate. Again, Kate was giddy about Tom: "I never saw any one more informed than he is—Tom has improved the advantages offered by travel & is a well read & quite an elegant young man." As always, he was a charmer.[48]

Following Tom's visit, the Gansevoorts had the Lansings to Christmas dinner, and on the last day of the year and the last day of his term, they had a small party for Governor Seymour, his staff, and some military men. During the winter, the Gansevoorts socialized with both ex-Governor Seymour and Governor Fenton, on one occasion entertaining both at the same function. On Christmas and New Year's Day, the three Melville brothers, their families, and their mother had a chance to celebrate together in the city. The holidays were lonely for Fanny and Gus in Gansevoort.[49]

On the first of March, Fanny left Gansevoort to visit the Griggses and the Hoadleys, leaving Gus alone. To keep Gus company, Kate Gansevoort brought Mrs. Van Rensselaer up to spend the night. Gus expected Tom to bring her mother back from the city by the middle of the month, but Mother Melville was having such a good time that she prolonged her stay. The only interruption was the death in early March of eighty-two-year-old Maria Peebles, her cousin and confidant over the years. The loss must have affected her deeply, but, since she was so far away, Uncle Peter substituted for her, driving to Lansingburgh for the funeral.[50]

On her arrival in New Bedford, Fanny reported that Lottie, whose illnesses had once again driven the Hoadleys to distraction, was better. Fanny did not mention seeing John's nephew Henry Pease, now a first lieutenant, though he was at home in Clinton. While on picket duty at Barrancas, Florida, he had contracted chronic diarrhea and had left on sick leave on February 14, 1865. Having been close to John in his youth, he must have seen him on this occasion and must have described his experiences with the U.S. Colored Troops. His sickness came at an inopportune time, during which his regiment participated in the siege of Fort Blakeley, near Mobile, and then occupied the city. After that it marched on Montgomery, Alabama, thus completing its only real campaigning of the war. Upon Henry's return, the regiment garrisoned Fort Morgan, whose guns Farragut had braved when he steamed into Mobile Bay, before returning to Florida.[51]

Surrounded by his family as in the old days, Herman spent his happiest winter since his mother and sisters had moved away from Pittsfield. Those he loved seemed safe now that the war pressed toward an end. The North had still to defeat the remaining Confederate forces before peace could come—that might take months, but there was little doubt now that it would happen. Then the rebuilding of the nation could begin. His day-to-day activities are sparsely recorded, but in addition to the attractions of art, literature, opera, drama, and friends, he could visit the waterfront, where the *Bengal* lay, and he could visit Allan and Richard Lathers (and Bruce, after his return from prison) in their offices downtown. Among the plays he may have seen, one stands out, Edwin Booth's triumphant *Hamlet*. Booth opened it on November 26, 1864, at the Winter Garden, with Mrs. J. W. Wallace, Jr., playing Ophelia. The play ran nightly for four months, closing on March 22, 1865.[52]

Other than that, the one surviving clue to his social life is an invitation from Bayard Taylor, the noted travel writer, to attend a meeting of the Travelers' Club on Monday, February 27. The agenda was to include talk, cigars, and "frugal refreshments." The frugality was a part of its ethos: the club was a modest organization formed in 1865 to bring together people of a certain sort who had traveled extensively outside the United States. It met in a house on the corner of 5th Avenue and 14th Street, often to listen to lectures by eminent travelers. Its membership, which included foreigners, was noteworthy. Taylor assumed that Herman knew many of them: Townsend Harris, who had been Minister to Japan from 1859 to 1861; Cyrus Field, who was laying his trans-Atlantic cable; Louis M. Gottschalk, the Southern pianist-composer who was one of the leading American musicians of the age (and who had played in Albany for Kate Gansevoort and in Pittsfield while Herman was there); Felix Darley, who had illustrated literary works and sketched Civil War scenes; and the painters Frederick Edwin Church, already famous, and Albert Bierstadt, who had just begun to gain acclaim for his western American scenes. Since Herman certainly knew Darley, there is no reason to question Taylor's belief that he was also acquainted with the others, and there is no reason to doubt that he attended the meeting. After all, the availability of precisely such society had helped to bring him back to the city.[53]

Professionally, Herman was infuriated by a demeaning event out of his literary past. In republishing *Israel Potter,* a Philadelphia firm, T. B. Peterson and Brothers, renamed it *The Refugee*. Although they had informed Herman of their intention, they had not honored his objection to the title change. To make matters worse, they listed him as "Author of 'Typee,' 'Omoo,'" which was the kind of puffery that he had wished to avoid in *Piazza Tales* and which he had asked Allan "for God's sake" not to include when he had attempted to publish the book of verse in 1860. But to cap the insult, Peterson attributed to him works he had never written, "The Two Captains" and "The Man of the World." In his outrage, Herman took pen in hand to sound thunder to the editor of the *New York World:* "I have never written any work by that title. In connection with that title Peterson Brothers employ my name without authority, and notwithstanding a remonstrance conveyed to them long ago." It took a great deal of insolence to smoke Herman out like that.[54]

Bummers

Now came the clutter of events and the high drama of the last months of the war. By the time of Lincoln's second inauguration, it was evident that the end was near. In New York, the tempo of military activity moderated. No longer were regiments filling and leaving for the front; the uniforms on the streets were largely those of garrison personnel, recruiters, and soldiers on leave. The pace of activity at the Brooklyn Navy Yard moderated, too. As early as December, Guert had been ordered to disarm the *Mobile* so she could be sold out of the service, and in late February he was advised that bombardment supplies for the South Atlantic Blockading Squadron were no longer needed. In March, Acting Volunteer Lieutenant Commander William Budd, who had spent the past two years terrorizing the South Atlantic coast, sailed the gunboat *Florida* from Brooklyn to the Western Gulf Blockading Squadron, but he did not arrive in time to fight. And Guert's career was ending. In February, a friend in the Bureau of Ordnance offered him a new post that might allow him to salvage something of his reputation, but Guert decided that for private reasons he would prefer to remain where he was until he was relieved. He was morose, he was weary, and, above all, he was ill.[55]

It was a strange, exultant period in which the long-static struggle between giant armies changed rapidly into a victory parade, then into an echo of stilled bugles, and then into peace. With Grant's forces checked before Petersburg, the momentum of the offense shifted to Sherman's army in Atlanta. The Confederates, now led by General Hood, decided to invade the North, thereby freeing Sherman's army through inadvertence. Delighted, Sherman sent Thomas to Nashville to oppose them and then set out to join Grant in Virginia by marching all the way across the South. On the way, he intended to deprive the Confederate army of its supplies and to ruin the South's railroads. Sherman destroyed much of Atlanta, abandoned his communication lines, and set out for Savannah. At that point, he all but disappeared from Herman's ken.

Following his ill-advised invasion plan, Hood marched on Nashville, but Thomas managed to collect his dispersed forces in time to oppose him. In the fighting along the approaches to the city, the 44th Illinois, including John Hobart, was heavily engaged. Then on December 15 and 16, 1864, with Hood's forces arrayed before Nashville, Thomas attacked. The battle, in which John won a commendation,[56] was a severe defeat for the Confederates. Hood retreated back to the Tennessee River with the 44th Illinois in hot pursuit. He had failed to capture Nashville, and more, his army was no longer a threat to the North.

On December 13, Sherman reappeared on the outskirts of Savannah, where he reestablished communications with the North. Behind his army came another one of slaves following the Union soldiers to freedom. On December 23, Sherman was able to telegraph Lincoln, "I beg to present to you, as a Christmas gift, the city of Savannah."[57] In a month and a week, Sherman had altered the entire countenance of the war. Only later did Herman discover what the western army had done along its line of march. Dividing his forces into two large columns that often marched many miles apart, Sherman had laid waste to a broad lane across Georgia, foraging and pillaging as he went. His progress was unstoppable, and, since he had the enemy population in his power, almost lighthearted. He had intended to treat the Southerners fairly, but his orders were so harsh that fairness was out of the question. Furthermore, fairness was hardly possible when the civilian population was treated as a single enemy class, with people of every loyalty, station, and color—including slaves—punished equally. One of his junior officers remarked that "we were expected . . . to destroy such property as was designated by our corps commander, and to consume everything eatable by man or beast." Ahead of the troops rode the bummers, whose business it was to seize crops, animals, and forage for the army, and who inevitably stole private property and inflicted indignities, injuries, and atrocities on civilians. Chivalry, civility, and sympathy were passé: what mattered to the army was crushing the enemy, soldiers and civilians alike. The officer quoted above described the bummers thus: "Before daylight, mounted on horses captured on the plantations, they were in the saddle and away, covering the country sometimes seven miles in advance." He noted that they stripped plantations of livestock and food and that they were especially adept at spotting provisions buried to save a little food from the armies of both sides.[58]

The North was ecstatic at this grand feat of Union arms achieved at such little cost. "What splendid news we have from Genl. Sherman," Kate Gansevoort wrote. To one anonymous Northern enthusiast, the sufferings of Southern families were sanitized by the idea that God had provisioned Sherman's army:

Like the tribes of Israel,
  Fed on quails and manna,
Sherman and his glorious band
Journeyed through the rebel land,
Fed from Heaven's all bounteous hand,
    Marching on Savannah.

A moment's thought might have reminded him that the intervention of "Heaven's all bounteous hand" implied that God was a scoundrel who stole food from the hungry.[59]

No other poem about the march could equal Herman's "The March to the Sea (December, 1864)," which captures in jaunty, swinging meter the swagger, the arrogance, the rhythms, and the facts of the march, including the thousands of slaves who joined it and the joy and exhilaration with which the North greeted the news of Sherman's audacious success: the columns

  streamed until their flashing
Met the flashing of the sea:
 It was glorious glad marching,
 That marching to the sea.

Why should one not share in this exultation? Who could nay-say success after such a long and bitter struggle? The stream across Georgia was an outpouring of Union strength that was winning the war by drowning the

South. But Herman was appalled that civilians were being persecuted, just as he had been appalled in "Running the Batteries" at the thought of the city of Vicksburg burning. At first, the pillage is brought into the poem so subtly that the reader is disarmed by the good-humored idea that the loot joined the army in order to participate in the fun:

> The flocks of all those regions,
>   The herds and horses good,
> Poured in and swelled the legions,
>   For they caught the marching mood.

The second reference, although not as ingenuous, is mitigated by the picture of the soldiers, the "Takers," enjoying their well-earned bounty:

> who should say them nay?
>   The regiments uproarious
>   Laughed in Plenty's glee;
>   And they marched till their broad laughter
>   Met the laughter of the sea.

With that preparation, the poem concludes in a condemnatory stanza with which generations of Southerners could agree:

>   behind they left a wailing,
>   A terror and a ban,
> And blazing cinders sailing,
>   And houseless households wan,
> Wide zones of counties paling,
>   And towns where maniacs ran.
> Was the havoc, retribution?
>   But howsoe'er it be,
> They will long remember Sherman
>   And his streaming columns free—

As Herman predicted, Sherman's name became an enduring reproach for Southerners. Here as elsewhere, Herman's ambiguity stemmed from the double vision that allowed him to see both the joy and the pain of experience; what is joy for Northerners is pain for Southerners, but the final vision is of the pain.

The real subject of the poem is the grim heartlessness that Grant had introduced into the war, a scorched-earth punishment of the entire South, children, granddams, and all. The Union could starve the Confederate armies by the grim expedient of starving the entire Confederacy. At the end of November 1864, Sheridan had ordered two brigades of cavalry into

Mosby's Confederacy to destroy all food and forage, to burn all barns and mills, and to drive off all livestock. Residences were not to be burned and civilians were not to be harmed, but the soldiers looted and pillaged nevertheless. The population was left in desperate want.

On February 1, Sherman disappeared once more as he marched north to invade South Carolina. Again his army moved in two separated columns, and again it sent out its bummers to seize the food of the inhabitants, but because many of the troops bore a vicious hatred for the South Carolinians, whom they blamed for instigating the war, they looted, burned, and committed mindless atrocities. One officer wrote that "it was sad to see this wanton destruction of property. . . . The country was necessarily left to take care of itself, and became a 'howling waste.'" As Sherman wrote, "The whole army is burning with an insatiable desire to wreak vengeance upon South Carolina. I almost tremble at her fate, but feel that she deserves all that seems in store for her." His army bypassed Charleston and headed for Columbia, the South Carolina capital, which surrendered on February 17. That night rampaging soldiers set fires that burned two-thirds of the city to the ground, and the next day Sherman destroyed what of any use remained and moved on. On March 23, he arrived at Goldsboro to find some eastern soldiers there awaiting him, and Herman again received news from his army.[60]

According to Herman's note, he composed "The Frenzy in the Wake: Sherman's advance through the Carolinas (February, 1865)" after the Western Army reached Goldsboro and before Lincoln's assassination. The passion of its Carolinian narrator suggests the deep hatred and impotent rage of the victims toward the men who vandalized their land, but Herman's note, which mentions both the march through Georgia and Sheridan's destruction in northern Virginia, reveals his intention to comment on the general devastation visited on the South.

A good reason for writing the poem at once and for imbuing it with the resentments of the Southerners was Herman's respect for Richard Lathers, who had never wavered in his loyalty toward his fellow South Carolinians or in his loyalty to the Union. Others could rejoice in the sufferings of the guilty authors of secession; Herman had only to look about him to see how shallow this attitude was. General Winfield Scott, Admiral Farragut, and Richard differed from other Southerners only in their allegiance to the Union. To revile those who had given their first loyalty to their own kind and to desire to reduce them to want was ungenerous, unwise, and unconsidered. In truth, there were only loyal Americans; for Southerners, to be loyal to one ideal was to be disloyal to the other.

Apart from the example of Richard, Herman was morally opposed to the policy. As he wrote, "There are those who can not but contrast some of the scenes enacted in Georgia and the Carolinas, and also in the Shenandoah, with a circumstance in a great Civil War of heathen antiquity. Plutarch relates that in a military council held by Pompey and the chiefs of that party which stood for the Commonwealth, it was decided that under no plea should any city be sacked that was subject to the people of Rome." True, he then mentioned a slight difference between the Roman and American civil wars that might "possibly" have justified the Union measures, though if that were the point he need not have mentioned Pompey's council at all. Thus without denying Sherman and Sheridan the credit for their successes, and without condemning them outright for their excesses, he made the case for the brotherhood of all Americans. He was opposed to Wise Draco, Sherman, Sheridan, and any other leader who would scourge Nature's Roman, because magnanimity was a necessary precondition to a viable restoration of the union. For the spirit of revenge aroused in blacks by slavery, as in "The Swamp Angel," no mitigation seemed possible, but Northern whites had no such justification. Forgetting that Atlanta and Columbia were cities of the United States, enthusiasts might welcome their destruction, but if the war was being fought to bring Americans back together, what end did such Draconian measures serve? If this was McClellanism, it was also Melvillism.

The poem, a dramatic monologue spoken by a Southerner, is a daring re-creation of the bitterness of the victims. The narrator sees the hellfire of war brought from the field of battle to the fields of peaceful toil: "With burning woods our skies are brass, / The pillars of dust are seen." The spoliation of Southern cities dishonors the scarred Confederate warriors who have fought and are fighting for these ruined homes: "O, the garments rolled in blood / Scorch in cities wrapped in flame." The North is like the biblical general Sisera, who "mightily oppressed the children of Israel" (Judg. 4:3), an analogy with which the Confederates, who saw themselves as freedom fighters, would have agreed. Behind the oppression of the Israelites lay its cause—their captivity was God's punishment for doing evil in his sight, but here the narrator refuses to admit that the South has done evil when he complains about the celebrating slaves: "the African—the imp! / He gibbers, imputing shame."

Surely the South was culpable for adhering to slavery and for severing the union. Nevertheless, had Sisera treated the Israelites humanely, they might have admitted their fault and Jael might not have driven the nail through his brow. Here in the Carolinas, the malice of the alien soldiers from Maine and Minnesota will similarly inspire the victims to hatred, to self-justification, and to a lust for revenge:

Shall Time, avenging every woe,
  To us that joy allot
Which Israel thrilled when Sisera's brow
  Showed gaunt and showed the clot?

The danger to a future reunion lies in the fact that "back from its ebb the flood recoils— / Back in a whelming sea." Revenge may beget a counterflood of vengeance. Even the South's recognition of its errors cannot now make it repentant: "We were sore deceived. . . . / Have we gamed and lost? but even despair / Shall never our hate rescind." Herman saw consequences of Sherman's march that have not yet run their course.

The Omega

While the stalemate at Petersburg broke with startling swiftness, Lincoln camped nearby. Ostensibly, little had changed. Lee was still strongly entrenched and Grant was still unable to breach his defenses. But the Union army was strangling the Confederates by interdicting their lines of supply. When Sheridan arrived, Grant reinforced him and placed him southwest of Petersburg. Lee sent a smaller force to oppose him, and in a furious attack Sheridan defeated it. The following morning, when Grant mounted a general assault on the city, the Confederate government evacuated Richmond. That night Lee marched his army out toward the west and Richmond formally surrendered. Some of the U.S. Colored Troops marched through the streets singing

Say, darkeys, hab you seen de massa,
  Wid de muffstash on his face,
Go long de road some time dis mornin',
  Like he gwine to leab de place?
He seen a smoke, way up de ribber,
  Whar de Linkum gumboats lay;
He took his hat, an' lef berry sudden,
  An' I spec he's run away!
    De massa run? ha, ha!
    De darkey stay? ho, ho!
    It mus' be now de kingdom comin',
    An' de year ob jubilo![61]

Thus they transformed a popular "darkey" tune into a triumphal march. On April fourth, Lincoln entered the Confederate capital to the cheers of local blacks and Union soldiers.

New York City went wild. When Petersburg was captured, the *New York*

Times gave over its entire front page to the story under the headline "Victory," and the following day, when Richmond fell, it did the same under the headlines "Grant. / Richmond and Victory." As tensions that had gripped people for four years relaxed, the city swelled with rapture. There were plenty of Melvilles present to celebrate the occasion—Mother Melville, her children, and their children—and they must have gathered to rejoice. Albany was so exultant that Uncle Peter could not resist going out on State Street to mingle with the crowds. One can only imagine the joy in the Hoadley and Griggs homes and in lonely Gansevoort. In Concord, Emerson was exultant: "Joy to you, in this joy of the land, & the world!"[62]

That Herman was describing the reaction of New York City in "The Fall of Richmond: The tidings received in the Northern Metropolis (April, 1865)" is patent in the poem's subtitle. According to the poem, all of the bells rang out and there were "crowds like seas that sway." The booming pulse of cannon manifested "the heart / Of the People impassioned." The poem does not express the thoughts of the poet but rather the emotions with which the news was received by the citizens on the street. It is couched in biblical terms: when the army suffered in the Wilderness, "Hell made loud hurrah"; Richmond fell as did Babylon; and the defeated enemy was "the helmed dilated Lucifer." Each stanza ends with an invocation either to prayer to a God who favored the Union or to a blessing on Grant's military prowess. The excesses of those feelings appear at the poem's end, where the two deities are conjoined: "But God is in Heaven, and Grant in the Town, / And Right through might is Law."

Yet this sentiment, read with care, is one with which Herman himself would have agreed. Read one way, it celebrates the victory of the God of the North over the Satan of the South, but read another, God's victory is the inevitable working out of the great plan, not His active involvement in men's affairs. The victory was won not by God but by Grant and his soldiers after "weary years and woeful wars, / And armies in the grave," and after "fainting we fought in the Wilderness." The Lucifer whose "Hell made loud hurrah" is the Satan of *Battle-Pieces,* not the Satan of the Bible; he is the "disciplined captain, gray in skill" of "The Conflict of Convictions," the personification of the malice and violence that war calls up from men's inner nature. God will not prevent men from fighting under Satan's banner, but "forever the scheme of Nature thrives," making possible "the final empire and the happier world" in which Satan is quelled. It is in this sense that "Right through might is Law."

With Lee on the march, Grant cut off his supply line and his escape route. On Sunday, April 9, Colonel Crowninshield, Chaplain Humphreys, just back from prison camp, and the rest of Lowell's old regiment sat in their saddles facing the starving but defiant Confederates, not knowing whether or not they would fight. But that day Lee surrendered. In Cambridge, Longfellow wrote, "So ends the Rebellion of the slave-owners." James Russell Lowell, who had lost so much, was gratified: "The news . . . is from Heaven. I felt a strange and tender exaltation. I wanted to laugh and I wanted to cry, and ended by holding my peace and feeling devoutly thankful." In Concord, Emerson again exulted: "What a joyful day is this & proud to Alleghany ranges, Northern Lakes, Missisippi rivers & all lands & men between the two Oceans, between morning & evening stars."[63]

Near midnight that day, the *New York Times* had an extra on the streets, and the next day the newspaper again gave over its front page to the story headed "Union Victory! / Peace!" It exhorted the populace to show their flags, and so they did. Despite the rain which fell throughout the day, the post office, the customhouse, all public buildings, all hotels, the principal offices and stores, and the ships in the harbor wore the national colors. The schools released their pupils, 100 gun salutes were fired, and the following day a grand "Te Deum" was sung at Trinity Church.[64]

But the celebration was tame compared with that which had followed the capture of Richmond. The abstractions Peace, Union, and Emancipation had been the aims of the war in people's minds, but the concrete goal had been Richmond. That is what the soldiers of the east had fought long and died miserably for, in McDowell's amateur campaign, in McClellan's push to within a few miles of the Confederate capital, in Pope's abortive campaign, in McClellan's slow pursuit of Lee after Antietam, in Burnside's disastrous assault on Fredericksburg, in Hooker's ill-fated end run at Chancellorsville, in Meade's failed winter campaign, and in Grant's bloody advance and siege. Peace was wonderful, but Richmond had been transcendent. In Albany, Uncle Peter, whose mind tended toward the abstract, thought that Lee's surrender was the great event of the war. He, Aunt Susan, and Kate were awakened at midnight by cannon fire and a pealing of bells that continued for two hours. "I never saw Albany as excited as it was," Kate wrote, "bon-fires, songs & ding dongs woke the slumbers." Overcome with joy, the whole family boarded a steamer for New York City and joined the celebrations of the populace and of their Melville relatives.[65]

Herman recorded the Union triumph and the city's response to it in "The Surrender at Appomattox (April, 1865)." Once more, he employed water imagery to suggest the irresistible masses of Northern troops: "As billows upon billows roll, / On victory victory breaks." In his mind, the manner of the surrender of the Southern "eagles" to the "eagles" of the North was equal in importance to the fact. Caesar's victory in the Roman civil war, which was followed by assassinations and tyranny, ended a struggle for power, but Grant's victory with its strict but humane terms was an end to "Treason." Herman did not mean that the Southern soldiers were treasonous, only that they had fought for treason. They were "a people for years politically misled by designing men, and also by some honestly-erring men, who from their position could not have been otherwise than broadly influential," as he wrote in his "Supplement" to *Battle-Pieces*. In other words, the point was not the defeat of the disaffected Americans, but the rejoining of the American states through the defeat of treason and, though muted in the poem, the end of slavery. With this, the great American experiment could recommence, making "all human tribes glad token see."

The Last Act at Ford's Theatre

During these triumphant months, Herman was in touch with Henry Gansevoort, who was still marooned in northern Virginia. Colonel Nelson B. Sweitzer succeeded Colonel Lazelle as commander of the 16th New York, and on November 21, 1864, the veteran 8th Illinois Cavalry joined what was now, with the addition of artillery, the First Separate Brigade. The Illinois colonel, William Gamble, was promoted to brigadier general and given command of the brigade, leaving Lieutenant Colonel David Clendennin to lead his regiment. Although the brigade headquarters was relocated to Fairfax Court House, Henry's regiment was moved to "Camp Lowell," a separate location at Prospect Hill, near the Potomac River, and his men were frequently appropriated for scouts led by others. Henry believed that he was being persecuted for political reasons, but General Halleck had a different explanation: the two New York regiments had been so often cut up by Mosby's men that "they are cowed and useless."[66]

The men of the 8th Illinois, who had fought with the Army of the Potomac from the Peninsular Campaign through Gettysburg, felt superior to the New Yorkers, who had never fought a regular battle. In addition, the voting scandal had given Henry's enemies an excuse to placard him as a Copperhead and as an opponent of emancipation who had flogged a black man. Henry did not deny the latter, but claimed that the man had "made it his business in my camp to steal pistols." As to the former, since before the election the provost marshal in Washington had been investigating the regiment. By turns, the inquisition opened, closed, and reopened, always with the threat that Henry might be dismissed from both the volunteers and the regular army. "It does no good for me to say I did not do it," he wrote. "They reply your Father is a McClellan man, your friends are Democrats Gov. Seymour, who appointed you is a Copperhead, you are charged by several of your officers with uttering disloyal sentiments, your Regt. voted against the war." Kate did not understand. "The word copperhead never should be applied to a true loyal man," she insisted.[67]

If, as Henry believed, his enemies had prevented him from being promoted to brigadier general and being ordered to the front, he could still obtain the rank by brevet, an honorary promotion awarded for distinguished service. "I want you to come down [to Washington] *at once*," he wrote his father, with as little luck as ever. Allan tried to help by arranging for Richard Lathers to call on Secretary Stanton. Stanton's secretary told Richard that he would have to wait, but after two hours Richard realized that Stanton did not intend to see him.[68]

Just after the middle of December, Henry's men nearly succeeded in ending Mosby's career. A detachment led by Major Frazar and including Captain Ed Lansing, who was now commanding a company of the 13th Cavalry, encountered him at the house of a rebel sympathizer. Mosby fired at them from the front door, then ran into a bedroom, where he was shot in the abdomen by a trooper outside the window. Despite the wound, he tore off the distinguishing parts of his uniform and hid them. When he told the troopers that he was a cavalry lieutenant from farther South visiting his home, Frazar, who was drunk, left him to die. After the detachment had ridden away, Mosby was carried to safety in an oxcart, and, before long, he returned to his command. Later, when a trooper produced Mosby's stolen uniform, the truth was out. General Gamble reported Frazar for misconduct and ordered the brigade to take all wounded Confederates into custody, "although I thought any officer ought to have brains and common sense enough to do so without an order." Frazar escaped by transferring to the command of a U.S. Colored regiment.[69]

There was also a brighter side to Henry's life. Georgie Bedell was in Washington to help him to find "pretty" girls, and the brigade was comfortable. A grand New Year's ball was held at headquarters, with guests invited from Washington and Virginia, and a few days later there was a great sleigh ride, though the horses bolted, scattering ladies about. When the news of the capture of Richmond arrived, General Gamble ordered thirty-six guns fired and conducted a grand review, and when the news arrived of Lee's surrender 200 guns were fired. Even though the rangers had not laid down their arms, a grand gala was planned for Saturday, April 15. Actor John Wilkes Booth was one of those who accepted the invitation.[70]

On Good Friday, the day before the party was to have been held, the Lincolns attended a performance of *Our American Cousin* at Ford's Theatre. Their guests were Senator Harris's daughter, Clara, and her fiancé, Harris's stepson, Major Henry Reed Rathbone of the regulars, both friends of Henry. During the course of the performance, Booth entered their box, wounded Lincoln fatally, and, before escaping, wounded Rathbone, who was grappling with him. Clara attended Lincoln on his deathbed.[71]

The Separate Brigade scoured the countryside in search of Booth. On Monday, General Gamble was ordered to Washington with the 8th Illinois and the 16th New York, which attended Lincoln's funeral and then continued the search for Booth. At Camp Lowell, Henry was left behind. The 8th Illinois was sent down the Maryland side of the Potomac while the 16th New York went down the Virginia side. While Henry sat idle, his regiment was divided, one part in Maryland accompanying the 8th, one part in the west toward the upper reaches of the Potomac, and one part in and around Camp Lowell. On April 24, when those in charge learned enough to put a patrol on Booth's track, Colonel Sweitzer sent Lieutenant E. P. Doherty of the 16th, two detectives, and twenty-five troopers south in Virginia. The party followed Booth's trail to a farm where, before dawn on May 26, they discovered Booth hiding in a barn. After futile negotiations, a sergeant fired at him through a crevice in the wall, wounding him mortally. The patrol brought Booth's body back to Washington, where Lieutenant Colonel Clendennin was appointed to a military commission to try Booth's fellow conspirators.[72]

Thus Henry Gansevoort was in the best possible position to inform Herman about the assassination. From Henry Rathbone, whom he visited at his sickbed,[73] he had an eyewitness account of the assassination itself, as, indeed, he had from Clara Harris. From Lieutenant Doherty he had an eyewitness account of the pursuit and slaying of Booth, and from Clendennin he had a participant's account of the trial of Booth's supposed confederates as well as an entree to the hearings.

The nation was shocked by its first presidential assassination. Whittier wrote, "In what times are we living! What great and awful events are written for eternity on the page of our generation. The assassination of the President has painfully affected me. I have been hardly able since to collect my thoughts, to fathom the extent of our loss, or to forecast the consequences."[74] In death, Lincoln became more popular than he had ever been in life. Despite the political bitterness of the past, it was a rare person who did not mourn him. Forgotten were the abrogations of civil rights, the civil and military measures which had offended Democrats, and the vacillations and blunders that had cost the lives of so many soldiers; remembered were the steadfastness of purpose and the fundamental decency of the man.

Peter Gansevoort, Susan, Kate, and, perhaps, Maria and Tom Melville, heard the news on Saturday afternoon when they arrived in Albany from their New York City visit. Albany was draped in funereal colors and cloaked with gloom. Kate was shocked and hoped that the guilty would be made to suffer. The four years of the war had prepared Lincoln for the difficult term to come, she thought, and she hoped that Andrew Johnson would be able to assume the burden. Like other Democrats, she had been encouraged by indications that Lincoln would bring the South back into the union as fully established states. The city mourned Lincoln's death with its usual excess. When Richard Lathers arrived in town and stopped at A. T. Stewart's department store to buy black bombazine with which to drape the Great Western office, he found that because of the demand the cloth was being rationed. A glance at the streets showed why: "Every building in the city was literally covered" with black.[75]

Then began the slow journey of Lincoln's funeral train to Springfield, Illinois. When his body reached New York City on April 24, the streets were decked with the national colors draped with black. The coffin was placed in a special hearse, one that had been built hurriedly but grandly for the occasion, and drawn through a multitude of spectators to City Hall, escorted by all of the city's militia regiments, all of the field and general officers in the area, which would have included Captain Guert Gansevoort and perhaps Surgeon Henry Thurston, local officials, and a mass of civic societies and deputations. It was placed in the City Hall rotunda while 800 or more voices of the United German Societies, accompanied by a band, intoned the "Pilgrims' Chorus" from Wagner's *Tannhauser.* While on display, Lincoln's body was attended by watches of high-ranking officers, including Guert's commander, Commodore Hiram Paulding, Brevet Major General Robert Anderson of Fort Sumter fame, and Herman's friend, Brevet Major General Robert O. Tyler, who had recovered somewhat from his wound, while the German chorus continued its sad chants. From noon to noon, crowds stood in line in City Hall Park to pass by the open casket. All was sadly grand—except that someone dropped a lighted cigar from the dome or thereabouts onto the drapery, which briefly caught fire. The following day, the body resumed its journey home.[76]

The North was bereaved, but it was also angry and vengeful. Mobs on the streets believed that the assassination was yet another atrocity committed by the South. Richard Lathers witnessed several violent attacks on persons suspected of being sympathizers with the South or secessionists and told Southerners who sought him out to lock themselves in their rooms for the day. Perhaps to reaffirm his loyalty one more time, he delivered a eulogy to Lincoln at Tammany Hall. Whittier wrote: "How black and hateful Slavery looks in the lurid light of this monstrous crime! We never hated it enough." Kate Gansevoort questioned why Grant had paroled the Confederate officers, thousands of whom, she believed, were now plotting against the government. But when the assailant was identified as a "madman," the violence abated and Whittier mended his attitude, writing to the *Friends' Review* that there was "much work to be done in the spirit of Christian meekness, in checking the fierce, vindictive feeling which has been awakened by the assassination of the President."[77]

Of the poems inspired by Lincoln's death, only a few were notable. Walt Whitman's "When Lilacs Last in the Dooryard Bloomed" was magnificent, and Thomas Bailey Aldrich's "A Great Man's Death" was a deft blend of the quiet pastoral with the unexpected heroic:

> A callow bird, of not so many days
> As there are leaves upon the wilding rose,
> Chirps from yon sycamore; this violet
> Sprung up an hour since from the fibrous earth:
> At noon the rain fell, and to-night the sun
> Will sink with its old grandeur in the sea,—
> And yet to-day a god died. . . . Nature smiles
> On our mortality. A sparrow's death,
> Or the unnoticed falling of a leaf,
> Is more to her than when a great man dies![78]

Herman would have agreed with the part of this vision, so like his own, that depicts nature smilingly indifferent to man's mortality.

Herman could be expected to react differently, but it is somewhat surprising that he did not mourn Lincoln poetically, that his interest lay, rather, in the response of the North to the assassination. The key to "The Martyr: Indicative of the passion of the people on the 15th of April, 1865," can be found in his note, in which he wrote that "the feeling which would have held the entire South chargeable with the crime of one exceptional assassin . . . has died away with the natural excitement of the hour." The narrator does hold the South responsible, making the poem one of those about which Herman said, in his "Supplement," "I have been tempted to withdraw or modify some of them, fearful lest in presenting, though but dramatically and by way of a poetic record, the passions and epithets of civil war, I might be contributing to a bitterness which every sensible American must wish at an end." Well might he worry that the spirit of revenge recreated in the poem might reawaken passions:

> the People in their weeping
> Bare the iron hand:
> Beware the People weeping
> When they bare the iron hand.

Nevertheless, the poem is a warning against such transient emotions.

The narrator's portrait of Lincoln, of the compassionate president, is

Herman's as well. "Pity," "clemency," "calm," and "kindness" are the marks of the "father" and "Forgiver" who is filled with "yearning . . . / To redeem the evil-willed." He is the leader who could have brought unity and hope to the shattered nation. Yet the narrator accuses "they"—the South, not the assassin—of the crime and calls for "the iron hand,"

The Avenger wisely stern,
  Who in righteousness shall do
  What the heavens call him to,
And the parricides remand.

The "Avenger wisely stern" calls to mind "wise Draco" of "The House-top." That is the purpose of the poem, to demonstrate, through irony, the wisdom of following Lincoln's example by avoiding "wise" sternness in the postwar era.

A second poem about the assassination, "'The Coming Storm': A Picture by S.R. Gifford, and owned by E.B. Included in the N.A. Exhibition, April, 1865," moves even farther from grief for Lincoln. It was inspired by Herman's later visit to the National Academy of Design exhibition, described in the following chapter, where he saw the painting that provided the title for the poem, a landscape by Sanford Gifford. The canvas was lent by its owner, Edwin Booth, the actor who had recently closed his production of *Hamlet* at the Winter Garden. What interested Herman was the fact that Booth's brother had assassinated Lincoln. Herman may have known Gifford, not only because he seems to have been acquainted with a number of New York artists but also because of Gifford's service with Henry Gansevoort in the Seventh Regiment. Herman may have attended one of Booth's performances of *Hamlet,* and the poem makes one suspect that he did. But he may also have known Booth, who maintained an elegant residence on 19th Street. Certainly the conjunction of the suggestive painting, the military service of the artist, the tragedy of Shakespeare, and the shocking event at Ford's Theatre made a powerful impression on him.

The coming storm was a conventional metaphor for impending war, but here it refers to the sudden tempest that had recently engulfed Booth: "A demon-cloud . . . / Burst on a spirit as mild / As this urned lake, the home of shades." But Booth is "Shakespeare's pensive child" who "never the lines had lightly scanned, / Steeped in fable, steeped in fate." He is protected from despair because "the Hamlet in his heart was 'ware":

No utter surprise can come to him
  Who reaches Shakespeare's core;
That which we seek and shun is there—
  Man's final lore.

The poem is a recognition by one man who had reached "Shakespeare's core" of a fellow initiate, a fraternal salutation to Booth, who had learned from Shakespeare that the black seed could germinate and flower even in his own brother. To understand Shakespeare is to know of the dark side of human nature, the side that allows men to run as wild as zebras on the pampas, in the wilderness, and in Ford's Theatre. As Milder has said, "To one who 'reaches Shakespeare's core,' particular evils like the assassination or the war itself fail to 'surprise,' for they appear as eruptions of a darkness always lurkingly present in human affairs."[79] In other words, what Booth had learned from Shakespeare was exactly what Herman hoped to teach in *Battle-Pieces*.

Moreover, the two Booth brothers focused in Herman's mind the fratricidal nature of the war and stirred something in his imagination. Since the early years of his literary career, he had envisioned paired, contrasting characters, such as, in *Moby-Dick*, Ishmael and Queequeg on the one hand and Ahab and Starbuck on the other. But henceforth these pairs would become brothers, symbolically or biologically. In his fragmentary "Rammon" he wrote an allegory of the postwar Reconstruction in which Rammon (a wise counselor) cautions his half-brother Rehoboam to be lenient with the rebellious Jeroboam, but without success. In "Timoleon" (209–15), the protagonist, Timoleon, saves Corinth from his brother's tyranny. And in *Billy Budd,* the good "master-at-arms" of the *Rights-of-Man* slays the evil master-at-arms of the *Bellipotent,* his symbolic brother.

Just as Lincoln's election had signalled the beginning of the war, so his death marked its end. The funeral train rolled on to Albany, where the Gansevoorts viewed it, and finally to Lincoln's home, where he was buried. But in Herman's family, the war would continue as long as Mosby and his rangers were still abroad. Kate Gansevoort heard that the guerrilla leader was planning to fight to the death, and, in truth, the rangers were giving some thought to continuing their struggle. But on a rainy April 21, the day Lincoln's funeral train left Washington, the rangers, in full uniform, formed ranks for the last time. With his beard newly shaven, Mosby rode up and down the lines as Willie Mosby read the order to disband. Then, without surrendering, they went home. And why should they have surrendered, when they had won their war?[80]

9

Battle-Pieces
1865-1866

As the fighting died away, Herman began sustained work on *Battle-Pieces.* In order to take commercial advantage of the public emotions evoked by the approach of victory, some writers had already rushed their war poems into print. George Henry Boker had published his *Poems of the War* in 1864, and, as has been noted, in September 1864, Walt Whitman was already marketing *Drum-Taps.* In contrast, the bulk of Herman's *Battle-Pieces* "originated in an impulse imparted by the fall of Richmond," according to his preface. His intention to write Civil War poems, and perhaps a book of them, dated from much earlier, at least as early as the period following the Battle of Fredericksburg, and by the time the Confederate capital fell he had probably composed versions of some of them. He delayed the main body of his book and the formulation of its final plan until the immediacy of the events on which most of the poems are based had dissipated and his emotions about them could be recollected from the more tranquil and more settled viewpoint of the war as a historical whole. As Hennig Cohen has described it, the book is a product "of the cool calculation which the passage of time makes possible."[1] Had it been otherwise, Herman could not have exercised firm control of his materials and methods. Like the violent upheavals of the war themselves, the immediate reactions of an artist to events were subject to excesses of grief, anxiety, anger, and exultation; it was necessary to wait until the flux of the conflict had subsided into a coherent memory. The end of the war, then, was the point at which Herman began to make his book.

He made use of newspaper accounts collected in *The Rebellion Record* as well as other contemporary materials, such as George Ward Nichols's *The Story of the Great March.* The influence of the *Record* has been detected in at least twenty of the poems, but the importance of the borrowings has been overstated, tempting readers to believe that *Battle-Pieces* is "versified journalism," and, therefore, that both the author and his poems were distant "from the actual events of the war." That idea is rooted in Raymond M. Weaver's conception of Herman as a "mariner and mystic" who stood aloof from earthly concerns, for a mystic looks only above and a mariner looks only beyond, at the inscrutable sea. That leaves unexplained the lively interest in the social and political issues of the time demonstrated in many of Herman's other works.[2]

A consequence of that biographical legacy has been the assumption that he was disengaged from and only marginally aware of the greatest national convulsion in American history as it occurred around him; that, while the rest of the population endured cataclysmic events in which the flames of war ignited and charred both North and South, he indulged in his lifelong metaphysical study of the nature of evil in some philosopher's cave, from which he emerged only at the time of the surrender of Richmond to discover in the *Record* what had been happening to his country. But as relatives, friends, and neighbors engaged in battles, as the telegraph and the newspapers and the casualty lists held the shocking news perpetually before the public eye, and as threats of invasion, domestic turbulence, celebrations of victories, the imposition of war taxes, and the upward spiral of prices claimed attention every day, essentially every citizen of the North was kept wide awake. Calling the war "the general heart-quake of the country," Hawthorne had written that "there is no remoteness of life and thought, no hermetically sealed seclusion, except, possibly, that of the grave, into which the disturbing influences of this war do not penetrate." Every major literary figure was at least to some degree forced to confront events on a daily basis: Thoreau, for the brief time before his death, Emerson, Whitman, especially, Longfellow, Lowell, and even Emily Dickinson. Herman was as involved as most authors of the time, if not more so: Arvin is correct in saying that "there was hardly a detonation of the great battles . . . that did not reach his ear," as is Shurr in saying that "he was fully involved, mentally, with the crises of a city and a country at war."[3]

To be sure, Herman was a borrower. For example, in *White-Jacket* he plundered the memoirs of others in order to add fictional interest to the record of his unexceptional experiences during his enlistment aboard the frigate *United States*. But *Battle-Pieces* is another matter. It deals with a war so lavish in emotion and so profligate in event that to the present day it affords historians an inexhaustible field for inquiry. Herman had no need to embellish what he already knew, nor did he. In fact, he may have used the *Record* somewhat less than has been supposed. It has been noted that in both "Donelson" and in a column reprinted from the *New York Times* the word "vim" appears; but at the time that word was in common use, as is demonstrated by General Sheridan's philippic against Jeff Hobart. Again, although a piece from the *Missouri Democrat* and "Donelson" both use the word "sortie," that is the kind of military term that war introduces to the civilian vocabulary.[4]

What use Herman did make of the *Record* is defensible. *Pace* Edgar Allan Poe, it was not unusual or unprofessional, then or later, for an artist to exploit existing written materials in his imaginative work, providing he refashioned them. Through the power of his imagination, Herman made his borrowings his own property. It is in part his use of Shakespearean materials in *Moby-Dick* that makes the work a triumph rather than an embarrassment. More to the point, he could not have written such a book as *Battle-Pieces* without supplementing his memory. To take the entire four years and the vast geographical panorama of the conflict as one's subject required research, since even the most experienced soldier or sailor had only limited personal knowledge of the war.

Herman's mind contained a rebellion record of its own. The newspapers he had read had followed the war in scrupulous detail. What was mere ink on their pages and pulses through telegraph wires was given life through his relationships with men who fought in many of the battles, and his own memories supplied images of the home front, of a revealing scout through Mosby country, and of a great army preparing for battle. He used the *Record* as a convenient source of information to jog his memory, to supply dates and detail, to avoid errors of fact, and to impose order on an imagination bloated with impressions, but he was the creator of the poems he wrote. The true starting point for many of them was a personal association with an event through a relative or friend who had participated in it or through some other special relationship. In other words, the poems come to the reader alive from Herman's imagination rather than secondhand.

The Big Parade

As Herman began his task, hostilities were fading into memory. On the day Booth was killed, Joseph Johnston, whose army opposed Sherman's westerners, surrendered, leaving only a few minor pockets of war to be eradicated. On May 9, Jefferson Davis was arrested in Georgia and taken to Fortress Monroe, where he was imprisoned. By early June, combat was only a sad memory. Sherman marched his army north through Virginia, where the awed westerners tramped through battlefields littered with bones. When they arrived near the capital they pitched their tents at Alexandria, not far from Henry Gansevoort's camp. They were to participate in a grand review through the streets of Washington on May 23 and 24, a review that defined for the armies and the public a point of demarcation between war and peace.

Abe Lansing suggested to Kate Gansevoort that they visit Washington, where they could combine the excitement of the pageantry with a visit to Henry's regiment. They arrived with Anna Lansing on the second day, having missed the "well and cleanly clad" Army of the Potomac—without its corps of Colored Troops, which was left behind—and its "fine marching," but they stood on the balcony of Willard's to watch Sherman's army parade by.[5]

Full of the pride of conquest, the westerners invented their own parade rules, marching through the capital with the same careless confidence with which they had marched through the South. Their columns were made doubly memorable by the bummers who followed each brigade. These specialists in felony trooped by "in their native ugliness," leading their pack mules and horses and showing off their pet gamecocks, raccoons, dogs, and goats. Walt Whitman was amazed by the

> solid ranks of soldiers, 20 or 25 abreast, just marching steady all day long . . . real war-worn *soldiers*, that have been marching & fighting for years—sometimes for an hour nothing but cavalry, just solid ranks, on good horses, with sabres glistening, & carbines hanging by their saddles, & their clothes showing hard service, . . . then great masses of guns, batteries of cannon, four or six abreast, . . . then great battalions of blacks, with axes & shovels & pick axes, (real southern darkies, black as tar)—then again hour after hour the old infantry regiments, the men all sunburnt—nearly every one with some old tatter all in shreds, (that *had been* a costly & beautiful *flag*)—the great drum corps of sixty or eighty drummers massed at the heads of the brigades, playing away—now and then a fine brass band . . . the different corps banners, the generals with their staffs &c.

After the Albany visitors had watched for a while, Abe hunted down Henry and his brother Ed. Later, they walked through the White House grounds and went to the generals' residences, where they listened to a band and heard speeches.[6]

The next day, they rode to Prospect Hill in Henry's ambulance. Henry met them at his headquarters, then conducted them to his tent, where his black servant, Moses, announced lunch in the dining tent. After they had eaten, Henry's colt, Beauty, appeared to share dessert with them. Then they visited the stables to see Henry's other horses, inspected Ed's tent, viewed the countryside from the signal tower, and toured the entrenchments, the blockhouses, a nearby artillery regiment, and the commissary, after which they were treated to a concert by Henry's regimental band and a dress parade. The day after that, Henry and Ed took Abe to the trial of the assassination conspirators at the old arsenal by the Potomac, with passes probably obtained from Clendennin. In the meantime, the ladies saw the sights, including Ford's Theatre, newly notorious. Then Kate and Anna returned to Albany, leaving Abe at camp with his brother and Henry. Kate warned Henry not to overdo Abe's "whiskey cure."[7]

As the review formalized the close of the war, so several of Herman's poems signify its end and summarize its meaning for *Battle-Pieces*. Recalling the "torrents [that] down the gorges go" of "Misgivings" and the "deep abyss" of "The Conflict of Convictions," the first two conclude the patterns of flowing water and ocean depths that pervade the book. If they are tinged with patriotic enthusiasm, it is because they reflect the mood of the victorious North and Herman's own hopes for the future—his idiosyncratic mix of realism and idealism. They also mark the beginning of a final phase of the battle section of the book in which, except for "The Martyr," Herman abandons dramatic irony to speak in what is, more or less, his own voice.

True to the times and the moment, "The Muster: Suggested by Two Days' Review at Washington (May, 1865)" is exultant. Ignoring for the moment the depths of war's grisly wilderness, it sees the waves of marching soldiers as "floods," the "watery multitudes" of men who have been gathering since the earliest poems of the book. They are "Abrahamic" because of the secular leadership of Lincoln and also because, like the Abraham of scripture, Lincoln was Father Abraham and the recipient of God's new covenant. They are the "quotas of the Nation, . . . / Eastern warriors, Western braves," rivulets and streams collected into an irresistible Mississippi.[8] The force of the united easterners and westerners stems from the "deep enforcing current" of "the God of floods." That current, like the "wind in purpose strong" of "The Conflict of Convictions," has ensured that the course of the war would drive in the direction of reunification regardless of its momentary diversions. Further, as an accumulation of the waters that washed casualty lists clean and that will level Donelson, this river has, it is to be hoped, cleansed the nation of the bitter rifts and divides of four long years as well as, perhaps, the follies of antebellum America.

The vision of the regiments parading "for hazy miles" inspires a momentary shift in metaphor from the river to the "Milky Way of armies— / Star rising after star." This constellation of the "eagles of the War" cancels any residual belief in the Raphaels and Michaels of a more innocent time, for the eagles, not the archangels, are the lofty champions of the nation. Returning to the metaphor of the flood, the poem concludes that, when congregated, the small rills from the states, even the primitive state of Kansas, have "evened" "Europe's marge." In fact, they have surpassed that marge. Never had Europe amassed such an army as had been raised to reunite the states. Thus America has taken its place as an equal to the nations of the Old World from which it sprang. Perhaps its destiny is to "even" Europe into nations of hope and promise for common people, like America.

In contrast to the footing in everyday events that anchors "The Muster" to reality, "A Canticle: Significant of the national exultation of enthusiasm at the close of the War" sees the victory—and the war as a whole—in wholly symbolic terms. It looks back in the fulfilled certainty that the union has survived and ahead with qualified hope to its future perfection. The opening vision depicts a great waterfall pouring from a "firmamental rim" into "the Gorge so grim." In acknowledging the "congregated Fall" of man implied in the shattered covenant that led to the war, it also characterizes the roil of waters at the bottom as Satan's war-world. This is what the picnickers on their way to Bull Run could not have imagined, that just as the rivulets of squads, companies, battalions, regiments, brigades, divisions, corps, and armies, they were brooks of people, purposes, and efforts joining to become streams, rivers, and finally a single massive torrent tumbling down to the sinister depths. For the individual soldiers and sailors the image is grim—many perished in the pool—but in terms of the "Mysterious" impulse of the nation, the force is gathered "in power, not in pride": it was Herman's hope that the victory would not be lost in hubris. The "Lord of hosts" is victorious, not because He led the armies into Satan's depths but because He found a "passage" to the outcome implicit in His divine plan.

Above the gorge floats Iris, the rainbow of America, its prewar essence and its promise. A wind from heaven, the stern decree of war, attacks it, "shivering and paling it / To blankness of the snows." Yet it is strong enough to survive and rekindle until "prevailing and transcending, / Lo, the Glory perfect there, / And the contest finds an ending." It has withstood the contrary winds of punishing events and renewed itself into a "Glory perfect." Then the Giant of the Pool, sculpted from the mists created by the torrent, rises (like the apotheosis of Bulkington in *Moby-Dick*) toward Iris. Its appearance marks a change in meaning of the rushing waters from the wartime army to "the Generations pouring / From times of endless date." It is the apotheosis of humanity, now growing "Toward the fullness of her fate" in the restored and renewed America. To realize that end, the narrator asks that

Thou Lord of hosts victorious,
  Fulfill the end designed;
By a wondrous way and glorious
  A passage Thou dost find.

As God had found a way to preserve the union, may He now find a way to the fulfillment of its destiny.

"The Apparition (A Retrospect)" was inspired by Frank Bartlett's experience in the great mine explosion at Petersburg. Herman could imagine the horror of the Confederate soldiers as they felt the solidity of the earth swell and burst beneath their feet, which suggested an important qualification of the meliorative tone of the latter part of *Battle-Pieces.* The poem is central to the meaning of the book in that it focuses and completes the initiation into war's horrors of earlier poems. It is final proof that the worldview of the "bachelor," who sees only the cheerful, comfortable side of the human condition, is incomplete and therefore false. That had been the error of those who had trusted in Raphael and Michael. This poem invokes a pastoral, Shenandoah-like America, a green and growing world signified here in Herman's poetic shorthand as "Solidity." Even after John Brown's shadow had fallen across the "pastoral green," the nation remained confident in its promise and its belief in an orgiastic future. But Solidity is not the way of the world, in the past or in the future. It is only an appearance concealing behind it a central fact of man's existence, Satan's "eruptions of a darkness always lurkingly present in human affairs." When the union is severed and the consequences are felt, America is blasted by an eruption of violence and malignity. In a convulsion, a "goblin-mountain" pushes up from beneath the verdure and fertility is replaced by marl, slag, and clinkers: "The unreserve of Ill was there," Satanic ill. Yet before the senses can fully absorb and the mind comprehend, the eruption disappears as though it had never existed, leaving behind it the great philosophical lesson of the war: "Solidity's a crust— / The core of fire below." The appearance of wholeness returns, but the existence of Satan has been established for all time; he retreats back to his abyss to await another moment when man's imperfection will renew his opportunity to seize the reins of events. Preserving the memory of the goblin-mountain is a major purpose of *Battle-Pieces*: if future fields for fight are congealing beneath the sea, awareness must protect the nation from again becoming the battleground. An entire people must be educated to distrust the illusion that Solidity is dependable and to prevent the apparition from appearing again.[9]

Similar in import but focused on a single individual is "Commemorative of a Naval Victory," a memorial poem and one that Warren was "tempted to call great."[10] The naval leader seems to be Admiral Farragut, since the first stanza bears a resemblance to the opening of "The Battle for the Bay" and since Farragut, who lived in New York City, was a "favored guest" in the "social halls" there when he was not lashed in the rigging running batteries. The nautical cynosure of the poem has been refined by the discipline of arms and tempered by the sea; gentle yet strong, he is entitled by his victories to bask in "woman's glance instinctive thrown" and to relish the plaudits "which make the barren place to shine." Yet what the College Colonel has learned from his suffering and what Edwin Booth has learned from Shakespeare's core, this sailor has learned from the sea, from battle, from the loss of the *Tecumseh*—in his thoughts there is "a light" and there are "October sunsets brown," but there are also "pensive pansies dark." Because of the ambiguity of the battles he has won, victory qualified by memories of carnage and death, "Elate he never can be." As with poets, "there's a light and a shadow on every man / Who at last attains his lifted mark— / Nursing through night the ethereal spark." And, as with the poet Herman Melville, the Colonel, and Booth, this warrior knows that "the shark / Glides white through the phosphorous sea."

"America" is more notable for its vision than it is for its originality. Embodying America in a conventional feminine figure, it is an allegory that the general public would have understood, and as such it has been criticized as tepid and derivative and as a "ritual of a sleazy sort." But when it is understood as a culminating point of *Battle-Pieces,* a counterpoint to "The Apparition," and the final appearance of the mother figure introduced in "Apathy and Enthusiasm," it gains purpose and dignity. To quote Milder, the poem "shapes the confusion of events [of the preceding poems] into an overarching national myth and clarifies the process of moral growth the poems have occasioned in the reader all along."[11]

If "The Apparition" invokes the dark side of the war experience, this poem is a reminder that there is also hope. It begins with a vision of an American flag "where the wings of a sunny Dome expand"—suggesting the Capitol dome as well as the firmamental dome—with the antebellum land reposing "in peace below." In this green world, the children (the states and the citizens alike) of the young mother were "folded to the exulting heart / Of young Maternity." Then in the earlier days of the war the flag streamed not in peace but "in fight / When tempest mingled with the fray," and over the flagstaff there was "ambiguous lightning." As her children strove "Valor with Valor" in their fierce Pride and Despair, "the lorn Mother speechless stood, / Pale at the fury of her brood." The children descend into Satan's primal world while the mother lapses into unconsciousness, seemingly dead and wrapped as on a bier in the flag that had once flown so grandly above. It is the dark night of the soul for America, as in sleep she sees the dark truths that *Battle-Pieces* has revealed. Her face is contorted by the vision "revealing earth's foundation bare, / And Gorgon in her hidden place." It is fearful to see "so foul a dream upon so fair a face." In short, she has glimpsed the "unreserve of Ill" of "The Apparition," the "core of fire" beneath Solidity. The "foul" dream serves the additional purpose of affirming that "the world's fairest hope linked with man's foulest crime" in "Misgivings" refers not to slavery but to the fratricidal battle which threatened "the Founders' dream."

The nightmare is necessary as a prelude to spiritual renewal.[12] Thus America awakens with slavery crushed ("At her feet a shivered yoke") and with "no trace of passion or of strife" in her "clear calm look." The hope for the future lies in the belief that the nation may not only survive the primitive passions of war but may also transcend them into greatness. America is no longer innocent; pain has purified her and knowledge has repressed her triumph; her power is dedicated and her hope informed. "Law on her brow and empire in her eyes. / So she, with graver air and lifted flag" stands on her promontory, the shadow that had fallen over her gone. The innocent and ineffective Raphael has been replaced on the pinnacle by the newly wise and mature America who, ideally, will never again fall victim to Satan. Thus the outcome of the war would justify its terrible suffering.

It is disquieting to read of an America with "empire in her eyes," since that suggests a nation vying with the crowns of Europe for colonial dominion in Africa, Asia, and the Pacific isles. Indeed, it would hardly be surprising, considering his late brother Gansevoort's oratory on behalf of the annexation of Texas, to learn that Herman's vision of America included Manifest Destiny in the sense of southwestern territorial expansion that would stretch the nation's borders from Atlantic to Pacific; *that* empire was already all but achieved, its borders essentially established. But he would not have approved of interference with primitive cultures, as on the island paradises of the Pacific, the spoliation of which by "Paul Pry" with his "Pelf and Trade" he lamented in his late poem, "To Ned" (200–201). Empire in this poem may be understood in terms of Frederick Merk's "Mission," as distinguished from territorial aggrandizement: the capture of men's minds rather than their lands. The Mission of America is "to redeem the Old World by high example": the example of liberty, democracy, human rights, public spiritedness, compassion, and all of the other ideals that the nation, however imperfectly, stood for. It is explained by White-Jacket thus: "We bear the ark of the liberties of the world. . . . God has given to us, for a future inheritance, the broad domains of the political pagans, that shall yet come and lie down under the shade of our ark, without bloody hands being lifted. . . . We are the pioneers of the world; the advance-guard, sent on through the wilderness of untried things, to break a new path in the New World that is ours" (151). The American empire would come to pass when, from one margin of the globe to the other, feudalism had given way to democratic equality. We will march at the fore while the rest of mankind follows, White-Jacket says.[13]

Mustering Out

After the victory parade, it was time for the great river of servicemen to divide again into rivulets and into individuals returning home. Those who had been unable or unwilling to remain to the end of the war were there already: Wendell Holmes, Charlie Longfellow, and Ned Curtis, who was working as a clerk. The others were still in ranks. On the fourteenth of July, Frank Bartlett, who had returned after the war's end to command the 1st Division of the Ninth Corps, left to prepare for his wedding to Agnes Pomeroy. On July 3, Toby Greene's battery reached Chicago, where he was mustered out. Toby did not re-enter either of his prewar occupations, telegraphy or journalism, but, content to be supported by his wife, who operated an art gallery, he sank into alcoholism, working only occasionally as a doorman at the gallery. In August, the 44th Illinois was sent to Camp Irwin, Texas, along the La Placida River, where, on September 25, John Hobart, now a corporal, was mustered out. The only Hobart to serve successfully, he returned to live with his father and brother but, instead of joining them in the carpentry trade, he became a mechanic. Acting Volunteer Lieutenant Commander William Budd was discharged on January 6, 1866, only to return later to the navy as an acting master. Henry Pease remained with the Colored Troops until April 10, 1866, when he came home. But for far too many, the widows and orphans, there was no returning veteran to greet. The war had ended for Charles Lowell many months before; now Effy and her infant daughter Carlotta wept while others celebrated.[14]

The dissolution of the armies inspired several *Battle-Pieces* poems. The first is the mystifying "Inscriptive and Memorial" poem, "Presentation to the Authorities, by Privates, of Colors captured in Battles ending in the Surrender of Lee." It is mystifying because it is difficult to discover a historical event on which the poem might be based, though captured colors are mentioned in "Lee in the Capitol." It is possible that the colors were presented as the title indicates, in the wake of the Confederate defeat, in which case this discussion is out of its proper place. It was customary, as when Charles Lowell carried the Antietam trophies to the capital, to send captured flags to Washington immediately after a battle, but if that was done in this instance it did not excite attention in the New York newspapers.[15]

It may be that Herman had in mind an event in Albany which did receive extensive coverage. In the afternoon of the Fourth of July, Uncle Peter, Judge Parker, and, probably, the rest of the Gansevoort family, went to the Washington Square parade ground to see the colors of the New York State volunteer regiments presented to Governor Fenton. With the governor and General Grant present, General Dan Butterfield presented about 200 flags, though, much to Uncle Peter's chagrin, Henry's was missing. As each flag was announced, a soldier paraded it before the dignitaries and the spectators, then took it to the rear to join the other flags. This ceremony was the precise antithesis of a presentation of captured Confederate flags, but perhaps Herman converted it in his imagination into a quite different ceremony. One reason may have been that the idea of the great Lost Cause was already incipient in the South, as the Rev. Abram J. Ryan, a Catholic priest, demonstrated in his poem "The Conquered Banner": "Furl it!—for the hands that grasped it, / And the hearts that fondly clasped it, / Cold and dead are lying low."[16]

But for Herman, the Confederate cause merited no such memorial. Much as he sympathized with the people of the South, and much as he wished them to resume their roles as fellow countrymen, the only true country was "Our Country." Because the flag of the United States was "the sovereign one," it was "foredoomed"—by God and by the power of the North—that the enemy flags should yield to it. The banners of the wrong must perish in order that the men who had served "Duty" could "go / To waiting homes with vindicated laws." This is a clear statement of the meaning of the terrible sacrifice. Loyal men died, not to enter heaven in a triumphal procession behind a warrior God but so that the United States should not, in Lincoln's words, "perish from the earth."

"Aurora-Borealis: Commemorative of the Dissolution of Armies at the Peace (May, 1865)" is a generalized tribute to the battle-weary army. It derives its controlling metaphor from the phrase "Milky Way of armies" in "The Muster" by comparing the flux of combat, attack and repulse, experienced by the Northern soldiers to "Northern Lights" and their "retreatings and advancings, / (Like dallyings of doom), / Transitions and enhancings." As the appearance and disappearance of the Aurora Borealis is an awesome demonstration of God's power, so the transition between "Splendor and Terror" and "pale, meek Dawn" also demonstrates this power. However much *Battle-Pieces* had refused to submit to the idea that the war was God's rather than man's, it was God who had done the "decreeing and commanding." While mortal generals had given the orders, it was God whose "old decree," as "The Conflict of Convictions" had said, had enforced "the scheme of Nature." Now He has decreed that after Satan's "Midnight" the nation will have its "Morn."[17]

The muskets and rifles that returned with the soldiers were now hunting pieces and mementos of the great cataclysm. In "The Returned Volunteer to his Rifle," the last poem of the "Inscriptive and Memorial" section, Herman devoted a few happy, relaxed lines to the peaceful retirement of such a weapon carried in the war by a New York veteran. As he mounts it above his hearth, he reminds his deadly companion of the despair they had shared: "Little at Gettysburg we thought / To find such haven; but God kept it green. / Long rest! with belt, and bayonet, and canteen." But for the cannon, which had no peaceful use other than as monuments in town squares, Herman composed "A Grave near Petersburg, Virginia," a delightful bagatelle that deserves to be better known, if only for its display of a fine comic talent otherwise little used in *Battle-Pieces*. A story (told in Herman's note) circulated that the Confederates at Petersburg had buried artillery pieces in graveyards with the intention of disinterring them later. Herman's comedy, which would have been impossible before the war's end, is achieved by treating one of them as a recently buried person and writing an elegy for it. "Daniel Drouth" is named for his metallic barrenness. He symbolizes the worst of war, its true spirit, the Satanic impulse to kill. In life, this "rebel of iron mould" was "full of his fire," a "fire of hell," but now, in death, he lies with "head-board and foot-board duly placed" and covered by a grassy mound. Although "many a true heart—true to the Cause, / Through the blaze of his wrath lies cold," the only atonement required of him is that he remain buried:

May his grave be green—still green
 While happy years shall run;
May none come nigh to disinter
 The—*Buried Gun.*

Many serious considerations are involved in that hope, since Satan remains hidden in his depths awaiting some new convulsion, but to dwell on these would be to violate the poem's carefree spirit.

Suddenly, Strangely, Peace

It was peace, a peace as unsettled and as unsettling after the routines of war as, in 1861, war had been after the routines of peace. It canceled the political controversies that the war had spawned. Now that the issues had been decided by force, it was futile to argue whether or how the war should have been fought or whether or not the South should have remained one nation with the North. Whichever sides of the questions one had espoused, history had provided unambiguous answers. For the same reason, those in the Democratic opposition were no longer Copperheads and traitors, though memory could be long, and every excuse for Draconian abrogations of civil rights, in the North, at least, had disappeared. With them disappeared Dix's secret police and the surveillance of Richard Lathers—and who knows who else?

The political dialogue, bitter and fraught with peril during the war, resumed on more civil terms. If the nation was deeply in debt, nothing could be done except to manage the best way possible. Now that such matters were returned to the traditional forum of political debate, Allan indulged himself by writing Henry Gansevoort a long, pedantic dissertation on the evil of specie payment, which, he said, was another name for universal bankruptcy. Even though the public refused to throw out of office those responsible, eventually there would be a demand for a stable currency, he prophesied.[18] It was an almost forgotten luxury to complain about governmental policies that did not leave thousands dead on battlefields.

Now that slavery had ended, there was no longer a choice to be made between union and emancipation, and many of those who had given first priority to union found that when emancipation was no longer a threat it was acceptable. Even Kate Gansevoort, who still believed that the North should not have intervened in the affairs of the South and that slavery would have died of natural causes within twenty-five years, said that "perhaps it was right to free one part of the darkies of this Continent." For Herman, no change of heart was necessary. To achieve both union and emancipation was an ideal outcome of the war, but with one qualification. He was not prejudiced against blacks, nor was he indifferent to their plight, but the United States had been guilty of many social injustices, of which slavery was only one. To his thinking, the union and its Constitution provided the only framework within which injustice, against blacks and whites alike, could be remedied, and for that reason he had believed that their preservation took precedence over all else. Now he was not certain that emancipation would bring the immediate blessings to the former slaves that many anticipated. In the abstract, he was satisfied with the "mustering out" from servitude of the hordes of Southern blacks, though they were victims as well as beneficiaries of the war. Because their experience had forced them to confront the blackness of darkness, liberty neither atoned for that darkness nor guaranteed them a bright future. While Northern radicals romanticized them as unfallen Adams and Eves, without considering their vulnerability to the challenges and pitfalls of a fallen world that was terra incognita to them, Herman saw them both as patient heirs of a wicked past and as parents of a race which might eventually know a good forever withheld from their elders, whose identities and fates were blighted by their history of thralldom.[19]

For the most part, Herman avoided the issue of slavery. He might not have written any poem at all on the subject had he not attended the National Academy of Design Exhibition held in May and June. It was a large show, made more attractive for Herman because of the association of Allan and

Jennie with it. Hundreds of paintings were hung in the North, South, East, and West Rooms and in a central corridor. It was in the corridor that Herman saw Sanford Gifford's "The Coming Storm," which inspired his poem about Edwin Booth. War illustrators, such as Thomas Nast and Winslow Homer, were represented by camp scenes, while other artists exhibited a large cross section of the most memorable works of a notable era in American art: Albert Bierstadt, Frederick Church, Eastman Johnson, William Sidney Mount, Asher B. Durand, William Bradford, George Innes, William M. Hunt, Jasper Cropsey, Thomas Hicks, and Elihu Vedder, among others.[20]

The paintings by Vedder, which included "The Arab Slave," "Jane Jackson, Formerly a Slave," "Lonely Spring," and "A Lost Mind," hung in the West Room. The *New York Times* critic was both impressed and perplexed by them. He admired their "absolute power," but he was put off by their darkness and by their enigmatic character. About the portrait of Jane Jackson, he decided that "the subject is not a very attractive one, but it is handled with great fidelity and strength." For Herman, the subject *was* attractive, and Vedder's dark vision was preferable to the conventionality of much of the show.

The inspiration for Herman's "'Formerly a Slave': An idealized Portrait, by E. Vedder, in the Spring Exhibition of the National Academy, 1865," then, was a rendering by a painter to whom he was particularly attracted of an old black peanut-seller encountered by Vedder on the streets of New York. Although "the sufferance of her race" is plain in her face, for her "too late deliverance dawns." Like the old crippled slave of "The Scout toward Aldie," she has no youth to squander on dreams, on education, and on personal fulfillment. For many like her, and even much younger, a past of servitude has bred a present of ignorance, dependence, and long-ingrained servility that makes them unemancipated slaves of fate. Even her son (a Union soldier, she told Vedder) may never gain full freedom. But "her children's children they shall know / The good withheld from her" as they break free of the yoke of the American black's special inheritance, and then emancipation will have come to an entire people. Thus from "down the depth of thousand years" she sees the good that is to come—not to her but to hers—and "her dusky face is lit with sober light."

As the many Northern men who had risked life and body on the battlefields, rivers, and oceans sought places in the postwar society, suddenly and ferociously Europe-fever struck the privileged who had remained at home. Kate Gansevoort reported that the bulk of the party that had accompanied her to Henry's camp had sailed for the Old World. Lemuel Shaw followed suit, as did the George Waleses, the Boston friends of Herman and

Lizzie, and Louisa May Alcott. While a new mansion was being constructed for them at Winyah, Richard and Abby Lathers ended the war by voyaging with their oldest daughter, Carrie, to England and France, leaving their relatives to care for the rest of their children. Allan and Jennie Melville, too, were contemplating a voyage.[21]

Herman's family celebrated the late spring, summer, and early fall in the new sunshine of tranquility. There was another innovation, too: Boston and Pittsfield supplanted New York City and Gansevoort as the centers of family activity, with the result that Herman was left almost alone. On the first of May, Commodore Paulding was relieved as commandant of the Brooklyn Navy Yard and work there slowed almost to its prewar pace. Guert received orders from Washington to economize in every area, to buy nothing that was not essential, and to reuse materials wherever possible. A week later, he was detached to await orders, a dignified way of sending him into retirement, and went home to Glens Falls. Then on June 25, his last command, the *Roanoke*, was decommissioned, to lie alongside a pier at the Brooklyn yard, a forlorn monument to his failed career.[22]

In the middle of the spring, Allan sold his house on 35th Street and moved his residence to Arrowhead. Bruce would have to look after the office while the senior partner luxuriated at his country estate, returning to the city occasionally to look in on the practice. At Arrowhead, Allan played the part that in times past Herman had envisioned for himself, the gentleman of leisure who enjoyed the cool weather with a glass of claret at his elbow. In transforming the old farm into a pleasure park, Allan and Jennie were planting Norway pines and fruit trees, laying out new paths, and building a new barn and new outhouses. They were probably redecorating and refurnishing the interior in rustic elegance, too, in anticipation of the

U.S. Frigate *Roanoke,* disarmed and decommissioned, Brooklyn Navy Yard. U.S. Navy Historical Center

many guests they expected. In one of her especially tactless moments, Mother Melville made an invidious comparison between the gentrified Arrowhead and its condition during the years when it had been home to Lizzie and Herman: "Arrowhead looks like a different place, it is now a beautiful place."[23]

One of Allan's first guests was young Miss Rachel Turner, of Savannah, Georgia, one of the many Southerners who fled the ruin and privation of home for the humming prosperity of New York City. So impressed was Herman by this Confederate lady in Puritan New England that he wrote about her in his poem "Iris (1865)," included in his unpublished collection "Weeds and Wildings" (276–78). A beautiful rainbow brought by the peace to "our mountains," this "loveliest invader" reverses the decree of history by conquering three New England colonels so that "three disenslavers / themselves embrace a chain!" But she has seen the darkness of war, leading the narrator to ask, "Was your gaiety your courage, / And levity its form?" No Puritan colonel can have her: it is her fate to die as the rainbow does, won by the "ravisher" who bears her to his "fastness" while her wooers are left with "tear-drops in the grass."[24]

Tom, too, was rarely present in the city. He spent some of the summer alternating between Gansevoort and Arrowhead and some of it in West Virginia, where John Hoadley had interested him in the petroleum speculations. One had to listen to John's advice—it was the year in which he was appointed a trustee of the new Massachusetts Institute of Technology. Through this gamble, John must have hoped to mend his fortunes, which had not recovered from the losses caused by secession, while Tom must have wished to multiply the savings he had accumulated during his years at sea. Family gossip had it that the two were making money "very rapidly."[25]

With Arrowhead now in favor, in the early summer Gansevoort was relatively deserted. Fanny had intended to return from New Bedford, bringing Helen Griggs with her, but she decided to remain with Kate Hoadley, who was pregnant. Mother Melville and Gus had some company when John Hoadley, with his two daughters, set out to visit his mother in Rochester, New York, after which the three intended to spend a few days in Gansevoort. On their way west they stopped in Albany, where they called on the Gansevoort family. Kate reported that John was "very deaf & very ultra," still the radical. While the Hoadleys were staying at the Temperance House that night, Minnie became ill, panicking John into rushing her to the haven of Gansevoort. The three remained for eight days, during which Lottie, too, fell ill, but Mother Melville was unimpressed, deciding that "they ate some thing that disagreed with them."[26]

While Allan entertained at Arrowhead, his girls spent much of the summer visiting relatives. Sometime around the middle of July, Allan and Jennie took two of them to New Bedford to visit Kate and Fanny and then went on to Brookline to leave them with Helen Griggs. Tom brought Allan's daughter Lucy to vacation at Gansevoort and later brought Florence and Kitty for a similar visit.[27]

Long after its end, the war finally took a member of Herman's family. On March 18, just as hostilities had been drawing to an end, Mary Thurston had presented Henry Thurston with a new daughter, Mary Bankhead. Three and a half months later, Henry was ordered to close Grant Hospital. But during his long service in the west and in Virginia he had contracted Bright's disease, and by July 27, when his mustering-out papers arrived, he was too ill to be informed. On August 2, he died at the New Rochelle home of his brother Charles, as much a victim of the war as any casualty on the field. Herman and Allan would have attended his funeral, if they were able to.[28]

The Poet at Work

Herman and Lizzie may have done some traveling in the early summer, since the two boys vacationed in the Boston area, Stanny with Helen Griggs[29] and Malcolm, on the last vacation of his youth, with Hope Shaw, most likely. While he was in New York City, Herman had the company of Gus for two days when, on the afternoon of Thursday, June 29, she burst in at his home with a crucifixion in her face. The servant problem in Gansevoort had become so desperate that she had been obliged to rush to the city in hopes of remedying it. The next day she was fortunate enough to find an immigrant couple just off the ship from Germany and took them home with her.

A few days later, the city celebrated its first Fourth of July after the victory. The holiday began on the third, when Wall Street and the schools played hooky and storekeepers wished that they had, too, the streets were so deserted. The day itself began with an artillery salute from the Battery, followed at noon by a serenade by the Trinity Church bells. Then came the parade, a raggle-taggle affair, since many of the soldiers in the veteran regiments were more anxious to go home than they were to march. However, some individual soldiers fell into ranks together with veterans of the War of 1812. The parade route passed near Herman's home, going up Madison Avenue from 23rd Street, then across 42nd Street, down Fifth Avenue, and up 14th Street to Union Square. At 3:30 in the afternoon there was a concert in Central Park, but the biggest daytime entertainment was at the customhouse. There the rotunda was decorated lavishly, with bunting and statues and a number of dedicatory inscriptions, lists of hero-generals, including Joe Hooker but omitting Ambrose Burnside, lists of heroes of lower rank, including Lieutenant Cushing, and lists of fallen generals, including McPherson and Lyon. Over all were slogans in large letters, "Freedom," "Victory," "Union," and "Peace." Those four words said everything that there was to say for this holiday. In the evening, there were fireworks displays throughout the city, including one at Madison Square. Herman and Lizzie had to celebrate the day without Tom and Allan, who were both at Arrowhead.[30]

Herman did not spend all of his hours working on his poetry. Although the city was "deserted," he had friends there. Another acquaintance was added when, shortly after Independence Day, Charles Brewster arrived to stay with Bruce. Very soon after Charles had been ordered from the Army of the Shenandoah to the local army headquarters at Richmond, he had been arrested in Washington for visiting without the required pass. Probably drunk and certainly disorderly, he told the patrol officer "that he would be damned if it [the pass] was [required], and that he would be damned if he would consider himself under arrest, nor would he report." On soberer consideration, he reported to the authorities, asserting that he had meant no disrespect to the arresting officer, that his statement on that occasion had been misunderstood, and that his orders to Washington had been left with the Commissary General of Subsistence. The Provost Marshal responded by turning the case over to Charles's superiors with a recommendation that he be discharged from the service.[31]

Relieved of his duties, temporarily, he thought, Charles brought his clerk to the city, where he made Bruce spend most of his time helping to make up his commissary accounts. With Bruce now an unofficial member of the family, Herman must have heard about Charles's adventures in the Cavalry Corps and in the Valley campaign, about Charles's escape from captivity the preceding fall, and about Lee's surrender. Then Charles made a futile voyage to New Orleans to join General Sheridan's expedition to Texas, only to receive the order mustering him out there. He returned to idle away his days at the Brewster family home in Goshen, New York, concocting get-rich-quick schemes in which Henry Gansevoort was to have a part.[32]

Around midsummer, Herman visited Gansevoort for several weeks while Lizzie, with Bessie and Fanny, probably visited Boston. Gansevoort was quiet except for Allan's three girls, the kind of quiet that would have allowed him to devote some of his time to his poems. But the visit was, after all, social. On August 15, the whole household went to a Sunday school picnic in the grove owned by Peter Gansevoort. It was a large affair, attended by 1,500 people, Mother Melville estimated, with young girls dressed in white frocks and entertainment provided by the red-coated Fort Edward Cornet

Band. A lavish refection of cakes, fruits, and nuts was served, but the affair ended at three o'clock when a storm commenced. With the sky suddenly black and sand blowing, Herman and the others "blew home for the wind was fair," just escaping torrents of rain.[33]

Solicitous about Guert's health, Herman must have visited Glens Falls during those weeks to see him, as Allan did a month or so later. Herman would have found the Curtises in the midst of a summer of discontent. Kate had been ill, a result, her physician said, of breathing the fumes of the lime kilns in the vicinity. Earlier in the summer, Mary accompanied her to Clarendon Springs, Vermont, not far from the place where Uncle Wessel had lived out his last years, for a change of air, but because temporary measures gave only temporary relief, all of the Curtises were now planning to board for the winter in Charlestown, a village on the New Hampshire side of the Connecticut River, and perhaps to buy a home there. Guert should not have had to move, situated as he was in the fine home that he had prepared for his retirement, but with his health deteriorating rapidly he decided to accompany Kate. With this in view, he sold his house for the considerable sum of $10,000 and disposed of most of his furniture, retaining only enough for the room he expected to occupy in the Curtis home. Soon after he reached Charleston, he became a semi-invalid with "water on the heart," the illness that had taken Leonard.[34]

While Herman was vacationing, the Albany Gansevoorts embarked on a trip through New England, Uncle Peter's biggest adventure since his return from Europe in 1860, in celebration of the salvation of the republic for which the hero of Fort Stanwix had fought. In Boston they visited the Griggses (and Stanny and Milie Melville) and called on Hope Shaw (and probably Malcolm), the widow of "my friend Chief Justice Shaw," as Uncle Peter put it. After Hope had gratified Uncle Peter by her curiosity about Henry, the Gansevoorts went on to Portsmouth, New Hampshire, where they inspected the "Navy Dock," and then on to Rye Beach to visit Fort Constitution. There "General" Gansevoort's vanity was satisfied by a salute from a band and an honor guard. Then it was back to Albany.[35]

Around August 20, Lizzie, Bessie, and little Fanny were scheduled to arrive in Gansevoort, bringing Allan's daughter Milie with them. If they came there from Boston, they may have traveled part of the way with Sam Shaw, who was to visit Arrowhead at about that time en route to the White Mountains. Assuming that Lizzie and the girls arrived when expected, Herman had about two weeks of vacation time remaining before his return to the city. That would have been two weeks of surviving six young girls. On or before September 8, he took his family back to the city, where Lizzie reported that he was unusually well after his visit. Stanny and Malcolm must have returned home by themselves—Malcolm was growing up.[36]

The General Lieutenant

When he arrived in New York, Herman found Henry Gansevoort there, staying with Bruce. The voting investigations had ended with the fighting, and while Mosby had practiced law in Culpepper, Henry had fought to salvage what glory he could from the war. In vain he attempted to have his regiment assigned to Sheridan's Texas expedition in the hope that something in the line of military distinction might turn up there. Then his brigade was broken up. General Gamble returned home with the 8th Illinois, leaving behind a damaging official evaluation that Henry managed to suppress, and the 13th and 16th New York were merged into a single regiment. Wanting brevet promotions in both the volunteers and the regulars, and wanting command of the consolidated regiment, Henry nagged his father mercilessly. Using all of his influence, Uncle Peter got him a brevet to brigadier general of volunteers but not a regular army brevet. The family was thrilled at his new rank, however honorary. Kate called him "Genl Gansevoort 3d!" and Mother Melville remarked that "Henrys vocation seems to be that of a soldier—May he in God's own time, become a soldier of the Cross." That seemed unlikely. About the regimental command, nothing could be done. That left Henry awaiting orders back to the 5th Artillery. They were issued on July 28, but he managed to remain in Washington in charge of some men and equipment. Then on August 27, he was again ordered to report to his battery, but he obtained a twenty-day leave to transact "important Private business."[37]

Bruce was just back from Arrowhead after ten days of flirting with Rachel Turner. Both Bruce and Allan promised Henry that he, too, could court the Southern belle when he visited Pittsfield, but before he could bask in her Confederate charms he was forced to return to Washington. Two of his three horses, his bay, Rouser, and his blood stallion, had been seized and were in the custody of the authorities. The problem was that in Mosby country horses had been stolen and restolen, captured and recaptured, hidden and found, and stabled by people who then claimed them as compensation for the fodder they had consumed. Though Henry had paid for his, everyone who had ever had anything to do with them claimed them. After much work and some stealth, he retrieved them and shipped them to New York.[38]

While he had been away, his father had fallen ill with dysentery, but that was not reason enough for him to visit Albany on his return. He recovered some of his belongings, which had been scattered around the city, but his civilian clothes had been eaten by moths and the price of replacements shocked him. "I fear that I shall have to emigrate to some isle of the ocean where native buff is fashionable," he quipped, taking his cue from *Typee*. Then the men of the 13th New York arrived to muster out, requiring his ceremonial presence.[39]

After Henry's return from salvaging his horses Herman was able to socialize with him. It was his first chance to see his cousin with the stars on his shoulders, which Henry was not above wearing, and to congratulate him on his brevet. It was also another opportunity to learn about the late days of the war. Henry could tell him about the end of the hostilities, of the deaths of Lincoln and Booth, of the grand review, and of the trial of the conspirators. Herman was proud of Henry, but he must also have been staggered by his cousin's churning discontent. Uncle Peter had prevented him from achieving greater glory by refusing to arrange his transfer to the victorious army, Henry felt, he had been persecuted mercilessly, he did not yet have his regular army brevets, and he thought that he might leave the army to pursue a career in politics. Was this the kind of self-sacrificing idealism that would reform and inspirit the new America? Did one fight a war for national survival only to grasp at the main chance, to be in the right place at the right time through the right kind of political influence? Herman must have harked back to Hawthorne's prediction: "What an incalculable preponderance will there be of military titles and pretensions for at least half a century to come! . . . military notoriety, will be the measure of all claims to civil distinction. One bullet-headed general will succeed another in the Presidential chair; and veterans will hold the offices at home and abroad, and sit in Congress and the state legislatures, and fill the avenues of public life." And yet there had been moments when this spoiled young man had fought as well as any other.[40]

Henry indulged his appetites, feasting on oysters for the first time since becoming a colonel and pursuing women. Georgie Bedell was there, and a friend found him another "pretty girl": "I have the address of a dev'lish nice girl here in N.Y. for you. She is stylish & *climbs right up*." Henry appreciated young women who climbed right up.[41]

Finally, Henry reported to his battery without having had a chance to test his luck with Miss Turner. Again he was a first lieutenant, wearing the single silver bar when on his post but changing to the single silver star as soon as he was off duty. He was in temporary command of the battery, and rumor had it going to the Southern coast, which he dreaded. "To be saved from all the dangers of the field and to perish perhaps by some deadly malaise or pestilence amid the everglades of the South is hardly desirable," he wrote. However, the battery was sent to Fortress Monroe, instead.[42]

Herman must have been amused when Bruce unexpectedly returned to Arrowhead. Henry's servant Moses and the three horses arrived at the New York City piers, whence they were to go to Allan's farm. As might have been expected, Allan was too busy to help, so the responsibility for them devolved upon Henry's faithful friend. Bruce decided that the former slave could not manage the trip up the Hudson Valley and across to Pittsfield by himself, so he had to ride one of the horses while Moses rode another, the two men leading the third. On his departure from Hudson, New York, the next day, Bruce must have felt as though he were back in the cavalry, and by the time he reached Arrowhead that night he must have been certain of it.[43]

Bruce found Allan, Jennie, Mother Melville, and especially Mattie Curtis there to soothe his way-weariness, and Mattie did the job so successfully that he remained for a number of days. Mattie had just graduated from an exclusive school in New Haven and was, as Mother Melville described her, "a charming girl 17 years old, very quiet and modest, a splendid performer on the piano." Before long, Mattie was riding Rouser with Bruce at her side. Rouser's checkered career, which had included service in both the Union and Confederate armies, had never before taken such a bizarre turn as when the beast who had galloped with Mosby was cantered by a young lady whose thoughts were centered on the "Broadway swell" beside her. Bruce thought Mattie pretty and Mother Melville noticed that "Mr Brewster is very careful & attentive to the ladies under his charge." Kate Gansevoort was quick to suspect romance. Was Bruce a marrying man? she asked. She had always feared that he was a drinker.[44]

On October 14, toward the end of Bruce's stay at Arrowhead, Frank Bartlett married Agnes Pomeroy. What might under other circumstances have been the wedding of a young man twenty-five years of age and of good family, perhaps a junior executive or a lawyer beginning his career, to a well-endowed young woman, was instead the marriage of Brevet Major General Bartlett to a woman who had been forced by war to bear the constant threat of a tragic end to her romance and to nurse her fiancé through the wounds of battle and the fever of prison. With his artificial leg, his shattered hand, his scarred brow, his nearly constant pain, and his memory of captivity, and with her thankfulness that at least something of him had been spared for her, the two were barred forever from that green and growing world created for the young. "There came— / Ah heaven! what *truth* to him." But they were determined to make the most of what bits and shards of joy remained for them. Frank had been permitted to retain his volunteer commission for the present, and on October 18 the two, accompanied by the Pomeroy family and their servant, left New York for Europe. Perhaps Herman was at the pier to bid bon voyage to his College Colonel.[45]

As the vacation season ended, Herman found himself amid a sudden swirl of relatives. Tom popped in and out between trips to West Virginia, and during the first week in October, Richard, Abby, and Carrie Lathers returned from Europe. On October 17, Allan, Uncle Peter, and Aunt Susan appeared. Allan had taken Mother Melville and Mattie Curtis back to Gansevoort and had then steamed down the Hudson River with his aunt and uncle. The Gansevoorts, who had come to celebrate Peter's recovery from his dysentery, were followed in a few days by Kate Gansevoort and Anna Lansing, escorted by Ed Lansing, who intended to seek his fortune in the city. After her arrival, Kate surprised Allan by appearing with Tom at Mrs. Hoffman's to visit Allan's girls, who had been put there to board.[46]

While Allan and Jennie made preparations for a trip to Europe and the Middle East, they stayed at the 19th Street house of a young lady from Raleigh, North Carolina, another refugee. While they were out of the country, Herman and Lizzie would look in on the girls at Mrs. Hoffman's, but the girls would spend the holidays at the Lathers estate. Prior to leaving, Allan sent a last-minute reminder to Henry Gansevoort that few things in life are free, asking him "what you propose in reference to those beasts and man [at Arrowhead]?" He explained (just before leaving on a grand tour that Herman and Lizzie could never have afforded) that he was no "nabob," that great demands were made upon his purse, including the education of his children. The costs of hay and feed were high, and if Henry wished his horses—and Moses, presumably—to stay at Arrowhead for the winter, he would have to pay for their upkeep. In response, Henry arrived in Pittsfield on November 2. It took only a day to straighten out the economics of the horses—together with Moses, the colt was to be shipped to Fortress Monroe, while Rouser and Beauty were to remain where they were. After that Henry went to Albany for a few days before returning to the city for the balance of his fifteen-day leave. Just how he entertained himself, between Herman, Allan, Bruce, Ed Lansing, Georgie Bedell, and the girl who climbed right up, is unknown. On the tenth of November, the family saw Allan and Jennie off for Havre and Brest on the *Europa*. Then when his leave expired Henry hurried back to Fortress Monroe.[47]

Malice toward None

After Lee's capitulation, many Northerners had cried for retribution, at first because of their horror at Booth's crime and their suspicion that a Confederate plot was behind it, then because they sought revenge for the damage done to heart, body, and mind by the war. When Henry Gansevoort invited John Hoadley to visit him at Fortress Monroe, John demurred but added, "I *would* go, to see Jeff. hung. . . . For my part, I would certainly hang Jeff. Davis, not because he is the most guilty, but because he is the most conspicuously guilty." John's humanity showed through when he admitted in the same letter that he would not mind seeing the former Confederate president receive a merciful pardon, but the hatred shared by hundreds of thousands of returned Union soldiers and sailors and by the loved ones of those who did not return was unqualified. Satan won the day with such radicals as Emerson, who enumerated the real and supposed crimes of the Southerners and condemned their very souls: "I charge Southern Morality with starving prisoners of war; with massacring surrendered men; with the St. Albans' raid; with the plundering railroad passenger-trains in peaceful districts; with plots of burning cities; with advertising a price for the life of Lincoln, Butler, Garrison, & others; with assassination of the President, & of Seward; with attempts to import the yellow fever into New York; with the cutting up the bones of our soldiers to make ornaments, & drinking-cups of their skulls." He did not exempt Lee: "General Grant's terms certainly look a little too easy, as foreclosing any action hereafter to convict Lee of treason, and I fear that the high tragic historic justice which the nation with severest consideration should execute, will be softened & dissipated & toasted away at dinner-tables." Originating in such self-righteousness, one's own idea of justice became the "high" justice.[48]

Despite the debasing influence of four Anarch years, others were tolerant of the defeated. Although Whittier had hated slavery passionately, he could still believe that "it would be sad now to have our good cause stained with cruelty and revenge." Contemplating the problems of the postwar period, James Russell Lowell demonstrated a crabbed generosity by forgiving the conservatives of the North for their wartime tolerance of the South: many opponents of the Republican war policies had been, he said, "moderate and modest men, many enlightened," who had not deserved the opprobrium of the Copperhead epithet. "It is precisely this class," he wrote, "dispassionate and moderate in their opinions, whose help we shall need in healing the wounds of war and giving equanimity to our counsels."[49]

The generosity of Herman and his conservative relatives and friends required no effort; they had opposed the Confederacy, but they had never lost their regard for its citizens. When the danger to the union ended, they embraced their Southern brethren once more. That was true of Herman in the best sense; it was true of the Albany Gansevoorts, but with an ugly qualification—they were still prejudiced against the African. When Henry offered to send his parents a black waiter, they hired an Irishman instead because, they said, the Irish women of their "downstairs" would not accept a black. At Fortress Monroe, Henry's prejudices were constantly renewed. He reported that the summer malarial conditions had been exacerbated by the 20,000 or so freedmen who had taken up residence in the vicinity. "These are hardly, since thrown on their own exertions to be found as cleanly and orderly as before." On April 16, 1866, a group of blacks in Norfolk paraded with muskets and attacked local whites, killing several, he heard. The next day he arrived there in command of a detachment of artillery, only to be greeted by volleys of bullets and random sniping. He was ready to "give the good people of Norfolk a taste of iron pills in the shape of canister." Later, he reported that detachments of troops were being sent from Fortress Monroe to various places to suppress interracial gunfights, though he admitted that "nobody is ever hurt." Thinking of the radicals in Washington, Bruce worried, tongue in cheek, that Henry's treatment of the black participants might damage him. "I hope that you did not hurt any of them," he wrote. "If you did you are little better than a dead duck." Henry was not amused: "God grant that the black fog that hangs over the destinies of the South may be speedily dispelled."[50]

But as Emerson had feared, time brought moderation, as was evidenced in the treatment of Jefferson Davis at Fortress Monroe. Initially, he had been chained and guarded by six sentries in his immediate vicinity, a line of them outside his casemate, guards in the casemates on either side, guards on the parapet above, and guards across the moat. Within Herman's own family, the man had been anathema. Kate Gansevoort had wished to see "that *arch traitor* Jeff Davis suffer for his crime—the blackest on Earth," and Henry had referred to him as "the fallen Lucifer of the rebellion." But by the time Henry fell into the habit of visiting with the old West Pointer, Davis's shackles had been removed, his guards had dwindled to a few, and he had been placed in healthier quarters—though pestilential enough to keep Henry, his next-door neighbor, constantly ill. Davis's courtliness and grace in adversity won Henry's admiration, so much so that the young man described him in flattering terms and conversed with him on matters that prudence did not allow him to commit to paper, even to his own family. Eventually, the former United States secretary of war was reminiscing with the young lieutenant about the old days when he had exercised authority over the fort in which he was now confined. "Poor Jeff," Henry wrote, "he bears his prison life patiently." He still wanted to see Davis tried and sentenced, but only so that treason could be defined and future rebellions discouraged. As time went by, Davis was paroled within the battlements so he could exercise and he was allowed to live with his wife, Varina. "He is feeble," Henry wrote, "but will I think soon revive."[51]

Herman worried that recalling the warfare in *Battle-Pieces* might rekindle passions. To guard against that, he muted phrases, descriptions, and attitudes that might have seemed provocative. But an event that occurred in the fall of 1865 caused him to do more, to end the battle section of the book with several poems which dramatize the national nature of the tragedy and advocate a future America free of interregional passion and strife. He knew that fierce enmities between the two sides were inescapable and that it was the function of the poet, as an unacknowledged legislator of the culture, to mitigate them.

After his return from Europe, Richard Lathers ended the war as he had sought to forestall it, by attempting to reconcile the two hostile peoples with whom he identified himself. He arranged social gatherings at Winyah and elsewhere "to bring the estranged of the two sections of our country together." He entertained jointly Northerners and former Confederates who had shared experiences and interests, in the hope that they would become friends or resume friendships "over their Madeira." He included such Union officers as Generals McClellan, Dan Sickles, Dix, Bartlett, and McDowell, and such Confederate generals as Joseph E. Johnston and John C. Breckinridge. He invited William Cullen Bryant to meet the Southern poet James R. Randall, and Horatio Seymour and ex-Governor Clifford of Massachusetts to meet Governor McGrath of South Carolina and Governor Gordon of Georgia. He invited Jefferson Davis's daughter Winnie to meet a host of Northern dignitaries, and he invited Robert E. Lee's daughter Mary to meet Grant's daughter-in-law. He was doing precisely what Emerson feared, softening and dissipating enmities by toasting them away at his dinner table. Quite possibly, Herman attended a number of these affairs—meetings with McClellan and "dark" Breckinridge would cast new light on *Battle-Pieces*—but, according to Lathers, he was certainly invited to one of them to meet William Gilmore Simms.[52]

The meeting occurred sometime during the month or so from late October to the end of November 1865. When Simms came north as a commissioner for the Charleston Masons, charged with literally begging their Northern Masonic brethren for aid, Richard invited him to a reconciliation dinner, probably in New York City. Richard gave Simms some literary assistance by inviting a number of prominent editors, and he also invited the mayor of the city, the president of the Chamber of Commerce, and some members of Congress. But in terms of regional symmetry, the most important guest was Herman. The two authors were not unknown to each other: Simms appears to have reviewed Herman's works favorably, though he had objected to the antislavery attitudes that he had found in them. Although the two authors had probably not met before, this encounter left them on terms of cordiality.[53]

Simms gave a speech in which he recalled the wartime complaints in Southern newspapers about Richard's loyalist activities in the North and the glee in the South when Northern newspapers copied the complaints with their own abuse appended, and he reported his discovery in Washington of the wartime surveillance to which Richard had been subjected. That was what Richard remembered of the occasion, but Simms must also have spoken, formally and informally, about his own desperate circumstances and the widespread suffering throughout the South. Whatever he said, his experiences and his plight brought to life in Herman's imagination the misery of the defeated. Simms had been an outspoken supporter of slavery and a strong advocate of secession, and he had proposed measures for reducing Fort Sumter and had watched enthusiastically as the bombardment had taken place, but he had paid a terrible price. During the war, and for reasons unconnected with it, he had lost two children, his wife, and his plantation house; but he had also nearly lost his eldest son, Gilmore, when the young man was terribly wounded in battle, he had lost his new house and his library of 10,700 books when they were torched by Sherman's marauders, and he had watched the senseless immolation of Columbia, South Carolina. Now a white-bearded mendicant, he owned next to nothing, and, like his children, he was living in a garret half-filled with lumber, without adequate clothing, furniture, and utensils. He had been able to make the trip north only because his expenses were paid by the desperate Masons of South Carolina, and he was able to report that the poet Henry Timrod was literally starving in Columbia. In the North, in addition to his Masonic mission, he was attempting to find whatever employment he could for his failing talent in order to provide himself with necessities.[54]

The meeting did not revolutionize Herman's attitude toward the South, but it did alert him to the acuteness of Southern sufferings and of their undoubted Americanness, if he needed such a reminder, and it did tell him once more that Anarch war had shattered Southern families as much as it had families of the North, though with a difference. Bereavement in victory was soul-wrenching; bereavement in defeat and humiliation was soul-destroying. For that reason, Southern war poems, which Simms was gathering for publication, sometimes conveyed a special pathos which victory denied Northern poets, as in the dignity and power achieved at the end, at least, of Mary Ashley Townsend's simple "A Georgia Volunteer":

He sleeps—what need to question now
If he were wrong or right?
He knows, ere this, whose cause was just
In God the Father's sight.
He wields no warlike weapons now,
Returns no foeman's thrust;
Who but a coward would revile
An honest soldier's dust?

Roll, Shenandoah, proudly roll
Adown thy rocky glen;
Above thee lies the grave of one
Of Stonewall Jackson's men.
Beneath the cedar and the pine,
In solitude austere,
Unknown, unnamed, forgotten lies,
A Georgia Volunteer.[55]

Such heartbroken energy was unavailable to Herman, but he could still hope to educate his readers about the dual nature of war's tragedy.

He began with the Confederate soldiers. Lee's army had been an array of formidable men at arms one moment, a pathetic column of defeated parolees trudging home the next. Herman examined their plight in "The Released Rebel Prisoner (June, 1865)," in which a Confederate soldier who, having endured imprisonment in the North, passes through New York City on his way home. There he is awe-struck by the vast crowds of Northerners whose very numbers had crushed the Confederacy. "Armies he's seen—the herds of war, / But never such swarms of men / As now in the Nineveh of the North." Dimly he begins to understand that he had been seduced by pleas of a just cause and promises of success in arms, that the pride that called him, the magnetism of the leaders who drew his steel to them, was a cruel deception that propelled him into a hopeless conflict.

His is an educated heart, one isolated "like a mountain-pool / Where no man passes by." He knows the cruel cost to the South in lost leaders like Hill, Ashby, and Stuart, and he sees the Northern soldiers—Americans, like him—healthy, well-clothed, and flushed with victory, returning from the destruction of his home to the arms of their women. But the defeated, "jail-worn," has no home and no brothers to whom to return, only the drear "cypress-moss" of his memories and a land bereaved, pillaged, starving, and despairing. Nothing invites him to remain in the city, where he is invisible to his former enemies, nor is there anything remaining to draw him back to the ruined land of his birth. Such was Herman's compassion, and such was his sense that the defeated Southerners were his kinsmen.

With colleges few and education treasured, the demagogue could fuel the fires of Northern hatred by bemoaning the loss of young students and graduates. Thus Julia Ward Howe indicted the South in her "Harvard Student's Song": "Oh! give them back, thou bloody breast of Treason, / They were our own, the darlings of our hearts."[56] But in his "On the Slain Collegians" (not a memorial but a battle-poem) Herman mourned the losses of both sides—in Henry Gansevoort's Princeton class more graduates had fought for the Confederacy than for the Union. Herman's poem is the antithesis of Howe's, contemplative, not shrill, philosophic, not angry. His college students, North and South, answered the same call, even if duty for one spoke through "the mask of Cain" and duty for the other was "Truth's sacred cause." Each was "enwrapped" in the fires of his own "social laws, / Friendship and kin, and by-gone days— / Vows, kisses." "What could they else," Herman asked, "North or South?" Even if one was right and the other wrong, "they both were young."

These were the special youth, the boys who, through the liberal arts and the nurture of college learned not the "underminings deep" of the world but rather the calm surface which "gives sunniness to the face." When they murdered each other, they were the best responding to the best, to the "golden mottoes" they had been given. What can we learn from them? That "the heavens all parts assign" and that these "striplings" had borne "their fated parts" well: their ends had been predestined. Further, their lives, like that of Charles Russell Lowell, had ended before they could be corroded by experience: they

> Never felt life's care or cloy.
> Each bloomed and died an unabated Boy. . . .
> They knew the joy, but leaped the grief,
> Like plants that flower ere comes the leaf—
> Which storms lay low in kindly doom,
> And kill them in their flush of bloom.

They can never be flogged by care and corrupted by the world, their autumns can never harvest the bitter fruits of wrinkles, cankers, disappointments, disillusionments, temptations, and falls—like the youths on Keats's Grecian urn, they are young fauns frozen forever in their Golden Age, never to be suborned by the direr knowledge.

"Rebel Color-bearers at Shiloh: A plea against the vindictive cry raised by civilians shortly after the surrender at Appomattox" is a direct response to hatemongers like Emerson and Howe. It was inspired by an anecdote of the Battle of Shiloh, found in *The Rebellion Record*, which must have reminded Herman of the Confederate order at Port Hudson not to fire at Frank Bartlett.

As he tells it in his note, a Union colonel, pressed hard by the enemy, ordered his sharpshooters not to fire on Confederate color-bearers who deliberately exposed themselves to danger because "they're too brave fellows to be killed." Herman's point was that if the heroic qualities of the Southerners deserved admiration in the heat of war, so much the more should the conqueror value them in the cool of peace.

The scene is of the precise type that appealed to Herman most. These Confederates, "martyrs for the Wrong," stood, like Farragut lashed to the mast, unprotected against the sleet of fire. (Herman still preferred frank bravery above prudence, Admiral Nelson above Captain Vere.) The poem begins with an admiring depiction of these men who, wrong in their cause, are right in their courage. The Union colonel who refused to harm them was also courageous: "He could dare / Strike up the leveled rifle there." Lest we forget, the poem says, the bloody days of Shiloh, of Stonewall charging, of McClellan invading the Peninsula, of Thomas holding fast at Chickamauga, and of the "cypress wreath" of the Wilderness. Now that the "daring color-bearers drop their flags, / And yield," should the North open fire on them? "Shall nobleness in victory less aspire / Than in reverse? Spare Spleen her ire, / And think how Grant met Lee." The point is made. Confederate courage in war should be matched by Northern courage in peace.

In the sense that it defines the problem of dealing with the postwar South, the final poem of this ilk, "Magnanimity Baffled," is the most likely to have been inspired by Herman's meeting with Simms. Except for the last line, it is a brief dramatic monologue. In a gesture of magnanimity, "the Victor bold," the only name given him, offers his hand to a recumbent Southerner who is given no name at all. Even when it is refused, he persists as a victor should: "I honor you; / Man honors man." Still unable to evoke a response, he asks, "Yet am I held a foe?" Willing to go the final distance, he grasps the hand of his former foe only to find that he has been speaking to a corpse. In this pointed allegory, the narrator represents the North at its generous best. By demonstrating his desire for renewed brotherhood, he satisfies the requirement of the "Rebel Color-Bearers at Shiloh" that grudges be forgotten. But the noblest gesture may be an empty one. Like Bartleby, the Southerner is beyond generosity, having perished before the cosmic wall of despair. How can one clasp the hand that one has destroyed? With slavery dead, with the social structure a rubble, and with an entire people humiliated, pauperized, and starved, what response to the offer of reconciliation is possible? The South must first be revived, brought back from the dead, rebuilt in society and government and production and distribution and self-respect without any thought of reciprocity: then there will be a living hand to grasp—in equality. Ah rebel! Ah humanity!

Chapter Nine

The Bard in Winter

As the year of triumph ended and 1866 began, Herman had been working to assemble his book for some seven or eight months. With Allan, Jennie, and Henry Gansevoort away, and with Tom occupied elsewhere much of the time, the city was an even quieter garret for a working poet than it had been. There were still distractions, however, periodic visits from family members passing through town, Allan's girls to look in on, and some nearby family members—the de Marinis, the Latherses and the Thurstons—to see occasionally.

He still had his old friends—Evert Duyckinck, Henry T. Tuckerman, and such—in the city. There were also acquaintances outside of his family and the literati. Titus Munson Coan had returned to his home on 5th Avenue, and there was Bruce, who, with both Henry Gansevoort and Allan away, must have turned to Herman for consolation. By this time, Bruce was not only a possible match for Mattie Curtis, as Kate Gansevoort thought, but he was also intimate enough with the family to call Tom by his first name.[57]

The Lansing brothers were in and out of town. While for several years there had been only two of them in Albany, Abe and Will, suddenly there were four. Ed ended his service in Washington with a relapse of malaria, then came home just before the middle of October 1865. He was at loose ends. Impatient with the slower rhythms of upstate Albany, he moved to New York City, where he stayed in Bruce's rooms and operated a shooting gallery before selling it and returning home. But with Albany no more appealing than it had been, he returned to secure a position as a clerk in a brokerage house. During this period, his brother, John T. Lansing, returned from Peru for a three-and-a-half-month visit to his native land. Herman must have seen John when all four Lansing brothers were in the city together, and he must also have seen quite a bit of Ed. But however much he may have been distracted by the presence of these friends, he had experimented with the isolation of Arrowhead and he preferred the city. At least Christmas was quiet—Herman gave his children volumes of *Harper's New Monthly Magazine*, which probably meant far more to Malcolm than to little Fanny and more, overall, to the giver than to the recipients.[58]

As his work on the poems neared completion, Herman succumbed to the nervous intensity that his family had come to expect when he was writing. It was this that he displayed at a Sunday evening reception at the home of Alice and Phoebe Cary, famed New York literary hostesses. It took place while he "was at work on his *Battle-Pieces*," probably during these winter months, since that was the most active season for city society. Although he disliked his reputation as the man who had lived with cannibals, he staged the kind of performance that had amazed the Hawthornes. It was thrilling, precisely the kind of moment that his acquaintances hoped for. During it, he returned to his late teens, aboard the *St. Lawrence* sailing for England and then ashore adventuring in Liverpool and London. The climax came when, "in true sailor fashion, and with picturesque detail," and with none of the stiffness that had chilled some of his lectures, he narrated for his rapt audience (with more skill than he had ever managed in his books, one thought) the story of his voyage to the South Seas in the *Acushnet*. Back went his mind to the "coarse brutality" of Captain Valentine Pease and to his desertion at Nukuheva with Toby Greene, and finally to the adventure that his auditors savored most, his voluptuous life among the Typees. It was a rare treat.[59]

No one outside of Herman's household knew that he was writing *Battle-Pieces* until the middle of January 1866, when the Harpers, who had agreed to publish it, began to preview some of the lyrics in *Harper's*. When Mother Melville found out, she alerted the rest so that they would not miss the anonymous "The March to the Sea" when it appeared. Kate Gansevoort thought it "very inspiriting," and John Hoadley thought it "splendid." John was so pleased that he read it aloud to Kate, the Hoadley girls, and his two visitors, Mother Melville and Tom. In subsequent months, *Harper's* published several other pieces, "The Cumberland" in mid-February, "Philip" ("Sheridan at Cedar Creek") in mid-March, "Chattanooga" in mid-May, and "Gettysburg" in mid-June.[60]

In the fall, both Herman and Tom had urged Mother Melville to visit the city with Gus, but the two women had decided to remain in Gansevoort until the end of the year—Gus wished to continue her Sunday School until then, and Mother Melville secretly preferred to go to New Bedford to see her new grandson, Francis W. Hoadley, who had arrived on October 24. The result was that on January 11, Tom brought them to Albany for an overnight visit with the Gansevoorts, after which they left for Boston. For the moment, Herman's mother and all of his siblings who were still in the country were congregated in and around the Boston area. Tom spent two weeks there, seeing the local relatives before going to New York on January 26 for a two-week visit with Herman, but well before the two weeks were up, he left for Parkersburgh, West Virginia. Things were not going well for him; from the tone of his letters, Kate Gansevoort surmised that his speculations had been less successful than they had promised to be. Gus spent less than a month in Brookline and New Bedford before returning alone to Gansevoort; Mother Melville stayed in the area about a week longer than that, most of the time in New Bedford with the Hoadleys and their baby, but visiting around Boston, as well. It was a special treat to have Mary

Captain Thomas Melville, Arrowhead, July 1865. By permission of the Berkshire Athenæum

D'Wolf, daughter-in-law of Uncle D'Wolf, drive her to visit her old friend, eighty-two-year-old Dorcas Dearborn. Mrs. Dearborn was the widow of General Henry A. S. Dearborn (the son of the Revolutionary War veteran and the uncle of Aunt Mary Melvill and Jeff Hobart). Mother Melville could not have seen Dorcas for many years, though she remembered well the days when her father and the elder General Dearborn had been friends. Dorcas remembered the time when her late husband and old Major Melvill had been colleagues at the Boston Custom House and when Andrew Jackson had fired them both.[61]

Although Herman had been left out of this activity, the situation changed as the winter wore on. Henry Gansevoort appeared during the earlier part of February, perhaps with a gift for Herman—a commemorative brick made from the clay of Malvern Hill. Then the Gansevoorts invited Herman and Lizzie (and Tom and Bruce) to a big party in Albany to be held on February 12, 1866. None of them attended, however: Herman and Lizzie because of the press of his work, perhaps, Tom because he was far away, and Bruce for no discoverable reason. In the middle of March, John Hoadley brought Mother Melville to the city for her belated visit with Herman and his family. She was full of gossip about Kate Hoadley, Helen Griggs, Hope Shaw, and other friends, and full of anecdotes about her new grandson. She had arrived just in time to help commemorate a recent event of great family importance, Malcolm's coming of age. Malcolm, who had celebrated his seventeenth birthday on February 16, went to work—for the moment, the only member of Herman's household who was gainfully employed. In the city, where work was so scarce that veterans were suffering severe privations, he was fortunate in having an uncle of a sort who was president of an insurance company. Richard Lathers had obligingly offered him a clerk's position at a salary of $200 a year, which Mother Melville thought generous. Working conditions were good, she reported: Richard provided his employees a substantial lunch, and if they were required to work after six he furnished a supper, too. It was an arrangement of which everyone approved. Richard was not only genial but also successful, the kind of model a young man should emulate, Mother Melville thought (perhaps with the hope that he would become a bigger success than his father). On the other hand, Malcolm was a bright youth of the sort whose work and character would repay an employer's investment.[62]

Mother Melville had been with Herman and Lizzie only a few days before she fell ill, seriously, Herman believed. When she did not improve, about March 19 he dashed off a panicky note asking Gus to come as soon as possible, in the belief, no doubt correct, that she knew best how to nurse their mother. The morning after the note arrived, Gus sped to the city, but Lizzie and Stanny were waiting at the depot to tell her that the patient was recovering. At Herman's home, she found Mother Melville pale and weak but sitting up, and the doctors had assured all that she would be well in a few days. Gus decided to stay anyway and was rewarded when, on March 23,

Uncle D'Wolf appeared. The worry about Mother Melville had been justified: on March 30, Jean Knight, Herman's aunt, died.[63]

In Albany, Uncle Peter also had not been well. On January 20, he had what seems to have been a minor stroke which paralyzed his right side, but by evening he had improved. A few days later, he was back at his desk, writing letters, but on February 27, Aunt Susan had an attack of erysipelas which lasted for several days. From March 15 to March 27, Uncle Peter was again the patient, bilious and suffering from dental ills which plagued him on and off for three months. Nevertheless, when Mother Melville arrived on April 11, he was ready to receive her. After waiting in vain for Tom to appear and escort them home, she and Gus had made the railroad trip up the Hudson Valley with only a manservant for company. Mother Melville stayed in Albany to visit while Gus and the servant continued on to Gansevoort to ready the house for the summer. Mother Melville stayed for almost three weeks of visiting and partying before returning to Gansevoort. Almost immediately after her departure, Uncle Peter and his family rushed to New York City to seek treatment for his teeth, though in early June they still hurt. In June, Aunt Susan was again ill, confined to her bed and still ailing in the first part of July.[64]

During the late winter and spring, Henry Gansevoort continued his relentless pursuit of self-advancement, and once more he demanded, with no success, that his father come to Washington. Henry still wanted his regular brevets, but now he had heard that an augmentation of the army would create new vacancies in the higher ranks. Threatening to resign because of "a due sense of honor and pride," he demanded that his father arrange his appointment to major in the cavalry. Wearily, Uncle Peter wrote back that Henry was old enough to make his own decision about resigning and suggested that, since he didn't like the law, he might have difficulty finding employment, but he promised to help.[65]

Allan and Jennie had not reported in since their arrival in Paris on the first of December, but in late March a letter arrived which the travelers had begun in Aswan, Egypt, on February 11, and ended on February 26, in Cairo. Enclosed was a journal they had authored entitled "Pencillings by the Way." It revealed that, together with a party of other Americans, they had voyaged up the Nile in a steamer. On their way they hoisted an American flag that Jennie had made with a ceremony that included a speech, a chorus of "Rally Round the Flag, Boys," cheers, a pistol salute, and a "tiger" for the seamstress. Jennie boasted that this was the first American flag that had ever waved over the Nile, and perhaps it was. In this mood of hilarity, the party visited Thebes, Karnak, and Luxor. After taking sailboats as far as the first cataract, Allan and Jennie returned to Cairo to continue their tour of the Near East. The family also learned, through a letter in a Boston newspaper, that Allan had made a speech in Egypt to commemorate Washington's birthday. If he envied Allan, Herman said nothing, but Henry Gansevoort, with Allan's plea that he was "no nabob" in mind, remarked, "Happy are they who can enjoy such a luxury as the gratification of curiosity in these days of depreciated currency."[66]

Later communications revealed that during the last week in Lent, in emulation of Herman's 1857 trip, Allan and Jennie had toured the Holy Land. But while staying in a convent in Jaffa, Allan became so ill that Jennie had to nurse him through two days of feverish delirium, a serious matter, considering his puny constitution. At the nearby home of a German doctor he recovered sufficiently to continue the tour, and the two went on to Messina, Naples, Rome, and Florence. The trip ended in London, where Allan was so garrulous about his experiences that the secretary of the American embassy pronounced him "exacting and inconsiderate" and "considerable of a bore," and in Paris, where he and Jennie found prices cheaper than in New York. Jennie's dedicated care of Allan won her some approval from her still-skeptical in-laws.[67]

Disturbing the Peace

As the winter progressed, Herman must have all but completed *Battle-Pieces* as it would have been had not political developments demanded that he supplement it—or so it would appear from its content and its typography. Without that additional material, it falls into five parts, a proem ("The Portent"), a historical battle section, the memorial and inscriptive verses, "The Scout toward Aldie," and the notes. It is a tragedy of a special type.[68] It depicts a fortunate fall through which the corrupted nation might be renewed. In its largest sense, it is founded on God's most recent covenant with man, the establishment by the Founding Fathers of a society of freedom, equality, and brotherhood. The violation of that covenant by a people who prospered "to the apoplex" and allowed the old European evils of caste, poverty, and oppression to pollute America brought on the chastisement of war. Through her suffering and bereavement, America is given an opportunity to rediscover the virtues on which the covenant depends.

Beginning with the "Portent" that throws its shadow across the green land, America undergoes the fated convulsion, particularized in the battle poems. Through it, she matures from a naif, as yet untested and unaware of the darkness of the world she inhabits, into a clear-eyed, pain-annealed adult. It is an awful convulsion demanded by an inexorable God: "The heavens all parts assign," he wrote in "On the Slain Collegians." Yet it operates to make rehabilitation possible; there is "a wind in purpose strong— / It spins *against* the way it drives."

But the truth, the apocalyptic demands of fate, is learned only gradually. In the early poems, Raphaelesque and Michaelesque delusions of chivalry and of divine protection, approval, and guidance blind the hopeful participants to the true nature of the ordeal they must endure. Men believe that it can be avoided through a reconciliation between the two adversaries and later they trust that God will lead and protect them in their just cause. When Raphael fails, youths march to war under what they believe to be the protection of Michael, to Bull Run and Ball's Bluff, to Shiloh and Malvern Hill. War is a picnic of glory and a communion of righteousness until, gradually, Michael is exposed as only another chimera. "Donelson," where the gallantry and fidelity of the troops result in long casualty lists at home, begins the process of revelation which the nation must undergo. But the full truth is not apparent until "The Armies of the Wilderness," where *"man runs wild on the plain, / Like the jennets let loose / On the Pampas—zebras again."* The cleansing cannot be complete until the nation is humbled by the knowledge that it has been following not a heavenly archangel but rather the "disciplined captain," Satan. He is the endower, spirit, and symbol of man's tragic flaw, original sin, the penchant for violence against one's fellow man. The true battlefield of Satan's war is the wilderness and the underworld—thus streams tumble down from Raphael's height to Satan's depth, streams of men hurtle toward underground mines, pools, and the ocean depths, and men march into the depths of the wilderness while underground eruptions of slag and marl squeeze up from below. The ordeal ends only after the monstrous appetite for suffering has been sated, when the mists from the accumulated streams of war dashing into the pool rise high into the air to greet the rainbow of the covenant.

To attain the new America, some of the old must be sacrificed. Much as one might yearn for chivalry, for blazoned knightliness, the democratic future belongs to plain-garbed, cigar-smoking Grant, and much as one might regret the stinking caloric and the crank-manipulating operatives of the *Monitor* and prefer the windblown, frank gallantry of the *Téméraire* and the *Cumberland*, America must turn away from youthful romance to grasp the majesty that awaits her. The war reveals the virtues that it demands, humility, self-sacrifice, Homeric character, bravery, and compassion, and the sacrifices are recorded in memory, America's children perishing in grand gestures denied to those of lesser breed. Their sacrifice allows Mother America to reawaken, the sins of slavery and greed forever (one hopes) abolished and atoned, ready to preside over the empire of the free. North and South will be one again, old passions and wounds will heal, and the iron dome, free of rust, will dominate the sky.

Had the book remained thus, the procession of battle and related poems in its earlier section would have been followed by "Verses Inscriptive and Memorial," in effect a poetic graveyard made up largely of simple, quiet epitaphs that honor the soldiers whose deaths brought the nation its greatest pain. That section would have been followed by the separate "The Scout toward Aldie," a recapitulation of the tragedy with its penetration of Satan's wilderness of war and its dramatization of Satan himself.

But the book did not end that way. In the final months of its composition, Herman saw its grand vision imperiled, forcing him to extend his poetic design in order to encompass the debate over the reconstitution of the union. For an understanding of his reaction to these developments, it is necessary to see them through his eyes, not through the retrospective vision of present-day historians. Therefore, the following events are narrated as far as possible in accordance with his perception of them without regard to the demands of historical rigor.

A reintegration of its recently alienated citizens was the best way to ensure the flowering of an America with "triumph repressed by knowledge meet, / Power dedicate, and hope grown wise, / And youth matured for age's seat." Above all, the country had to guard against redividing itself. Thus far, the actions of the new president had been encouraging. They had accorded with a principle that had commonly been cited since the beginning of the war as its justification, that because secession had never been legal, the Southern states had never actually seceded. Therefore, the victory of the North had not altered their position in the union; it had merely settled the argument about slavery and corrected the misapprehension that secession was possible. There was no need to readmit states that had never departed, and there was no need to reconstruct what had, since the ratification of the Constitution, remained constructed. Furthermore, Johnson had acted as though he agreed with Herman's belief that the white community of the South would respond, however reluctantly, to fair and just treatment by being fair and just to the freedmen. During the immediate postwar era, while Congress was out of session, Johnson had begun to reinstitute the Southern political structure along those lines, that is, to reconstitute the prewar United States. He had permitted new state governments to form and representatives to Congress to be elected. The Southerners had responded badly by opposing black suffrage and enacting "Black Codes" which all but reinstituted servitude—that did not surprise Herman—but it was within the power of the central government to correct that behavior. Had "restoration" (Johnson's word) proceeded along those lines, a healthy portion of the burden of creating a new order out of defeat would have rested on those who would have to live with it. Perhaps full justice would be achieved slowly, but Henry Gansevoort had spoken for most of Herman's family when he had hoped for "the full rehabilitation of the States."[69]

If the prewar white establishment were to reassume its former position, it followed that blacks would attain the full rights of citizenship only gradually, and then only when they had satisfied whatever requirements might be imposed by the states. From the enlightened vantage point of today, the idea of denying any portion of the population the vote is unthinkable, raising the question of why Herman would favor such treatment of four million black people. But it was a time when universal suffrage was unknown. Since a variety of qualifications were imposed by the various states and communities and since women were generally disqualified completely, only a minority of Americans were allowed to vote. Not only that, but the principle of suffrage for blacks had not greatly exercised the consciences of Northerners, not even those of the Republican Congress. As Senator John Sherman, a moderate Republican from Ohio, pointed out at just this time, "There were only six of the Northern States in which negroes had the right to vote, and until the present session the proposition to give negroes this right in the District of Columbia had never been seriously considered, although Congress had unrestricted jurisdiction over the district. Even in the Territories, also under the unrestricted jurisdiction of Congress, the franchise had never been extended to the colored race." Two years earlier, he added, the Congress had expressly refused to include black suffrage in reconstruction legislation it had attempted to enact. Granted that situation, the idea that freedmen should grow and mature into full civil equality did not seem alien or severe. Emancipation was a fact; civil rights would grow according to natural rhythms. That seemed true to the entire Gansevoort family, the Melville women in Gansevoort, and Herman and his brothers, all of whom supported Johnson.[70]

Considering Herman's philosophical stake, it is understandable that he was drawn into the political conflict that began after the Congress reconvened in December 1865. It was a battle that even Whittier sought to forestall. His crusade against slavery having ended with the institution itself, he was now anxious to ensure an equitable future for the freedmen but wise enough to know that their interests would not be served by treating Southern whites as defeated enemies. In his poem "To the Thirty-Ninth Congress," he advocated both restoring the Southern leaders to power and promoting the welfare of the freedmen. He did not wish to see the defeated humiliated nor the victors bloated with triumph. By restoring their lands and privileges and exhorting them to act justly toward the freedmen, including the institution of black suffrage, the Congress could encourage the former Confederates to be "men, not beggars." Having been faithful to the abolitionist cause for many a weary year, Whittier had the right to urge on his fellow radicals the pleas of enlightened generosity and Christian forgiveness.[71]

But Congress did not listen. With their numbers swollen by the Democratic disaster in the 1864 election and with the Southern states still disenfranchised, the Republicans were unwilling to concede to the president the broad power that he had assumed. Empowered by the Constitution to govern its own membership, the Congress refused to seat the newly elected Southerners. Instead, it formed a joint Select Committee on Reconstruction to resolve the issue of membership and to deal with a broad spectrum of postwar issues. Thus the shape of the new union that would emerge was to be dictated without the participation of the South, hardly even that of the Northern Democrats. That, together with Johnson's inflexibility and his political clumsiness, set the stage for a bitter power struggle between the executive and legislative branches.

Both of the most influential radical leaders, Herman's friend Sumner in the Senate and Thaddeus Stevens, of Pennsylvania, in the House, rejected the idea that the Southern states were states at all. Because they had committed political suicide, they were no more than conquered provinces that the North could do with what it wished. The attitude of Stevens, an intemperate and acrimonious fanatic, was especially dangerous. Since before the war, he had ached to wipe off the face of North America the Southern culture that he despised. Now in his "foolish violence," as James Russell Lowell termed it, he advocated expropriating the property of the large landholders and driving them into exile, if need be. In a notorious statement of his intentions on December 18, 1865, he came directly to the point: "I take no account of the aggregation of whitewashed rebels who, without any legal authority, have assembled in the capitals of the late rebel states and simulated legislative bodies." Pretending that the "late" states were states in being was a charade "intended to delude the people, and accustom Congress to hear repeated the names of these extinct states as if they were alive; when, in truth, they have now no more existence than the revolted cities of Latium, two thirds of whose people were colonized, and their property confiscated, and their right of citizenship withdrawn by conquering and avenging Rome." Now he wished Congress to "assume something of the dignity of a Roman senate" by treating the South as Rome had treated Latium.[72]

In opposing the president, Sumner and Stevens also opposed Herman, though Herman demonstrated his intellectual complexity by his refusal thereafter to repudiate Sumner. He knew of Stevens's pronouncement and his policies, as everyone seemed to, and he intended to respond to them. Stevens's allusion to Rome and Latium was inept and therefore a point of vulnerability against which a counterattack might be mounted. In 340 B.C., the Latins had rebelled against Roman domination under circumstances far different from those of the rebellion of 1861. The Latins had never been partners of the Romans, as the Southerners had been of the Northerners, but rather had been compelled to allegiance. To use an analogy that suggested that the Southern states had always been vassals of the North, and therefore that victory entitled the North to uproot persons, seize property, and revoke citizenship, was to twist history out of any recognizable shape and to advocate an antique and foreign vengeance that was contrary to the values of rationality and equality on which the nation was based. As Herman knew, during the Revolution the American colonies had been more or less in the position of Latium, while the British Empire had been the equivalent of Rome. Had the Americans lost their war, would Britain have been justified in following the example of Rome? That is what Stevens seemed to be saying.[73]

So certain was Stevens of the righteousness of his course that he viewed Johnson, the former War Democrat, as an enemy agent. Johnson's usurpation of power, he said, was as heinous a crime as the one that had justified the execution of Charles I. Johnson's growing fear of a conspiracy against him was revealed in his response. In an impromptu speech in front of the White House, he called Sumner and Stevens enemies and referred to Stevens as one "who has assassination broiling in his heart." Warming to his subject, he said, "Does not the blood of Lincoln appease the vengeance and wrath of the opponents of this government? Is their thirst still unslaked? Do they want more blood? Have they not honor and courage enough to effect the removal of the presidential obstacle otherwise than through the hands of the assassin?" With that strident rhetoric, the hope of cooperation between administration and legislature waned. Congress proceeded to pass its own Reconstruction program, bills that, in effect, demanded a reordering of the cultures of the Southern states as a precondition to their readmission. Johnson vetoed them, and, as often as not, the Congress passed them over his veto. After the passage of one such bill, Kate Gansevoort wrote that the radicals thought only of the "*Nubians*" and themselves; after another, she wrote that "the Radicals are trying to ruin this Magnificent Government." Herman would have agreed.[74]

The North split into pro-Congress and pro-Johnson factions—precisely the kind of Anarch squabbling that Herman had feared. In New York City, the reunited conservatives met on February 21. John A. Dix, a civilian and a partisan Democrat once more, was chairman. The participants vowed to support Johnson's policies and to consult with him about assisting "in the measures which he proposed to take, and aiding him in his patriotic efforts to restore harmony to the Union, while guarding against an evident tendency to enlarge the powers of the Federal Government to an extent far beyond what they considered safe." Richard Lathers was not an official of the meeting, nor was he appointed a delegate to call on Johnson—his Southern background might have furnished ammunition to Johnson's opponents, though it is also possible that the birth of his last child, Edward, on March 24, prevented him from joining the delegation. No doubt, however, he attended the meeting, as he was accustomed to do, and, since it occurred at about the time when he hired Malcolm, no doubt he discussed with Herman the anxieties of the conservatives and the measures adopted at the meeting.[75]

That was the day before Johnson's assassination speech and, by chance, the day after General Lee had completed his testimony before a subcommittee of the Committee on Reconstruction. Perhaps until that moment, Herman had not fully realized the severity of the threat to his dream. However desultory his past participation in politics, he was now ready to join the battle. He began to expand and revise his book by adding three new pieces after "The Scout toward Aldie."

The appearance of Lee inspired Herman's first "Reconstruction" poem (placed in a separate section after "The Scout toward Aldie"). The subcommittee was taking testimony from prominent Confederates, in its innocence expecting them to be remorseful and apologetic about their rebellion. This may be why, in substantive terms, Lee's appearance was unremarkable. He answered questions about the probable loyalties of Southerners in the postwar period, particularly in hypothetical situations in which they might be tempted to renew the rebellion, but his testimony was not illuminating. In his retirement as president of Washington College, the wily old soldier said, he did not communicate with the Virginia politicians nor even read the newspapers regularly. At the end of his testimony, he declined an opportunity to make a further statement. But to Herman, it seemed that, as the one notable living Confederate whose reputation remained unimpeached, Lee had lost a valuable opportunity to speak for his defeated comrades and countrymen. Herman would rectify the omission in "Lee in the Capitol (April, 1866)" by "moulding what has been into what should have been ideally," as Fogle has put it. The poem is one of his fictions built upon fact, but it is more, an audacious recreation of Lee as a Melville character—while the real person was still alive and able to respond and remonstrate. However,

Herman must have felt confident that the admiration implicit in his portrait and the justice of the words that he put into Lee's mouth, if noted by the defeated leader, would not be objectionable.[76]

Herman's depiction of Lee in defeat, when "the hour is come of Fate," is from his own imagination, however biographically accurate it may be. Stripped of "station and riches," bereaved of comrades and friends, he accepts, perhaps stoically, his condition and the "asserted laws" of the reestablished union. That picture of power surrendered with dignity is central to the poem's appeal for understanding and tolerance. In his secluded "seminary," Lee might have lived out his life in chastened peace had not the Senate summoned him, but the summons reaggravates hurts and rekindles his pride of conquest. After riding through the ruins of the state to which love had bound him, he must pass his former home and lands, confiscated and converted into a national cemetery: *now* these senators command his appearance, though *once* they had shrunk in terror of him

on the day
Of Pope's impelled retreat in disarray—
By me impelled—when toward yon Dome
The clouds of war came rolling home.

As he nears the Capitol, where flags captured from his army are still displayed, the narrator breaks in to speculate on how different Lee's condition might have been had this "intrepid soldier" fought on the side of the Union. Then he would have come to the Capitol "in pageant borne," honored and cheered at "close of the war and victory's long review." Herman little doubted that, had Lee fought for the Union, he, not Grant or Sherman, would have been the foremost.

Even now, Lee intimidates his questioners, for "who looks at Lee must think of Washington; / In pain must think, and hide the thought, / So deep with grievous meaning it is fraught." Hold what prejudices one will, *this* former rebel is "allied by family" to the Father of the Country, and because he represents the South he reminds all that the recent enemies have deep roots in the common American experience. The idea is inescapable that the rebellion was inherent in the great experiment, was born into the character of Mother America, was fated.

Because Lee's words are really Herman's, Herman himself becomes the "voice or proxy" for the South, assuming the duty "the flushed North from her own victory [to] save." The ruined South, he says, is filled with doubt and dread, desiring peace and law again so that she can go about the task of rebirth. It is useless to ask her to recant: "she yields," and, like the dead of both sides intermingled in the earth and equally mourned, she "would blend anew." A ghostly voice from the terrible slaughter cries out, *"Died all in vain? both sides undone?"* In respect for these buried legions, Lee warns, "Push not your triumph; do not urge / Submissiveness beyond the verge." If the North insists on more, she will create an enduring enemy within the nation's borders, "eleven sliding daggers in your side." Although some in the North may blame the South for what has happened, "Common's the crime in every civil strife." Even more, "this I feel, that North and South were driven / By Fate to arms."

Lee then illustrates his meaning with a story of a Moorish woman who, after becoming a Christian, is told that she must renounce her pagan father. The hope of redemption is weaker than the pull of family, causing her to remain loyal to her father even if she must burn in hell with him. This same loyalty led men of the South to war against the North. "True to the home and to the heart," they fought on the side on which nature had placed them. "Was this the unforgivable sin?" These large hearts can yet be won for the nation. Then Herman speaks directly to Thaddeus Stevens: "Shall the great North go Sylla's way? / Proscribe? prolong the evil day?" This was the parry that he had been preparing against Stevens's allusion to the civil war between the Latins and the Romans. Substituting the later internecine wars in which Sulla was victorious was the same strategy that he had used in "The House-top" when he had introduced the despised name of Draco. Stevens's allusion was not likely to arouse sympathetic assent from his listeners—the Latin war had occurred so early in history that the names of both the revengers and their victims had been lost and the events were recorded only in general terms. But history had preserved the name of Sulla by associating it with a postwar blood-letting so odious that his name has ever since connoted rabid revenge. Thus when Herman speaks of "Sylla's way," the force of his allusion dwarfs the murky intent of Stevens's. The point is reinforced when Lee leaves the Capitol "through vaulted walks in lengthened line / Like porches erst upon the Palatine." The Congress has the choice of emulating the vicious Sulla or of following that other Roman principle which held that the American, even the former Confederate, "is Nature's Roman, never to be scourged." For Herman, the Lee of the poem is a prophet of America's fate: "Faith in America never dies; / Heaven shall the end ordained fulfill, / We march with Providence cheery still."

Although Lee's testimony had actually been taken in February, Herman dated the poem in April, when the process of legislating, vetoing, and overriding was at its apogee. The message is clear: the interests of America will be best served by a victory of the philosophy of Johnson over that of

Stevens. "Faith in America" comes perilously close to being a campaign slogan.

The final poem of *Battle-Pieces*, "A Meditation: Attributed to a Northerner after attending the last of two funerals from the same homestead—those of a National and a Confederate Officer (brothers), his kinsmen, who had died from the effects of wounds received in the closing battles," is set in a separate section following "Lee in the Capitol," thereby suggesting, along with its content and tone, that it is another late addition. Its heavily contrived dramatic situation refers back to the brothers who had parted in hatred in "Apathy and Enthusiasm," but where another poet might have focused his attention on the sentimental cliché of the fraternal deaths, Herman chose instead to dwell on the brotherly bonds that the war never sundered.

It is largely a compendium of recorded incidents of the war, and there were many, in which the bond of common humanity reasserted itself. An emissary from one army finds old friends in the other with whom to spend a warm social hour. Soldiers fronting each other at close range exchange compliments and food instead of bullets. In an event that occurred before Marye's Heights at Fredericksburg, a Confederate soldier risks his life to bring water to a Union soldier lying gravely wounded between the battling armies. Generals who had been schoolmates at West Point battle one another, and when armies pause during a truce, friends and relatives glimpse each other across the chasm of divided loyalties: "And something of a strange remorse / Rebelled against the sanctioned sin of blood, / And Christian wars of natural brotherhood." At such moments they feel "the god within the breast" and doubt "each plea and subterfuge of earth," asking rebelliously, "Can Africa pay back this blood / Spilt on Potomac's shore?"

In 1866, while the nation was searching for the means of reunification, this godly pull of brotherhood had special significance. If the two sides were to become one again, it would be necessary to abandon the vindictiveness of Emerson and Stevens: "*'The South's the sinner!'* Well, so let it be; / But shall the North sin worse, and stand the Pharisee?" To feel the old bonds now is as manly—and at least as easy—as it was to feel them during the bloodiest moments of the war. Southerners inspired admiration for their bravery in battle; so much the more should they be treated with dignity now: "When Vicksburg fell, and the moody files marched out, / Silent the victors stood, scorning to raise a shout." If Herman had refused to celebrate the starvation of the Vicksburg defenders in his battle poems, now he could find in their surrender a trenchant example of respect for the defeated to guide the North.

The Last Salvo

As this last bit of work on *Battle-Pieces* was concluding, Herman saw a great deal of his brothers. Tom arrived, too late to escort Gus and Mother Melville home, to spend the week between May 11 and May 17 with Herman, after which he went to Gansevoort for two weeks to help his mother with the farm. He then returned to spend another week and a half with Herman before returning around the tenth of June to West Virginia. Gus wished that he could have remained to welcome Allan and Jennie back from their tour, but that was not to be. On the twenty-seventh of June, just about the time when Mrs. Hoffman closed her school for the summer, the *Java* arrived with the two tourists. Allan must have given Herman a complete account of their adventures, providing him with yet another opportunity to be generous about Allan's considerable affluence. Not so Bruce, who wished that he, too, could travel abroad. Shortly before their return, he had written that he would like to attend the 1867 Paris Exhibition with Henry Gansevoort.[77]

Despite Augusta's invitation to visit Gansevoort before settling into Arrowhead, Allan took his family to Pittsfield on July 3 to open the farm and to begin a sociable season there. Once again Rachel Turner, the late Confederate belle, was a house guest, joined by "the New Rochelle party"—the Latherses and some of the Thurstons, most likely. When he could spare time from the office, Bruce, too, visited, as did young Rachel Barrington, Allan's niece. Rouser was much in demand, particularly with Milie, and the visitors reveled in rural delights—riding and a circus.[78]

On July 10, Tom returned for a three-day stay with Herman, then went on to Gansevoort. Herman, too, was planning to vacation there, but he did not accompany Tom. He was probably readying his book and delivering it, in the form of a fair copy made by Lizzie, to the Harpers, who had it in press by the twentieth—without the supplementary essay, it would seem. Lizzie must have been exasperated, as always. She hated these tense periods when Herman was wrestling with the angel Art, in part because he was fussy and bad-tempered, but this time because the publication of a book of poems gave her little hope of family income. It must have been a relief for her to pack up the three younger children for Boston—the girls were to visit with Helen Griggs and Malcolm would join her when his two-week vacation began. Visiting in Boston allowed her to parade her marital grievances before her sympathetic family and to be reassured that she deserved better than life with Herman afforded her.[79]

With the proofreading completed and the making of the volume well along, Herman was ready for his vacation. That week Allan and, it would

Allan Melville. By permission of the Berkshire Athenæum

seem, John Hoadley, arrived in the city to accompany him to Gansevoort, but business detained Allan. On Saturday, July 21, Herman and John left for Albany without him, then boarded the evening train for Gansevoort without making the customary stop to see Uncle Peter. That left Malcolm at home to take the train to Boston by himself.[80]

The Gansevoort family thought that Herman looked "very thin & miserable," but the rural atmosphere and pace were good medicine for that. Aside from Mother Melville, Gus, and Fanny, Kate Hoadley was there with Minnie, Lottie, and baby Frank, and Tom had brought Kate Gansevoort up for a visit. Herman had just missed Kate Curtis. She had left her daughter Mary in charge of Guert, whose illness was now referred to as "neuralgia in his spine" that was "gradually killing him," so she could come over from New Hampshire for several days, and that had inspired Stanwix Gansevoort to visit from Glens Falls. It was the first time that Kate Gansevoort had met either of them; she was taken by Kate Curtis, but thought Stanwix out of "his sphere." When Herman arrived, Kate Curtis had already returned home to take her turn nursing Guert. If the news of Guert's declining health worried Herman, the baby was a cheering sight, "a comical likeness of his grand-mother," Kate Gansevoort wrote.[81]

When the sun came out after a rainy Monday morning, Tom, Kate Gansevoort, Kate Hoadley, and John left in high spirits for a trip up Lake George. ("I never met such a joking happy fellow as Tom Melville," Kate wrote that morning.) After checking in at a hotel, they went for a moonlight row on which Tom and John did the work while the two Kates reclined and enjoyed. The next day they took the steamer *Minnehaha* to Fort Ticonderoga, John lecturing along the way on the local geology according to the theory of Professor Agassiz. On their arrival, the two men and Kate Gansevoort hiked to the ruins of the fort while Kate Hoadley languished. On Wednesday, they returned to Gansevoort.[82]

It was unusual for Herman to remain behind when such an outing beckoned, and almost as strange that neither Fanny nor Gus went on the excursion. But despite his bucolic surroundings, Herman was still at work. For several days he had been exposed to the hot radicalism of John Hoadley, which was little different from listening to Sumner. One did not take offense at John, but one paid attention to what he said to learn the mood and thought of the opposition. What Herman heard warned him of the need for supplementing the last two poems of *Battle-Pieces* with a direct statement of advocacy. The result was a political essay, the only one he ever wrote, the composition of which confined him to the house while his sisters made fair copy for him.[83]

His task was similar to that of Whittier in his "To the Thirty-Ninth Congress," to urge on the Congress a generous and workable settlement of the conflict. The resulting "Supplement," "a deeply impressive document, . . . subtle in its analysis of the difficulties of Reconstruction," is one of the most unusual and unexpected of Herman's works. It is remarkable in several ways. It is a forthright exposition, without irony or other literary subterfuge, of the views on public policy of a notoriously reticent author. Herman thought that this kind of exposure was dangerous for a writer, and he understood the special risk of injecting his opinions into the venomous political dialogue of the moment: "In times like the present, one who desires to be impartially just in the expression of his views, moves as among sword-points presented on every side." Another remarkable fact is that, in its content and its tone of conciliation, the essay shows how firm was Herman's grasp of contemporary events and how well suited were his talents for public debate. Finally, the essay is an impressive achievement in American letters, one which, as Howard P. Vincent has said, deserves a place among the "American Scriptures."[84]

One senses the hot immediacy in which the essay was written when one encounters a simile inspired by Allan's recent vacation in Egypt: "Effective benignity, like the Nile, is not narrow in its bounty, and true policy is always broad." That is the tenor of the entire essay, which addresses its audience through metaphor, aphorism, and appeal to high-mindedness. That it was directed toward those at the highest level of government is made clear by the question, "We have sung of the soldiers and sailors, but who shall hymn the politicians?"

Herman believed that the war had been fated; perhaps "nothing could ultimately have averted the strife," since "human actions" are always "second causes." He thought that "Secession, like Slavery, is against Destiny," and he maintained that the war would be justified only if it resulted in "an advance for our whole country and for humanity." He admitted that in his wartime loyalties he "never was a blind adherent," that he never subscribed uncritically to the loyalist dogma of the moment. As a conservative, he did not believe that the Union flag was the standard of God: "The mourners who this summer bear flowers to the mounds of the Virginian and Georgian dead are, in their domestic bereavement and proud affection, as sacred in the eye of Heaven as are those who go with similar offerings of tender grief and love into the cemeteries of our Northern martyrs." Yet he differed from other conservatives in that he "always abhorred slavery as an atheistical iniquity" and he joined "in the exulting chorus of humanity over its downfall." The blacks were his "fellow-men" who, in their new adventure in freedom, "appeal to the sympathies of every humane mind." Yet one could not win a bright future for the freedmen by legislating for them alone, apart from the rest of the population. Thus "the future of the whole country, involving the future of the blacks, urges a paramount claim upon our anxiety."

Herman did not hesitate to instruct the Committee on Reconstruction. Pacification with justice, for which Americans yearned, was not won by the war, nor can legislation alone, "however anxious, or energetic, or repressive," achieve it. Some laws required by the changed condition of the nation are required, "but with this should harmoniously work another kind of prudence, not unallied with entire magnanimity. Benevolence and policy—Christianity and Machiavelli—dissuade from penal severities toward the subdued." Such a policy is as essential and wise as is benevolent care of the newly freed slaves, for "the great qualities of the South, those attested in the War, we can perilously alienate." The burden of the argument is, then, that the policies and legislation of the North should do justice both to the late rebels and to the new freedmen. But Herman knew that this Congress would look after the well-being of the blacks without further argument; it was the Southern whites who needed his advocacy.

Are the Southerners not penitent? If they were not during the war, then to ask it of them now is to demand "contrition hypocritical." Did they fight for slavery? Some did, but most fought out of "the most sensitive love of liberty." Are the names of Southern heroes blackened by Northern partisanship? In time, that will cease to be so: loyal Americans of the South will cherish the memories of the great Confederate leaders. Did the Southerners lose the war because of a lack of art or courage? No, "our triumph was won not more by skill and bravery than by superior resources and crushing numbers." Did Confederates commit atrocities? Yes, but the Southern people cannot be held collectively responsible for acts of individuals. Above all, the North should be as generous to the Southerners as to the freedmen because the whites "stand nearer to us in nature." "In our natural solicitude to confirm the benefit of liberty to the blacks, let us forbear from measures of dubious constitutional rightfulness toward our white countrymen."

The blacks, he said, were infant pupils of freedom. One had to imagine oneself "in the unprecedented position of the Southerners" in relation to the millions of freedmen to whom it was now proposed to give the vote. Herman looked into the future relationship between the two races inhabiting the same region and worried about what he saw:

> Benevolent desires, after passing a certain point, can not undertake their own fulfillment without incurring the risk of evils beyond those sought to be remedied. Something may well be left to the graduated care of future legislation, and to heaven. In one point of view the coexistence of the two races in the South . . . [is a] calamity. Especially in the present transition period for both races in the South, more or less of trouble may not unreasonably be anticipated. . . . With certain evils men must be more or less patient. Our institutions have a potent digestion, and may in time convert and assimilate to good all elements thrown in, however originally alien.

It was better to resolve the racial confrontation through time than to enact radical laws, since God's plan had provided a political system that could accommodate the freedmen.

The problem of Reconstruction, Herman believed, "demands little but common sense and Christian charity," but it was also true, he warned, continuing his metaphor of "The Apparition," that the Satanic crater may only have shifted. If the radicals had their way, he could foresee bitter regional and political passions that would divide the nation far into the future. Northern conservatives would be bitter enemies of the radicals, and white Southern representatives in Congress—he knew that there would eventually be such—would fight the war over and over with their Northern counterparts. What future woes he foresaw for the black man he did not say, but something lurks in his statement that "benevolent desires" to cure evils, if pressed too far, "can not undertake their own fulfillment" without creating yet greater evils. If only the Congress would act with prudence and generosity, the new America would be born.

If today Herman's argument seems less than considerate of those who had long been yoked in slavery, one could argue that its absence of malice toward any party was the noblest attitude of all. When he said that in nature the Southerners stood closer to the Northerners than did the freedmen, he was not necessarily referring to race. He was referring to the bond of nationality that had originated when Northerner and Southerner together had created the nation and given it form, and that bond probably extended to those black men who had already been assimilated into free society. To use the excuse of rebellion to substitute, in political terms, the freedmen for the former Confederates would be to disable a portion of the body politic in order to give immediate suffrage to men who were of necessity ignorant, both in terms of education and in terms of the truncated experience of civil life permitted them by their servitude. That would impoverish the land, he thought. Citizenship and full political investiture were due the former slave, but they had to be given so as to produce the best future for men of both colors.

In its final form, *Battle-Pieces* was now complete. Herman had originally intended that its finale be Shakespearean in its vision of order restored and rancor reconciled, but the marauding Reconstruction Committee and its clients had rendered that outcome uncertain. Herman could only end his book with a prayer for wisdom: "Let us pray that the great historic tragedy of our time may not have been enacted without instructing our whole beloved country through terror and pity; and may fulfillment verify in the end those expectations which kindle the bards of Progress and Humanity." He could do no more, except to dedicate the labor of his pen to the Union dead.

If this chronology of composition is correct, the essay was completed in a little less than two weeks, during which Kate Gansevoort returned to Albany, John Hoadley apparently left, as well, and relays of laborers, under Tom's supervision, worked on Mother Melville's dam and mill. On Saturday, August 4, Tom went to Lansingburgh to visit Augustus Peebles and his family, and Allan was supposed to make an appearance in Gansevoort, though he was held up by business. On Sunday, Herman set out in the rain for New York City, stopping in Albany to spend the night with Uncle Peter, a trip that he probably would not have made had he not had business to transact with the Harpers. Only a week and a half before the publication of the book he would have delivered his essay, to be placed at the end following the notes. Then he returned to Gansevoort for his real vacation.[85]

In Herman's absence, Allan had finally arrived in Gansevoort and he was trying to persuade Mother Melville to go to Arrowhead with him. When Herman returned, with less than a week of vacation left, he made up for the recreation time he had missed. His change of mood was remarkable. While Gus swung idly in the hammock, Herman played croquet, giving a demonstration to Tom, Allan, Fanny, and Kate Hoadley of how the game should be played. The following day, he and Tom went off by themselves for a day at Saratoga Lake. Then on Thursday, August 9, Allan left for Pittsfield, taking Mother Melville with him. Malcolm's return from Boston on Monday, August 13, meant that Herman was needed back in the city to play the parent. That was the week when *Battle-Pieces* was published.[86]

10

Postscript
1866

On August 17, 1866, *Battle-Pieces* was published. However much Melville may have masked his excitement, he must have been anxious for its success. Although he deplored those who played the game of literary lionism, he wanted the recognition to which his achievements entitled him. More than he was willing to admit, he was proud and ambitious; his disparagement of *Mardi* to General Tyler had been no more than a contrary witticism, cut from the same stuff as his "trunk-maker" badinage with Tom two years earlier. Without arrogance or self-serving comparisons, he believed that he belonged with the greatest authors. He felt that he understood Shakespeare, Milton, Homer, Plato, Camõens, and Montaigne as only one of their peers could, and he hoped for a like understanding of his works. He was devastated by hostile criticism that measured his works by inapplicable standards, criticism that condemned him for his failure to conform to the freaks and fads of the marketplace.

He might have predicted its reception from the reaction of some members of his family. After buying it in Boston instead of awaiting a presentation copy, loyal Tom described it as "a very pretty volume" and added his hope that it would succeed, but Henry Gansevoort predicted that it would fail. "Have you seen Herman Melvilles new work 'Battle Pieces,'" he wrote. "There are some beautiful things in it. Unfortunately he has so much of Emerson & transcendentalism in his writing that it never will really touch the common heart. Still I must say that this work shows him to be a poet of high order & certainly of originality." Kate Gansevoort's comments show how valid was her brother's pessimism: "I must say I cannot get interested in his style—of Poetry. It is too deep for my comprehension."[1]

As Daniel Aaron put it, in *Battle-Pieces* Melville "defied consensus and took one further step toward popular oblivion." Readers were unprepared for the demands of its poetics and many did not agree with its message when they did understand it. Of the thirty-nine or so announcements and reviews thus far discovered, most were concentrated in New York City and New England, with a few appearing in Philadelphia (3), Cincinnati (2), and San Francisco (2). Some of the notices were favorable, some were not. *Harper's*, which was guilty of special pleading, boasted that some of the poems would "stand as among the most stirring lyrics of the war," while the *New York Herald,* moved by political considerations, praised the supplement and defended the roughness of the poems as consistent with the ruggedness of the nation's experience. The *Philadelphia Inquirer* thought the poems better than Brownell's, and the *Boston Traveller* said that because of their vigor and sweetness they were an exception to the rule that the poetry of the war was of little worth, though the reviewer objected to Melville's talk about generosity toward the South. But others were unfavorable. *Albion* put a negative construction on a positive truth in saying that "no one but Mr. Melville could have written it, and few besides himself would have cared to write it." The complaints of the other reviewers are summed up in the words of the *American Literary Gazette and Publisher's Circular:* "He has written too rapidly to avoid great crudities. His poetry runs into the epileptic. His rhymes are fearful." Writing in the *Atlantic Monthly,* William Dean Howells showed why Melville would not become the poet of the coming age of literary empiricism: "Is it possible . . . that there has really been a great war, with battles fought by men and bewailed by women? Or is it only that Mr. Melville's inner consciousness has been perturbed, and filled with the phantasms of enlistments, marches, fights in the air, parenthetic bulletin-boards, and tortured humanity shedding, not words and blood, but words alone?" Several reviewers maintained that Melville was not a poet and one questioned whether he was even an artist.[2]

With the passing of the weeks and months, Melville's aspirations for *Battle-Pieces* foundered. That meant another disappointment. His opportunity to instruct voters and politicians in the necessity for postwar compassion and fair-mindedness and for earnest dedication to the building of a new, better America was directly proportional to the sales of his book, since an unread argument would sway no one. In part, he was to blame: he always overestimated the abilities of his intended readers to comprehend, and his book appeared too late to ride the crest of postwar excitement and to avert the Reconstruction mess in Washington. In its first year and a half, fewer than 500 copies were sold, some to his own friends and relatives. The days when he could influence government power brokers, as he could believe he had done with *White-Jacket,* were over.

What kind of response had Melville expected? What did he believe he had written? What *had* he written? Perhaps all three amount to a single question with two answers. First, *Battle-Pieces* is the maiden offering of an important new American poet, no longer the casual versifier of the *Mardi* interludes but the earnest, self-taught bard who had brought to fruition a pioneering volume of lyric and narrative poetry. In this sense, the book can be likened to Walt Whitman's 1855 *Leaves of Grass* and to the poems on scraps of paper that Emily Dickinson was at that moment writing in the seclusion of her boudoir. Some new literary breeze was blowing; it is not a coincidence that in just over a decade these three innovators began to delineate a new territory in American poetry, a territory that would belong to them, whether or not the public acknowledged it, from just after the middle of the century until its last decade. It was as though all three had heard the call of Emerson for a new, democratic poetry. Still, no one of them followed the path of either of the other two. Whitman was the iconoclast who reshaped the tradition of versification and verbal protocol until it was scarcely recognizable as the vehicle of Bryant, Whittier, Longfellow, Lowell, and Holmes. In her rough ballads Dickinson despoiled the fluid line, the elegant cliché, and the genteel sentiment. Melville employed in part and on occasion the democratic zeal and idiosyncratic vocabulary of the one and the metric crudity, the "colloquialism, the prosaic, the anti-poetic, the ironical," as Newton Arvin has put it,[3] of the other, but he differed from them both in that he was the romancer-turned-poet who translated his symbolic habit, his mastery of dialogue, and his skill at manipulating point of view into a poetics of his own.

In the politics of literary reputation, he differed from them in that he had already concluded a brilliant if inadequately recognized and rewarded career as a writer of fiction, leaving behind him a body of work that, had he written nothing more, would have assured his future recognition. That has encouraged his audiences, then and now, to see him not as a poet but as a novelist whose venture into poetry was an invasion of alien literary territory. Even today, *Battle-Pieces* is often measured against nineteenth-century conventions as the verse of Whitman and Dickinson is not, and thus it has not been accorded the serious study that it deserves. But, as Shurr has said, "If he had written no prose at all, we would still have a poet in the American pantheon named Herman Melville." There is little question that the quality of his war poems is uneven, ranging from "Lyon," which at the present stage of critical understanding appears to be a failed experiment according to any criterion, to many fine achievements, including, but not limited to, "The Portent," "A Utilitarian's View of the Monitor's Fight," "Shiloh," "The House-top," "The College Colonel," and "Commemorative of a Naval Victory." But in terms of the overall merit of the volume, most criticism has echoed what was once said about the work of the other two pioneers, as when readers dismissed *Leaves of Grass* as prosy and when Colonel Higginson felt obliged to polish Dickinson's suspect meter. On the other hand, there is now a stirring of recognition. Admitting that the book is uneven, Robert Milder has noted its importance: "Its achievement lies in the artfulness of design by which Melville patterns his readers' shared experience of the war into national myth and leads his audience, without their knowing it, toward an understanding of history and experience."[4]

It has not been the purpose of this study to provide a foundation for a new evaluation of Melville's poetics, but rather to follow his biographical footsteps as he gathered his materials and made *Battle-Pieces,* to locate the source of the poems in his experiences, and to suggest what he intended them to accomplish. His achievement will become fully available only when the critical tools needed to measure it are forged by others. That work has barely begun, most notably by Newton Arvin, who sees Melville's poetic attention focused on the "unideal Actual" and his ear "capable of great feats of harmony and rhythm, and capable too of cacophonies that suggest the tone-deaf." Arvin cites as typical Melville's "slow, weighty, tight, and rather toneless line" which is well-suited to his subject matter, and his "powerfully prosaic vocabulary of terms that suggest business, industry, the law, and even mathematics" that allies him with the seventeenth-century English metaphysical poets. Yet Arvin protests against his use of "stale poetic archaisms" that sprinkle his pages like withered leaves.[5] That use of archaisms must be understood better. In many of the war poems he did not employ them, and an explanation of his vulgar diction and his inkhorn words is equally needed. His awkward poetics cannot be dismissed as a result of a bad poetic ear, since his blank verse in "The House-Top" is as deft and as gripping as one is likely to find in the nineteenth-century canon. There is also a need for a broader analysis of his imagery, including Grant's cigar and his back heaping to a hump. So, too, the functionality of his heavy allusiveness—to the Bible and to the ancient Romans and Greeks, for example—must be better understood. And if his work owes something to the seventeenth-century metaphysical poets, that, too, requires more investigation. When such work has been done, when readers are confident of understanding Melville's poetic strategies, they will come into full possession of the third participant in the mid-nineteenth-century American poetic revolution.

Second, like *Moby-Dick, Clarel,* and *Billy Budd, Battle-Pieces* is the only book of its type ever written or ever likely to be written in America. Calling him "the Brady of Civil War verse," Arvin claims that "Melville is the first poet in English to realize the meaning of modern technological warfare."[6] But the book is more. In the realm of imaginative literature, it is the only important attempt ever made to grapple intellectually with a distinctly *American* war, which is not to deny that there are other notable war books with different aims. There have been only two *American* wars, wars in which Americans battled to create and define their political identity, the Revolutionary War and the Civil War. All others have been foreign expeditions. But these two were truly national, the first the crucible from which the new country was poured and the second the agony that seems to have been necessary to resolve unanswered questions about the national identity. Of the Revolutionary War, it is safe to say that it inspired no literary work of distinction other than prose advocacy. Those who experienced it left that task to future writers, such as Harold Frederic, who in 1891 included Melville's Gansevoort grandfather as a character in *In the Valley.* But these later works have never attained the first rank of literary merit.

Near the end of the eighteenth century, Americans had yet to develop the kind of cultural identity that leads to vigorous literary expression. But it is less understandable that a mature literary community that was transfixed by the experiences of the Civil War should have produced only one work of the type of *Battle-Pieces.* Minor poets, such as Boker, Howe, Brownell, and Stedman, devoted their talents to answering public demands for description, inspiration, beatification, bathos, Philippic, and satire. Far from addressing the phenomenon of a nation sundered by conflicting principles and searching for the origin and the significance of the resulting conflagration, their works were little more than events of the war. Had he lived, Hawthorne could not have written a war romance about the American experiment because his faith in it was too feeble, his loyalties too narrowly confined to New England—and because his imagination did not work that way. Many other celebrated writers of the time were too partisan for broad vision and judicious expression. The abolitionists, Emerson, Whittier, and Lowell, were too blinded by the single issue of slavery to look beyond it, and Whittier's Quaker convictions forbade him to commemorate battles. Even when the Brahmin poets wrote about the war, their verses differed from newspaper poetry mostly in tact and polish, although Lowell's losses inspired him to write the one memorable poem, "Ode Recited at the Harvard Commemoration." Bryant, old and long since exhausted creatively, wrote no significant war poetry. Holmes, an acute analyst, might have written such a book had his intellect been more profound and his ego less self-consuming. Dickinson was not shallow, but she wrote of a different world. The young Henry James did not choose the moment to begin his career, and the other youths—Howells comes to mind—did not find in the war a useful subject. As can be seen from the poems quoted in earlier chapters, Thomas Bailey Aldrich gave promise of being an important war poet, but that promise found fruition in only a few lyrics that he did not consider important. His temperament was not suited to the work, he abandoned poetry for prose fiction, and he omitted most of the war poems from late collections of his verse. What of literary interest was written came largely from fiction writers of the second rank, such as Ambrose Bierce and John William DeForest.

Nevertheless, when one thinks of Civil War literature the name of Walt Whitman leaps to mind. Indeed, one commentator has said that "Walt Whitman alone . . . contemplated a book about the war," and, speaking of Melville's achievement in *Battle-Pieces*, he dismissed the book as no more than "a volume of his poems."[7] There is no need to deny that *Drum-Taps* is a literary achievement of the first order and that Whitman based his poems on far greater personal experience of the front than went into Melville's book. Some of Whitman's poems are even similar in content to poems in *Battle-Pieces*, and that he might have written the same kind of book can be seen in his early poetic jotting, "Come now we shall see what stuff you are made of Ship of Libertad." Had his curiosity led him to subject his war experiences to political analysis, to examine the "stuff" of "Libertad" as Melville did, *Drum-Taps* might have been a second Civil War book of the sort defined here. But it is not. As it pictures New York City springing to action after Sumter, the opening poem, "First O Songs for a Prelude," points in a direction that the other poems do not follow. What does follow is largely subjective response, not objective examination. The poems are mostly detached lyrics, snapshots, and grains of life in which the battles and the men who fought them become anonymous types. Specificity is so rare that the reader frequently depends on his knowledge of Whitman's biography to remind himself that the war of *Drum-Taps* is the American Civil War, rather than the Crimean War or the Franco-Prussian War; most of the scenes could as well have occurred at another time and place. If one exempts the Lincoln poems, there are no specific battles or people, little suggestion that North is pitted against South, and scarcely any mention of the issues being decided. The principal significance of *Drum-Taps* is that it is a subsection of *Leaves of Grass*. *Leaves of Grass* is a vision of America, but *Drum-Taps* is not a vision of America searching in battle for its soul. That is not to deny its greatness, but to suggest its nature. Whitman was a romantic, Melville a romancer.

In contrast to *Drum-Taps*, the vision of *Battle-Pieces* is entire unto itself. It is a political book, Whitman's is not. Fogle has described Melville's "public role" as "an unofficial poet laureate of the American nation, who tries to register in poetry the impact and the scope of the Civil War in all representative aspects." Melville asked what nation this was, why Fate had dashed it against the rocks of war, and what sort of future might await it. That future could be bright if the author were permitted to enter the "historical breach" caused by the war "to help refound America upon a worthier ideal of character." The resulting poetry is the product of restless wisdom, sharp sight and insight, high patriotism, unfailing compassion, religious fatalism, both tragic and epic intentions, and the poetic will to weave these elements into a single, unified expression. It is a revolt against the genteel and ideal sentiment that told readers what they wished to hear about the nobility and sanctity of their cause and their warriors, substituting grittiness that told readers who they were, what they had done and why, in what direction they might be headed, and what hope remained that the American experiment might yet ennoble mankind. It is a literary achievement that could have come only from Herman Melville.[8]

A Few Observations

The topic in *Battle-Pieces* that may most concern the modern reader, slavery, is given little attention; it is only in the "Supplement" that the reader is reminded of what he could have learned from reading Melville's earlier works, that the author had always abhorred the institution as an atheistical iniquity and that he believed that it was fated to perish. In view of his muted treatment of the subject, it is hardly surprising that he argued in favor of a conservative reestablishment of the union and against a punitive Reconstruction, even though such a course meant a delay in granting the full prerogatives of citizenship to the freedmen.

The conservatives with whom he aligned himself were often prejudiced against the black man, and even when they were not, their defense of their white brethren in the South distracted them from their obvious duty to assist the freedmen who had been cast adrift in an alien world. But prejudice and neglect were common failings of men of all persuasions. Although the radicals deserved credit for ending slavery, many of them did not regard black people as the equals of whites. Many were puritanical bigots who disdained Catholics, Jews, immigrants, Indians, and conservatives. They hated the Southern rebels passionately, and those Northerners who disagreed with them they smeared as Copperhead traitors. Using the power of the state, they wished to impose their own morals and manners on everyone. Some of them had wished, even before the war, to destroy the South, even if that meant destroying the nation, and in the wake of the war they turned on the former Confederates, bereaved by battle and by the pestilential Northern prison camps, wasted by blockade and by pillage, bereft of industry and agriculture, and drained of treasure, to exact revenge. Still some, notably Whittier, based their hatred of slavery in a broad love of humanity that did not exclude sects, ethnic groups, races, or regions. That was radicalism at its best.

Melville represented conservatism at its best. He could not be narrow, he was unable to classify the human race in terms of communities and types, heroes and villains, and his mind worked holistically. He cherished all of the various people of his country and desired the orderly rehabilitation of former enemy and former slave alike. It was for that reason that he sought a new America in which the defeated children of Washington, Jefferson, and Jackson, and the newly freed children of black men and women stolen from the nations of Africa, could prosper together.

How did he imagine that the great and mutual tragedy of the war might lead to a unified America in which the Mason-Dixon Line and the Color Line would become dim memories? Like Hawthorne, he believed that civic reform cannot be legislated, that it can come only as a result of a reform of the human heart. Something, he said, may be left to gradualism and to heaven. What was needed, he believed, was compassion and generosity in victory, a full restoration of the rights of citizenship to those lately in rebellion which would reunify the country and place the future of the freedmen in the hands of their former masters. That would mean that the Southern whites would create the new South of which the freedmen would be citizens. A new growth of Southern enlightenment and generosity would be required, but the generosity of the conqueror would, he believed, breed reciprocal generosity in the conquered: Christianity and Machiavelli. He was not alone in this; it is precisely the message of Whittier in his "To the Thirty-Ninth Congress."

Well-intended legislation, Melville had told the Congress, may have dire unforeseen consequences, and he lived to see history confirm his warning. The radical Reconstruction resulted in what Melville's Lee had warned against, "eleven sliding daggers" in the nation's side, and the gulfs between South and North and between white and black yawned for another 100 years or more. Yet it is possible that the measures adopted by the Congress, even with their deficiencies, were the best possible response to the dilemma in which the nation found itself at the war's end, and that the moderate policy advocated by Melville would have had even more dire unforeseen consequences without preventing the daggers and gulfs. Nevertheless, one cannot say with certainty that the power of magnanimity would not have succeeded in doing what Melville thought it would do, simply because it was not tried. The nation did not learn the grim necessity of charity toward the vanquished until it looked aghast at the consequences of the vindictive Versailles Treaty that ended the first World War and nurtured the second.

Melville felt deeply that his warning should have been heeded. In the uncompleted "Rammon," the title character warns his half-brother, the king of the Israelites, that the repentant "Jereboam is valorous, a mighty man. If you make him hopeless of lenity, he will stir up mischief, perchance a rebellion." But the king rejects Rammon's advice, leading the latter to mourn, "But now as then he hold[s] me for an imbecile. He surrounds himself with those whom he calls practical men." There is little doubt that the king stands for the radical government that spurned the mendicants of the late Confederacy and that Rammon is a mask through which Melville speaks. Rammon's rejection makes him turn away from public affairs toward Buddhism and visions of "enviable isles," a withdrawal that Melville made his own. Significantly, an embittered Confederate appears in *Clarel*.[9]

Although many of his family and friends must have wished to see the nation restored, as much as possible, to its prewar condition, Melville wished to see a new nation refined from the shattered remains of the old. He prayed that the pity and fear of the unprecedented tragedy would instruct the *whole* of the country, to the end that the nation would fulfill his visionary hope for progress and humanity. He wished for an America purified by her pain, her triumph subdued by prudence gained from her experience, her power dedicated, and her hope grown wise.

For that goal to be reached, it was necessary that his allegorical abstraction of a purified Mother America find living form in sage leaders and a chastened people, but that did not happen. At the moment, the radicals in the Congress were depleting their moral treasury through narrow vision and bitter rancor. Where else could the leaders of the future be found? The foremost men of the South were disqualified from office and the Northern Democrats were discredited. Had Melville named a suitable candidate, it might have been General McClellan, a thoughtful, capable, articulate, charismatic leader and one dedicated to the reestablishment of the union, though McClellan might not have done justice to the needs of the freedmen and history had already rendered its verdict on him in the 1864 election.

In theory, the great military leaders who had won the war should have been prepared to lead the nation in peace. Who more than they had reached Shakespeare's core and had seen the white shark glide through the phosphorus sea? Who better than the man whose shoulders had humped in silent grief at Chattanooga could lead a chastened America? As Melville had written in "The Armies of the Wilderness," Grant's strength, wisdom, honesty, and calm promised the kind of leadership that would permit the happy world to disarm. But to the extent that he believed that the generals had been ennobled by their war experiences Melville was victimized by the very heresy he had exposed in *Battle-Pieces,* the idea that war is somehow glorious. However inescapable it may be, and however justifiable it may be, war is the great atrocity that spawns a host of other atrocities. In his outrage, Emerson had catalogued atrocities committed by the Confederates, not realizing, perhaps, that the list of Union atrocities was equally long, however much they had been sublimated in the Northern imagination through the mitigative excuse of military necessity. Prisoners had been brutalized and killed; sanctioned and unsanctioned arson, looting, starvation, and even more unspeakable crimes had been visited on civilians; and the war had resulted in a slaughter and piteous suffering on the battlefields beyond the comprehension of ordinary men, as Henry Gansevoort had found out when he had revisited the battlefield at Bull Run.

However much they had earned the gratitude of the nation, the virtues of Grant, Sherman, and Sheridan were inappropriate for peace. In prewar civil life, both Grant and Sherman had been mediocrities, and Sheridan was never more than a war machine. Men who without a war to fight might have made no impression on history, they found their true calling on the battlefield. They practiced the brutality to which they had been called by commanding armies, planning and executing campaigns, and stomaching the destruction of men and treasure which they ordered or which befell them. Grant became president, a reward to which he was entitled for having captured Richmond, but he had little interest in reconciling the regions late at war and he does not seem to have had any vision at all of a better nation. Sherman and Sheridan continued to do what they had done best, making war on a new enemy, the plains Indians. After Grant's two administrations, the nation was led by the parade of veteran officers that Hawthorne had foreseen, none of whom were capable of fulfilling Melville's hopes. Probably the first postwar president satisfactory to him was Grover Cleveland, the first who was not a veteran and the first to accept the late Confederates as fellow Americans.

Nor did the vast army of returning veterans bring home the kind of sad virtue for which Melville had hoped, for war does not improve men. Their wartime degradation was described by Rebecca Harding Davis, who saw, at the border, "the actual war; the filthy spewings of it; the political jobbery in Union and Confederate camps; the malignant personal hatreds wearing patriotic masks, and glutted by burning homes and outraged women; the chances in it, well improved on both sides, for brutish men to grow more brutish, and for honorable gentlemen to degenerate into thieves and sots. War may be an armed angel with a mission, but she has the personal habits of the slums."[10] Men who had been coarsened by life in camp had also learned on the field that deception and dishonesty are useful weapons, that power is the supreme virtue, and that rewards are given not for selfless virtue and brotherhood but for survival and success.

Many returning veterans were pathetic husks whose earlier promise had foundered in the war. Many nurtured hatreds for the Southerners and for the rest of their lives yearned for vengeance. Still others had learned lessons of cynicism and craft that benefited them—but only them—in the bloated, belching days of the Gilded Age. For all of Melville's hopes, out of the millions who had fought on both sides it is difficult to remember one man who grew into the sort of great American he had envisioned—save the one who had abandoned the war because he could no longer bear it, Wendell Holmes.

Some civilians—Melville was one—may have been chastened, but others had learned ugly lessons. Among them were the profiteers for whom the war had been a windfall. After its end, these nouveaux riches joined the established nabobs in an orgy of materialistic folly, inspiring Herman's pastor, Henry Bellows, to deplore the failure of decorum, refinement, moderation, and morals. "What kind of sentiments are to have power with the new time and the new civilization?" he pleaded.[11] In the postwar years, they made the "mart's intrusive roar" (334) endemic. There was no escaping the crass impudence which surrounded Melville, the greed of robber barons and the shame of their arrogance, the burgeoning of massive fortunes and of massive deprivation, the vicious class wars between striking laborers and hired strikebreakers—a renewal and intensification of the social ills of which he had complained in the 1850s and a failure of his vision for America.

After witnessing this failure, Melville turned to the idea that the nation would be better served by natural leaders than by winners of nominations and elections. His allusive imagination articulated that belief in the poem "The Age of the Antonines" (235–36), based on that line of nonhereditary Roman emperors under whom, he believed, Rome had most flourished: "A halcyon Age, afar it shines, / Solstice of Man and the Antonines . . . No demagogue beat the pulpit-drum / In the Age of the Antonines!" he wrote, but now, "We sham, we shuffle while faith declines— / They were frank in the Age of the Antonines." That was because the Antonines so clearly merited their power that men willingly followed them:

> Under law made will the world reposed
> And the ruler's right confessed,
> For the heavens elected the Emperor then,
> The foremost of men the best.

"Ah," he added, "might we read in America's signs / The Age restored of the Antonines."

If the postwar era led Melville to despair of ever seeing a satisfactory America, he lost faith in some other ideas of *Battle-Pieces,* as well. Advancing technology, as he encapsulated it in his ironclad poems, had been a useful weapon against secession. As the ugly little *Monitor* had gone where the tall ships could not go, he had given it his grudging approval while bidding a reluctant farewell to the great age of sail. If instinct kept the *Téméraire* and the *Cumberland* in his heart, he recognized that the chivalry of the past was an ideal of the aristocratic South, not of the democratic North. Further, the feats of the Nelsons and the Decaturs had lent romance to bloodshed and carnage, seducing men into loving war too much. The stink and clank, the hiss and grumble of the *Monitor* presented war as it really is, the assemblyline of Satan. Thus it was possible for Melville to accept technological progress, even though he disliked it.

But the industrial growth and innovation of the war years evolved into an age of sophisticated machinery and product development—the age of Edison—that further encouraged American materialism. In his old age Melville could turn on electric lights, speak into a telephone, and ride an elevated railway while the nation seemed oblivious of the values that he had espoused. It is not too much to suppose that he recognized in William Dean Howells's call for a literature of empirical fact an analogue to that materialism, and that he doubly resented Howells's denunciation of the romancers of his era. Thus after he had paid a one-day visit to the Centennial Exposition in Philadelphia, swollen with technology, merchandise, and gewgaws, he wrote Kate Gansevoort, now Kate Lansing, that it was "a sort of tremendous Vanity Fair."[12] The comment was good-humored in tone, but that was his way. His critical attitude was unmasked when, in "Bridegroom Dick," he caused his protagonist to say, "But better, wife, I like to booze on the days / Ere the Old Order foundered in these very frays, / And tradition was lost and we learned strange ways" (174). Certain it is that he turned against the age of the *Monitor* that had seemed so promising and returned in sympathy to the tall ships he had loved and the free-spirited, honest sailors who had manned them, as in this, also from "Bridegroom Dick":

> Nor brave the inventions that serve to replace
> The openness of valor while dismantling the grace.
> Aloof from all this and the never-ending game,
> Tantamount to teetering, plot and counterplot;
> Impenetrable armor—all-perforating shot;
> Aloof, bless God, ride the war-ships of old,
> A grand fleet moored in the roadstead of fame;
> Not submarine sneaks with *them* are enrolled. (181–82)

He mourned the old sailor spirit lost in an age of crank and caloric, and when he re-created it in *Billy Budd* he did so in a coal black Handsome Sailor, his ideal man.

It is doubtful that the war revolutionized Melville's religious beliefs, but it affected them by subjecting them to the severest of tests. If one believed in a god at all, one was forced to reconcile the ravages and sufferings of war, and even the outbreak of the war itself, to that belief. What kind of god would decree such suffering? Melville's lifelong search for theological certainty ensured that he would attempt to answer that question. Many years later, in the far different mood of "Bridegroom Dick," Herman's narrator described the heavenly forces that presided over the war:

so spins the whizzing world,
A humming-top, ay, for the little boy-gods
Flogging it well with their smart little rods,
Tittering at time and the coil uncurled. (173)

But that is not the theological paradigm that emerges from *Battle-Pieces*.

His insistent allusions to the Old Testament and to Milton, added to his frequent resort to a dramatic irony that deals with religion in conventional terms, imperils any attempt to discern a belief in his poems. But despite the fact that the actors in his ecclesiastical drama have Judeo-Christian names, they belong to a somewhat different order of belief such as Zoroastrianism, for want of a better point of reference. Perhaps that is why Rowland Morewood objected to his religious conversation.[13] Like Ormuzd the supreme, his God is not anthropomorphic, does not, that is, incorporate human traits and values. To seek compassion from this all-powerful intellectual abstraction is to misunderstand His role. He is Nature, in the form of the elms of Malvern Hill which are unaffected by human tragedy; Fate, in the form of the "strong Necessity" of "The Conflict of Convictions"; Divine Plan, as in the "scheme of Nature" of the same poem; He who has predestined, in the broadest of terms, all that comes to pass, as in the destiny that, in the "Supplement," decreed the end of secession and slavery. Daily events are irrelevant to Him, since His will is effected through the "deep enforcing current" of "The Muster." Therefore, the infinite folly and tragedy of a country at war is folly and tragedy to its human participants alone; they are the ones who, in the "Conflict of Convictions," "bring to pass" the events that afflict them.

In *Battle-Pieces,* the analogues to Ormuzd, the son, and Ahriman, his evil twin, the subordinate gods of constructive good and anarch evil in Zoroastrianism, are, to further confuse matters, named Christ and Satan. In a book of war poems, there is little room for Christ except as "the Forgiver" of "The Swamp Angel," whose wish it is to convert those who would celebrate the sufferings of the innocent. He appears most frequently in the "Supplement," where both charity and benevolence are Christian principles. The war is the province of Satan, its instigator. He is the god of dissonance, malignancy, disruption, derangement, and suffering. He is the author of original sin, of which war is the ultimate celebration. In "Misgivings," he is the spirit of Nature's "dark side." Yet he cannot prevent even war from having a favorable outcome—because in the end God's plan governs.

It is difficult to determine precisely what Melville meant Christ and Satan to be. It is possible that they are intended to be genuine deities—or angels—but it is equally possible that they represent elements, good and evil, of man's moral or psychological nature. In the latter case, Christ would represent man's higher values, his compassion, forgiveness, conscience, while Satan would represent his innate malevolence, belligerence, hatreds, bigotries, callousness. Nevertheless, in *Billy Budd* Melville implicitly deplored the decline of "that lexicon which is based on Holy Writ" and protested against the idea that a theological explanation of evil would be "subject to the charge of being tinctured with the biblical element" (75). Other members of Melville's celestial host are canards. Raphael and Michael are human fabrications, and the holy angels who stand behind the Union sailors at Mobile Bay are no more than baroque figurines introduced for ornament. Thus the population of Melville's unseen world numbers three, at most.

It is safe to say that, other than Father Mapple, Melville never created a clergyman that he liked, and at the time of *Battle-Pieces* this anticlericism was in full flower. If the battle-poems offered him little opportunity to introduce clerics as dramatic characters, in "The Battle of Stone River" he did so by allusion, recalling that during the Wars of the Roses "monks blessed the fratricidal lance, / And sisters scarfs could twine." He would take up that theme again in *Billy Budd*, in which the chaplain, a man of Christ who should oppose war, permits himself to be enlisted in the ranks of Satan's warriors. He is the "church" in "church and state," an instrument of feudal tyranny. In "The Scout toward Aldie," the chaplain, far from sustaining others spiritually, is intent on curing his own spiritual ailments. Melville's complaint was not that these clergymen were evil or ill-intentioned men, only that they were inadequate to the daunting task they undertook.

The principal religious uncertainty of *Battle-Pieces* concerns the afterlife. For most casual Christians such a belief was a necessity, mitigating the gross slaughter through the certainty that God honored and rewarded the victims—the Union victims, at least—by receiving them into his heaven. Sometimes this confidence was awesome, as in the case of one poet who wrote of a militia lad, killed while passing through Baltimore with the 6th Massachusetts, that, as he lay dying, God bestowed upon him a "Vision apocalyptical" of "the seeds that sages cast / In the world's soil in cycles past, / Spring up and blossom at the last."[14] That was heaven with a bonus access to futurity thrown in, but it was not Melville's belief. If God were as cold and as indifferent as Melville believed, then eternal life in His celestial city was a chancy matter at best. Refusing to accept the common belief in this crucial issue—crucial when men were slaughtered by the hundreds of thousands—Melville referred to it only twice in poems of *Battle-Pieces* that are not clearly ironic and once in his Fredericksburg poem. The patriot ghosts of the Union soldiers slaughtered before Marye's Heights ascend transfigured, but that idea, which he may have believed in late 1862 and early 1863, did not survive in the book. General McPherson's final sleep was to be rent by heaven's trumpet, but that may have been a concession to Toby Greene. More trustworthy is his hope for the sailors who died passing the forts on the Mississippi, that there must be a better world in store for them—not *will* be, but, if there is fairness in the cosmos, *must* be. The most telling statement of all occurs in his epitaphs, the earlier of his "Verses Inscriptive and Memorial," which, in mourning the slain soldiers, make not the slightest reference to an afterlife. No doubt Melville alternated between optimism and pessimism on the subject, but by the time he finished *Clarel* he could do no better than to guess that "even death may prove unreal at the last, / And stoics be astounded into heaven" (499).

Herman Melville's Civil War

When John Brown's raid startled North and South, Melville's reaction was complex. However much he liked and admired Southerners, he opposed slavery as a manifestation of the principal fault line in the nation, the transplantation of the inequities of the Old World to the New and the consequent oppression and repression of the powerless. Yet he could not accept the peril into which such revolutionary measures as Brown's placed the nation. The hope for the future lay in the United States inherited from the Founding Fathers, including his own grandparents, and if the price of union was the delay of corrective measures, that delay was a part of the gradualism through which, he believed, true progress is attained. The election of a Republican administration was even more disastrous. It guaranteed the secession that he feared and made fratricidal war likely. Yet Lincoln's aims, preservation of the union and the abolition of slavery, were, ultimately, his aims, too.

Despite his pacifism, he was stimulated and enthused by the outbreak of war. He joined his fellow Northerners in the "gesture into which patriotic passion surprised the people in a utilitarian time and country," as he put it in his "Supplement," since no other reaction was thinkable. Once begun, the war must have seemed historically inevitable, the necessary climax to the decades of growing schism between North and South. If the union survived, it would be the stronger for the repair of that fault. Patriotic passion demanded its survival, allowing Melville to become what Whittier could not be, a pacifist who cheered troops, anxiously read bulletin boards for news of successes in arms, and toured the armies in the field. A different president might have prevented the tragedy, but when nature's dark side appeared there was no refuge from the darkness. When emancipation did come, he did not oppose it: the schism that it would otherwise have caused had already occurred.

There was only one antidote to the pain and suffering, the prospect that fear and pity would guide the nation toward a better future in which it would abandon the follies and vanities of the past to embrace faith, humility, Christian charity, and its destiny of leading the world toward a future of moral progress. At some midwar point, Melville dedicated his artistry to that future, and when the government divided and faltered over the proper postwar path, he was ready with his pen to lead the way toward justice and tolerance. He was wrong in believing that he would be heard, but that miscalculation does not invalidate the achievement of *Battle-Pieces*.

Thus for five intense years Melville was a man dedicated to a cause, not the man of uncertainty and clouded aims he had been before the war. His subsequent fall was as precipitous as his ascent had been steep. A new America was emerging, but it was not his chastened mother. His hopes for national rededication were shattered and his poetic aspirations were crushed. Never again would he delude himself into thinking that he might be recognized in his own time, nor would he ever again see himself as the bard of national destiny.

Notes

Abbreviations

B&L	Robert Underwood Johnson and Clarence Clough Buel, eds., *Battles and Leaders of the Civil War,* 4 vols. (1887–88; reprint, Secaucus, N.J.: Castle, 1982)
Dyer	Frederick Henry Dyer, comp., *A Compendium of the War of the Rebellion . . . ,* 3 vols. (Des Moines, Iowa: Dyer, 1908)
FANY	Federal Archives and Records Center, New York
GL	Gansevoort-Lansing Collection, Rare Books and Manuscripts Division, New York Public Library, Astor, Lenox, and Tilden Foundations
LC	Library of Congress
Log	Jay Leyda, *The Melville Log: A Documentary Life of Herman Melville, 1819–1891,* 2 vols. (New York: Gordian Press, 1969)
MFPA	Melville Family Papers Addition, GL
NA	National Archives
NYHS	New-York Historical Society
NYPL	New York Public Library, Astor, Lenox, and Tilden Foundations
NYT	*New York Times*
RG	Record Group
Sun	*Pittsfield Sun*
U&CA	U.S. War Department, *The War of the Rebellion: A Compilation of the Official Records of the Union and Confederate Armies,* 1st ser., 53 vols., 2d ser., 8 vols., 3d ser., 5 vols., 4th ser., 3 vols., and index (Washington, D.C.: Government Printing Office, 1889–1901)
U&CN	U.S. Navy Department, *Official Records of the Union and Confederate Navies in the War of the Rebellion,* 1st ser., 27 vols., 2d ser., 3 vols., and index (Washington, D.C.: Government Printing Office, 1894–1922)

Introduction

1. Quotations from *Battle-Pieces* are from the first edition text in *Battle-Pieces and Aspects of the War,* ed. Sidney Kaplan (Amherst: University of Massachusetts Press,

1972), emended to reflect corrections in Melville's copy (listed xxv–xxviii). The most eloquent modern edition is *The Battle-Pieces of Herman Melville,* ed., intro., notes Hennig Cohen (New York: Thomas Yoseloff, 1964), the invaluable notes to which I have borrowed with and without acknowledgment. (Quotations of Melville's minor poems are from *Collected Poems of Herman Melville,* ed., intro., notes Howard P. Vincent (Chicago: Hendricks House, 1947); for the sources of quotations from other works of Melville, see Bibliography.)

2. Letters: *The Letters of Herman Melville,* ed. Merrell R. Davis and William H. Gilman (New Haven, Conn.: Yale University Press, 1960), 197–227. Little recorded: what memoirs are available, chiefly by J. E. A. Smith, a Pittsfield newspaper editor and author, Titus Munson Coan, a New York City physician, and Arthur Stedman, a New York City literary figure, are reprinted in Merton M. Sealts, Jr., *The Early Lives of Melville: Nineteenth-Century Biographical Sketches and Their Authors* (Madison: University of Wisconsin Press, 1974). Bits and snatches: much of the available information about Melville from the fall of 1859 to the middle of 1866 is in *Log,* 2:609–82, 944–48, which will not be cited except in the case of quotations.

3. "Introduction," *Herman Melville: Representative Selections,* intro., bibl., notes Willard Thorpe (New York: American Book, 1938), lxxxviii.

4. Joel H. Silbey, *A Respectable Minority: The Democratic Party in the Civil War Era, 1860–1868* (New York: W. W. Norton, 1977), 5–6. The following discussion is based on this study.

5. The following family sketches are largely from standard biographical dictionaries and from Alice P. Kenney, *The Gansevoorts of Albany: Dutch Patricians in the Upper Hudson Valley* (Syracuse, N.Y.: Syracuse University Press, 1969).

6. Politics of Revolutionary War General Gansevoort: he supported George Clinton, later vice-president under both Jefferson and Madison, for the postwar governorship of New York, to Major Fonda and Zephaniah Batchellor, 20 April 1783, Misc. Mss., Gansevoort, Peter, NYHS; and in 1801 Thomas Jefferson made him military agent for the Northern Department, Letters of Application and Recommendation during the Administration of Thomas Jefferson, 1801–1809, RG 59, Department of State, NA. Old Major Melvill's war service: Thomas Melvill Pension Application, Revolutionary War Pension and Bounty-Land Warrant Application Files, Veterans Administration, RG 15, NA. Politics of Major Melvill: he was kept in office by Jefferson, Madison, and Monroe, and from the wartime activities of his son, Major Thomas Melvill, Jr., it is likely that he supported "Mister Madison's war." See Stanton Garner, "The Picaresque Career of Thomas Melvill, Junior," parts 1, 2, *Melville Society Extracts,* nos. 60, 62 (November 1984, May 1985): 1–10, 1, 4–10.

7. Henry Gansevoort to Catherine Gansevoort, 17 January, 2 February 1859, GL.

8. Patron of the arts: Allan was interested in acquiring two paintings from the Freeman Collection, Henry Gansevoort to Catherine Gansevoort, 19 March 1861, GL; he was a sponsor of the 1865 exhibition of the National Academy of Design; and as a result of a $500 donation, his wife was a National Academy of Design Fellow for Life, Cohen, "Introduction," *Battle-Pieces of Herman Melville,* 14.

9. Gruff, parsimonious: Eleanor Melville Metcalf, *Herman Melville: Cycle and Epicycle* (Cambridge, Mass.: Harvard University Press, 1953), 214. Difficult to please: Frances Melville asked her sister Augusta not to show her letter to "critical George," 18 [May] 1863, MFPA. Able to afford a home, living with brother: Eighth Census of the United States, 1860, Brookline, Norfolk County, Mass., dwelling

435, family 541, 14 July 1860, Records of the Bureau of the Census, RG 29, NA, lists his real estate at $4,000, his personal estate at $15,000. George and John brothers: Clarence Winthrop Bowen, *The History of Woodstock Connecticut: Genealogies of Woodstock Families,* 8 vols. (Norwood, Mass.: Plimpton, 1935), 6:121.

10. Metcalf, *Cycle and Epicycle,* 28.

11. John Hoadley biography: John Chipman Hoadley, "Sketch of John Chipman Hoadley, Written by Himself in Response to the Request of the Magazine," *American Machinist* 9 (27 November 1886): 1–2; Hoadley obit., *American Machinist* 9 (13 November 1886): 1; Francis Bacon Trowbridge, *The Hoadley Genealogy: A History of the Descendants of William Hoadley of Branford, Connecticut, Together with Some Account of Other Families of the Name* (New Haven, Conn.: Trowbridge, 1894), 87–88, 146–47. Family tradition: *Log,* 1:xxvii. Prosperous: Census, 1860, Lawrence, Essex County, Mass., dwelling 445, family 588, 16 June 1860, NA, lists his personal estate as $8,000.

12. A number of his manuscript poems are contained in the Hoadley box, GL. "Destiny" volume: John Hoadley to Alfred B. Street, 11 July 1853, Misc. Mss., Street, Alfred B., NYHS.

13. Kenney, *Gansevoorts of Albany,* 260.

14. Hawthorne and Holmes: Fanny Melville said, "I have met them both several times at Pittsfield when they have been at our house to see Herman. Mr. Hawthorne once passed several days with us," to Catherine Gansevoort, 5 April 1862, GL.

15. Allan Melville as a Thurston: Charles Myrick Thurston, *Genealogy of Charles Myrick Thurston and of His Wife, Rachel Hall Pitman, Formerly of Newport, R.I., after December, 1840, of New York* (New York: John F. Trow, 1865), states on the title page that it is for the "families of Mrs. Rachel H. Thurston, Mrs. Rachel H. Barrington, Charles M. Thurston, Dr. A. Henry Thurston, Deceased, Richard Lathers, and Allan Melville." Other information about the Thurstons: Charles Myrick Thurston, *Descendants of Edward Thurston, the First of the Name in the Colony of Rhode Island* (New York: Trow and Smith, 1868); Brown Thurston, *Thurston Genealogies* (Portland, Me.: Brown Thurston and Hoyt, Fogg and Donham, 1880).

16. Richard Lathers biography: Richard Lathers, *Reminiscences of Richard Lathers: Sixty Years of a Busy Life in South Carolina, Massachusetts and New York,* ed. Alvan F. Sanborn (New York: Grafton Press, 1907); *Life and Services of Col. Richard Lathers of New Rochelle, New York* (n.p., 1897); [Charles F. Canedy,] *This Discursive Biographical Sketch, 1841–1902, of Colonel Richard Lathers Was Compiled as Required for Honorary Membership in Post 509, Grand Army of the Republic . . .* (Philadelphia: J. B. Lippincott, 1902); Richard Lathers obit, *NYT,* 18 September 1903; Abby Pitman Lathers obit., *NYT,* 4 February 1904; Richard Lathers Papers, LC. Duyckinck circle: "Mr. Lathers married Miss Thurston sister of Allan Melville's wife—through whom my acquaintance with Mr L comes," Evert A. Duyckinck Diary, 23 June 1859, Duyckinck Family Papers, NYPL, courtesy Donald Yannella. *Reminiscences* is sometimes woefully inaccurate, perhaps because of Sanborn's editing of materials unfamiliar to him.

17. Wealth, household: Census, 1860, New Rochelle, Westchester County, N.Y., dwelling 2307, family 2583, 2 September 1860, NA, values his real estate at $20,000, his personal estate at $5,000. Intimacy between Herman and Lathers: suggested by Herman Melville to Richard Lathers, "Lord of Winyah," 9 April [1854]; Lynn Horth, "Letters Lost Letters Found: A Progress Report on Melville's *Correspondence,*" *Melville Society Extracts,* no. 81 (May 1990):5, in which Herman invited himself to Winyah without a previous invitation and invited Richard and Abby to visit Arrowhead.

18. Cincinnati: Allan Melville to Henry Gansevoort, 27 June 1862, GL. Uncle Herman as active Democrat: Hershel Parker, "Melville and Politics: A Scrutiny of the Political Milieux of Herman Melville's Life and Works" (Ph.D. diss., Northwestern University, 1963), 116. Strange man: Catherine Gansevoort Diaries, 11 August 1862, GL. Danby: Census, 1860, Danby, Rutland County, Vt., dwelling 202, family 203, 11 June 1860, NA. Wessel is listed as "J. Gansevoort" and his place of birth as "unknown."

19. Curtis genealogy: Harlow Dunham Curtis, comp., *A Genealogy of the Curtiss-Curtis Family of Stratford, Connecticut* (Stratford, Conn.: Curtiss-Curtis Society, 1953), 218ff.

20. Census, 1865, Third Election District, Queensbury, Warren County, N.Y., household 282/351 (a local census), courtesy John Austin. Ages accurate to within a year.

21. Guert Gansevoort biography: Abstracts of Service of Naval Officers, Bureau of Naval Personnel, RG 24, Department of the Navy, NA. I am grateful to the late Wilson Heflin for providing me with extensive information about Guert's service.

22. DuPont: Guert Gansevoort to Samuel F. DuPont, 20 January 1843, Admiral Samuel Francis DuPont Papers, Hagley Museum and Library. Quotations: *Autobiography of Thurlow Weed,* ed. Harriet A. Weed (Boston: Houghton Mifflin, 1883), 515–19.

23. Notes, Naval Reform Board, 1855, DuPont Papers.

24. *NYT*, 29 November, 29 December 1855, 28 February 1856 (quotation).

25. Squadron commander: Captain William Mervine to Secretary of the Navy, 18 September 1856, Letters Received by the Secretary of the Navy from Commanding Officers of Squadrons, Naval Records Collection of the Office of Naval Records and Library, RG 45, Department of the Navy, NA. Home at Glens Falls: 2/12 (1858), 2/132 (1858), 3/112 (1859), Deed Grantees to 1876, Land Records, Warren County, N.Y., courtesy John Austin, show that he purchased three properties in 1858 and 1859; Augusta or Frances Melville to Catherine Gansevoort, 7 October 1865, GL., reported that Guert had sold his house for $10,000, a large amount.

26. See note 18, Cincinnati.

27. Memorabilia: Kenney, *Gansevoorts of Albany,* 262–63; unidentified newspaper clipping, 23 March 1912, concerning donations to the National Museum, Washington, D.C., GL; unidentified newspaper clipping, 31 May 1910, concerning Gilbert Stuart paintings, GL; Peter Gansevoort to Henry Gansevoort, 15 April 1862, GL; Catherine Gansevoort Diaries, 12 May 1862, GL. Fortune: Peter Gansevoort Diaries, 31 January 1861, GL. Household: Census, 1860, Albany, Albany County, N.Y., 9th Ward, dwelling 516, family 665, 1 February 1860, NA.

28. Fanny terrified: Metcalf, *Cycle and Epicycle,* 211. Cliosophic Society: Peter Gansevoort folder, Princeton University Archives.

29. Princeton: Henry S. Gansevoort folder, Princeton University Archives.

30. Census, 1860, Albany, Albany County, N.Y., 1st Ward, dwelling 373, family 467, 8 July 1860, NA.

31. Captain D'Wolf and his family: Calbraith B. Perry, *Charles D'Wolf of Guadaloupe, His Ancestors and Descendants . . .* (New York: T. A. Wright, 1902), 48–50. Aunt Helen: Census, 1860, Hingham, Plymouth County, Mass., dwelling 211, family 193, 11 June 1860, NA. It is possible that there were other Souther children who were not living at home in 1860.

32. Amos Nourse civil service: *Register of Officers and Agents, Civil, Military, and Naval, in the Service of the United States on . . .* (*Register of All Officers . . .*) (*Biennial Register of All Officers . . .*) (Washington, D.C.: Government Printing Office and others, biennial), passim. This publication, which will not be cited further, is the source of information about federal employment, civilian, army, and navy—for example, that of Oakes Shaw, below. Admired yarns: *Log,* 1:361. Daughters and grandchildren: Helen Griggs to Augusta Melville, 22 March 1863, MFPA. Mary in or near Boston: around the beginning of 1863, she rented her house and boarded in Roxbury, where Helen Griggs saw her often, Lucy Nourse [to Augusta and Frances Melville,] 2 January 1863, MFPA.

33. Hobart family: Census, 1860, Rockford, Winnebago County, Ill., dwelling 1420, family 1437, 21 July 1860, NA. Carpenter: ibid. and Rockford city directories. Republican: Thomas J. Hobart obit., *Galena Weekly Gazette,* 6 June 1879. It is possible that the Hobarts had other daughters who were no longer living at home, but it is unlikely that they had other sons.

34. Shaw biography: Elijah Adlow, *The Genius of Lemuel Shaw: Expounder of The Common Law* (Boston: Massachusetts Law Quarterly, 1962); Frederic Hathaway Chase, *Lemuel Shaw: Chief Justice of the Supreme Judicial Court of Massachusetts, 1830–1860* (Boston: Houghton Mifflin, 1918); and Leonard W. Levy, *The Law of the Commonwealth and Chief Justice Shaw* (Cambridge, Mass.: Harvard University Press, 1957). Ben Butler: ibid., 26.

35. Carolyn L. Karcher, *Shadow over the Promised Land: Slavery, Race, and Violence in Melville's America* (Baton Rouge: Louisiana State University Press, 1980), 10.

36. Unmarried, living with parents: Census, 1860, Boston, Suffolk County, Mass., 6th Ward, dwelling 298, family 310, 9 June 1860, NA. Lemuel Shaw, Jr., on *Confidence-Man: Log,* 2:574.

37. "Democratic family": to Peter Gansevoort, 7 April 1857, Metcalf, *Cycle and Epicycle,* 165. Armageddon: Henry Gansevoort to Catherine Gansevoort, 29 December 1861, Catherine Gansevoort to Henry Gansevoort, 2 January 1862, GL.

38. "Disgusting object": Catherine Gansevoort Diaries, 20 August 1861, GL. "Refuse of Gods Creation": to Catherine Gansevoort, 12 August 1864, GL. Slavery would die: Catherine Gansevoort to Henry Gansevoort, 8 November 1859, GL. Lathers's story: *Reminiscences of Richard Lathers,* 21–22. Vesey conspiracy: Richard C. Wade, *Slavery in the Cities: The South 1820–1860* (New York: Oxford University Press, 1964), 228–41.

39. The only evidence linking the Morewoods to the Democratic Party is the fact that—as will be seen—Sarah was a frequent contributor to the Democratic *Sun.*

40. Uncle Peter quotation: Metcalf, *Cycle and Epicycle,* 148. Never voted: ibid., 165.

41. Merton M. Sealts, Jr., *Melville as Lecturer* (Cambridge, Mass.: Harvard University Press, 1957), 105.

42. Karcher: *Shadow over the Promised Land,* 17. Paludan: Phillip Shaw Paludan, *"A People's Contest": The Union and the Civil War, 1861–1865* (New York: Harper and Row, 1988), xx. Strong: 11 January 1860, *The Diary of George Templeton Strong,* ed. Allan Nevins and Milton Halsey Thomas, 4 vols. (New York: Macmillan, 1952), 3:4.

43. Chase: Richard Chase, *Herman Melville: A Critical Study* (New York: Macmillan, 1949), 230–31. Mumford: Lewis Mumford, *Herman Melville: A Study of His Life and Vision,* rev. ed. (New York: Harcourt, Brace and World, 1962), 204.

44. Interest in Herman's works, *Typee:* Henry Gansevoort to [Catherine Ganse-

voort,] 30 May 1868, J[ohn]. C[hipman]. Hoadley, *Memorial of Henry Sanford Gansevoort, Captain Fifth Artillery, and Lieutenant-Colonel by Brevet, U.S.A.: Colonel Thirteenth New York State Volunteer Cavalry, and Brigadier-General of Volunteers by Brevet* (Boston: Franklin Press and Rand, Avery, 1875), 265. *Omoo: Log,* 1:250. *Moby-Dick:* Henry Gansevoort to Susan L. Gansevoort, 27 October 1851, GL. *Piazza Tales: Log,* 2:515. *Confidence-Man:* Henry Gansevoort to Catherine Gansevoort, 11 April 1857, GL. *Battle-Pieces: Log,* 2:682, 686. Griggs calling, walk, dinner: Henry Gansevoort to Catherine Gansevoort, 25 May 1857, GL. Herman and Shaw visiting, sumptuous banquet: *Log,* 2:579. Dana chauffering: Henry Gansevoort Diaries, 27 May 1857, GL. Note about Aunt Melville: Henry Gansevoort Diaries, 4 June 1857, GL. Dining with Aunt Melville: *Log,* 2:580. Thanksgiving with Shaws: Henry Gansevoort to Catherine Gansevoort, 28 November 1857, GL.

45. Allan looking in on Henry: Henry Gansevoort Diaries, 3 November 1858, GL. Henry looking in on Allan: Henry Gansevoort Diaries, 26 November 1858, GL. Hoadleys' baby: Henry Gansevoort to Catherine Gansevoort, 17 January 1859, GL. Tour of *Meteor:* Henry Gansevoort to Catherine Gansevoort, 24 February 1859, GL. Saw Herman: Henry Gansevoort to Catherine Gansevoort, 8 December 1858, GL. Saw Aunt Melville, bothering Allan: Henry Gansevoort to Catherine Gansevoort, 9 March 1859, GL. Continued visits to Allan: Henry Gansevoort Diaries, 14 March, 10, 12, 13 May 1859, GL.

46. One-day service: letters between the yard and the bureau in Washington were normally delivered in one day, Records of the New York Navy Yard, N.Y., Records of Naval Districts and Shore Establishments, 1826–1953, RG 181, FANY, and the correspondence in MFPA shows the same. "Comfort and blessing": Helen Griggs to Catherine Gansevoort, 14 September 1872; Metcalf, *Cycle and Epicycle,* 214.

47. Eagerness: Newton Arvin, *Herman Melville* (New York: William Sloan, 1950), 259. "Unusual intensity": Mason, *Spirit above the Dust,* 211.

48. "Iron Nerves": Oliver Wendell Holmes, "Bread and the Newspaper (September 1861)," *The Works of Oliver Wendell Holmes,* 13 vols. (Boston: Houghton Mifflin, 1892), 8:7. Daily ride into town: *Log,* 1:401. During the period of Herman's residence in and near Pittsfield, there was no home mail delivery, *Berkshire County Eagle,* 17 March 1967, courtesy Alan B. Grieve.

49. Paludan, *"A People's Contest,"* 328.

50. Fogle: Richard Harter Fogle, "Melville and the Civil War," *Tulane Studies in English* 9 (1959): 61. "Crow's-nest": Daniel Aaron, *The Unwritten War: American Writers and the Civil War* (New York: Alfred A. Knopf, 1973), 77.

51. Shurr: William H. Shurr, *The Mystery of Iniquity: Melville as Poet, 1857–1891* (Lexington: University Press of Kentucky, 1972), 7. "Entity": Ronald Mason, *The Spirit above the Dust: A Study of Herman Melville* (London: John Lehmann, 1951), 211.

52. Warren, violence, distortions, wrenchings: "Melville the Poet," *The Kenyon Review* 8 (Spring 1946): 210. Stein: *The Poetry of Melville's Late Years: Time, History, Myth, and Religion* (Albany: State University of New York Press, 1970), 4. Karcher: *Shadow over the Promised Land,* 260. Warren, nervous, maculine: "Introduction," *Selected Poems of Herman Melville: A Reader's Edition,* ed., intro. Robert Penn Warren (New York: Random House, 1970), 12.

53. Stewart: Rachel Whitesides Stewart, "The Conditional Mood of Melville's Poetry" (Ph.D. diss., University of Colorado, 1975), 76. Karcher: *Shadow over the Promised Land,* 263. See also Stewart, "The Conditional Mood," 79, 87–88, 96.

Chapter 1 Before the Fall

1. Frances Melville recalled that Herman railed "at conditions in the country at large, to anyone who would listen, with much heat and oratory," Metcalf, *Cycle and Epicycle,* 216. The words are Eleanor Metcalf's, not Frances's.

2. Reporter: *Log,* 2:591. Height: Metcalf, *Cycle and Epicycle,* 251. Militia census: Pittsfield, Mass., Town Records.

3. According to J. E. A. Smith, Metcalf, *Cycle and Epicycle,* 33–34.

4. Suppers, dresses: Metcalf, *Cycle and Epicycle,* 133, 204. In 1856, his family "had begun to suffer not only from insufficient funds for daily needs, but far more from his bursts of nervous anger and attacks of morose conscience," ibid., 159. Without understanding: Lizzie spoke of the "fogs" of *Mardi* and wrote Hope Shaw, "if the mist ever does clear away, I should like to know what it [*Mardi*] reveals to *you,*" ibid., 61. Emotional crises: during its proofreading, Lizzie said that *Clarel* "has undermined all our happiness," *Log,* 2:747.

5. Sell Arrowhead: *Log,* 2:580. Vere de Vere: J. E. A. Smith, "Herman Melville," Sealts, *Early Lives of Melville,* 139. Brooklyn: Merton M. Sealts, Jr., *Melville's Reading: Revised and Enlarged Edition* (Columbia: University of South Carolina Press, 1988), 103. Herman not gifted: Metcalf, *Cycle and Epicycle,* 160. Lizzie and housework, party slippers: ibid., 98. Hat and dresses: ibid., 80. Whist: ibid., 56. *Eagle: Log,* 1:479. The name "Vere" commonly signified one who is inordinately proud of his aristocratic origins. See Tennyson's "Lady Clara Vere de Vere" ("I know you proud to bear your name") and Hawthorne's "The Great Carbuncle" ("besides his own share, he [Lord de Vere] had the collected haughtiness of his whole line of ancestry").

6. Herman and Morewoods, facts of Broadhall: Smith, "Herman Melville," 129–30; Morewood family: Census, 1860, dwelling 1887, family 2016, 17 August 1860, Pittsfield, Berkshire County, Mass., NA. Naming Broadhall, cows: Metcalf, *Cycle and Epicycle,* 126. Herman underestimating Sarah: ibid., 124. Pressures: *Log,* 1:271.

7. Popular notion: Paludan, *"A People's Contest,"* 22–25, 342.

8. Herman's lecturing: the subject of Sealts, *Melville as Lecturer,* required reading for those interested in this period of Melville's life. Mesmerizing Hawthornes: Julian Hawthorne, "Tribute to Hawthorne," *The Berkshire Hills: An Historic Monthly* 2 (1 February 1902): 214, reprinted from "Hawthorne at Lenox," *The Booklovers Weekly,* courtesy Alan Grieve; Metcalf, *Cycle and Epicycle,* 57. Henry Gansevoort quotations: ibid., 167, 172. Rockford: Sealts, *Melville as Lecturer,* 88–90.

9. Nervous temperaments: Metcalf, *Cycle and Epicycle,* 208. Allergies, Herman being left alone: ibid., 262–63. Herman challenging Lizzie: ibid., 259. Herman incapable of handling "head work": ibid., 263. Frederika: Census, 1860, Pittsfield, Berkshire County, Mass., dwelling 674, family 709, 28 June 1860, NA. Overseeing cooks, ordering coffee: Metcalf, *Cycle and Epicycle,* 216. Drinking: "His countenance is slightly flushed with whiskey drinking," *Log,* 2:605. Nerves taut: Metcalf, *Cycle and Epicycle,* 150–51.

10. Metcalf, *Cycle and Epicycle,* 283.

11. Sealts, *Melville's Reading,* 108, 166, 185–86, 175–76.

12. Concord meeting: Otto J. Scott, *The Secret Six: John Brown and the Abolitionist Movement* (New York: Times Books, 1979), 281. Stedman: "How Old Brown Took Harper's Ferry," *Poetry of America: Selections from One Hundred American Poets from*

1776 to 1876, ed. W. J. Linton (London: George Bell and Sons, 1878), 288. Longfellow: journal, 2 December 1859, Samuel Longfellow, ed., *Life of Henry Wadsworth Longfellow with Extracts from His Journals and Correspondence,* 3 vols., vols. 12–14 of *The Works of Henry Wadsworth Longfellow* (1896; reprint, New York: AMS Press, 1966), 2:396.

13. Alcott: December 1859, *The Journals of Louisa May Alcott,* ed. Joel Myerson, Daniel Shealy, and Madeleine B. Stern, intro. Madeleine B. Stern (Boston: Little, Brown, 1989), 95. Emerson: James M. McPherson, *Battle Cry of Freedom: The Civil War Era* (New York: Oxford University Press, 1988), 209. "Servile insurrection": to Henry Gansevoort, 8 November 1859, GL. Bessie to city: Augusta Melville to Catherine Gansevoort, 4 January 1860, GL. Sarah: *Log,* 2:609. Illness: Eleanor Metcalf said that "a fluctuation little understood by Melville's family (and perhaps no better by himself) could bring about marked changes in his health," Metcalf, *Cycle and Epicycle,* 171.

14. *Reminiscences of Richard Lathers,* 72–73.

15. Whitman's first poem: "Year of Meteors (1859–60)," *Leaves of Grass,* ed. Sculley Bradley and Harold W. Blodgett (New York: W. W. Norton, 1973), 238. Second: "Premonition," *Whitman's Manuscripts: Leaves of Grass (1860): A Parallel Text,* ed., notes, intro. Fredson Bowers (Chicago: University of Chicago Press, 1955), 10. Hawthorne in public: "Chiefly about War Matters," *The Complete Works of Nathaniel Hawthorne,* intro., notes George Parsons Lathrop, 12 vols. (Boston: Houghton Mifflin, 1883), 12:327–28. In private: to Horatio Woodman, 22 June 1862, Nathaniel Hawthorne, *The Letters, 1857–1864,* ed. Thomas Woodson, James A. Rubino, L. Neal Smith, and Norman Holmes Pearson, vol. 18 of *The Centenary Edition of the Works of Nathaniel Hawthorne* ([Columbus:] Ohio State University Press, 1987), 463.

16. *Log,* 1:410.

17. Element of time: Joyce Sparer Adler, *War in Melville's Imagination* (New York: New York University Press, 1981), 136–37. "Fateful": Laurence Barrett, "The Differences in Melville's Poetry," *PMLA* 70 (September 1955): 613. "Wyrd": Shurr, *The Mystery of Iniquity,* 17.

18. "Valley": Stein, *Poetry of Melville's Late Years,* 7; Cohen, "Notes," *Battle-Pieces of Herman Melville,* 204.

19. Children's activities: *Log,* 2:602.

20. Abstracts of Service of Naval Officers, NA, Letters and Telegrams Received from the Bureau of Ordnance, Series 265, Records of the New York Navy Yard, Records of Naval Districts and Shore Establishments, Series 265, RG 181, Department of the Navy, FANY.

21. Mansion House: Census, 1860, Brooklyn, Kings County, N.Y., 1st District, 3rd Ward, dwelling 618, family 883, 28 July 1860, NA; Budd: *ibid.,* dwelling 190, family 234, 25 June 1860.

22. *Log,* 2:614.

23. Republican regionalism: Randall C. Jimerson, *The Private Civil War: Popular Thought during the Sectional Conflict* (Baton Rouge: Louisiana State University Press, 1988), 11–14. Conversation: Alfred H. Guernsey and Henry M. Alden, *Harper's Pictorial History of the Civil War* (1866, 1868; reprint, 2 vols. in 1, of *Harper's Pictorial History of the Great Rebellion*, New York: Fairfax Press, 1977), 16. Although not

named, Lathers must have been the only New York City insurance executive who habitually arranged meetings between prominent New Yorkers and Southerners.

24. Health: Howard C. Horsford and Lynn Horth, "Historical Note," Herman Melville, *Journals*, ed. Howard C. Horsford and Lynn Horth, vol. 15 of *The Writings of Herman Melville* (Evanston, Ill., and Chicago: Northwestern University Press and Newberry Library, 1989), 194. Herman's journal of the cruise, reprinted in this edition, is the source of the route and the events of his voyage, below.

25. Pipes: Metcalf, *Cycle and Epicycle*, 216. Reading material: Sealts, *Melville's Reading*, 109, 155, 171, 198, 186, 162, 211, 227, 183, 155–56. Dewey: Horsford and Horth, "Historical Notes," Melville, *Journals*, 201. Bessie's bag: Herman Melville to Elizabeth Melville (daughter), 2 September 1860, *Letters of Herman Melville*, 204. Miss Property: Metcalf, *Cycle and Epicycle*, 206.

26. Everett admiring Herman: Metcalf, *Cycle and Epicycle*, 65. Dickinson's nomination: Jay Leyda, *The Years and Hours of Emily Dickinson*, 2 vols. (New Haven, Conn.: Yale University Press, 1960), 2:15–16.

27. Facts about *Meteor*: Horsford and Horth, "Historical Note," Melville, *Journals*, 198. Decor: to Catherine Gansevoort, 24 February 1859, GL.

28. Sealts, *Melville's Reading*, 162, 183.

29. Ibid., 211, 198, 186, 155–56.

30. Glauco Cambon, *The Inclusive Flame: Studies in American Poetry* (Bloomington: Indiana University Press, 1963), 13.

31. Reading: Sealts, *Melville's Reading*, 155, 227, 198, 171, 186. "Savage Tuscan": "Herman at Christie's: On the Block—Again," *Melville Society Extracts*, no. 63 (September 1985): 10. "Gentleman": Horsford and Horth, "Historical Note," Melville, *Journals*, 199n.

32. Herman punctuating: *Log*, 1:276. Quotations: *Log*, 2:618. Derby and Toby Greene: Amy Elizabeth Puett, "Melville's Wife: A Study of Elizabeth Shaw Melville" (Ph.D. diss., Northwestern University, 1969), 119–20.

33. 15 January 1857, Hawthorne, *Letters, 1857–1864*, 8.

34. Arrival, respects: Peter Gansevoort Diaries, 31 August, 8 September 1860, GL. Henry to City: Peter Gansevoort Diaries, 20 September 1860, GL; Abraham Lansing to Henry Gansevoort, 26 September 1860, GL. Truckling expedients: Robert Sanford to Henry Gansevoort, 10 April 1862, GL. Pressured: Peter Gansevoort to Henry Gansevoort, 5 October 1860, GL. Appointment: Abraham Lansing to Henry Gansevoort, 2 November 1860, GL.

35. Rockford Zouaves: Michele Y. Spray, "Lincoln's 'Wide Awake' Leader," *Nuggets of History* (Rockford, Ill.) 18 (Spring 1981): 1.

36. *Meteor*'s cargo and destination: Horsford and Horth, "Historical Note," Melville, *Journals*, 203n.

37. Touring: "I want to see what I can while here," Herman Melville to Samuel Shaw, 16 October 1860, *Log*, 2:628. Frémonts: Horsford and Horth, "Historical Note," Melville, *Journals*, 201–2.

38. Sketch: reproduced in Horsford and Horth, "Historical Note," Melville, *Journals*, 642–44.

39. *Cortes*, *North Star*: ibid., 205–6; weather, arrival date: *NYT*, 14 November 1860, courtesy John M. J. Gretchko. Schiller: *Log*, 2:629.

40. Whittier: 30 October 1860, *Letters of John Greenleaf Whittier*, ed. John B. Pickard,

3 vols. (Cambridge, Mass.: Harvard University Press, 1975), 2:474. Henry's belief: Catherine Gansevoort to Henry Gansevoort, 7 November 1860, GL. Pittsfield vote: *Sun*, 8 November 1860. Block radicals: to Peter Gansevoort, 7 November 1860, GL.

41. Whittier: to Hannah Lloyd Neall, 8 November 1860, *Letters of John Greenleaf Whittier*, 2:476. Henry: see note 40, block radicals.

42. *Sun*, 15 November 1860.

43. Curious occurrences: *Sun*, 22 November 1860. Visits to the Griggses, the Hoadleys, and the Melvill aunts are inferred; in Boston, Herman and Lizzie saw George W. Wales several times, George Wales to Henry Gansevoort, 3 December 1860, GL. Revealed by chance in an unrelated letter, these visits suggest that Herman's social circle exceeded significantly the limits indicated by the dearth of other evidence.

44. Visited Gansevoort: Catherine Gansevoort to Henry Gansevoort, 23 November 1860, GL. Thanksgiving: in the same letter, Kitty said that "All [Aunt Melville and Fanny] are to Dine with us on Thursday next—[for] Thanksgiving dinner." Since the departure of Uncle Peter, Aunt Susan, and Kitty for Europe, Herman and Lizzie had not seen them. To return to the Shaw home for Thanksgiving not only would have meant cutting short their visit to Herman's mother and sisters, but also it would have injured feelings in Albany.

45. Neither to blame: for a proposal that in the matter of blame Herman was not referring to Hawthorne, see the note to the discussion in chapter 7 of Herman's poem "Monody." Emerson: Ralph Waldo Emerson, *The Journals and Miscellaneous Notebooks of Ralph Waldo Emerson, 1860–1866,* ed. Linda Allardt, David W. Hill, and Ruth H. Bennett, vol. 15 of *The Journals and Miscellaneous Notebooks of Ralph Waldo Emerson* (Cambridge, Mass.: Harvard University Press, 1982), 60.

46. Hawthorne: Metcalf, *Cycle and Epicycle,* 160–62.

47. Recent voyage: Cohen, "Notes," *Battle-Pieces of Herman Melville,* 206–7. Beecher: in *Billy Budd,* 122, a man-of-war chaplain is "as incongruous as a musket would be on the altar at Christmas." A note (187) relates Beecher to that quotation, but explains that muskets were referred to as "Beecher's Bibles" for an unrelated reason.

48. Milder: Robert Milder, "The Rhetoric of Melville's *Battle-Pieces," Nineteenth-Century Literature* 44 (September 1989): 178.

49. Princeton friend: J. P. Lovejoy to Henry Gansevoort, 16 November 1860, GL. Lathers: *Reminiscences of Richard Lathers,* 74–91.

50. Whittier: to Edward Gilman Frothingham, 21 November 1860, *Letters of John Greenleaf Whittier*, 2:478. Silbey: *Respectable Minority,* 34. New York meeting: *Reminiscences of Richard Lathers,* 91–112; Morgan Dix, *Memoirs of John Adams Dix,* 2 vols. (New York: Harper Brothers, 1883), 1:347–60. The Dix account, written by Richard Lathers, is probably the more reliable.

51. Judge Shaw: *Sun*, 20 December 1860. Pittsfield petitions: *Sun,* 23 January 1861. Lemuel Shaw, Jr.: *Sun*, 31 January 1861. "Too droll": to Charles Sumner, 10 February 1861, *The Letters of Henry Wadsworth Longfellow*, ed. Andrew Hilen, 6 vols. (Cambridge, Mass.: Harvard University Press, 1972), 4:216.

52. Longfellow: to Charles Sumner, 20 December 1860, 29 January 1861, *Letters of Henry Wadsworth Longfellow,* 4:201, 212. Whittier: John Greenleaf Whittier, *The Works of John Greenleaf Whittier,* 7 vols. (Boston: Houghton Mifflin, 1892), 3:218–19. Hawthorne quotation: to Henry A. Bright, 17 December 1860, N. Hawthorne, *Letters,*

1857–1864, 355. Hawthorne and newspapers: to William D. Ticknor, 28 December 1860, ibid., 358.

53. The innovations were "useless *trash* foisted on the Service and the World," NYNS to Navy Department, 6 May 1861, Letters Received from Navy Yards, Navy Yard New York, Naval Records Collection of the Office of Naval Records and Library, RG 45, Department of the Navy, NA.

54. When Uzziah, King of Judah, became proud and trespassed in the temple, he was stricken with leprosy and, according to one tradition, the land was afflicted by an earthquake, 2 Chron. 26:16–23.

55. Lathers: *Reminiscences of Richard Lathers,* 38–40. Endorsed Herman: *Log*, 1:234.

56. Henry: to Catherine Gansevoort, 19 March 1861, GL. Hoadley's difficulties: *Reminiscences of Richard Lathers,* 252.

57. See note 56, Henry.

58. Henry joining: Certificate of Membership, Seventh Regiment of New York State Militia, 11 February 1861, GL. Members of regiment: William Swinton, *History of the Seventh Regiment, National Guard, State of New York, During the War of the Rebellion . . . ,* Ill. Thomas Nast (New York: Fields, Osgood, 1870), 141–58. Shaw as Herman's publisher: when Dix and Edwards failed in August 1857, Shaw took charge of the firm, making the decisions on the terms of Herman's contracts, *Log*, 2:582.

59. Scott: 9 January 1861, Strong, *Diary*, 3:88. Rockford: Charles A. Church, *Past and Present of the City of Rockford and Winnebago County, Illinois* (Chicago: S. J. Clarke, 1905), 86–87. Emerson: to Charles Sumner, 27 February 1861, *The Letters of Ralph Waldo Emerson*, ed. Ralph L. Rusk, 6 vols. (New York: Columbia University Press, 1939), 5:241.

60. Richard's journey: *Reminiscences of Richard Lathers,* 120–67.

61. Abe: Abraham Lansing to Henry Gansevoort, 20 February 1861, GL. Kitty: Catherine Gansevoort Diaries, 18 February 1861, GL.

62. To Parker Pillsbury, 10 April 1861, *The Correspondence of Henry David Thoreau,* ed. Walter Harding and Carl Bode (New York: New York University Press, 1958), 611.

63. Allen Guard: *Sun,* 31 January, 28 March 1861. Guns, low temperature: *Sun,* 17 January 1861. Roofs collapsed: *Sun,* 24 January 1861.

64. Well-wrought: Fogle, "Melville and the Civil War," 65, calls it "Melville's finest achievement in the elaborate pseudo-Pindaric ode at which he occasionally tried his hand." T. S. Eliot: Rachel Whitesides Stewart, "The Conditional Mood of Melville's Poetry" (Ph.D diss., University of Colorado, 1975), 27–28.

65. "Rhetoric of Melville's *Battle-Pieces,*" 179.

66. Brownell: Henry Howard Brownell, *War-Lyrics and Other Poems* (Boston: Ticknor and Fields, 1866), 35–36. Lowell: "The Pickens-and-Stealin's Rebellion," *The Complete Writings of James Russell Lowell,* 16 vols. (Boston: Houghton Mifflin, 1904), 6:109.

67. Lincoln: Paludan, *"A People's Contest,"* 372. Louisiana woman: Kate Stone, 4 July 1861, Jimerson, *Private Civil War,* 20.

68. [1?] June 1851, *Letters of Herman Melville*, 129.

69. "Iron age to come": Fogle, "Melville and the Civil War," 62.

70. Milder, "Rhetoric of Melville's *Battle-Pieces,*" 180.

71. Herman passing the winter: Catherine Gansevoort to Henry Gansevoort, [early January 1861], GL. Henry's visit, Aunt Melville's arrival: Catherine Gan-

sevoort Diaries, 12 January 1861, GL. Whirl of activity: Peter and Catherine Gansevoort Diaries, 12 January to 5 February 1861, GL.

72. Herman's health, message to Henry: Catherine Gansevoort to Henry Gansevoort, 13 February 1861, GL. Uncle Herman's health: this was so on 12 March 1861, Maria G. Melville to Catherine Gansevoort, GL. "Infirmity of jocularity": to George Duyckinck, 20 December 1858, *Letters of Herman Melville*, 193.

73. Whittier: to [Anson Burlingame?] 2 March 1861, and to Charles Sumner, 13 March 1861, *Letters of John Greenleaf Whittier*, 3:13–15. Strong: 19 March 1861, *Diary*, 3:111.

74. Campaign: Harrison Hayford and Merrell Davis, "Herman Melville as Office-Seeker," parts 1, 2, *Modern Language Quarterly* 10 (June, September 1949): 2:380–86. Allan absent: Jane Melville to Henry Gansevoort, Saturday Evening [23 February?] 1861, GL; Hoadley: on 21 March 1861 he had just returned from the visit to Washington, Augusta Melville to Catherine Gansevoort, GL.

75. Hope Shaw: Hope Shaw Diary, 21 February 1861, courtesy Jay Leyda.

76. Storm: *Sun,* 28 March 1861. Strong: 19 March 1861, *Diary,* 3:111. Capital weather: *Washington Intelligencer*, 25 March 1861.

77. Disgrace: *Sun*, 28 March 1861. Hotel lobbies: see note 76, Strong. Number of applications: *Sun*, 21 March 1861. Dozens of congressmen: *Sun*, 16 March 1861. Lincoln statement: Carl Russell Fish, *The Civil Service and the Patronage* (New York: Russell and Russell, 1963), 169.

78. "Shoot a rebel": see note 74, Hoadley. Uncle Nourse: Herman Melville to Elizabeth S. Melville, 24, 25 March 1860, *Letters of Herman Melville*, 209–10.

79. Whitman: to Thomas Jefferson Whitman, 13 February 1863, *Walt Whitman: The Correspondence*, ed. Edwin Haviland Miller, 6 vols. (New York: New York University Press, 1961), 1:75. Strong: 5 January 1861, *Diary,* 3:86. Herman and paintings: old General Gansevoort had been at Saratoga, and the family treasured a souvenir flag that his men had brought him from Yorktown.

80. Senate, here and below: *Washington Intelligencer*, 23, 25, 26, 27 March 1861. Nothing interesting: see note 78, Uncle Nourse.

81. Herman to Lizzie: see note 78, Uncle Nourse. Emerson on Lincoln's taste: Lindeman, *Conflict of Convictions,* 161. "Leaders of the low": R. Emerson, *Journals and Miscellaneous Notebooks,* 390.

82. See note 79, Strong.

83. Hideous Washington monument: see note 76, Strong. Penguins and lizards: see note 79, Strong.

84. *Washington Intelligencer,* 26, 27 March 1861. Herman may have seen Jefferson's parents on the Galena stage in 1840, Garner, "Picaresque Career of Thomas Melville," 2:7–8, and if so he may have wished to see their famous son.

85. Strong: 28 March 1861, *Diary,* 3:113. Letter of thanks: courtesy Jay Leyda. Good Friday weather: *Washington Intelligencer*, 30 March 1861.

86. Snow: *Sun*, 14 April 1861. Shaw's last hours, storm, funeral, burial: F. Chase, *Lemuel Shaw*, 270–72.

87. Strong: 5 April 1861, *Diary,* 3:114. Tyler biography: [George W. Cullum,] *Memoir of Brevet Major-General Robert Ogden Tyler, U.S. Army, together with His Journal of Two Months' Travels in British and Farther India* (Philadelphia: J. B. Lippincott, 1878) and standard biographical dictionaries.

Chapter 2. War

1. Thunderstorm: *Sun,* 18 April 1861. Whitman: "Specimen Days," *Prose Works 1892,* ed. Floyd Stovall, 2 vols. (New York: New York University Press, 1963), 1:24.

2. Organ, war prayers: 14 April 1861, *Diary,* 3:120. Hawthorne: Arlin Turner, *Nathaniel Hawthorne: A Biography* (New York: Oxford University Press, 1980), 363. Rockford: Church, *Past and Present of the City of Rockford,* 86. Spotty church attendance: Metcalf, *Cycle and Epicycle,* 72, 253.

3. Lowell, "Pickens and Stealin's," 6:107.

4. Lowell: ibid., 108. Douglas: to Virgil Hickox, 10 May 1861, Silbey, *Respectable Minority,* 45. Only two parties: ibid., 40.

5. Whitman: "Ship of Libertad," Walt Whitman, *Notebooks and Unpublished Prose Manuscripts,* ed. Edward F. Grier, 6 vols. (New York: New York University Press, 1984), 1:437. Longfellow: to Anne Longfellow Pierce, 25 April 1861, *Letters of Henry Wadsworth Longfellow,* 4:236. Whittier: to Lucy Larcom, 27 April 1861, *Letters of John Greenleaf Whittier,* 3:18. Hawthorne on Emerson: to Henry A. Bright, 14 November 1861, N. Hawthorne, *Letters, 1857–1864,* 422. Hawthorne exalted: to Horatio Bridge, 26 May 1861, ibid., 380–81. Volunteering: to William D. Ticknor, 16 May 1861, ibid., 379.

6. Arvin, *Herman Melville,* 258.

7. Stedman: "The Twelfth of April," Ralph E. Hitt, "Controversial Poetry of the Civil War Period, 1830–1878" (Ph.D. diss., Vanderbilt University, 1955), 215. Rain, editorial, Guards: *Sun,* 18 April 1861. Other information: *Sun,* 25 April 1861.

8. Vilified: for example, *New York Evening Post,* 17 April 1861, *Reminiscences of Richard Lathers,* 169–70. Quotation: ibid., 168. Half-truth: ibid., 171. Flag at Winyah, defense fund: undated clipping, *White Plains Journal,* Richard Lathers Papers, LC. Major Anderson: [Canedy,] *This Discursive Biographical Sketch,* 16. New Orleans newspaper: unidentified clipping, Lathers Papers, LC.

9. Catherine Gansevoort Diaries, 23 April 1861, GL.

10. Guard: J. E. A. Smith, *The History of Pittsfield (Berkshire County), Massachusetts,* 2 vols. (Boston and Springfield, Mass.: Lee and Shepard and C. W. Bryan, 1869, 1876), 2:612–13. Departure: Herman witnessed such scenes with his family, Stanwix Melville to Maria G. Melville, 8 June 1862, MFPA.

11. Seventh Regiment, here and below: Swinton, *History of the Seventh Regiment,* 23–224; William J. Roehrenbeck, *The Regiment That Saved the Capital,* intro. Allan Nevins (New York: Thomas Yoseloff, 1961).

12. Lincoln: Roehrenbeck, *Regiment That Saved the Capital,* 107. McDowell: ibid., 130.

13. Henry Thurston: Frederick Phisterer, *New York in the War of the Rebellion, 1861 to 1865,* 3rd ed., 5 vols. and index (Albany, N.Y.: F. B. Lyon, 1912), 1:576. Henry Gansevoort in Albany: Peter and Catherine Gansevoort Diaries, 20 April 1861, GL. Revolver, trip: Henry Gansevoort to George Henry Brewster, 1 May 1861, GL. Trip: Henry Gansevoort to Peter Gansevoort, 30 April 1861, GL. Gifford: courtesy Ila West.

14. Departure of Rockford Zouaves: Spray, "Lincoln's 'Wide Awake' Leader," 1; Church, *Past and Present of the City of Rockford,* 86–88. Mustered: Dyer, 3:1048.

15. Meeting: U. S. Grant, *Personal Memoirs of U. S. Grant,* 2 vols. (New York: Charles L. Webster, 1885), 1:230–32 (inaccurate); *Galena Daily Advertiser,* 17 April

1861. Departure of Guards: *Galena Weekly Northwestern Gazette,* 30 April 1861. Departure of Grant: statement of Thomas M. Roberts, *Galena Weekly Gazette,* 30 December 1926, courtesy Jean Melvill. Station of regiment: Dyer, 3:1048.

16. Bartlett: Francis Winthrop Palfrey, *Memoir of William Francis Bartlett* (Boston: Houghton Mifflin, 1881), 1–2. Holmes, Jr., and Melville: Catherine Drinker Bowen, *Yankee from Olympus: Justice Holmes and His Family* (Boston: Little, Brown, 1944), 103. Crowninshield: Caspar Crowninshield, "Journal of Brevet Brigadier General Caspar Crowninshield" (typescript), Boston Public Library, 1.

17. Poem: "Harvard Student's Song," Julia Ward Howe, *Later Lyrics* (Boston: J. E. Tilton, 1866), 29. Fort Independence: Mark DeWolf Howe, *Justice Oliver Wendell Holmes,* 2 vols. (Cambridge, Mass.: Harvard University Press, 1957), 1:68.

18. Longfellow, birds and children: to Catherine Jane Norton, 26 April 1861, *Letters of Henry Wadsworth Longfellow,* 5:237. Longfellow watching musters, reading: journal, 16, 17, 30 April 1861, S. Longfellow, *Life of Henry Wadsworth Longfellow,* 2:414–16. Emerson: to Edith Emerson, 20 April 1861, *Letters of Ralph Waldo Emerson,* 5:246. Alcott: April 1861, *Journals of Louisa May Alcott,* 105. War interrupting Hawthorne: see note 5, volunteering. Hawthorne reading and listening: Hawthorne, "Chiefly about War Matters," 12:300.

19. *Sun* quotation, promulgating telegraphic information, rumor of Seventh Regiment: *Sun,* 25 April 1861. Selden: *Sun,* 5 June 1862.

20. Pollock Guard: *Sun,* 2 May 1861. Camp: *Sun,* 9 May 1861. Rifle company: *Berkshire County Eagle,* 9 May 1861. Military clubs: *Sun,* 13 June 1861. Julian Hawthorne: see note 5, Hawthorne exalted. Zouave camp: *Sun,* 4 July 1861.

21. Pierce, flags: *Sun,* 2 May 1861. Flags, celebration, Everett: *Sun,* 9 May 1861.

22. Fire: *Sun,* 13 June 1861. Uniforms: *Sun,* 16 May 1861. Departure of Pollock Guard, presentation of flag: *Sun,* 20 June 1861.

23. Sarah Morewood: to George Duyckinck, 23 June 1861, Daniel C. Nascimento, "Melville's Berkshire World: The Pastoral Influence upon His Life and Works" (Ph.D. diss., University of Maryland, 1971), 254. Fortress Berkshire: speech by Governor Andrew, 1 September 1861, M. Howe, *Justice Oliver Wendell Holmes,* 1:87–88.

24. Umbrella: Warren Lee Goss, "Going to the Front," *B&L,* 1:153. Needlebooks: *Sun,* 13 June 1861. Alcott: May 1861, *Journals of Louisa May Alcott,* 105. Alcott states erroneously that 300 women were present.

25. Agatha Young, *The Women and the Crisis: Women of the North in the Civil War* (New York: McDowell, Obolensky, 1959), 68. Fenn: L. P. Brockett and Mary C. Vaughan, *Woman's Work in the Civil War: A Record of Heroism, Patriotism, and Patience* (Philadelphia and Boston: Zeigler, McCurdy and R. H. Curran, 1867), 666–75; Smith, *History of Pittsfield,* 2:624–26.

26. Visitor to Washington: Goss, "Going to the Front," 1:158. *Sun,* 13 June 1861.

27. Common soldier: 9 May 1861, GL. Brady: Roehrenbeck, *Regiment That Saved the Capital,* 236. Winthrop: he reported to the *Atlantic Monthly,* ibid., 235. Gifford: he painted "Sunday Morning at Camp Cameron," "The Bivouack of the Seventh Regiment at Arlington Heights," and "Baltimore 1862," obit., *NYT,* 30 August 1880. Nursery for brigadiers: Goss, "Going to the Front," 1:159.

28. Spoof: George Henry Brewster to Henry Gansevoort, [1 June 1861], GL. Henry to Washington: Catherine Gansevoort Diaries, 6 June 1861, GL.

29. Winthrop: Roehrenbeck, *Regiment That Saved the Capital,* 180–81, 235. Curtis: to Charles Eliot Norton, 30 July 1861, Edward Cary, *George William Curtis*

(Boston: Houghton Mifflin, 1894), 146–47. Longfellow: to George William Curtis, 20 June 1861, *Letters of Henry Wadsworth Longfellow,* 4:240.

30. Norfolk yard: Frank M. Bennett, *The Steam Navy of the United States: A History of the Growth of the Steam Vessel of War in the U.S. Navy, and of the Naval Engineer Corps* (Pittsburgh, Pa.: Warren, 1896), 230–42. 3rd Massachusetts: Dyer, 3:1249. "Confederate States": U.S. Navy Department, *Civil War Naval Chronology, 1861–1865* (Washington, D.C.: Government Printing Office, 1971), VI–318.

31. Five steamers: 21 April 1861, *Civil War Naval Chronology,* I–11. "Cmmdr. Gansevoort": 6 May 1861, Letters Received from Navy Yards, Navy Yard New York, NA.

32. Planning flotilla: James H. Ward to Secretary of the Navy, 22 April 1861, *U&CN,* ser. 1, 4:420. Approval of flotilla, Budd assignment: Secretary of the Navy to New York Navy Yard, 27 April 1861, ibid., 430. Budd appointment: 17 May 1861, Thomas H. S. Hamersly, comp., "Complete General Navy Register," in *Complete Army and Navy Register of the United States of America from 1776 to 1887* (New York. T. H. S. Hamersly, 1888), 111. Ward's ships: 12 May 1861, Letters and Telegrams Sent to the Secretary of the Navy, Series 249, Records of the New York Navy Yard, Records of Naval Districts and Shore Establishments, 1826–1953, RG 181, Department of the Navy, FANY. Pirate: after 18 June 1861, "the vandal" Budd torched the home of a Doctor Howe, *U&CN,* ser. 1, 4:553; on 20 June 1861 the Secretary of the Navy told Commodore Dahlgren to release the *Bachelor* and the *H. Day,* which Budd had captured, ibid., 519; and on 11 August 1861 Commander T. T. Craven ordered Budd to explain to the Secretary of the Navy his capture of ten blacks, ibid., 603. Mathias Point: Guernsey and Alden, *Harper's Pictorial History,* 162–63; *NYT,* 29 June 1861.

33. Ward, here and below: *NYT,* 1, 2 July 1861. "War comet": *NYT,* 6 July 1861. Dazzling: *Sun,* 11 July 1861. More ordnance: 10 June 1861, Letters and Telegrams. Sent to the Secretary of the Navy, FANY.

34. *Log,* 2:641.

35. Strawberry festival: Nascimento, "Melville's Berkshire World," 254. Winyah: *Reminiscences of Richard Lathers,* 53–56; [Canedy], *This Discursive Biographical Sketch,* 44. Children: all of the Lathers children were educated at home, ibid., 40.

36. *NYT,* 4, 6 July 1861.

37. Edgewater: Allan began his summer vacation at this time in 1862, and on 21 September 1861, he wrote Henry Gansevoort that he was "Still in the cottage," GL. Forty-five minute ride: *Reminiscences of Richard Lathers,* 53.

38. Longfellow: journal, 20 May 1861, S. Longfellow, *Life of Henry Wadsworth Longfellow,* 2:417. Hawthorne: to Rose Hawthorne, 5 August 1861, Hawthorne, *Letters, 1857–1864,* 399.

39. Tuckerman: "The Battle Summer," Frank Moore, ed., *Lyrics of Loyalty* (New York: G. P. Putnam, 1864), 110. Longfellow: journal, 12 September 1861, S. Longfellow, *Life of Henry Wadsworth Longfellow,* 2:422. Hawthorne: see note 5, Hawthorne on Emerson.

40. Morgan Dix: *Memoirs of John Adams Dix,* 2:18. Hawthorne: to William D. Ticknor, 26 May 1861, N. Hawthorne, *Letters, 1857–1864,* 382.

41. To Catherine Gansevoort, 13 July 1861, GL.

42. Whitman: "Specimen Days," 1:28. Allan: Allan Melville to Catherine Gansevoort, 25 July 1861, GL.

43. "Upon the Hill before Centreville," Hitt, "Controversial Poetry of the Civil War Period," 206.

44. First quotation: to James Russell Lowell, 23 July 1861, N. Hawthorne, *Letters, 1857–1864,* 394. Second: N. Hawthorne, "Chiefly about War Matters," 12:320.

45. Epitaphs: Stewart, "Conditional Mood of Melville's Poetry," 114–15.

46. Sister Lucy Marie Freibert, "Meditative Voice in the Poetry of Herman Melville" (Ph.D. diss., University of Wisconsin, 1970), 87–88.

47. Randolph Hobart: Illinois Adjutant General's Office, *Report of the Adjutant General of the State of Illinois, 1861–1866,* rev. J. N. Reece, 9 vols. (Springfield, Ill.: Phillips Brothers, 1900), 1:324–26. Harvard boys: M. Howe, *Justice Oliver Wendell Holmes,* 1:74–77. 11th Illinois: Dyer, 3:1048. 12th Militia: ibid., 1410. Allen Guard: *Sun,* 8 August 1861.

48. Dix, *Memoirs of John Adams Dix,* 1:337.

49. McClellan: George B. McClellan, "The Peninsular Campaign," *B&L,* 2:160–62. "Finest army": James V. Murfin, *The Gleam of Bayonets: The Battle of Antietam and the Maryland Campaign of 1862,* intro. James I. Robertson, Jr. (1965; reprint, Baton Rouge: Louisiana State University Press, 1982), 39. Henry: to Catherine Gansevoort, 4 August 1861, GL.

50. Bryant: *Sun,* 5 December 1861. Holmes: *Sun,* 3 October 1861. Root: "The Battle-Cry of Freedom," Richard Crawford, ed., *The Civil War Songbook* (New York: Dover Publications, 1977), 1–4.

51. Lathers: *Reminiscences of Richard Lathers,* 172–73. Thorpe: Milton Rickels, *Thomas Bangs Thorpe: Humorist of the Old Southwest* (Baton Rouge: Louisiana State University Press, 1962), 211. Strong: 16 April 1861, *Diary,* 3:122. Whitman: *Leaves of Grass,* 678.

52. Thurston appointment, orders: Brown Thurston, *Thurston Genealogies,* 326. Aldrich: Ferris Greenslet, *The Life of Thomas Bailey Aldrich* (Boston: Houghton Mifflin, 1908), 56–58.

53. Tyler: [Cullum,] *Memoir of Brevet Major General Robert Ogden Tyler,* 13. Hodge's Cornet Band: "Berkshire Brass Bands," parts 1, 2, *The Berkshire Hills* 1 (1 March, 1 April 1901): 1:74, courtesy Alan Grieve. Bartlett: Palfrey, *Memoir of William Francis Bartlett,* 4–5. Other officers: "Journal of Brevet Brigadier General Caspar Crowninshield," 2–25.

54. Place of birth: Tenth Census of the United States, 1880, Soundex microfilm T746, roll 50, Fulton, Fulton Township, Whiteside County, Ill., RG 29, NA; Richard T. Greene Pension Application and Pension Application (widow), Civil War Pension Application Files, Veterans Administration, RG 15, NA. Lecturing, newspaper accounts: Clarence Gohdes, "Melville's Friend 'Toby,'" *Modern Language Notes* 59 (January 1944): 52–55. Sign painter: *Log,* 1:221. *Sandusky Mirror*: Gohdes, "Melville's Friend 'Toby,'" 53–55. Move to Chicago, difficulty finding work, return to New York: Metcalf, *Cycle and Epicycle,* 194–95. Physician: Chicago municipal directory, courtesy Lynn Horth. Information about Greene's life and service not otherwise documented below is from Richard T. Greene Compiled Service Record, Records of the Record and Pension Office, 1784–1917, Records of the Adjutant General's Office, RG 94, War Department, NA, and pension applications.

55. Russ: *Log,* 2:630. Toby's duty: Robert J. Rombauer, *The Union Cause in St. Louis in 1861: An Historical Sketch* (St. Louis, Mo.: Nixon-Jones, 1909), 298–99.

56. Jeff recruiting, made major: Church, *Past and Present of the City of Rockford,*

045. Joining 44th Illinois: *Report of the Adjutant General of the State of Illinois*, 3:328. St. Louis: ibid., 326. Information about the service of the Hobarts not otherwise documented is from Thomas J. Hobart Compiled Service Record, Randolph Hobart Compiled Service Record, and John A. Hobart Compiled Service Record, NA.

57. Lowell's appointment: Charles A. Humphreys, *Field, Camp, Hospital and Prison Camp in the Civil War, 1863–1865* (Boston: George H. Ellis, 1918), 181–82.

58. Uncle Peter's alarm: to Henry Gansevoort, 13 May 1861, GL. Henry's request: to Peter Gansevoort, 17 May 1861, GL. Influence: Peter Gansevoort Diaries, 24 May 1861, GL; Catherine Gansevoort Diaries, 6 June 1861, GL; letter of recommendation, Greene C. Bronson, 8 June 1861, GL. Dix: Henry Gansevoort to Susan L. Gansevoort, 10 June 1861, GL. Treacherous and uncongenial world: to Peter Gansevoort, 16 June 1861, GL. Uncle Peter's response: to Henry Gansevoort, 24 June 1861, GL.

59. Received appointment: see note 49, Henry. Transfer: Henry Gansevoort to Thomas A. Scott, 7 August 1861, GL. Could remain in army: Meredith [Henry?] to Henry Gansevoort, 10 August 1861, GL. Hoadley: to Henry Gansevoort, 8 August 1861, GL.

60. Washington news: to Abby Larkin Adams, 24 July 1861, *Letters of Ralph Waldo Emerson*, 5:251. Sarah Morewood: *Sun*, 11 July 1861. Independent Zouaves: *Berkshire County Eagle*, 18 July 1861. Phalanx: *Sun*, 18 July 1861. Phalanx disbanded: *Sun*, 15 August 1861. Mary Downer: Perry, *Charles D'Wolf of Guadaloupe*, 189. Return of Allen Guard, weather: *Sun*, 8 August 1861.

61. Robert Melvill move: obit., Susan B. Melvill, *Galena Weekly Gazette*, 27 March 1885. Gansevoort and Glens Falls socializing: Frances Melville was invited to stay with the Curtises, Stanwix Melville to Peter Gansevoort, 5 September 1861, GL. Henry ill: Peter and Catherine Gansevoort Diaries, 12 August 1861, GL; Catherine Gansevoort to Susan L. Gansevoort, 13 August 1861, GL. Uncle Peter leaving for New York: Peter Gansevoort Diaries, 15 August 1861, GL.

62. Tom Thumb: *Sun*, 5 September 1861. Briggs tragedy: *Sun*, 19 September 1861.

63. Uncle Herman walking: Catherine Gansevoort to Henry Gansevoort, 17 September 1861, GL. Kate Curtis, Mary Curtis, Maria Melville: John Hoadley to Henry Gansevoort, 7 September 1861, Augusta Melville to Susan L. Gansevoort, 13 September 1861, GL. Able young man: Maria G. Melville to Peter Gansevoort, 15 March 1862, GL. "Georgie": Helen Griggs to Augusta and Frances Melville, 25 January 1863, MFPA.

64. National hymn: *Sun*, 23 May 1861. Exhibition: *Sun*, 10 October 1861.

65. Order to report: William E. Van Reed to Henry Gansevoort, 25 August 1861, GL. Epaulets, sword: Peter Gansevoort Diaries, 28 August 1861, GL. Departure: Catherine Gansevoort Diaries, 29 August 1861, GL. Hoadley: John Hoadley to Henry Gansevoort, 31 August 1861, GL. Reporting: Henry Gansevoort to Peter Gansevoort,
10 September 1861, GL.

66. Bruce's move: George Henry Brewster to Henry Gansevoort, 11 May 1861, GL. Partnership with Allan: George Henry Brewster to Henry Gansevoort, 13 September 1861, GL; note 37, Edgewater. Bruce visiting Allan: George Henry Brewster to Henry Gansevoort, 9 October 1861, GL.

67. Henry received appointment: Abraham Lansing to Henry Gansevoort, 18 April 1861, GL. Wakeman's promise: George Henry Brewster to Henry Gansevoort, 17 October 1861, GL. Cousinly ragging: see note 66, partnership. Resignation: George Henry Brewster to Henry Gansevoort, 1 October 1861, GL.

68. Presentiment: *Sun,* 31 October 1861.

69. Crowninshield's coat, casualties: ibid.

70. Abe Lansing: to Henry Gansevoort, 1 November 1861, GL. Hawthorne: see note 5, Hawthorne on Emerson. Longfellow: journal, 25 October 1861, Jack Lindeman, *The Conflict of Convictions: American Writers Report the Civil War—A Selection and Arrangement from the Journals, Correspondence, and Articles of the Major Men and Women of Letters Who Lived through the War* (Philadelphia: Chilton, 1968), 48.

Chapter 3. The Anaconda and the Asp

1. Sarah Morewood: to George Duyckinck, 17 August 1861, Nascimento, "Melville's Berkshire World," 254. Fanny Kemble: to Arthur, 15 September 1861, Frances Anne Kemble, *Further Records, 1848–1883: A Series of Letters,* 2 vols. (1891; reprint, New York: Benjamin Blom, 1972), 2:229–30.

2. Emerson: to James Elliot Cabot, 4 August 1861, *Letters of Ralph Waldo Emerson,* 5:253. Dickinson: to Mrs. Samuel [Mary Schermerhorn] Bowles, ca. August 1861, *The Letters of Emily Dickinson,* ed. Thomas H. Johnson and Theodora Ward, 3 vols. (Cambridge, Mass.: Harvard University Press, 1958), 2:377.

3. Procuring ships: Gideon Welles, quoted in *NYT,* 17 January 1862; Bennett, *Steam Navy of the United States,* 214–17. Guert examining: 20 August 1861, Letters and Telegrams Sent to the Secretary of the Navy, FANY.

4. Ned's commission: Bennett, *Steam Navy of the United States,* app. A. *Sciota*'s characteristics: ibid., 221; *U&CN,* ser. 2, 1:203. Guert, quotation: Catherine Gansevoort to Henry Gansevoort, 4 November 1861, GL.

5. *Ellen:* 19 October 1861, Letters and Telegrams Sent to the Secretary of the Navy, FANY.

6. DuPont and *White-Jacket:* Frederick J. Kennedy and Joyce Deveau Kennedy, "Some Naval Officers React to *White-Jacket:* An Untold Story," *Melville Society Extracts,* no. 41 (February 1980): 3–11.

7. Rosenberry: Edward H. Rosenberry, *Melville* (London: Routledge and Kegan Paul, 1979), 141. Covenant: suggested by Adler, *War in Melville's Imagination,* 144.

8. Freibert, "Meditative Voice in the Poetry of Herman Melville," 77–78, relates this poem to Emerson's "Merlin." Merton M. Sealts, Jr., "Melville and Emerson's Rainbow (1980)," *Pursuing Melville, 1940–1980* (Madison: University of Wisconsin Press, 1982), 250–77, discusses Herman's circles, this poem, and the larger influence of Emerson on Herman.

9. Catherine Gansevoort to Henry Gansevoort, 16 January 1862, GL.

10. Emerson, Herman's comment: *Log,* 2:648.

11. Uncle Peter and family, weather fine: 21 October 1861, Peter Gansevoort Diaries, GL. Books: Sealts, *Melville's Reading,* 112, 188, 218. Allan Melvilles: Allan would have moved back to the city shortly after Bruce's 6 October visit, his usual time. Acting commandant: Catherine Gansevoort Diaries, 1 November 1861, GL. Guert well: see note 4, Guert. Seeing *Adirondack,* Guert's hope for command: Peter Gansevoort to Henry Gansevoort, 31 March 1862, GL.

12. Gansevoorts' return to Albany: Catherine Gansevoort Diaries, 1 November 1861, GL. Wessel: Wessel Gansevoort to Peter Gansevoort, 6 November 1861, GL. Van Buren: Peter Gansevoort Diaries, 21 November 1861, GL. Henry's arrival: Catherine Gansevoort Diaries, [2]7 November 1861, GL. Augusta's visit: Peter

Gansevoort Diaries, 29 November 1861, GL. Allan's taunt: Allan Melville to Henry Gansevoort, 29 November 1861, GL. Henry dining with Allan: Catherine Gansevoort to Henry Gansevoort, 18 December 1861, GL.

13. Elections, Cameron: *Sun,* 14 November 1861. Davis, Lee: *Sun,* 21 November 1861. Thanksgiving, snow: *Sun,* 28 November 1861.

14. Tom's route: see note 9.

15. Ale: Augusta Melville to Peter Gansevoort, 26 December 1861, GL. Stanwix's mental training, growth: Catherine Gansevoort to Henry Gansevoort, 2 January 1862, GL. Knitting: Augusta Melville to Catherine Gansevoort, 6 January 1862, GL. Leonard and the navy: Catherine Gansevoort to Henry Gansevoort, 20 March 1862, GL.

16. Emerson: to William Emerson, 6 December 1861, *Letters of Ralph Waldo Emerson,* 5:259. Visits to Boston: see note 15, knitting. Uncle D'Wolf: Sealts, *Melville's Reading,* 112, 174. Mother Melville's holiday: see note 15, Ale.

17. *Exploring Expedition:* Sealts, *Melville's Reading,* 30–32, 223. *Omoo, Typee, Mardi:* Charles Roberts Anderson, *Melville in the South Seas* (New York: Columbia University Press, 1939), 217, 328, 342. *Moby-Dick:* Howard P. Vincent, *The Trying Out of Moby-Dick* (1949; reprint, Carbondale: Southern Illinois University Press, 1965), 181–84, 366.

18. R. Emerson: *Journals and Unpublished Notebooks,* 15:153, 174. Whittier: to James T. Fields, 20 December 1861, *Letters of John Greenleaf Whittier,* 3:26.

19. Tom's arrival: see note 9. Tom in New York: see note 15, knitting.

20. Tom to Gansevoort: he was scheduled to arrive on the 7th, note 15, knitting. Tom in Albany, St. Peter's, talk of Henry, left for Boston: Catherine Gansevoort Diaries, 11, 12, 13 January 1862, GL. Quotation: see note 9. Ed Lansing and Zouave Cadets: Lansing Letterbook, Richard Manney private collection. Ed and West Point: see note 15, Stanwix. Engagement: Catherine Gansevoort Diaries, 9 January 1862, GL. Mother Melville's desire: Maria G. Melville to Catherine Gansevoort, 11 January 1862, GL.

21. Sailing date postponed, weekend in Lawrence: Thomas Melville to Catherine Gansevoort, 19 January 1862, GL. Lunch aboard *Bengal:* Maria G. Melville to Catherine Gansevoort, 4 February 1862, GL. *Bengal* sailed: Frances Melville to Catherine Gansevoort, 11 February 1862, GL.

22. Gloom: Ernest A. McKay, *The Civil War and New York City* (Syracuse, N.Y.: Syracuse University Press, 1990), 116–41. N. Hawthorne: "Chiefly about War Matters," 12:301. Longfellow and newspapers: journal, 4 February 1862, S. Longfellow, *Life of Henry Wadsworth Longfellow,* 3:2. Allan's illness: George Henry Brewster to Henry Gansevoort, 6 February 1862, GL.

23. Allan better: George Henry Brewster to Henry Gansevoort, 20 February 1862, GL. Quotation: 1? February 1862, *Letters of Herman Melville,* 213.

24. Sealts, *Melville's Reading,* 113, 228, 172–73, 175, 184, 216, 196, 200, 186–87, 177, 185, 169, 151, 161, 167–68, 226; Merton M. Sealts, Jr., "A Supplementary Note to *Melville's Reading* (1988)," *Melville Society Extracts,* no. 80 (February 1990): 7–8.

25. Whale: *Sun,* 5 December 1861. Ferries: Metcalf, *Cycle and Epicycle,* 259.

26. Arming *Monitor:* Robert MacBride, *Civil War Ironclads: The Dawn of Naval Armor* (Philadelphia: Chilton Books, 1962), 14. *Monitor* to be ready, *Adirondack:* 22 February 1862, Letters and Telegrams Sent to the Secretary of the Navy, FANY.

27. Had it not been for the presence of Evert Duyckinck, there would be no

record of Herman's visit to the Navy Yard described in chapter 2. Therefore, it is reasonable to assume that he made other unrecorded visits when notable events occurred there.

28. To Bureau of Construction, 18, 20 March 1862, Letters and Telegrams Sent to Navy Department Bureaus, series 252, Records of the New York Navy Yard, Records of Naval Districts and Shore Establishments, RG 181, Department of the Navy, FANY.

29. Boker: "The Sword-Bearer," George Cary Eggleston, ed., *American War Ballads and Lyrics: A Collection of the Songs and Ballads of the Colonial Wars, the Revolution, the War of 1812–15, the War with Mexico and the Civil War,* 2 vols. (New York: G. P. Putnam's Sons, 1889), 2:45–47. Longfellow: "The Cumberland," *The Poetical Works of Henry Wadsworth Longfellow,* vol. 3, vol. 3 of *The Works of Henry Wadsworth Longfellow* (1896: reprint, New York: AMS Press, 1966), 69. Hawthorne: "Chiefly about War Matters," 12:336–39.

30. "Grim and characterless": Fogle, "Melville and the Civil War," 73. Cohen: "Notes," *Battle-Pieces of Herman Melville,* 227.

31. Quotation: Fogle, "Melville and the Civil War," 62. Turner painting: Cohen, "Notes," *Battle-Pieces of Herman Melville,* 224–25.

32. Thomas Bullfinch, *Bullfinch's Mythology: The Age of Fable, The Age of Chivalry, Legends of Charlemagne* (New York: Thomas Y. Crowell, 1913), 181.

33. Whittier: to Hannah Lloyd Neall, 24 January 1862, *Letters of John Greenleaf Whittier,* 3:27. City celebration: McKay, *Civil War and New York City,* 118. Glorious news: Catherine Gansevoort to Henry Gansevoort, 22 February 1862, GL. Albany celebration: Peter Gansevoort Diaries, 17 February 1862, GL.

34. Fogle, "Melville and the Civil War," 72, calls this poem "a reworking of the New York *Times* account as reprinted in the *Rebellion Record.*" Herman's use of that account and of a report in the *Missouri Democrat,* also reprinted in *The Rebellion Record,* are noted in Frank L. Day, "Herman Melville's Use of *The Rebellion Record* in His Poetry" (master's thesis, University of Tennessee, 1959), 19–20. Herman's use of the *Record* will be discussed in chapter 9.

35. "Bread and the Newspaper," *Works of Oliver Wendell Holmes,* 8:7.

36. William Ross Wallace, "Keep Step with the Music of Union," Moore, *Lyrics of Loyalty,* 137–38.

37. Parallels of experience: Cohen, "Notes," *Battle-Pieces of Herman Melville,* 219–20. "Shard": for example, see Herman's "The Ravaged Villa," 222.

38. Symbol of war: suggested by Cohen, "Notes," *Battle-Pieces of Herman Melville,* 221; amplified by Adler, *War in Melville's Imagination,* 145–46.

39. Water imagery: Cohen, "Notes," *Battle-Pieces of Herman Melville,* 220; Adler, *War in Melville's Imagination,* 147.

40. 6 May 1862, Brown Thurston, *Thurston Genealogies,* 326.

41. Mason, *Spirit Above the Dust,* 216.

42. 44th Illinois during this period: Franz Sigel, "The Pea Ridge Campaign," *B&L,* 1:314–34. Regiment suffering: *Report of the Adjutant General of The State of Illinois,* 5:326. Randolph: Randolph Hobart Compiled Service Record, NA. Jeff: Thomas J. Hobart Compiled Service Record, NA.

43. 26th Massachusetts to Butler: William Schouler, *A History of Massachusetts in the Civil War,* 2 vols. (Boston: E. P. Dutton and William Schouler, 1868, 1871), 1:275. Pease family: David Pease and Austin W. Pease, comps., *A Genealogical Historical Record of the Descendants of John Pease, Sen., Last of Enfield, Conn.* (Springfield, Mass.:

Samuel Bowles, 1869), 238–39. Moved into Hoadley's house: Andrew E. Ford, *History of the Origin of the Town of Clinton, Massachusetts, 1653–1865* (Clinton, Mass.: W. J. Coulter, 1896), 399. Henry's age, employment: Massachusetts Adjutant General, comp., *Massachusetts Soldiers, Sailors, and Marines in the Civil War,* 8 vols. and index (Norwood, Mass., and Boston: Norwood Press and Wright and Potter, 1931–37), 3:92. Presentation of flag, departure: *Sun,* 13 February 1862. 26th Massachusetts at Ship Island: it arrived 3 December 1861, Dyer, 3:1257. 14th Maine: it arrived 8 March 1862, Dyer, 3:1224. "Camp Morewood": *Sun,* 29 May 1862.

44. Capture of *Margaret: Civil War Naval Chronology,* II–18. News of *Sciota* joining Farragut: Frances Melville to Catherine Gansevoort, 1 April 1862, GL.

45. *Sciota* casualties: "The Opposing Forces in the Operations at New Orleans, La.," *B&L,* 2:73. Western Bay State Regiment: *Sun,* 5 June 1862. Henry Pease's regiment: *Massachusetts Soldiers, Sailors, and Marines,* 3:61.

46. Brownell, *War-Lyrics and Other Poems,* 23–34.

47. *Works of Oliver Wendell Holmes,* 13:63.

48. Thomas Alexander Little, "Literary Allusions in the Writings of Herman Melville" (Ph.D. diss., University of Nebraska, 1948), 46.

49. Hoadley's job: Hoadley, "Sketch of John Chipman Hoadley," 1–2. Women in Lawrence: Kate Hoadley went house hunting in New Bedford on 1 April, note 44, *Sciota.*

50. Washington, assignment to command: Peter Gansevoort to Guert Gansevoort, 20 March 1862, GL. Quotation: John S. Almy to Henry A. Wise, 21 March 1862, Naval History Society Collection, BV Wise, LB2, #246, Manuscript Department, NYHS.

51. Heart failure ("dropsy"): Peter Gansevoort to John J. Hill, 3 April 1862, GL. Funeral: Catherine Gansevoort Diaries, 19 March 1862, GL. Funeral, Allan present, Allan's game leg, receiving vault, events in Albany: see note 15, Leonard, and note 50, Washington. Allan's return, Herman's visit: Maria G. Melville (Allan's daughter) to Stanwix Melville, 25 March 1862, MFPA. Ida Lathers: Brown Thurston, *Thurston Genealogies,* 296.

52. Fort Stanwix, madeira: see note 50, Washington. Guert's neglect: Peter Gansevoort to Guert Gansevoort, 10 June 1862, GL.

53. *Reminiscences of Richard Lathers,* 191.

54. Crittenden-Johnson, Confiscation Act: Paludan, *"A People's Contest,"* 63–65. *Freeman's Journal:* McKay, *Civil War and New York City,* 93.

55. "Abo Bo Lition": *Sun,* 5 June 1862. Washington: Catherine Gansevoort to Henry Gansevoort, 11 November 1861, GL. Democrats in Congress: Silbey, *Respectable Minority,* 54.

56. *Sun,* 19 December 1861.

57. To Harriet Winslow Sewall, 31 July 1861, *Letters of John Greenleaf Whittier,* 3:21–22.

58. Gallagher: "Move on the Columns!" Francis F. Browne, ed., *Bugle-Echoes: A Collection of Poems of the Civil War: Northern and Southern* (New York: White, Stokes, and Allen, 1886), 54. Boker: "Tardy George," Eggleston, *American War Ballads and Lyrics,* 2:86. Hamlet's soliloquy: A Daughter of Georgia, "McClellan's Soliloquy," Frank Moore, ed., *The Civil War in Song and Story, 1860–1865* (New York: P. F. Collier, 1889), 358.

59. "Republican tinge": 17 May 1862, Hawthorne, *Letters, 1857–1864,* 457. The description of Hawthorne's trip is based on his "Chiefly about War Matters."

60. 9 March 1862, N. Hawthorne, *Letters, 1857–1864,* 434.

61. Bit of flag: to Julian Hawthorne, 27 March 1862, ibid., 441. Gloriously forlorn: to James T. Fields, 2 April 1862, ibid., 445.

62. Southern atrocities: suggested in N. Hawthorne, "Chiefly about War Matters," 12:320–21, but described explicitly (with the matter quoted here) in a lesser essay, "Northern Volunteers. From a Journal," *Monitor* (Concord) 1 (7 June 1862): 1–2, courtesy Thomas Woodson.

63. 7 May 1862, N. Hawthorne, *Letters, 1857–1864,* 455.

64. N. Hawthorne, "Chiefly about War Matters," 12:311. Richard N. Current, *The Lincoln Nobody Knows* (New York: Hill and Wang, 1958), 1–6, describes Lincoln's appearance.

65. McClellan shot: to Una Hawthorne, 16 March 1862, Hawthorne, *Letters, 1857–1864,* 437–38. Praise: N. Hawthorne, "Chiefly about War Matters," 12:324.

66. N. Hawthrone, "Chiefly about War Matters," 12:307.

67. Wild beast: ibid., 330. Regeneration: ibid., 331. Present thoughts about blacks: ibid., 319. Year earlier: to Horatio Bridge, 26 May 1861, N. Hawthorne, *Letters, 1857–1864,* 381.

68. Truth: to James T. Fields, 23 May 1862, N. Hawthorne, *Letters, 1857–1864,* 461. Curtis: to Charles Eliot Norton, 26 June 1862; Cary, *George William Curtis,* 156.

69. Clifford Dowdey, *The Seven Days: The Emergence of Robert E. Lee* (1964; reprint, New York: Fairfax Press, 1978), 11.

70. Catherine Gansevoort to Henry Gansevoort, 12 March 1862, GL.

71. Low rank: for example, Henry Gansevoort to Peter Gansevoort, 23 November 1861, GL. Healthy and exciting life: Henry Gansevoort to Peter Gansevoort, 10 September 1861, GL. Remount blade: Henry Gansevoort to Catherine Gansevoort, 15 September 1861, GL. Rumble: Catherine Gansevoort to Henry Gansevoort, 17 September 1861, GL. Abandoned the idea: Henry Gansevoort to Peter Gansevoort, 9 October 1861, GL. Uncle Peter pleased: Peter Gansevoort to Henry Gansevoort, 17 October 1861, GL.

72. Service ideals: M. Howe, *Justice Oliver Wendell Holmes,* 1:83. Chapeau: as evidenced by all of the extant photographs of him in which he is wearing a hat.

73. Battery M: 1 December 1861, Hoadley, *Memorial of Henry Sanford Gansevoort,* 77. Makeup of battery: Henry Gansevoort to Catherine Gansevoort, 10 March 1862, GL.

74. See note 11, *Adirondack.*

75. Other officers, Henry in charge, steamer: Henry Gansevoort to Peter Gansevoort, 29 March 1862, GL. Arrival: Henry Gansevoort to Catherine Gansevoort, 30 March 1862, GL.

76. Henry's camp: see note 75, arrival. Bartlett: Palfrey, *Memoir of William Francis Bartlett,* 40–44.

77. To Horatio Bridge, 19 April 1862, Hawthorne, *Letters, 1857–1864,* 451.

78. Camp "No Where": H. M. Baldwin to Henry Gansevoort, 25 May 1862, GL. Pompeii, call on Wool: Henry Gansevoort to Peter Gansevoort, 8 April 1862, GL. Romantic posture: see note 75, arrival. Instruction to call on Wool: see note 11, *Adirondack.* Peter incredulous: Peter Gansevoort to Henry Gansevoort, 15 April 1862, GL.

79. Thompson P. McElrath to Catherine Gansevoort, 22 June 1873, GL.

80. Visit to Albany: Peter Gansevoort Diaries, 21 April 1862, GL. Saw Bruce: Henry Gansevoort to George Henry Brewster, 24 April 1862, GL. Volunteer battery, rank and deed: Henry Gansevoort to Peter Gansevoort, 27 April 1862, GL. Asking Bruce for help: Henry Gansevoort to George Henry Brewster, 27 April 1862, GL.

81. Applied for transfer: Truman Seymour to Henry Gansevoort, 8 April 1862, GL. Henry visiting Barry: see note 78, Pompeii.

82. Battery C: Henry Gansevoort to Peter Gansevoort, 9 May 1862, GL. Flag: see note 78, incredulous. Homily: Peter Gansevoort to Henry Gansevoort, 31 May 1862, GL.

83. Henry Gansevoort to Catherine Gansevoort, 25 May 1862, GL. Quotation: Francis Winthrop Palfrey, *The Antietam and Fredericksburg* (1882; reprint, New York: Jack Brussel, n.d.), 8.

84. Longfellow: to Luigi Monti, 20 May 1862, *Letters of Henry Wadsworth Longfellow,* 4:285. Lowell: to James T. Fields, 5 June 1862, *Letters of James Russell Lowell,* ed. Charles Eliot Norton, 2 vols. (New York: Harper Brothers, 1894), 1:321. Kate: to Henry Gansevoort, 3 June 1862, GL. Colonel Bunkum: *The Works of Herman Melville,* ed. Raymond M. Weaver, 16 vols. (London: Constable, 1924), 13:376. Letter to Tom: 25 May 1862, *Letters of Herman Melville,* 215.

Chapter 4. Wreck and Wrack

1. Shortened visit: according to Fanny, Herman had intended to remain until early May, to Catherine Gansevoort, 15 April 1862, GL. To Pittsfield, Newton, Lizzie sick, house, school: Stanwix Melville to Augusta Melville, 24 [25], 30 April, 8, 24 May 1862, MFPA. School: Stanwix Melville to Maria G. Melville, 8 June 1862, MFPA. Letter to Tom: 25 May 1862, *Letters of Herman Melville,* 215.

2. Amusements of boys, visits to village, walking excursions: see note 1, to Pittsfield. Herman's stamina: he could not walk from Arrowhead to town, Elizabeth S. Melville to Augusta Melville, 11 February 1863, MFPA. Morewood: Sarah Morewood to George Duyckinck, 26 April 1862; Nascimento, "Melville's Berkshire World," 256–57.

3. "Trunk-maker": see note 1, letter to Tom: Inside joke: Stanton Garner, "Herman Melville and the Trunkmaker," *Notes and Queries* n.s. 26 (August 1979): 307–8.

4. On 2 May 1862, Hawthorne read Sophia his related piece, "Northern Volunteers," courtesy Thomas Woodson.

5. Lizzie's improvement: Elizabeth S. Melville to Augusta Melville, verso of Stanwix Melville to Augusta Melville, 8 May 1862, MFPA. Herman's instructions to Gus: [29 April 1862?] courtesy Jay Leyda. Visit of Fanny and Helen: Stanwix Melville to Augusta Melville, 24 May 1862, MFPA.

6. Bust of Shaw: *Sun,* 1 May 1862. Riding, girls' lessons: Elizabeth Melville (daughter) to Augusta Melville, 26 May 1862, MFPA. Ladies gathering: *Sun,* 1 June 1862. Mary rehired: see note 5, Lizzie's improvement.

7. Wintergreens: see note 1, school. Circus: *Sun,* 1 May 1862. Sanford's troop: *Sun,* 12 June 1862. Bessie's birthday: see note 6, riding. Fireworks: *Sun,* 19 June 1862.

8. Allan Melvilles to Gansevoort: Catherine G. Melville (Allan's daughter) to Augusta Melville, 9 May 1862, MFPA. Hoadley to Washington: Frances Melville to Catherine Gansevoort, 1 April 1862, GL. Lathers in Washington: *Reminiscences of*

Richard Lathers, 184–88. Kate sewing: Catherine Gansevoort to Henry Gansevoort, 8 May 1862, GL. Awaiting news from Henry: Catherine Gansevoort to Henry Gansevoort, 16 June 1862, GL.

9. Information about the *Adirondack* not otherwise documented, here and later: Guert Gansevoort, Capt., USN, Court of Inquiry 3135, Court of Inquiry into the Loss of USS ADIRONDACK, 23 August 1862, 22 September 1862, and Guert Gansevoort, Capt., USN, General Court-Martial 3144, Loss of USS ADIRONDACK, 15 October 1862, Records of General Courts-Martial and Courts of Inquiry of the Navy Department, Records of the Judge Advocate General, RG 125, Department of the Navy, NA. Allan's report: Catherine Gansevoort to Henry Gansevoort, 16 November 1862, GL. Characteristics of *Adirondack*: Bennett, *Steam Navy of the United States,* 211 and Appendix B. Crew: 19 July 1862, Letters and Telegrams Sent to the Secretary of the Navy, FANY.

10. Allan's visit: Allan Melville to Henry Gansevoort, 27 June 1862, GL. Cincinnati rules and records: Bryce Metcalf, *Original Members and Other Officers Eligible to the Society of the Cincinnati, 1783–1938, with the Institution, Rules of Admission, and Lists of the Officers of the General and State Societies* (Strasburg, Va.: Shenandoah Publishing, 1938), 133. Despite the will, on Guert's death the order passed to Uncle Peter.

11. Sail in two weeks, Bruce: see note 10, Allan's visit. Fourth of July: Jane Melville to Henry Gansevoort, 11 November 1862, GL.

12. Move to New Rochelle: see note 10, Allan's visit. Cottage, routine: Catherine G. Melville (Allan's daughter) to Augusta Melville, 2 September 1862, MFPA. Visit to Guert: see note 11, Fourth of July.

13. Orders: Secretary of the Navy to Guert Gansevoort, 11 July 1862, *U&CN,* ser. 1, 1:399–400. *Emma* and *Herald,* below: Guert Gansevoort to Secretary of the Navy, 23 July 1862, ibid., 403–5.

14. Letter from *Greyhound*: from H. D. Hickley, 25 July 1862, ibid., 408–9. Reply: to H. D. Hickley, 25 July 1862, ibid., 409–10. "Dixie": Guert Gansevoort to Secretary of the Navy, 4 August 1862, ibid., 406–8. *Herald* sailors: Samuel F. DuPont to Sophie M. DuPont, 24, 25, 28, 29 August 1862, *Samuel Francis Du Pont: A Selection of His Civil War Letters,* ed. John D. Hayes, 3 vols. (Ithaca, N.Y.: Cornell University Press, 1969), 2:202.

15. See note 14, "Dixie."

16. Duty with DuPont: Secretary of the Navy to Guert Gansevoort, 12 August 1862, *U&CN,* ser. 1, 13:250. Emergency orders: Secretary of the Navy to Guert Gansevoort, 1, 13 August 1862, ibid., 1:416–17. Pirate: see note 14, *Herald* sailors.

17. Bennett, *Steam Navy of the United States,* 332.

18. "Almost distracted": ibid. Salvaged photographs: see note 11, Fourth of July.

19. Loss of *Adirondack:* Samuel F. DuPont to Sophie M. DuPont, 31 August, 2 September 1862, DuPont, *Civil War Letters,* 2:208. Guert drinking: see note 14, *Herald* sailors. *Adirondack* on fire: J. F. Green to Samuel F. DuPont, 5 September 1862, *U&CN,* ser. 1, 1:425–26.

20. Request for Court: Guert Gansevoort to Samuel F. DuPont, 5 September 1862, *U&CN,* ser. 1, 1:422–24. DuPont's support: Samuel F. DuPont to Guert Gansevoort, 7 September 1862, ibid., 1:426.

21. Lieutenant: James Parker, 23 September 1862, Court of Inquiry. Surgeon: John Rudenstein, 24 September 1862, ibid. Midshipman: Governeur K. Haswell, 25 September 1862, ibid.

22. Quotation: Secretary of the Navy to William B. Shubrick, 8 October 1862, Court-Martial. Ordnance duties: 20 November 1862, Abstracts of Service of Naval Officers, NA.

23. Sympathy, photographs: for example, Henry Gansevoort to Peter Gansevoort, 8 September 1862, GL, and note 11, Fourth of July. Kate's information from Allan: see note 9, Allan's report. Henry concerning court-martial: 23 October 1862, GL. Kate concerning court-martial: 6 November 1862, GL.

24. Lincoln quotation: McClellan, "Peninsular Campaign," *B&L,* 2:175. McDowell quotation: *Sun,* 18 December 1862.

25. Seventh Regiment: Ralph Waldo Emerson to Nathaniel Prentiss Banks, 29 September 1862, *Letters of Ralph Waldo Emerson,* 5:288. Departure of Allen Guard: see note 1, school, and *Sun,* 29 May 1862. Return of guard: *Sun,* 5 June 1862.

26. Hodge's Band, Briggs: "Berkshire Brass Bands," 1:74.

27. Rejoined battery: 20 June 1862, Henry Gansevoort to George Henry Brewster, 9 July 1862, GL. Letter to Wool: Peter Gansevoort Diaries, 2 June 1862, GL. Ed's adventures: Edwin Lansing to Abraham Lansing, 21 June 1862, GL.

28. Joke: John S. Bowman, ed., *The Civil War Almanac,* intro. Henry Steele Commager (New York: W. H. Smith, 1983), 367. Halleck's nicknames: Warren W. Hassler, Jr., *General George B. McClellan: Shield of the Nation* (Baton Rouge: Louisiana State University Press, 1957), 180–81.

29. 25 June: Henry Gansevoort to Peter Gansevoort, 25 June 1862, GL. Confederate casualties: McPherson, *Battle Cry of Freedom,* 467. Henry during the Seven Days: see note 27, rejoined.

30. Ferris Greenslet, *The Lowells and Their Seven Worlds* (Boston: Houghton Mifflin, 1946), 282.

31. Shurr: William H. Shurr, "Melville's Poems: The Late Agenda," in *A Companion to Melville Studies,* ed. John Bryant (New York: Greenwood Press, 1986), 356. "Accomplices": Thomas Bailey Aldrich, *The Poems of Thomas Bailey Aldrich* (Boston: Ticknor and Fields, 1865), 240.

32. Kate: to Henry Gansevoort, 19 August 1862, GL.

33. "Unhappy" state: *Sun,* 26 June 1862. Other information: *Sun,* 10 July 1862.

34. 7 July 1862 meeting: *Sun,* 10 July 1862; Smith, *History of Pittsfield,* 2:622. 2 August 1862 meeting: Pittsfield Town Records.

35. Camp: *Sun,* 7 August 1862. Colonel Lee at town meetings: *Sun,* 21 August 1862. Adjutant Edwards: Smith, *History of Pittsfield,* 2:618. March into town: *Sun,* 28 August 1862.

36. Allan Melville family: see note 12, cottage. Kate: see note 8, Kate sewing. Gus: Augusta Melville to Catherine Gansevoort, 15 September 1862, GL.

37. "Clarke": *Sun,* 31 July 1862. Sam Houston, Jr.: *Sun,* 21 August 1862. "Dombrofsky": *Sun,* 18 September 1862.

38. Worry about Henry, support of McClellan, Fourth of July, Gottschalk: Catherine Gansevoort to Henry Gansevoort, 3 July 1862, GL. Departure for vacation: Peter Gansevoort Diaries, 20 July 1862, GL. Experiences during vacation, Abe in Canada: Catherine Gansevoort to Henry Gansevoort, 2 August 1862, GL.

39. Return: Peter Gansevoort Diaries, 2 August 1862, GL. Letter from Wessel: Wessel Gansevoort to Peter Gansevoort, 22 July 1862, GL. Wessel's and Peter's movements: Peter Gansevoort Diaries, 7 August 1862, GL. "Blame": Catherine Gansevoort Diaries, 11 August 1862, GL. "Lonely life," Catskill trip: see note 32.

Message from Danby: C. M. Bruce to Peter Gansevoort, 7 August 1862, GL. Messages and invitations: Wessel Gansevoort folder, GL. Funeral: Peter Gansevoort Diaries, 9 August 1862, GL.

40. Desertion: Richard T. Greene Pension Application, NA.

41. Thomas J. Hobart Compiled Service Record, NA.

42. Ed reporting: Edwin Y. Lansing Compiled Service Record, NA. Ed ill: Edwin Lansing to Henry Gansevoort, 19 July 1862, GL. Lowell's appointment: [Elizabeth Cabot Putnam,] *Memoirs of the War of '61: Colonel Charles Russell Lowell, Friends and Cousins* (Boston: Geo. W. Ellis, 1920), 5. Henry's promotion, transfer, regret: Henry Gansevoort to Catherine Gansevoort, 3 August 1862, GL.

43. McClellan: Hassler, *General George B. McClellan,* 196. Lowell: to James T. Fields, 2 August 1862, *Letters of James Russell Lowell,* 1:322. Emerson: *Journals and Miscellaneous Notebooks,* 15:207. Bruce: to Henry Gansevoort, 28 July 1862, GL.

44. Hassler, *General George B. McClellan,* 195.

45. Henry's experiences through Bull Run: see note 23, sympathy.

46. Ibid.

47. William H. Powell, in John Pope, "The Second Battle of Bull Run," *B&L,* 2:489n–90n.

48. Truce: *Sun,* 3 September 1862. Henry's experiences: Henry Gansevoort to Peter Gansevoort, 8 September, 1 October 1862, GL.

49. See note 23, sympathy.

50. Halleck's message: 30 August 1862, Murfin, *Gleam of Bayonets,* 61. Meeting: *Reminiscences of Richard Lathers,* 191–92.

51. Hordes of officers: eyewitness account, *Sun,* 11 September 1862. Bars, money, Lincoln's steamer: Murfin, *Gleam of Bayonets,* 35. McClellan taking command: George B. McClellan, "From the Peninsula to Antietam," *B&L,* 2:549–52. McClellan's presence: see note 47.

52. Lee quotation: McPherson, *Battle Cry of Freedom,* 536. Meetings in Pittsfield: *Sun,* 3 September 1862.

53. Henry to Leesburg, right flank: Palfrey, *Antietam and Fredericksburg,* 10–13. Condition of armies: see note 23, sympathy.

54. Henry, South Mountain and Antietam: Henry Gansevoort to Peter Gansevoort, 22 September 1862, GL. Lincoln: 15 September 1862, McPherson, *Battle Cry of Freedom,* 534.

55. M. Howe, *Justice Oliver Wendell Holmes,* 1:126–27.

56. 22 September 1862, *U&CA,* ser. 1, 19 (part 1):271.

57. Although the subject battle is not specified, the chronological placement of the poem suggests that it is Antietam.

58. Wendell's request: M. Howe, *Justice Oliver Wendell Holmes,* 1:130. Expedition: Holmes, "My Hunt after 'The Captain,'" *Works of Oliver Wendell Holmes,* 8:16–77.

59. Holmes, "My Hunt after 'The Captain,'" 8:24.

60. Dickinson: poem 502, *The Complete Poems of Emily Dickinson,* ed. Thomas H. Johnson (Boston: Little, Brown, 1960), 243–44, Paludan, *"A People's Contest,"* 366. Hawthorne: to Francis Bennoch, 12 October 1862, N. Hawthorne, *Letters, 1857–1864,* 501.

61. Allan Melvilles at wedding: see note 11, Fourth of July. Intended visit to Gansevoort: Augusta Melville to Susan L. Gansevoort, 5 September 1862, GL.

62. Picnic: Stanwix Melville to Augusta Melville, 30 September 1862, MFPA.

Regiment departed, withheld from Antietam: Smith, *History of Pittsfield,* 2:618. Canceled services, Sarah's flag: *Sun,* 11 September 1862. Rev. Todd: Henry T. Johns, *Life with the Forty-Ninth Massachusetts Volunteers,* [rev. ed.] (Washington, D.C.: Ramsey and Bisbee, 1890), 17. Hodge's band and Peninsula: "Berkshire Brass Bands," 1:74. Hoadley: Peter Gansevoort Diaries, 17, 18 September 1862, Catherine Gansevoort Diaries, 17 September 1862, GL.

63. School, Herman to New York: see note 62, picnic. Lizzie Thurston's death: *NYT,* 14 September 1862. Allan communicated to family: see note 36, Gus. Stanny gave the date of Herman's trip as "the other day."

64. Allan and Richard attended the funeral: Allan Melville and Richard Lathers deposition, 27 May 1869, A. Henry Thurston Pension Application (widow), NA.

65. Attempted reassignment: on 19 November 1862, General W. B. Franklin, commanding the Left Grand Division of the Army of the Potomac, requested Henry as his medical director, A. Henry Thurston Compiled Service Record, NA. Bruce's letter: see note 11, Fourth of July. Peaches: see note 62, picnic.

66. Bartlett taking command: Palfrey, *Memoir of William Francis Bartlett,* 51. Severe but popular: Smith, *History of Pittsfield,* 2:619. Quotation: Palfrey, *Memoir of William Francis Bartlett,* 298. Neither uniforms nor arms: Johns, *Life with the Forty-ninth Massachusetts,* 36, 39. Standing on single leg, riding in carriage: ibid., 65.

67. Appearance of camp: Johns, *Life with the Forty-ninth Massachusetts,* 20–21. Profanity, women invading tents: ibid., 56. Style of uniforms: ibid., 60–61. Uniforms arrived: *Sun,* 23 October 1862.

68. Lizzie working regularly: Nascimento, "Melville's Berkshire World," 259. Scraping linen: Frances M. Thomas to Eleanor M. Metcalf, 30 April 1925, courtesy Jay Leyda.

69. Move, fair: see note 62, picnic. Helen passing through: Helen Griggs to Catherine Gansevoort, 6 October 1862, GL. Fair in progress: from 1 to 3 October, *Sun,* 18 September 1862. Living in town enjoyable and the information in the following paragraph: Stanwix Melville to Augusta Melville, 28 October 1862, MFPA.

70. Wessel's estate, Maria's request, quotation: to Peter Gansevoort, 26 September 1862, GL. Gus's plea: to Peter Gansevoort, 5 November 1862, GL. Refusal: Peter Gansevoort to Maria G. Melville, 6 November 1862, GL.

71. Parker, Harris: Ira Harris to Peter Gansevoort, 29 September 1862, GL. *Argus:* clipping, 3 October 1862, GL. Pictures of Henry's battery: Frances Melville to Catherine Gansevoort, 13 December 1862, GL. Henry's rebuke: 2 November 1862, GL.

72. Regenerate: see note 54, Henry. Remained at battlefield: see note 71, rebuke.

73. To Peter Gansevoort, 1 October 1862, GL.

74. Dix negotiations, here and below: *Reminiscences of Richard Lathers,* 176–80.

75. Clipping, *Putnam County Courier,* Carmel, N.Y., 3 November 1877, Richard Lathers Papers, LC.

76. Meeting with Seymour, Republicans, trumped-up charges: *Reminiscences of Richard Lathers,* 180–81.

77. Democrats' tactics: Silbey, *Respectable Minority,* 67–68. Treatment of McClellan: M. Howe, *Justice Oliver Wendell Holmes,* 1:134–35. Republican misdemeanors: *Sun,* 2, 9 October 1862. Bryant: Parke Godwin, *A Biography of William Cullen Bryant, with Extracts from his Private Correspondence,* 2 vols. (New York: Appleton, 1883), 2:176.

78. Pittsfield's vote: *Sun,* 6 November 1862. Jennie: see note 11, Fourth of July.

79. Henry: to Peter Gansevoort, 10 November 1862, GL. One volunteer, Meade, historian: Hassler, *General George B. McClellan,* 317, 328.

80. Departure: George Ticknor Curtis, in Richard B. Irwin, "The Removal of McClellan," *B&L,* 3:104n. Quotation: ibid., 104.

81. Reception at Winyah: *Reminiscences of Richard Lathers,* 192–94.

82. Curtis: to Charles Eliot Norton, 3 August 1862, Cary, *George William Curtis,* 156. Kate: Catherine Gansevoort to Henry Gansevoort, 2 December 1862, GL. Contemporary: Palfrey, *Antietam and Fredericksburg,* 135.

83. Flawed poetry: Fogle, "Melville and the Civil War," 71, claims that the poem "falls flat, from general poor judgment, [and] the relative meaningless of the praise bestowed," and Milder, "Rhetoric of Melville's *Battle-Pieces,*" 197, says that this is "an odd poem to include given McClellan's equivocal reputation." Grant: Hassler, *General George B. McClellan,* 325. Critic: Palfrey, *Antietam and Fredericksburg,* 134–35.

84. Hill: "Chickamauga—The Great Battle of the West," *B&L,* 3:638n. Lee: as told to Cazenove Lee and quoted by Robert E. Lee, *Recollections and Letters of General Robert E. Lee* (1904; reprint, Garden City, N.Y.: Garden City, n.d.), 416. In defense of "The Victor of Antietam," one may note the opinion of Richard N. Current (*Lincoln Nobody Knows,* p. 151), still valid today, that the passions and prejudices of the Civil War are still alive and that an impartial assessment of McClellan will not be possible until they subside.

Chapter 5. Defeat, Dander, and Victory

1. Priscilla died alone: Lucy Nourse to [Augusta and Frances Melville,] 2 January 1863, MFPA. "English Women": *Sun,* 6 November 1862.

2. Accident: *Sun,* 13 November 1862.

3. Ibid.

4. Visited city: Peter Gansevoort Diaries, 5 November 1862, GL. Melvilles' call, met Jennie: Jane Melville to Henry Gansevoort, 11 November 1862, GL. Return visit, offended by Bruce: Catherine Gansevoort to Henry Gansevoort, 16 November 1862, GL. Decor of St. Nicholas: Nat Brandt, *The Man Who Tried to Burn New York* (Syracuse, N.Y.: Syracuse University Press, 1986), 97–98. Temper cooled: Catherine Gansevoort to Henry Gansevoort, 2 December 1862, GL.

5. Kate and Guert: See note 4, temper cooled. Kate and Mary Curtis: Frances Melville to Catherine Gansevoort, 13 December 1862, GL. Gansevoorts' return: Peter Gansevoort Diaries, 22 November 1862, GL.

6. Johns, *Life with the Forty-ninth Massachusetts Volunteers,* 71–72.

7. Illness: to Augusta Melville, undated, MFPA. Sarah and Berkshire Regiment: letter from S. B. S., 27 December 1862, *Sun,* 1 January 1863.

8. Henry's illness, Ed's visit: Henry Gansevoort to Catherine Gansevoort, 2 December 1862, GL. Sick leave: Henry Gansevoort to J. A. Haskins, 3 June 1865, GL.

9. Aunt Melville: Catherine Gansevoort Diaries, 9 December 1862, GL. Henry home: Peter Gansevoort Diaries, 8 December 1862, GL. Henry looking well: Catherine Gansevoort Diaries, 8 December 1862, GL. Lieutenant: Gulian V. Weir to Henry Gansevoort, 9 December 1862, GL.

10. Stephen Longfellow: Henry Wadsworth Longfellow to Sarah Fisher Clampit Ames, 18 December 1862, *Letters of Henry Wadsworth Longfellow,* 4:304. Curtis:

George William Curtis to Charles Eliot Norton, 15 December 1862, Cary, *George William Curtis*, 160, 160n–61n.

11. *Poems of Thomas Bailey Aldrich*, 239.

12. George Whitman: Phisterer, *New York in the War of the Rebellion*, 3:2394. Walt Whitman: "Specimen Days," *Prose Works 1892*, 1:32–33. Alcott in Washington: Young, *Women and the Crisis*, 228–32. Coan: Titus M. Coan Pension Application, NA.

13. Whitman: to Thomas Jefferson Whitman, 16 January [1863,] *Walt Whitman: The Correspondence*, 1:68. Bryant: Allan Nevins, *The Evening Post: A Century of Journalism* (1922; reprint, New York: Russell and Russell, 1968), 297. Holmes: M. Howe, *Justice Oliver Wendell Holmes*, 1:136.

14. Poem: Eggleston, *American War Ballads and Lyrics*, 2:105. J. R. Lowell: Leslie Stephen to Charles Eliot Norton, 11 February 1892, *Letters of James Russell Lowell*, 1:410. Charley's service: *Massachusetts Soldiers, Sailors, and Marines in the Civil War*, 6:179. Charley's illness, Longfellow's visit, war terrible: to Ernest Wadsworth, Edith, and Anne Allegra Longfellow, 13 June 1863, *Letters of Henry Wadsworth Longfellow*, 4:332–33. First gunshot wound: Henry Wadsworth Longfellow to Ernest Wadsworth Longfellow, 22 June 1863, ibid., 342.

15. Herman improved: see note 5, Kate and Mary Curtis. War work: Brockett and Vaughan, *Woman's Work in the Civil War*, 669–70; Sam Shaw, house not settled, excuse for living, lengthening mother's visit: 10 December 1862, *Log*, 2:656–57.

16. Children's activities, dog, and Christmas, below: Stanwix Melville to Augusta Melville, 30 December 1862, MFPA. Black Newfoundland: J. Hawthorne, "Hawthorne at Lenox," 214.

17. Henry L. Abbott, M. Howe, *Justice Oliver Wendell Holmes*, 1:145.

18. Sewing: Elizabeth S. Melville to Augusta Melville, [4] March [1863], MFPA. Wednesdays and Fridays: *Sun*, 5 February 1863. Malcolm, happy in town: Helen Griggs to Augusta and Frances Melville, 25 January 1863, MFPA. Stanny ill: Elizabeth Melville (daughter) to Augusta Melville, 10 February 1863, MFPA. Illness of Hoadley girls: for example, Catherine Hoadley to Augusta Melville, 23 February 1863, MFPA.

19. Heterodox lady: see note 5, Kate and Mary Curtis. Later adventures: Thomas Melville to Maria G. Melville, Augusta Melville, and Frances Melville, 22 January, 8 February 1863, MFPA.

20. Activity of family, "imbeciles": Catherine Gansevoort to Henry Gansevoort, 2 January 1863, GL. Uncle Peter's illness: Catherine Gansevoort to Henry Gansevoort, 26 January 1863, GL. Hoadley: see note 18, Hoadley girls.

21. Guert elusive: "Guert seems to be no where," Jane Melville to Catherine Gansevoort, [27 February] 1863, GL. Yard business: Frances Melville to Catherine Gansevoort, 7 January 1863, GL. Allan and Guert: Catherine Gansevoort to Henry Gansevoort, 16 November 1862, GL. Ned's health: on 25 March, the Curtises had just received a letter from Ned saying that his resignation had been accepted, Frances Melville to Augusta Melville, [29? March 1863,] MFPA.

22. Mary Curtis: Jane Melville reported that Mary had been there for a month, note 21, Guert elusive. Gertrude and Alice Downer: Nancy Downer to Augusta Melville, 28 December 1862, MFPA, and note 1, Priscilla. Alice's visit to Allan Melvilles: Catherine G. Melville (Allan's daughter) to Augusta Melville, 29 December 1862, MFPA. Downer family information: Perry, *Charles D'Wolf of Guadaloupe*, 152, 189–90.

23. Aunt Mary's letter: Mary A. A. Melvill to Maria G. Melville, 16 January 1863, MFPA. Allan Melvill's adventure: Allan C. Melvill to Mary A. A. Melvill, 11, 18, 20, 24 May, 17 June, 18 July, 9 August 1862, courtesy Jean Melvill.

24. See note 1, Priscilla.

25. Longfellow: journal, 1 January 1863, S. Longfellow, *Life of Henry Wadsworth Longfellow,* 3:19. Fear of driving: Smith, "Herman Melville," 136.

26. Elizabeth S. Melville to Augusta Melville, 11 February 1863, MFPA.

27. Elizabeth S. Melville to Augusta Melville, 29 June 1863, MFPA.

28. Poem: S., "The Rebellion," *Sun,* 15 January 1863.

29. 8 December 1862, Thomas Carlyle and Ralph Waldo Emerson, *The Correspondence of Thomas Carlyle and Ralph Waldo Emerson, 1834–1872,* 2 vols. (Boston: James R. Osgood, 1883), 2:280–81.

30. "Chattanooga": Cohen points out the relationship between these two poems, "Notes," *Battle-Pieces of Herman Melville,* 243–44.

31. Jimerson, *Private Civil War,* 41.

32. Harvard Regiment groaning: M. Howe, *Justice Oliver Wendell Holmes,* 1:148. Senator: Wilson, of Massachusetts, *Sun,* 22 January 1863.

33. Gulian V. Weir to Henry Gansevoort, 24 January 1863, GL.

34. Not hankering, volunteers: Henry Gansevoort to Peter Gansevoort, 1 October 1862, GL. Safely do it: Gulian V. Weir, 26 December 1862, GL. Returning to army: Peter Gansevoort Diaries, 22 December 1862, GL. Fort Hamilton, explanation, Dix, Bruce, Wakeman: Henry Gansevoort to Peter Gansevoort, 30 December 1862, GL.

35. Eleanor Wilson to Henry Gansevoort, 27 January 1863, GL.

36. Curtis: to Charles Eliot Norton, 25 September 1862, Cary, *George William Curtis,* 158. Emerson: to Matilda Ashurst Briggs, 8 April 1863, *Letters of Ralph Waldo Emerson,* 5:322. Hawthorne: to Henry A. Bright, 8 March 1863, N. Hawthorne, *Letters, 1857-1864,* 543-44.

37. Miserable administration: to William D. Ticknor, 8 February 1863, N. Hawthorne, *Letters, 1857–1864,* 535. Honest man, suspected by radicals: see note 36, Hawthorne. Care a fig, negro-question: to Elizabeth P. Peabody, 20 July 1863, ibid., 591–92.

38. Dedication: C[laude]. M. S[impson]., "Introduction to *Our Old Home,*" *Our Old Home: A Series of English Sketches,* ed. William Charvat, Roy Harvey Pearce, Claude M. Simpson, Matthew J. Bruccoli, Fredson Bowers, and L. Neal Smith (Columbus: Ohio State University Press, 1970), xxii–xix. Quotation: to James T. Fields, 18 July 1863, N. Hawthorne, *Letters, 1857–1864,* 586.

39. Secret correspondence: *Sun,* 20 August 1863. Norton: to George William Curtis, 21 September 1863, N. Hawthorne, *Letters, 1857–1864,* 561n. Stowe: 3 November 1863, courtesy Thomas Woodson.

40. Caricature: *Sun,* 12 February 1863. Poem: *Sun,* 22 January 1863.

41. Brawl: on 17 January, *New York Herald,* 1 February 1863, courtesy Hershel Parker. Helen: see note 18, Malcolm.

42. Kate: 30 January 1863, GL. Henry: to Catherine Gansevoort, 27 January 1863, GL.

43. Paludan, *"A People's Contest,"* 236.

44. *Reminiscences of Richard Lathers,* 194–95.

45. Clara's illness, Jeanie, Mary: Helen Griggs to Augusta Melville, 22 March 1863, MFPA. House, school, Burnside, Pittsfield: see note 27.

46. New York Democratic leaders, "implied treason": Stewart Mitchell, *Horatio Seymour of New York* (New York: Da Capo Press, 1970), 289–91.

47. Most city newspapers, drumhead law, newspapers proscribed and banned: *Sun,* 4 June 1863. *Times* seized: *Sun,* 11 June 1863.

48. Meeting, resolutions, signatories, Lincoln's response: Guernsey and Alden, *Harper's Pictorial History,* 645n–46n.

49. Henry Gansevoort: Catherine Gansevoort to Henry Gansevoort, 6 April 1863, GL. Downers: see note 22, Gertrude. Latherses: Frances Melville to Augusta Melville, 25? March 1863, MFPA. Allan Melvilles: see note 21, Guert elusive, and note 18, Malcolm. Griggses: Helen Griggs to Catherine Gansevoort, 12 April 1863, GL. Curtises: Catherine Curtis to Catherine Gansevoort, 13 February 1863, GL. D'Wolfs: Catherine Hoadley to Augusta Melville, 23 February 1863, MFPA. Kate Hoadley: Catherine Hoadley to Helen Griggs, [1863], MFPA. Album: see note 21, yard business.

50. Inflation: McKay, *Civil War and New York City,* 216. Helen: to Augusta Melville, 25 February 1863, MFPA. Repairs: Frances Melville to Augusta Melville, 11 June 1863, MFPA. Sadler: see note 49, D'Wolfs. Priscilla: Frances Melville to Augusta Melville, 16 [March] 1863, MFPA. Taxes heavy: Frances Melville to Augusta Melville, 20 March 1863, MFPA.

51. Give Allan a shaking: see note 50, taxes heavy. Allan's defense: see note 18, Malcolm. "The Repairs": see note 50, Priscilla. Allan's note: see note 49, Latherses.

52. Seeing Glens Falls family: George Curtis to Augusta Melville, 3, 24 January 1863, MFPA, and note 50, taxes heavy. Long visit: see note 49, Curtises, and Maria G. Melville to Augusta and Frances Melville, 13 February [1863,] MFPA. Mountain home: George Curtis to Augusta Melville, 24 January 1863, MFPA. Leonard ill, report of Ned's resignation, Kate Curtis looking younger: see note 21, Ned's health. Ned's resignation: Abstracts of Service of Naval Officers, NA. Ned's poor health has been inferred from his illness after he returned home.

53. See note 18, Stanny ill.

54. Two week visit: on 17 February 1863, probably immediately after his return from the city, Herman wrote Kate Gansevoort about seeing Henry, *Log,* 2:658. Allan not well: see note 21, Guert elusive. Summer residence in New Rochelle: see note 4, Melvilles' call. Financial arrangements: Puett, "Melville's Wife," 124. Sam Shaw: Maria G. Melville to Augusta Melville, 11 May 1863, MFPA.

55. Visit of 7 February: Henry Gansevoort to Catherine Gansevoort, [8 February 1863,] GL. Herman's description of Henry: 17 February 1863, *Log,* 2:658. Henry writing Kate: see note 42, Henry.

56. Herman envisioned old General Gansevoort "looking down upon this dishonorable epoch," see note 55, description.

57. Walk: see note 26. Two-hour journey: Henry Gansevoort to Catherine Gansevoort, 2 March 1863, GL.

58. Fanny and Bessie: see note 18, Stanny ill. Never able to leave home again: see note 26. "Goings-on": see note 18, sewing.

59. Gus's offer, haggling: see note 18, sewing. Helen's intervention: to Elizabeth S. Melville, 6 March [1863], MFPA. Gus agrees: note by Gus, 7 March, on the envelope of Lizzie's [4] March letter, MFPA.

60. Shaw in New York: see note 21, Guert elusive. Drawing up documents: Helen

Griggs sensed that something was up and that Sam Shaw was involved, note 50, Helen.

61. Cheerful: see note 55, description. Minstrel show: Stanwix Melville to Augusta Melville, 3 March 1863, MFPA; *Sun,* 5 March 1863. Malcolm's vacation: see note 58, "goings on." Malcolm on stage: see note 59, Helen's intervention. Examination, snowstorm: *Sun,* 12 March 1863. Church, buckwheat, packed and ready, maid: Elizabeth S. Melville to Augusta Melville, 8 March 1863, MFPA.

62. John's arrival: Catherine Hoadley to Augusta Melville, 20 March 1863, MFPA. Difficulty hiring servants: Catherine Hoadley to Augusta Melville, 23 February 1863, MFPA. Leaving New Bedford: see note 61, cheerful, and Maria's letter. Old friends, recitations: see note 50, taxes heavy. Maid ill: Elizabeth S. Melville to Augusta Melville, 25 March 1863, MFPA. "Miss Gusty": Elizabeth S. Melville to Augusta Melville, 16 April 1863, MFPA.

63. All Lizzie had hoped: Elizabeth S. Melville to Augusta Melville, 22 March 1863, MFPA. Distribution of children, Stanny peaked, visit to Brookline: see note 45, Clara's illness. Oakie and Stanny: Stanwix Melville to Augusta Melville, 19 March 1863, MFPA. Willie Griggs: John William Griggs, Junior, the son of George Griggs's brother John, 1860 Census. Frog pond: see note 62, maid ill.

64. Reluctant return: see note 62, maid ill. Maid, stamps: see note 62, "Miss Gusty." Northern lights: on 9 April, *Sun,* 16 April 1863.

65. Resignation, Sheridan quotations: Thomas J. Hobart Compiled Service Record, NA. Bringing John: John was discharged on 26 January 1863, when Jeff departed for home, John A. Hobart Compiled Service Record, NA.

66. McPherson, *Battle Cry of Freedom,* 626.

67. *Typee:* Anderson, *Melville in the South Seas,* 118. "Encantadas": Cohen, "Notes," *Battle-Pieces of Herman Melville,* 237.

68. Toby deserting and returning to original regiment: Richard T. Greene Compiled Service Record, Richard T. Greene Pension Application, NA.

69. Battle: Palfrey, *Memoir of William Francis Bartlett,* 81–85; Johns, *Life with the Forty-Ninth Massachusetts Volunteers,* 252–68.

70. Herman in New York: see note 62, "Miss Gusty." Richard's departure: Maria G. Melville to Augusta and Frances Melville, 7 April 1863, MFPA. Voyage: *Reminiscences of Richard Lathers,* 197–219. Letter to Adams: clipping, *White Plains Journal,* Richard Lathers Papers, LC.

71. Rowland: Elizabeth S. Melville to Frances Melville, [7?] May 1863, MFPA.

72. Helen's invitation, health of George and Leonard: Mary Curtis to Augusta Melville, 10 April 1863, MFPA. Ned expected: Frances Melville to Augusta Melville, 4 May 1863, MFPA. Ned's arrival: he first visited the Melvilles in Gansevoort on 10 June, see note 50, repairs. Tom's gifts: Frances Melville to Augusta Melville, 25 April 1863, MFPA. Herman informing mother: see note 71. Quotation: see note 54, Sam Shaw. Pittsfield station: see note 62, "Miss Gusty." John's trip: Catherine Hoadley to Helen Griggs and Augusta Melville, 24 April 1863, MFPA. Little girls: Catherine Hoadley to Augusta Melville, 9 April 1863, MFPA.

73. Visit, here and below: see note 71.

74. Lizzie's fatigue: ibid. Allan's return: Jane Melville to Elizabeth S. Melville, 2 June 1863, MFPA.

75. Weather: *Sun,* 28 May, 11, 25 June 1863. Sarah spending the night: Stanwix

Melville to Augusta Melville, 30 May 1863, MFPA. Gottschalk: *Sun,* 28 May, 4 June 1863. Varian, Hoffman, Porter, income tax: *Sun,* 4 June 1863.

76. Rabbits, catechisms: see note 75, Sarah. Lizzie arranging: see note 74, Allan's return.

77. Poor, simple *Arrowhead:* see note 74, Allan's return. Madam satisfied: Helen Griggs to Augusta Melville, 14 June 1863, MFPA.

78. Melville activities, quotation: Elizabeth S. Melville to Frances Melville, 14 June 1863, MFPA. Beautiful day: *Sun,* 11 June 1863. Rain: *Sun,* 18 June 1863.

79. See note 27.

80. Summer allergies: Lizzie said only that her wits were not clear, ibid. "Greely & the nigger": ibid.

81. Quotation: *Log,* 2:659. Herman's letter, visit to Gansevoort: implied in Frances Melville to Augusta Melville, 22 June [1863,] and Maria G. Melville to Catherine Hoadley, 22 June 1863, MFPA.

82. See note 27.

83. Tom: Frances Melville to Augusta Melville, 15 June 1863, MFPA. "Allabamas," Mother Melville's reaction to Hoadley's poetry, Fanny's copy: see note 81, Herman's letter. Evade commerce raiders: Catherine Gansevoort to Henry Gansevoort, 30 June 1863, GL. Uncle Peter's copy: inscribed 6 July 1863, *National Union Catalogue,* 248:486.

84. Children: Frances Melville to Augusta Melville, 29 June [1863], MFPA. Glens Falls family: Helen Griggs to Augusta Melville, [27 June 1863,] MFPA.

85. M. Howe, *Justice Oliver Wendell Holmes,* 1:154–55.

86. Morgan Dix: journal, 6 May 1863, *Memoirs of John Adams Dix,* 2:57. Whitman: to Thomas P. Sawyer, 27 May 1863, *Walt Whitman: The Correspondence,* 1:106. *Times: Sun,* 21 May 1863. Southern newspapers: *Sun,* 4 June 1863.

87. Henry to father: 16 February 1863, GL. Peter calling on adjutant-general: Peter Gansevoort Diaries, 19 February 1863, GL. Adjutant-general's assurance: Peter Gansevoort to Henry Gansevoort, 19 February 1863, GL. Assignment to position: Special Order No. 140, New York State Adjutant General, 10 March 1863, GL. Battery pressing: Special Order No. 89, War Department, 24 February 1863, GL. Lathers and Allan: telegram, Richard Lathers to Edwin Stanton, 16 March 1863 (actually sent by Allan Melville, Allan Melville to Catherine Gansevoort, 16 March 1863), stating that Lathers had written on 11 March, GL. Leave: Special Order No. 122, War Department, 16 March 1863 (signed 2 April 1863), GL. Took rooms: Henry Gansevoort to Catherine Gansevoort, 1 April 1863, GL. Abe's vision: to Henry Gansevoort, 23 March 1863, GL. Kate's worry: to Henry Gansevoort, 17 March 1863, GL.

88. Abe's first sermon: see note 87, Abe's vision. Battery-mate: Gulian V. Weir to Henry Gansevoort, 24 April 1863, GL. Abe's second sermon: to Henry Gansevoort, 3 May 1863, GL.

89. Camp Sprague: inquiry form submitted by Henry to the Bureau of Military Statistics, New York, GL. Abe's interest: see note 87, Abe's vision. Health not good enough: to Henry Gansevoort, 23 June 1863, GL. Civilian enemies: the entire intrigue, including Charles Brewster's 1 April 1863 letter to Lincoln, is detailed in Charles Brewster Compiled Service Record, NA.

90. Arrival of family: Peter and Catherine Gansevoort Diaries, 23 May 1863, GL. Henry ill: Catherine Gansevoort Diaries, 24 May 1863, GL. Webb ill: Daniel Webb to

Henry Gansevoort, 26 May 1863, GL. Webb's death: Catherine Gansevoort Diaries, 28 May 1863, GL. Henry in Albany: Peter Gansevoort Diaries, 29 May 1863, GL. Will: Catherine Gansevoort to Henry Gansevoort, 3 June 1863, GL. Appointed colonel: Special Order No. 259, New York State Adjutant General, 1 June 1863, GL.

91. Consolidation order, new ranks: Henry Gansevoort to Peter Gansevoort, 26 June 1863, GL. Adjutant-general: Peter Gansevoort Diaries, 18 June 1863, GL. Col. Lansing: H. Seymour Lansing to Catherine Gansevoort, 30 July 1878, GL.

92. Regiment mustered: Henry S. Gansevoort mustering papers, GL. Ordered to Washington: Special Order No. 325, New York State Adjutant General, 21 June 1863, GL. Lockwood: Henry Gansevoort to Peter Gansevoort, 2 November 1864, GL. Woodward: George Woodward to Henry Gansevoort, 7 July 1863, GL. Allan: Allan Melville to Henry Gansevoort, 24 June 1863, GL. Departing strength: inquiry form, Board of Military Statistics, New York, GL.

93. Catherine Gansevoort to Henry Gansevoort, 30 June 1863, GL.

94. *Sun:* 2 July 1863. Tyler: [Cullum,] *Memoir of Brevet Major-General Robert Ogden Tyler,* 13. Barry's offer: Henry Gansevoort to Peter Gansevoort, 23 July 1863, GL.

95. Return of Allan Melvilles: George Henry Brewster to Henry Gansevoort, 13 July 1863, GL. Suspension of celebration: *Sun,* 25 June 1863. Rain, news: *Sun,* 9 July 1863.

96. John Hoadley to Augusta Melville, 10 July 1863, MFPA. I am indebted to the late Jay Leyda and to Hershel Parker for their aid in reading this almost illegibile letter.

97. For valuable annotations to this poem, some of which have been used here, see Cohen, "Notes," *Battle-Pieces of Herman Melville,* 238–39.

Chapter 6. Farewell to Berkshire

1. Aunt Lucy: Elizabeth S. Melville to Augusta Melville, 29 June 1863, MFPA. Shaws, Augusta: Elizabeth S. Melville to Augusta Melville, 30 July 1863, MFPA.

2. Coan: Titus M. Coan Pension Application, NA. Company G: Charles Brewster to Henry Gansevoort, 19 July 1863, GL.

3. Income distribution: McKay, *Civil War and New York City,* 216. Life of rich, condition of poor, riots: Adrian Cook, *The Armies of the Streets: The New York City Draft Riots of 1863* (Lexington: University Press of Kentucky, 1974), 3–31.

4. Irish attitudes: Iver Bernstein, *The New York City Draft Riots: Their Significance for American Society and Politics in the Age of the Civil War* (New York: Oxford University Press, 1990), 100–24. Businessmen profiting, rich man's war, poor man's fight, wages: Paludin, *A People's Contest,"* 145, 190, 113. Freed slaves and jobs: McPherson, *Battle Cry of Freedom,* 609. Population figures: Brandt, *Man Who Tried to Burn New York,* 82.

5. Democrats: Silbey, *Respectable Minority,* 73. *Argus: Sun,* 2 April 1863.

6. Draft law: James W. Geary, *We Need Men: The Union Draft in the Civil War* (DeKalb: Northern Illinois University Press, 1991), 66. Confederate law, Northern soldiers: Jimerson, *Private Civil War,* 192, 197–98.

7. Radical enrollment officers, Irish in war: Paludan, *"A People's Contest,"* 236, 281–84. Enrollment period violence: Eugene C. Murdock, *One Million Men: The Civil War Draft in the North* (Madison: State Historical Society of Wisconsin, 1971), 26–61. *Register: Sun,* 9 July 1863. Quotations: Catherine Gansevoort to Henry Gansevoort, 15 July 1863, GL.

8. Riots: described in Cook, *Armies of the Streets,* and analyzed in Bernstein, *New York City Draft Riots.* Bennett: Mitchell, *Horatio Seymour of New York,* 307. Cook, 60, believes that as few as a hundred effective troops might have been enough.

9. Halted: see note 2, Company G, and Cook, *Armies of the Streets,* 162–64. Offices of 13th, Lockwood, Frazar: Douglas Frazar to Henry Gansevoort, 24 July 1863, GL.

10. Fighting subsiding: Swinton, *History of the Seventh Regiment,* 353, 355.

11. Bernstein, *New York City Draft Riots,* particularly 43–60 and 125–61, outlines the division among the city leaders. "Old New York": ibid., 126. "American aristocracy": ibid., 55. Quotations about Irish and blacks: Strong, 19 July 1863, *Diary,* 3:342. Infuriating mob: Bernstein, *New York City Draft Riots,* 46–47.

12. Conciliating mob: Bernstein, *New York City Draft Riots,* 47.

13. Ibid., 48–49, 54–56, 60.

14. Fabrications: for example, Dix, *Memoirs of John Adams Dix,* 2:72. Historian: McPherson, *Battle Cry of Freedom,* 610. During the Battle of Gettysburg, the 5th, 8th, 11th, 13th, 22nd, 37th, 65th, 71st, and 74th militia regiments had been assigned to the Department of the Susquehanna, primarily for the defense of Harrisburg; the 7th and 84th militia regiments to the defenses of Baltimore (but the 84th after the battle had begun); the 8th U.S. Infantry to the provost guard of the Army of the Potomac headquarters, in Taneytown, Maryland; the 162nd New York Volunteers and the 26th Michigan Volunteers to the Seventh Corps on the James Peninsula: Dyer, *Compendium of the War of the Rebellion,* and Phisterer, *New York in the War of the Rebellion,* passim. The one unit that *had* fought at Gettysburg was Henry Gansevoort's Battery C, 5th Artillery, which, decimated in the battle, was sent to the city to reform. It appears to have arrived on 18 July, after the end of the riots, *NYT,* 19 July 1863.

15. Allan at Arrowhead, Bruce: George Henry Brewster to Henry Gansevoort, 13 July 1863, GL. Whitman: to Louisa Van Velsor Whitman, 15 July 1863, *Whitman Correspondence,* 1:117. Uncle Peter: Peter Gansevoort Diaries, 16 July 1863, GL.

16. Rosenberry: *Melville,* 140. Stewart: "Conditional Mood of Melville's Poetry," 221–22. Fogle: "Melville and the Civil War," 74. Connor: Marian Connor, "The Abysm and the Star" (Ph.D. diss., Boston University, 1977), 74n. Freibert, "Meditative Voice in the Poetry of Herman Melville," 63–64.

17. Silbey, *Respectable Minority,* 83.

18. Whittier: to Mary Curzon, 24 December 1862, *Letters of John Greenleaf Whittier,* 3:33. Dickinson: to Thomas Wentworth Higginson, February 1863, *Letters of Emily Dickinson,* 2:423.

19. Ford, *History of the Origin of the Town of Clinton,* 647.

20. Ranks: Peter Burchard, *One Gallant Rush: Robert Gould Shaw and His Brave Black Regiment* (New York: St. Martin's Press, 1965), 79–80, 83–86. Stanton's prohibition: Schouler, *History of Massachusetts in the Civil War,* 1:407.

21. Longfellow: journal, 28 May 1863, S. Longfellow, *Life of Henry Wadsworth Longfellow,* 3:22. Douglass: Schouler, *History of Massachusetts in the Civil War,* 1:409–10.

22. Heaviest casualties: Hondon B. Hargrove, *Black Union Soldiers in the Civil War* (Jefferson, N.C.: McFarland, 1988), 156.

23. Higginson: Thomas Wentworth Higginson, *Army Life in a Black Regiment,* intro. Howard Mumford Jones (1870; reprint, East Lansing: Michigan State University Press, 1960), 4. Whitman: "November Boughs," *Prose Works 1892,* 2:587. *New York Tribune:* McPherson, *Battle Cry of Freedom,* 686.

24. Allan Melville to Catherine Gansevoort, 16 March 1863, GL.

25. Details of *Roanoke,* here and below: MacBride, *Civil War Ironclads,* 40–41. Guert's orders: Abstracts of Service of Naval Officers, NA.

26. Defects: MacBride, *Civil War Ironclads,* 41; Bennett, *Steam Navy of the United States,* 354, 357. Firing guns: B. F Sands to S. P Lee, 14 July 1863, *U&CN,* ser. 1, 9:125. Better suited: B. F Sands to Secretary of the Navy, 11 July 1863, ibid., 119–20. Uncle Peter: 16 July 1863, GL.

27. Seward's visit: *Sun,* 30 July 1863.

28. General's request: telegram Guert Gansevoort to Secretary of the Navy, 3 August 1863, *U&CN,* ser. 1, 9:145. Excursion: Guert Gansevoort to Secretary of the Navy, 8 August 1863, ibid., 146–47. Explosion: Samuel Huse to Guert Gansevoort, 7 August 1863, ibid., 147–48. Davidson: *Civil War Naval Chronology,* III–123.

29. Allan to New York: Allan Melville to Catherine Gansevoort, 26 July 1863, GL. Repairs: John Hoadley to Augusta Melville, 13 August 1863, MFPA. Rain: *Sun,* 6 August 1863. Shaws in Pittsfield: see note 1, Shaws. Shaws in Gansevoort: Maria G. Melville to Augusta Melville, 24 July 1863, MFPA.

30. House crowded, meet Gus at station: see note 1, Shaws. Visit of Nourses: Jane Melville to Maria G. Melville, 25 September 1863, MFPA. Clear days: *Sun,* 6 August 1863. Hot spell: *Sun,* 13 August 1863. Gus's travels in Berkshire: see note 29, repairs.

31. Jane Melville to Elizabeth S. Melville, [7 August 1863,] MFPA.

32. This and the following about the trip: Elizabeth S. Melville to Augusta Melville, 16 August 1863, MFPA. I am indebted to Alan Grieve for assistance in identifying and locating some of the landmarks mentioned in Lizzie's letter.

33. Peru Hill: probably present-day Peru. Malcolm's school: in the fall, he attended a boarding school in Newton Center, a Boston suburb, Puett, "Melville's Wife," 125, but it is not clear what school was meant in this instance.

34. Mrs. Fenn, flag: *Sun,* 6 August 1863. Preparations: *Sun,* 23 July 1863. Sanitary Rooms, soldier: *Sun,* 20 August 1863.

35. Bartlett's return: *Sun,* 6 August 1863. Arrival: *Sun,* 27 August 1863. Liederkranz: "Berkshire Brass Bands," 2:86. Sarah's health: see note 32, trip.

36. Bayou La Fourche: *Sun,* 30 July 1863. Return: *Massachusetts Soldiers, Sailors, and Marines,* 4:471; *Sun,* 27 August 1863; Johns, *Life with the Forty-ninth Massachusetts Volunteers,* 75, 422, 425–35; Smith, *History of Pittsfield,* 2:620. Different numbers are given in different sources.

37. Sick to Sanitary Rooms, Lizzie: Johns, *Life with the Forty-ninth Massachusetts Volunteers,* 411, and Brockett and Vaughan, *Women's Work in the Civil War,* 674, say "the hospital," but *Sun,* 27 August 1863, specifies the Sanitary Rooms. Beef tea: Frances M. Thomas to Eleanor M. Metcalf, 30 April 1925, courtesy Jay Leyda. Naming Lizzie, among others, Johns says that "many a stricken soldier will ever think with gratitude, and many a soldier's widow will, in her loneliness, invoke Heaven's blessings on them who so tenderly handed *their* loved ones to God and His mercy."

38. Johns, *Life with the Forty-ninth Massachusetts Volunteers,* 403.

39. Bust of Shaw: *Sun,* 1 October 1863. Photographs: Elizabeth S. Melville to Augusta Melville, 16 October 1863, MFPA. Malcolm's baptism: *Log,* 1:315. Clara Nourse: see note 1, Aunt Lucy.

40. Liederkrantz, Wilkes: *Sun,* 17 September 1863. Bartlett at Learneds': Palfrey, *Memoir of William Francis Bartlett,* 138. At Pomeroys': *Sun,* 24 September 1863.

41. John Hoadley, Allan: Catherine Hoadley to Augusta Melville, 9 September 1863, MFPA. Visit to Gansevoort: Maria G. Melville to Catherine Gansevoort, 11 September 1863, GL; Catherine and Peter Gansevoort Diaries, 15 September 1863, GL; Catherine Gansevoort to Henry Gansevoort, 17 September 1863, GL. Helen Griggs: Helen Griggs to Augusta and Frances Melville, 29 September 1863, MFPA.

42. Mission to England: Schouler, *History of Massachusetts in the Civil War,* 1:518–19; Hoadley obit., *American Machinist,* 1. Helen: Helen Griggs to Catherine Gansevoort, 5 October 1863, GL. Fanny's arrival: Allan Melville to Augusta Melville, 12 October 1863, MFPA. *Scotia: NYT,* 4 September 1863.

43. Allan's return, Jennie to Gansevoort, Henry Thurston in New York: see note 30, Nourses. Herman's hope: see note 32. Allan Melvilles to New York: George Henry Brewster to Henry Gansevoort, 8 October 1863, GL. Herman to New York, plans to return: see note 42, Fanny's arrival. Henry Thurston's leave: A. Henry Thurston Compiled Service Record, NA.

44. Sarah's last days, death: see note 39, photographs. Shock to family: for example, Frances Melville to Augusta Melville, 21 October 1863, MFPA; *Sun,* 22 October 1863.

45. Elizabeth S. Melville to Augusta Melville, 28 October 1863, MFPA.

46. Hoadley: see note 44, shock. Herman's return, move: see note 45.

47. Date and details of move: Helen Griggs to Maria G. Melville, 9 November 1863, MFPA. Helen heard this from Hope Shaw on Friday, 6 November, which means that the Melvilles had arrived in New York and had begun work before that date. Paid for, girls' school: Puett, "Melville's Wife," 124–25.

48. Church: Walter Donald Kring, *Liberals among the Orthodox: Unitarian Beginnings in New York City, 1819–1839* (Boston: Beacon Press, 1974), 9; Donald Yannella and Hershel Parker, eds., *The Endless, Winding Way in Melville: New Charts by Kring and Carey* (Glassboro, N.J.: Melville Society, 1981), 7.

49. Lathers's visit to Allan's family: Maria G. Melville (Allan's daughter) to Augusta Melville, 1 November 1863, MFPA. Representation on Confederate raids: 28 October 1863, reply, 14 November 1863, *Reminiscences of Richard Lathers,* 219–23.

50. Proprietors of *Baltimore Republican: Sun,* 17 September 1863. Republican party and contractors: *New York World,* 6 September 1863, in Silbey, *Respectable Minority,* 72.

51. Henry Gansevoort to Peter Gansevoort, 30 December 1862, GL.

52. Troops: Cook, *Armies of the Streets,* 174, states that on 25 August there were twelve regular infantry regiments, eight volunteer artillery regiments, and twenty-three volunteer regiments in the city, with five more volunteer infantry regiments on the way, but these figures are not reliable. For example, Dyer, 3:1711–15, lists only ten regular infantry divisions there. Secret police: Dix, *Memoirs of John Adams Dix,* 2:94.

53. *Reminiscences of Richard Lathers,* 256.

54. Gentian: "To Major John Gentian, Dean of the Burgundy Club," *Works of Herman Melville,* 13:359.

55. "Melville and the Civil War," 75.

56. Mother Melville: Catherine Gansevoort to Henry Gansevoort, 21 April 1864, GL. Aunt Helen: see note 47, move. Ned Curtis: E. M. Greenleaf to Maria G. Melville, 2 November 1863, MFPA. Aunt Helen, Ned: Frances Melville to Augusta Melville, 16 [November] 1863, MFPA.

57. John's departure, Stanny's toys: Frances Melville to Augusta Melville, 8 De-

cember 1863, MFPA. *Hecla:* the only steamer scheduled to leave England for New York on 1 December. John's arrival: *NYT,* 21 December 1863. Children home: Puett, "Melville's Wife," 125. Party: *Log,* 2:665.

58. Toby's assignments, movements: Richard T. Greene Pension Application, NA. Letter to Herman: implied in Richard T. Greene to Herman Melville, 20 October 1863, Metcalf, *Cycle and Epicycle,* 202.

59. Herman visited Grant in April, 1864, then in a *Battle-Pieces* note repeated a remark Grant had made in that month to "a visitor"—a typical Melville device for masking his own identity.

60. *NYT,* 25 May 1865.

61. "The Flag of the Sky," Moore, *Lyrics of Loyalty,* 55.

62. Moslem and biblical allusions: Cohen, "Notes," *Battle-Pieces of Herman Melville,* 242.

63. Resign: for example, Henry Gansevoort to George Henry Brewster, 18 July 1863, Henry Gansevoort to Peter Gansevoort, 23 July 1863, GL. Hoadley: *Memorial of Henry Sanford Gansevoort,* 31n. Description of officers, immigrants: Edwin Y. Lansing to Allan Melville, 29 May 1871, GL.

64. Opposing Stuart: inquiry form relating to New York regiments, Board of Military Statistics, New York, GL. Companies to Cavalry Corps: Henry Gansevoort to George Henry Brewster, 6 June [July] 1863, GL. Compassionate general: Nathaniel Coles to Henry Gansevoort, 9 July 1863, GL.

65. Henry's return to the city: Catherine Gansevoort Diaries, 4 August 1863, GL. Dr. Woodward: Catherine Gansevoort to Henry Gansevoort, 18 March 1864, GL. Henry with Allan: Catherine Gansevoort to Henry Gansevoort, 17 September 1863, GL. Henry at the seashore: Peter Gansevoort Diaries, 15 August 1863, Catherine Gansevoort Diaries, 30 August 1863, GL. Return to regiment: Henry Gansevoort to Peter Gansevoort, 1 October 1863, GL. Not magnificent: Charles Russell Lowell to Josephine Shaw, 2 August 1863, Edward Waldo Emerson, *Life and Letters of Charles Russell Lowell, Captain Sixth United States Cavalry, Colonel Second Massachusetts Cavalry, Brigadier-General United States Volunteers* (Boston: Houghton Mifflin, 1907), 289.

66. Henry drinking liquor, gold for ransom: see note 65, return to regiment. Ambush: "Capt. Gillingham's Adventure," Moore, *Civil War in Song and Story,* 155–56. Sutler's wagon: Archibald McKinley to Charles Russell Lowell, 13 August 1863, Cavalry Brigade Records, Corcoran's Division, Department and Defense of Washington, Records of Geographical Departments, Divisions, and Military (Reconstruction) Districts, 1821–1920, Records of United States Army Continental Commands, 1821–1920, RG 393, War Department, NA. Capture of horses: Major William H. Forbes to War Department, 25 August 1863, Cavalry Brigade Records, NA. Henry commanding brigade: Henry Gansevoort to Catherine Gansevoort, 8 October 1863, GL. Because all of the regimental, brigade, division, and department archives cited below belong within the Department and Defenses of Washington, citations to them will henceforth be skeletal.

67. Henry happier: see note 65, return to regiment. Ed accepting commission: Edwin Y. Lansing to Henry Gansevoort, 7 October 1863, GL.

68. Charles's amusements in Washington: Charles Brewster to Henry Gansevoort, 22 September 1866, GL. Warning, rather late: Georgia Bedell to Henry Gansevoort, 25 November 1866, GL.

69. Henry Gansevoort to Catherine Gansevoort, 30 October 1863, GL.

70. Henry's house: Henry Lazelle to Tyler's Division, 30 March 1864, Tyler's Division Records, NA. Horses and mules: Virgil Carrington Jones, *Ranger Mosby* (Chapel Hill: University of North Carolina Press, 1944), 175.

71. Losing men, help from father and Abe: Henry Gansevoort to Peter Gansevoort, 17 December 1863, GL. Lockwood's dishonesty: Nathaniel Coles to Henry Gansevoort, 16 August 1863, Douglas Frazar to Henry Gansevoort, [12 July 1863?] Charles Lyell to Henry Gansevoort, 27 October 1863, Douglas Frazar to Henry Gansevoort, 3 December 1863, George F. Woodward to Henry Gansevoort, 12 December 1863, George Ferguson to Henry Gansevoort, 31 December 1863, GL. Lockwood fired: on 16 January 1864, Phisterer, *New York in the War of the Rebellion,* 2:974. Help from Allan and Bruce: Henry Gansevoort to George Henry Brewster, 29 December 1863, GL. Petition: 11 December 1863, GL.

72. Purloined, group of officers: Henry Gansevoort to Peter Gansevoort, 27 December 1863, GL. Plot to have another officer appointed, Coles surprising conspirators, conception of plot, Woodward, Woodward's conviction: Nathaniel Coles to Henry Gansevoort, 5 February 1864, GL. Lowell's letter: Charles R. Lowell to Nathaniel Coles, 2 February 1864, Henry S. Gansevoort Compiled Service Record, NA. Influence: Henry Gansevoort to Peter Gansevoort, 2 February 1864, GL. Coles in Albany: Peter Gansevoort Diaries, 5 February 1864, GL. Peter's opinion: Peter Gansevoort Diaries, 6 February 1864, GL. Woodward's certification: on 6 February 1864, George F. Woodward to Amasa Parker, 3 March 1864, GL. Henry's leave: 6 February 1864, letter not transcribed but listed, Tyler's Division Records, NA. Arrival in New York City and Albany: Peter Gansevoort Diaries, 8, 9 February 1864, GL. Rumors, Frazar: Edwin Y. Lansing to Henry Gansevoort, 15 February 1864, GL.

73. The antipodes: to George Henry Brewster, 11 March 1864, GL. Invitation to camp: on 29 December 1863, Henry had written Bruce, "I had hoped to see one of you [Bruce or Allan] here before this," GL.

74. Woodward's withdrawal: see note 72, certification. Benjamin Rush Taylor: Henry Gansevoort to Catherine Gansevoort, 14 March 1864, GL.

75. Henry's blessing: petition to Lincoln, Charles Brewster Compiled Service Record, NA. Received appointment: Nathaniel Coles to Henry Gansevoort, 3 March 1864, GL. Bruce joining: Henry Gansevoort to J. T. Sprague, 26 March 1864, GL.

76. Keeping regiment snug: Nathaniel Coles to Henry Gansevoort, 17 February 1864, GL. Officer preferring charges, withholding resignation, muster in New York: Nathaniel Coles to Henry Gansevoort, 5 March 1864, GL. Substance of charges: see note 70, house, and Henry Lazelle to Henry Gansevoort, 27 March 1864, GL. Buffoon: Henry Gansevoort to Peter Gansevoort, 11 March 1864, GL.

77. Peter in Seymour's office: Peter Gansevoort Diaries, 25 March 1864, GL. Henry mustered in: 13th New York Volunteer Cavalry muster sheet, GL. Triumphant return: Memorandum 63, 29 March 1864, 13th New York Volunteer Cavalry, GL. Asking that charges be dismissed: E. E. Gillingham to Tyler's Division, 31 March 1863, Tyler's Division Records, NA. Frazar's offer: Douglas Frazar to Henry Gansevoort, 2 April 1864, GL. Henry agrees: Henry Gansevoort to Douglas Frazar, 8 April 1864, GL. Henry on Ed Lansing: to Peter Gansevoort, 30 March 1864, GL.

78. George Henry Brewster to Henry Gansevoort, 4 April 1864, GL.

79. Hawthorne's letters: Nathaniel Hawthorne to George McLaughlin, 11 December 1863, N. Hawthorne, *Letters, 1857–1864,* 621. Details of volume: Robert C.

Winthrop to Nathaniel Hawthorne, 15 February 1864, ibid., 636n. Revised version: enclosure to Herman Melville to Alexander Bliss, 22 March 1864, *Letters of Herman Melville,* 224.

80. Patroness, U.S. booth, Holland booth: Dudley Alcott to Susan L. Gansevoort, 16 March, 21, 23 January 1864, GL. Kate's afghan: Catherine Gansevoort to Henry Gansevoort, [3?] February 1864, GL. Mother Melville's ticket: Augusta Melville to Catherine Gansevoort, 29 February 1864, GL. Woodward's: see note 65, Woodward. Letters: invitation and list of officers, 9 February 1864, GL. U.S. booth costume: Catherine Gansevoort to Henry Gansevoort, 25 January 1864, GL.

81. Bazaar opened: Catherine Gansevoort Diaries, 22 February 1864, GL. Herman, Allan, Fanny: see note 80, Mother Melville.

82. Clipping, *Albany World,* 27 February 1864, GL.

83. McKay, *Civil War and New York City,* 239–40.

Chapter 7. A Portrait of the Artist as a Man of War

1. Longfellows to Washington, Charley's wound: Henry Wadsworth Longfellow to Alice Mary Longfellow, 5 December 1863, *Letters of Henry Wadsworth Longfellow,* 4:371; journal, 5 December 1863, S. Longfellow, *Life of Henry Wadsworth Longfellow,* 3:25. Commission: Henry Wadsworth Longfellow to George Washington Greene, 20 February 1864, *Letters of Henry Wadsworth Longfellow,* 4:396.

2. Bellows recruiting: McKay, *Civil War and New York City,* 128. The fair is described in *NYT,* beginning 1 April 1864, the art exhibit in *NYT,* 11 April 1864.

3. Peter Gansevoort Diaries, 16 March 1864, GL.

4. Dix, *Memoirs of John Adams Dix,* 2:245.

5. Autographs and holographs: *NYT,* 14, 17 April 1864. Vote after three days: *NYT,* 7 April 1864. Thereafter, the paper reported the tally every day.

6. Emerson: R. Emerson, *Journals and Miscellaneous Notebooks,* 15:60. Sophia: to Horatio Bridge, 5 April 1864, Horatio Bridge, *Personal Recollections of Nathaniel Hawthorne* (1893; reprint, New York: Haskell House, 1968), 190–91.

7. Trip: Caroline Ticknor, *Hawthorne and His Publisher* (Boston: Houghton Mifflin, 1898), 311–25. Washington: Sofia Hawthorne thought they were headed there, note 6, Sophia. Ticknor's illness: Nathaniel Hawthorne to James T. Fields, [9 April 1864,] N. Hawthorne, *Letters, 1857–1864,* 651–52.

8. Bruce's letters: 4, 5 April 1864, GL. Except as noted, the story of Herman's journey is adapted from Stanton Garner, "Melville's Scout toward Aldie," parts 1,2, *Melville Society Extracts,* nos. 51, 52 (September, November 1982): 5–16, 1–14.

9. Allan Melville to Richard Lathers, 8 April 1864, Richard Lathers Papers, LC.

10. Improved railroad connections: *Washington Intelligencer,* 5 April 1864. Description of journey: B. W. to editor, 28 March 1864, *NYT,* 1 April 1864.

11. Longfellow: to George Washington Greene, 18 December 1863, *Letters of Henry Wadsworth Longfellow,* 4:372.

12. See note 9.

13. 7 April 1864 (the previous day), Whitman, "Some War Memoranda," *Prose Works 1892,* 2:584–85.

14. Senate: *Washington Evening Star,* 9 April 1864. Note: *Log,* 2:666.

15. Entertainments: *Washington Intelligencer,* 8 April 1864. Lincoln and Seward: *Washington Evening Star,* 8 April 1864.

16. Bruce mustering in: 9 April 1864, 13th New York Volunteer Cavalry Regiment Order Book, GL. Reception, weather: see note 14, Senate. Entertainments: *Washington Intelligencer,* 9 April 1864.

17. Storm: *NYT,* 12 April 1864. Departure: Jane Melville to Henry Gansevoort, 13 April 1864, GL.

18. *Civil War Naval Chronology,* IV–39; *Washington Intelligencer,* 13, 14 April 1864.

19. Actions of Jennie and Milie: see note 17, departure. Glimpse: Catherine Gansevoort to Henry Gansevoort, 3 May 1864, GL.

20. Letter unclaimed: listed as undelivered, *Washington Evening Star,* 15 April 1864. Had Henry picked it up that weekend, he would have known where she was.

21. *Washington Intelligencer,* 14, 15 April 1864.

22. Herman presented Ed Lansing with a copy of *Battle-Pieces* inscribed "As a souvenir of his soldier hospitality at the cavalry camp in the Virginia woods, April 1864," courtesy of Serendipity Books, in whose possession the volume came to light.

23. "Model in arms": to Peter Gansevoort, 31 October 1864, GL.

24. Greenslet, *Lowells and Their Seven Worlds,* 289.

25. Regimental library: Humphreys, *Field, Camp, Hospital and Prison in the Civil War,* 24. Curtis: after marrying Effy's sister, Curtis lived in or near the Shaw mansion on Staten Island, Cary, *George William Curtis,* 118.

26. Capture, trial, execution of Ormsby: Cavalry Brigade General Order No. 10, 7 February 1864, 16th New York Volunteer Cavalry Records, NA. Details about Ormsby: Humphreys, *Field, Camp, Hospital and Prison Camp in the Civil War,* 19-22.

27. Lowell quotation: see note 26, capture. Ed Lansing: to Henry Gansevoort, 15 February 1864, GL.

28. *History of the Connecticut Valley in Massachusetts, with Illustrations and Biographical Sketches of Some of Its Prominent Men and Pioneers,* 2 vols. (Philadelphia: Louis H. Everts, 1879), 2:1063.

29. Garner, "Melville's Scout toward Aldie," based on offical reports and records and on the poem "The Scout toward Aldie," is here supplemented and corrected by Humphreys's *Field, Camp, Hospital and Prison Camp in the Civil War,* 24–33, an eyewitness account which had not come to light when that essay was published.

30. Lazelle present: after the scout had departed, he communicated Lowell's last-minute changes of plan to General Tyler.

31. Quotations: Greenslet, *Lowells and Their Seven Worlds,* 291.

32. Meeting Herman, soldier's life: *Field, Camp, Hospital and Prison Camp in the Civil War,* 24–25. *Moby-Dick:* ibid., 305n.

33. Because the key location in Humphreys's account, Ball's Mill, is not shown on the contemporary map available to the author, U.S. War Department, *The Official Military Atlas of the Civil War,* comp. Calvin D. Cowles (1891; reprint of *Atlas to Accompany the Official Records of the Union and Confederate Armies,* New York: Crown, 1978), plate vii, the route has been difficult to establish. Humphreys gives the distance as twenty-five miles which, together with other clues, suggests the destination given here. The dwelling closest to this point was owned by M. Ball.

34. Hotbed of secessionism: Humphreys, *Field, Camp, Hospital and Prison Camp in the Civil War,* 25. Charge: ibid., 27.

35. Maltreatment, neglect: Jimerson, *Private Civil War,* 72–73.

36. Quotation: Humphreys, *Field, Camp, Hospital and Prison Camp in the Civil War,* 33. Philosophy and social sciences: ibid., 186. Humphreys implies that the

discussion occurred between himself and Lowell, but knowledge of Herman's habits suggests that he took an active part. Years earlier, he had discussed "East India religions and mythologies" with Oliver Wendell Holmes, Senior, "with the most amazing skill and brilliancy on both sides," Maunsell B. Field, *Log,* 2:506.

37. Edmund Wilson, *Patriotic Gore: Studies in the Literature of the American Civil War* (New York: Oxford University Press, 1962), 326, sees the parallel between Mosby and Moby-Dick, among other things.

38. "Head of the Column," Moore, *Lyrics of Loyalty,* 67.

39. Humphreys, *Field, Camp, Hospital and Prison Camp in the Civil War,* 33.

40. "In your tent you introduced him [the doctor] to Gen. Tyler," Herman Melville to Henry Gansevoort, 10 May 1864, *Letters of Herman Melville,* 224–26.

41. "Remarkable poems": Cambon, *Inclusive Flame,* 10. "Lycidas": F. O. Matthiessen, *American Renaissance: Art and Expression in the Age of Emerson and Whitman* (London: Oxford University Press, 1941), 494.

42. Robert O. Tyler to Department and Defense of Washington, 28 February, 1 March 1864, Tyler's Division Records, NA.

43. Meeting: see note 40. Jonathan Edwards: [Cullum,] *Memoir of Brevet Major-General Robert Ogden Tyler,* 91.

44. Letter: advertised *Washington Evening Star,* 22 April 1864, but not advertised 29 April 1864. Account of scout: ibid., 22 April 1864.

45. Whitman: to John Townsend Trowbridge, 8 February 1864, to Louisa Van Velsor Whitman, 12 February 1864, to Dr. Le Baron Russell, February 1864, *Walt Whitman: The Correspondence,* 1:195–200.

46. Fun: to Louisa Van Velsor Whitman, 12 February 1864, ibid., 198. Spirit of soldiers: to Dr. LeBaron Russell, February 1864, ibid., 200.

47. 2 May 1864, GL.

48. Lizzie claimed, *Log,* 2:667, that on this trip Herman called on Grant, and his note to "Chattanooga" supports her claim.

49. Whitman's description: Walter Lowenfels, ed., *Walt Whitman's Civil War* (New York: Alfred A. Knopf, 1961), 250. "Imperial Caesar": attributed to A. R. Waud, inset note, Ulysses S. Grant, "Preparing for the Campaigns of '64," *B&L,* 4:97.

50. Football: probably not a genuine recollection, since Herman first wrote "baseball." His information about the Confederate dispositions is accurate: the ten unidentified camps were Louisianians.

51. To Louisa Van Velsor Whitman, 10 April 1864, *Walt Whitman: The Correspondence,* 1:209.

52. Proceeds: *NYT,* 26 April 1864. Mrs. Bennett: *NYT,* 22 April 1864. Republican plot: McKay, *Civil War and New York City,* 243. Final vote: *NYT,* 24 April 1864.

53. Quotations, here and below: see note 40.

54. Allan Melvilles: see note 19, glimpse. Maria's visit: Peter Gansevoort to Henry Gansevoort, 15 April 1864, GL.

55. A. Henry Thurston Compiled Service Record, NA; A. Henry Thurston Pension Application (Widow), NA; Brown Thurston, *Thurston Genealogies,* 326. In his General Order No. 1, Twentieth Army Corps, 16 April 1864, Hooker listed "Surgeon A. H. Hurston" as medical officer of his staff, *NYT,* 28 April 1864.

56. Whitman: Walt Whitman to Louisa Van Velsor Whitman, 26 April 1864, *Walt Whitman: The Correspondence,* 1:211–12.

57. Stephen Longfellow: Henry Wadsworth Longfellow to William Pitt Fes-

sendon, 25 November 1864, *Letters of Henry Wadsworth Longfellow,* [illegible] Whittier: to Harriet Minot Pitman, 12 May 1864, *Letters of John Greenleaf Whittier,* 3:69, 69n. Bartlett's mother, Harriott Plumber Bartlett, had been a classmate of Whittier at Haverhill Academy.

58. Greeley: Bowman, *Civil War Almanac,* 201. Kate: to Henry Gansevoort, 20 June 1864, GL.

59. Garbage: Maria G. Melville to Peter Gansevoort, 24 May 1864, GL. Hoax: *Reminiscences of Richard Lathers,* 223–26; Dix, *Memoirs of John Adams Dix,* 2:96–100; McKay, *Civil War and New York City,* 248–51.

60. To Gail Hamilton, [May 1864,] *Letters of John Greenleaf Whittier,* 3:71.

61. Family's loss: see note 59, garbage.

62. Harrison Hayford, *Melville's "Monody": Really for Hawthorne?* (Evanston, Ill: Northwestern University Press, 1990), demonstrates that the poem cannot be assumed to be about Hawthorne and argues that Herman's friendship with him may have been less important than it is widely supposed to have been.

63. Inheritance, mortgage: Puett, "Melville's Wife," 124. Judge Shaw's mother, Susanna Hayward, was a sister of Doctor Lemuel Hayward, which may have led Puett to conclude that Doctor George Hayward was Lizzie's uncle.

64. To parents, 16 May 1864, Mark DeWolf Howe, ed., *Touched with Fire: Civil War Letters and Diary of Oliver Wendell Holmes, Junior, 1861–1864* (Cambridge, Mass.: Harvard University Press, 1946), 121–22.

65. [Cullum,] *Memoir of Brevet Major-General Robert Ogden Tyler,* 13.

66. Confederate officers and general: E. M. Law, "From the Wilderness to Cold Harbor," *B&L,* 4:142–43. Sherman: McPherson, *Battle Cry of Freedom,* 744. Holmes: to parents, 24 June 1864, M. Howe, *Touched with Fire,* 150. High-ranking comrade: Martin T. McMahon, "Cold Harbor," *B&L,* 4:220.

67. Abe: K, "The Soldier Bird," Moore, *Civil War in Song and Story,* 193–94. Herman was influenced by the anonymous "The Eagle of the Eighth Wisconsin," Cohen, "Notes," *Battle-Pieces of Herman Melville,* 255, and Henry Howard Brownell's "The Eagle of Corinth," Brownell, *War-Lyrics and Other Poems,* 51–55, 237–39.

68. "The Custom-House," *The Scarlet Letter,* ed. William Charvat, Roy Harvey Pearce, Claude M. Simpson, Fredson Bowers, and Matthew J. Bruccoli, intro. W[illiam]. C[harvat]., textual preface and intro. F[redson]. B[owers]., vol. 1 of *The Centenary Edition of the Works of Nathaniel Hawthorne* ([Columbus:] Ohio State University Press, 1962), 5.

69. Excellent officer: to Peter Gansevoort, 26 April 1864, GL. Patrol: Henry Gansevoort to Peter Gansevoort, 11 May 1864, GL; Roster of Officers, 13th New York Volunteer Cavalry Regiment, GL. Effy's return: Josephine Lowell to Henry Gansevoort, 22 January 1866, GL.

70. Henry's health: Henry Gansevoort to Peter Gansevoort, 31 May 1864, GL. Unable to leave quarters: 13th New York Volunteer Cavalry Regiment Records, NA. Bruce discharged: Roster of Officers, 13th New York Volunteer Cavalry Regiment, GL.

71. Soldier work: Catherine Gansevoort to Henry Gansevoort, 25 May 1864, GL. The Negro: to Henry Gansevoort, 29 July 1864, GL. West Point: Catherine Gansevoort Diaries, 15 June 1864, GL. Saratoga: Catherine Gansevoort to Henry Gansevoort, 9 July 1864, GL.

72. Hoadleys: see note 59, garbage, and Frances Melville to Catherine Ganse-

voort, 24 May 1864, GL. Griggs plans: Maria G. Melville to Catherine Gansevoort, 4 August, 5 September 1864, GL. Helen's refusal: Maria G. Melville to Catherine Gansevoort, 9 September 1864, GL. Allan Melvilles: see note 19, glimpse. Following the Fourth of July: an assumption based on their usual date of departure. Henry Thurston: Brown Thurston, *Thurston Genealogies,* 326.

73. Boston: when Herman returned to the city, Lizzie and the girls were absent.

74. Leonard: Maria G. Melville to Catherine Gansevoort, 4 August 1864, GL.

75. Ibid.

76. Lizzie's arrival in Gansevoort: she was expected on 20 August, Maria G. Melville to Catherine Gansevoort, 19 August 1864, GL. Lizzie to New York, Gus to Gansevoort: Maria G. Melville to Catherine Gansevoort, 5, 9 September 1864, GL.

77. Bartlett in Pittsfield: Palfrey, *Memoir of William Francis Bartlett,* 108, 129. Crater, here and below, Bartlett's leg: ibid., 119; William H. Powell, "The Battle of the Petersburg Crater," *B&L,* 4:545–60; Charles H. Houghton, "In the Crater," *B&L,* 4:561–62. Colored Troops: Henry Goddard Thomas, "The Colored Troops at Petersburg," *B&L,* 4:563–67.

78. "Rhetoric of Melville's *Battle-Pieces,"* 184.

Chapter 8. De Year ob Jubilo

1. John Hobart: John A. Hobart Compiled Service Record, NA. Toby's discharge, Sherman's march: Richard T. Greene Pension Application, NA. Enlistment in 1st Illinois Artillery: *Report of the Adjutant General of the State of Illinois,* 8:604.

2. Toby's alcoholism nearly cost him his pension, Richard T. Greene Pension Application, NA.

3. An apparent error in the poem, calling McPherson a Sarpedon to Sherman's Achilles, is discussed by Cohen, "Notes," *Battle-Pieces of Herman Melville,* 256.

4. *Tallahassee:* McKay, *Civil War and New York City,* 272–73.

5. Joined the navy: Titus Munson Coan Pension Application, NA. *Sebago: U&CN,* ser. 2, 1:204. Coan and Herman: *Log,* 2:787.

6. Farragut "desired to secure the moral effect of a victory," John Coddington Kinney, "Farragut at Mobile Bay," *B&L,* 4:385.

7. Brownell, *War-Lyrics and Other Poems,* 3.

8. Telegram, Secretary of the Navy to Guert Gansevoort, 2 July 1864, telegram, Guert Gansevoort to Secretary of the Navy, 3 July 1864, Secretary of the Navy to Samuel P. Lee, 2 July 1864, *U&CN,* ser. 1, 10:222–25.

9. Confederate plan: telegram, Commanding Officer *Minnesota* to Secretary of the Navy, 18 July 1864, ibid., 5:467; *Roanoke* to Point Lookout: Secretary of the Navy to Guert Gansevoort, 30 July 1864, ibid., 5:472. Guert detached: Abstracts of Service of Naval Officers, NA. Guert's option: Maria G. Melville to Catherine Gansevoort, 4 October 1864, GL.

10. Henry J. Hunt, "The First Day at Gettysburg," *B&L,* 3:268.

11. Humphreys: *Field, Camp, Hospital and Prison Camp in the Civil War,* 92–109. Brother: Georgia Bedell to Henry Gansevoort, undated, GL.

12. Humphreys, *Field, Camp, Hospital and Prison Camp in the Civil War,* 149.

13. Resign commission, casualties among officers: to parents, 16 May 1864, M. Howe, *Touched with Fire,* 121–22. Not the same man: to parents, 30 May 1864, ibid., 135. Promotion: to Mother, 7 June 1864, ibid., 143.

14. Lowell's command: [Putnam,] *Memoirs of the War of '61,* 8. Lazelle in command: 31 July 1864, *U&CA*, ser. 1, 37 (part 2):546. Lansing adjutant: Lansing Letterbook, 76. Every means: Henry Gansevoort to Catherine Gansevoort, 12 August 1864, GL. Charles Brewster: to Henry Gansevoort, 4 July 1864, GL. Lowell: to Henry Gansevoort, 11 October 1864, GL. Harris, Parker, artillery: Henry Gansevoort to Peter Gansevoort, 15 August 1864, GL.

15. Butcher: Henry Gansevoort Journal, 14 September 1864, GL; Hoadley, *Memoir of Henry Sanford Gansevoort,* 170. Wounding: Jones, *Ranger Mosby,* 203.

16. Wise: Catherine Gansevoort Diaries, 27 September 1864, GL. Coles: ibid., 5 October 1864, GL. Quotation: Henry Gansevoort to Catherine Gansevoort, 2 November 1864, GL.

17. Moore, *Civil War in Song and Story,* 399–400.

18. Sheridan's statement: Humphreys, *Field, Camp, Hospital and Prison Camp in the Civil War,* 188. J. R. Lowell: "Ode Recited at the Harvard Commemoration, July 21, 1865," *Complete Writings of James Russell Lowell,* 13:26–27.

19. Lowell: to Charles Eliot Norton, 1 August 1864, *Letters of James Russell Lowell,* 1:339. Whittier: to Theodore Tilton, 10 September 1864, *Letters of John Greenleaf Whittier,* 3:77.

20. Uncle Peter in the city: Peter Gansevoort Diaries, 18, 27 August 1864, GL. Albany meeting: ibid., 14 September 1864, GL. City enthusiasm: McKay, *Civil War and New York City,* 271.

21. Purists, Legitimists: Silbey, *Respectable Minority,* 93–109. Whittier: see note 19, Whittier.

22. Lowell: to John Lothrop Motley, 28 July 1864, *Letters of James Russell Lowell,* 1:336. Uncle Peter: "voted as always the whole Democratic ticket," Peter Gansevoort Diaries, 8 November 1866, GL. Mother Melville: to Catherine Gansevoort, 5 September 1864, GL.

23. Maria G. Melville to Catherine Gansevoort, 9 September 1864, GL.

24. Whitman: "November Boughs," *Prose Works 1892,* 2:619. Emerson: to Thomas Carlyle, 26 September 1864, *Correspondence of Thomas Carlyle and Ralph Waldo Emerson,* 2:287.

25. Letter to Allan: 3 November 1864, GL. Henry's regret: Henry Gansevoort to Peter Gansevoort, 31 October 1864, GL. Henry and platform: to Catherine Gansevoort, 10 November 1864, GL. Piatt: Linton, *Poetry of America,* 303.

26. Whitman, Copperheads: to William D. O'Connor, 11 September 1864, *Walt Whitman: The Correspondence,* 1:242. Largest rally: McKay, *Civil War and New York City,* 266. Whitman, display: to Charles W. Eldridge, 8 October 1864, *Walt Whitman: The Correspondence,* 1:243.

27. Lazelle's resignation: Hamersly, *Complete Army and Navy Register,* 573. Guarding railroad: Henry Lazelle to Henry Gansevoort, 7 October 1864, GL.

28. Commended: Henry Gansevoort to C. C. Augur, 15 October 1864, GL; C. C. Augur to Henry Gansevoort, 15 October 1864, GL; Henry S. Gansevoort Compiled Service Record, NA. Lowell: E. Emerson, *Life and Letters of Charles Russell Lowell,* 67.

29. Henry Gansevoort draft letter, 3 November 1864, Henry Gansevoort to Peter Gansevoort, 23 May 1865, GL.

30. Democratic whiskey: 4th Delaware Volunteer Infantry Regiment Records, NA. Copperheadism: Henry Gansevoort to Peter Gansevoort, 18 September 1864, GL.

31. Julia Lathers: Brown Thurston, *Thurston Genalogies,* 296. Leonard's death: George Curtis to Peter Gansevoort, 9 October 1864, GL. Burial, Guert behaving strangely: Catherine Gansevoort to Henry Gansevoort, 19 October 1864, GL. Kate sulking: to Henry Gansevoort, [ca. 7 October 1864,] GL. Although Kate gave the burial date as 10 October, her family did not leave for the city until 11 October, Peter and Catherine Gansevoort Diaries, GL, suggesting that the funeral did not take place until 12 October at the earliest.

32. These events and those that follow: Garner, "Melville's Scout toward Aldie," supplemented and corrected by Charles Brewster; "Captured by Mosby's Guerrillas," in Military Order of the Loyal Legion of the United States, Missouri Commandery, *War Papers and Personal Reminiscences, 1861–1865: Read before the Commandery of the State of Missouri, Military Order of the Loyal Legion of the United States* (St. Louis, Mo.: Becktold, 1892), 74–107; V. Jones, *Ranger Mosby*, 221–28; an account by Private George H. Soule, reported from Winchester, 7 November 1864, by E. A. Paul, *NYT*, 10 November 1864; an account by Corporal and Acting Commissary Sergeant Charles E. Marvin, ibid.; Charles Brewster Compiled Service Record, NA. In Brewster's memoir, his brother's name is concealed behind the pseudonym "G. B. H———."

33. Order of the day: Brewster, "Captured by Mosby's Guerrillas," 97. Red-bearded ranger: ibid., 93.

34. Richmond news item reprinted in the *New York Herald*, 17 November 1864.

35. Election in the city: Dix, *Memoirs of John Adams Dix,* 2:94–96. Plot: Brandt, *Man Who Tried to Burn New York,* 87–91. Longfellow: journal, 10 November 1864, S. Longfellow, *Life of Henry Wadsworth Longfellow,* 3:47.

36. Allan: Allan Melville to Henry Gansevoort, 21 November 1864, GL.

37. Allan's first letter: see note 36. Charles's letter: 18 November 1864, GL. Allan's second letter: GL.

38. Charles's letter: 17 December 1864, GL. Alexander: William Best Hesseltine, *Civil War Prisons: A Study in War Psychology* (New York: Frederick Ungar, 1964), 246–47. Hero: description when the dog was displayed in the city, *NYT,* 24 May 1865.

39. Various people, Custer: Charles Brewster to Henry Gansevoort, 27 January 1865, GL.

40. Escape attempt: *New York Herald,* 9 January 1865. Bruce's escape: George Henry Brewster obit., *NYT*, 13 May 1903. Visit to Henry: Allan Melville to Henry Gansevoort, 18 February 1865, GL.

41. Prisoner-of-war poem: George Frederick Root, "Tramp! Tramp! Tramp! or the Prisoner's Hope," Crawford, *Civil War Songbook,* 45–48. *Aeneid:* Cohen, "Notes," *Battle-Pieces of Herman Melville,* 253.

42. Composed before 17 August 1865, Cohen, "Notes," *Battle-Pieces of Herman Melville,* 283.

43. Date of arrival: 19 November 1864 in *Log,* 2:671, but Kate Gansevoort specified that it was on 17 November, to Henry Gansevoort, 23 November 1864, and on 21 November Allan wrote Henry Gansevoort that Tom had arrived "within a few days past," GL. Year at home: see note 9, Guert's option.

44. See note 40, visit to Henry.

45. Catherine Gansevoort to Henry Gansevoort, 23 November 1864, GL.

46. Brandt, *Man Who Tried to Burn New York,* 13–20, 109–20, 123–24.

47. Visiting Herman, dancing school: Catherine Gansevoort to Henry Gansevoort, 22 December 1864, GL. Visiting Allan: ibid., 23 January 1865, GL. Sleighing, vaccination: Maria G. Melville to Susan L. Gansevoort, 16 February 1865, GL. *Bengal*: Augusta Melville to Catherine Gansevoort, 15 March 1865, GL.

48. Visit to Gansevoort, Albany: Peter Gansevoort Diaries, 17 December 1864, GL. Presents to Gansevoort: an assumption. Presents to Albany, quotation: see note 47, visiting Herman.

49. Christmas, party for Seymour: Catherine Gansevoort to Henry Gansevoort, 31 December 1864, GL. Both governors: Peter Gansevoort Diaries, 27 February 1865, GL.

50. Fanny's departure: Peter Gansevoort Diaries, 1 March 1865, GL. Kate and Mrs. Van Rensselaer: Catherine Gansevoort Diaries, 11 March 1865, GL. Tom to bring mother back: see note 47, vaccination. Death of Mrs. Peebles, Uncle Peter at funeral: Peter Gansevoort Diaries, 5, 7 March 1865, GL.

51. Fanny's arrival: Frances Melville to Catherine Gansevoort, 8 March 1865, GL. Henry Pease home: Henry Pease Pension Application, NA.

52. *NYT,* 28 November 1864, 22, 24 March 1865.

53. Details of club: James Grant Wilson, ed., *The Memorial History of the City of New-York from Its First Settlement to the Year 1892*, 4 vols. (New York: New-York History Company, 1893), 4:256–57. Acquaintance with Darley: Metcalf, *Cycle and Epicycle,* 148–49.

54. *Piazza Tales*: *Log,* 2:937. Request to Allan: ibid., 2:616. To *World*: ibid., 2:672.

55. *Mobile:* 15 December 1864, Letters Sent to Naval Officers, series 274, FANY. Supplies: 20 February 1865, Letters and Telegrams Received from the Bureau of Ordnance, FANY. Budd: *New York Herald,* 25 March 1865. Offer to Guert: Guert Gansevoort to Henry A. Wise, 13 March 1865, Naval History Society Collection, NYHS.

56. Brigadier General W. L. Elliot to headquarters, 4th Army Corps, 6 January 1865, *U&CA*, ser. 1, 45 (part 1):237.

57. Oliver O. Howard, "Sherman's Advance from Atlanta," *B&L,* 4:666.

58. Quotations: Daniel Oakey, "Marching through Georgia and the Carolinas," *B&L,* 4:672. Punishing slaves: Jimerson, *Private Civil War,* 72.

59. Kate: to Henry Gansevoort, 21 February 1865, GL. Poem: "Sherman's in Savannah," Moore, *Civil War in Song and Story,* 194.

60. Officer's quotation: Oakey, "Marching through Georgia and the Carolinas," 678. Sherman quotation: 1 February 1865, Bowman, *Civil War Almanac,* 248.

61. Henry C. Work, "Kingdom Coming," Crawford, *Civil War Songbook,* 145–48.

62. *Times*: 3, 4 April 1865. Uncle Peter: Peter Gansevoort Diaries, 3 April 1865, GL. Emerson: to Frederic Henry Hedge, 3 April 1865, *Letters of Ralph Waldo Emerson,* 5:411.

63. Lowell's regiment: Humphreys, *Field, Camp, Hospital and Prison Camp in the Civil War,* 284–85. Longfellow: journal, 7 April 1865, S. Longfellow, *Life of Henry Wadsworth Longfellow,* 3:56. Lowell: to Charles Eliot Norton, 13 April 1865, *Letters of James Russell Lowell,* 1:344. Emerson: to Caroline Sturgis Tappan, 10 April 1865, *Letters of Ralph Waldo Emerson,* 5:412.

64. News arriving, celebration: *NYT*, 11 April 1865.

65. Tame celebration: ibid. Albany: to Henry Gansevoort, 10 April 1865, GL. Family to city: Peter Gansevoort Diaries, 11 April 1865, GL.

66. Herman in touch: in a letter to Allan Melville, 3 November 1864, GL, Henry asked for a reply to his letter to Herman. 8th Illinois: Abner Hard, *History of the Eighth Cavalry Regiment, Illinois Volunteers, during the Great Rebellion* (Aurora, Ill.: n.p., 1868), 316. Prospect Hill: Edwin Lansing to Abraham Lansing, 3 April 1875, GL. Regiment separated: Henry Gansevoort to Peter Gansevoort, 23 May 1865, GL. Politics: ibid., 6 February 1865, GL. Halleck: Jones, *Ranger Mosby*, 214.

67. Voting scandal, injustice: see note 66, regiment separated. Admitting flogging: see note 30, Copperheadism. Kate: to Henry Gansevoort, 11 December 1864, GL.

68. Come to Washington: 16 February 1865, GL. Richard and Stanton: see note 40, visit.

69. Incident: note 66, Prospect Hill; Jones, *Ranger Mosby,* 246–50; *New York Herald,* 29 December 1864. Quotation: George Baylor, *Bull Run to Bull Run: or, Four Years in the Army of Northern Virginia . . .* (1900; reprint, Washington, D.C.: Zenger, 1983), 284.

70. Georgie Bedell: she apologized to Henry that a Miss Owens had gone to Baltimore, November 1864, GL. Celebrations, Booth: Hard, *History of the Eighth Cavalry Regiment,* 318–20.

71. Assassination and pursuit of Booth: Louis J. Weichmann, *A True History of the Assassination of Abraham Lincoln and of the Conspiracy of 1865,* ed. Floyd E. Risvold (New York: Random House, 1977). Rathbone's friendship with Gansevoorts: Peter Gansevoort to Henry Gansevoort, 8 May 1865, GL, and note 67, voting scandal.

72. Brigade movements: Hard, *History of the Eighth Cavalry Regiment,* 321–22. Henry's regiment: Henry Gansevoort to Catherine Gansevoort, 25 April 1865, GL.

73. See note 66, regiment separated.

74. To William Allinson, 20 April 1865, *Letters of John Greenleaf Whittier,* 3:87–88.

75. Arrival in Albany: Peter Gansevoort Diaries, 15 April 1865, GL. Kate: to Henry Gansevoort, 16 April 1865, GL. Quotation: *Reminiscences of Richard Lathers,* 231.

76. *NYT*, 23–26 April 1865.

77. Lathers: *Reminiscences of Richard Lathers,* 231. Whittier blaming slavery: to ?, 14 April [1865], *Letters of John Greenleaf Whittier,* 3:86. Whittier on feeling toward South: 23 May 1865, ibid., 3:91. Kate on plotting: see note 75, Kate.

78. *Poems of Thomas Bailey Aldrich,* 180.

79. "Rhetoric of Melville's *Battle-Pieces,"* 187.

80. Gansevoorts viewing funeral train: Catherine Gansevoort to Henry Gansevoort, 29 April 1865, GL. Kate on Mosby: see note 75, Kate. End of the rangers: Jones, *Ranger Mosby,* 269–71.

Chapter 9. Battle-Pieces

1. "Introduction," *Battle-Pieces of Herman Melville,* 15.

2. *Rebellion Record:* Day, "Herman Melville's Use of *The Rebellion Record*"; Cohen, "Introduction," *Battle-Pieces of Herman Melville,* 15–19. "Actual events of the war": ibid., 19. "Versified journalism": Geoffrey Stone, *Melville* (New York: Sheed and Ward, 1949), 261. "Mariner and mystic": *Herman Melville: Mariner and Mystic*, intro. Mark Van Doren (1921; reprint, New York: Cooper Square, 1968).

3. Hawthorne: "Chiefly about War Matters," 12:299. Dickinson's awareness: Aaron, *Unwritten War,* 355–56. Arvin: *Herman Melville,* 259. Shurr: "Melville's Poems: The Late Agenda," 355.

4. Supposed use of *Record:* Day, "Herman Melville's Use of *The Rebellion Record,*" 19–20. After studying the influence of George Ward Nichols's *The Story of the Great March* on *Battle-Pieces,* R. D. Madison, "Melville's Sherman Poems: A Problem in Source Study," *Melville Society Extracts,* no. 78 (September 1989): 8–11, recommends caution in the matter of Herman's borrowings.

5. Abe's suggestion: Catherine Gansevoort Diaries, 16 May 1865, GL. Army of the Potomac, without Colored Troops: *NYT,* 24 May 1865. Arrival in Washington, events of the day: Catherine Gansevoort Diaries, 24 May 1865, GL.

6. Western army, "native ugliness": H. W. Slocum, "Final Operations of Sherman's Army," *B&L,* 4:758. Bummers' pets: *NYT,* 25 May 1865. Whitman: to Louisa Van Velsor Whitman, 23 May 1865, *Walt Whitman: The Correspondence,* 1:261.

7. Visit to camp: Catherine Gansevoort Diaries, 25 May 1865, Catherine Gansevoort to Susan L. Gansevoort, 25 May 1865, GL. Events in Washington: Catherine Gansevoort Diaries, 26 May 1865, GL. Whiskey cure: Catherine Gansevoort to Henry Gansevoort, 28 May 1865, GL.

8. Mississippi: Cohen, "Notes," *Battle-Pieces of Herman Melville,* 271.

9. David Cody, "'So, then, Solidity's a crust': Melville's 'The Apparition' and the Explosion of the Petersburg Mine," *Melville Society Extracts,* no. 78 (September 1989): 1, 4–8, believes that its source is an A. R. Waud illustration of the mine explosion. "Eruptions of a darkness": Milder, "Rhetoric of Melville's *Battle-Pieces,*" 187.

10. "Introduction," *Selected Poems of Herman Melville,* 23.

11. Tepid, derivative: Connor, "Abysm and the Star," 25. Sleazy ritual: Warren, "Introduction," 31. Milder: "Rhetoric of Melville's *Battle-Pieces,*" 189.

12. R. Chase, *Herman Melville,* 236.

13. Gansevoort's oratory: Parker, "Melville and Politics," 117. Merk: *Manifest Destiny and Mission in American History: A Reinterpretation* (New York: Random House, 1966, 3 (quotation), 261–[266].

14. Bartlett: Palfrey, *Memoir of William Francis Bartlett,* 149–52. Ned Curtis as clerk: census, 1865, Third Election District of Queensbury, N.Y., courtesy John Austin. Toby mustered out: Dyer, 3:1035. Toby after the war: Richard T. Greene Pension Application, NA. John Hobart mustering out: Dyer, 3:1066. Hobart family's postwar occupations: *Rockford City Directory and County Gazeteer for 1869 . . .* (Rockford, Ill.: Kauffman and Burch, 1869), 244. Budd's discharge, return to navy: Hamersly, "Complete General Navy Register," 111. Pease: Ford, *History of the Origin of the Town of Clinton,* 647.

15. *NYT* does not index any such event, nor does it record one adjunctive to the grand review. This poem escaped annotation in both the Vincent and the Cohen editions.

16. Peter, Parker: Peter Gansevoort Diaries, 4 July 1865, GL. Ceremony: *NYT,* 6 July 1865. Poem: Browne, *Bugle-Echoes,* 279.

17. Cohen, "Notes," *Battle-Pieces of Herman Melville,* 272, speculates that Herman was inspired by Guido Reni's fresco, "Aurora."

18. Allan Melville to Henry Gansevoort, 11 July 1865, GL.

19. Kate: to Henry Gansevoort, 9 April 1865, GL.

20. Exhibition: *NYT*, corridor, 12 May 1865, North Room, 29 May 1865, East Room, 7 June 1865, South Room, 13 June 1865, West Room, 27 June 1865.

21. Bulk of party: Catherine Gansevoort to Henry Gansevoort, 14 July 1865, GL. Lemuel Shaw, Waleses: Catherine Gansevoort to Henry Gansevoort, 27 August

1865, GL. Alcott: journal, July 1865, *Journals of Louisa May Alcott,* 141. Latherses: their return was reported in Maria G. Melville to Catherine Gansevoort, 12 October 1865, GL. Allan and Jennie: Catherine Gansevoort to Henry Gansevoort, 3 May [1865], GL.

22. Order to economize: 9 May 1865, Letters and Telegrams Received from the Bureau of Ordnance, FANY. Guert detached: 15 May 1865, Abstracts of Service of Naval Officers, NA. Return to Glens Falls: Maria G. Melville to Catherine Gansevoort, 18 July 1865, GL. Roanoke decomissioned: MacBride, *Civil War Ironclads,* 41.

23. Allan selling house: see note 21, Allan and Jennie. Enjoying Arrowhead, claret: Allan Melvillle to Henry Gansevoort, 4 July 1865, GL. Work on Arrowhead, quotation: Maria G. Melville to Catherine Gansevoort, 18 October 1865, GL.

24. Rachel Turner: Allan Melville to Henry Gansevoort, 9 September 1865, George Henry Brewster to Henry Gansevoort, 12 September 1865, GL. She did marry, since "Iris" memorializes Rachel Turner Pond, *Log,* 2:737. Southerners in New York: McKay, *Civil War and New York City,* 308–9.

25. Gossip: *Log,* 2:674. Hoadley and MIT: Hoadley, "Sketch of John Chipman Hoadley," 1–2.

26. Fanny expected: Thomas Melville to Catherine Gansevoort, 9 May 1865, GL. Fanny staying with Kate, illnesses: Maria G. Melville to Catherine Gansevoort, 5 July 1865, GL. John's visit in Albany: see note 21, bulk of party.

27. To New Bedford and Brookline: see note 18 and note 22, return. Tom, Lucy: see note 26, Fanny with Kate. Allan's girls: Maria G. Melville to Catherine Gansevoort, 5, 18 July 1865, GL.

28. Daughter, Thurston's death: Brown Thurston, *Thurston Genealogies,* 326; A. Henry Thurston Pension Application (widow), NA.

29. See note 21, Lemuel Shaw.

30. Events: *NYT*, 4 July 1865. Tom: see note 26, Fanny with Kate. Allan: see note 23, enjoying Arrowhead.

31. City deserted: see note 18. Washington, quotation, other information: Provost Marshal, Washington, to Commissary-General of Subsistence, 13 May 1865, Charles Brewster Compiled Service Record, NA.

32. Charles in the city: see note 18 and Charles Brewster to Henry Gansevoort, 12 July 1865, George Henry Brewster to Henry Gansevoort, 15 July 1865, GL. Charles to New Orleans: Charles Brewster Compiled Service Record, NA. Goshen, schemes: Charles Brewster to Henry Gansevoort, 12 September 1865, GL.

33. *Log,* 2:675.

34. Allan to Glens Falls, Curtis move, Guert's house: [Augusta Melville] to Catherine Gansevoort, 7 October 1865, GL. Lime kilns, Clarendon Springs: see note 22, return. Guert's illness: Catherine Gansevoort to Henry Gansevoort, 14 November 1865 (quotation), Maria G. Melville to Catherine Gansevoort, 21 December 1865, GL.

35. Peter and Catherine Gansevoort Diaries, 22 August to 2 September 1865, GL.

36. Sam Shaw to Arrowhead: Maria G. Melville to Catherine Gansevoort, 17 August 1865, GL. To White Mountains: see note 21, Lemuel Shaw. Return of Herman's family to city: on 12 September 1865, a Tuesday, Frances Melville said she had heard the preceding Friday that they had left Gansevoort, to Catherine Gansevoort, GL.

37. Henry's leave: Department of Washington Special Order No. 219, 4 September 1865, GL. Staying with Bruce: Henry Gansevoort to Catherine Gansevoort,

17 September 1865, GL. Texas expedition: Henry Gansevoort to Catherine Gansevoort, 25 April 1865, GL. Poor evaluation: Henry Gansevoort to Adjutant General, U.S. Army, 10 September 1865, GL. Nagging for brevet: beginning with Henry Gansevoort to Peter Gansevoort, 30 April 1865, GL. Nagging for command: beginning with Peter Gansevoort Diaries, 16 May 1865, GL. Brevet to general awarded: Ira Harris to Peter Gansevoort, 24 June 1865, GL. Mother Melville: see note 21, bulk of party. Nothing could be done: Abraham Lansing to Henry Gansevoort, 5 July 1865, GL. Awaiting orders: Henry Gansevoort to Peter Gansevoort, 5 July 1865, GL. First order: Assistant Adjutant General, U.S. Army, Special Order No. 405, 28 July 1865, GL. Henry remaining in Washington: [Henry Gansevoort] to Adjutant, Artillery Brigade, 25 August 1865, GL. Second order: Assistant Adjutant General, Department of Washington, Special Order No. 209, 27 August 1865, GL. Leave: ibid., Special Order No. 219, 4 September 1865, GL.

38. Bruce back from Arrowhead, Miss Turner: Allan Melville to Henry Gansevoort, 9 September 1865, GL, and note 24, Rachel Turner. Henry in Washington, struggle for horses: see note 37, staying with Bruce. Shipping horses: Henry Gansevoort to Catherine Gansevoort, 26 September 1865, GL.

39. Peter ill: Catherine Gansevoort to Henry Gansevoort, 16 September 1865, GL. Locating belongings: see note 24, Rachel Turner. Clothing, quotation: see note 37, staying with Bruce. 13th mustered out: see note 38, shipping horses.

40. General's stars: Henry's mail was being addressed to "General Gansevoort." Peter prevented glory: see note 37, nagging for brevet. Persecution, leave the army: see note 37, nagging for command. Hawthorne: N. Hawthorne, "Chiefly about War Matters," 12:303.

41. Oysters: see note 37, staying with Bruce. Quotation: E. L. Townsend to Henry Gansevoort, 16 September 1865, GL.

42. Leave not extended: Henry Gansevoort to Catherine Gansevoort, 30 September 1865, GL. In command, rumor, quotation: Henry Gansevoort to Catherine Gansevoort, 6 October 1865, GL. Fortress Monroe: Henry Gansevoort to Catherine Gansevoort, 14 October 1865, GL.

43. Bruce's ride: George Henry Brewster to Henry Gansevoort, 7, 13 October 1865, GL.

44. Affairs at Arrowhead: see note 23, work on Arrowhead. Kate: to Henry Gansevoort, 16 October 1865, GL.

45. Marriage: Palfrey, *Memoir of William Francis Bartlett,* 159. Retained commission: ibid., 152, 196. Departure for Europe: *NYT,* 19 October 1865.

46. Tom in and out: Bruce reported that he was "in town sometimes," to Henry Gansevoort, 22 December 1865, GL. Latherses' return: "last week," note 21, Latherses. Allan, Uncle Peter, Aunt Susan: Allan Melville to Henry Gansevoort, 20 October 1865, GL. Catherine to the city: Catherine Gansevoort to Susan L. Gansevoort, 22 October 1865, GL. Kate and Tom at Mrs. Hoffman's: Allan Melville to Henry Gansevoort, 28 October 1865, GL.

47. Plans of Allan and Jennie: see note 34, Allan to Glens Falls, and note 21, Latherses. Lady from Raleigh: see note 42, leave not extended. Allan's daughters to Winyah: see note 21, Latherses. "Beasts and man," no nabob: see note 46, Allan, Uncle Peter. Henry's leave: Headquarters, Department of Virginia, Special Order No. 281, 23 October 1865, GL. Henry's arrival at Pittsfield: Allan Melville to Henry Gansevoort, 2 November 1865, GL. Colt and man to Fortress Monroe, Henry at

Fortress: Henry Gansevoort to Catherine Gansevoort, 17 November 1865, GL. Rouser and Beauty still at Arrowhead in summer: Allan Melville to Henry Gansevoort, 20 July 1866, GL. Henry to Albany, New York City: Peter Gansevoort Diaries, 3, 6 November 1865, GL. *Europa*: *NYT*, 11 November 1865.

48. Hoadley: 24 November 1865, GL. Crimes of Southerners: R. Emerson, *Journals and Miscellaneous Notebooks*, 15:471–72. Grant's terms: ibid., 471.

49. Whittier: to William Allinson, 20 April 1865, *Letters of John Greenleaf Whittier,* 3:88. Lowell: James Russell Lowell, "Reconstruction," *Complete Writings of James Russell Lowell,* 6:285.

50. Black servant: Catherine Gansevoort to Henry Gansevoort, 8 June 1866, GL. Blacks, malarial conditions: to Catherine Gansevoort, 4 January 1866, GL. Norfolk incident, "black fog": to Catherine Gansevoort, 17 April 1866, GL. Detachments of troops: to Catherine Gansevoort, 17 July 1866, GL. Bruce's response: 28 July 1866, GL.

51. Arch traitor: to Henry Gansevoort, 7 July 1865, GL. "Lucifer," Henry ill: see note 50, blacks, malarial. "Poor Jeff": Henry Gansevoort to Catherine Gansevoort, 7 April 1866, GL. Friendship with Davis, prudence, treason defined, future rebellions: to Catherine Gansevoort, 7 March 1866, GL. Old days: see note 50, detachments. Davis feeble: to Catherine Gansevoort, 27 May 1866, GL.

52. *Reminiscences of Richard Lathers,* 406–7.

53. Ibid., 255–57. This account, which does not mention Herman, conforms with the facts of Simms's visit to the city (especially his stop in Washington en route) contained in his letters between 20 September and 5 December 1865, *The Letters of William Gilmore Simms,* ed. Mary C. Simms Oliphant and T. C. Duncan Eaves, 5 vols. (Columbia: University of South Carolina Press, 1955), 4:520–27. The statement (note 52) that Lathers entertained "Herman Melville of Massachusetts" and Simms together specifies that it occurred at Abby Lodge, across the road from Arrowhead, but it is probable that he entertained Simms only once, in New York. Lathers bought the property for Abby Lodge in 1867, but moved to Charleston that year. After summering at Abby Lodge from 1868 to 1873, he moved there in 1874, four years after Simms's death. His editor apparently believed that after he built Abby Lodge Herman Melville, rather than Allan Melville, was his neighbor (328–29), which may account for the confusion. Cordiality: in a letter to Evert Duyckinck, 18 May 1867, ibid., 5:53, Simms regretted missing a Charleston Board of Trade dinner at which Allan Melville was present because he was Herman's brother.

54. Simms's wartime losses, want: William P. Trent, *William Gilmore Simms* (Boston: Houghton Mifflin, 1892), 268–96; J. V. Ridgely, *William Gilmore Simms* (New York: Twayne, 1962), 125–26, and all postwar letters to Duyckinck.

55. Eggleston, *American War Ballads and Lyrics,* 2:237–38.

56. J. Howe, *Later Lyrics,* 30.

57. Coan present: Titus M. Coan Pension Application, NA. Tom's name: George Henry Brewster to Henry Gansevoort, 22 December 1865, GL.

58. Ed ill: see note 37, staying with Bruce. Ed to Albany: see note 44, Kate. Ed staying with Bruce: see note 57, Tom's name. Selling shooting gallery, return to Albany, arrival of John Lansing: Catherine Gansevoort to Henry Gansevoort, 14 November 1865, GL. Ed as clerk: Catherine Gansevoort to Henry Gansevoort, 12 March 1866, GL. Lansings in the city: Catherine Gansevoort to Henry Gansevoort, 12 December 1865, GL.

59. *Log,* 2:676–77.

60. Mother Melville, Kate's opinion: Catherine Gansevoort to Henry Gansevoort, 20 January 1866, GL. John's reaction: Thomas Melville to Catherine Gansevoort, 29 January 1866, GL.

61. Hoadleys' new baby: Maria G. Melville to Catherine Gansevoort, 27 October 1865, GL. Mother Melville, Tom, Gus in Albany: Peter Gansevoort Diaries, 11, 12 January 1866, Catherine Gansevoort Diaries, 12 January 1866, GL. Tom's two-week visit to the city: see note 60, John's reaction. Visit cut short: Frances Melville to Catherine Gansevoort, 8 February 1866, GL. Tom's speculations less successful: to Henry Gansevoort, 1 July 1866, GL. Gus's return to Gansevoort, Mother Melville to the city, Mary D'Wolf, Dorcas Dearborn: Maria G. Melville to Catherine Gansevoort, 6 [8?] March 1866, GL.

62. Henry in city: he returned from leave in New York and Washington on 22 February, Henry Gansevoort to Peter Gansevoort, 3 March 1866, GL. Commemorative brick: see photograph in Cohen, "Notes," *Battle-Pieces of Herman Melville,* 232. Invitation to Herman and Lizzie: Elizabeth S. Melville to Catherine Gansevoort, 9 January [February] 1866, GL. Invitation to Tom: Thomas Melville to Catherine Gansevoort, 23 May 1866, GL. Invitation to Bruce: Catherine Gansevoort to Henry Gansevoort, 8 May 1866, GL. Mother Melville to city: see note 61, Gus's return. Work scarce for veterans: Mary R. Dearing, *Veterans in Politics: The Story of the G.A.R* (Baton Rouge: Louisiana State University Press, 1952), 54–55.

63. Mother Melville's health, Gus: Augusta Melville to Catherine Gansevoort, 23 March 1866, GL.

64. Stroke, improvement: clipping, *Albany Argus,* 21 January 1866, GL. Writing letters: Peter Gansevoort to Henry Gansevoort, 26 January 1866, GL. Aunt Susan's erysipelas: Peter Gansevoort Diaries, 27 February, 3 March 1866, Catherine Gansevoort to Henry Gansevoort, 3 March 1866, GL. Uncle Peter again a patient: Peter Gansevoort Diaries, 15 to 27 March 1866. GL. Waiting for Tom: see note 63. To Albany, to Gansevoort, manservant: Catherine Gansevoort to Henry Gansevoort, 12 April 1866, GL. Mother Melville partying: Peter Gansevoort Diaries, 16, 24 April 1866, GL. Mother Melville's departure: Peter and Catherine Gansevoort Diaries, 30 April 1866, GL. Dental trip to city: see note 62, invitation to Bruce. June dental problems: Peter Gansevoort Diaries, 4 to 11 June 1866, GL. Aunt Susan ill in June and July: Catherine Gansevoort to Henry Gansevoort, 19 June 1866, Henry Gansevoort to Catherine Gansevoort, 8 July 1866, GL.

65. Uncle Peter to Washington: see note 64, writing letters. Henry's demands: for example, see note 62, Henry in city, note 51, friendship, and especially to Peter Gansevoort, 7 May 1866, GL. Uncle Peter's response: 9 May 1866, GL.

66. Arrival in Paris: see note 57, Tom's name. Allan's letter, newspaper: see note 63, and Catherine Gansevoort to Henry Gansevoort, 3 April 1866, GL. Henry: to Catherine Gansevoort, 7 April 1866, GL.

67. Itinerary, illness: see note 66, Allan's letter, note 62, invitation to Bruce, GL. Messina: Catherine Gansevoort to Henry Gansevoort, 24 May 1866, GL. Cheaper prices: Catherine Gansevoort to Henry Gansevoort, 15 June 1866, GL.

68. *Battle-Pieces* as tragedy: Adler, *War in Melville's Imagination,* 133–58.

69. Politics of this period: Patrick W. Riddleberger, *1866: The Critical Year Revisited* (Carbondale and London: Southern Illinois University Press and Feffer and Simons, 1979). Henry: see note 50, malarial.

70. Sherman: as paraphrased in Guernsey and Alden, *Harper's Pictorial History,* 816. Supported Johnson: Herman, because of the Supplement to *Battle-Pieces,* Tom, as evidenced in his letter to Kate Gansevoort, 23 September 1866, GL, and Allan, the women in Gansevoort, and others in the Gansevoort family because of their consistent politics.

71. *Works of John Greenleaf Whittier,* 3:261–63.

72. "Foolish violence": "The Seward-Johnson Reaction," *Complete Writings of James Russell Lowell,* 6:374. "Whitewashed rebels": Guernsey and Alden, *Harper's Pictorial History,* 813. "Roman senate": Riddleberger, *1866,* 36.

73. Respect for Sumner: describing Major Jack Gentian's attitude toward Sumner, Herman wrote, "for what was sterling in him, thou didst so sincerely honour [him], though far from sharing in all his advocated measures," "To Major John Gentian, Dean of the Burgundy Club," 359.

74. Johnson quotations: Guernsey and Alden, *Harper's Pictorial History,* 819. Kate quotations: see note 64, erysipelas, and note 64, to Albany.

75. Quotation: Dix, *Memoirs of John Adams Dix,* 2:126. Lathers baby: Brown Thurston, *Thurston Genealogies,* 296.

76. Fogle: "Melville and the Civil War," 83. Melville character: Freibert, "Meditative Voice in the Poetry of Herman Melville," 66, compares Lee to Timoleon.

77. Tom's arrival, Paris Exhibition: George Henry Brewster to Henry Gansevoort, 11 May 1866, GL. Tom's departure, 17 May: see note 62, invitation to Tom. Tom's return to city, 31 May: Thomas Melville to Catherine Gansevoort, 30 May 1866, Peter Gansevoort Diaries, 31 May 1866, GL. Tom's departure ca. 10 June, Gus's wish, Mrs. Hoffman's school: Augusta Melville to Catherine Gansevoort, 7 June 1866, GL. Arrival of *Java*: *NYT,* 28 June 1866.

78. Invitation to Gansevoort: see note 77, Tom's departure 10 June. Allan to Pittsfield: George Henry Brewster to Henry Gansevoort, 27 July 1866, GL. Allan's failure to visit Gansevoort, Milie, Rouser: see note 47, Rouser and Beauty. Bruce, "New Rochelle party," Miss Turner, riding, circus: Augusta Melville to Catherine Gansevoort, 9 August 1866, GL. Rachel Barrington: George Henry Brewster to Henry Gansevoort, 17 September 1866, GL.

79. Tom's return, departure for Gansevoort: Thomas Melville to Catherine Gansevoort, 7 July 1866, GL. Book completed, copy by Lizzie: Puett, "Melville's Wife," 126. Book in press: see note 47, Rouser and Beauty. Lizzie, Malcolm to Boston: Catherine Gansevoort to Henry Gansevoort, 23 July 1866, GL. Girls with Helen: Thomas Melville to Catherine Gansevoort, 2 September 1866, GL. Malcolm: in her 23 July 1866 letter, Kate noted that he was in Boston, and his two weeks were up on 13 August, note 78, Bruce. It is possible that the "concluding essay" was written earlier, but the following reconstruction of events is consistent with the known facts of this period.

80. Proofreading completed: unless he brought the sheets to Gansevoort, which is unlikely. His subsequent movements preclude any later date. Puett believes that he had finished proofreading before Lizzie left for Boston, "Melville's Wife," 127. Allan to New York and plan to visit Gansevoort: see note 47, Rouser and Beauty. Herman and John to Gansevoort: see note 79, Lizzie, Malcolm.

81. Visitors, Guert's spine, Stanwix, Herman's appearance: see note 79, Lizzie, Malcolm. Gradually killing Guert, comical likeness: Catherine Gansevoort to Susan L. Gansevoort, 18 July 1866, GL. Kate Curtis's departure: ibid., 21 July 1866, GL.

82. Trip: Catherine Gansevoort Diaries, 23 to 25 July 1866, GL. Quotation: see note 79, Lizzie, Malcom. Rowing, visit to fort: Catherine Gansevoort to Henry Gansevoort, 2 August 1866, GL.

83. He had probably brought with him a book that expressed views much like his, John William Draper's *Thoughts on the Future Civil Policy of America,* which he had purchased only ten days before going to Gansevoort.

84. "Deeply impressive document": Fogle, "Melville and the Civil War," 85. "Scriptures": "Explanatory Notes," *Collected Poems of Herman Melville,* 460.

85. Kate to Albany: Peter Gansevoort Diaries, 27 July 1866, GL. Dam and mill: Thomas Melville to Catherine Gansevoort, 8, 21 August 1866, GL. Tom to Lansingburgh: Peter Gansevoort Diaries, 4 August 1866, Thomas Melvillle to Catherine Gansevoort, 8 August 1866, GL. Allan: ibid., and Augusta Melville to Catherine Gansevoort, 9 August 1866, GL. Herman to city: Peter Gansevoort Diaries, 5, 6 August 1866, Catherine Gansevoort Diaries, 6 August 1866, GL.

86. Activities at Gansevoort, return to city of Herman and Malcolm: Augusta Melville to Catherine Gansevoort, 9 August 1866, GL. Mother Melville and Allan to Arrowhead: Peter Gansevoort Diaries, 9 August 1866, GL.

Chapter 10. Postscript

1. Tom: to Catherine Gansevoort, 2 September 1866, GL. Henry: to Peter Gansevoort, 1 September 1866, GL. Kate: to Henry Gansevoort, 17 September 1866, GL.

2. Aaron: *Unwritten War,* 90. Reviews: *Log,* 2:682–85; Kevin J. Hayes and Hershel Parker, *Checklist of Melville Reviews* (Evanston, Ill: Northwestern University Press, 1991), 111–13; Gary Scharnhorst, "More Nineteenth-Century Melville Reviews," *Melville Society Extracts,* no. 89 (June 1992): 1–6; Richard E. Winslow III, "New Reviews Trace Melville's Reputation," ibid., 7–12.

3. "Melville's Shorter Poems," *Partisan Review* 16 (October 1949): 1035.

4. Shurr: "Melville's Poems: The Lat Agenda," 351; Milder: "Rhetoric of Melville's *Battle-Pieces,"* 175.

5. Arvin, *Herman Melville,* 262–69.

6. Ibid., 267.

7. Lindeman, *Conflict of Convictions,* vii, ix.

8. Fogle: "Melville and the Civil War," 63. "Worthier ideal of character": Milder, "Rhetoric of Melville's *Battle-Pieces,"* 174–75.

9. "Rammon": Eleanor M. Tilton, "Melville's 'Rammon': A Text and Commentary," *Harvard Library Bulletin* 13 (Winter 1959): 66–67.

10. Aaron, *Unwritten War,* 41–42.

11. McKay, *Civil War and New York City,* 295.

12. *Log,* 2:756.

13. Ibid., 1:441.

14. Clarence Butler, "APOCALYPSE: *'All Hail to the Stars and Stripes!'"* Moore, *Civil War in Song and Story,* 164–65 (in Browne, *Bugle-Echoes,* 31–33, attributed to Richard Realf).

Selected Bibliography

Archival Sources

Berkshire Athenæum
Herman Melville Memorial Room
Erwin H. Kennedy Collection
Boston Public Library
"Journal of Brevet Brigadier General Caspar Crowninshield" (typescript)
Federal Archives and Records Center, New York
Records of the New York Navy Yard, Records of Naval Districts and Shore Establishments, 1826–1953, Record Group 181, Department of the Navy
Letters Sent to Naval Officers, series 274
Letters and Telegrams Received from the Bureau of Ordnance, series 265
Letters and Telegrams Sent to Navy Department Bureaus, series 252
Letters and Telegrams Sent to the Secretary of the Navy, series 249
Hagley Museum and Library, Eleutherian Mills, Delaware
Admiral Samuel F. DuPont Papers
Library of Congress
Richard Lathers Papers
Richard Manney, private collection
Edwin Y. Lansing Letterbook
National Archives
U.S. Bureau of the Census
Eighth Census of the United States, 1860, Record Group 29
Tenth Census of the United States, 1880, Record Group 29
U.S. Department of State
Letters of Application and Recommendation for Appointment to Federal Office, Record Group 59
U.S. Navy Department
Abstracts of Service of Naval Officers, Record Group 24
Naval Records Collection of the Office of Naval Records and Library, Record Group 45
Letters Received from Commanding Officers of Squadrons

Letters Received from Navy Yards, Navy Yard, New York
Records of the Judge Advocate General (Navy), Record Group 125
Records of General Courts-Martial and Courts of Inquiry of the Navy Department
U.S. Veterans Administration, Record Group 15
Revolutionary War Pension and Bounty-Land Application Files
Civil War Pension Application Files
U.S. War Department
Records of the Adjutant-General's Office, 1780–1917, Record Group 94. (Records of the Record and Pension Office, 1784–1917, contain compiled service records for volunteers, and General Records, 1784–1917, contain regular army service records.)
Records of the Surgeon-General (Army), Record Group 112. (Other General Records contains personnel records of surgeons.)
Records of United States Continental Commands, 1821–1920, Record Group 393. (Records of Geographical Departments, Divisions, and Military [Reconstruction] Districts, 1821–1920, contains records of Department and Defense of Washington, 22nd Corps.)
New York Public Library, Astor, Lenox, and Tilden Foundations, Rare Books and Manuscripts Division
Duyckinck Family Papers
Gansevoort-Lansing Collection
New-York Historical Society
Alfred B. Street Collection
Gansevoort Papers
Naval History Society Collection
Princeton University Archives
Pittsfield, Mass., Town Records
Queensbury, N.Y., Town Records
Warren County, N.Y., Land Records

Books and Articles

Aaron, Daniel. *The Unwritten War: American Writers and the Civil War.* New York: Alfred A. Knopf, 1973.

Adler, Joyce Sparer. *War in Melville's Imagination.* New York: New York University Press, 1981.

Adlow, Elijah. *The Genius of Lemuel Shaw: Expounder of the Common Law.* Boston: Massachusetts Law Quarterly, 1962.

Alcott, Louisa May. *The Journals of Louisa May Alcott.* Edited by Joel Myerson, Daniel Shealy, and Madeleine B. Stern. Introduction by Madeleine B. Stern. Boston: Little, Brown, 1989.

Aldrich, Thomas Bailey. *The Poems of Thomas Bailey Aldrich.* Boston: Ticknor and Fields, 1865.

Anderson, Charles Roberts. *Melville in the South Seas.* New York: Columbia University Press, 1939.

Arvin, Newton. *Herman Melville.* New York: William Sloan, 1950.

———. "Melville's Shorter Poems." *Partisan Review* 16 (October 1949): 1034–46.

Barrett, Laurence. "The Differences in Melville's Poetry." *PMLA* 70 (September 1955): 606–23.

Baylor, George. *Bull Run to Bull Run: or, Four Years in the Army of Northern Virginia. . . .* 1900. Reprint. Washington, D.C.: Zenger, 1983.

Bennett, Frank M. *The Steam Navy of the United States: A History of the Growth of the Steam Vessel of War in the U.S. Navy, and of the Naval Engineer Corps.* Pittsburgh, Pa.: Warren, 1896.

"Berkshire Brass Bands." Parts 1, 2. *The Berkshire Hills: An Historic Weekly* 1 (1 March, 1 April 1901): 73–77, 85–91.

Bernstein, Iver. *The New York City Draft Riots: Their Significance for American Society and Politics in the Age of the Civil War.* New York: Oxford University Press, 1990.

Bowen, Catherine Drinker. *Yankee from Olympus: Justice Holmes and His Family.* Boston: Little, Brown, 1944.

Bowen, Clarence Winthrop. *The History of Woodstock Connecticut: Genealogies of Woodstock Families.* 8 vols. Norwood, Mass.: Plimpton, 1935.

Bowman, John S., ed. *The Civil War Almanac.* Introduction by Henry Steele Commager. New York: Gallery Books, 1983.

Brandt, Nat. *The Man Who Tried to Burn New York.* Syracuse, N.Y.: Syracuse University Press, 1986.

Brewster, Charles. "Captured by Mosby's Guerrillas." In Military Order of the Loyal Legion of the United States, Missouri Commandery, *War Papers and Personal Reminiscences, 1861–1865: Read before the Commandery of the State of Missouri, Military Order of the Loyal Legion of the United States,* 74–107. St. Louis, Mo.: Becktold, 1892.

Bridge, Horatio. *Personal Recollections of Nathaniel Hawthorne.* 1893. Reprint. New York: Haskell House, 1968.

Brockett, L. P., and Mary C. Vaughan. *Woman's Work in the Civil War: A Record of Heroism, Patriotism, and Patience.* Introduction by Henry W. Bellows. Philadelphia and Boston: Zeigler, McCurdy and R. H. Curran, 1867.

Browne, Francis F., ed. *Bugle-Echoes: A Collection of Poems of the Civil War: Northern and Southern.* New York: White, Stokes, and Allen, 1886.

Brownell, Henry Howard. *War Lyrics and Other Poems.* Boston: Ticknor and Fields, 1866.

Burchard, Peter. *One Gallant Rush: Robert Gould Shaw and His Brave Black Regiment.* New York: St. Martin's Press, 1965.

Cambon, Glauco. *The Inclusive Flame: Studies in American Poetry.* Bloomington: Indiana University Press, 1963.

[Canedy, Charles F.] *This Discursive Biographical Sketch, 1841–1902, of Colonel Richard Lathers Was Compiled as Required for Honorary Membership in Post 509, Grand Army of the Republic . . .* Philadelphia: J. B. Lippincott, 1902.

Carlyle, Thomas, and Ralph Waldo Emerson. *The Correspondence of Thomas Carlyle and Ralph Waldo Emerson, 1834–1872.* 2 vols. Boston: James R. Osgood, 1883.

Cary, Edward. *George William Curtis.* Boston: Houghton Mifflin, 1894.

Chase, Frederic Hathaway. *Lemuel Shaw: Chief Justice of the Supreme Judicial Court of Massachusetts, 1830–1860.* Boston: Houghton Mifflin, 1918.

Chase, Richard. *Herman Melville: A Critical Study.* New York: Macmillan, 1949.

Church, Charles A. *Past and Present of the City of Rockford and Winnebago County, Illinois.* Chicago: S. J. Clarke, 1905.

Cody, David. "'So, then, Solidity's a crust': Melville's 'The Apparition' and the

Explosion of the Petersburg Mine." *Melville Society Extracts,* no. 78 (September 1989): 1, 4–8.

Connor, Marian. "The Abysm and the Star: A Study of the Poetry of Herman Melville." Ph.D. diss., Boston University, 1977.

Cook, Adrian. *The Armies of the Streets: The New York City Draft Riots of 1863.* Lexington: University Press of Kentucky, 1974.

Crawford, Richard, ed. *The Civil War Songbook.* New York: Dover, 1977.

[Cullum, George W.] *Memoir of Brevet Major-General Robert Ogden Tyler, U.S. Army, together with His Journal of Two Months' Travels in British and Farther India.* Philadelphia: J. B. Lippincott, 1878.

Current, Richard N. *The Lincoln Nobody Knows.* New York: Hill and Wang, 1958.

Curtis, Harlow Dunham, comp. *A Genealogy of the Curtiss-Curtis Family of Stratford, Connecticut.* Supplement to the 1903 edition. Stratford, Conn.: Curtiss-Curtis Society, 1953.

Day, Frank L. "Herman Melville's Use of *The Rebellion Record* in His Poetry." Master's thesis, University of Tennessee, 1959.

Dearing, Mary R. *Veterans in Politics: The Story of the G.A.R.* Baton Rouge: Louisiana State University Press, 1952.

Dickinson, Emily. *The Complete Poems of Emily Dickinson.* Edited by Thomas H. Johnson. Boston: Little, Brown, 1960.

Dix, Morgan. *Memoirs of John Adams Dix.* 2 vols. New York: Harper Brothers, 1883.

Dowdey, Clifford. *The Seven Days: The Emergence of Robert E. Lee.* 1964. Reprint. New York: Fairfax Press, 1978.

DuPont, Samuel Francis. *Samuel Francis Du Pont: A Selection from His Civil War Letters.* Edited by John D. Hayes. 3 vols. Ithaca, N.Y.: Cornell University Press, 1969.

Dyer, Frederick Henry, comp. *A Compendium of the War of the Rebellion . . .* 3 vols. Des Moines, Iowa: Dyer, 1908.

Eggleston, George Cary, ed. *American War Ballads and Lyrics: A Collection of the Songs and Ballads of the Colonial Wars, the Revolution, the War of 1812–15, the War with Mexico and the Civil War.* 2 vols. New York: G. P. Putnam's Sons, 1889.

Emerson, Edward Waldo. *Life and Letters of Charles Russell Lowell, Captain Sixth United States Cavalry, Colonel Second Massachusetts Cavalry, Brigadier-General United States Volunteers.* Boston: Houghton Mifflin, 1907.

Emerson, Ralph Waldo. *The Journals and Miscellaneous Notebooks of Ralph Waldo Emerson, 1860–1866.* Edited by Linda Allardt, David W. Hill, and Ruth H. Bennett. Vol. 15 of *The Journals and Miscellaneous Notebooks of Ralph Waldo Emerson.* Cambridge, Mass.: Harvard University Press, 1982.

———. *The Letters of Ralph Waldo Emerson.* Edited by Ralph L. Rusk. 6 vols. New York: Columbia University Press, 1939.

Fish, Carl Russell. *The Civil Service and the Patronage.* New York: Russell and Russell, 1963.

Fogle, Richard Harter. "Melville and the Civil War." *Tulane Studies in English* 9 (1959): 61–89.

Ford, Andrew E. *History of the Origin of the Town of Clinton, Massachusetts, 1653–1865.* Clinton, Mass.: W. J. Coulter, 1896.

Freibert, Sister Lucy Marie. "Meditative Voice in the Poetry of Herman Melville." Ph.D. diss., University of Wisconsin, 1970.

Garner, Stanton. "Herman Melville and the Trunkmaker." *Notes and Queries*, n.s. 26 (August 1979): 307–8.

———. "Melville's Scout toward Aldie." Parts 1, 2. *Melville Society Extracts,* nos. 51, 52 (September, November 1982): 5–16, 1–14.

———. "The Picaresque Career of Thomas Melvill, Junior." Parts 1, 2. *Melville Society Extracts,* nos. 60, 62 (November 1984, May 1985): 1–10, 1, 4–10.

Geary, James W. *We Need Men: The Union Draft in the Civil War.* DeKalb: Northern Illinois University Press, 1991.

Godwin, Parke. *A Biography of William Cullen Bryant, with Extracts from his Private Correspondence.* 2 vols. New York: Appleton, 1883.

Gohdes, Clarence. "Melville's Friend 'Toby.'" *Modern Language Notes* 59 (January 1944): 52–55.

Grant, U. S. *Personal Memoirs of U.S. Grant.* 2 vols. New York: Charles L. Webster, 1885.

Greenslet, Ferris. *The Life of Thomas Bailey Aldrich.* Boston: Houghton Mifflin, 1908.

———. *The Lowells and Their Seven Worlds.* Boston: Houghton Mifflin, 1946.

Guernsey, Alfred H., and Henry M. Alden. *Harper's Pictorial History of the Civil War.* 1866, 1868. Reprint, 2 vols. in 1, of *Harper's Pictorial History of the Great Rebellion.* New York: Fairfax Press, 1977.

Hamersly, Thomas H. S., comp. *Complete Army and Navy Register of the United States of America from 1776 to 1887. . . .* New York: T. H. S. Hamersly, 1888.

Hard, Abner. *History of the Eighth Cavalry Regiment, Illinois Volunteers, during the Great Rebellion.* Aurora, Ill.: n.p., 1868.

Hargrove, Hondon B. *Black Union Soldiers in the Civil War.* Jefferson, N.C.: McFarland, 1988.

Hassler, Warren W., Jr. *General George B. McClellan: Shield of the Nation.* Baton Rouge: Louisiana State University Press, 1957.

Hawthorne, Nathaniel. *The Complete Works of Nathaniel Hawthorne.* Introduction, notes by George Parsons Lathrop. 12 vols. Boston: Houghton Mifflin, 1883.

———. *The Letters, 1857–1864.* Edited by Thomas Woodson, James A. Rubino, L. Neal Smith, and Norman Holmes Pearson. Vol. 18 of *The Centenary Edition of the Works of Nathaniel Hawthorne.* [Columbus:] Ohio State University Press, 1987.

———. "Northern Volunteers. From a Journal." *Monitor* (Concord) 1 (7 June 1862): 1–2.

———. *Our Old Home: A Series of English Sketches.* Edited by Roy Harvey Pearce, Claude M. Simpson, Matthew J. Bruccoli, Fredson Bowers, and L. Neal Smith. Introduction by C[laude]. M. S[impson]. Textual introduction by F[redson]. B[owers]. Vol. 5 of *The Centenary Edition of the Works of Nathaniel Hawthorne.* Columbus: Ohio State University Press, 1970.

———. *The Scarlet Letter.* Edited by William Charvat, Roy Harvey Pearce, Claude M. Simpson, Fredson Bowers, and Matthew J. Bruccoli. Introduction by W[illiam]. C[harvat]. Textual preface and introduction by F[redson]. B[owers]. Vol. 1 of *The Centenary Edition of the Works of Nathaniel Hawthorne.* [Columbus:] Ohio State University Press, 1962.

Hawthorne, Julian. "Tribute to Hawthorne." *The Berkshire Hills: An Historic Monthly* 2 (1 February 1902): 213–14. Reprinted from "Hawthorne at Lenox," *The Booklovers Weekly.*

Hayes, Kevin J., and Hershel Parker. *Checklist of Melville Reviews*. Evanston, Ill.: Northwestern University Press, 1991.

Hayford, Harrison. *Melville's "Monody": Really for Hawthorne?* Evanston, Ill.: Northwestern University Press, 1990.

Hayford, Harrison, and Merrell Davis. "Herman Melville as Office-Seeker." Parts 1, 2. *Modern Language Quarterly* 10 (June, September 1949): 168–83, 377–88.

"Herman at Christie's: On the Block—Again." *Melville Society Extracts,* no. 63 (September 1985): 10.

Hesseltine, William Best. *Civil War Prisons: A Study in War Psychology*. New York: Frederick Ungar, 1964.

Higginson, Thomas Wentworth. *Army Life in a Black Regiment*. Introduction by Howard Mumford Jones. 1870. Reprint. East Lansing: Michigan State University Press, 1960.

History of the Connecticut Valley in Massachusetts, with Illustrations and Biographical Sketches of Some of Its Prominent Men and Pioneers. 2 vols. Philadelphia: Louis H. Everts, 1879.

Hitt, Ralph E. "Controversial Poetry of the Civil War Period, 1830–1878." Ph.D. diss., Vanderbilt University, 1955.

Hoadley, John Chipman, ed. *Memorial of Henry Sanford Gansevoort, Captain Fifth Artillery, and Lieutenant-Colonel by Brevet, U.S.A.: Colonel Thirteenth New York State Volunteer Cavalry, and Brigadier-General of Volunteers by Brevet*. Boston: Franklin Press and Rand, Avery, 1875.

———. "Sketch of John Chipman Hoadley, Written by Himself in Response to the Request of the Magazine." *The American Machinist* 9 (27 November 1886): 1–2.

———, obituary. *American Machinist* 9 (13 November 1886): 1.

Holmes, Oliver Wendell. *The Works of Oliver Wendell Holmes*. 13 vols. Boston: Houghton Mifflin, 1892.

Horth, Lynn. "Letters Lost Letters Found: A Progress Report on Melville's *Correspondence*." *Melville Society Extracts,* no. 81 (May 1990): 1–8.

Howe, Julia Ward. *Later Lyrics*. Boston: J. E. Tilton, 1866.

Howe, Mark DeWolf. *Justice Oliver Wendell Holmes*. 2 vols. Cambridge, Mass.: Harvard University Press, 1957.

———, ed. *Touched with Fire: Civil War Letters and Diary of Oliver Wendell Holmes, Junior, 1861–1864*. Cambridge, Mass.: Harvard University Press, 1946.

Humphreys, Charles A. *Field, Camp, Hospital and Prison Camp in the Civil War, 1863–1865*. Boston: George H. Ellis, 1918.

Illinois Adjutant General's Office. *Report of the Adjutant General of the State of Illinois, 1861–1866*. Revised by J. N. Reece. 9 vols. Springfield, Ill.: Phillips Brothers, 1900–1902.

Jimerson, Randall C. *The Private Civil War: Popular Thought during the Sectional Conflict*. Baton Rouge: Louisiana State University Press, 1988.

Johns, Henry T. *Life with the Forty-ninth Massachusetts Volunteers*. [Rev. ed.] Washington, D.C.: Ramsey and Bisbee, 1890.

Johnson, Robert Underwood, and Clarence Clough Buel, eds. *Battles and Leaders of the Civil War*. 4 vols. 1887–88. Reprint. Secaucus, N.J.: Castle, 1982.

Jones, Virgil Carrington. *Ranger Mosby*. Chapel Hill: University of North Carolina Press, 1944.

Karcher, Carolyn L. *Shadow over the Promised Land: Slavery, Race, and Violence in Melville's America*. Baton Rouge: Louisiana State University Press, 1980.

Kemble, Francis Anne. *Further Records, 1848–1883: A Series of Letters*. 2 vols. 1891. Reprint. New York: Benjamin Blom, 1972.

Kennedy, Frederick J., and Joyce Deveau Kennedy. "Some Naval Officers React to *White-Jacket:* An Untold Story." *Melville Society Extracts,* no. 41 (February 1980): 3–11.

Kenney, Alice P. *The Gansevoorts of Albany: Dutch Patricians in the Upper Hudson Valley*. Syracuse, N.Y.: Syracuse University Press, 1969.

Kring, Walter Donald. *Liberals among the Orthodox: Unitarian Beginnings in New York City, 1819–1839*. Boston: Beacon Press, 1974.

Lathers, Richard. *Reminiscences of Richard Lathers: Sixty Years of a Busy Life in South Carolina, Massachusetts and New York*. Edited by Alvan F. Sanborn. New York: Grafton Press, 1907.

Lee, Robert E.[,Jr.] *Recollections and Letters of General Robert E. Lee*. 1904. Reprint. Garden City, N.Y.: Garden City, n.d.

Levy, Leonard W. *The Law of the Commonwealth and Chief Justice Shaw.* Cambridge, Mass.: Harvard University Press, 1957.

Leyda, Jay. *The Melville Log: A Documentary Life of Herman Melville, 1819–1891*. 2 vols. New York: Gordian Press, 1969.

———. *The Years and Hours of Emily Dickinson*. 2 vols. New Haven, Conn.: Yale University Press, 1960.

Life and Services of Col. Richard Lathers of New Rochelle, New York. N.p., 1897.

Lindeman, Jack, ed. *The Conflict of Convictions: American Writers Report the Civil War—A Selection and Arrangement from the Journals, Correspondence, and Articles of the Major Men and Women of Letters Who Lived through the War.* Philadelphia: Chilton, 1968.

Linton, W. J., ed. *Poetry of America: Selections from One Hundred American Poets from 1776 to 1876*. London: George Bell and Sons, 1878.

Little, Thomas Alexander. "Literary Allusions in the Writings of Herman Melville." Ph.D. diss., University of Nebraska, 1948.

Longfellow, Henry Wadsworth. *The Letters of Henry Wadsworth Longfellow*. Edited by Andrew Hilen. 6 vols. Cambridge: Harvard University Press, 1966–1983.

———. *The Poetical Works of Henry Wadsworth Longfellow.* 6 vols. Vols. 1–6 of *The Works of Henry Wadsworth Longfellow.* 1896. Reprint. New York: AMS Press, 1966.

Longfellow, Samuel, ed. *Life of Henry Wadsworth Longfellow with Extracts from His Journals and Correspondence*. 3 vols. Vols. 12–14 of *The Works of Henry Wadsworth Longfellow.* 1896. Reprint. New York: AMS Press, 1966.

Lowell, James Russell. *Letters of James Russell Lowell.* Edited by Charles Eliot Norton. 2 vols. New York: Harper Brothers, 1894.

———. *The Complete Writings of James Russell Lowell.* 16 vols. Boston: Houghton Mifflin, 1904.

Lowenfels, Walter, ed. *Walt Whitman's Civil War.* New York: Alfred A. Knopf, 1961.

MacBride, Robert. *Civil War Ironclads: The Dawn of Naval Armor.* Philadelphia: Chilton Books, 1962.

McKay, Ernest A. *The Civil War and New York City.* Syracuse, N.Y.: Syracuse University Press, 1990.

McPherson, James M. *Battle Cry of Freedom: The Civil War Era.* New York: Oxford University Press, 1988.

Madison, Robert D. "Melville's Sherman Poems: A Problem in Source Study." *Melville Society Extracts,* no. 78 (September 1989): 8–11.

Mason, Ronald. *The Spirit above the Dust: A Study of Herman Melville.* London: John Lehmann, 1951.

Massachusetts Adjutant General, comp. *Massachusetts Soldiers, Sailors, and Marines in the Civil War.* 8 vols. and index. Norwood, Mass., and Boston: Norwood Press and Wright and Potter, 1931–37.

Matthiessen, F. O. *American Renaissance: Art and Expression in the Age of Emerson and Whitman.* London: Oxford University Press, 1941.

Melville, Herman. *Battle-Pieces and Aspects of the War.* Edited by Sidney Kaplan. Amherst: University of Massachusetts Press, 1972.

———. *The Battle-Pieces of Herman Melville.* Edited, introduction, and notes by Hennig Cohen. New York: Thomas Yoseloff, 1964.

———. *Billy Budd, Sailor (An Inside Narrative).* Edited, introduction, and notes by Harrison Hayford and Merton M. Sealts, Jr. Chicago: University of Chicago Press, 1962.

———. *Clarel: A Poem and Pilgrimage in the Holy Land.* Edited by Harrison Hayford, Alma A. MacDougall, Hershel Parker, and G. Thomas Tanselle. Historical and critical note by Walter E. Bezanson. Historical supplement by Hershel Parker. Vol. 12 of *The Writings of Herman Melville.* Evanston, Ill., and Chicago: Northwestern University Press and Newberry Library, 1991.

———. *Collected Poems of Herman Melville.* Edited, introduction, and notes by Howard P. Vincent. With corrigenda. Chicago: Hendricks House, 1947.

———. *Herman Melville: Representative Selections.* Introduction, bibliography, and notes by Willard Thorpe. New York: American Book, 1938.

———. *Journals.* Edited by Howard C. Horsford and Lynn Horth. Vol. 15 of *The Writings of Herman Melville.* Evanston, Ill., and Chicago: Northwestern University Press and Newberry Library, 1989.

———. *The Letters of Herman Melville.* Edited by Merrell R. Davis and William H. Gilman. New Haven, Conn.: Yale University Press, 1960.

———. *Moby-Dick: or, The Whale.* Edited by Harrison Hayford, Hershel Parker, and G. Thomas Tanselle. Vol. 6 of *The Writings of Herman Melville.* Evanston, Ill., and Chicago: Northwestern University Press and Newberry Library, 1988.

———. *Pierre: or, The Ambiguities.* Edited by Harrison Hayford, Hershel Parker, and G. Thomas Tanselle. Vol. 7 of *The Writings of Herman Melville.* Evanston, Ill., and Chicago: Northwestern University Press and Newberry Library, 1971.

———. *Poems of Herman Melville.* Edited by Douglas Robillard. New Haven, Conn.: College and University Press, 1976.

———. *Selected Poems of Herman Melville: A Reader's Edition.* Edited and introduction by Robert Penn Warren. New York: Random House, 1970.

———. *White-Jacket: or, The World in a Man-of-War.* Edited by Harrison Hayford, Hershel Parker, and G. Thomas Tanselle. Vol. 6 of *The Writings of Herman Melville.* Evanston, Ill., and Chicago: Northwestern University Press and Newberry Library, 1970.

———. *The Works of Herman Melville.* Edited by Raymond Weaver. 16 vols. London: Constable, 1924.

Merk, Frederick. *Manifest Destiny and Mission in American History: A Reinterpretation.* New York: Random House, 1966.

Metcalf, Bryce. *Original Members and Other Officers Eligible to the Society of the Cincinnati, 1783–1938, with the Institution, Rules of Admission, and Lists of the Officers of the General and State Societies.* Strasburg, Va.: Shenandoah Publishing, 1938.

Metcalf, Eleanor Melville. *Herman Melville: Cycle and Epicycle.* Cambridge, Mass.: Harvard University Press, 1953.

Milder, Robert. "The Rhetoric of Melville's *Battle-Pieces.*" *Nineteenth-Century Literature* 44 (September 1989): 173–200.

Mitchell, Stewart. *Horatio Seymour of New York.* New York: Da Capo Press, 1970.

Moore, Frank, ed. *The Civil War in Song and Story, 1860–1865.* New York: P. F. Collier, 1889.

———, ed. *Lyrics of Loyalty.* New York: G. P. Putnam, 1864.

Mumford, Lewis. *Herman Melville: A Study of His Life and Vision.* Rev. ed. New York: Harcourt, Brace and World, 1962.

Murdock, Eugene C. *One Million Men: The Civil War Draft in the North.* Madison: State Historical Society of Wisconsin, 1971.

Murfin, James V. *The Gleam of Bayonets: The Battle of Antietam and the Maryland Campaign of 1862.* Introduction by James I. Robertson, Jr. 1965. Reprint. Baton Rouge: Louisiana State University Press, 1982.

Nascimento, Daniel C. "Melville's Berkshire World: The Pastoral Influence upon His Life and Works." Ph.D. diss., University of Maryland, 1971.

Nevins, Allan. *The Evening Post: A Century of Journalism.* 1922. Reprint. New York: Russell and Russell, 1968.

Palfrey, Francis Winthrop. *The Antietam and Fredericksburg.* 1882. Reprint. New York: Jack Brussel, n.d.

———. *Memoir of William Francis Bartlett.* Boston: Houghton Mifflin, 1881.

Paludan, Phillip Shaw. *"A People's Contest": The Union and the Civil War, 1861–1865.* New York: Harper and Row, 1988.

Parker, Hershel. "Melville and Politics: A Scrutiny of the Political Milieux of Herman Melville's Life and Works." Ph.D. diss., Northwestern University, 1963.

Pease, David, and Austin W. Pease, comps. *A Genealogical Historical Record of the Descendants of John Pease, Sen., Last of Enfield, Conn.* Springfield, Mass.: Samuel Bowles, 1869.

Perry, Calbraith B. *Charles D'Wolf of Guadaloupe, His Ancestors and Descendants. . . .* New York: T. A. Wright, 1902.

Phisterer, Frederick. *New York in the War of the Rebellion, 1861 to 1865.* 3rd ed. 5 vols. and index. Albany, N.Y.: F. B. Lyon, 1912.

Puett, Amy Elizabeth. "Melville's Wife: A Study of Elizabeth Shaw Melville." Ph.D. diss., Northwestern University, 1969.

[Putnam, Elizabeth Cabot.] *Memoirs of the War of '61: Colonel Charles Russell Lowell, Friends and Cousins.* Boston: Geo. H. Ellis, 1920.

Register of Officers and Agents, Civil, Military, and Naval, in the Service of the United States, on . . . (Register of All Officers . . .) (Biennial Register of All Officers . . .). Washington, D.C.: Government Printing Office and others, biennial.

Rickels, Milton. *Thomas Bangs Thorpe: Humorist of the Old Southwest.* Baton Rouge: Louisiana State University Press, 1962.

Riddleberger, Patrick W. *1866: The Critical Year Revisited*. Carbondale and London: Southern Illinois University Press and Feffer and Simons, 1979.

Ridgely, J. V. *William Gilmore Simms*. New York: Twayne, 1962.

Roehrenbeck, William J. *The Regiment That Saved the Capital*. Introduction by Allan Nevins. New York: Thomas Yoseloff, 1961.

Rombauer, Robert J. *The Union Cause in St. Louis in 1861: An Historical Sketch*. St. Louis, Mo.: Nixon-Jones, 1909.

Rosenberry, Edward H. *Melville*. London: Routledge and Kegan Paul, 1979.

Scharnhorst, Gary. "More Nineteenth-Century Melville Reviews." *Melville Society Extracts*, no. 89 (June 1992): 1–6.

Schouler, William. *A History of Massachusetts in the Civil War*. 2 Vols. Boston: E. P. Dutton and William Schouler, 1868, 1871.

Scott, Otto J. *The Secret Six: John Brown and the Abolitionist Movement*. New York: Times Books, 1979.

Sealts, Merton M., Jr. *The Early Lives of Melville: Nineteenth-Century Biographical Sketches and Their Authors*. Madison: University of Wisconsin Press, 1974.

———. *Melville as Lecturer*. Cambridge, Mass.: Harvard University Press, 1957.

———. *Melville's Reading: Revised and Enlarged Edition*. Columbia: University of South Carolina Press, 1988.

———. *Pursuing Melville, 1940–1980*. Madison: University of Wisconsin Press, 1982.

———. "A Supplementary Note to *Melville's Reading* (1988)." *Melville Society Extracts*, no. 80 (February 1990): 5–10.

Shurr, William H. "Melville's Poems: The Late Agenda." In *A Companion to Melville Studies*, 351–74. Edited by John Bryant. New York: Greenwood Press, 1986.

———. *The Mystery of Iniquity: Melville as Poet, 1857–1891*. Lexington: University Press of Kentucky, 1951.

Silbey, Joel H. *A Respectable Minority: The Democratic Party in the Civil War Era, 1860–1868*. New York: W. W. Norton, 1977.

Simms, William Gilmore. *The Letters of William Gilmore Simms*. Edited by Mary C. Simms Oliphant, Alfred Taylor Odell, and T. C. Duncan Eaves. Introduction by Donald Davidson. Biographical Sketch by Alexander S. Salley. 5 vols. Columbia: University of South Carolina Press, 1952–56.

Smith, J. E. A. *The History of Pittsfield, (Berkshire County,) Massachusetts*. 2 vols. Boston and Springfield, Mass.: Lee and Shepard and Clark W. Bryan, 1869, 1876.

Spray, Michele Y. "Lincoln's 'Wide Awake' Leader." *Nuggets of History* (Rockford, Ill.) 18 (Spring 1981): 1–2.

Stein, William Bysshe. *The Poetry of Melville's Late Years: Time, History, Myth, and Religion*. Albany: State University of New York Press, 1970.

Stewart, Rachel Whitesides. "The Conditional Mood of Melville's Poetry." Ph.D. diss., University of Colorado, 1975.

Stone, Geoffrey. *Melville*. New York: Sheed and Ward, 1949.

Strong, George Templeton. *The Diary of George Templeton Strong*. Edited by Allan Nevins and Milton Halsey Thomas. 4 vols. New York: Macmillan, 1952.

Swinton, William. *History of the Seventh Regiment, National Guard, State of New York, During the War of the Rebellion. . . .* Illustrated by Thomas Nast. New York: Fields, Osgood, 1870.

Thoreau, Henry David. *The Correspondence of Henry David Thoreau*. Edited by Walter Harding and Carl Bode. New York: New York University Press, 1958.

Thurston, Brown. *Thurston Genealogies*. Portland, Me.: Brown Thurston and Hoyt, Fogg and Donham, 1880.

Thurston, Charles Myrick. *Descendants of Edward Thurston, the First of the Name in the Colony of Rhode Island*. New York: Trow and Smith, 1868.

———. *Genealogy of Charles Myrick Thurston and of His Wife, Rachel Hall Pitman, Formerly of Newport, R.I., after December, 1840, of New York*. New York: John F. Trow, 1865.

Ticknor, Caroline. *Hawthorne and His Publisher.* Boston: Houghton Mifflin, 1898.

Tilton, Eleanor M. "Melville's 'Rammon': A Text and Commentary." *Harvard Library Bulletin* 13 (Winter 1959): 50–91.

Trent, William P. *William Gilmore Simms*. Boston: Houghton Mifflin, 1892.

Trowbridge, Francis Bacon. *The Hoadley Genealogy: A History of the Descendants of William Hoadley of Branford, Connecticut, Together with Some Account of Other Families of the Name*. New Haven, Conn.: Trowbridge, 1894.

Turner, Arlin. *Nathaniel Hawthorne: A Biography.* New York: Oxford University Press, 1980.

U.S. Navy Department. *Civil War Naval Chronology, 1861–1865*. Washington, D.C.: Government Printing Office, 1971.

———. *Official Records of the Union and Confederate Navies in the War of the Rebellion*. 1st ser., 27 vols., 2d ser., 3 vols., and index. Washington, D.C.: Government Printing Office, 1894–1922.

U.S. War Department. *The Official Military Atlas of the Civil War.* Compiled by Calvin D. Cowles. 1891. Reprint of *Atlas to Accompany the Official Records of the Union and Confederate Armies*. New York: Crown, 1978.

———. *The War of the Rebellion: A Compilation of the Official Records of the Union and Confederate Armies*. 1st ser., 53 vols., 2d ser., 8 vols., 3d ser., 5 vols., 4th ser., 3 vols., and index. Washington, D.C.: Government Printing Office, 1880–1901.

Vincent, Howard P. *The Trying Out of Moby-Dick*. 1949. Reprint. Carbondale: Southern Illinois University Press, 1965.

Wade, Richard C. *Slavery in the Cities: The South 1820–1860*. New York: Oxford University Press, 1964.

Warren, Robert Penn. "Melville the Poet." *The Kenyon Review* 8 (Spring 1946): 208–23.

Weaver, Raymond M. *Herman Melville: Mariner and Mystic*. 1921. Reprint. New York: Cooper Square, 1968.

Weed, Thurlow. *Autobiography of Thurlow Weed*. Edited by Harriet A. Weed. Boston: Houghton Mifflin, 1883.

Weichmann, Louis J. *A True History of the Assassination of Abraham Lincoln and of the Conspiracy of 1865*. Edited by Floyd E. Risvold. New York: Random House, 1977.

Whitman, Walt. *Leaves of Grass*. Edited by Sculley Bradley and Harold W. Blodgett. New York: W. W. Norton, 1973.

———. *Notebooks and Unpublished Prose Manuscripts*. Edited by Edward F. Grier. 6 vols. New York: New York University Press, 1984.

———. *Prose Works 1892*. Edited by Floyd Stovall. 2 vols. New York: New York University Press, 1963–1964.

———. *Walt Whitman: The Correspondence*. Edited by Edwin Haviland Miller. 6 vols. New York: New York University Press, 1961–1977.

———. *Whitman's Manuscripts: Leaves of Grass (1860): A Parallel Text*. Edited, notes, and introduction by Fredson Bowers. Chicago: University of Chicago Press, 1955.

Whittier, John Greenleaf. *The Works of John Greenleaf Whittier.* 7 vols. Boston: Houghton Mifflin, 1892.

———. *The Letters of John Greenleaf Whittier*. Edited by John B. Pickard. 3 vols. Cambridge, Mass.: Harvard University Press, 1975.

Wilson, Edmund. *Patriotic Gore: Studies in the Literature of the American Civil War.* New York: Oxford University Press, 1962.

Wilson, James Grant, ed. *The Memorial History of the City of New-York from Its First Settlement to the Year 1892*. 4 vols. New York: New-York History Company, 1893.

Winslow, Richard E., III. "New Reviews Trace Melville's Reputation." *Melville Society Extracts,* no. 89 (June 1992): 7–12.

Yannella, Donald, and Hershel Parker, eds. *The Endless, Winding Way in Melville: New Charts by Kring and Carey.* Glassboro, N.J.: Melville Society, 1981.

Young, Agatha. *The Women and the Crisis: Women of the North in the Civil War.* New York: McDowell, Obolensky, 1959.

Index